THE SOCIOLOGY OF GAMBLING

ABOUT THE AUTHOR

Mikal Aasved is a Research Associate at the Center for Addiction Studies in the School of Medicine and an Adjunct Assistant Professor in the Department of Sociology and Anthropology at the University of Minnesota in Duluth. He has degrees in the behavioral and social sciences with academic specializations including human motivational theory, human social theory, and addiction studies. The findings of his gambling, alcohol, and barroom behavior research have been presented as papers read at professional conferences and as articles published in scholarly journals. This is his third book.

Cover design by Lin Tuschong: *typewitch@attbi.com.*

The Gambling Theory and Research Series

Volume II

THE SOCIOLOGY
OF GAMBLING

By

MIKAL AASVED, PH.D.

Center for Addiction Studies
University of Minnesota-Duluth

CHARLES C THOMAS • PUBLISHER, LTD.
Springfield • Illinois • U.S.A.

Published and Distributed Throughout the World by

CHARLES C THOMAS • PUBLISHER, LTD.
2600 South First Street
Springfield, Illinois 62704

ISBN 0-398-07380-5 (hard)
ISBN 0-398-07381-3 (paper)

Library of Congress Catalog Card Number: 2002040857

With THOMAS BOOKS *careful attention is given to all details of man-ufacturing and design. It is the Publisher's desire to present books that are sat-isfactory as to their physical qualities and artistic possibilities and appropri-ate for their particular use.* THOMAS BOOKS *will be true to those laws of quality that assure a good name and good will.*

Printed in the United States of America
CR-R-3

Library of Congress Cataloging-in-Publication Data

Aasved, Mikal J.
    The sociology of gambling / by Mikal Aasved.
        p. cm. -- (The gambling theory and research series ; v. 2)
    Includes bibliographical references and index.
    ISBN 0-398-07380-5 (hard) -- ISBN 0-398-07381-3 (paper)
    1. Gambling--Research--United States. 2. Gambling--United
States--Psychologial aspects. 3. Compulsive gambling--United States.
I. Title. II. Series.

HV6715 .A37 2003
306.4'82--dc21

                                                2002040857

To my Mother

This one's for you, Mom

PREFACE TO THE SERIES

This series of books was written primarily to fill what I perceived as a conspicuous gap in the gambling literature: Some years ago when I first entered the field of gambling studies and tried to locate a single source which would provide the necessary background on the motivations for normative and excessive gambling, no such source existed. For some puzzling reason, no similarly extensive review and synthesis of the voluminous published materials on gambling theory and research had ever been undertaken. With the exception of a few "handbooks" on gambling and some hard-to-find anthologies of papers presented at various symposia, the necessary source materials were scattered throughout a plethora of academic journals and books. Moreover, most existing reviews of the gambling literature are far from exhaustive. Instead, they are all too often cursory overviews appearing either as relatively brief journal articles or as chapters or even smaller sections of books whose authors usually then go on to profess the superiority of their own favored theory.

This series therefore represents a synthesis of the major ideas and findings of leading theoreticians and researchers in their quest to discover and explain the human propensity for gambling. It is evident that just as many writers in the field of alcohol studies often fail to distinguish among drinking, drunkenness, and alcoholism, so do many writers in the field of gambling studies fail to acknowledge that there are also different degrees of gambling involvement. It is therefore extremely important to distinguish among normative or moderate recreational gambling which is harmful to none, heavy or immoderate gambling which may or may not be harmful to a particular gambler, and compulsive or pathological gambling which is generally harmful not only to all those who are afflicted with it but also to their families, friends, and sometimes even to the greater society in which they live. Addressing primarily the etiological issues related to both normative and excessive gambling, this series includes the speculative thoughts of armchair scholars as well as the empirical findings of front-line scientific researchers in all disciplines including the behavioral, social, and medical sciences.

It is intended to benefit both students and professionals. One goal is to provide students with the introductory background they need to embark on a career in gambling studies. A second is to remind those who are already established in the field not only that many possible explanations for normative and pathological gambling have been proposed, but also that the authority of those who have advanced them should always be questioned. Toward this end, another aim of this more extensive review is objectivity. Rather than champion a particular theoretical orientation as so many others have done, it includes critical assessments of many of the theoretical ideas and research findings that are discussed. This has been done to help readers become more critical not only in their appraisal of the ideas of others but also in their own thinking. Many of the "experts" in any field are firmly convinced that they have discovered the absolute truth and then write as though their explanation for any phenomenon constitutes the final, definitive answer to that particular question. Many such explanations have an initial intuitive appeal that may "sound good" but that can blind the unwary reader to all other possibilities. In this way some theories have become very much like religions that are sustained more by the faith of the zealots who follow them than by any unbiased scientific observations. Since so many different and competing final "truths" have been propounded, it is clear that not all of them can claim the prize. This is particularly evident in the field of addiction studies, but it is also true of other disciplines. Occasionally a purportedly scientific treatise or explanation will turn out to be merely a guise that its author has used to promote some hidden agenda. The propagandistic tracts of the "creation scientists" are prime examples of this. Readers of all scientific works–including those by reputable authors–are therefore strongly encouraged always to question their validity and never to accept any idea or argument solely on the basis of its author's credentials, reputation, position, or salesmanship since it may turn out to be entirely baseless. The ultimate truth or falsity of any proposition must always be determined by empirically derived facts.

MIKAL AASVED

ACKNOWLEDGMENTS

A work of this nature and scope is clearly not the product of a single author but of many, all of whom deserve credit. I therefore want to thank all the theoreticians and researchers in gambling studies upon whose ideas, analyses, and conclusions the entire contents of this series are based.

I am especially grateful to my parents, Harry and Lucille Aasved, for their undying encouragement and support throughout this project. Although severely tried, they were never wanting.

William Madsen, my mentor, friend, and author of the highly popular *The American Alcoholic*, not only introduced me to addiction studies but also provided the inspiration necessary to undertake this project. Thanks for everything, Bill, including all those prime rib dinners.

I would also like to thank a number of friends and colleagues including Jim Schaefer, with whom I first entered into gambling studies, who introduced me to the hidden world of pull tab gambling, and who demonstrated that it can sometimes be more profitable not to raise when you are holding a nut hand; J. Clark Laundergan not only for his help and encouragement but also for making this work possible; and Henry Lesieur for his sage advice, assistance, direction, and willingness to share any information he has.

I am immeasurably grateful to William Eadington whose review and expert commentary on the chapter on economic theories of gambling spared me a great deal of embarrassment, to Michael Emerson for taking the time to solve what was for me a perplexing problem in statistical analysis, and to Ken Winters for sharing his collection of professional journals.

I am also indebted to the entire staff of the University of Minnesota/Twin Cities interlibrary loan office for tracking down countless source materials and to my friend Merlin Spillers, thespian, terpsichorean, and librarian extraordinaire, who generously provided me with source materials I would not otherwise have been able to review. I am especially grateful to my friends Skylar Rupp, who came to my rescue with a computer when my old one died, and computer wizard Kip Barkley who was able to recover all the data I thought I had lost with it. Assistant Dean John Hamlin of the College of Liberal Arts at the University of Minnesota/Duluth was kind enough to submit the required paperwork and cut through all the other red tape required to procure a newer and much faster "obsolete" computer for me from the campus "boneyard." J. Laundergan then undertook the arduous task of boxing it up and shipping it to me. I thank you all profusely.

Finally, but foremost in my life and thoughts, my beloved Star, my soulmate and lifemate, gave me all the love and support necessary to see this endeavor through to its completion. Mo grà thu, my Goddess.

CONTENTS

Part III: QUANTITATIVE APPROACHES
The Role of Survey Research and Statistical Analysis

TABLES

THE SOCIOLOGY OF GAMBLING

INTRODUCTION TO THE SERIES

Why do people gamble? Why do some continue to gamble even when they consistently lose more than they win? Why do some continue to gamble even when they have lost everything they have? Many theories have been proposed by various clinicians, laboratory and field researchers, and participant observers in their attempts to discover and explain the reasons for gambling. This series of books was written to review and evaluate the most popular and influential of these explanations and the extensive amount of research that has been undertaken to test them.

Gambling, according to most definitions, means risking something of value on the unknown outcome of some future event. The ultimate goal—or, more accurately, the ultimate hope—of gambling is to realize a value greater than that risked. When we hear the word most of us think of a friendly (or not so friendly) poker game, or of betting on competitive events like horse racing or football games, or of casino games like roulette, blackjack, and slot machines. However, gambling also has other guises. Any speculative business venture, commodities investment, or insurance purchase is just as much a "crap shoot" as playing the dice tables in Las Vegas. Historical and archaeological records provide ample evidence that gambling has also been popular throughout the world for a very long time. Almost since the dawn of human existence people have gambled for the possessions of their dead, for the possessions of their living friends and relatives, to settle legal disputes and establish rights to various resources, and on the outcome of athletic contests and other competitive events.

Gambling is increasingly being recognized by national and local governments throughout the United States and the world as an effective means of generating revenues. Whereas most gambling activities were unlawful in many states and countries until quite recently, many forms of gambling are now becoming accepted and, as a result, national trends toward the legalization of gambling in one form or another are on the rise. Not only has "lottery fever" swept many nations, but many are also allowing on- and off-track parimutuel betting, electronic video gaming machines, and other forms of lawful gambling. In the United States, as some of the states along the

Mississippi River and other major waterways began to legalize riverboat gambling as it existed in the nineteenth century, others quickly followed suit. Indian reservations across the country and rural communities in such states as Colorado and South Dakota are now offering Las Vegas, Atlantic City, and even Monte Carlo some stiff competition for the tourist's discretionary income.

Many specialists are convinced that as opportunities for gambling continue to increase, so will the problems associated with it. Salient among these potential problems is the anticipated increase in the incidence of excessive or problem gambling which is commonly referred to as compulsive or pathological gambling. Whether one considers pathological gambling to be an individual, social, or public health problem, it is one which must be confronted if it is to be prevented and treated. To do so effectively will of course require a thorough understanding of the phenomenon. Unfortunately, with our currently limited knowledge of the mechanisms and motivations underlying gambling, we have a long way to go before achieving this goal.

While our current understanding of the causes of pathological gambling is insufficient, its ramifications are well known. It can have disastrous consequences not only for the individual, but also for his or her immediate family, employer, and society. Among its most well-known consequences are the calamitous losses and severe personal and family debts it can cause. Individual debts for pathological gamblers seeking help have been reported to average from about $53,000 to $92,000.[1] Considered together, the sum of individual gambling debts can be extraordinary. One estimate placed the annual debt accrued by pathological gamblers in New Jersey alone at $514 million.[2] The debt levels of many pathological gamblers can become so high at the individual level that the stress and depression they produce can cause actual physical ailments which require medical treatment. At the domestic level pathological gambling and its consequences can disrupt home life to such an extent that it causes the breakup of families. In its more advanced stages pathological gambling frequently results in absenteeism and loss of productivity on the job. Eventually the need for gambling money can lead to such crimes as theft, embezzlement, insurance fraud, and other kinds of illegal activities. In its final stages the only apparent course of action remaining is all too often suicide.[3]

Because gambling usually involves money, many people believe that therein lies the answer to its attraction and popularity–that this motivation alone explains why people gamble. People are thought to gamble in the hope of winning money they don't already have, of winning more money than they already have, or, in the case of insurance, of protecting what money they already have. But is acquisitiveness really the only reason for gambling? While many card games are played for money, many people play these same games among friends purely for enjoyment or as an opportunity to socialize with friends and relatives, often with no money involved. While many adults become mesmerized by the electronic gambling games they play in casinos in hopes of winning money, countless children and adolescents become equally mesmerized by electronic video games in public arcades and on home computers that are played for amusement only. Technically, friendly card parties and children's video games do not constitute gambling since they do not involve money, but they certainly have many other elements in common with gambling. On the other hand, many risky behaviors like sky-diving, auto racing, Russian roulette, motorcycle jumping, and driving while intoxicated do not involve money but they certainly constitute gambling. There may very well be more to gambling than just the prospect of mone-tary gain.

A number of competing theories have been proposed by various psychia-trists, psychologists, sociologists, economists, anthropologists, lay people, and others in their attempts to explain the "real" motivations for gambling. A number of the more popular and influential of these approaches will be reviewed in this series. Theories, it will be seen, are often little more than opinions, and nearly everyone who studies gambling behavior has a favored opinion. It will be clear that many of those which have been advanced are frequently little more than the standard, stock-in-trade ideologically inspired answers that specialists in various disciplines typically call upon to explain all behavioral phenomena. Thus, in the past and sometimes even today it has generally been assumed that all instances of gambling–normal and patho-logical–have the same underlying cause irrespective of individual prefer-ences. Many authorities have even proposed single, monolithic explanations to account for excessive or uncontrolled behaviors of all kinds, and a num-ber of the approaches that will be discussed reflect this tendency toward "grand theorizing." It should be obvious that some of these theories may, indeed, offer some insights into certain instances of gambling behavior while the utility of others may be extremely limited. Most importantly, however, since the individual motivations for gambling appear to be so many and var-ied, it should also be obvious that no single theoretical approach, despite the most fervent aspirations, proselytizations, and diatribes of its adherents, will ever be able to account for all cases.

A QUESTION OF MORALS?

The earliest theoretical approach viewed drinking, drug use, and gambling from a moral perspective.[4] Throughout most of human history the social mores, religious doctrines, and ethical standards of a society have provided the only criteria by which to gauge the behavior of its members. Islamic tradition forbade beverage alcohol and gambling at the same time since both were regarded as tools of Satan. In India the great spiritual leader Mahatma Ghandi also compared the habit of gambling to that of drinking: it is a vice that destroys men's souls and makes them a burden on the earth.[5] Similar views have a long standing in the Western cultural and Judeo-Christian religious traditions. Aristotle himself equated gamblers with thieves and plunderers in his treatise on ethics. In describing those who take what they are not entitled to he wrote:

> meanness is not the term we apply to those who operate in this way on a grand scale—high and mighty persons, for example who sack cities and plunder temples. Such we prefer to call wicked or impious and unrighteous. But the dicer, the thief, the footpad may be reckoned among the mean, because their own hope is to turn a dishonest penny. That is why they labour in their vocation regardless of the world's reproach; the thieves running the greatest risk for the sake of the haul, the gamblers by skinning their friends, who ought rather to benefit by their connexion. Both sorts are unscrupulous profit-hunters, looking to the main chance in discreditable circumstances.[6]

In fourteenth-century England Geoffrey Chaucer's Pardoner condemned gambling as

> . . . the very mother of all lies,
> And of deceit, and cursed false swearing,
> Blasphemy of Christ, manslaughter, and waste also
> Of property and of time; and furthermore,
> It is shameful and dishonorable
> To be known as a common gambler.[7]

In the American colonies Cotton Mather censured gambling as "unquestionably immoral and, as such, displeasing to God."[8] Despite a remarkable lack of any concrete evidence, both legal and illegal forms of gambling in the modern United States are commonly believed to be under the firm control of vast organized criminal networks. According to a sociologist who has thoroughly examined the issue, this myth is often perpetuated, exaggerated, and exploited by self-serving politicians and other government officials whose public support and personal fortunes are predicated on an illusory commitment and adherence to the principles of law, order, capitalism, and Christianity.[9]

These moralistic attitudes persist because one of the most cherished core values in Western European Protestant capitalistic societies is that wealth should be acquired only through hard work, sacrifice, and frugality. Any money that has been acquired through other means such as theft or gambling was considered to be ill-gotten and tainted, the cause of hardship and ruin for others, and thus a blemish on the Puritan complexion. Indeed, criminologists, treatment providers, and other gambling researchers have often claimed an association between pathological gambling and criminal activities of one form or another[10] although this is rarely the case among non-problem or normal gamblers. Nevertheless, gambling, whether pathological or non-pathological, has therefore been condemned as an unChristian and uncapitalistic tool of the devil.

Interestingly, gambling has been denounced as an agent of moral decay equally by representatives of both capital and labor. Since winning eliminates the need for honest labor as a means for social advancement, the religious and ruling elite have seen gambling as a threat to the existing "divinely instituted" social order. Since losing what wealth one does manage to accumulate through wage labor eliminates all chances for honest social advancement, labor leaders have seen gambling as a greater enemy of the working classes than capitalism itself. Thus, "To the guardians of public morality gambling is Gambling and Wrong; so labeled it has been filed safely away, along with Drugs and Homosexuality, under the headings of 'Vice' and 'Deviance.'"[11]

A fundamental assumption of this "simplistic"[12] prescientific "moral model" of human behavior is that gambling, drinking, and other "degenerate" behaviors are solely a matter of willpower. In the traditional popular view, any activity which does not conform to established behavioral norms and conventions is often condemned as a deliberately deviant and immoral flouting of the standards and values of propriety. Thus, the gambler, drinker, drug user, roué, or homosexual, always in full control of himself (women were generally excluded from considerations of such possibilities), is a willful sinner who, owing to his spiritual weakness and moral depravity, freely chooses to indulge himself for his own hedonistic pleasures. Since he is entirely responsible for his "vice" he must be held fully accountable for any and all consequences which may ensue, and should expect no help or sympathy from others. In the past, "treatment" for these self-indulgences consisted of spiritual, moral, and theological counseling and exhortation. When these methods failed, the individual was often subjected to such secular punishments as public ridicule, restraint, corporal punishment, and imprisonment to insure his future conformity to accepted social conventions.

The moralistic view of gambling has the longest history of any approach and is still held by large segments of the general public.[13] Although this attitude predates the development of the scientific method by millennia it is still very much alive in the popular press and today's cultural moralist continues to regard excessive, and even nonexcessive, gambling as a moral deficiency rather than a consequence of cultural, social, psychological, and/or biological factors over which the individual may or may not have any personal control. Nevertheless, owing to the widespread popularity and acceptance of gambling, others argue that it is a normal, everyday psychologically beneficial activity which should be regarded as neither socially or personally harmful.[14] For those who prefer to view gambling from a more scientific perspective, all moral, religious, and ethical arguments against it "are essentially matters of belief and, as such, unanswerable.[15]"

AN ADDICTION?

Many specialists in the field feel that pathological gambling, like alcohol and other drug dependence, is an addiction and therefore a major public mental health problem which must be dealt with by medically trained personnel.[16] The inclusion of pathological gambling in the 1980 and subsequent editions of the *Diagnostic and Statistical Manual of Mental Disorders* (DSM-III, DSM-III-R, DSM-IV), published by the American Psychiatric Association[17] and the *International Classification of Disease* (ICD-9-CM; ICD-10), of the World Health Organization[18] is responsible for much of this agreement.

The Definitional Issue in Addiction Research

It is important to note, however, that the conception of pathological gambling as an addiction is not universally shared, especially since the DSM and the ICD have always classified pathological gambling as a disorder of impulse control rather than an addiction. Nevertheless, many authorities from many different disciplines tend to agree that compulsive or pathological gambling is, indeed, an addiction. However, there is relatively little agreement as to what this term signifies. Among professionals in the field the definitional issue alone is therefore monumental but relatively few find it necessary to provide a formal definition of what they mean by "addiction." Many simply leave it to their readers to infer their intended meanings from the contexts in which the term is used.[19] Apparently, most feel that a formal definition is unnecessary since they seem to assume that their own particular use of the term enjoys universal acceptance even though this is clearly not the case. Moreover, many specialists are convinced that the idea that gamblers can be neatly dichotomized as either "normal" or "pathological" is entirely groundless since, apart from their differing levels of involvement, there are no observable qualitative differences between them. They argue that excessive or problem gambling is that point along a continuum of involvement–progressing from zero, through light and moderate, to extremely heavy involvement–at which an individual begins to encounter negative consequences. Since people live in a wide variety of financial and social circumstances, some will reach this point much sooner than others.

Not only are existing terms being used inconsistently to convey different meanings for different addiction specialists, but new terms are continually being coined in the hope that taxonomy alone might somehow resolve the issue. Many specialists in the field of substance abuse adhere to a narrow definition in which "addiction" refers only to physiological dependence on a chemical substance, as in cases of nicotine or opiate addiction. On the other hand are those who hold an equally narrow definition by seeing it as an entirely psychological phenomena with no physiological basis whatsoever. Thus, the expressions "monopolistic activities"[20] and "addictive-like preoccupations"[21] have been proposed to describe such behaviors as pathological gambling, compulsive hair pulling (trichotillomania), nail biting, and even such involuntary nongoal-directed behavioral phenomena as facial tics. Advocates of this view refer to these and other nonchemical dependencies as "pure addictions" since the addict's functioning is not influenced by the effects of chemical substances.[22] However, some specialists prefer a less restricted usage in which the term refers to physiological and psychological dependence, or to persistent behaviors which are in any way harmful to the "addict" irrespective of the presence or absence of physical dependence as in "problem drinking" and certain eating disorders. Those who wish to avoid taking sides in the debate suggest the term "driven behaviors"[23] or "appetitive behavior problems"[24] to account for all types of behavioral excesses irrespective of whether they are psychological or physiological in origin.

A number of authorities feel there is no need to distinguish chemical from behavioral addictions since they have so much in common that no distinction is necessary. (One cannot help but wonder if they might also suggest that arson be regarded and treated the same as spontaneous combustion since they also have so much in common.) Still others, including many lay people, have adopted a very broad definition in which "addiction" includes indulgence in any behavior, whether goal oriented or not, which is thought to exceed culturally normative standards, as in the case of "workaholics," "exercise nuts," and blues or bluegrass music "junkies." While one specialist in the field distinguishes "positive addictions" such as jogging and meditation which are deemed to have beneficial effects from "negative addictions" which have harmful consequences,[25] another feels that the term is being used so broadly and inclusively that it is in danger of becoming meaningless[26] since even such hobbies as hang gliding, racing, painting, poetry, gardening, needlepoint, knitting, and reading are sometimes referred to as "addictions."

Perhaps none trivialize the concept so much as those who speak of individual and societal addictions to other people, love, pets, religion, music, television programming, coin and stamp collecting, a particular standard of living, and externally structured lives.[27] This situation has been characterized as follows:

> . . . it is not impossible to see two [addiction] researchers using the same terms but coming to entirely different conclusions about the same subject. There is, consequently, no accumulated body of knowledge informed by previous research in the field. Hence the fundamental purpose of the scientific process, the accumulation of a body of knowledge based on systematic and consistent research, is largely unfulfilled in this field.[28]

Among gambling specialists there is little agreement not only as to how "addiction" should be defined, but also as to what constitutes an addiction or how addictions of any sort originate and develop.[29] One addiction specialist has referred to this unfortunate situation as a "conceptual crisis" which plagues the entire field of addiction studies.[30] Consequently, some gambling authorities, particularly those with moralistic inclinations, fail to distinguish normal or nonharmful gambling from that which is excessive or harmful by treating all degrees of gambling as equivalents. Others, who see no qualitative difference between compulsive gambling and any other form of steady and harmful or potentially harmful gambling, prefer to speak of "immoderate,"[31] "heavy,"[32] "excessive,"[33] "intensive,"[34] "troubled,"[35] "habitual,"[36] "high-frequency," "persistent,"[37] "dysfunctional,"[38] "dysfunctionally persistent,"[39] or "disordered"[40] gamblers in their research and writing. Those who dispute the validity of such concepts as "compulsive" or "pathological" gambling speak only of "problem" or "problematic" gambling,[41] a term which has been described as a semantic "wastebasket" since it has been invested with so many different meanings.[42] Likewise, steady but nonpathological gamblers have been referred to by a variety of designations including "obsessive,"[43] "habitual" or "control,"[44] and "serious social"[45] gamblers. Finally, at the low end of the spectrum, those who gamble only lightly and periodically have been called "casual,"[46] "social,"[47] "occasional,"[48] and "infrequent"[49] or "low-frequency"[50] gamblers.

Unfortunately, politics rather than scientific objectivity often determines which particular definition is adopted for which particular addiction by which particular interest group at which particular time under which particular set of circumstances. These choices are more than occasionally influenced by the researcher's need for funding, a highly competitive funding process, and the perspectives of particular funding agencies or government administrations. Thus, it has been observed that

Drug abuse is viewed, even by professionals as a crime, alcoholism as a disease, smoking as a bad habit, and obesity [i.e., compulsive overeating] as either simple gluttony and laziness, a learned behavior pattern, or a metabolic disorder. These different ways of conceptualizing addictive behavior patterns are more related to historical/political phenomena than to factual information.[51]

As will be shown, gambling has been, and often still is, considered in the same light as all of the above. Since the course of addiction research often appears to be guided by the same tides of emotionalism that currently surround human fetal tissue research, the definitional question will no doubt remain unresolved for a long time to come, just as it has in the past.

Co-Addiction

A large number of empirical studies have confirmed the existence–though not necessarily the cause–of a strong association between pathological gambling and other addictions, a phenomenon known as co-addiction, cross addiction, multi-addiction, poly-addiction, or co-morbidity. However, this association was not always evident. One of the first studies to investigate this phenomenon found that eight percent of a sample of Gamblers Anonymous members were alcoholic and two percent were addicted to other drugs. It also found that four percent of a sample of hospitalized pathological gamblers were also alcoholic and six percent were addicted to other drugs.[52] Although the low frequencies that were initially reported did not arouse much concern, many later studies employing modern screening techniques have reported much higher occurrences of co-addiction.

More recent studies have reported that rates of problem gambling (7% to 64%) among adult substance abusers are much higher than those (.23% to 3%) which have been reported for general adult populations.[53] For example, an earlier study of 70 alcoholics reported that 17 percent also admitted having "gambling difficulties" as opposed to only 3 percent of an equal number of nonalcoholic controls.[54] A later study of 100 substance abusers reported 14 percent rates of both pathological and problem gambling.[55] A much larger survey of 458 patients undergoing treatment for substance abuse found that nearly one-fifth of these subjects also had gambling difficulties: 40 (8.7%) were diagnosed as pathological and 47 others (10.3%) were problem gamblers.[56] An even larger and more recent study of 2,171 substance abusers reported that 7.2 percent were also probable and 5.8 percent were severe pathological gamblers.[57] A smaller study of 85 males found that 21.3 percent of the Caucasians and 41 percent of the Native Americans who had entered a U.S. Veterans Administration treatment center for alcohol dependence also had gambling problems.[58] After 100 alcoholic prisoners were screened for gambling problems, 18 were referred to Gamblers Anonymous.[59] Recent studies of heroin addicts enrolled in methadone maintenance treatment programs have reported similar findings. One of these found that three percent of the 220 methadone patients sampled were problem gamblers while seven percent were classed as probable pathological gamblers.[60] Substantially higher rates were reported in a similar study of 117 methadone patients which found that 19 or 16 percent of those sampled were probable pathological gamblers and another 18 or 15 percent were potential pathological or problem gamblers.[61] Two years later a larger study of 462 methadone patients identified 21.4 percent as probable pathological gamblers and 8.9 percent as potential problem gamblers.[62] Likewise, of 93 homeless veterans admitted to an outpatient treatment program for alcohol and heroin addiction, 17 percent were diagnosed as probable pathological gamblers and 34 percent as potential problem gamblers. This study also made the interesting observation that those who were addicted to both heroin and alcohol were even more likely to have a gambling problem than those who were addicted to only one of these substances.[63] A third study of military veterans admitted for substance abuse treatment reported that fully one-third (33.3%) were also pathological gamblers.[64] A fourth found that 25 percent of the veterans admitted to a substance abuse treatment center in Minnesota had mild gambling problems while 15 percent were pathological gamblers, a rate that is approximately ten times that of the state's general population.[65]

Rates of psychoactive substance abuse among problem gamblers are also inordinately high. Modern research has found that from 36 percent[66] to 88 percent[67] of the pathological gamblers studied also abused alcohol and/or other drugs. One recent survey of 246 mostly male (85%) pathological gamblers found that over one-quarter (26%) of the sample had a concurrent drug problem while over half (50.8%) admitted that they also had an alcohol problem.[68] Studies of co-addiction among female compulsive gamblers reported that well over half (56%) of those who were members of Gamblers Anonymous either abused or were dependent upon alcohol and/or other drugs[69] and that nearly all (88%) of a sample of female prisoners who were pathological gamblers were also chemically dependent.[70] As many as 52 percent of the members of two additional Gamblers Anonymous groups demonstrated evidence of alcohol and other drug addiction.[71] In one of these, a group of 50 females, 24 percent also considered themselves to be compulsive spenders, 20 percent admitted they were also compulsive overeaters, and 12 percent claimed to be sexually addicted.[72] Of 51 successive males admitted for inpatient treatment for pathological gambling at the Veterans Administration Hospital in Brecksville, Ohio, nearly half (47%) met medical criteria for chemical dependency at some time in their lives and nearly two-fifths (39%) met these criteria within the previous year.[73] A similar study reported that over one-third (36%) of a separate group of 50 consecutively admitted male pathological gamblers were also chemically dependent (32% alcoholics; 4% drug abusers).[74] A later study of 100 pathological gamblers admitted to this program reported that 14 percent were also diagnosed as sex addicts.[75] In another gambling treatment center 34 percent of those enrolled also were alcoholics, 6 percent were drug addicts, and 31 percent abused both alcohol and drugs.[76] A subsequent study of prison inmates found that 30 percent of this population exhibited clear signs of pathological gambling. Of this sample population, over half (58%) the women and nearly half (44%) the men were also alcoholics. Two-fifths of both the men (39%) and women (40%) who were drug addicts, and nearly two-thirds of the men (64%) and two-fifths (39%) of the women who were alcoholics, were also pathological gamblers.[77] A study of 136 hospitalized male pathological gamblers found that 81, or 60 percent, were also diagnosed as alcoholic.[78] Of 58 patients admitted to a pathological treatment unit in Germany 29 (50%) were also addicted to alcohol while another eight (13.8%) were addicted to more than one drug; only two (3.4%) did not smoke.[79] An epidemiological survey of the general population of Edmonton, Alberta reported that 63.3 percent of those identified as pathological gamblers were also alcoholics and 23.3 percent were also drug addicts.[80] A study of 298 patients receiving treatment for cocaine abuse found that 15 percent (n=44) were also pathological gamblers. The authors noted that this frequency was ten times that reported in general population studies.[81] Likewise, of 64 veterans seeking treatment for chemical dependency, 17 percent were diagnosed as probable and 14 percent as potential pathological gamblers.[82] A study of 25 male and 14 female pathological gamblers receiving outpatient treatment in Minnesota found that 60 percent of both sexes also had a substance abuse or dependence disorder of some kind, the most common of which was alcoholism.[83] Similar findings have been reported by many other researchers.[84] However, some who have investigated this phenomenon found no differences in the levels of drug use between normative and pathological gamblers with the exception of a higher lifetime rate of tobacco use among the latter.[85] Others who have found no co-addictive relationship between substance abuse and pathological gambling in clinical populations have suggested that they are independent addictions.[86]

One of the more interesting studies to posit an association between problem gambling and other addictions employed an epidemiological approach: it reported that those cities in Galicia (northwestern Spain) which have the highest rates of pathological gambling also have the highest rates of addictive substance consumption.[87] However, a study of 46 patients admitted to a German gambling treatment facility suggested that substance abuse may be differentially associated with different types of gambling. Although 22 or nearly half (48%) of these patients were either periodic or chronic substance abusers only two (4.3%) subjects in the entire sample were diagnosed as alcohol dependent or addicted. Nevertheless, far more slot machine players (42%) than roulette players (16%) abused alcohol while more roulette players (21%) than machine players (4%) abused pain killers or sleeping medicines after gambling.[88] While this hypothesis is intriguing, it will require further testing with larger samples.

Some findings suggest that among alcoholics and drug addicts, gambling that was once merely problematic often becomes fully pathological when they quit drinking and using drugs. For this reason one treatment specialist warns that "One should always be cautious of the recovering alcoholic who starts to gamble."[89] A previously mentioned study of incarcerated female gamblers also found an interesting pattern of drug use and gambling among these women: although the majority used these substances while they gambled, they tended to gamble less when drugs were available but to gamble more when they were not. This pattern suggested that these individuals simply alternated between drugs and gambling to satisfy a generalized addictive drive.[90] A somewhat similar pattern was reported in a study which found a low (8%) incidence of drinking among pathological gamblers before treatment but an increase in alcohol use after they had stopped gambling.[91] Similar reciprocal patterns of drug use have also been reported among substance abusers.[92]

Although the authors of some of these studies have interpreted their findings to mean that the source of all addictive and polyaddictive behaviors can be traced to the same underlying personality and/or learning factors, this same body of evidence could also point to the influence of genetic, biological, or sociocultural factors as common causes.[93] However, one medical researcher has suggested two other possibilities for this association: if gambling is primary, chemical dependency may represent the gambler's means of mustering the courage necessary to continue gambling; conversely, if chemical dependency is primary, gambling may represent the addict's means of obtaining the money necessary to continue drinking or using drugs.[94] Due to the lack of certainty, some investigators feel that further research will be required before this evidence can be considered conclusive.[95] Nevertheless, no matter what its cause may be, "multiple addiction appears to be a fact of life for many pathological gamblers."[96]

THE NATURE-NURTURE CONTROVERSY IN MENTAL HEALTH AND ADDICTION STUDIES

Developments in addiction theory appear to be based on those which have taken place in the study of other psychiatric disorders. For example, the search for the cause of schizophrenia has led to the emergence of countless theoretical explanations. However, more than a generation ago all of these approaches were seen to fall into three broad categories which were referred to as life experience theories, monogenic-biochemical theories, and diathesis-stress theories.[97] Essentially, the first referred to explanations that attributed the disorder to environmental causes, the second to biological or genetic causes, and the third to a combination of biological and environmental influences. More specifically, diathesis-stress theory maintains that it is not the abnormality *per se* that is inherited, but merely a predisposition for it. Thus, development of the latent disorder must be triggered by a sufficiently stressful experience. Each of these major categories has its analogue in theories which attempt to explain addictive behaviors.

Despite the many different views of addiction, modern etiological or causal theories of gambling are also of several major types, each of which claims explanatory primacy. As has been the case among students of other addictions,[98] the "nature-nurture" controversy over why human beings behave as they do has not bypassed the field of gambling studies. Consequently, many researchers have tended to align themselves with one or the other of these two camps. On one hand are those who believe that all addictive behaviors are purely a matter of "nurture," or of learning and experience; on the other are those who are equally convinced that all addictions are largely a consequence of "nature," or of biology and genetically determined predisposition. It has generally been the case that most "talk therapists," behavioral psychologists, and sociologists who see these behaviors as lying along a continuum from moderate to severe align themselves with the first camp. This viewpoint assumes that, biologically, all people are basically the same and that pathological gambling and other addictive behaviors are essentially a matter of degree commensurate with one's life experiences. Conversely, medical professionals who endorse the precepts of biopsychiatry and biopharmacology tend to favor the second approach since they regard addicts as qualitatively (physiologically and/or genetically) different from social or occasional participants in these behaviors. Members of Gamblers Anonymous, Alcoholics Anonymous, and other self-help groups which have come into being to provide help and understanding for addicts of all kinds also tend to regard addictions as organically-based illnesses.

The strength of the convictions of some of those in either camp that theirs is the only valid approach sometimes borders on the religious. It has therefore been suggested that

The most serious problem of definition seems to be its usual sequel–an attempt to provide **the** explanation of gambling, that is to seek a single underlying process, mechanism, set of factors or whatever that accounts for gambling in all its manifestations. This is a well-known state of affairs in Psychology, and can often be misguided.[99]

For this reason gambling researchers have been warned that theories can act as perceptual filters which serve to limit our research and treatment options: exclusive adherence to any single theory cannot only lead to misconceptions concerning the nature of gambling but can also blind one to the value of any other approach.[100] More recently, therefore, a number of researchers and clinicians from both camps have begun to regard addiction as the consequence of a combination of environmental and biological influences.

SCIENTIFIC APPROACHES

Whether "it" is merely a form of entertainment, a habit, an impulse control disorder, a form of physiological dependence, a combination of these factors, or something else entirely has yet to be decided. Nevertheless, in the face of this confusion a number of scientific approaches to gambling and pathological gambling have emerged.

Most theories seeking to explain pathological gambling define it as symptomatic of either a sick mind, a sick body, or a sick society; more recent approaches attribute it to various combinations of these causes. One of the earliest and most persistent theoretical explanations for pathological gambling is the psychoanalytic, psychodynamic, or Freudian model which regards all addictions, including pathological gambling, as a deep-seated intrapsychic or basic personality problem.[101] Learning, behavioral, or reinforcement models regard all behaviors, whether excessive or not, as a matter of learning or habituation and explain persistent gambling in terms of rewards, reinforcements, and learned associations.[102] Cognitive psychological models explain gambling persistence as a consequence of the erroneous beliefs gamblers have about gambling and the false hopes they have about their ability to win.[103] The sociological, environmental, or subcultural model postulates that all potentially addictive behaviors, whether "normal" or pathological, result from the temporary pleasure, satisfaction, or relief they provide the participant in the face of stressful crisis situations,[104] or as the result of social expectations where such behaviors are accepted and encouraged.[105] The medical, disease, or physiological model seeks the cause in human biology.[106] The most recent multicausal, multifactorial, or biopsychosocial, approach attributes pathological gambling and other addictive disorders to various combinations of endogenous and exogenous factors.[107]

Statistical models employ mathematical methods for measuring and ascertaining the nature and extent of various behaviors including normative and pathological gambling. Some statistical studies such as prevalence surveys are primarily descriptive in nature since they focus almost exclusively on the frequencies of these behaviors in a given population.[108] Others such as risk-factor analyses are primarily correlational in that they attempt to ascertain which psychological, personality, demographic, social, and other environmental variables are associated with these behaviors and may therefore be considered at least partially responsible for them.[109] Still other statistical studies are undertaken to test hypotheses that have been advanced by others.[110]

The general features of each of these approaches and a number of specific examples will be reviewed in this series. Many of these theories will strike the reader as highly plausible, some as questionable, and others as patently ludicrous. Since each of these approaches has had its vociferous and highly persuasive champions, all competing with one another to attract the greatest number of adherents, all have at one time or another gained wide but often uncritical acceptance as entirely valid explanations. Consequently, many of the more popular theories, as well as some of the research studies designed to test them, will also be critically examined to point out some of their more obvious weaknesses and strengths.

The goal of this endeavor is to draw the reader's attention to the many divergent explanations which have been proposed to account for both moderate and immoderate gambling and, hopefully, to equip the reader to avoid some of the hazards of blind adherence to any single approach. It will be seen that gambling theorists can be every bit as partisan and intolerant of opposing viewpoints as any politician or preacher. In the past the explanations of many were derived almost exclusively from the precepts of their own particular field. Thus, behavioral scientists tended to look for and find answers to the phenomena they investigated in psychological maladaptations, social scientists attributed theirs to various social forces, and medical scientists contended that biological factors lay at the heart of these matters. As a consequence, many specialists were often reluctant to see any value in those coming from any other discipline. Fortunately, however, recent years have seen a move away from such parochialism.

A NOTE ON GENDER BIAS

The male-orientated gender bias which has tended to dominate gambling research, particularly in its earlier days, has been justifiably criticized.[111] Apparently, many early clinicians, researchers, and other authorities believed either that most women avoided potentially addictive behaviors, or that they were somehow immune to many addictive disorders, or that the occurrence of these disorders among women was so rare as to be negligible. In fact, one early psychologist and gambling researcher reflected the strong gender bias of his day by attributing the differences he observed in the willingness of young males and females to take risks to their inherent evolutionary biological differences:

> The fact that the boys' curve rises, as the ages approach those of maturity, we believe to be in line with the general biological thesis of the male being the more iconoclastic, exploiting and venturesome element, while the fact, that the curve of the girls falls, is, on the other hand, in line with the biological thesis, that woman is the conservative and cautions element.[112]

In reality, as many women gamble as men. Although women tend to gamble less frequently than men overall, certain forms of gambling such as electronic machines attract high-frequency gamblers in equal numbers from both sexes[113] while bingo and video poker machines appear to be particularly attractive to women. Moreover, population studies have determined that at least one-third of all pathological gamblers are women.[114] In Las Vegas, the traditional gambling capital of the United States, more than half the members of Gamblers Anonymous are women.[115] Nevertheless, the gender bias of many gambling researchers, particularly those of earlier generations, will be reflected in the extensive use of male pronouns throughout much of the discussion. This bias has been retained so that the original tenor of the ideas, perspectives, and thought processes of the various theoreticians under discussion might be more accurately conveyed.

INTRODUCTION TO THIS VOLUME

This is the second in a series of books intended to review and evaluate the most popular and influential explanations for gambling and the many research studies that have been conducted to confirm or refute them. This volume focuses on the contributions of specialists in the social sciences, most of whom are convinced that gambling is a consequence of the social or sub-cultural environment in which the gambler lives.

Theoretical explanations for gambling in the social sciences have been generated primarily from two distinctly different approaches: qualitative studies involving observational, participant observational, and interview research methods with relatively few informants and quantitative studies involving survey research methods and statistical analyses of the responses obtained from larger population samples. However, the ideas of a number of earlier social scientists appear to have been influenced by the medieval philosophical notion that all questions can be answered through reason alone without any need for field research. As a consequence, the contributions of these "armchair" pedagogues were based more on speculation than empirical observation. In contrast to the views of contemporary economists who see gambling as a form of entertainment which is paid for by gambler's losses, the ideas of earlier economists who attempted to describe human risk-taking behavior in terms of precise mathematical formulas might also be considered "armchair" theory.

The early lack of empirical research prompted later investigators to go to places where gambling occurs and actually spend time among and interact with the gamblers who frequent them. While their research offers valuable insights, many were more observers than participants in the forms of gambling they studied. To further our understanding of why people gamble, others became participant observers in various gambling establishments by becoming employed as roulette croupiers or card dealers. Some attended meetings of Gamblers Anonymous as an adjunct to their investigations. However, like the nonparticipant observers who preceded them, their conclusions also represent the perspective of the detached social scientist.

A few intrepid social scientists entered the field not as observers but as actual gamblers. They often spent years at racetracks, cardrooms, casinos, and sometimes even in illegal gambling situations. In most cases they were already so involved in gambling that their research was conducted almost as an afterthought. Through the lasting friendships they made with other gamblers they become thoroughly enmeshed in the gambling subculture before writing about their experiences. These insiders are able to offer highly insightful descriptions of gambling from the unique perspective of the committed gambler.

Statistical studies of gambling, which began to appear in the mid-1960s, generally attempt to determine not only what proportion of a population gambles, but also which demographic groups are the most and least active gamblers and, often, why they are so. Some studies are largely descriptive while others are largely correlational in nature although most incorporate elements of both statistical approaches. Information for these studies is generally obtained from questionnaire surveys, some of which include sections on the respondents' attitudes toward gambling.

Initially, most statistical studies of gambling behavior were designed to test specific hypotheses. The conclusions of correlational studies are typically based on the presence or absence of statistically significant, hence, possibly causal, relationships between the incidence of gambling and certain cultural, demographic, socioeconomic, behavioral, and attitudinal variables. Statistical significance means that the associations that emerge between rates of gambling and other variables are probably not due to chance alone. Research scientists determine significance by subjecting their numerical data to various mathematical tests which are then accepted as rigorous scientific proof of their hypotheses concerning the causes of human behavior. When a correlation meets a standard test of statistical significance, the hypothesis it was designed to test can be accepted, at least temporarily; if significance is not attained, the hypotheses must be rejected.

Some quantitative studies are designed purely for market research to assess the gambling frequencies, intensities, and preferences of various demographic groups. Such studies are generally sponsored by commercial gaming interests to help them target potential customers. Others focus on special populations such as females, children, and adolescents to determine the extent to which they are involved in gambling and the impacts that it may be having on their lives. Irrespective of their goals, however, the results of almost all quantitative studies have at least some theoretical relevance, even though it may be incidental to their original intent.

In their quest to quantify gambling behaviors, habits, and preferences, countless investigators have administered countless survey questionnaires to countless respondents. It would therefore be beyond the scope of this volume to attempt to review all of them. The following discussion will instead be limited to summaries of the most important of these studies and a representative number of those of lesser importance.

PART I

EARLY "ARMCHAIR" APPROACHES

The Role of Speculation

Chapter 1

GAMBLING AND SOCIAL STRUCTURE

Despite its tremendous popularity in Western and non-Western societies alike, gambling initially received relatively scant attention from social scientists. This early lack of interest in scientific studies of gamblers and gambling has been attributed to the general disapproval of, and stigma associated with, gambling in general. According to one characterization of this situation, "The professional literature on gambling. . .largely ignores gambling as a normal part of human behavior, treating it much as the Victorians treated sex."[1] Even in academic circles the *study* of gambling was for a long time deemed to be unacceptable merely because the *act* of gambling was unacceptable.[2] Those who did deal with the subject were generally "armchair" sociologists who did little actual fieldwork and assumed it to be a deviant behavior. The last several decades have witnessed a definite shift in attitude and approach, and a profusion of empirically-based scholarly publications on gambling which demonstrate that it is an entirely normal and sometimes even a culturally mandated behavior.

THORSTEIN VEBLEN: GAMBLING AS A DIVERSION FOR THE LEISURED UPPER CLASSES

One of the earliest sociological approaches to gambling was that of Thorstein Veblen who attempted to explain its popularity among the upper classes.[3] In so doing he adopted the cultural evolutionary orientation of nineteenth-century social scientists who looked to the prehistoric past in their quest to discover the origins of all present social customs and conventions. These "armchair anthropologists" were firmly convinced that all societies–including those of Western European derivation–had passed through the identical sequence of sociocultural developmental stages, beginning with savagery and passing through barbarism before attaining the fully civilized status they now enjoyed. From this perspective Veblen postulated that gambling is a behavioral survival from our barbarian heritage during which human beings gave full vent to their inherent predatory impulses.

Although gambling itself may be a survival from our barbaric past, Veblen, on the basis of early anthropological thought,[4] believed that our modern day belief in luck represents a cultural survival or vestige from a much earlier primeval age when the belief in and manipulation of spiritual forces were integral parts of daily life. Since today's gamblers still believe that the outcome of future events can be foreseen and influenced, Veblen argued that modern forms of gambling are ultimately an outgrowth of ancient divinatory rites which had their basis in the animistic beliefs of our most primitive savage ancestors. As our forbears abandoned their old beliefs the rites that were once associated with them gradually became more secularized. Consequently, these rites eventually lost their original sacred meanings and assumed new and increasingly more profane ones pertinent to emerging social and cultural developments. Thus, Veblen maintained, in modern stratified and highly class-conscious Western society, gambling has taken on connotations appropriate to this situation.

Since Veblen's focus was on the values and behaviors of the upper class—which to the nineteenth-century mind obviously represented the most highly civilized segment of modern society—Veblen suggested that gambling, like many other customary pursuits of the idle rich, had survived primarily as a means for demonstrating conspicuous consumption and conspicuous leisure and, hence, their inherent superiority over the less affluent classes. Since "esteem is awarded only on evidence,"[5] the mere possession of wealth and power is not enough to maintain it. He therefore saw gambling and the apparent indifference to money it entails as having an important prestige value. As an overt indicator of wealth it constitutes a powerful symbolic affirmation of one's elevated social status through which one gains entrée into, and reaffirms one's standing among, the ranks of the social elite.

Veblen may well have been influenced by Fyodor Dostoevsky who, some 30 years earlier, had described in *The Gambler* the cool, unemotional gambling demeanor of the wealthy aristocrats he had personally witnessed in the casinos of Europe:

> A gentleman . . . may bet five or ten louis d'or, rarely more, though he may bet as much as a thousand francs if he is very rich, but solely for the sake of the game as such, simply for amusement, and actually only in order to watch the process of winning or losing, but must on no account display an interest in winning per se. If he wins, he may, for instance, laugh aloud, he may remark something to one of the bystanders, he may even place another bet or double his stakes, but solely out of curiosity, for the sake of watching the chances or even calculating them, never out of a plebian desire to win. In a word, he must look

upon all these gaming tables, roulette wheels, and trente et quarante sets as no more than a pastime, arranged entirely for his amusement.[6]

Veblen, who felt that the extent of people's gambling would be commensurate with the size of their income and therefore positively related to social class, was apparently unaware of the popularity and extent of gambling among the masses. Dostoevsky, however, was very much aware of gambling's other side since he had also written,

> One thing that struck me as particularly unpleasant . . . about the riffraff lining the roulette tables, was their respect for the business at hand, the seriousness and even reverence with which they all were crowding around the tables. This is why a sharp distinction is drawn here between the kind of game which is called *mauvais genre*, and the kind which a decent person might indulge in. There are two kinds of gambling: the genteel kind, and the plebian or mercenary, such as that played by all sorts of riffraff. The distinction is observed here and how base it really is![7]

> He [the aristocratic gambler] must not even suspect the existence of the mercenary motives and snares upon which the bank is founded and built. In fact, it wouldn't be a bad idea at all if he thought, for instance, that all this rabble, trembling over a gulden, were men of great wealth and gentlemen entirely like himself, and that they too, were gambling solely for diversion and entertainment.[8]

Despite his failure to recognize that gambling attracted people from all levels of society, Veblen did manage to attract a limited following as his ideas are echoed in the work of several later sociologists. Thus, it has been more recently proposed that "the higher the social class, the greater the propensity to gamble."[9] Although Veblen's explanations were entirely speculative and largely fanciful, his greatest contribution to the science of society is that he generated considerable empirical research by others who have attempted to confirm or repudiate his ideas.

GAMBLING AS A PURSUIT OF THE SOCIALLY DEVIANT AND DISENFRANCHISED LOWER CLASSES

Later sociologists, in their attempts to understand and explain a variety of major social problems, also focused on class differences but held that gambling is negatively related to social class. Such aphorisms as "Nothing ventured, nothing gained," and "If at first you don't succeed, try, try, again," demonstrate that gambling and persistence are positive values that are deeply entrenched in the Western capitalistic sociocultural tradition. Nevertheless, many early sociologists, apparently strongly influenced by the moral model, portrayed gambling negatively as a deviant, escapist, criminal, or some other antisocial form of behavior typical of lower class behaviors in general. One reason for this is that in Victorian England gambling was perfectly legal for the wealthy who could attend the Derby and other well-publicized races but illegal for all others who could only bet through bookmakers.[10] Some sociologists included professional gamblers among society's core social deviants along with prostitutes, delinquents, criminals, jazz musicians, bohemians, gypsies, carnival workers, show people, homosexuals, hobos, winos, and the urban poor. Such marginal types were described as failures not only lacking in piety but also exhibiting a flagrant disrespect for their social superiors.

Legalized commercial gambling was commonly believed to be just one of the many enterprises promoted and controlled by a vast organized criminal network. Academic as well as popular writers have held gambling accountable for irresponsibility, indolence, financial ruin, poverty, divorce and the breakup of families, graft, criminal activities, and a host of other social ills. After reviewing the literature on gambling, one sociologist wrote, "That gambling, particularly when legally sanctioned, and criminality, racketeering, extortion, and corruption travel hand in hand has long been held as an article of faith by social scientists."[11] Another expressed the opinion that "There is, indeed, scarcely an evil in human society for which gambling has not, at one time or another, been blamed."[12] It was therefore condemned as a major social problem along with such vices as the sale and use of narcotics, prostitution, extortion, confidence schemes, labor racketeering, and police and political corruption.[13]

Because so many early social scientists were just as given to armchair speculation as the early psychoanalysts, many of their thoughts on human motivation and behavior were derived more from inference and contemporary ideology than from empirically obtained facts. And like the psychoanalysts, many sociologists also justified their stance on the basis of anecdotal evidence and individual case histories of pathological gamblers whose gambling had, indeed, ruined their lives.[14] Little consideration was given to the fact that such sensationalistic reports were in no way descriptive of the gambling practices of the general population. In the words of a sociologist who studied gambling in a working-class neighborhood of London, "To try . . . to enumerate the personality characteristics of *The Gambler*, when this group forms approximately 75 percent of the population under review, would not seem very illuminating."[15]

The limited amount of early sociological research on gambling was reviewed by James Frey[16] who recognized alienation, anomie, and structural-functional approaches to the problem. These theories attempt to explain the purpose or "function" that a social activity or institution serves in society. A number of social structural theories incorporate both sociological and economic dimensions and frequently include a decision-making dimension. Deviant behaviors such as gambling, it was held, are exhibited in reaction to the socioeconomic deprivations to which members of the lower classes are subjected.[17] Some advocates of these approaches[18] assumed that gamblers, as working class industrial wage-earners, are the hapless victims of capitalism. As such they have very little control over their own destiny, particularly in everyday life on the job, and so rarely have the opportunity to make any of their own decisions. Gambling, however, was thought to provide one of the few opportunities that these deprived members of society have for exercising control by weighing choices and making independent decisions. Although these approaches generally attribute gambling to the intellectual stimulation and gratification it provides, many also have Marxist and/or psychoanalytic overtones and there is often a great deal of overlap among them.

ALIENATION THEORY

Alienation, as the term is used by sociologists, refers to a condition in which certain individuals are removed from the decision-making processes which govern the greater part of their daily lives. Although this term has sometimes been equated with the lack of job satisfaction in general, it has more often been used in a specifically Marxian sense to describe the impotence of the working classes in complex industrialized and impersonal urban capitalistic societies. Many sociologists believe that the advent of modern industrialization, with its time clocks, monotonous assembly line labor, and large bureaucratic organizations, has caused workers to feel uncreative, isolated, unable to exercise any initiative, and lacking any meaning of control in their lives.[19] Consequently, many of the first sociologists to consider gambling attributed it to the strong feelings of alienation encountered by a large segment of society. Some also incorporated a variant of the psychoanalytic frustration-aggression hypothesis into their explanations. These approaches maintained that those in Western industrial society who feel the greatest boredom, alienation, powerlessness, and frustration on the job will be those most likely to seek alternative means for restoring some meaning to their lives. For these individuals, trapped as they are at the low end of the industrial capitalistic social order, gambling provides an "escape hatch." It offers not only the possibility of wealth, but also a means of self-expression, thrill-seeking, an escape from a monotonous routine existence and poverty, and the attainment of power and prestige not normally available to them in their everyday lives.[20] According to this view, those who have the least control over their own lives–those in most menial positions and, hence, in the lowest socioeconomic strata–will be the heaviest gamblers:

> Gambling is an escape from the routine of boredom characteristic of much of modern industrial life in which the sense of creation and the "instinct of workmanship" have been lost. "Taking a chance" destroys routine and hence is pleasurable, particularly in a culture where the unchanging and predictable routines of employment are sharply separated from "leisure "–the time when the individual *really* lives.[21]

More recently this explanation has been proposed to account for gambling by an increasingly alienated middle class[22] and by children and adolescents.[23]

ANOMIE OR DEPRIVATION THEORY

Anomie, a sociological concept akin to alienation, refers to a condition in which a society's normative goals and the social values, behavioral standards, and customary means for attaining them are absent or unattainable due to inherent social inequalities. The inability of some people to realize these goals through the prescribed methods is believed to be a primary cause of social deviance. Sociologist Robert Merton's[24] initial exploration of anomie theory explained gambling and other "deviant" behaviors by reference to a conventional economic value-maximizational decision making model. According to Merton and the tenets of anomie theory, the ultimate goal of life in capitalistic society is financial success, but the existing socioeconomic system denies certain segments of society equal access to this goal. Among the options available to those who are unable to achieve success through approved channels (again, referring primarily to the lower socioeconomic classes) are illegal or unethical ones, such as crime, gambling, prostitution, etc. For Merton, then, it is the lack of opportunity for attaining financial success in socially sanctioned ways that accounts for the popularity and prevalence of gambling and other socially deviant pursuits among the socially and economically deprived segments of the population. In the words of another anomie theorist,

> gambling provides a function in well-organized societies where the stress of competition is great, and where, in contrast, the regimen of economic and

social life is rigorous. Such a society, placing a premium upon "risk" and "taking a chance," provides through gambling an outlet for many individuals who, hedged in by social restrictions and limited or no opportunity, would otherwise find little satisfaction for the need for new experience and pecuniary success.[25]

In short, anomie theory predicts that since gambling provides at least the possibility of social advancement, it should be more prevalent among those for whom access to material success is more restricted, but less prevalent among those for whom it is not restricted. Rates of gambling should therefore be inversely correlated with social class and with income levels within classes. In other words, anomie theory predicts that the more impoverished you are, the more likely you are to gamble.

STRUCTURAL-FUNCTIONAL ANALYSES

Structural-functional analyses draw heavily from drive-reduction theory. One of the fundamental assumptions of structural-functionalism is that all social customs and institutions necessarily serve some positive purpose or "function" in society: if this were not the case they would either be successfully eradicated by the social pressures brought to bear against them or they would simply disappear by themselves due to their lack of utility. Some structural-functionalists have employed an "organismic" or "organic" analogy to describe the situation as they saw it. Like the human body, they insisted, society is a living organism whose different social institutions are comparable to different vital organs (heart, lungs, liver, brain, etc.) Each and every organ (institution) is so essential to the life of the whole organism (society) that it would be unable to survive without them. It was the task of the structural-functional theorist to discover and describe the ways in which an institution contributed to the preservation of society.

The positive functions that sociologists most often ascribed to any social institution were (1) reducing the overall levels of stress and anxiety of a group (tension-reduction models) and (2) maintaining the existing social structural order or *status quo* by strengthening the social cohesion of its members (social solidarity or structural equilibrium models). Many structural-functionalists ascribed both functions to various social phenomena by claiming that societal equilibrium is maintained by an institution's ability to reduce tension.

EDWARD DEVEREUX: SOCIETY'S SAFETY VALVE

The most extensive sociological study of gambling, and one which incor-porated many of the tenets of earlier sociologists, was undertaken in the mid-twentieth century by Edward Devereux whose doctoral dissertation repre-sented a classic structural-functional analysis.[26] Essentially, Devereux sought to explain why gambling was so strongly condemned in Western society and why it persisted so tenaciously despite this condemnation. In accordance with the principles of structural-functionalism, Devereux rejected the notion that gambling is always a negative, irrational or deviant individual behavior and attempted to determine the ways in which gambling, gamblers, and gambling organizations are structurally integrated into society. He therefore felt that gambling must fulfill one or more strong, basic social needs. In keep-ing with the typical structural-functionalistic orientation of the day, and drawing heavily from Weber's ideas on the relationship between capitalism and the Protestant ethic, he determined those needs to be the reduction of tension and the maintenance of social equilibrium and solidarity. He then offered a standard psychoanalytic frustration-aggression explanation tinged with Marxism in defense of these conclusions.

Gambling and the Protestant Ethic. Devereux noted that the values of modern Western industrial society are inconsistent with the realities of life for most of its members. Contradictions between the values of capitalist eco-nomics and those of the puritan Protestant ethico-religious system generate a great deal of tension, ambivalence, and conflict among a large segment of the population. More specifically, the highest values of capitalism are competi-tion and individualism, acquisitiveness and consumption, hedonism and self-aggrandizement, and wealth and leisure for their own sake. However, these values are in direct opposition to those of Protestant Christianity which stress cooperation and love of one's neighbor, hard work and thrift, humility and self-denial, charity and other altruistic good works, and contentment with one's lot in life. Even some values within capitalism—consumption as opposed to thrift, risk as opposed to caution, competition as opposed to cooperation—conflict with one another to create social tensions and attitudi-nal ambivalence. Furthermore, in theory anyone living in a capitalistic sys-tem can become financially independent. In reality, however, not everyone can accomplish this since the proper, socially sanctioned avenues for advancement are not equally accessible to all people. The inability to attain success is therefore frustrating and stressful to the majority of society's mem-bers but prevailing Christian values act to prevent any overt expression of the hostile and aggressive emotions that this frustration engenders. Finally, entrepreneurial pursuits provide opportunities for independent decision making, risk-taking, thrill-seeking, and, of course, the accumulation of wealth which are in accord with the dictates of capitalism but which most members of Western society are denied. The frustration and tension that result from these conflicting social values must somehow be reduced and dispelled.

Gambling, in which rewards are derived from chance instead of hard work, is condemned by its censors since it is antithetical to the principles of capitalism and puritanism.[27] By fostering sloth, indolence, and superstition it threatens the Protestant ethical doctrine that rewards and advancements must always derive from hard work, rationality, and devotion to Judeo-Christian dictates and deities. Nevertheless, gambling has many features in common with capitalism since it involves decision making, risk, and the potential for large returns that are not ordinarily available to common people. Moreover, the winnings that do happen to befall a few lucky working class gamblers are never wisely invested in business ventures; they are quickly squandered on frivolities, unnecessary luxuries, and additional betting.

Gambling and hope. Its negative sanctions notwithstanding, gambling has not disappeared and, Devereux assumed, it must therefore serve some positive functions apart from the chance of winning money and accumulating wealth. For the lower classes, he argued, it offers hope for those otherwise unable to escape from the life of toil and budgetary requirements they must constantly observe. It also represents a symbolic means of protest against the economic inequities of capitalism, against the need for unremitting rationality, and against the Puritanical Christian ethical constraints that are inherent in Western society. Moreover, some forms of gambling are socially sanctioned. Horse racing in particular not only provides a temporary escape from the vicissitudes of a reality that is otherwise inescapable, but it also constitutes a sublimated expression of entrepreneurial decision making, speculative risk-taking, and hedonistic thrill-seeking which are ordinarily denied most people (**alienation theory**). Legitimated as a "sport," horse racing is also an enjoyable form of entertainment which is readily available to all classes of people and through which one can interact with a particular social group in the particular context of one's choice.

Gambling and the status quo. Devereux concluded that since the true nature of capitalism cannot be acknowledged by its beneficiaries or revealed to its victims, gambling provides an ideal scapegoat which is blamed for keeping the masses in a state of perpetual impoverishment. It is therefore essential to the middle and upper class defenders of capitalism since it provides an indispensable tool that serves to preserve a social system which will permit their continued exploitation of the masses. Thus, Devereux argued, gambling is good for everyone since it serves all classes of society: it not only allows the low-paid worker to blow off a little steam, but it lets him have a little fun and feel like a big shot in the process; it also lets his exploitative employer sleep with a clear conscience.

Residence, anomie, and deviance. Devereux also made a number of predictions concerning the incidence of gambling. Since it has always been so strongly condemned by the Calvinistic tradition, he advanced a **rural-urban residence** or **community size hypothesis** which predicts that gambling will be less prevalent in small towns and rural areas. He explained this phenomenon by reference to a **religion hypothesis** which predicts that gambling will be less prevalent where the Protestant ethic has deeper roots and still prevails. It should also tend to become more common as one moves out of these areas and into larger and more cosmopolitan urban centers where this religious orientation is weakest. However, even in larger population centers gambling should be less common among a community's middle class religious and business leaders who endeavor to transmit their conservative puritan values, but more prevalent among the lower and working classes who have become disillusioned by them. Since gambling is inconsistent with the traditional middle class commitment to one's job, family, neighborhood, church, and the idea that rewards accrue through one's efforts and achievements, it will be most common among those who do not share these values (**anomie theory**). On this basis, and because most forms of gambling were illegal at the time, Devereux speculated that it would be heaviest among the criminal element and slum dwellers who have rejected or have never adopted middle-class values (**deviance theory**). However, he also thought it would be relatively heavy among the upper classes who have no need of these values and who regard gambling as a symbolic indicator of their wealth and status (Veblen's **leisure class theory**).

Decision making. Despite his emphasis on the social functions and influences of gambling, Devereux[28] also gave some thought to individual considerations. Racetrack bettors, he believed, are not likely to ascribe either their successes or failures to fate or chance alone but to strengths and weaknesses in their own knowledge and abilities. In this respect Devereux anticipated the ideas of later attribution theorists who stress the importance of one's locus of control orientation in the genesis of problem gambling. He also anticipated some of the ideas of others including play theorist Roger Caillois and interactional theorist Erving Goffman.

Summary

In the final analysis, Devereux argued that gambling functions positively as Western society's "safety valve" and "shock absorber" since it offers hope, an explanation that appealed strongly to some later theorists.[29] It persists among the masses since it affords them fantasies and opportunities that capitalism cannot. It is tolerated by the ruling elite since it not only provides a ready scapegoat for the social inequalities inherent under capitalism, but it also serves as an effective means of social control for its censors by defusing the hostile and aggressive impulses of the lower classes. In this way, Devereux maintained that gambling contributes toward the preservation and maintenance of the existing social order by providing a substitute for other, more disruptive forms of protest against Western society's inherent inequities and attitudinal ambivalence.[30] In essence, he concluded, gambling protects the privileged and maintains the status quo by reducing tension among the masses.

CRITIQUE OF SOCIAL STRUCTURAL ANALYSES

All social structural models, including alienation, anomie, deprivation, and deviance theories, are essentially structural-functional approaches since they all relate the motivations for gambling to the existing social system. Although these approaches are intuitively attractive, they are seriously flawed. According to one critic[31] the greatest defects of these approaches are that (1) like psychoanalytic theory, they are empirically untestable, and (2) they treat the consequences of an activity as its causes or "functions." Furthermore, such terms as "boredom," "alienation," and "frustration" as they are employed in sociological analyses are imprecisely defined and, hence, inconsistently used. He asked, for example, at what point do these conditions motivate gambling? Why should different people react differently to these conditions? Why exactly should they lead to gambling instead of a multitude of other alternatives? Consequently, such terms are of "meagre analytical value."[32] Moreover, a study which correlated attitudes toward gambling with alienation found that those who were more alienated tended to hold significantly stronger antigambling attitudes than those who were less alienated.[33] Another, which correlated self-esteem with a number of addictive behaviors, found no relationship between gambling and low self-esteem,[34] a factor which some theorists assumed to be of primary motivational importance.[35] Nevertheless, alienation, anomie, and deprivation are still held by some social researchers to be the primary motivations for gambling among the socially marginal disenfranchised classes.[36]

It has also has been pointed out that Devereux's functionalistic "safety valve" hypothesis could account for the rapid expansion of state lotteries, but its utility in explaining such middle- and upper-class casino games as blackjack and baccarat is highly questionable.[37] Moreover, if gambling did serve as a "safety valve" for lower income groups, then overall rates of gambling should be expected to rise during economic depressions and to decline in times of prosperity. However, this phenomenon has not been observed. Perhaps the most realistic but still untested view of the purported relationship between gambling and current economic situations is that different forms of gambling will be affected differently by different conditions.[38] Thus, lottery expenditures might be expected to increase in hard times while casino expenditures might be expected to decrease.

The logical fallacy of *non causa pro causa*, or false cause, refers to arguments that incorrectly ascribe the cause of an event to something that is not its real cause. Social scientists have frequently been guilty of mistakenly attributing the consequences of the activities and social institutions they study for their causes when, in reality, the behavior in question may or may not have been initially motivated or continue to be motivated by any of the "functions" it is said to serve. The faulty logic inherent in the structural-functional paradigm is clearly illustrated when it is reduced to the level of absurdity. Driving while intoxicated, for example, often results in death but nevertheless persists despite strong negative sanctions against it. Therefore, it could be argued, it must have some positive value or "function" which outweighs its negative costs. It might then be proposed that despite the general disapproval with which it is met, drunk driving "functions" positively to reduce the stress of overcrowding and to preserve society as it now exists by serving as an effective and socially beneficial population control mechanism, and by creating employment in the fields of law enforcement, health care, and auto body repair. As another critic so cogently pointed out, while most such behaviors have both positive and negative ramifications, the "bad" clearly outweigh the "good" in such cases.[39]

Finally, the very antiquity of gambling invalidates social structural explanations. Having been widely practiced under all types of economic and religious systems in such diverse places as ancient Greece, Rome, Germany, Egypt, Mesopotamia, sub-Saharan Africa, China, India, and the pre-Columbian Americas, gambling predates the advent of stratified society, Christianity, and industrial capitalism by millennia. Its global popularity in tribal societies throughout the ages refutes any claim that its universal "functions" are in any way related to boredom, alienation, anomie, capitalism, or Christianity in modern Western societies.[40]

Nevertheless, structural-functionalism was so popular an approach and attracted such a wide following that its influence is still quite strong. Consequently, some recent social scientists have insisted that gambling serves an important function in modern affluent middle-class American society:

> We argue that commercial gambling caricatures the nineteenth-century ideology of enterprise—sober individual risk-taking, thrift, effort, and self-denial—that legitimated investment capitalism in a democracy. These values constitut-

ed what Max Weber called "the Protestant ethic," which is caricatured insofar as the gambler invests in the present—in a chance for immediate, materialistic rewards in an atmosphere of self-indulgence. Gambling thus exemplifies a reversal of American values: the ethic of saving, of self-denial and capital accumulation has been replaced by an ideology of hedonistic consumerism. . . . Today Americans eagerly consume disposable time and wealth. The accumulation of capital is no longer as important to most people as the search for ways to use money in pursuit of pleasure and status. The emphasis on consumption is quite functional in a modern capitalistic society. By embracing gambling and so enthusiastically caricaturing the work ethic of our parents, mainstream Americans truly mirror a historic cultural change.[41]

Although the tension-reduction and social solidarity explanations for gambling may be wanting, the "exercise of rationality" function of gambling found some support in the anecdotal evidence provided by Marvin Scott's[42] ethnographic study of racetrack gamblers. When asked why they played the horses, several of Scott's informants claimed they did so for the mental exercise it offered. In the words of one handicapper, "Why? I'm a tailor with a nice place and two helpers. So in the afternoons, maybe twice a week, I come to the track and buy a *Racing Form*, and make picks. For 40 years I do tailoring and don't have to think about it. . . . Here I can use my *kopf*."[43] Likewise, in reference to his skill at handicapping with the aid of the *Form*, a storeroom clerk responded, "I only went to the eighth grade, but I'd like to see the college boy that reads them little numbers like me."[44] According to Scott, these and the other examples he presented offered a serious challenge to the prevalent view of racetrack betting as a deviant occupation pursued solely for economic gain as Merton and other early sociologists maintained.

Chapter 2

GAMBLING AND ECONOMICS

Because economics makes up a branch of the social sciences, economic theories are closely related to sociological theories and the two are often complementary. The assumption that the prospect of acquiring money is the primary motivation for gambling and other forms of risk-taking is basic to many early economic theories of gambling just as it was to many early sociological theories. One of the most commonly held opinions about gambling is that it reflects the universal human desires to "get something for nothing" and to "get rich quick" thereby permitting the lucky winner to escape the insecurity and tedium of the work a-day world in which most people must live.[1] These ideas appear to garner a great deal of support from studies which conclude that gambling, particularly in forms which have low costs and potentially high payoffs, is primarily a lower class pursuit.[2] It is therefore commonly held that gambling

> offers a chance, however slender, of economic mobility to those who have no other means of transforming their circumstances. The vast majority simply have no legal way to procure a fortune, no matter how hard they work or how intelligent they are. Against this background, lotteries with small costs and high winnings seem a sensible alternative.[3]

Some researchers maintain that the appeal of lotteries derives solely from the chance they offer their players to win very large amounts of money while risking only very small amounts. Any psychological or social aspects of lottery playing are purely secondary.[4] In the words of a Canadian economist who has studied the phenomenon, "the typical Canadian lottery buyer seems to be a person who seeing all other avenues of success closed turns to lottery as his chance of improving his lot; buying some tickets means a few bottles of beer less. But winning the big prize means a great deal."[5]

The economic approach also receives considerable support from the responses of actual gamblers who were asked to explain their own reasons for gambling. A large survey of 60,000 respondents found that 70 percent of those who gambled said that they did so for money.[6] A similar study of 25,000 people some years later found that 75 percent of the gamblers and 20 percent of the nongamblers also cited economic motivations for their respective choices.[7] A more recent study of lottery players found that nearly all (93%) of those surveyed played in hopes of winning and becoming rich.[8] Likewise, according to a sociologist who studied gambling among Britain's working classes,

> The plain fact is that, within the situational reality of the majority of working men, gambling makes sense. Their avowed reason is almost exclusively pecuniary, the primary articulated motivation is overwhelmingly the quest for money. Ask the working man why he gambles and he will justify his action in economic terms. Is not, after all, the daily loss of his small sums an insignificant price to pay for the hope of a big strike. . . ?[9]

As will soon be evident, in their attempt to achieve scientific rigor and precision, economic theories also introduced mathematics into the study of human behavior.

VALUE-MAXIMIZATIONAL OR EXPECTED UTILITY THEORIES AND DECISION MAKING

Value-maximizational decision models of human behavior assume that people always act in their own self-interest. Adherents of these models contend that whenever they are faced with an economic decision, people will choose whichever option they perceive as being the most potentially rewarding or, in the language of economics, as having the greatest expected value or utility. Thus, a further assumption of these models, which are also known as *rational choice theories*, is that nearly all people, including gamblers, are rational decision makers who carefully weigh three factors before making any choice involving money and other valued commodities: the initial cost, the potential payoff, and the probability that the desired outcome will occur. It is therefore assumed that whether he is in an executive board room or a casino, the rational or "economic man" will endeavor to maximize the value of his expenditure by choosing a course of action having the lowest cost, the greatest payoff potential, and the highest probability of occurrence.

A number of economists have felt that human economic behavior is generally guided by certain scientific "laws" of consumption which can be described by rigorous mathematical formulas. Based on the assumptions that, as a group, "consumers are self-interested, goal oriented, and rational,"[10] and that they seek to derive as much satisfaction or "utility" from their purchases and investments as possible, these formulas have been devised to provide a means of distinguishing potential decisions that are more rational from those that may be less so. Adjustable for the different risk tolerances of different individuals, a number of such formulas, incorporating initial costs, potential payoffs, and outcome probabilities, have therefore been proposed to calculate the expected value or utility of all potentially risky ventures. It should be emphasized that these formulas are descriptive rather than predictive. They were not intended to suggest that economic decision makers actually calculate every possible choice and compare every imaginable outcome before acting. Rather, they behave "as if" they know all the odds and act accordingly in much the same way that billiards players behave "as if" they calculate the trajectory and outcome of every possible shot and then act accordingly. Viewing economic behavior in this way circumvents the criticism that expected utility formulas are unrealistic.[11]

Most of the formulas that attempt to describe risk-taking behavior are based on Expected Value or Expected Utility Theory. Although they may appear as complex and imposing aggregates of arcane algebraic symbols to those who are not mathematically inclined, they merely state that ventures in which one's chances for gain are greater than one's chances for loss are rational while those in which one is more likely to lose are irrational. Put even more simply, they suggest that people will gamble if they think their chances of winning are better than their chances of losing or, as in the case of lotteries, if the likelihood of a small loss is counterbalanced by the possibility, no matter how remote, of a large win. Since the assumption that people risk capital or gamble to acquire wealth is often accepted as a given, what these formulas for risk are really attempting to describe is a process of rational economic decision making. Several of these formulas will be presented and briefly discussed below to provide a sense of their evolution from simpler to more complex forms.

Elementary expected utility theory. One of the simplest formulas for describing risk-taking behavior,

$$EV = P_W V_W + P_L V_L$$

states that the Expected Value or Utility (payoff) of a bet is a function of the Probability of Winning times the monetary Value of Winning plus the Probability of Loss times the monetary Value of Loss.[12] Like most expected value theories, it assumes that the goal of all speculation is the maximization of utility or wealth while the purpose of avoiding it is to minimize loss. When the result of the calculation is greater than zero or has a positive value the venture would be rational; when it less than zero or has a negative value it would be irrational.

The expected value or utility of any venture can also be understood as the average return it will yield if the same risk were taken repeatedly. Perhaps one of the simplest and most meaningful illustrations of all expected utility formulas is the common coin toss in which two parties each risk the same amount—one dollar, for example. Since there are only two possible outcomes (either the gain or loss of a dollar) and since the probability of either outcome is .5 (a "50-50" chance) the expected value for both parties is (.5 x $1) + (.5 x -$1) or zero, which makes it a "fair" bet. That is, neither party can expect to lose more than it can expect to win since the calculated result falls at a point precisely midway between gain and loss, or rationality and irrationality.

Casino games in which the expectation of winning is less than .5 for the player and greater than .5 for the house are "unfair" since they yield a negative expected utility for the player and a certainty of gain for the house. In other words, casino games are irrational from the point of view of the player but quite rational from the point of view of the house. This is evident in the fact that table games retain an average of about three cents out of every dollar wagered on them, which means that every player can expect to lose about three percent of all money wagered. Less rational games are slot machines which retain about 11 percent of all the money that is fed into them and bingo whose players lose an average of 26 percent of their money. Lottery games, which are the least rational or most "unfair" of all gambling games, cost the players an average of roughly half of all the money spent on them.[13] Any such house advantage means simply that the house is guaranteed to win while, as a group, the players are guaranteed to lose. It also means that even initially lucky players who experience an early big win must eventually lose if they continue to play long enough.

The Bernoulli model of multiple possibilities. One of the earliest economic models of risk was formulated in the mid-eighteenth century by Daniel Bernoulli.[14] Bernoulli proposed that the sum of *all* possible outcomes of a venture, $\Sigma(U)$, would provide a more accurate estimation of its utility than its expected value, EV, which he considered to be a naive measure. His formula for assessing the utility of a venture,

$$\Sigma(U) = \Sigma[U_1(X_1) \times P_1 + U_2(X_2) \times P_2 + \bullet\bullet\bullet + U_n(X_n) \times P_n]$$

(where $U_1(X_1)$, $U_2(X_2)$, $U_n(X_n)$ refer to the utility or value of outcomes 1, 2, etc., and P_1, P_2, and P_n refer to the probability of outcomes 1, 2, etc., respectively), appears to be far more complex than the simple EV model illustrated above but, in reality, it is not.

Bernoulli's model simply means that the expected utility of any venture can be calculated by multiplying the value of each possible outcome by its probability of occurrence and totalling the results. Like the simpler EV model, the venture would be rational if the result has a positive value and irrational if it is less than zero. If the data from our coin toss example were plugged into this formula the sum of the two expected utilities or $\Sigma(U)$ would also be +\$.50 -\$.50 or zero. In cases where many outcomes are possible, an average utility or expected value would be determined by dividing the sum of these products by the number of possible outcomes. On the basis of this formula Bernoulli argued that diversification of risk is rational and that since a monetary unit (Euro, dollar, pound, yen, etc.) has more value to poor than to wealthy people, bets between people of different degrees of wealth would be rational whereas those between people of equal wealth would be irrational. These ideas form the basis of modern investment theory.

Half a century later, in his classic economic treatise *The Wealth of Nations* Adam Smith[15] introduced a cognitive element when he argued that people participate in such irrational ventures as lotteries and other long shot bets, in which the probabilities of gain are highly negative, because their conceit and biased estimations of their own abilities or luck prompt them to overvalue their likelihood of gain and undervalue their likelihood of loss. Thus, the expected value of money often meant its *subjective* value which means that people's decisions are not always based on objective assessments. Some decision-making models since Bernoulli's have therefore incorporated this idea so that rather than calculating for *EU*, the economist calculates for *SEU*, or subjective expected utility. For example, the formula

$$SEU = S(P_W) \times U(\$_W) + S(P_L) \times U(\$_L)2$$

differs from the simple expected value formula only in that the variables represent subjective expectations[16] and means only that gamblers will bet on those outcomes which they believe will have the greatest payoff value. This also means that the decision-making process can become quite complex for some gamblers. For example, by strictly following his own rational betting system, the racetrack handicapper will sometimes bet on a horse that is more likely to lose than to win:

> Even if a player expects to lose a bet, the expected value of the play may be positive. For example, if the subjective probability of horse A is 2 to 1 and the odds are 5 to 1, and if the subjective probability of horse B is 1 to 1 and its odds are 1 to 1, the player will have a greater expected value from horse A, even if he is more certain that horse B will win.[17]

Adam Smith also pointed out that two parties might have different expectations or probabilities of gain and loss. In the example of the coin toss, if one
party stands to lose a dollar per toss while a second party stands to lose only
half a dollar, the gamble would be irrational for the first party but highly
rational for the second since the first party could expect to lose an average
of $.25 for every dollar wagered while the second party could expect to win
an average of $.50 per dollar wagered. The odds offered by most lotteries are
even longer and less fair since the sponsors risk nothing yet retain about half
of everything that is staked. The results of a number of scientific investigations of risk since then appear to verify the importance of subjective assessments, the relative importance that different people place on different values
and probabilities, and the importance of different and changing circumstances.[18]

The von Neumann and Morgenstern model of base wealth. One of the principal contemporary theories for explaining economic behavior under conditions of uncertainty is the Expected Utility Theory of John von Neumann
and Otto Morgenstern.[19] Unlike the models of Bernoulli and others, this
model incorporates a person's base wealth or net worth at the time of the
proposed venture. Stated in its formal formulaic fashion

$$V(\{w;p\}) = \Sigma_i p_i U(w_i)$$

this model predicts that an individual's decision to participate in any risk-
laden venture will be determined by his or her base wealth, the expected cost
of the venture, its potential reward, and the probability of realizing that
reward. A fundamental assumption of this theory is that, subjectively, a dollar holds more value for the poor than for the wealthy or, in the language of
economics, the marginal utility of wealth decreases as wealth increases. This
means only that the wealthy should be more prone to risk while the poor,
being more concerned about possible losses, should be more averse to risk.
The poor should therefore avoid it altogether or risk only small amounts.
This basic theme has a number of variations with different economists giving
more weight to one variable over another but all are intended to explain
rational economic decision-making behavior in general rather than gambling
behavior in particular.

The Friedman-Savage model of gambling and social climbing. The above
models have a common flaw in that they fail to take into account the tendency of so many people to engage in economic activities that tend to reduce
their net worth and therefore appear to violate the principles of expected utility theory. Specifically, the fact that so many people choose both to play lotteries and to take out insurance is inconsistent. People pay to take risks when
they gamble and pay to avoid risks when they buy insurance. In either case,

the end result is generally a monetary loss. Because expected utility theories predict that people are motivated to maximize their value, both gambling and buying insurance appear to be irrational. Nevertheless, both have a very strong appeal to many otherwise rational people.

This paradoxical situation was first addressed by Milton Friedman and L. J. Savage[20] who attempted to explain why people might make such "unfair" bets or otherwise assume risks in which a negative return can be expected. The answer, they reasoned, is that gambling offers hope while insurance offers protection and security: gambling offers hope for a level of wealth that is unattainable for most people while insurance offers protection against catastrophic losses which could obliterate one's present resources. The Friedman-Savage hypothesis which has become the "standard economic explanation of gambling"[21] therefore assumes risk-taking and risk-reduction to be functions of initial as well as potential (hoped for) levels of wealth. The formula

$$\bar{U}(A) = aU(I_1) + (1\text{-}a)U(I_2)$$

proposes that a person's expected utility after a wager can be calculated by adding (1) the probability of winning multiplied by the expected utility of his wealth if he wins to (2) the probability of losing multiplied by the expected utility of his wealth if he loses. According to this model, a proposed bet would be rational if the result is positive or greater than his present wealth but irrational if it is negative or less than his present wealth. The decision to jeopardize any money at all will also be enhanced as initial costs decrease and potential payoffs increase. To graphically illustrate their approach, Friedman and Savage plotted an "S-shaped" rather than a linear utility curve which could be used to chart the degrees of risk and likelihoods of success, hence, the rationality, of all proposed ventures. If the possible payoff or expected value fell above the utility curve it would be rational and should be taken; if it fell below the curve it would be irrational and should be avoided.

In essence, this model sees the different income levels and risk tolerances of different people as important considerations when economic decisions are made. Thus, those at lower levels of the socioeconomic ladder are far more likely to play lotteries in hopes of advancing socially than those who are already at the top and can climb no higher. Those at the very lowest level whose existence is already compromised should also tend to avoid buying lottery tickets since even small losses could mean severe hardship. However, even a modest increase in discretionary income should then encourage participation. Those at the higher levels will be more likely to take out insurance to protect themselves against losing their assets and slipping down the social ladder while those at the bottom who have relatively little to lose will tend to avoid insurance. The majority of society's members, those in the middle classes who want to protect what they already have and to climb even higher, will be most likely to buy both lottery tickets and insurance.

Some contemporary economic theorists, still contending that gambling is motivated primarily by the desire to climb the social ladder through the accumulation of wealth, feel that proclivities for gambling are determined more by particular social demographic conditions than by individual psychological or personality differences. Some, after considering the influence of such variables as income, household size, and age on people's decisions to gamble for greater wealth, have therefore added their own propositions to the Friedman-Savage hypothesis. It has been suggested, for example, that those of any class who have never played lotteries may suddenly begin to do so if they should happen to lose a portion of their wealth. Conversely, former players may abruptly stop once they have won a prize large enough to propel them into the desired status. Given similar household incomes, families with many children will have less money per member and will feel relatively poorer than families with fewer children. Since money has more value for the poor, people living in larger households should be more prone to gamble in hopes of raising their living standards than those living in smaller households. Likewise, since the elderly often have incomes that are smaller and more fixed than those of younger people who are still in the labor force, older people should feel poorer and therefore be more likely to gamble than younger.[22]

SUMMARY AND CRITIQUE OF EXPECTED UTILITY THEORY

All expected utility theories are intended to explain the decision-making behavior of the "economic man" and, by extension, the "economic gambler." According to the tenets of these models, "no 'economic man' would freely and willingly accept a decline in his level of utility because there is no self-interest in doing so."[23] Consequently, economically rational people are presumed to risk money for the sole purpose of maximizing utility. They are thought to act as though they had carefully considered every variable, had exhaustively reviewed every possible option and outcome, had weighed the likelihood of gain and how much they stand to gain against the likelihood of loss and how they stand to lose, and then to assume only those risks that they deem to be rational and profitable.[24] These theories therefore predict that whether they are investing, speculating, or gambling, people will tend to avoid risks that threaten to severely diminish their current level of wealth and will tend to take risks that offer the possibility of substantial gains but minimal damage to their present level of wealth. In reality, however, people will be more likely to gamble when their probability of winning is small–even millions to one against them–if the amount of money they stand to win is large compared to the amount they stand to lose, especially if they are in the lower and middle socioeconomic classes. Thus, lottery games among the working and middle classes are far more popular than stock options and commodities markets.

Some laboratory studies of risk-taking behavior appear to support utility theory. Studies of risk involving several variations of a carnival coin toss game reported that most players chose the variation from which they could derive the greatest expected value or return and had the least likelihood of loss.[25] The Friedman-Savage hypothesis has found at least some support in several large-scale statistical surveys. For example, at the macroeconomic or intersocietal level it was supported by an anthropological cross-cultural study which found that, in general, societies having the greatest degrees of social inequality also have the most highly evolved forms of gambling.[26] At the microeconomic level it was supported by a recent survey of lottery players in Cameroon which revealed that "the poorer elements of the population are the ones that are gambling relatively more. . . . Moreover, the nongambling population is somewhat richer."[27] The researchers therefore concluded that people whose means of advancement are limited will "turn to the lottery as a rational response that may be their only means of bettering themselves."[28] In another study a group of test subjects were asked to choose from a selection of different gambles to determine their payment for participating in the experiment. When their decisions were purely hypothetical they chose riskier gambles having higher potential payoffs but also having higher probabilities of loss. However, when they knew their choices would be binding they made less risky gambles having lower payouts but lower chances for loss.[29] The expected utility model also received at least partial support from an earlier study which found that Americans who spent the most money on lotteries were, in fact, those who expressed the greatest dissatisfaction with their present income.[30] Apparently, despite their astronomical odds against winning, many people of even the most modest means regard the price of a lottery ticket as cheap in comparison with the potential payoff of winning. However, income dissatisfaction failed to correlate with other kinds of gambling. In fact, among bingo, poker, and sports betting enthusiasts, those who were more satisfied with their current incomes were most likely to gamble.

While expected utility models may accurately describe the motivations and decision-making processes of the executives of profit-oriented commercial gaming and betting industries, they certainly do not apply to those of their customers since the behavior of gamblers is often far from rational. As noted above, Adam Smith's observation over 200 years ago that gamblers tend to overvalue long shots and undervalue safer, low odds bets provides one such example. As was also noted above, all casino games are "unfair" since they are designed to have a negative expected value for the player and a positive expected value for the house. Because these situations are far more likely to be costly than profitable, one critic maintains that "the gambler is incurring an expected cost (in the mathematical sense) every time he makes a wager."[31] Even though casino patrons may carefully allocate a certain amount for their visits, many end up spending more than they initially planned.[32]

Other critics[33] also argue that economic theories are incapable of providing an adequate explanation for gambling since the observable behavior of many gamblers does not conform to their hypothesized predictions. They maintain, for example, that gambling behavior does not alter dramatically with differences in wealth nor do gamblers always avoid high-risk situations to minimize their losses. Moreover, when they are in possession of essential information they often dismiss it as irrelevant. As noted above, a number of studies have reported that horse players tend to prefer the high paying but riskier and less rational "long shots" to the less risky and lower paying but more rational favorites. These observations are also apparent in other commercial gaming enterprises, whether they are privately owned or government sponsored, which offer only games that favor the house. From a purely economic standpoint, all lottery and casino games represent irrational risks for the players yet continually attract throngs of people from all walks of life. "Thus," one critic concluded, "economic explanations of gambling, though insightful, cannot fully explain this phenomenon."[34]

It has also been pointed out that the expected value models proposed above generally make several assumptions that are clearly not always valid. In the first place, they assume that the gambler will always choose one of the gambling alternatives available to him rather than deciding not to gamble at all. They further assume that the investor or gambler is always in full possession of the essential information pertaining to the costs, potential payoffs, and probabilities of occurrence of every venture and that they will carefully and exhaustively consider each of these variables. In reality, however, many economic and wagering decisions are based on incomplete or erroneous information.[35] It is also important to remember that the choices actual gamblers continually face and the decisions they must ultimately make are always subject to unforeseeable contingencies which do not remain constant and which cannot, therefore, be expressed in a rigid formulaic fashion.[36] These include time and money constraints, individual differences in the players' anticipated wins and losses, house rules governing minimum and maximum allowable bets, the randomness of the cost per dollar bet which continually changes with one's wins and losses, and the individual's ability to process all the information necessary to make an informed decision. These are all highly influential factors which not only vary over time for any single gambler, but which are never the same for all gamblers at any single time.

Finally, value-maximization theories appear to have no bearing at all on pathological or compulsive gamblers who appear to gamble only for the sake of gambling irrespective of their base wealth, of whether they can expect to win or lose, and of whether they actually are winning or losing. In the words of one prominent economic theorist, "when the discussion stretches into the area of pathological gambling, the concept of rationality that economic models take for granted must clearly come into question."[37]

Despite these problems, economic models of gambling and risk have become increasingly more complex as attempts have been made to replace the objective mathematical probabilities of gambling with people's subjective assessments of its "utility." Even then these models cannot take into account the biases interposed by such cognitive factors as hunches, wishful thinking, and the degree to which skill or luck is held to be a determining factor. Since different people gamble for different reasons, and since typical gamblers are constantly reevaluating their strategies and readjusting their expenditures, none of these factors can be held constant and therefore cannot be organized into precise mathematical formulas.[38] Thus, after reviewing the issue one critic characterized these models as a "sort of *ex post facto* accounting for empirical data" through "mathematical tinkering which obscures rather than provides explanation."[39] His investigation of them forced him to conclude that apart from lottery playing, "expectation theories have not had much success at providing satisfactory explanations for many types of gambling behavior."[40]

Assuming that all human beings face every situation as rational decision makers, some theorists have nevertheless persisted in devising incredibly complex formulas to explain not only gambling,[41] but *all* addictions as rational behaviors.[42] Advocates of **rational addiction models** argue that since most people are able to drink, use drugs, and gamble with no adverse consequences, the risks of becoming addicted are low. Therefore, the initial decision of whether or not to engage in any of these activities, made prior to the onset of addiction, is a rational voluntary choice based on the anticipated costs and benefits of doing so. Addiction is therefore an unintentional, unforeseen, and unwanted result of experimenting with a substance or behavior that is known to provide instant gratification but expected to cause little harm.[43]

CONSUMER THEORY: THE ENTERTAINMENT
VALUE OF GAMBLING

Because so many gamblers–particularly patrons of casinos and other commercial gaming establishments–participate in games in which the expected value is clearly negative, factors other than the simple desire for wealth must be involved in motivating them to gamble. Consequently, not all gambling researchers accept purely economic explanations or "expected value" models of gambling. Although value-maximizational decision-making models may sound reasonable in theory, one noted theorist observed that, "In practice, it is unusual for gambles to be chosen in terms of the highest expected value. This is, of course, one of the most important reasons why the gambling trade is able to make a large profit."[44] Others have made the equally irrefutable observation that "Many participants in gambling games realize that the odds are set against them, yet this realization does not stop them from gambling."[45] Consequently, some later researchers have begun to realize that the "expected value" or "utility" of gambling is not only a monetary one: people may visit and derive value from casinos for any of a number of noneconomic and, hence, nonquantifiable reasons. Some advise that if winning money is the only goal of gamblers, they should avoid commercial gaming altogether. This was precisely the conclusion of researchers who conducted an extensive study of blackjack in the casinos of Amsterdam:

> Our experience in the casinos and interactions with large numbers of players suggests that maximizing expected value, though important, is not the only goal of the player. Indeed, players who have only this goal in mind should not play; not playing has a higher expected value than any strategy except [card] counting. The mere fact that players continue to visit the casino despite the accumulating losses is a strong indication for the presence of other goals.[46]

Investigators have also noted that the gambler's subjective expectations of success do not necessarily accord with the economist's objectively determined probabilities.[47] As demonstrated by research into the cognitive psychology of gambling, the betting decisions of many gamblers are often influenced more by their own individual personality characteristics, irrational thought processes, "hunches," beliefs, misperceptions, and emotionally charged hopes for risky "long shots" than by detached, objective mathematical calculation.

A number of modern economic theorists have therefore begun to think of gambling as a consumptive rather than productive activity. In so doing they have added another dimension to their equations by postulating that the two fundamental motivations for gambling are (1) a desire for greater wealth and (2) the entertainment value that it provides.[48] Adherents of this view feel that people with different motivations for gambling are attracted to different kinds of gambling:

> Certain types of gambling opportunities lend themselves more strongly toward either the entertainment motive or the wealth motive. Lotteries which have low intrinsic entertainment value but very large prizes relative to the cost of participation are the ideal wealth motive gambles. Fixed odds games with even money pay-offs, on the other hand, are more likely to attract entertainment motivated players than wealth seekers. Certain wagers whose expected values can be influenced by the analytical skills of the gambler, such as horse race betting, sports betting, poker, and blackjack might be quite rewarding to an individual, independent of the financial outcome of the wagers.[49]

Thus, as the earlier economic theorists predicted, those who are older, poorer, less well educated, lacking job security, have larger families, or recently lost some of their wealth may very well gamble for the money they hope to win. However, those who are younger, better educated, more affluent, have greater job security, have smaller families, or have recently experienced an enhancement of their wealth may seek out gambling for its entertainment value. In neither case is the gambler's behavior regarded as irrational.[50]

Those who are motivated to gamble primarily for entertainment are regarded no differently than other consumers who, according to consumer theory, are "self-interested, goal oriented, and rational. They purchase and consume commodities for the ultimate purpose of generating 'utility' or satisfaction."[51] From this perspective gamblers are consumers of entertainment, losses are its cost, and utility becomes a measure not of expected wealth but of personal enjoyment. Examples of the nonmonetary utility or satisfaction that gambling might provide would be the opportunity to socialize with one's friends, excitement, a means of escaping reality, an opportunity for decision making and the challenge of testing one's intellectual abilities, or merely the satisfaction of one's curiosity. According to one economist, "In effect, the gambler is buying 'action' by making wagers, but the actual price will not be known until after the wagering has been completed."[52] Despite this uncertainty, some economists feel that three hours of casino gambling is cheap entertainment compared to the total cost of attending professional sporting events such as football and baseball games. Therefore, "Analyzed as an entertainment rather than an investment, roulette does not seem irrational."[53]

MARXIAN THEORY: GAMBLING AS EXPLOITATION

In his well-known literature review James Frey maintained that a purely Marxian analysis of gambling had never been published. Such an analysis, he pointed out, would have to insist upon the sanctioning of gambling by the economic and social elite as part of their continuing effort to exploit the masses.[55] Although a Marxian analysis of gambling may never have appeared in the sociological literature prior to Frey's review, at least one such analysis was published elsewhere. In condemning the promotion of legalized gambling Peter Fuller, a psychoanalyst with an obvious comprehension of sociological issues, expressed a clearly Marxist orientation when he suggested that lower class gambling is encouraged by the upper classes because it is so profitable to them:

> At best, gambling involves the reallocation of wealth within a given class, without affecting the total wealth available to that class. More often, the reallocation is the result of a pooling of limited economic resources, which are skimmed by both the state and the entrepreneurs, before being handed back to the winners. It emerges as just another form of economic exploitation. Far from providing a lever with which the capitalist machine can be disrupted or overthrown, gambling is another channel for its reinforcement. In Western industrial society, the working class is always the gross loser.
> .... Gambling is a safety valve in the capitalists' system. By offering apparent potential wealth to a tiny minority, it seduces the mass of the people, and deadens inclinations which they might have towards organized, revolutionary activity. As long as a worker believes that he, individually, has a chance of freeing himself from the oppression of capital, however remote that chance, he will be less likely to feel class solidarity, or to engage in political activity. Gambling divides the working class against itself, substitutes for the development of revolutionary perspectives, and tends to further enrich those who are already rich through the exploitation of labour.[55]

Fuller referred to structural-functionalists who fail to recognize that gambling can be neurotic or addictive as "bourgeois sociologists." Although they know full well that gambling serves to maintain the oppression of the working classes, they dare not acknowledge its "hegemonizing function." Instead, they explain gambling as a positive cohesive element which serves to preserve the existing social order. Since they profit from this capitalistic social order, they must deny that gambling can be at all harmful or abnormal.[56]

A quite different point of view was taken by a later Marxian social class theorist who suggested that instead of promoting lower class gambling to maintain their profits, the middle and upper class merchants and entrepreneurs have always endeavored to repress it for precisely the same reason. According to this view, gambling among the working classes is antithetical to the interests of the middle and upper classes since it serves to reduce the surplus labor pool upon which capitalism depends. The working class penchant for gambling must therefore be checked by legal restrictions not only to insure that their energies will not be diverted from productive labor, but also to prevent them from losing the discretionary income they would otherwise spend on the consumer goods that the middle and upper classes produce and sell at such handsome profits.[57]

CRITIQUE OF ECONOMIC THEORIES

In the blunt words of one critic, "Whatever else we might say, gambling is not a rational economic activity."[58] Value-maximization and other purely economic theories which postulate that gambling is motivated only or principally by the desire for wealth coincide nicely with the Skinnerian approach but they do not accord with reality. In the first place, they fail to take into account the motivations for gambling among those who are already wealthy or the self-destructive nature of pathological gamblers and the irrationality of their gambling behavior. In the second place, betting decisions are often subjective and do not always fall into the objective pattern described by mathematical formulae. This is particularly true of "hunch" and "long shot" bettors whose betting behavior appears to be controlled more by superstition and wishful thinking than by judgment and reason. Consumer theory, which explains gambling as an amusement that gamblers purchase with their losses, may indeed account for many instances of normative gambling but it is incapable of explaining pathological or even irresponsible gambling.

Nevertheless, some research into people's expressed motivations for gambling appears to lend some support to economic motivations. For example, one such study of racetrack bettors reported that the prospect of winning money was given as the main reason for betting among 63 percent of its respondents.[59] Similarly, a study of slot machine gamblers reported that 58 percent of those sampled gave winning money as one of their primary reasons for playing.[60] However, only 35 percent of the subjects of a third study indicated that they played primarily to win money; most said they did so for amusement or entertainment[61] as did nearly one quarter (22%) of the first study and nearly half (48%) of the second. Moreover, some specialists seriously question the scientific merit of people's expressed motivations for gambling as they are often merely rationalizations for their behavior.[62] In truth, 85 percent of the subjects in the first study and four out of every five players in the second study admitted that they lost more money than they had ever won.

If all average gamblers gambled only to maximize the value of their stake and went about it as rationally as many economic theorists assume they must, then Las Vegas would be a ghost town. The casino gambler's stake is always automatically devalued by the built-in "house advantage" of all casino games. Furthermore, the larger the anticipated win, the greater the percentage that is retained by the house. Thus, the overall return of such even-money games as blackjack and roulette may range from about 90 percent to 95 percent, slot machines return an average of perhaps 80 percent to 85 percent, pull tabs typically return from 70 percent to 85 percent, and various lotto and lottery games which offer the largest prizes return only 45 percent to 64 percent.[63] Therefore, no rational "Economic Man" would ever consider playing them since "the expected values of most commercially available gambles are negative, which means that they should never be preferred to the simple alternative of not gambling."[64] The same argument would hold true for horse or sports betting through a bookie who, as a broker, always retains a portion of every bet as his broker's fee or "vigorish." A noted cognitive psychologist stated the problem very simply but cogently when he wrote, "in the vast majority of cases, each dollar invested in gambling loses value. For this reason, the heavy involvement of people in the various gambling forms is difficult to understand in purely economic terms."[65] Obviously, then, other factors are such as its entertainment value and the irrationality of many gamblers are involved.

Decision making, Marxist, and other economic explanations for gambling also suffer the same weaknesses and are subject to the same criticisms as structural-functional approaches since they, too, are basically structural-functional analyses. They suffer, for example, from the same "false cause" error and from the fact that gambling was popular throughout the world in tribal and other early historical societies long before the development of the highly stratified social systems and capitalistic economic systems that exist today. Proponents of these models also assume that acquisitiveness is the primary motive for gambling. Furthermore, these approaches, and the Marxian model in particular, erroneously assume that *all* gamblers, otherwise impotent as decision makers or living at or near the poverty level, must have lower and working class origins. As Veblen and others have pointed out, gambling is also a popular pastime among the upper and middle classes.

PART II

QUALITATIVE APPROACHES

The Role of Observation

Chapter 3

TESTS OF "ARMCHAIR" THEORIES

In an effort to test the "armchair" theories and rectify the shortcomings of their predecessors, later social scientists began to insist on more empirical research. Since valid theory can be based only on valid, factual data, they sought to obtain it more directly. In their attempts to learn why people gamble some employed qualitative methods by conducting field research among active gamblers while others conducted reviews of the literature on gambling in an effort to synthesize existing knowledge.

Despite their more empirical approach, relatively few in the next generation of sociologists to study gambling questioned the explanations formulated by their mentors: instead, they continued to interpret their own observations and findings by reference to the theories printed in their textbooks. Consequently, the position that gambling allows independent decision making, relieves the stress of anomie and alienation, and therefore "functions" as a "safety valve" retained its wide popularity among younger sociologists who adapted these ideas to suit their own particular research arenas. Only later was the structural-functional approach seriously questioned and eventually challenged.

In keeping with the structural-functionalist tradition, however, some of the findings and conclusions of this newer breed of investigator stand in stark contrast to the negative attitudes and ideas of their more moralistically-inclined predecessors. Whereas most of the early sociologists had presented gambling of any kind as a serious social problem which must be controlled, a number of later researchers presented it as a socially beneficial activity which should be encouraged. It has been suggested, for example, that the attraction of the bingo parlor for many working class British women, particularly the elderly, is not the game itself but the opportunity it provides for meeting and socializing with others.[1] A participant observer of gambling in Las Vegas went so far as to claim that "by and large, gambling is beneficial to the gambler and increases rather than decreases his efficiency and productivity."[2] As an avid gambler herself, she went on to suggest that "accident rates could be cut and absenteeism reduced if the workers were given gambling breaks, perhaps run by the firm, much as they are given coffee breaks today."[3] She also felt that slot machines should be placed in nursing homes to provide stimulation for those whose lives are lacking in other forms of excitement. Most, however, were substantially more subdued in their suggestions even though they, too, saw gambling as serving a variety of beneficial purposes. Representative examples of their research and ideas are outlined below.

FIELD STUDIES

Irving Zola: Bettors, Bookies, and Peer Group Prestige

The conclusions of alienation theorist Irving Zola,[4] who studied illegal off-track betting, closely conformed to the ideas proposed by Devereux. Zola conducted his study as a participant observer at Hoff's, a bar in a lower class Italian-American and Polish-American neighborhood of a large New England city. Because this was the first study to be based on empirical, first-hand observation, it has been hailed as a landmark in sociological research.[5] Like Devereux, Zola suggested that while the opportunity to compete and win money may have contributed to the continual betting that went on in the bar, they were of only secondary importance to the gamblers he observed. He felt that the primary functions of gambling were to enable these men to affirm their attachment to, and gain prestige among, a core group of regular bar patrons who also lived in the neighborhood, and to provide them a means of releasing their pent-up aggressive hostilities.

Zola first eliminated the possibility that the members of this group bet for the thrill or excitement of gambling. Social interaction among the men at Hoff's revolves entirely around betting since even the core group of daily regulars speak to one another only in this context. The bar radio stays tuned to the track as the men of the group place their bets with the illegal bookmakers who occupy booths of their own. Nonbettors are treated as outsiders and coldly rejected by the regulars who refuse to interact with them. Only after they start betting themselves are they accepted and treated as insiders. Even so, between races the men of the group drink in silent isolation largely ignoring each other until several minutes before the broadcast of each new race. At this time those who have gone outside reenter the bar and those who had been silent begin talking about the various horses or jockeys and their chances in the upcoming event. The men and their conversation become more animated as the bookie begins taking their bets. Although the men are intensely interested in each race, they are expected to refrain from showing any emotion whether they win or lose. Even during the race their cheering is subdued. To Zola it was clear that the element of excitement is strongly deemphasized in this setting.

He then found that although these men gamble for money, they do not gamble for profit. For them the environment at Hoff's represents a sphere of existence entirely separate from their lives outside the bar. They tolerate no intrusion into their barroom activities even by their wives. In fact, they are neither expected to share any money they might win with their families nor even to inform them of it. Gambling and everything associated with it, including any money they might win, stay inside the bar. The men of the core group never quit when they are ahead but bet the same or even larger amounts on subsequent races. Quitters are disliked by the bookies who chastise them for being cheap as well as by the core bettors who bar them from the group. They are instead expected to buy a round of drinks for their associates and continue betting. Peer pressure allows a bettor to quit only when no more races are being run. Gambling for profit would be impossible under these circumstances.

Gambling also creates an opportunity for the attainment of status and prestige. Unlike the "numbers" game in which selection of a winner is purely a matter of chance and requires no skill, picking a winning horse is seen to require superior mental acuity since this process involves a rational application of intelligence and skill. Horse race betting therefore provides the men an opportunity to make the kinds of independent decisions and choices which they rarely have outside the bar (**alienation theory**). Those who successfully demonstrate these attributes by picking winners gain the recognition and respect of their peers who make poorer choices. To the clientele at Hoff's, successful off-track betting through a bookie is even more prestigious than successful on-track betting since success is achieved only through the exercise of one's wits and abilities rather than through the "hot tips" and "inside information" that abound at the track. All winning bettors are therefore expected to explain the reasoning they employed in choosing a particular horse. Typical responses might be that he had been following the weight and track record of the horse or its jockey. Consequently, the greatest prestige accrues to those who are not only able to win more often than the others, but who are also able to provide the most reasonable explanations for doing so. According to Zola, the importance of any monetary reward pales in comparison to the social and emotional satisfaction of picking a winner.

As a typical structural-functionalist, Zola therefore concluded that if the regulars at Hoff's did not gamble for excitement or profit, they must gamble for purposes of social solidarity and tension reduction. He was particularly struck by the observation that members of the group do not compete against each other but against the bookie who personifies "the system" they are trying to beat. The residents of the lower class neighborhood in which Hoff's bar is located do not perceive themselves as having a great deal of mastery over their own lives and destinies but to be governed primarily by external forces emanating from a "system" over which they have very little control. As part of this "system" the bookie is their enemy and gambling is the weapon with which they hope to defeat him. Thus, their primary goal is not to become wealthy through gambling but to "beat" or "crack" the system and keep it from beating them. Much of their hostility is directed against bookies they particularly dislike and hope to break. In this way the men are able to deny the futility of any attempts to alter their daily existence by demonstrating that there are some areas in life over which they do have some control. Bookies therefore serve two functions: they symbolize an inequitable "system" that the gamblers wish to beat using purely rational means and, as scapegoats for the hostility the feel toward this unjust system, they also serve to unify the men against a common enemy.

In brief, Zola argued that gambling "functions" primarily as a means of providing social solidarity, tension reduction, and prestige. The men identify with the core group and conform to its norms not only through their common interest and activity (racing and betting), but also through their disdain for any emotional displays while engaged in it, their determination not to quit, their lack of interest in profit, and their common enemy, an unfair "system" which is symbolized by the bookie. Gambling also allows these men a means of making decisions and earning or losing prestige that poses no threat to their actual status outside the bar. Finally, their common goal of "beating the system" by beating the bookie provides a "safety valve" through which they are able to vent the hostility they feel toward an unjust world. A more modern variant of these ideas has been advanced to explain the appeal of gambling among the working class habitués of a casino in Edmonton, Alberta.[6]

Robert Herman: Different Functions for Different Classes

Despite the popularity of "deviance" theory, not all sociologists were swayed by it. Whereas his predecessors had concentrated primarily on the functions of gambling among the lower classes, Robert Herman[7] attempted to explain its value in all classes when he conducted his sociological study of betting at large racetrack in California. He was also among the first to give any consideration to gender differences in discussing the different functions of gambling. Herman undertook his study to test the widely held beliefs that gambling lures an innocent public into "(a) the reckless expenditures of scarce resources on events of great risk in the naive hope of (b) 'making a killing,'" and that it represents "(c) an escape from rationality, even where pathological addiction is not at issue."[8] His study was unable to confirm any of these popular moralistic arguments.

Through his observations of, and interviews with track officials and bettors, Herman found that gambling in real life does not conform to its popular stereotype as an irresponsible or irrational activity. Studies of track betting both before and after Herman's investigation have an irrational "bettor bias" since they contend that most players prefer the riskier but higher paying "long shots," whose true chances of winning are unlikely, over the less risky but lower paying favorites, whose chances of winning are greater. Specifically, these studies have reported that the overall amounts wagered on the favorites are less than their true odds of winning would warrant while the amounts wagered on the "long shots" are greater than their objective probabilities should justify.[9] They claim that this is particularly evident in the last race of the day since, according to one researcher, it is at this time that the losers attempt to recoup their losses.[10] Herman observed instead that high paying but much riskier long shots are played only rarely. Moreover, nearly 80 percent of all bets are for fifteen dollars or less, much of which is "house money" (that won on previous bets) as opposed to "fresh money," and players of both genders in all classes and tend to place their bets on low-risk favorites paying at relatively much lower odds. The responses of 100 track "loners" who were asked how they handle their winnings suggested that these men were conservative gamblers since only three percent indicated that they eventually rebet it all on subsequent races. Herman therefore concluded that racetrack betting is "more characteristic of self-control and caution than recklessness."[11]

Armed only with the knowledge that most racetrack bettors play favorites and place relatively small bets, Herman proceeded to speculate on the motivations for gambling and the "functions" it serves. He began by stressing that racetrack gambling is not at all like roulette, dice, slot machine, and other casino games which are entirely dependent on chance; it is an intellectual exercise involving knowledge, strategy, and rational choice which requires substantial mental effort:

> Decision making requires of players that they study the past performance records, ponder the tote board, consider reasonable lines of action, estimate probabilities, risk money, and collect the fruits of their action. Though on a smaller scale, *they emulate traditional, entrepreneurial roles*–weighing alternatives, making decisions, and signalling these decisions by attaching money to them.[12]

Although money is used, Herman insisted that it does not constitute the primary motivation for gambling. Money is merely the vehicle through which people from all social classes become involved in the activity and the decision making it requires:

> I suggest that *the function of money*, in the context of the gambling institution, *is primarily to reify the decision-making process*. Money establishes the fact of a decisive act, and in its being lost or returned, it verifies the involvement of the bettor in the "action." Thus, the player, even the "little guy," is brought into meaningful association with processes beyond himself.[13]

Marvin Scott,[14] one of Herman's contemporaries who also studied racetrack betting as a participant observer, arrived at similar conclusions regarding the rationality of the activity and the conservative betting practices of the participants who generally attempt to maximize profits while minimizing risk.

Herman clearly adopted the decision-making interpretation of the **alienation theorists** when he described the racetrack as an arena for making individual choices and taking independent actions by men who ordinarily lack these opportunities. However, while his predecessors had limited this explanation only to lower class gambling, Herman extended it to explain gambling by middle class men, as well, since those working in the many large, automated, and impersonal bureaucratic organizations that were rapidly emerging "may also be increasingly separated from traditional sources of self-esteem."[15]

Herman also adopted the **safety valve** or **escape hatch hypothesis** of the structural functionalists when he suggested that racetrack betting provides a break from the routine and boredom of daily lives of lower class women. He obtained this idea from a sociological study in which working class women were described as leading "dull, sparkless, unfulfilled lives in routinized settings bereft of social-emotional rewards but heavy with responsibility."[16] Both men and women play the favorites and therefore employ the same betting strategy but women place more "Show" bets (bets that a horse will finish in either first, second, or third place) and do not study the racing form as much as men. Thus, where men formulate and act on their own decisions, women tend to act on the advice and decisions of others. To Herman this meant that for women the attraction of gambling must not lie in any desire for independent decision making. Since the attraction of "Show" bets is not that they are rewarded greatly but that they are rewarded frequently, he concluded that for lower class women, "Show payoffs are frequent sparks against a background of dreariness."[17]

Middle class women bet no differently than lower class women but, according to Herman, they do so for an entirely different reason: for them it is a direct consequence of their early socialization. From another sociological study Herman took the idea that middle class women are not raised to be competitive, aggressive, and independent as men are. As they grow up, women of this class are taught to be "more dependent than men on the authority of their parents."[18] This early training is reflected in the betting habits of women who rely on the judgment of public handicappers rather than make their own decisions. Thus, Herman maintained that while playing the favorites represents an expression of, and desire for, independent thought and autonomous action for men, for middle class women the identical strategy represents just the opposite: it not only reflects their denial of independence, but it also expresses their traditional acceptance of, and desire for, dependence.

Finally, Herman took an obvious cue from Veblen's **leisure class theory** when he ascribed the motivations for gambling by members of the upper classes to the desire to express their wealth through conspicuous consumption. Although the wealthy bet large amounts of money, they play the favorites to an even greater degree than gamblers of other classes. This suggests that they are not so indifferent to potential monetary loss as Veblen had claimed. But because their gambling takes place "in a setting of conviviality, sociability, and exclusiveness,"[19] Herman concluded that they do so not to express independence, but to express their desire for solidarity and conformity to group choices.

In summary, then, Herman felt that difficult gambling decisions are actively sought by middle and lower class men, they are irrelevant to women, and they are consciously avoided by the entire upper class. Some later researchers have ascribed the same motivation to gambling by children and adolescents.[20] As a structural-functionalist who saw institutionalized gambling as having only positive functions, he could not resist a final assault on the negative moralistic arguments his study was undertaken to assess:

> What other cultural devices are available to middle-class and lower-class men that can be as effective in bolstering a sense of independence and self-determination and that so compellingly exercise mental skills and rational powers? What else might be done to brighten the lives of working-class women? How else might the wealthy engage in the open consumption of leisure in ways that [appear to be] "harmless."
>
> In short, commercialized gambling offers to many people efficient means of enhanced self-esteem and gratification in a culture in which satisfactions are increasingly likely to be found in enterprises of consumption rather than production.[21]

In the final analysis, Herman's analysis of gambling has the same defects as other structural-functional explanations. This is perhaps most evident in his interpretation of a single betting strategy in three entirely different ways. His conclusions were based entirely on the armchair theorizing of others without any factual evidence whatsoever to support them.

LITERATURE REVIEWS

Joseph Scimecca's Typology: Not All Gamblers Are Neurotic Deviants

Dissatisfied with the ideas of most early social and behavioral scientists who saw gambling as a deviant, neurotic, or compulsive behavior, sociologist Joseph Scimecca[22] proposed his own classification of gamblers. He felt that distinguishing among types of gamblers would provide a better conceptual frame of reference than the narrow range of ideas offered by traditional sociological and psychoanalytic theories. Such a typology would represent merely the first stage of research. By introducing a scheme based on systematic observation he hoped to lay the foundation upon which a general theory, "which is almost completely lacking in the sociological study of gambling,"[23] could be built. Since his ideas were based entirely on the work of others, he adamantly insisted that his formulation was tentative and required substantiation by future empirical research.

On the basis of the existing literature, Scimecca distinguished among seven types of gamblers: the professional gambler, the percentage gambler, the cheater, the economic gambler, the compulsive gambler, the thrill gambler, and the functional gambler. Each was defined according to five distinguishing characteristics: primary motivation, degree of ego involvement, degree of skill required, degree of superstition, and society's reaction to them. Although the owners of gambling establishments make their living in the gambling business, Scimecca felt that they could not legitimately be considered gamblers since all games favor the house and they therefore risk none of their own money on uncertainties. Like any other business people, they profit from providing a service for which there is a public demand. Writing at a time when most forms of gambling were illegal in the United States, Scimecca characterized proprietors of commercial gambling establishments along with bookmakers as organized criminals.

Committed *professional gamblers*, like professionals in other fields, learn their occupational skills and attitudes through training, practice, and experience. However, since most forms of gambling were illegal when Scimecca was writing, he felt that professionals necessarily learn their trade in a deviant subculture which also helps to shape their attitudes. Since their whole life and livelihood depend on gambling, professionals must adhere to a "code" of unwritten rules that govern this way of life. Foremost among them is that the payment of gambling debts takes precedence over all other obligations. The reason for this is simply that gambling would be senseless if winning were not profitable.

Percentage gamblers are part-time players who have not internalized the values and attitudes of professionals. Since they gamble only to make some extra money, gambling is not their whole life and they lack the ego involvement of the professional. Nevertheless, whether they are playing poker, betting on a horse, or shooting dice, percentage players know the odds of placing any bet or making any play. Unlike professionals they avoid games with their peers and only look for "suckers" who lack their specialized knowledge.

Cheaters are dishonest, fraudulent gamblers. They employ marked cards, loaded dice, and other deceitful means to take unfair advantage of their opponents. However, since gambling is also their way of life, they are more deeply involved than the percentage player for whom gambling is an avocation but not as involved as the committed professional. Although cheaters rely heavily on manual dexterity, they also have a great deal of technical knowledge though not as much as the professional.

Scimecca classed percentage gamblers and cheaters as subsets of the professional category since the motivations of all three are purely economic. All three of these types require a great deal of skill whether in the form of an intimate knowledge of the game or sleight-of-hand techniques. Professional gamblers are more skillful in applying their knowledge than percentage players who are essentially accomplished amateurs. Since superstition is the mark of suckers and losers, neither the professional, the percentage player, or the cheater are superstitious. Society regards professionals and percentage players as "heros" since they are able to do what everyone would like to do—get something for nothing. Cheaters are condemned as criminals.

The *economic gambler* is motivated by the same desire as the professional, percentage gambler, and cheater since he, too, is attracted by the lure of fast money without the necessity of working for it. However, the main distinctions of the economic gambler is that he lacks gambling skill. He therefore puts his hopes and his money on long odds risks such as exotic horse races and lotteries and, consequently, rarely wins. Since his livelihood is not dependent on gambling his degree of ego involvement is low. He is a highly superstitious person whose gambling is based more by hope than reality. Society condones the economic gambler as someone who is merely trying to realize the American dream of getting rich quick.

In describing *compulsive gamblers*, Scimecca adopted the psychoanalytic theories of Bergler, Lindner, and others who characterized them as masochists with an unconscious desire to lose. Because they are motivated to lose, compulsive gamblers have a high degree of ego involvement in gambling. Since they are so successful at this they either possess very little skill or they unconsciously direct the skills they do have to losing. They are seen as highly superstitious since their gambling is so ritualistic and so closely oriented toward manipulating and appeasing Fate. Society regards them sympathetically as the victims of an uncontrollable societal disease, much as it does alcoholism and drug dependence.

Thrill gamblers, who are motivated by the "pleasurable-painful sensations" that gambling provides, are also a product of Bergler's psychoanalytic scheme. However, Scimecca insisted that thrill gamblers are not compulsive gamblers since they do not gamble in order to lose; they gamble purely for amusement. Scimecca speculated that most thrill gamblers would be members of the upper classes who see gambling as a way to relieve boredom. Their degree of ego involvement would depend on how much they depend on gambling to relive their boredom. Since they are not concerned with winning, very little skill is involved but since gambling for thrills represents an appeal to irrationality, they would be highly superstitious. The reaction of those who gamble for thrills and excitement is one of neutrality: they are neither condemned or condoned.

Finally, Scimecca took his definition of the *functional gambler* from earlier sociologists who advocated anomie and alienation theories. The functional gambler is a lower class male who finds in gambling a means of self-expression and an avenue for the success and recognition he is ordinarily denied. He is therefore motivated by the functions that gambling serves as a means of expressing individual masculinity and group solidarity. There is a high degree of ego involvement since gambling symbolizes the gambler's identification with a primary reference group of men who are trapped in the same inescapable socioeconomic circumstances. Since winning accrues status and prestige, there is a high degree of reliance on skill and no place for superstition in gambling. Society also views the functional gambler with neutrality since his gambling harms neither himself nor others.

In formulating his typology Scimecca attempted to synthesize the limited amount of information that was then available on gamblers and gambling and to expand his colleagues' narrow views on the subject. Specifically, he hoped to alert his peers to the facts that different people gamble for different reasons and that not all gamblers are despised and condemned by greater society; some are lauded and envied. He was therefore one of the first sociologists to suggest that not all gamblers are driven by the same exclusive motivations that his predecessors had decreed and consequently that gambling does not necessarily constitute a deviant or neurotic behavior that always has detrimental social and individual consequences. Instead, he proposed that in many instances gambling is a normative pastime that harms no one. Since he conducted no original research, he was unable to estimate how many gamblers are represented by each class. As will be shown, however, such statistics were compiled by a number of later researchers.

In essence, while most of his predecessors had advocated monocausal explanations for gambling, Scimecca advanced an early psychosocial multicausal approach which he hoped would broaden our perspective on the subject. For many years relatively few gambling researchers shared this view. However, the notion that all gambling is motivated by a single monolithic cause is being rejected by growing numbers of modern researchers.

Henry Lesieur: The Positive and Negative Functions of Pathological Gambling

Whereas his predecessors investigated the social functions of *normative* gambling, modern sociologist Henry Lesieur was interested in the functions of *pathological* gambling. Citing functionalist Robert Merton who admonished his colleagues to seek out the positive as well as the negative functions of any social institution or behavior, Lesieur[24] listed a number of each. However, in looking over those he listed as positive, one wonders whether his intent was tongue-in-cheek or otherwise. The positive functions include:

1. Increased overtime work. In striving to come up with gambling money, pathological gamblers who work overtime inadvertently contribute to a nation's overall productivity.

2. Increased business profits and employment. Pathological gambling is responsible for generating most of the profits of commercial gaming and at least ten percent of all jobs in commercial gaming industries.

3. Upward social mobility for those involved in criminal activities. Organized crime is commonly believed to be highly involved in all sorts of gambling and gambling-related activities. If so, pathological gambling would support and create opportunities for social advancement for such underworld types as crime bosses, loan sharks, bookmakers, numbers runners, and other criminal types—provided, of course, that the pathological gambler does not welsh on his debts.

4. Greater tax revenues. Barring tax evasion and fraud, any tax revenues that are derived from legalized gambling would be substantially increased by pathological gambling.

5. Increased profits for legitimate lending institutions. Barring bankruptcy, bank robbery, suicide, and defaulting on loans, pathological gambling would be highly profitable for banks, loan companies, credit unions, etc.

6. Increased employment opportunities in the law enforcement, finance, and related businesses. Since pathological gamblers do commit such crimes as loan defaults, forgery, robbery, insurance fraud, tax evasion, etc., they are directly responsible for increasing employment in such areas as insurance investigation, credit agencies, law enforcement, collection agencies, the legal profession, etc.

7. Enhanced sense of morality and promotion of the spirit of capitalism in greater society. By labeling some people as pathological gamblers and comparing them to one's self, members of greater society are able to reaffirm their cherished values of hard work and thrift and condemn those who appear to disdain them.

8. Increased profits and employment opportunities for treatment providers. Since more gambling opportunities create more pathological gamblers, more treatment facilities, counselors, and administrators will be needed to meet the increasing demand for their services and insurance providers are being lobbied to pay for them.

9. Increased employment in the construction and corrections industries. By increasing the size of prison populations, pathological gamblers who fail to receive treatment and continue to commit crimes will provide ongoing needs and benefits for those who build, maintain, and staff our regional and national penitentiaries.

There is clearly nothing insincere or humorous in Lesieur's list of the negative functions of pathological gambling. Included among them are:

1. Family disruption. Pathological gambling is responsible for the deception and financial exploitation of close family members; it can lead to disagreements, arguments, mistrust, mental and physical abuse, family dysfunction, separation, divorce, and serious problems among the children in such families.

2. Lost productivity and business failure. Pathological gamblers not only miss days of work because of gambling, they also embezzle and otherwise steal or divert funds from their employers or their own businesses for purposes of gambling.

3. Suicide. Compared to the general population, rates of suicidal thoughts, attempts, and actual acts are higher not only for pathological gamblers, but also for their spouses.

4. Increased crime rates. Pathological gamblers commit a variety of crimes to fund their gambling.

5. Increased insurance costs. Theft and insurance fraud schemes by pathological gamblers raise insurance premiums for everyone. Pathological gamblers also cash in policies and default on insurance payments.

6. Loan defaults. Pathological gamblers are notorious for borrowing large amounts of money and defaulting on their debts thereby denying credit to and increasing lending fees for others.

7. Strained health care delivery services. Pathological gambling has many medical consequences including depression, anxiety, psychosomatic problems, and the aftermath of suicide attempts. Because gambling is so often overlooked as the reason for these problems, psychiatrists and other treatment specialists waste a great deal of their time and resources treating symptoms rather than their cause.

8. Increased tax levies and appropriations for treatment. Publicly funded gambling treatment programs will burden taxpayers by consuming tax revenues.

9. Increased tax levies and appropriations for law enforcement and correctional institutions. The public must not only bear the costs of investigating, arresting, and prosecuting pathological gamblers who commit gambling-related crimes, but they must also pay the costs of imprisoning those convicted of these offenses.

Lesieur made it patently obvious that pathological gambling is not motivated by any of its social "functions" no matter how beneficial they may seem since the "positive" consequences of pathological gambling are clearly outweighed by the negative. His primary purpose in contrasting them was to alert researchers to the possibility that by focusing exclusively on either the "good" or the "bad" aspects of gambling, they may actually be adopting and promoting a moral stance either for or against it. As has already been demonstrated, a number of sociologists have done precisely that by claiming that gambling is a major social problem; as will be shown elsewhere, others have done so by claiming that since gambling is normative behavior (i.e., there are more gamblers than abstainers), it is *not* a social problem.[25]

Chapter 4

THE RESEARCHERS' POINT OF VIEW

SMALL-GROUP INTERACTIONAL APPROACHES

Those who favor a small-group approach see gambling as an activity that provides a means of role-playing through which certain desirable personality and behavioral traits can be expressed. From this perspective the gambling environment (the betting shop, card table, racetrack, casino, etc.) is viewed as a stage upon which gamblers are granted license to assume a desired identity, act out their wish-fulfillment fantasies, or play a particular role. Many interactional theorists are functionalists who argue that gambling provides social opportunities and benefits that are ordinarily unavailable: it "functions," they contend, to meet the gambler's personal demands for self-expression or self-presentation which would otherwise remain unsatisfied. The explanations of some interactional theorists can therefore be seen to have close affinities with those of the earlier alienation and anomie theorists. As noted in the discussion of psychoanalytic theory,[1] many of the ideas of later interactional theorists were also anticipated by Wilhelm Stekel.

Erving Goffman: You Are What You Pretend To Be

Small-group explanations are based largely upon the work of Erving Goffman[1] who studied temporary, focused interactional situations during his investigation of "action." Goffman viewed gambling as a metaphor which would be useful in explaining many other kinds of established social interactive rituals that regularly take place in competitively-oriented Western capitalistic societies. For example, gambling, like all other conventional social activities, involves specific sets of culturally prescribed rules and roles to which all participants are expected to adhere. Like the earlier macrotheorists, Goffman believed that most people in Western society are prevented from exercising a great deal of choice in their lives except when they are engaged in voluntary risk-taking enterprises like gambling. But unlike them, he did not see gambling as a reactionary response to the frustrations encountered in everyday life. Instead, Goffman[2] regarded risk-taking as one of Western society's highest values and saw in it a means for an observer to gauge another person's true character–that revealed under highly stressful conditions. Many of his ideas on gambling and human social life in general resulted from his work as a Las Vegas croupier and blackjack dealer.

Goffman maintained that the "action" derived from any kind of gambling involves four distinct phases. The first, "squaring off," refers to the initial decision to gamble. "Determination," the process through which this decision is carried out, refers to the toss of the coin, the roll of the dice, the spin of the wheel, the deal of the cards, the run around the track, and any other means of resolving a wager. "Disclosure" refers to the actual outcome of the wager and "settlement" refers to the exchange of stakes once the outcome is known. Actors in the gambling drama appraise one another's character as well as their own on the basis of their individual performances throughout each phase or act of this play.

According to Goffman, the "action" of gambling derives not only from the stimulation derived from risk, but also from the fact that it constitutes a test of one's conduct or character when the pressure is on. "Character" is a personal quality akin to a capital resource that can be gambled, gained, and lost. It is under stressful circumstances generated by such activities as gambling that those seeking to be judged have an opportunity to present their persona of choice–generally one of daring, courage, integrity, composure, self-confidence, dignity, and even gallantry under fire–to those around them. Goffman[3] referred to the effort expended in displaying these personal qualities as "face work," a concept he derived from the Chinese concern with "losing face" and "saving face." He felt that such character displays are among the principal "tacit" purposes underlying all risky behaviors.[4] Thus, "character" is even more important than money since gains in this quality can, and often do, accrue with the favorable performances that accompany loss.

The influence of Goffman's ideas is evident in many later studies. In his discussion of gambling in the betting shops of London's East End, Otto Newman described the betting shop as a place "where the bettor, in the company of his comrades and peers, is offered the opportunity of displaying characteristics of steadfastness, valour, and coolness; where he is able to exhibit the qualities of modesty in his moments of triumph and imperturbability in times of despair; . . . where roles are rehearsed and refined."[5] Among the many roles a gambler can play are those of "Sage, Jester, Barrackroom Lawyer, Neophyte, Rebel, Greek Chorus."[6] Irving Zola[7] drew similar conclusions from his observations of off-track betting in an American working class bar. Marvin Scott, who studied on-track betting behavior, felt that racetrack betting creates entirely new personas by allowing the bettor to practice new skills and make his own decisions. Thus, "At the track, Sammy the painter becomes Sammy the handicapper."[8] Louis Zurcher,[9] who studied poker playing among a small group of regular participants, described the temporary character displays or personas that gamblers adopt as "ephemeral roles" which serve to meet social-psychological needs that are left unsatisfied by the roles they ordinarily play in daily life. Vicki Abt and her colleagues described the committed gambler's social reality in this way:

> The gambler who is a *poor loser* is even more so a *poor gambler*. Manifest discontent and complaining about losing a bet on a race or a roll of the dice, for example, is a deviation from the gambling norm which calls for a stoic, and perhaps even cavalier, acceptance of loss as an inevitable part of the action. Accepting loss gracefully shows character and style which is itself a basis for winning respect from fellow gamblers. As with many other forms of social behavior, the loss of personal worth in the judgment of peers because of failure to *play by the rules* may be experienced as a far greater loss than a financial loss on a series of gaming outcomes. In the same respect, it is important to win with a display of composure if the gambler wishes to be regarded by fellow gamblers as someone who knows how to handle the chips.[10]

Psychologist Thomas Holtgraves[11] attributed the "risky-shift" phenomenon, the tendency of individual gamblers to increase their bet sizes along with others at the gaming table, to their desire to present a favorable appearance to those around them: most gamblers do not want to be regarded as cautious, hence, penurious, by their fellows. Casinos in New Jersey and Nevada exploit these feelings by promoting a "carefree, reckless, free-wheeling image"[12] of extravagance and conspicuous consumption. David Spanier, a popular writer on gamblers and gambling, expressed the slightly different opinion that the gambler himself, rather than those around him, is object of his character displays: "In seeking where the action is, part of what one is doing, I believe, is putting one's qualities of character on trial, not for other people, but for oneself. It is a test of each individual's mettle, a test of how far a man can go in gambling, knowing that basically the chances are against him. . . ."[13]

Holtgraves,[14] who adopted and developed many of Goffman's ideas, insisted that the kind of image one presents while gambling is as important to oneself as it is to others. His thoughts are based on the assumptions that an actor's overt behavior carries certain social meanings that influence others' perceptions of him and that all actors make a conscious or unconscious effort to control the images they present to others. Holtgraves' own research into the character assessments that casino gamblers make of others on the basis of their responses to various gambling situations led him to conclude that "character" can be displayed, gained, and lost in a number of different ways while gambling. Since different games vary in complexity, expected odds ratios, the degree to which chance and skill are involved, and the degree to which others are involved, the type of game one chooses to play–craps, slot machines, blackjack, roulette, baccarat, etc.–can communicate something of the gambler's character. One's comportment while playing is also important. Perhaps the most important character signals are the gambler's reactions to winning and losing. Others include the avoidance of bragging or complaining, limiting extraneous conversation, and a thorough knowledge of the formal and informal rules of the game such as the use of correct terms and knowing when to tip. However, the appropriateness of certain behavioral displays also differ from one game to another: loud emotional outbursts are permitted and even encouraged at the craps table but not at the baccarat table where cool nonchalance is the rule. Wagering itself communicates certain nonverbal messages. Large, risky bets and calm indifference to them mark one as a "high roller" while small conservative bets convey trepidation and suggest a small bankroll. Confidence, competence, sound betting strategies, and, of course, winning are sure to secure the favorable evaluation of oneself and one's peers. However, character can also accrue through losing: consistent losses that are accepted with equanimity can convey the impression that they are easily affordable and beneath consideration.

According to advocates of the small-group interactional approach, then, people do not gamble to gain money, they do so to make a favorable impression and gain a reputation through their character displays. They insist that it is one's conduct and appearance while gambling rather than a desire for money or the excitement it provides that is most important to the gambler. It has therefore been argued that the reason casino gamblers continue to play despite the negative consequences so many of them inevitably suffer is not an economic but a social one. They might not gamble at all if this activity did not allow them to express their exhibitionistic inclinations.[15] Here, too, Dostoevsky provided an example by exploiting his reader's belief in the "gambler's fallacy":

> But I, having noticed that red had been up seven times in succession, by strange perversity, made a point of putting my money on it. I am convinced that half of it was vanity; I wanted to impress the spectators by taking mad risks.[16]

This approach is also reflected to a certain degree in the Big Book of *Gamblers Anonymous*: "We realize we had the urge to be 'big shots,' to enjoy the feeling of being all-powerful. We were willing to do anything . . . to main-tain the image of ourselves we wanted others to see."[17] Some researchers and treatment specialists feel that the unwillingness to abandon their "big shot" and "graceful loser" images constitutes a major impediment to the recovery of at least some pathological gamblers.[18]

David Oldman: Gambling Appearances and Secret Identities

Many social scientists, including other advocates of the small-group and interactional theories, have also conducted gambling studies which are based upon observational and participant observational research at commercial gambling establishments. Another to do so was David Oldman[19] who spent two years as a casino croupier. Oldman's personal experiences led him to conclude that gambling persistence despite consistent loss often results from the erroneous beliefs that many gamblers entertain. However, this same experience convinced him that compulsive gambling is motivated by some-thing else entirely.

During his review of the scientific literature, Gamblers Anonymous publi-cations, and religious tracts on gambling, Oldman found that a desire for money is most commonly believed to be the primary cause of compulsive gambling. Moral judgments notwithstanding, Oldman felt, this purely eco-nomic perspective recognizes little difference between entrepreneurial spec-ulation and risk, which are sanctioned and encouraged in Western society, and gambling which is reviled and censured.[20] Compulsive gambling is often thought to be precipitated by a financial crisis which results from spending more on gambling than one can afford. In the popular view, this occurs when the gambler begins to borrow money and continues to do so until his debts so greatly exceed his assets that he cannot possibly repay them, and then feels forced to continue to gamble in the hope of winning enough to offset his losses and debts. Since the chances of this are unlikely, sooner or later a crisis situation develops.

According to the sources Oldman reviewed, compulsive gambling is char-acterized by three essential features. These are: (1) the "addiction" itself which is believed to be chronic and incurable and which is expressed in the gambler's compulsive need for risk taking and "action"; (2) the gambler's "dream world" which consists of his "rationalization" that he must continue to gamble to recoup his losses and pay his debts—a phenomenon which is commonly referred to as "chasing" an evasive big win[21]—and his "irrational or hopeless optimism"[22] that he will eventually win enough money to do this; and (3) the gambler's self-punishing "love of losing." These sources, many of which advocate the medical model, argue that compulsive gambling should be regarded as a disease[23] rather than a form of social deviance or victimless crime.

On the basis of his own observations, however, Oldman could not entirely agree with this characterization. Although gambling often leads to an economic crisis, this in itself is not sufficient to explain compulsive gambling. According to Oldman, it is widely known that since the odds in any casino situation do not favor the player, the gambler himself realizes the futility of hoping for a big win. Instead of monetary gain, Oldman reasoned, the rewards of gambling must be largely social: entering the casino means leaving the outer world behind; it allows the gambler to check all the worldly cares and problems at the door and enter "an entirely controllable world"[24] in which these concerns no longer exist and where he can become the person he would really like to be.

More specifically, Oldman attributed habitual gambling not merely to the social intercourse it provides, but primarily to the gambler's desire to assume the identity he would like to have but cannot otherwise present. During his years as a croupier Oldman became very familiar with many of the regular players. He noticed that although the opportunities for social interaction among casino gamblers are limited by the physical setting and the business at hand, the situation does permit some expression of individuality. Of particular interest to Oldman were the types of social relationships that develop among regular casino patrons as well as the various playing strategies, individual personality characteristics, and general demeanor they display.[25] As one of a group of regulars at a gaming table, "One can show fortitude, cool, generosity, calculation, disinterest, sociability—and one can do this with essentially simple and easily recognized performances."[26]

From Oldman's sociological perspective, the characterization and language of the medical model are inappropriate to what he sees as the true gambling situation. He felt that the medical approach and its terminology were adopted in an effort to decrease the social stigma attached to irresponsible gambling since it is preferable to be thought of as a treatable medical patient than as a social deviant. Thus, Oldman found the term "compulsion" to be a misnomer since the term is applied by clinically-based treatment providers only after the "compulsive gambler" has encountered a financial crisis and has sought their help in dealing with it. He therefore felt the term "habitual gambler" would be more suitable in describing the situation as he saw it as it does not distinguish the postcrisis from precrisis gambler. Moreover, "habituation is partly a matter of choice, in that the casino does indeed offer itself as a stage for the simple, and easily authenticated, presentation of virtually *any* desired identity."[27] However, in the absence of any vocabulary to describe the actual situation, and since many gamblers do encounter financial difficulties, "the label of compulsion easily extends to cover the gratification they experience in this social haven."[28]

Psychoanalytic explanations for the habitual gambler's often-reported "love of losing" are also in error. According to Oldman, the habitual gambler gambles neither to gain money, nor to lose money, nor for the "thrill" it provides; he gambles to gain a sense of interpersonal security in a world where he is always in full control of his persona. Losing is therefore inconsequential and may even be a necessary precondition for the portrayal of the gambler's idealized alter-ego. The desire to project a certain image, Oldman felt, explains the gambler's "love of losing" far better than theories which postulate a masochistic need for self-punishment over some guilt-laden childhood experience. In Oldman's view, "Losing large amounts of money may demonstrate one's self-control. . ., or may reinforce a 'good-guy' image, or may demonstrate that one is successful in business-life so that one can be seen as being able to afford to throw one's money about."[29] In fact, Oldman contended, during a gambling episode when the habitual gambler is "on stage" and immersed in the role he has assumed, an unexpected big win may be every bit as undesirable as a big loss since either would be disruptive to the identity he is trying to establish. He believed that "In all such cases 'wanting to lose' is either a formulation by outsiders of a state of affairs which appears incomprehensible, or a formulation by insiders of the otherwise morally unspeakable."[30]

Finally, although Oldman felt that habitual gamblers are not really playing for money, the economic realities of gambling cannot be avoided. The habitual gambler (i.e., loser) does not irrationally entertain any "hopeless optimism" when he continues to gamble but is merely facing his financial problems in the only way that he knows. Because he has outstanding debts he must win to pay them. Although he realizes that the chances of a big win are slight, it is not entirely outside the realm of possibility. So while he may expect to lose he nevertheless hopes to win. Arguing against the psychoanalytic model, Oldman therefore concluded that uncontrolled gambling "is a consequence not of personality defect but of a defective relationship between a strategy of play on the one hand and a way of managing one's finances on the other."[31]

Playing strategies. Unfortunately, Oldman did not provide good explanations of what he meant by either effective or defective gambling and money management strategies; fortunately, others did. Robert Ladouceur and his associates found in a series of studies that both regular and nonregular roulette players tend to escalate the size of their bets during the course of play.[32] This has been explained as a result of two betting strategies, the "law of effect" and "chasing," that gamblers commonly employ.[33] Each is related to a particular "streak" of luck, either good or bad. The first, the "law of effect," (representing a "Type II" fallacy) suggests to the gambler that when he or she has been winning, the streak is likely to continue and so larger bets are made to capitalize on this trend. Thus, during a winning streak bets are based on the way "things are running."[34] The second, a system in which the gambler doubles the size of his or her previous bet after each even-money (i.e., red or black) bet loss, is commonly employed during a losing streak. This strategy, which actually represents the "gambler's fallacy," (or "Type I" fallacy) is used in the belief that the gambler must ultimately win and therefore end up slightly ahead of the game. In this case, bets are determined on the basis of what the gambler thinks is "overdue" simply because it hasn't happened for some time.[35]

The doubling strategy is quite feasible in theory, but quite impossible in practice. This is because two very real restrictions, the house table limits and the size of the gamblers bankroll, are inexorably imposed after even a short run of bad luck.[36] Since the casino establishes a maximum bet, doubling is prohibited beyond a certain point. If that point is $500, as it once was in many Las Vegas casinos, full doubling of an initial $1 bet would be allowable only through the ninth consecutive loss, at which point $256 would have been staked. If this were also lost, the tenth bet would be restricted to $500 which is $12 less than the amount required by the doubling strategy. At this point a win would put the gambler $11 behind while another loss would mean that he or she would be out a total of $1,012. Relatively few gamblers who visit Las Vegas have that much money to risk at one time. Gamblers with limited stakes of only a few hundred dollars would be ruined and could do nothing to recoup their losses while the aspirations of those with larger bankrolls would be frustrated by the $500 house limit. Furthermore, the house advantage on American roulette with its two green zeros is a constant 5.4 percent (in Europe, with only one green zero, it is 2.7%). Since there is no way for a player to gain an odds advantage over the house, this means that players will lose an average of 5.4 percent (or 2.7%) of every bet. But because the outcome of every spin is a purely random event, a few lucky gamblers will be able recoup their losses or even win enviable amounts. In reality, however, the majority of those who adhere to this strategy are destined to lose and, of course, the larger the initial bet, the sooner the doubling system will fail. With an initial bet of $5, for example, the system would break down after the seventh straight loss. Such a system, to which many gamblers adhere, exemplifies the defective money management or chasing strategies to which Oldman referred.

According to one gambling specialist,[37] reverse systems represent much wiser money management strategies. Under one such system even-money bettors should begin with an initial wager of $8 or $12, for example, then reduce it by half after each loss but double it after every win. Following the third consecutive loss, at which time $2 or $3 would have been bet, the gambler starts over with the original $8 or $12 bet. In this way losses are minimized while wins are maximized. However, this strategy can also be seen to follow the "law of effect." Since gamblers double the size of their bets after every win, they are actually risking all their "house money" (any money they have accumulated in excess of their original stake) on every play if they follow this system to the letter. But here, too, the strategy is flawed by house limits and the inevitability of loss at some point. To be successful, gamblers must therefore decide at which point to quit doubling or, perhaps even more wisely, be willing to quit when they are modestly ahead.

John Rosecrance: Casino "Regulars" and The Social Worlds of Gambling

Another interactional theorist, John Rosecrance,[38] was especially antagonistic to economic and psychological models of gambling and "compulsive" gambling. Economic theories, he believed, are refuted by research demonstrating that the motivations of frequent gamblers are determined more by recreational than by economic concerns.[39] Studies by treatment providers and experimental psychologists are flawed by serious sampling errors: those of clinicians are based solely on self-admitted problem gamblers who are actively seeking treatment while those of psychological researchers are derived largely from the responses of college students who are tested in artificial laboratory environments. Consequently, he argued, the conclusions of these studies could not possibly apply to actual gamblers in real-life gambling situations. Finally, he felt that although a number of ethnographic studies of active gamblers in natural gambling environments succeeded in refuting the compulsion model,[40] they failed to provide an acceptable alternative explanation of persistent gambling despite consistent loss.

Rosecrance felt that the social rewards of gambling are among its greatest attractions since few gamblers are able to make money at it. In developing his interactional explanation for gambling persistence Rosecrance[41] studied "regular" casino gamblers who are committed to gambling despite its costs. Since the house always wins while gamblers rarely do, occasional gamblers and nongambling outsiders fail to see any rational basis for persistent gambling. But because regular gamblers do lose more often than they win, he reasoned that the rewards of gambling must be other than economic and that these rewards must outweigh the economic costs. Rosecrance therefore proposed that the rewards of persistent or excessive gambling must be social since quitting would mean abandoning long-standing social relationships with other regulars. He suggested that "the sustaining mechanisms of regular gambling are not rooted in individual pathology or economic rationality but instead can be located in the social networks that have developed among the participants."[42]

To test his hypothesis Rosecrance[43] initially selected three distinct subject groups: 60 off-track bettors, 45 sports bettors, and 40 poker players most of whom were men. All were self-designated regulars at two large gambling casinos in Nevada. He later extended his study to include lottery and other casino game players.[44] An avid gambler himself, Rosecrance was readily accepted by his subjects since he was already an established regular. His research methods included participant observation, nonparticipant observation, interviews, and the "implicit knowledge" he had gained during a lifetime (over 30 years) of regular gambling.

Rosecrance rejected the psychological and economic reasons that casino regulars frequently give—the need for "action" or money—as superficial, but readily accepted "more searching" verbal comments about the importance of their social networks—"All my friends are here. When I don't come there's nothing for me to do"—as more valid explanations of persistent gambling.[45] He stressed that horse players and sports bettors commonly form cliques of four to six members who habitually sit together and talk about the various racing and athletic events of the day. Thus, "Gambling is conducted in settings that can be considered social worlds. Within these worlds, gambling is the central activity and the main topic of discussion."[46] Moreover, when they are in their particular social world, gamblers rely far more on shared information, rational decision making procedures, and sound money management skills to minimize their losses than they do on chance or luck in the hope of making a killing.

The social bonds that develop among regular gamblers are strengthened through four primary binding social arrangements which serve to establish and reinforce group membership and gambling participation. One of these is the sharing of valuable gambling information among all members. Since horse players and sports bettors do not compete with one another nor profit at one another's expense, shared information—the "inside dope" on a race or the "momentum" of a team—can benefit the entire group. Although poker players do compete, regulars do not try to beat each other. Their goal is to take as much money as they can from newcomers and others from outside the group. News of an outsider's "loose action" circulates rapidly among the regulars.[47] Other regulars can also act as sounding boards or devil's advocates for those planning to bet on certain horses or sports teams, and for poker players who may be planning to participate in a "big game" but know nothing about the skills of the other players. Gamblers who specialize in certain types of races, athletic events, or poker games also seek information and advice from specialists in other areas. Many gamblers refuse to bet or play before discussing the prospects with their friends. Because it is so vital, "The gamblers' desire for information binds them to the social networks that have formed with other gamblers."[48]

Mutual money lending among regulars is a second binding social arrangement that reinforces gambling participation. Regulars who have the cash are also expected to provide interest-free loans to their gambling friends who need money but are unable to secure it from other sources. In fact, it is considered a serious breach of gambling etiquette for a regular who has the money to refuse such a loan. Since today's lender may be tomorrow's borrower, money lending serves to strengthen social bonds by creating reciprocal obligations: those who loan money when they have it can expect to be able to borrow money when they need it. Social bonds are strengthened within any group which provides a mutual financial support system for its members.

Shared contingencies also reinforce the social bonds and gambling participation among regulars who live in a world of their own from which outsiders are excluded. Regular gamblers will periodically encounter heavy, unexpected losses which nongamblers never have to face. Most gamblers appreciate a sympathetic ear following a run of bad luck but most feel that only other gamblers can identify with them and provide the sort of mutual understanding and encouragement required to restore a loser's confidence and self-esteem. The knowledge that other regulars share these contingencies and provide the only source emotional support necessary for dealing with them also increases the gambler's commitment to the group and its interests.

A final binding social arrangement among regular gamblers is social interaction to a degree which would otherwise be limited since their specialized existence also restricts the number of people with whom they have interests in common. Rosecrance felt that as regulars become more deeply involved in gambling their relationships with other gamblers steadily intensify due to their shared interests while those they once had outside the gambling situation gradually disintegrate. As they are drawn more deeply into this world and continue to withdraw from their outside associations they become increasingly dependent upon fellow gamblers for all their social needs. Eventually other regular gamblers constitute their only circle of friends. Rosecrance claimed that when no outside sources of social contact remain, the need for simple human interaction becomes the primary reason for maintaining one's association with fellow gamblers:

> In many cases, through a process of socialization, gamblers have disengaged from other social groupings and maintain only a limited number of relationships outside of the gambling milieu. Because membership in betting groups can be maintained only by continuing to participate, quitting gambling can be extremely disruptive.[49]

In the words of one informant, "In the end you're left with your track buddies."[50]

According to Rosecrance, then, the gambler's commitment to persistent gambling despite financial loss originates in and is continually reinforced by the four primary binding social arrangements of information sharing, money lending, shared contingencies, and unlimited social interaction that accompany regular participation. Instead of the economic, structural-functional, and psychological explanations that have been proposed, his sociological approach and first-hand observations led him to conclude that "the sustaining dynamic of gambling is not the game itself, but the interaction of the players. The seemingly complex issue of why regular gamblers don't quit is that, for them, the rewards of social interaction outweigh the cost of participating."[51] So committed was he to his explanation that Rosecrance later ascribed social interactional motivations even to such individual forms of gambling as machine and lottery playing.[52]

FAMILY DYNAMICS

The related transactional or "game" and family systems approaches claim that pathological gambling and other addictive behaviors are caused by strained and unhealthy dysfunctional family relationships.[53] According to these explanations, which draw heavily from psychoanalytic and social learning theories, excessive eating, drinking, drug use, gambling, and similar behaviors become associated with certain social contexts which generally involve the members of one's own nuclear family. Thus, some transactional theorists believe that an addict may eat, drink, or gamble to excess in emulation of a parent who does so in order to win the love and approval of the other parent. In these cases it is believed that the addict is unconsciously acting on the irrational belief, for example, that if Father behaves in a certain way and Mother loves him, then she will also love me if I behave in the same way. However, most transactional and family systems theorists believe that addicts are merely playing their part in a social interactional "game" which they find rewarding. It is "played" in a maladaptive effort to control and manipulate others, particularly members of their own family.

Robert Ingram: Transactional Script Theory

Robert Ingram[54] combined elements of psychoanalytic theory with transactional analysis to develop a "transactional script theory" of pathological gambling. Like the psychoanalysts he assumed that the life experiences of all children play a key role in their later personality development and like the small- group interactional theorists he assumed that human behavior is also shaped by the positive and negative reactions, judgments, and opinions of others. Ingram argued that all gamblers know that they will inevitably lose if they play in places such as casinos, card rooms, and racetracks where the "house" always takes a cut. Because gamblers can choose between winning and losing venues, he felt that those who persist in gambling in such places must want to lose. He further maintained that any gambler's desire to win or lose can be traced to the judgments made by his parents and other influential authority figures in childhood, particularly to those who continually expressed the opinion that he would always be a success or a failure. With constant repetition of these attributions the child soon comes to believe this of himself. At about three and one-half years of age, children who are constantly exposed to such attributions write their own "life script" to fulfill these predictions. Those who have received approval and praise for their successes will adopt the life script of a winner while those who have been harshly criticized for their failures will adopt the life script of a loser. This choice, which children are said to see as a matter of survival, represents a lifelong commitment to actually becoming a winner or loser since this is what they have come to believe is expected of them. Therefore, pathological gamblers who persistently lose do not do so to alleviate the guilt they are supposed to feel over their unconscious masturbatory fantasies and parental death wishes as the psychoanalysts maintained; according to Ingram they do so to realize the "life script" of loser that they adopted in childhood to fulfill the negative expectations of their parents.

W. H. Boyd and D. W. Bolen: Family Systems Theory

Advocates of the "family systems" approach to marital counseling attribute the development and maintenance of addictions to dysfunctional family relationships in which addicts and their spouses have adopted the respective roles of "scapegoat" and "martyr."[55] In cases of pathological gambling, the gambler or "scapegoat" is usually the husband who is blamed for creating all the family's financial and other difficulties. The "martyr," generally the wife, laments her situation but stoically bears her burden often by turning to religion and prayer and constantly providing the necessary "bailouts," lies, and coverups for her unrepentant husband who misinterprets her behavior and the hardships she endures as love. As the situation deteriorates, the growing anger and resentment she feels toward the man whose incessant exploitation and deception have placed her in this position further strain the family relationship. In the meantime, however, the "martyr" gradually assumes more and more of the responsibility for running the family and making its decisions.

The modern family systems approach to pathological gambling was pioneered by W. H. Boyd and D. W. Bolen[56] who were among the first psychotherapists to hold group sessions with pathological gamblers and their wives. Their initial sessions involved two separate groups of four couples each. As these sessions progressed, Boyd and Bolen noted an emotional "seesaw" or alternation of symptoms between the marriage partners. In each case, as the family situation deteriorated with gambling, the wife gradually assumed a position of dominance within the household.

Boyd and Bolen repeatedly observed that whenever the "sick one" quit gambling and began to demonstrate assertiveness, independence, and other signs of "wellness," the wife's mental stability began to deteriorate. The ultimate purpose of the wife's behavior, the therapists determined, was to reestablish her own position of dominance. Throughout their husbands' lengthy "sick" period the wives had grown to enjoy a clearly defined degree of authority and control within their respective relationships, a role they preferred to that of submissive, compliant housewife. A wife, fearing that she might lose her hard-won control should the husband regain his former position as household head, reacted accordingly, sometimes by threatening a nervous breakdown. When a husband witnessed this irrational behavior he, in turn, felt threatened that he might lose his strong and capable wife. He then fell back into his "sick" role and resumed gambling in order to salvage his precarious marriage. Time and again, the therapists insisted, the chaotic and symbiotic nature of the marital relationships, the complementary pathology present in the marriages, and the vicious villain-victim style of interactions were reflected in a turbulent group process and phasic alternations of therapeutic progression and regression."[57] Such strained family relationships can persist only so long before they break down entirely. They point out that gambling is sometimes wrongly blamed for perpetuating marital discord when it is in fact an effect rather than a cause of family dysfunction:

> In this confusing circus of marital acrobatics and ploys, there exists the endless scapegoating involved in the projective identificatory processes, the simultaneous victim-villain interactions, and the ubiquitous threats, accusations, and fears of abandonment. Finally, in order to simplify and understand the endless intrapsychic confusion and marital chaos, both marital partners fraudulently and inaccurately label gambling as the cause and reason for it all.[58]

Valerie Lorenz: The Phases of Family Breakdown

The origin and development of the various kinds of family dysfunction that pathological gambling can generate have been more recently described by Valerie Lorenz.[59] In her view, women who have joined GamAnon tend to conform to a particular pattern, share a common personality, and are attracted men who have an addictive personality. GamAnon is an organization of close family members–generally the wives–of pathological gamblers. As a group they have been described as "passive, dependent, impulsive, loving, nurturing, responsible, and law abiding."[60] They typically grew up in homes in which the father was an alcoholic or gambler himself and the mother was strict, demanding, and rejecting. Since they feel unloved, insecure, and have no self-confidence, they are drawn to men who are aggressive, flamboyant, colorful, glib, generous, and exciting.

As the gambler's addiction and the resulting dysfunctional relationship progress, the spouse–most often the wife–passes through a series of developmental stages:[61]

The denial phase. The first is the "denial" or "discovery" phase during which the wife first learns of her husband's gambling, confronts him about it and the monetary losses, believes his demonstrations of remorse and his promises to cut down or quit, and forgives him. When the inevitable relapse occurs she begins to make excuses for her husband in whom she wants to believe and whose gambling, she tells herself, will only be temporary. Although the problem mounts as the cycle of gambling, accusation, and forgiveness continually repeats itself, her denial of it is still so strong that she may even accompany her husband to the track or casino. During this first phase the spouse therefore accepts the gambling and its escalation as relatively minor difficulties.

The stress phase. The second is the "stress" phase which is marked by an obvious reduction in the time her husband is at home, the realization that he has continually lied to her, feelings of rejection and isolation, arguments over family finances and other problems, attempts to control her husband's gambling, and "bailouts" or covering his losses and debts for him. This is also the stage at which the gambler takes the offensive by adopting a "See what you make me do?" strategy and accusing his wife, with her lack of understanding and constant nagging, of being the ultimate cause of the problem. If he is at all successful, his wife will even begin to accept part of the blame and guilt for her husband's gambling and her family's difficulties. Nevertheless, the resentment she feels toward her husband continues to grow along with her humiliation over the family's unpaid bills and lack of necessities. Toward the end of this stage she often begins to avoid her own friends and associates in an effort to hide her own embarrassment.

The exhaustion phase. The third or "exhaustion" phase marks the limit of her endurance. It involves impaired thinking and confusion, rage, anxiety, and panic as well as feelings of betrayal, hopelessness, helplessness, and doubts about her own sanity. Even she begins to take out her frustrations on her children who now bear the brunt of the family discord and suffer verbal, and often physical, abuses at the hands of both parents. The wife may experience a host of psychosomatic problems, resort to alcohol or pills, or have a mental breakdown. By this time she is seriously contemplating divorce and possibly even suicide. It is also at this point that she seeks help for her plight, usually through mental health and religious professionals, the legal system, and various social service agencies few of which ever refer women in her situation to GamAmon.

When they finally do discover GamAnon their own recovery involves passage through another series of developmental stages. During the "critical" phase she accepts the fact that compulsive gambling is an illness, refuses to provide any additional bailouts, and begins to reestablish old social relationships. In the "rebuilding" phase, the spouse regains some of her self-confidence, begins to make realistic decisions and plans, recognizes her own needs, and improves communications and becomes closer with the other members of her family. The final or "growing" phase finds the wife relaxed, sharing, helping others, and feeling a much stronger sense of accomplishment.[62] When the pathological gambler is a woman, the resultant family dysfunction is much the same though it often develops at a greatly accelerated pace and a husband is generally less tolerant of this behavior than a wife.

The Control Game

A variation of this theme was provided by a psychoanalytically-oriented psychologist who conducted an eight-month participant observational study of Gamblers Anonymous.[63] He suggested that the principle reason the wives of so many gamblers show so much interest in the program and in maintaining their husbands' abstinence is not because they are afraid the men will gamble and lose, but because they are afraid they may gamble and win. Despite the lack of any evidence, he assumed that these women were all motivated by a need to manipulate and control their husbands, a condition they were able to impose as long as they were losing. Therefore, he speculated, since a large win would threaten their dominance, the wives must have unconsciously hoped their husbands would lose whenever they gambled. He felt that the men perpetuate this situation for much the same reason. For them, "gambling represents an abortive attempt at emancipation which must fail because independence from the wives cannot be sustained."[64] Abstinence, the goal of Gamblers Anonymous, now becomes essential for both parties since it is as effective as loss in preventing the big win that would destroy the dominant-submissive relationship that they were already enjoying.

Valerie Lorenz[65] also observed that parents of pathological gamblers often fall into a similar trap which puts a severe strain on their own relationship. Typically, they, too, pass through a denial phase during which they make excuses, lie for their son, and lend him money. Believing the stories they have heard about the bodily harm that unpaid loan sharks are capable of causing, they may even mortgage their home to pay his gambling debts. Lorenz described the fathers of compulsive gamblers as typically "hard-working, a taskmaster, nonaccepting, and undemonstrative."[66] Only after his patience and resources are exhausted, and he finally realizes that his harsh and incessant lectures on maturity, responsibility, and self-control have been useless, does he refuse any more bailouts. However, when this happens the mother, who is generally described as "loving, protective, overly emotional, dependent, and controlling"[67] becomes even more protective and begins to provide the gambler with money and support behind the father's back. The mother, who is now forced to choose between her husband and son, becomes increasingly resentful of her husband's rejection and angrier at her own failure to make her son give up gambling. This new mother-son relationship serves to further alienate the father and to create even more tension and discord between father and son, and now also between husband and wife. The husband, who invariably learns of his wife's actions, feels that he has lost the ability to control her and becomes filled with self-doubt for which he also blames the son. In the meantime, the gambler's siblings also feel anger, jealousy, and resentment since they interpret all the attention that he is receiving as their own rejection by the parents. Although this nearly intolerable situation may continue for years, the marriage survives precisely because of the son's gambling. The attention the parents' focus on their son's gambling and the problems it is causing blinds them to the realization of their own dysfunctional relationship. Therefore, like the wife of the gambler, "the parents have a vested interest in maintaining their son's pathology, thus avoiding awareness of unhappiness in their own marriage."[68]

CRITIQUE OF INTERACTIONAL APPROACHES

Although small group, interactional, transactional, and family systems theorists seldom speak of the "functions" of gambling, their approaches are essentially functionalistic. As noted above, structural-functional analyses generally attribute the persistence of all institutionalized social behaviors to one of two primary functions: reducing anxiety and the promotion of social solidarity through the reinforcement of social bonds. In fact, Lorenz used this very term in describing the dysfunctional relationship that develops between the parents of pathological gamblers:

The son's gambling and the turmoil caused by the gambling, in reality, tend to serve *a very useful function*, unacknowledged by the parents. The son's pathology enhances the symbiotic relationship of the parent's own pathological marriage.[69]

This orientation is also evident in Rosecrance's discussion and analyses of the various ways in which an individual's commitments to gambling are fostered and strengthened by the "binding social arrangements"[70] that develop among regular gamblers. In the final analysis, Rosecrance claimed nothing more than that information sharing, money lending, shared contingencies, and the opportunity for social interaction all "function" to promote social interaction and solidarity among regular gamblers. Implicit in the explanations of other interactional theorists is that gambling serves to reduce anxiety by providing gamblers with identities and role behaviors of their own choosing. Unfortunately, neither Oldman nor the other researchers provided any empirical data by which their claims could be verified; they offered only opinions which were shaped by their prior theoretical indoctrinations.

Social interactional explanations for gambling persistence are therefore subject to the same basic criticism that applies to structural-functional analyses of any other social phenomenon, the false cause. To use Rosecrance's example, regular gamblers may indeed form cohesive social groups and membership in these groups may indeed provide certain benefits. However, these things tell us nothing about the true origins and motivations underlying persistent gambling since a person must already be a persistent or "regular" gambler before even being considered for acceptance by the group. Likewise, while many gamblers may adopt a certain persona or play a certain role after they start gambling, we do not know that they were initially motivated to gamble or that regulars are currently motivated to continue gambling primarily for that reason. Thus, while identity adoption, role-playing, mutual support group formation, and the functions they serve may very well be among the *consequences* of persistent gambling, they are certainly not its *causes*.

Perhaps the most obvious failing of the small-group explanation is that it cannot account for solitary gambling: the arguments of its proponents are entirely invalidated by most lottery and gaming machine players, the loners of the gambling world. Even in crowded casino settings many video poker and slot machine gamblers avoid conversation or social interaction of any other kind. Furthermore, many such gamblers have their own favorite machines and are aggressively territorial in keeping others from playing them. If they gambled primarily to socialize, any machine would do.[71]

Transactional and family systems explanations suffer many of the same failings as the other interactional approaches. The idea that pathological gambling somehow "functions" to reinforce marriage bonds between gambler and spouse or between the parents of the gambler is highly unlikely. Although this idea may be supported by a few case histories, given the high rates of divorce in this population–twice that of other groups[72]–it seems to be grounded far more on faith than in fact. The frequency of parental divorce among the cases that Lorenz herself cited and the quality of the marital relationship among the others also belie this contention:

> In case records for twenty-one patients at the Gambling Treatment Center of the National Foundation for the Study and Treatment of Pathological Gambling, the marital relationship of twenty sets of parents was extremely discordant; divorces were actualized in seven cases and the remaining marital relationships were described as very argumentative, emotionally barren, and limited in communications.[73]

The fact that more divorces do not occur could easily be explained by moral values and religious proscriptions that were internalized in childhood. For example, some clinicians[74] have reported that fully half the pathological gamblers they have treated were raised in Catholic homes and attended parochial schools where they would have been steeped in the teachings of a church that forbids divorce. An additional one-quarter belonged to the Jewish faith which also takes a dim view of divorce. Some treatment providers have reported that the frequencies of Catholics (41%) and Jews (19%) in their patient population were disproportionately high in comparison with the general population[75] while others have reported that nearly all the participants in their group therapy sessions came from Catholic backgrounds.[76] Nevertheless, even if pathological gambling somehow does serve to deter divorce in some cases, the knowledge that family dysfunction is one of its consequences again tells us nothing about how the problem arose in the first place. Lorenz's scenario in which the wives of pathological gamblers are all passive-dependent nurturing types who are initially attracted to the addictive personalities of their future husbands means that the disorder must already be established before the marriage takes place.

Henry Lesieur[77] has also criticized a number of Lorenz's generalizations. For example, the high rates of spousal abuse and spousal suicide attempts she reported have little meaning in isolation since they were not compared with the rates of these behaviors either in a control group or in the general population. Are the physical ailments that spouses of pathological gamblers experience due to stress or some other problem such as alcoholism? Since GamAnon members are primarily females, Lesieur also felt that Lorenz's data may be more representative of women than of men. Do husbands of pathological gamblers go through the same developmental phases of denial, stress, and exhaustion that women do? Is the situation any different in cases of poly-addiction? Since family research has so far tended to focus on the spouses of pathological gamblers, far too little is known about effects of gambling on the development of their children. It is clear, Lesieur argued, that our existing knowledge of family influences on the course of pathological gambling must be augmented by detailed ethnographic studies of family life and by comparative data from larger populations.

Like psychoanalytic theory, the family systems approach appears to be highly procrustean. That is, since its advocates insist on ascribing all addictive behaviors to dysfunctional nuclear family relationships, they go to great lengths to force every case of pathological gambling into this mold whether the "scapegoat" is single or married. Moreover, it is highly doubtful that the childhood experiences and personality traits of all pathological gamblers and spouses (or parents or children) are so similar that they all fall into the single "typical" patterns of "scapegoat" and "martyr" that Lorenz described. Finally, cases which do not fit the orthodox theory—such as those presented by single orphans and all others whose behavior could not possibly be influenced by family members—are simply not discussed. In the final analysis, although family systems theory may perhaps offer some insight into how dysfunctional family relationships develop and why they persist, they, in fact, reveal nothing about the ultimate origin of any addiction.

PLAY THEORY: SOCIOLOGICAL PERMUTATIONS

As discussed in the first volume of this series, a number of behavioral and social scientists have contended that gambling satisfies one or more basic human needs or drives. To reiterate, around the turn of the twentieth century it was suggested that the need for play, like the needs for food and sex, is an ancient instinctive drive that can be satisfied through gambling.[78] In the mid-twentieth century play, theorist Johan Huizinga agreed with his predecessors that play was an important evolutionary biological adaptation but he took their initial speculations several steps further by adding several new ideas of his own. He described play as an activity which is neither serious nor a part of our ordinary existence, but nevertheless has the ability to completely absorb its participants.[79] As voluntary contests for some material or symbolic reward, all play activities are constrained by sets of binding but freely accepted rules. An early need-state theorist, Huizinga felt that play activities serve both to relieve tension and to inspire states of euphoria that are otherwise unattainable. He then suggested that the play instinct was also the catalyst which allowed ancient societies to evolve from states of savagery to civilization. His rationale was that the spirit of play is suppressed by work but flourishes with leisure. Since greater leisure time is associated with higher levels of sociocultural development, leisure rather than hard work was responsible for all the greatest human achievements. He therefore saw evidence of the purported "play instinct" in all the legal, philosophical, socioeconomic, technological, and artistic accomplishments of civilized societies since, as far as he was concerned, they could not have become fully developed in the absence of leisure. Although he saw gambling as one form of play, he felt that it was neither profitable nor associated with any material interests.

These conclusions were later challenged by Roger Caillois[80] who disputed the assertion that modern games, contests, and other forms of play are vestigial cultural survivals of archaic instincts or that they are merely substitutes for real-life learning experiences. Although Caillois agreed that play produces nothing of material value, he maintained that it often results in the exchange of value and therefore subsumed all forms of gambling under his definition of play. Like Huizinga, Caillois saw play as a voluntary activity which is governed by numerous rules but is nevertheless quite detached from ordinary life.

Caillois divided the various forms of play into four fundamental categories: *agôn* includes competitive games such as billiards and athletic contests which involve skill and strategy; *alea* includes games of pure chance such as dice, roulette, and lotteries; *mimicry* involves role-playing situations in which the participants pretend to be and assume the behavioral and character traits of others; *ilinx* involves the pursuit of mood altering experiences which result in sensations of dizziness, euphoria, or panic. Because gambling provides amusement, enjoyment, a challenge, and "action," a term which includes both emotional arousal and escape, some modern researchers still regard it as a psychological drive-reduction mechanism which satisfies the hypothetical drive for play.[81] Some play theorists feel that our reliance on gambling to satisfy or reduce this need is learned in childhood through such games as marbles, card playing, and other games in which no actual money is staked.[82] According to Caillois, when people become so deeply involved in any recreational activity to the extent that it begins to dominate their thoughts and lives, it can no longer be considered play: when the pursuit of pleasure becomes an obsession, when the pursuit of escape becomes an obligation, or when a pastime becomes a compulsion, the activity has become pathological. Thus, according to Caillois, any form of play, including gambling, can become addictive.

Since Caillois' description of play applies to so many forms of gambling, his ideas have appeared in a number of motivational theories of gambling whose architects see this activity primarily as a form of adult play.[83] For example, *mimicry*, which allows players to cast off their own identity and personality and pretend to be someone else, is central to interactional theories of gambling. *Ilinx* or vertigo, which alters the players emotional state, is central to arousal theory. Thus, many play theorists see gambling more as a form of entertainment than a means of acquiring personal wealth. Marvin Scott's ethnographic description of racetrack life[84] would place this form of gambling under Caillois' *agôn* category of play. According to Scott, the "racing game" involves skill, strategy, and the careful consideration of data from a wide variety of sources. Successful racetrack betting not only requires the participants to acquire the crucial information necessary to win, but also to conceal this information from others and even to give out false information intended to cause their opponents to lose. Both the acquisition of useful information and the dissemination of useless information require guile, deceit, and connivance with such "backstage" actors as horse owners, trainers, grooms, jockeys, and other track employees. Although he called it a "game," Scott made it perfectly clear that serious daily bettors, for whom the racetrack is a way of life, are motivated only by the prospect of winning money. He contrasted these gamblers, who he described as "regulars," with the "occasionals" who visit the track only periodically and regard betting as a form of recreation: the regulars expect to win whereas the occasional merely hope to win. Other social scientists have also adopted Caillois' ideas in developing their theories.

Play and Structural-Functionalism

Some social scientists such as Vicki Abt and her colleagues[85] emphasized the play theory of Roger Caillois when they contended that the appeal of most common forms of gambling can be explained by their entertainment value. They were particularly antagonistic to the earlier psychological explanations which proposed that gambling of any sort serves only negative individual needs:

> This approach largely ignores the social system-maintaining dynamics of gambling which enable the *action* to continue through the socialization of players into the properties of the gambling situation. It places an excessive emphasis on the formal outcome of the game–economic gain or loss–while neglecting the process of the game itself. It ignores the leisure gambler who gambles for recreation and it exaggerates the influence of individual motivation to the neglect of the social context of gambling . . . such investigations . . . ignore the social and cultural functions of gambling behavior, especially at a track or casino.[86]

Although they stressed the play and entertainment value of gambling, Abt and her colleagues combined the principles of play theory with the ideas of earlier sociologists. In their synthesis they were careful to distinguish normative or conventional styles of gambling, which offer excitement, safe risk, and diversion, from abnormal, irresponsible, or pathological forms and insisted that their explanation of gambling as play applied only to the former. Like the earlier structural-functionalists they claimed that gambling often meets positive social as well as individual needs and therefore serves a very important purpose in modern Western society. Like the interactional theorists they also maintained that by establishing new roles and confirming new identities, casino and racetrack gambling can create their own distinct social worlds with their own particular symbolic meaning systems. Thus, in these contexts gambling is "simultaneously an escape from the 'real world' as well as a 'world building activity.'"[87] Like the play theorists they felt that gambling is a remedy for despair and a source of hope.[88]

As play theorists, Abt and her associates insisted that conventional gamblers do not play for money, they play for fun: for them, gambling provides entertainment, excitement, safe risk, escape, and an alternative social reality. Like modern economic theorists they insisted that cash, while it is important to gambling, is merely the medium through which this form of entertainment is enjoyed while player losses are voluntary outlays of discretionary consumer income which are spent to cover its cost. Although their explanation incorporated elements of interactional theory, unlike the earlier interactional theorists Abt and her colleagues claimed that play allows people to express their true personalities rather than the idealized personalities of those they are trying to imitate. Therefore, the numerous compulsions which psychologists so often claim as the motivations for all forms of gambling do not apply in these cases: "It does not intrude itself into 'ordinary' life nor does it impair the gambler's ability to function in the domain of work or to carry out personal responsibilities. It is voluntary behavior."[89]

Play as a Vehicle for Culture Change

Some anthropologists working with non-Western tribal groups agree that gambling is merely a recreational pastime but add functional elements of their own. For example, gambling was unknown to Australia's aboriginal peoples until European contact after which it was readily adopted and rapidly diffused. Anthropologist Jon Altman,[90] who lived among some of these peoples, maintained that the primary function of gambling among the Gunwinggu of Arnhem Land, is entertainment. An elderly native of Queensland's Biri tribe verified that gambling with cards initially became popular among his people solely for its entertainment value. Although the native players would sit on a blanket and gamble for hours, their individual gains and losses were relatively small. This was because they did not gamble for profit and the winners always returned a portion of their winnings to the losers so that they could continue to play.[91] Altman noted that cash, formerly unknown to the Gunwinggu, was still a relatively scarce commodity at the time of his study. Moreover, since it was derived primarily from social security payments and the sale of artifacts, its appearance among them was arbitrary and sporadic. Consequently, younger men and women of the tribe devoted considerable time to card playing in gambling bouts which sometimes continued for two weeks. Altman pointed out that since their principal game was a one of pure chance, the stakes tended to circulate continually among the players. Whenever any big winners emerged they would generally redistribute their winnings to others as gifts or, failing this, they would be pressured to continue playing until they inevitably lost. Altman explained that since the Gunwinggu had only recently been introduced to Western capitalism with its emphasis on individualism and the accumulation of wealth, they had not yet abandoned their traditional hunter-gatherer values of egalitarianism and sharing. He argued that during the transitional period in which they were undergoing rapid economic and social changes, gambling provided a vehicle for the redistribution cash in a way that accorded more closely with their traditional cultural values than those of Western society. Altman therefore saw aboriginal gambling not only as a form of play, but also as a mechanism which functioned to facilitate the transition from a subsistence to a cash economy.

Play and Interactional Theory

Other social scientists did not entirely reject interactional theory but incorporated some of its elements into Caillois' explanation for gambling. Sociologist Robert Herman also maintained that play theory would provide a much better explanation for gambling than psychoanalytic theory since it is grounded in reality as opposed to purely specious speculation. Play theory is preferable "not because the former is less outlandish or parsimonious, but [because] it is based on an evaluation of games played by children and adults, games generally and properly understood to be thoroughly interlaced with the normal, the typical, the *mainstream* life of larger culture."[92] Moreover, this approach relegates the roles of risk-taking and acquisitiveness to positions of minor importance in explaining peoples motivations for gambling. Caillois' classification suggested to Herman that the *fun* or *entertainment* function of gambling can be understood to be one or more of these variables in combination . . . that mimicry and vertigo account for the ostentation of *high rollers*; that mimicry efficiently describes much of what is meant in various writings by "role playing," "preparation" or "rehearsal". . . for adult life, or display of "character". . . in casinos. Vertigo may subsume such categories as the release of "*pleasurable-painful tension*, thrills and *expressive self-testing*, as well as many of the fanciful sexual metaphors that have plagued this field since Freud conjured up his essay on Dostoevsky and his father. . . . Competition, chance-taking, mimicry, vertigo and rule-making are all conventional, acceptable, mundane aspects of life. They are learned the same way anything else is learned, and they can be expressed in hundreds of different ways, including gambling.[93]

Play, Social Learning, and Drive-Reduction

Play theorists who emphasize the importance of *mimicry* are actually proposing a variant of social learning theory which incorporates a strong element of drive-reduction theory. However, the drive does not represent an instinctive need for play or recreation as some behavioral scientists have suggested. It is instead the contention of some social scientists that the need gambling serves to reduce is a learned or acquired drive for social status and prestige.

As advocates of this approach, James Smith and Vicki Abt[94] agreed with many of Herman's ideas but rejected his suggestion that monetary considerations are only of minor importance in gambling. Specifically, they felt that play constitutes one of the primary socialization mechanisms through which our cultural values are transmitted, reinforced, and eventually learned. Like Herman, they maintained that although the world of play is distinct from the world of reality, it is "consonant with the world around us"[95] in that it is often grounded in, and is a reflection of reality. It is through the games played in childhood and adolescence, they insisted, that people learn to gamble. This is thought to be particularly true in capitalistic societies where wealth is the principal measure of one's social worth. As a central value in modern American culture, the desire for wealth through risk-taking is mirrored in many of the games and pastimes of American children. According to Smith and Abt:

A person does not magically become a gambler at a certain age. Various cultural signals actually condition would-be gamblers. The media participate by romanticizing stories about gambling and gamblers, frequently showing daring, larger-than-life heroes thriving on risk, and also by giving enormous publicity to game show contestants or gamblers who win substantial prizes. American cultural myths and values ironically reinforce the materialism, the longing for material reward, and the excitement of pursuing dreams that characterize many gamblers' fantasies. Finally, the ritualized play of several childhood games provides training for future gambling activity and in some cases may be seen as a kind of gambling in itself. In this way, the reflecting and teaching functions of culture may actually predispose Americans to gambling behavior; thus it comes as no surprise that commercial gambling occupies the significant social, economic, and cultural position that it does in American society today.[96]

Like Herman, Smith and Abt also stressed that competitiveness, aggressiveness, courage, bravery, and independence, all of which are necessary for the acquisition of wealth, are core values of American males. They maintain that all of these highly valued qualities are cultivated and reflected in the games of children and adolescents, particularly in athletic events. Owing to strong cultural pressures to compete and win, those who are not physically endowed or athletically inclined will seek other ways of expressing these necessary masculine characteristics. Gambling games, which combine skills which are not dependent on strength with a strong element of chance, provide a ready means of doing so. Smith and Abt therefore regard aggressive competition and acquisitiveness as expressions of a socially learned or acquired drive. This drive for success is fueled by the culturally-imposed sanctions and incentives which all Americans assimilate as they grow up. Those who cannot otherwise satisfy this drive may learn that it can be reduced, at least in part, through gambling. These ideas are probably nowhere better expressed in the following description of an adolescent poker game:

> The subsurface habits, whether verbal or physical, which these adolescents brought to the poker table, are essentially those which they bring to the dinner table, the classroom, their other play. They are part of the maturative process. When the adolescent approached the card table, he brought his "inner manliness" with him. It is this kind of "man-to-man" relationship, where adolescent striving for asserting maturity and achieving recognition thereof from his peers, can genuinely be observed, stripped of fraud, of role playing his adolescence in front of his seniors.[97]

Chapter 5

THE GAMBLER'S POINT OF VIEW

Although Goffman, Oldman, Herman, Abt, Smith, and others conducted their research in gambling settings, they were more outside observers of gambling and its consequences than they were actual gamblers. However, a number of others felt that while detached, objective scientific observation may allow some insights that elude the armchair theorist, observation alone does not permit the researcher to "get inside the head" of the gambler. Like Rosecrance, they employed different research methods by becoming participant observers in natural gambling environments and conducting in-depth interviews with actual gamblers. These approaches often led to quite different conclusions.

THOMAS MARTINEZ AND ROBERT LAFRANCHI: POKER PLAYERS IN NORTHERN CALIFORNIA

Thomas Martinez and Robert LaFranchi[1] studied active poker players in the cardrooms of northern California. Martinez, a professor of sociology with a fondness for poker, entered the field to discover not only why people play poker, but also why some people remain consistent losers even after years of experience with the game. "Why didn't they learn how to win?", he asked.[2] To answer these questions Martinez became a participant observer, an approach he preferred to structured interviews and other forms of nonparticipant observation. As an active gambler himself, he simply kept his eyes and ears open and engaged other gamblers in casual conversation while playing poker with them. At the time, LaFranchi was a business student who was financing his education by working as a dealer and part-time manager at the cardroom that Martinez frequented. After four years of study, collaboration, and synthesizing their respective observations, they arrived at their own conclusions about why people gamble and why some never learn to win.

Like Bergler, Martinez and LaFranchi felt that different people were driven by different motivations. Unlike him, however, they rejected psychoanalytic explanations with their emphasis on sex. Instead, they adopted a more eclectic approach by drawing from a number of popular sociological and psychological theories.

A Typology of Poker Players

Martinez and LaFranchi not only pioneered the use of participant observation in the study of gambling behavior but they were also among the first to construct a typology of active gamblers. Their principal subjects were 60 poker players who regularly patronized the cardroom. All were men, most of whom were middle-aged, had at least a high school education, enjoyed steady employment, and earned lower-middle class incomes. For these reasons the researchers also rejected the earlier moralistic and sociological notions that cardroom gambling attracted the transient, criminally inclined, and otherwise "deviant" lower-class elements of society. Despite the apparent homogeneity of their subjects, they were able to distinguish four distinct types of poker players: action players, losers, break-evens, and winners. The behaviors and motivations for playing in all four groups appeared to be closely related to their gambling attitudes, particularly those toward winning and losing.

Action players appear to be compulsive gamblers who want to lose. Action players, who represent about two percent of all regulars, rely more on blind luck than reason and good playing skills: they typically play extremely poor hands, bluff transparently, bet wildly, and lose consistently. Although they observe the formal rules of poker, they continually violate the informal rules of the cardroom. Action players are poor losers who breach the customary standards of sportsmanship and other principles of cardroom etiquette: they curse their luck, curse the winners, throw their cards and insults at the dealer, and otherwise disrupt the usually polite and cordial atmosphere of the game. Although the others cannot comprehend such reckless and rude behavior, the action player is tolerated because he loses so much money. According to the authors, "If he wants to be granted privileges, he has to pay the price."[3] Although their losses "make" the game, the extent to which their offensive conduct is endured is directly related to how much they lose and how fast they lose it.

Martinez and LaFranchi felt that tension-reduction is the primary reason that action players gamble. During their research they were struck by the fact that all the action players they encountered were small businessmen who gave the distinct impression of lacking the full degree of success and status to which they aspired. While playing they repeatedly complained about their customers, the demands of their job, and their lack of satisfaction in it. Since they were unable to discharge their frustrations at work they did so in the cardroom:

> Forced to keep their emotions in check at work, action players apparently use poker to give vent to built-up tensions. Since, as big losers, they felt free to let off almost as much steam as they cared to, poker for the action player is a sort of therapy, a release.[4]

However, the cardroom also provides a stage upon which the action player can don the persona of his idealized self. According to the authors, the action player behaves as he does in an attempt to gain the respect and esteem of the other players. Since he cannot earn the respect he desires in the larger world outside, he seeks it inside the cardroom by attempting to convey the impression that for him poker is merely a game and monetary losses are insignificant. By playing recklessly and plunging wildly he believes that the others will regard him as a highly successful businessman who can easily afford to squander his resources. He also believes that the others tolerate his unmannerly behavior because they secretly admire and envy him. In reality, however, although he actually can afford his losses, "the others do not care about what he may be or earn outside the cardroom, while inside it, he is someone to be laughed at when he is not around, but highly valued when he is."[5]

Losers are typically social isolates whose main interest in life is the cardroom and nothing outside of it is as important as playing poker. They were the least well educated of all the men in the sample and had the least prestigious occupations. In terms of their overt behavior, losers are very similar to action players with several important differences. In the first place, they are genuinely trying to win but lack the ability to do so and they are playing with money they cannot afford to lose. They do not lose as much as the action players since they do not gamble as recklessly and, consequently, the other players are less tolerant of their offensive behavior. For these reasons, and because they do not want to be held in the same foolish regard as the action players, losers tend to exert greater control over their behavior and are therefore somewhat less unmannerly and disruptive. Nevertheless, like the action players they behave badly whenever they lose, and they lose consistently. Although both losers and action players complain about losing, only the losers become nervous about it. Their play therefore becomes particularly reckless once they have lost about a hundred dollars. They also tend to drink more than the other players, especially when they have lost large amounts of money, and this, too, affects their play. Drunk or sober, action players always play in the same irresponsible way.

Rather than assume responsibility for their losses, losers attempt to preserve their self-image by rationalizing them. They do so by attributing their losses to "bad luck" since they hold the firm conviction that luck alone is responsible for winning or losing. Unaware of the statistical probabilities of the game, losers believe they could become winners if only they had the right luck. However, losers also place far more importance on the status and prestige that come with winning than do other players. This makes them poor winners as well as poor losers since they credit the few wins that they do manage to enjoy to a triumph of their own superior playing skills over the bad luck that ordinarily plagues them. Even action players are reluctant to make such outrageous claims. Nevertheless, losers will be more likely to continue playing if they can blame their losses on bad luck. Therefore, even though they know better, the more experienced players enthusiastically reinforce the loser's false beliefs and perceptions surrounding the importance of luck since by doing so they can relieve him of even more of his money. The authors added another cognitive dimension to their analysis when they wrote, "It is probably a safe assumption that the same people who blame their gambling losses on bad luck rather than lack of skill will also blame bad luck for their other failures."[6]

Martinez and LaFranchi looked to earlier sociological thought to explain why losers gamble when they concluded that, for them, gambling not only represents an attempt to bolster a low self-image but it also serves as a substitute for satisfactory social relationships. The main complaints that losers voice at the poker table concern their jobs and family lives, and usually center around arguments with their bosses and wives. Losers also make frequent ideological statements about what they consider to be proper gender roles in marriage. The nature of their complaints, in conjunction with their false beliefs about winning and losing, suggested to the authors that poker provides them means of counteracting or escaping from anomic relationships. Martinez and LaFranchi also felt that the strength of the loser's belief in luck is directly responsible for his persistence while losing, and that this general outlook—which attribution theorists would describe as an external locus of control orientation—probably extends into other areas of life outside the cardroom. However, since they were unacquainted with modern cognitive psychology and its explanations for gambling, they placed greater emphasis on the sociological theories with which they were familiar.

Winners and *break-evens* are quite similar. They consistently exhibit a rational approach to the game by combining sound playing techniques with good emotional control and they have little faith in luck and seldom lose control since they have learned through experience the patience needed to wait out a losing streak. They also make a conscious effort to adhere to the unwritten rules of play and tend to be good winners as well as good losers. Good sportsmanship is especially easy for winners since they consistently win more than they lose. Therefore, even more so than the break-evens, consistent winners are model players in terms of the exemplary standards of conduct and card-room etiquette they maintain. Both winners and break-evens are far more satisfied with their jobs than the others, make far fewer complaints about them, and enjoy a rich and active social life outside the cardroom.

However, there are some differences between them. While winners consistently win more than they lose, break-evens generally lose about as much as they win since they have not yet developed the playing skills and self-control that come with experience. Consequently, winners have greater confidence, patience, composure, and a more secure self-image. Break-evens are more satisfied with their marriages than action players and losers, and make few complaints about their home lives. Winners, who are generally younger than the other players, tend to be single or divorced and therefore have no domestic problems at all. Winners appear to be particularly extroverted, sociable, and self-confident people who like their jobs, have many friends, and enjoy many leisure pursuits apart from poker.

Both winners and break-evens place far less reliance on luck than losers since they know that good and bad runs of cards are inevitable: what really counts is how the hand is played. Moreover, the self-image of winners and break-evens is not dependent on the opinions of others: winning alone is expression enough of their self-worth. In order to reduce the frustration and anger of other players, winners may publicly attribute their success to luck. They know privately, however, that winning is a matter of skill and self-control.

Martinez and LaFranchi contended that winners and break-evens play for the challenge and entertainment that poker provides:

> They seem to play primarily for the satisfaction of succeeding through personal skill. Winners and break-evens also enjoy the gamesmanship of being the good winner and good loser; under this kind of stress they pride themselves on keeping their "cool." At poker they have a fateful situation for highlighting and reinforcing this much-admired quality.[7]

Winners and break-evens appear to have an outlook on life that attribution theorists would refer to as an internal locus of control orientation. They therefore approach the poker table with the same attitude they have in approaching other areas of life: "For the winners," the authors wrote, "poker is neither a release nor an escape, but a way of life, a continuation of a gamble they thoroughly enjoy and master."[8]

The Importance of Emotional Control

Since consistent losers are rarely able to control their outbursts, Martinez and LaFranchi felt that the key to winning lay in mastering one's emotions. Winners and break-evens see the behavior of the action players and losers as an important object lesson: "it highlights the importance of rational, patient control over betting as the superior guide for winning."[8] It is precisely the command that the better players have over their emotions and playing style that keeps them from losing:

> When the average player finds himself acting like a bad loser, he often knows it is time to quit playing for a while, because such behavior is associated with a consistent loser. Players with sufficient insight realize the importance of detachment and coolness to winning. Quite often they will get up to "cool off" for a few minutes, and then return after getting back into the frame of mind that will help him resist the pressure of losing until he gets a good run of cards. Winners do this the most, then the break-evens, the losers, and action players not at all.[10]

The authors therefore concluded that success is a direct consequence of the gambler's self-image, sportsmanship, and behavior. Even some losers are eventually able to realize that their personal conduct can lead to poor playing and therefore make a conscious effort to remain calm as they play. Thus,

> It is this growing ability to recognize one's behavior in response to losing and winning that is a transitional stage between being a consistent loser and a break-even. Few consistent losers, however, ever develop this ability to see that it is their reaction to losing that causes them to lose.[11]

This, they felt, is because the social significance that poker holds for losers and action-players is so great that it takes precedence over any desire to develop the skills and self-discipline necessary to win.

Although few would dispute their conclusion that good emotional control can reduce a poker player's losses, Martinez and LaFranchi eventually carried this line of thought beyond the bounds of reason. So convinced were they of the causal relationship between a player's character displays and accomplishments that they went so far as to claim that merely effecting a winning attitude and demeanor can itself become the key to success:

> Poker is a game which helps some men shape ideas about themselves. If a player is able to create an image of the calm, self-assured winner, he is likely to become a winner.[12]

Motivations

In summary, Martinez and LaFranchi felt that different kinds of people gamble for different reasons and that these reasons are social rather than sexual. Despite the fact that some poker players consistently lose, they found no overt evidence that people gamble as a substitute for sex or to allay any sexually-related guilt feelings as Bergler and the other psychoanalysts proclaimed.

They called upon both **tension-reduction** and **interactional theory** to explain the motivations of *action players* who gamble not only to vent their frustrations as some learning theorists maintain, but also to display a particular kind of persona or "character," as Goffman and other interactional theorists claimed. Thus, their purpose in reckless playing and intentionally losing is to communicate the impression that they are "big shots" who can afford to lose.

The investigators explained the motivations of *losers* by reference to **anomie theory** since they felt that losers gamble in an attempt to gain the social recognition and status that come with winning. They also echoed the ideas of contemporary **personality** theorists and anticipated the ideas of later **cognitive** psychological theorists when they attributed the loser's persistence to the strength of his external locus of control orientation and irrational beliefs concerning the importance of luck in a game that requires a large measure of skill.

Winners and *break-evens*, the authors felt, are motivated by their enjoyment of the game, and especially by the challenge of competition and the opportunity to exercise their own skill and intelligence in playing a winning game. Although they also stressed the good character traits that winners and break-evens commonly display, their discussion suggested that these displays were more genuine than affected. Thus, the gambling of winners and break-evens was not motivated by the opportunity to feign good character, as Goffman argued. Rather, their character displays appeared to be more a consequence of their preexisting attitude concerning the importance of skill over luck and their rational, pragmatic playing styles. While the authors therefore adopted Caillois' **play theory** to explain the motivations of winners and break-evens, they also implied that these players possess a strong **internal locus of control orientation** with which they approach all facets of their lives.

DAVID HAYANO: POKER PLAYERS IN SOUTHERN CALIFORNIA

David Hayano,[13] an anthropologist with a love for poker, was an active participant long before he became a scientific observer. Hayano freely admitted that he was so avid a poker player in the cardrooms of southern California that he had seriously considered resigning from his tenured university faculty position to become a full-time professional gambler.[14] Only after he had already spent "thousands of long, hard hours in the cardroom,"[15] had become well-known and accepted by the cardroom staff and other regular players, and had begun to socialize with these people even outside the cardrooms did he begin to think about his situation from the perspective of a social scientist.

The result of Hayano's deep personal involvement in the lives and lifestyles of professional gamblers was *Poker Faces*, a richly detailed "auto-ethnography" of the social scientist's "own people" written from the point of view of a true "inside member" of this unique subculture.[16] As an ethnographer, Hayano presented more a descriptive analysis of the California cardroom scene and the professional poker players who frequent these establishments than a theoretical treatise on gambling motivations. Nevertheless, one major point he stressed throughout his work is that these gamblers play to win, not to lose.

Gambling as Work

Although Hayano touched only lightly on the phenomenon of compulsive gambling, he clearly disagreed with the earlier psychoanalytic and sociological explanations for it.[17] In doing so he showed as much concern for what compulsive gambling is *not* as with what it might be. He acknowledged, for example, that "Winning brings on a feeling of power and the sensation that the run of cards and the attack of opponents are well under control"[18] but he did not subscribe to power theory as the cause of compulsive gambling. Instead, Hayano described these feelings as a consequence of gambling rather than its cause. He also became convinced that "the single causal factors normally advertised in the literature, such as a lonely childhood, the alleviation of guilt, the desire for self-punishment, escapism, or masturbatory substitutes, do not seem to provide sufficient explanation."[19] Hayano agreed with Goffman and other small-group interactional theorists that many players do, indeed, adopt certain self-images and present them to others but he did not endorse **interactional** or **game theory** explanations as the cause of gambling. Instead, Hayano also explained the adoption of the gambler's persona as a consequence rather than a cause of gambling. Such displays are not performed to act out wish-fulfillment fantasies but to deceive, intimidate, or otherwise influence the play of their opponents and to keep losers and reckless players in the game. As part of an overall playing strategy they represent just one of many tactics that serious and professional players employ in their quest to win.[20] Finally, and perhaps most importantly, the playing strategies of all the poker players that Hayano observed demonstrated only their keen desire to win: he has never seen a gambler play to lose as the psychoanalysts maintain.[21]

Since cardroom regulars come from all walks of life and represent all socioeconomic classes, Hayano also disagreed with the moralists and deprivation theorists who categorized all serious and professional gamblers as lower-class cultural deviants.[22] Neither are the professional card players that he has encountered all cheats and scoundrels as has been commonly thought: obvious cheaters, drunks, and thieves are not welcome in the cardroom.[23] Nor are they all of the most honest and ethical sort: some may steal chips, others "forget" to ante or how much they owe the pot after a series of raises, and friends sometimes play in collusion with one another. Hayano felt that the overall level of cardroom dishonesty falls at some indeterminate point between these extremes[24] but he nevertheless believed that "most commercial cardroom poker games are completely straightforward."[25] He admitted that some professionals deliberately adopt the persona of social misfits, if only to shock outsiders. However, most attempt to show a positive image of respectability, stability, and legitimacy to a disapproving public outside the cardroom. "Face work" of this sort is therefore performed in an effort to gain social approval and acceptance for an unconventional, stigmatized way of life.[26]

Most full-time poker players think of their occupation as hard work. Professional gambling involves long hours at the poker table, intense concentration and self-discipline, and the constant threat of heavy losses. Only a few players win large amounts while many go broke. The phrase, "It's a hard way to make an easy living"[27] is commonly voiced. Although some professionals describe themselves as "sick" or abnormal for spending so much time in the cardroom and attempting to earn a living in such a difficult way,[28] Hayano did not regard their gambling as necessarily compulsive or pathological since they are there primarily to make money. He therefore felt that it may be more accurate to think of professional poker players as "compulsory" rather than compulsive gamblers.[29] While gambling may cause financial ruin, for many it also provides the only recognizable means of salvation from insolvency and debt. He therefore maintained that "the decision to gamble may be a *realistic* appraisal of the individual's situation and a reasonable way to dig himself out of debt."[30]

Cardroom Jargon

Cardroom regulars have their own jargon. They refer to losers as "feeders" since their losses support the professionals.[31] Loose, uncontrolled players who lose large amounts without seeming to care are known as "berserkos" and "desperados."[32] Those who continue to play after winning large amounts but are unable to walk away from the table until they have "blown back" their winnings and lost all their own money are "sickies" or "degenerates."[33] Persistent losing in and of itself does not necessarily signal compulsive gambling since many regular but controlled gamblers have no difficulty in limiting their daily, weekly, or monthly losses to no more than they can afford.[34]

Normally controlled players who become angry, depressed, and careless after a particularly painful loss or during losing streaks are said to be "on tilt." Painful losses or "bad beats" include not only large losses but also situations in which a good, potentially winning hand loses to an even better hand.[35] A "bad beat" in poker is therefore analogous to an unexpected "fluke" situation in racetrack and sports betting. Even long-time regulars and professionals can find themselves "on tilt" for periods of only a matter of minutes to those lasting several months or years. According to Hayano, "being on tilt is *always* accompanied by visible moods such as anger, depression, hostility, or anxiety when a player changes from calm to erratic behavior and loses his patience and composure."[36] This is especially dangerous for professionals since when they are "on tilt" they may begin to play in the self-destructive style of a "berserko" or "sickie" and thus threaten their playing future. For Hayano, though, being "on tilt" represents a potentially disastrous but temporary mental state and not a permanent, uncontrollable gambling compulsion.

Impediments to Success: Compulsive Gambling as Irresponsible Gambling

Like Oldman, Hayano felt that compulsive gambling is largely a matter of **poor money management**. He believed that the primary difference between the professional from the compulsive gambler is that professionals consistently win more than they lose while compulsives consistently lose more than they can afford: "The compulsive gambler . . . is a poor player and consistent loser who does not possess the psychological makeup for skillful, controlled, play."[37] "Sickies" and "degenerates" who cannot quit when they are ahead appear most closely to fit Hayano's definition of compulsive gamblers.

All gamblers, whether professional or amateur, are vulnerable to three primary money management risks which may lead to "chasing," financial problems, and problem gambling. These are the failure to set limits on one's time and money (playing too long and borrowing more money to play than one is able to repay), the escalation of playing stakes (playing beyond one's means), and betting on games and events outside of one's specialty (taking chances on riskier games).[38] These three dangers often operate at the same time to wipe out a gambler's bankroll and create large debts. "More often than not," Hayano found, "when these dangers deplete a player's stake, the professional as well as the regular and loser must search for practical alternatives in order to stay in action. And so the downward spiral of playing, losing, and raising a stake takes hold."[39] After they have borrowed all they can from cardroom friends, from the cardroom's resident loan shark, or from outside sources, the final alternative for persistent losers is to stop gambling entirely and get outside help for their problem.

In addition to poor money management, the success of many inexperienced and less sophisticated gamblers may also be jeopardized by other dangers.[40] One obvious reason for the losses and failures of many aspiring gamblers is a **lack of basic playing skills**. Novices frequently play too many unlikely hands and fail to alter a consistently loose or conservative playing style to accommodate different games and different players.

Erroneous cognitions represent a third factor since even the most seasoned gamblers are vulnerable to a lack of knowledge or unrealistic beliefs concerning luck and the laws of probability. Gamblers often erroneously believe in winning and losing streaks and in false probabilities rather than a purely random occurrence of events. Hayano also agreed with Oldman[41] when he observed that "cardroom gamblers rely on two contradictory beliefs: (1) when things run bad, they've got to change, and (2) when things run bad, they've got to stay that way."[42] By simultaneously holding and acting upon these two contradictory beliefs, a gambler can never make a wrong prediction but can still continue to lose more often than win.

Finally, **locus of control orientation** is also an important factors in any gambler's success or failure. Hayano felt that most consistent losers tend to ascribe their failures in the cardroom and in life in general to outside influences—bad luck, fate, etc.–over which they have no personal control. Thus, losers not only expect to lose, but they look for and find external reasons for doing so. Even their few successes are credited to such external factors as good luck or good timing.[43]

All of these risk factors—poor money management, inept card playing, acting upon false beliefs, and a fatalistic outlook on life–combine to prevent a gambler from winning consistently. Hayano considered "compulsive gambling" to be a consequence of the co-occurrence of these factors rather than the result of any unconscious desires or uncontrollable social conditions. Thus he argued, "My position avoids the tautology that compulsion causes losing and losing causes compulsion because I have focused directly on various observable game, metagame, and coping strategies created not by the desire to lose but by the desire to stay in action."[44]

The way a committed gambler's mind works is probably nowhere better communicated than in Hayano's final paragraphs which describe an actual incident involving the author and another poker player:

> It is 7:15 in the morning, a Monday morning, and the sun, bright and clear, is a stark visual contrast to the inside of the cardroom. After sixteen hours of solid poker playing I have just stepped outside of the Rainbow Club. Bone weary and depressed, I'd been trying to get even the whole night but never succeeded. I'm looking forward to a good ten hours' sleep.
>
> Walking to the car a friend approaches and says, "Look. I've got an idea. We're both stuck. Let's have some breakfast and then start the game at nine. The day crew is easy. We'll both get even."
>
> I think about his offer for a short second, but all I can see is bad hand after bad hand dancing before my eyes. Uncertain feelings about the gains and losses of poker, and over ten thousand hours of ethnography-cum-poker-playing (or is it the reverse?) merge into one confusing mess. I take a deep breath and find some comfort in the crisp air. I straighten my back.
>
> "You're on . . . let's go!"[45]

JOHN ROSECRANCE: PROBLEM GAMBLING AND ATTRIBUTION THEORY

Whereas sociologist John Rosecrance called upon **interactional theory** to explain "persistent" gambling,[46] he called upon **cognitive psychology**, and **attribution theory** in particular, to explain "problem gambling." He believed that this condition, which others refer to as "compulsive" or "pathological" gambling, results from a shift in the gambler's cognitive orientations.[47] Rosecrance's attribution theory is strikingly similar to the **learned helplessness theory** of McCormick and his colleagues[48] although the two approaches appear to have been developed independently.

Like Hayano, Rosecrance was himself an avid gambler before deciding to conduct field research. Whereas Hayano was a poker player, Rosecrance was an avid horse racing fan with a preference for off-track betting although he also spent a considerable amount of time at the track. Rosecrance claimed a thirty-year history of involvement in gambling activities, nearly half of which were spent at racetracks in Southern California and more than half of which were spent as a regular bettor at legal race books or off-track betting parlors in the casinos of Lake Tahoe, Nevada. To emphasize that he was no armchair theorist, Rosecrance reported that during his lifetime he had undergone

> ... a gambling odyssey that [took] me throughout the world, from palatial gaming clubs to back-room poker games and rundown, outlaw racetracks. During my gambling career, I have both experienced the dizzying heights of winning streaks and unbeatable rushes and suffered agonizing losses and confidence-shattering bad beats. I have come to know all manner of gamblers and their social worlds; those of poker players, horse racing devotees, sports bettors, casino gamesters, and lottery participants. Some could be considered occasional bettors; some, regular players; some, professionals; others, degenerates.[49]

Rosecrance also entertained thoughts of becoming a professional gambler and, at times, had even considered himself to be one.

The purpose of his studies was to investigate gambling and problem gambling in natural settings as opposed to the artificial environments of clinical and experimental psychologists. As noted previously, Rosecrance felt that his status as a racetrack and race book "insider" allowed him access to qualitative information which would be entirely unavailable to researchers outside the betting fraternity. His subjects were other "regulars" with whom he had already developed a close relationship. His study methods included a great deal of participant observation, many informal conversations, and even some interviews of a more formal nature with his many "horse playing buddies."

A Typology of Racetrack Bettors

Like others who had formulated typologies of gamblers,[50] Rosecrance[51] was disturbed that so many of his predecessors and colleagues viewed gambling as a social problem and therefore emphasized only its negative aspects and consequences. Like Scimecca, he stated that the purpose of his classification was "to demonstrate that racetrack behavior should be considered from a broad social perspective and not exclusively from a social problems orientation."[52] During his own long career as a horse player, Rosecrance became familiar enough with the racetrack and its devotees to distinguish among various kinds of gamblers. Since about 95 percent of all track bettors lose more money than they win, Rosecrance reiterated his earlier conviction that most gamblers must attend the track not to win money, but for other noneconomic reasons. By observing and interviewing 87 other serious track bettors over a 16-month period, he was able to describe five distinct types of gamblers and several different motivations for gambling. Using the "ethnoscientific" approach developed by anthropologists, the categories that Rosecrance enumerated were those that were devised and employed by the racetrack bettors themselves.

Regulars, who make up about 45 percent of all track bettors, are not problem gamblers but attend the track for purely social and entertainment purposes. Many regulars are older, retired men who had been weekend bettors for many years and, since their retirement, continue to enjoy track betting as a daily pastime. Since their incomes are now limited, however, most bet smaller amounts than previously and play favorites more often. Like Oldman,[53] Rosecrance believed that most players regard their losses as the price of the entertainment: while they all may hope to win, they generally expect to lose. Their primary goal in betting this way is therefore not to "make a killing" but to lose as little as possible. For them, racetrack betting and the social atmosphere they enjoy are amusements for which they are prepared and willing to pay. Like Newman, Rosecrance also found a substantial number of regulars to be younger men who were self-employed or employed as taxi drivers or shift workers whose flexible and nonstandard working hours allow them to spend time at the track. Since they are still earning regular incomes they are not so cautious in their betting as the retired regulars but tend to make more elaborate combination bets and bet more recklessly on long shots in hopes of making a big win. All regulars bet within their means and are able to weather their losses.

Part-timers are weekend players who make up about 35 percent of all participants. Although they enjoy the track as much as the regulars, their regular full-time employment prevents them from attending as often as they would like. Many therefore look forward to retirement so they can join the ranks of the regulars. Like the regulars, most part-timers do not play to win and keep their stakes within their means. Although participation is purely recreational for most part-timers, a minority take it more seriously. They hope eventually to start winning enough money at the track that they can quit their regular jobs and become professionals. For the aspiring professionals, however, losing streaks present more serious setbacks which they are less able to tolerate. Consequently, few realize their ambitions.

Pros, or professional horse players, who make up about 5 percent of all track-goers, are those few who have given up other employment and are able to support themselves through consistently successful racetrack betting. Since they win more often than they lose, and have been self-supporting for a number of years, they have built up enough of a stake to be able to sustain the periodic losing streaks they must inevitably face. Even when they are losing, pros will adhere to consistent, disciplined betting strategies which include playing the odds to the best advantage.

According to Marvin Scott[54] who also studied racetrack gamblers as a participant observer, pros are distinguished from other types of handicappers because they know the horsemen as well as the horses. That is, because they know that horses are not always entered in a race to win, they also try to determine the trainer's intentions. To accomplish this, the pros go to the paddock when the trainer finally reveals his intentions to the jockey immediately before the race. Although trainers attempt to conceal their intentions from the onlookers, the pros, through years of experience, are able to detect any inconsistencies in a trainer's normal interaction with a jockey. Any deviation from the typical pattern enables the pro to read the trainer's true intentions and alter his bet accordingly.[55] Moreover, since they view the racing game as a business, pros are far more disciplined in their demeanor and betting behavior than other kinds of horse players.

Serious players, about 10 percent of the track population, are nascent professionals who have also quit their regular employment to earn a living at the track. Serious players are distinguished from established pros by the fact that most have relatively recently quit their regular jobs or are actually semi-professionals who often resort to supplemental outside employment. Moreover, the undisciplined betting patterns of serious players frequently result in financial difficulties when they encounter the inevitable losing streak. When this occurs many will lose the control that marks the true professional. They abandon their usual betting strategies, bet inconsistently, and play dangerously by increasing their bets and chasing their losses in hopes of getting even with a spectacular big win.

Bustouts, who make up about 5 percent of all horse players, are primarily interested in action. Bustouts are not regularly employed but generally take part-time or temporary work when they need money. They therefore have relatively little to spend and what they do have is for betting. Bustouts most closely resemble the stereotypical Damon Runyon character. They are generally as knowledgeable about racing and handicapping as the regular and serious players but they rarely apply their knowledge. Instead, they use no consistent winning strategy but will bet on any race, generally choosing long shots over favorites, in hopes of making a killing. Consequently, they are resigned to their many losses but when they do realize an occasional win their money soon evaporates and they are once again reduced to hustling for their next stake. However, Rosecrance insisted that bustouts do not fit the clinical description of compulsive gamblers since they feel no compulsion to gamble, see nothing wrong in what they are doing, and have no desire to quit. Like Oldman, Rosecrance maintained that their primary problem is that they employ defective betting strategies and lack sound money management skills. Thus, the question that must be answered is why do they consistently bet so unwisely?

"Bad Beats," Going "On Tilt," and Problem Gambling

Attribution theory, Rosecrance's[56] approach to "problem gambling" is in direct opposition to those who argue that an early winning phase generates the initial optimism that leads to "compulsive gambling" as many advocates of the medical model insist. Not only did Rosecrance refuse to accept the notion that gambling can be "compulsive" but, like Hayano, he was also convinced that gambling problems originate with devastating losses resulting from "bad beats" or "flukes" that are entirely unexpected and extremely difficult for the gambler to rationalize and accept. He based his conclusions on first-hand observations and conversations with 65 race book regulars.

Attribution theory was developed by cognitive psychologists in their effort to explain the processes through which people attempt to understand, order, predict, and control the events that affect their lives. According to Rosecrance, attribution theorists see individuals as "intuitive scientists" who are always seeking to discover the reasons underlying various events and outcomes. The reasons they give for these occurrences reveal a great deal about their basic approach to life. One of the primary concerns of attribution theory is whether the perceived locus of control of any actor is internal or external; do people see themselves as controlling or controlled? Those whose locus of control orientation is internal generally attribute the outcomes of events to their own actions and therefore think of themselves as masters of their own destiny. Conversely, those who have an external locus of control orientation tend to perceive events as the result of such uncontrollable forces as luck or chance and therefore think of themselves as hapless pawns of fate.[57]

Attribution theorists maintain that people's causal attributions–their interpretations and explanations of their past successes and failures–can strongly influence their later actions. They also maintain that a person's normal locus of control orientation can be reversed by certain unexpected traumatic events, and that the changes in one's normal locus of control orientation can, in turn, alter his or her usual pattern of behavior. The duration of the emotional disorientation and abnormal behavior which follow such events varies not only with the individual, but also with the type, strength, and impact of any particular traumatic experience. Some attribution theorists therefore regard people's locus of control orientations as a gauge of the mental state which governs their actions. Thus, an internal locus of control orientation indicates a level of mental competence which is essential for rational behavior while an external locus of control orientation suggests a temporary emotional disruption or long-term maladjustment which can, and often does, precipitate irrational behavior.[58]

Rosecrance believed that regular racetrack bettors normally have an internal locus of control orientation and that their betting choices are rationally made on the basis of their past experiences and present handicapping skills. For this reason they rarely play casino games which they consider to be games of chance over which they have no personal control. Although they realize that some racing losses are inevitable, in the long run they expect to win more than they lose. They are able to explain away and cope with their losses—even extended periods of loss—since their causal attributions, which may or may not be based in reality, provide them with at least an illusion of control and allow them to maintain an optimistic outlook. In the words of one race book regular, "There's always a logical explanation for a losing bet"[59]—the saddle slipped, the filly was in heat, the race was fixed, etc. Rosecrance argued that such "Retrospective manipulation of data sustains horse-players' beliefs in the rationality of the actions and assures them that handicapping the horses is a skillful activity."[60] Thus, "An assumed under-standing of race results, even if erroneous, reinforces the gambler's sense of personal control."[61] On this point Rosecrance was in complete agreement with other adherents of **cognitive theory** who referred to such rationaliza-tions as the gambler's "biased evaluation of outcomes."

The "bad beats" that racetrack bettors experience can range from mildly disturbing to severely traumatic depending on the circumstances and the size of the bet. "Bad beats" are especially devastating when they result from such unexpected causes as an electrical power failure, a horse that stumbles or hits the rail, or a foolish mistake of the jockey.[62] According to Rosecrance, these catastrophic and seemingly inexplicable losses can trigger a chain of events leading directly to problem gambling. First, a "bad beat" can be so traumat-ic that it disrupts the gambler's normal locus of control orientation causing it to switch from internal to external: "Distraught losers no longer assume they have control and tend to attribute the success of future wagers to a 'cruel fate.'"[63] This severe cognitive disorientation then provokes dramatic changes in the gambler's usual betting and money management strategies which only serve to bring about even greater losses. The gambler then goes "on tilt" and begins to chase his losses by betting large sums in a highly irrationally man-ner—on long shots and improbable combinations—blindly appealing to fate but with no real hope of winning. He is now a problem gambler. In the words of one veteran horse player, "Nobody can keep cool when a really bad beat strikes. It's as if the fates are out to screw you personally. You can't help but get a little crazy."[64]

Most gamblers who encounter bad beats generally exhibit a distinct three-stage pattern of coping behavior before they are able to overcome these experiences. They initially undergo a "manic reaction" during which their normally internal locus of control orientation shifts to external and they start betting in an entirely uncontrolled manner. This is the "on tilt" phase described above. They then enter a "realization" phase during which they begin to acknowledge the irrationality and futility of this betting behavior, to regain some of their self-control, and to employ sounder betting strategies. This is known as "coming to your senses." Gamblers enter the final stage, "regaining internal control," when they have completely recovered their internal locus of control orientation and resume betting in their normally controlled manner. This is known as "putting it all behind you."[65]

Since most gamblers eventually do overcome these periods of emotional distress, Rosecrance felt that most problem gamblers (i.e., compulsive or pathological gamblers) can eventually resume responsible gambling. All serious gamblers sustain "bad beats," experience attributional shifts, and go "on tilt" at one time or another but the desire to stay "in action" eventually forces most of them to take the steps necessary to regain control of their emotions and betting behavior. Since the duration of any "on tilt" period of problem gambling will vary with each individual and circumstance, not all gamblers pass through these stages at the same rate and some will not pass through them at all. For certain individuals a "bad beat" can be so devastating and ruinous that they can never regain control and will continue to gamble in a problematic manner.

Rosecrance provided two real-life illustrations of the kinds of "super bad beats" that racetrack bettors can experience. The first involved a man who was prevented by a traffic jam from arriving at the track in time to place a $5,000 bet on his pick which paid over ten-to-one when it won the race. The second involved a man who bet $10,000 on a horse paying eight-to-one to win. It won the race but the man was unable to collect his $80,000 when the winner was disqualified on a foul caused by another horse. Until these experiences both men had been capable handicappers and careful bettors but these "bad beats" were so devastating that they immediately lost all control. In trying to obtain the money they "should have won" they foolishly bet all their remaining money on long shots in later races and continued betting irresponsibly for some time thereafter. The man in the first example was able to regain control and resume his normal betting pattern after a period of several months. The second was never able to overcome the emotional trauma of his "bad beat" and continued betting irrationally and losing consistently for the next 13 years.

Getting off "Tilt"

The specific reasons that some gamblers can overcome a "bad beat" and regain their normal locus of control orientation while others cannot are unknown although they probably involve a variety of financial, circumstantial, and psychological factors. Rosecrance suggested, however, that one key to overcoming the trauma of a "bad beat" and minimizing the length of the "on tilt" period lies in the support that is available from one's peers, other race book regulars. This support usually takes the form of "empathetic interaction" during which they can make objective assessments of the problem gambler's playing practices and call his attention to the irrationality of his bets. In this way one's peers "provide a touchstone to reality which can bring disoriented gamblers to their senses."[66] Those who utilize this network of "race book shrinks" have the greatest chance of regaining their internal locus of control. Those who disdain the advice and support that is offered are left to their own devices and may never be able to regain their emotional equilibrium. Rosecrance maintained that these are the ones who remain problem gamblers.

Somewhat earlier Rosecrance[67] had also described four additional strategies that veteran horse players commonly employ to help them ameliorate their gambling problems, stay off "tilt," and remain in action. He felt that "An understanding of these mechanisms can offer valuable insights into the phenomenon of problem gambling"[68] since, by applying them in a satisfactory manner, many committed gamblers have overcome their problems without having to quit.

The first of these strategies is the exercise of "voluntary external controls." After experiencing a particularly bad beat, some handicappers will temporarily abandon all gambling activities. They find that taking a hiking or skiing trip serves to distance them from the racing scene enough to "recharge their batteries" and gain a fresh perspective. Some gamblers deposit a portion of all winnings into an inviolable trust where it cannot possibly be used for gambling. For example, some gamblers make advance mortgage payments while others invest in long term treasury notes which carry substantial interest penalties for early withdrawal. Still others solicit the involvement of a spouse or significant other who is voluntarily given control of the gambler's income and allots only a predetermined amount of money each week for gambling.

A second adaptive strategy, "goal reorientation," involves an alteration of the gambler's basic betting strategy. Switching from riskier high-odds bets to more conservative low-odds bets represents an orientation away from a purely monetary goal to one of sustained participation.

A third strategy, the use of "aligning actions," represents the attempt to maintain a particular self-image. Aligning actions usually take the form of verbal disclaimers intended to communicate the gambler's reduced commitment to a particular bet or outcome. Knowing full well that they are more likely to lose than to win, many gamblers voice prospective disclaimers which are meant to express a degree of uncertainty in their betting choices thereby negating any appearance of overconfidence. As noted above, after losing they also have ready access to an arsenal of retrospective accounts or excuses—including flukes—which they can call upon to help them avoid any personal responsibility for the outcome and to maintain their illusion of control.

Finally, many horse players resort to "techniques for increasing short-term rewards." For example, after a series of losses many gamblers begin to bet on more than one horse or place a number of exotic combination bets (quinellas, exactas, and trifectas) per race. Although such practices increase short-term rewards by producing more winners, they also decrease the amount that can be won and eventually lead to even greater long-term losses. Rosecrance advised against this practice since "straight" betting–betting to win on only one horse per race–is generally less costly in the long run: while straight betting results in more overall losses, the occasional win is more likely to offset them.

Rosecrance's studies–which were based on the two case histories described, the work of other ethnographers, and his own observations of regular horse players–led him to draw two primary conclusions: problem gambling is reversible and one's peers in the gambling world–other *active* gamblers–are the best source of help in overcoming these problems. He added that these observations directly contradict the assertion of Gamblers Anonymous that the most effective counselors are former problem gamblers who are now abstinent.[69]

In sum, Rosecrance believed that "attributions of cause and locus of control play a central role in the development of problem gambling."[70] A devastating "bad beat" can seriously disrupt a gambler's emotional stability which, in turn, can change his normal locus of control orientation from internal to external. The gambler then goes "on tilt": he abandons his rational playing strategies and attempts to recoup his losses by betting irrationally. This emotional disruption is the primary cause of "problem gambling" which can be curtailed and reversed through the support and wise counsel of one's peers. Since problem gambling among horse race bettors can be reversed, Rosecrance contended that his findings contest the validity of conventional approaches which maintain that abstinence is the only acceptable solution. Instead, he recommended the establishment of treatment programs using active controlled gamblers as peer counselors to teach out-of-control gamblers some of the better gambling strategies and money management skills he described. Such programs, he speculated, would be highly successful in getting problem gamblers off "tilt" and keeping them from going "on tilt" again in the future.[71]

BASIL BROWNE: "ON TILT," EMOTIONAL CONTROL, AND PROBLEM GAMBLING

Sociologist Basil Browne's[72] thoughts on problem gambling were quite similar to those of Rosecrance. Like Rosecrance, Browne felt that the most perplexing question facing gambling researchers is why some people persist despite losing and, to arrive at an answer, he also studied active gamblers in a natural setting. Unlike Rosecrance, however, Browne also studied compulsive gamblers as they were involved in the attempt to quit gambling. Browne's observations of active gamblers were made during three years of employment as a card dealer at a legal poker parlor in northern California; his observations of recovering compulsive gamblers were made during one year's attendance at open meetings of Gamblers Anonymous. Thus, while Rosecrance did not acknowledge any severe losses by the active problem gamblers he studied, Browne wrote of the loss of jobs, of families, and the occasional loss of life that, according to GA members, can and do result from problem gambling.

Browne did not see problem gambling as an internal personality or addictive problem; he explained it as a combination of the external environmental or learned factors that shape gamblers' cognitions and their emotional reactions to the situations they face. Like advocates of the medical model, Browne felt that "loss of control" is central to the development of problem gambling. By definition, he pointed out, problem gambling means loss of control over one's gambling. Although this is often accepted as axiomatic, he also felt that the "loss of control" concept has not been adequately developed: as used by clinicians whose only contact with gamblers is in a therapeutic setting, it fails to include the experiences of active problem gamblers who have not sought treatment.

A thorough knowledge of the game and good money management skills are essential to the good gamesmanship necessary for retaining control over one's gambling. Although novices lacking in knowledge and experience are prime candidates for problem gambling, poor playing and money management skills are not its only causes as Oldman, Lesieur, and others suggested. "Logically," Browne argued, "it follows that if one learns good playing strategy and good money management one should be able to avoid gambling crises."[73] However, this is not always the case since experienced, skillful gamblers with a history of good money management skills sometimes do experience financial crises. Browne therefore felt that some other important but unseen factor must also be involved in the development of problem gambling. On the basis of his research, he became convinced that this factor is poor emotional management.

To explain loss of control over one's emotional equilibrium and gambling behavior, Browne also adopted the expression "on tilt," which gamblers commonly use to describe both the periods of loose, irrational playing and the mental state that accompanies such periods. Some researchers claim that subjective experience of being "on tilt" can include "blackouts, memory loss, dissociative states, or simply playing mindlessly without thinking of strategy."[74] Browne's use of the term in describing temporary deviations from gamblers' normal playing patterns and their obvious "intense internal emotional struggle"[75] was very similar to that of Hayano and Rosecrance. He noted that all gamblers go "on tilt" at some points in their career and that it is during these periods that they sustain the greatest losses. The length of time a player can be "on tilt" ranges from minutes to days but it can sometimes persist for months. Because gambling becomes a problem for those who are frequently "on tilt," Browne believed that "Problem gamblers' careers are characterized by tilting rather than by chasing."[76]

Inducing "Tilt"

Going "on tilt" involves three developmental phases: an initial encounter with a "tilt-inducing situation," an "internal emotional struggle to regain control," and "the deterioration of the player's game if he or she does not regain control."[77] Although inexperience and poor money management can lead to problem gambling, the way in which players deal with the tilt-inducing situations they encounter is the most decisive factor. Browne therefore believed that the most common tilt-inducing situations are unexpected "bad beats" (highly improbable losses) and "needling" (verbal criticism, provocation, and baiting) by other players who, for their own advantage, deliberately try to force their opponents into going "on tilt."

Other tilt-inducing situations include escape gambling, sustained losing streaks despite skillful playing, long playing sessions, and intoxication, all of which can adversely affect any player's normal game. The gambling establishments themselves are also responsible for some tilt-inducing situations. The cardroom management is sometimes called upon to settle disagreements among players and the word of the arbitrator is final. Frequently, however, the "house rules" are either unknown, or they are applied in some instances but not others, or they are applied to some players but not others. Additionally, poker parlors typically offer a number of different games, some of which are considered "beatable" and some of which are not. "Unbeatable" games are those that are structured in such a way that even the most skillful players are certain to lose. Both inconsistent or "bad" decisions by the house management and "unbeatable" games can also put a player "on tilt" and cause problem gambling.

Avoiding "Tilt"

Whereas Rosecrance believed that "tilt" and problem gambling are manifestations of a shift in locus of control orientation from internal to external,

Browne believed that they are primarily matters of frustration. He therefore suggested that one key to avoiding "tilt" is avoiding frustrating and other tilt-arousing situations. Because adversities and frustrations originating outside the cardroom impair one's game, no one should ever play as a means of escaping them. Because losing streaks are inevitable, all gamblers should be prepared for them by having enough money–enough for 500 to 1,000 table limit bets–to continue playing as they normally would; playing with "short money" invites financial disaster. During a losing streak gamblers should never play aggressively just because they think they are "overdue" for a win. Because everyone's game deteriorates with fatigue, no gambler, whether winning or losing, should play for extended periods. For every session gamblers should set and adhere to limits on both the amount of money they will allow themselves to lose and the amount of time they will allow themselves to play. When they are "on tilt" many gamblers will violate both of these fundamental strategies. Since intoxicants are detrimental to every gambler's game, one should always avoid drugs and alcohol while playing: "Many skilled players," Browne claimed, "only go on tilt and lose huge amounts of money while intoxicated." Finally, since the gambling establishment itself is sometimes responsible for problem gambling, "unbeatable" games should be avoided, house rules should always be consistently enforced and applied to all players, and service should be discontinued to all patrons who are obviously uncontrolled and "on tilt" through either intoxication or frustration.

Getting and Staying off "Tilt"

The key to getting off "tilt" once it has progressed to the second phase is learning to manage the frustration-arousing contingencies that all gamblers must inevitably face. Browne suggested that the most logical response to "bad beats" and "needling" is simply to leave the game. To do so requires that a gambler, especially one who has been losing, ignore the pressure by other players to stay–and lose even more. However, instead of leaving a game some players try to do "emotion work" by making a conscious effort to control their negative emotions. This is effective for some players but not others. Browne has observed that those who are the most successful at "emotion work" tend to win consistently while those having the least success are consistent losers. The main difference between them, he believed, is that winners acknowledge their feelings but are able to suppress them whereas losers try to deny or ignore these feelings which will not simply dissolve. Winners who are alert to the statistical probabilities and contingencies of the game expect to encounter occasional "bad beats" and "needling." Consequently, they are fully prepared when these situations arise and are able to take them in stride while losers are not. Winners who are successful at "emotion work" are therefore able to get "off tilt" and resume their normal playing after only a few hands while those who are unsuccessful remain "on tilt" and continue to play poorly for days, weeks, and sometimes for months at a time. "Consistent losers," Browne asserted, "become problem gamblers."[79] Gamblers can therefore stay "off tilt" by having a "complete game." This means beginning a session with enough money to meet all contingencies, maintaining a consistent (winning) playing strategy, and, most importantly, having good emotional management which includes avoiding all intoxicants.

SUMMARY AND CRITIQUE OF "ON TILT" THEORIES

As Lesieur has pointed out, the explanations of sociologists such as Oldman, Hayano, Rosecrance, and Browne "tend to recognize that rather than being a state, pathological gambling is the end on a continuum which includes social gamblers at one end and suicide attempters at the other."[80] The reason for this, he suggested, is that "This approach is the logical consequence of doing research in gambling settings and through intensive interviews with gamblers of all types rather than focusing solely on those in treatment."[81] Thus, these investigators all felt that the poor judgment, hence, the poor playing, that accompanies emotional disequilibrium–commonly referred to as being "on tilt"–provides the key to understanding problem gambling. However, whereas Rosecrance felt that this disequilibrium is caused primarily by "bad beats" or flukes, Browne felt that "bad beats" constitute just one of a number of possible causes: others include "needling," differentially enforced and inconsistent house rules, "unbeatable" house games, extended losing streaks, long gambling sessions, playing with "short money," escape gambling, inexperience, and intoxication. Another point of departure is that Rosecrance attributed emotional disequilibrium to a change in the gambler's locus of control orientation while Browne attributed it primarily to frustration.

Both Browne and Rosecrance saw problem gambling as a temporary and correctable phenomenon. Since "tilt" equates with problem gambling, and since all gamblers experience "tilt," they agreed that all gamblers alternate between periods of controlled and uncontrolled or problem gambling. Rosecrance contended that the "tilt" period can be reduced only with the help of one's friends. Browne felt that consistent losers are those who become problem gamblers. Winners and normal gamblers, he maintained, have learned to avoid the most obvious tilt-inducing situations and when they do encounter them they are able to reduce the length of the time they are "on tilt" through successful "emotion work." Thus, Browne argued that getting "off tilt" is an individual responsibility while Rosecrance saw it as a social responsibility. They shared the opinion that the difference between normal and problem gamblers is quantitative: normal or successful gamblers are "on tilt" less frequently and for shorter durations than problem gamblers who are "on tilt" more frequently and for longer periods.

Because Rosecrance and Browne both regarded problem gambling as primarily a matter of learning involving cognitions, reactions, and emotional management, they both adopted the outlook of learning theorists regarding its treatment. Both also questioned the abstinence doctrine of Gamblers Anonymous. Browne boldly suggested the alternative:

> Logically, if one could change this mind-set, it follows that one could become a normal gambler. This implies the possibility of treatment strategies other than abstinence, the treatment imperative of Gamblers Anonymous. Educating problem gamblers about correct strategy might possibly lead to controlled gambling.[82]

He cautioned, however, that by the time gamblers seek help from GA, their gambling has probably progressed to the extent that "abstinence is probably a necessary first step to alleviate the many pressing problems they have."[83] Rosecrance argued not only that controlled gambling was possible, but that "a successful controlled gambling program is currently in operation."[84] Its source, he maintained, lies in one's network of gambling acquaintances. However, his proposal of establishing treatment programs in which active gamblers would act as peer counselors to teach controlled gambling is questionable. It may, indeed, have a greater chance of success with racetrack bettors, the type of gamblers he studied, than with other kinds of gamblers since their handicapping skills could conceivably be improved and their "hunch" and desperation betting curtailed. But it is extremely difficult to imagine such a program helping casino, slot machine, and other kinds of gamblers who play games in which the built-in house advantage assures that, overall, they will lose more than they will win.

The studies of Rosecrance and Browne and, hence, the validity of their conclusions, suffer from several flaws. In an endnote Browne revealed that most of his key informants were winning "props" or proposition players, the salaried professionals who are paid to play poker by the cardroom management. Since winners are rarely "on tilt," relatively few, if any, of his key informants would have been active problem gamblers. Thus, none of his key cardroom informants would have been able to discuss problem gambling, the phenomenon he attempted to explain, from first-hand experience.

Similarly, Rosecrance's informants were all active gamblers none of whom considered themselves to be problem gamblers. Although Browne attended meetings of Gamblers Anonymous whose members do consider themselves to be problem or compulsive gamblers, he failed to distinguish the data he obtained from active poker players in the cardroom from any data he may have obtained from abstinent gamblers at GA meetings. It is therefore unclear whether any self-admitted problem gamblers acknowledge that their gambling problems arose only from temporary periods of being "on tilt," as both Rosecrance and Browne contended, or whether they feel that problem gambling is a permanent condition, as GA maintains. Some critics of this approach feel that the presence of certain preexisting psychiatric disorders may make it impossible for all gamblers to recover from the "on tilt" condition in the ways described by Rosecrance and Browne:

> It is likely that individuals with attention deficit disorder, depression, or other kinds of mental illness may have a more difficult time stopping gambling. . . . Perhaps some gamblers can revive from this state with peer support. But individuals with other emotional difficulties such as poor impulse control and low frustration tolerance may be less able to get "off tilt" and may continue in the vicious cycle of destructive gambling.[85]

Furthermore, the studies of both sociologists were each limited to one kind of gambler: off-track horse players and cardroom poker players. Browne's description of most members of Gamblers Anonymous as "unskilled gamblers" who "played badly"[86] suggests that they, too, were primarily poker players. Unfortunately, he gave no other indication of which kinds of gambling may have caused their problems or, as noted, whether or not their interpretations of problem or pathological gambling, on the basis of their first-hand experiences with it, accord with the concept of "tilt." Therefore, while the "on tilt" approach may be able to account for the heavy losses and temporary emotional upsets of some racetrack and poker enthusiasts who tend to attribute success more to skill than to chance, it may be entirely inapplicable to persistent or compulsive bingo, dice, roulette, numbers, lottery, slot machine playing, or other games of pure chance. As has been pointed out, "It is hard to imagine a bad bet [sic] in a lottery drawing or an instant game leading to problem gambling."[87]

The explanations of Rosecrance and Browne are contradictory to those of other attribution theorists. They proposed that "bad beats" are responsible for problem gambling because they cause gamblers to lose control of their emotions which in turn, causes them to relinquish their normally controlled rational betting style and to begin gambling in a reckless uncontrolled manner. However, attribution theorists offer an entirely different explanation when they argue that such "fluke" events contribute to problem gambling precisely because they allow gamblers to rationalize their losses and, by implication, to avoid losing emotional control.[88] The opportunity to blame their failures on factors beyond their control allows gamblers to remain faithful to a gambling system that was faulty to begin with. Despite the consistent losses that it produces they refuse to abandon their chosen systems not only to defend the cherished fantasy that success lies just within their grasp, but also to protect their own sensibilities: acknowledging the failure of their system would be tantamount to admitting that they were wrong all along.

Finally, it is highly doubtful that social scientists engaged in field research would be able to assess pathological gambling in their subjects with any degree of accuracy or consistency, and it is even more doubtful that they would then be able to explain the phenomenon solely on the basis of their observations. To think otherwise would be as unrealistic as expecting an anthropologist or sociologist to be able to determine how many regular patrons of their favorite bar could be clinically diagnosed as alcoholics and then to be able explain the phenomenon of alcoholism solely on the basis of their observations of barroom behavior. This would be as unlikely as expecting a social scientist to be able to explain nicotine addiction by becoming a tobacconist. In fact, one of the objectives of an observational study of pull tab gambling in Minnesota's drinking establishments was to test the "co-addiction" hypothesis which proposes that addictive drinking and gambling often accompany or substitute for one another. Although the researchers were trained and experienced in addiction and barroom behavior studies, they were unable to support or refute the existence of any such relationship on the basis of their field observations alone.[89]

Far more information is needed to diagnose and explain pathological gambling than can be obtained from merely watching a group of gamblers in action. A temporary display of irrational betting behavior after a "bad beat" may be no more an indicator of pathological gambling than getting drunk after losing one's job or spouse is an indicator of chronic alcoholism. In the words of a prominent addiction specialist, "bad luck 'heavy gamblers' can be mistaken too easily for pathological gamblers."[90] Moreover, since alcoholics can sometimes conceal the extent of their involvement from even close family members for long periods, it is likely that pathological gamblers are able to do likewise. If gambling is indeed a "social world" unto itself which gamblers endeavor to keep entirely separate from other areas of their personal lives, it is even more likely that they would try to conceal any gambling-related problems from their gambling peers. Others have also commented on the invisibility of pathological gamblers. As one researcher observed, "it would be difficult if not impossible to pick out a group of compulsive gamblers in their natural setting. It is hard to tell them apart from the rest of their colleagues at the track, and by definition, they usually deny their addiction."[91] Another expressed similar reservations when he wrote, "unlike drug or alcohol abusers, pathological gamblers are not readily discernable."[92] This means that the observer—even a highly trained one—will be able to see only a limited portion of any subject's overall gambling picture.

Specifically, a detailed clinical and family knowledge of any subjects' degree of involvement, gambling-related indebtedness, ability or inability to pay bills, sources of gambling money, criminal activities, domestic discord, and the like would also be necessary before determining that his or her gambling is pathological. This is information to which dice, card, and horse players are rarely granted access even though they may be highly trained social scientists. Information of this nature is often available only in settings apart from the gambling situation and only after the gambler or a close family member has acknowledged the existence of a gambling problem. Such assessments require a much more intimate knowledge of the subjects' gambling history and behavior including their personal finances, their individual motivations, and the consequences of these activities in other areas of their lives. The social scientist must have access either to clinical test results or to the gambler's case history including his personal life outside the card room, track, or casino and be able to chronicle the consequences that his gambling has on his family, marriage, friends, employment situation, and other social relationships. Consequently, it has been argued that any assessment of pathological gambling must include (1) the gambler's perception of self, (2) the perceptions of clinical professionals, (3) the perceptions of the gambler's friends and close family members, (4) time spent gambling, (5) money spent on gambling, and (6) whether the gambler is winning or losing.[93] Any attempt to make an accurate assessment otherwise would be analogous to attempting to make an observational determination of early pregnancy on the basis of a woman's behavior or appearance rather than clinically on the basis of conception and hormonal or other internal physiological evidence that is not available to the casual observer.

HENRY LESIEUR: CHASING, THE DRIVE TO GET EVEN

The need for more empirically-derived knowledge of compulsive or pathological gambling as opposed to social, professional, or periodic irrational betting led sociologist Henry Lesieur to conduct detailed life history interviews with 70 compulsive gamblers, many of whom had been clinically diagnosed as such. Roughly half of these subjects, as members of Gamblers Anonymous, were abstinent while the others, which included college students, probationers, and prisoners, were active gamblers. Lesieur also interviewed six spouses (all wives) of compulsive gamblers. His resulting book *The Chase*[94] is one of the most fascinating and influential accounts of compulsive gambling behavior ever written. While it describes the increasing involvement in gambling activities that compulsive gamblers experience, it focuses primarily on the concomitant progression of strategies and methods they employ in their endless quest for the new funding sources they need to pay old debts and make new bets. "Chasing" refers specifically to the need gamblers feel to continue gambling in order to "get even" for previous losses. Once again, Dostoevsky's gambler, during a conversation with an insightful friend, provides an excellent example:

> "To hell with gambling! I'll quit immediately, as soon as. . ."
> "As soon as you've won back what you lost? That's what I thought. You don't have to tell me–I know. . . . Tell me, besides gambling, is there anything else you're doing?"
> "No, nothing at all. . . ."[95]

"Another name for the 'chase,'" Lesieur contended, "is compulsive gambling."[96]

Although Lesieur acknowledged that such psychological factors as the excitement and "action" that gambling provides are also important causal influences, his explanation is primarily an economic one which includes a strong cognitive element. Chasing, he maintained, is a defensive strategy which is reinforced by periodic chance-determined wins.[97] It begins with a need for quick money to pay overdue bills or to recover a larger than normal loss. But since gambling, by its very nature, is most often a losing proposition, the stakes continue to escalate until the compulsive gambler becomes enmeshed in a vast web of gambling, losing, then heavier gambling in a futile effort to "get even." Clearly, not every bet is lost but even when a compulsive gambler wins it is never enough: gambling inevitably continues until all is lost and once again the chase resumes. Ironically, as the need for gambling money increases, more and more of the gambler's funding sources disappear.

To distinguish compulsive gambling from noncompulsive but heavy gambling, Lesieur differentiated between long-term and short-term chasing. Short-term chasers may try to get even during the course of a gambling session but if the effort fails they concede that their money as gone for good and forget about it. However, long-term chasers cannot forget any past losses and continually hope and try to get even for all of them. Long-term chasers are the compulsive gamblers who firmly though erroneously believe that chasing is the only possible way to make up for their losses and eventually make the elusive big win they are so desperately hoping for. In later publications Lesieur attempted to build a bridge between his own ideas and those of Hayano, Rosecrance, and Browne who felt that the "on tilt" condition accounted for compulsive or problem gambling. "It is possible." he wrote, "that going on tilt is but the first stage in the compulsive gambler's career. While on tilt, the gambler may then chase his or her losses to such an extent that it has devastating consequences."[98]

The Career of the Compulsive Gambler

Lesieur divided the course of the compulsive gambler's career into three distinct stages.[99] Since his sample consisted mostly of married men, the progression is described from a married male's point of view. In the early *attainment of money stage* the gambler's paycheck is enough to support this "recreational" activity. However, with deeper involvement and continued losses both his personal savings and his wife's assets are tapped. As the family's financial difficulties mount, the wife becomes aware of the problem and discovers that gambling is the cause. The gambler invariably promises to quit gambling and may even do so for a while but his inevitable relapse is only a matter of time. The wife's questions and accusations often provide the only excuse a gambler needs to continue gambling, or, as soon as his wife's initial anger has subsided, the lure of the "sure thing" is felt, or the gambler may resolve only to gamble "sensibly" from now on and, once again, the "chase" resumes.

The middle stage of the gambling career, which Lesieur referred to as the *moving, manipulating or juggling money stage*, begins when household resources are exhausted and the gambler seeks other options. Initially, outside loans from friends, banks, finance companies, bookies, and loan sharks are easily obtained. But as these debts mount the gambler must often "juggle" or "move" money (borrow from one source to pay another) to keep his creditors pacified and to "buy time" for himself. This strategy enables him not only to delay payment but also to keep several lines of credit open at all times. At this stage of his career, as the old saying so astutely describes the situation, the gambler is literally "robbing Peter to pay Paul." As old money sources dry up new ones must constantly be found and the juggling continues. Naturally, the gambler makes every effort to conceal these debts from his spouse and other family members for fear of having to "face the music" and the conditions which would then be required of him. However, with mounting pressure to make restitution, loans from parents and in-laws may eventually be solicited with remorseful confessions and promises to quit gambling permanently. But even though his increasingly heavier losses and debt loads are the direct result of gambling, the gambler knows of only one way to repay them: more gambling. Thus, the "chase" continually accelerates as the gambler discovers new sources of money and bets harder, faster, and with higher stakes.

The escalating costs of gambling eventually lead to an inability to repay old debts which, in turn, leads to a denial of credit. This lack of access to the critical sources of funding marks the late or *closure stage* of the gambling career. The gambler, who by this time is probably separated or divorced, may now "gamble madly" in an last ditch effort to bail himself out of his predicament and, like a desperate quarterback's last second "Hail Mary" pass, this occasionally works. But with no money and no legitimate lines of credit remaining, some desperate gamblers turn to illegal and criminal activities to repay debts and finance an out-of-control gambling habit. Others, tired of being confronted and threatened by collection agencies, employers, and legal authorities may turn to Gamblers Anonymous or some other treatment source for help. For some, the final resort of suicide is the only conceivable way out.

In summary, Lesieur described the career of the compulsive gambler as a "spiral of options and involvement"[100] which continually narrows as his involvement in gambling activities increases and his options for obtaining the money to pay for them decrease. Lesieur therefore saw compulsive gambling or "chasing" as a self-destructive cyclical activity: gambling leads to losses and debts which the gambler, in his quest to "get even," attempts to relieve through more gambling, which only leads to greater losses and higher debts, which he believes can only be relieved through even more gambling, etc. This cyclical spiral involves three repeated steps: attaining money, "juggling" or "moving" money, and the constriction of resource options or "closure" state.[101] New options are found when the old ones are no longer available and the cycle is repeated until all options are exhausted. When this strategy fails the gambler can either seek help, resort to crime, or attempt suicide, the ultimate bailout.[102] Similar self-destructive "vicious cycle" explanations have also been proposed to account for alcoholic drinking.[103]

Critique of The Chase

For Lesieur the motivation for chasing, which he equated with compulsive gambling, was economic: the need to get even for past losses continually drives gambling to progressively higher levels. Few critics felt negatively about Lesieur's explanation. One pointed out that while many gamblers feel a desire to chase their losses, "there is at present no evidence that at some point some high-frequency gamblers come to believe that chasing is correct,"[104] as

Lesieur maintained. Browne's study of active regular gamblers and abstinent compulsive gamblers verified this criticism when he reported that "no one, including G.A. members, asserted that 'chasing' is correct."[105] Although his study also confirmed the relationship between long-term chasing and problem gambling, Browne went on to stress that "Chasing, however, is not the single factor that distinguishes problem gamblers from nonproblem gamblers."[106] This was suggested by Lesieur himself when he reported that compulsive gamblers are unable to stop even when they are winning. Nevertheless, irrespective of whether they perceive chasing as "correct" or not, a recent study of pathological gamblers in Sweden found that nearly all, in fact, did chase their losses: fully 95 percent admitted that they had done so while 73 percent admitted that they did so "often" or "always."[107] Another recent study of adults seeking treatment for gambling problems in Manitoba also found that chasing was typical in this population.[108]

On the positive side, Lesieur has been commended for discussing pathological gambling as a long-term developmental process or "career" while others[109] tended to think of it in terms of discrete incidents. His use of the terms "spiral of options" and "the chase" to describe the funding arrangements and gambling styles that emerge also focus on broad developmental trends rather than isolated wagers or gambling episodes. These terms, in turn, serve to direct the reader's attention to the overall behavioral patterns that are characteristic of the pathological gambler and away from the specific bets and incidents such as "bad beats" and "tilt" situations that occasionally trouble social and professional gamblers.[110]

Clinical Observations. At least one attempt has been made to reconcile the approaches of Lesieur and the "on tilt" theorists. In doing so, psychiatrist Richard Rosenthal[111] expanded upon Rosecrance's explanation. On the basis of his clinical observations, Rosenthal felt that Rosecrance's "manic reaction" actually consists of four distinct defensive responses which can occur individually or simultaneously. The first is *denial,* the gambler's refusal to accept the reality of his "bad beat." The second is *personalization and anger,* his failure to understand why this should happen to *him.* The third is *external attribution and increased superstitiousness* as Rosecrance described. The fourth is *undoing,* the phase of irrational "on tilt" betting during which the gambler tries to reverse his misfortune "all at once."

Rosenthal suggested that gamblers who have experienced a "bad beat," which he has also heard referred to as a "major burn," feel cheated. He claimed that such an occurrence represents "an insult to one's sense of 'how things should be.'"[112] When this happens, the gambler feels that he has been unjustly served or betrayed even though he has diligently played by the rules. In order to undo the outrage that has been done to them, gamblers begin chasing not only to make up for the money they should have won, but to eradicate their feelings of shame, humiliation, and injustice.

Adding an element of psychoanalytic theory to his synthesis, Rosenthal proposed that pathological gambling can often be traced to some previous life trauma. Specifically, he suggested that events similar to bad beats but occurring in earlier nongambling situations might set the stage for going on tilt while gambling. Such events, which would indicate psychological vulnerability, would constitute "precursors" to irrational betting behavior. As an example, Rosenthal cited the case history of a patient who, due to circumstances beyond his control, had suffered several traumatic experiences earlier in life and eventually became a pathological gambler. According to Rosenthal, "The similarities between his gambling behavior and his earlier experience with an improbable and psychologically unacceptable event, is something that I have been noticing in other gamblers."[113]

SUE FISHER AND MARK GRIFFITHS: YOUTHFUL FRUIT MACHINE GAMBLERS

Fruit machines are slot machines which British law euphemistically refers to as AWPs or "amusements with prizes" rather than gambling devices. These machines, which usually have three reels printed with symbols of various kinds of fruit, are found in the amusement arcades and other venues of Great Britain where they are legal for and readily available to minors. As a consequence, fruit machines represent the most popular form of gambling among adolescents in the United Kingdom. One survey of Exeter students 13 and 14 years of age found that over four-fifths (81%) of them played these machines.[114] A second survey of 1,332 Birmingham school children reported that 35.4 percent of those 11 to 12 years of age and 45.5 percent of those 14 to 15 years old did so; of these 39.6 percent played the machines at least once a week and 15.7 percent did so four times or more per week.[115] Fruit machines are especially popular among the young people who haunt the amusement arcades of British seaside resort towns where children have unrestricted access to them. These amusement arcades have therefore become the focus of a number of studies of adolescent gambling behavior by sociologist Sue Fisher and psychologist Mark Griffiths.

Unlike many of their predecessors and colleagues who attributed persistent or problem gambling to a single motivating factor, Fisher[116] and Griffiths[117] both supported the conclusions of Martinez and LaFranchi[118] when they also found that different people gamble for different reasons. Fisher conducted her 14-month observational and interview study of young fruit machine players while working as a cashier in a seaside amusement arcade. Griffiths conducted his 28-month participant observational and interview study in several different arcades. Both researchers undertook their respective studies not to test any existing hypotheses, but to generate new ones. Through their observations and interactions with arcade patrons, largely adolescents and young adults, they were able to distinguish several types of players on the basis of their knowledge, "skill," and motivations.

British fruit machines are similar to other kinds of slot machines but they also include such features such as mechanical reels whose symbol sequences can be memorized, and "nudge," "hold," and "gamble" buttons. German slot machines that are equally appealing to the youth of that country have analogous "stop," "start," and "risk" buttons.[119] Certain machines are also thought to have their own particular idiosyncrasies which can be learned and exploited. These features, which offer a degree of choice which is not available on machines in the United States, engender some rather elaborate playing strategies. Those few serious players who "know the reels" have memorized the symbol sequences on all three reels of certain machines and therefore know how many "nudges" it will take before a winning symbol sequence appears. Experienced players also know when to push or how long to hold down the "gamble" buttons of different machines to obtain the highest payout ratios.[120] Earlier researchers had also commented on the ability of regular players to "read" a machine by trying one after another until they find one that "feels right" and of "getting to know" particular machines.[121]

Experienced players therefore believe that "skillful playing involves good tactile, auditory, and visual perception and coordination."[122] Later, researchers argued that this knowledge does not really enhance one's playing ability but merely creates an illusion of control and a skill attribution since the outcome of each play is electronically predetermined.[123] Nevertheless, the *belief* that some players are more skillful than others is an accepted article of faith among the arcade regulars. Thus, whether a specialized knowledge of these machine features and peculiarities provides any real playing advantage or merely reinforces an illusion of control is irrelevant to the fact that the *perceived* skill level of different players is precisely what determines their relative positions in the status hierarchy of the amusement arcade. Those who have the greatest knowledge of fruit machine play in general as well as a detailed knowledge of specific machines are deemed to be the most skillful and are therefore accorded the highest status.[124]

A Typology of Fruit Machine Players

The most skillful of all fruit machine players are known as the "Arcade Kings."[125] Members of this select group are generally young men in their late teens and early twenties who have mastered all playing skills and are highly proficient. Enjoying the highest status of all players, Arcade Kings are particularly revered by their entourage of juveniles who adopt the role of "Slaves" or "Apprentices" by performing such menial tasks as fetching change, food, drinks, cigarettes in return for the knowledge, expertise, and the occasional monetary rewards they receive from their older mentors.[126] Although the Arcade Kings play separately to increase their chances of winning, they comprise a cohesive social group of "quasi-professional" gamblers whose members share new knowledge, playing skills, and often their winnings with one another. Arcade Kings are heavy but controlled, rational gamblers who do not chase their losses and are not gambling addicts. Moreover, whether winning or losing, they maintain an air of nonchalance by keeping their emotions in check. According to Fisher, their primary motivation for gambling is a social one. Like Goffman, she maintained that they play principally to achieve and maintain their status which she described as "a positive gain in *character* . . . resulting from the timely production of phenomenal playing skills in the public arena of an arcade; and the self-control to carry off win or loss without circumspection."[127] Since they are also described as semiprofessional gamblers who often win relatively large amounts of money, monetary gain is also a major motivational factor. However, since Arcade Kings often show a disregard for money (in keeping with their attitude of proper indifference), Fisher believes it to be secondary to their interest in ego-enhancement and status maintenance:

> while the contest appears to be against the machine, indirectly the contest is against other members of a peer group, so that the machine becomes a vehicle for participation in a status game. Thus a specific subculture emerges which is organized around participation in an interpersonal contest, and which results in a hierarchy of performance and consequent status roles.[128]

The Arcade Kings, and those who are attempting to emulate them, therefore appear to lend support to Goffman's **small-group interactional theory**.

"Machine Beaters" are also extremely skillful players who "know the reels" and the idiosyncrasies of individual machines but avoid any type of social interaction while playing. Thus, while the Arcade Kings play for social reasons, the Machine Beaters play for asocial ones. According to Fisher, they see the machine as a challenge and play purely for the enjoyment of beating it: "Their abiding concern is interaction with the machine and opportunities for technical decision making which are on offer as long as their money holds out."[129] Griffiths felt that such players are motivated by their need for "control" since beating the machines gives them "a sense of mastery, control, competence and achievement."[130] A common tactic is to watch while others play a favorite machine, make mental notes of the number of payouts, and wait for it to "fill up with other people's money"[131] until it is primed for a big payout before playing it themselves. Unlike the Arcade Kings who are always in control of their emotions, Machine Beaters often express frustration and rage when they lose and these emotions can profoundly affect their playing decisions: "While they may play the technical game well, poor emotional management leads to poor money management in the form of chasing losses and 'problem gambling' results."[132] This obsession can be costly: whereas the Arcade Kings often cut their losses and change machines in an effort to win more money overall, Machine Beaters frequently go "on tilt" and lose all their money in an attempt to beat a particular machine. Some Machine Beaters have gambled away their college tuition in the arcades, some have sold their possessions, and some have even resorted to theft to support a fruit machine habit.

"Rent-a-Spacers" are teenage girls who patronize the arcades for purely social reasons. They gamble occasionally but lack playing skills and have no desire to acquire any. When they do play they do so only to keep the management from asking them to leave. Rent-a-Spacers are not there to gamble; they are there to socialize with their friends and meet boys. The money they do spend on gambling constitutes an obligatory fee or payment for being allowed to remain on the premises. Griffiths reported that while some teenage girls did go to the arcades in social groups, most of those that he observed were there merely as "girlfriends" or "cheerleaders" for the young male players.[133]

"Action Seekers" gamble primarily for the thrill and excitement gambling provides. Because the "action" of fruit machine play is so fast, it is especially suited to this type of gambler: "the affective states of thrill, excitement and tension which accompany the cycle of wagering, anticipation and outcome are recharged every few seconds."[134] Griffiths reported that some of those he studied claimed that they played the machines to "get a buzz."[135]

In addition to their fast action, fruit machines have a number of other built-in physical or structural characteristics that contribute to this effect and possibly to the development of addictive playing. These machine characteristics include the low initial stakes, the active involvement and feeling of control (whether illusory or actual) that the various play buttons provide, the different stakes and odds ratios afforded by the "gamble" button, the relatively high frequency of small wins, and the prospect of a large win.[136] As a socially marginalized adult activity, gambling also allows some adolescents to act and feel older and more experienced than they actually are. The arcade environment itself, which provides freedom from parental supervision, also allows adolescents to experience directly or vicariously such marginalized and potentially dangerous activities as smoking, drinking, fighting, and other "forbidden" but affect-arousing adult diversions. Many young people are attracted to the arcades for these reasons alone.[137]

"Escape Artists" are socially isolated and depressed youngsters of either sex who "gamble primarily as a means of escape from overwhelming prob-lems."[138] Escape Artists find solace in the arcade environment as well as in actual fruit machine gambling. The arcade itself is a haven which offers escape from the unpleasant realities of the outside world and the opportuni-ty to associate with others while avoiding social intimacy. Fruit machines become a narcotic whose play can be so absorbing that by immersing them-selves in it troubled teens can temporarily forget their domestic problems. Some of Griffiths' subjects actually admitted to him that they gambled to "escape from reality."[139]

As a result of her study, Fisher concluded that because different people gamble for different reasons, none of the existing sociological theories can account for all cases and, therefore, none is able to explain gambling in gen-eral. She rejected Skinnerian and economic theories by pointing out that although all players endeavored to make their money last as long as possi-ble, none of the types she observed gambled primarily to win money. However, while they are gambling, "huge amounts of money relative to income may be wagered and peers impressed by consequential risk tak-ing."[140] Thus, Arcade Kings are motivated primarily by their desire for social status and ego-enhancement; Machine Beaters, by their drive to solve tech-nical problems and beat the machine; Rent-a-Spacers, by their desire for social interaction; Action Seekers, by their quest for excitement; and Escape Artists, by their need to shut out a troubled home life. Fisher maintained that monetary considerations are merely "an extrinsic end, which unified all play-ers and provided a rational justification for their involvement."[141] She also stressed that although the Machine Beaters and Escape Artists might be con-sidered "problem" or "addicted" gamblers, the motivations she outlined are not mutually exclusive. Since the dominant characteristics of each type are present to some degree in all arcade patrons, the primary orientations of individual players can and do shift over time with the result that more chil-dren and young adults are becoming members of Gamblers Anonymous.

Fruit Machine Addiction

To clarify some of the questions raised by his more general study of fruit machine players, Mark Griffiths turned his attention to some of the young addicts who haunt Great Britain's many amusement arcades. In a prelimi-nary study[142] he focused on eight adolescent and young adult males, two of whom had once sought help from Gamblers Anonymous and all of whom met the standard medical (DSM-III-R) criteria for pathological gambling.[143] All reported that they felt a constant "need" to play, that they had engaged in truancy to do so, and that they spent all their own money as well as all they could borrow at every opportunity on these machines. For example, a subject once lost all the money he was given for Christmas at the arcade the very morning he received it. They all wished they could stop playing and many felt that the machines, which they frequently described as "deadly" and "life-destroyers," should be outlawed. All had gone into debt from gambling at some point in their lives. Seven members of the group were unemployed and, although none admitted to stealing to obtain gambling money, all claimed to know other fruit machine addicts who regularly stole to support their habit. Griffiths later learned that two of his subjects had been arraigned on four counts of burglary.

Most of Griffiths' subjects said they started playing in order to win money but that they now played only "for the sake of playing."[144] Although all eight of these subjects admitted to being addicted to fruit machines, none were excessively involved in other forms of gambling such as football pools, sports betting, racing, bingo, or cards. They all began playing fruit machines by the age of 11. Five claim to have been addicted by the time they were 13 and the others by age 15. Most began playing in cafes, fish and chip shops, or other nonarcade settings since, unlike the owners of amusement arcades, the owners of these businesses rarely stopped them from playing.

For this group of addicts, fruit machine gambling was a purely solitary rather than a social activity. Although three reported that they began playing with parents or friends and five reported that had always played by themselves, by the time of the study all were solitary players. None engaged in any conversation with their peers once they began playing a machine and none gambled with females in order to impress them as some others players did. Consequently, "Peer group pressure to play fruit machines only seemed to be relevant once the player was established in a group of other players."[145] Nevertheless, they claimed that they and their friends met at the arcade only because "there was nowhere else to go" and "nothing else to do"; all alternative activities are considered "near useless" once a player has become addicted.[146]

Griffiths' efforts to discover whether there were any circumstances under which these subjects might play more heavily than others were largely unrewarded. For example, only one of the subjects claimed to play less when he was dating a girl and needed money for this. Two of the group stated that they played less when they were unemployed because they had less money but three claimed to play more when they were unemployed because they had more time to do so. Another said that when he was employed he would play only once a week on payday. However, each week he would play all evening until he had lost all his wages. Three subjects claimed to play more heavily when they were depressed. At such times, they stated, gambling offered an "escape from reality" and "relief of worry and tension."[147] Their correspondence to Fisher's "Escape Artists" is obvious.

According to Griffiths, "By far the major factor mentioned in relation to persistence in fruit machine playing was the excitement experienced during play."[148] All subjects claimed that they experienced a "high" when they were playing and that this feeling intensified and their heartbeats increased when they were winning or close to winning. When they were asked to describe the "high" they felt, most gave somewhat vague responses but two members of the group compared it to a sexual experience. However, they adamantly rejected any comparison of this feeling with those induced by alcohol or other drugs since their mood altering effects are long-term while those of fruit machine gambling are immediate. Conversely, when they were losing or after they had lost all their money they felt a "low." All insisted that no other form of gambling could produce these effects and half claimed to be able to enjoy a secondary though less intense "high" once they had lost all their own money merely by merely watching the play of others. Bouts of anger or extreme depression, which sometimes led to a realization that outside help for problem gambling was needed, were common whenever large sums of 50£ or more were lost.

Griffiths stressed the importance of money over merely playing in the addictive process since "none of the group said they would enjoy playing a fruit machine if they had one in their bedroom which gave free plays on the push of a button."[149] However, reiterating the thoughts of his predecessors, Griffiths stressed that once they had become addicted his subjects "were fully aware that they would spend every penny they possessed playing *with* money rather than *for* it."[150] Although they were motivated by the opportunity to win money when they first started playing, once they were addicted their primary motivation, like Fisher's subjects, was to "stay on the fruit machine for as long as possible using the least amount of money."[151] The only times that any of these players left the arcade with any money at all was when they still had some left at closing time. Consequently, Griffiths agrees with Fisher that experienced fruit machine players, with their knowledge and use of the nudge, hold, and gamble buttons, perceive their activity as one for which success requires a great deal of skill.

Griffiths made it clear that the findings of this exploratory study required further empirical verification, particularly in measuring changes in levels of physiological arousal before, during, and after play. Similar measures of the "secondary" or vicarious "high" and increased excitement arousal after a "near miss" that a number of his subjects reported should also prove valuable in determining the extent to which self-arousal may reinforce persistence. Additionally, if experienced players are indeed able to play for longer periods than inexperienced players with the same amount of money, this would demonstrate that playing skill is a genuine rather than a perceived attribute. Finally, since he and others have reported a co-incidence of video games and other arcade amusements with fruit machine playing, Griffiths also suggested that the possibility of a causal link between the two (with video games acting as a precursor to gambling) should be explored.

In an effort to answer at least some of the questions raised by his preliminary study, Griffiths later conducted a postal survey of 19 former fruit machine addicts who were attempting to quit playing.[152] Unlike many surveys which are designed primarily for ease of data entry and computer analysis, the questionnaire for this study included a number of open-ended questions. Therefore, despite his small sample size, Griffiths was rewarded with many rich and poignant anecdotal vignettes which described, in their own words, some of the real-life experiences of these young self-admitted fruit machine addicts. His findings revealed that nearly all of them fed hundreds of pounds into the machines each week, often losing it all in a single gambling session. Some actually spent far greater amounts.[153] For these young people pathological gambling is not a debatable hypothetical construct but a stark and inescapable reality. To emphasize the severity of problem gambling among young fruit machine addicts, Griffiths provided a number of frank admissions by these adolescents which reveal the lengths to which they will go to obtain the money they need for gambling. In the words of an 18 year old male,

> As for obtaining money, I did this in any way possible no matter who I might hurt or what I may destroy. If I wasn't actually gambling I was spending the rest of my time working out clever little schemes to obtain money to feed my habit. These two activities literally took up all my time. . . . When my financial resources ran out I would simply depend on someone else's, no matter who or how close to me this person was. . . . I sold a great deal of my possessions to subsidize my [fruit machine] addiction. . . . This led me to selling my motorbike after owning it for just three months. The four hundred pounds that I received for the bike lasted just a day.[154]

Likewise, a 16 year-old female addict admitted that she spent any money her parents gave her for school lunches or bus fare on fruit machines that she played while school was in session. The 75£ in wages that she earned each week from her job as a cashier disappeared in a matter of hours. When she needed more she stole it from the cash register till. This behavior continued until she was arrested.

When these adolescents were asked why were attracted to fruit machine gambling the most commonly given reason involved the desire to win money (63.2%). Other responses included attraction to the lights and sounds of the machines (31.6%), to escape depression (31.6%), to alleviate boredom (31.6%), for the challenge (10.5%), for the thrill or excitement (10.5%), to chase losses (5.3%), and because their friends played (5.3%). Some respondents described the depression they felt before gambling and the relief that the machines provided. A 16 year-old male admitted that he was initially drawn to the arcades by the idea of winning. Later, however, he was attracted by the lights and sounds, the spinning wheels, and new machines with novel themes. He admitted that he could not quit until he had spent everything he had.[155] One respondent, a 16 year-old female who preferred video games to fruit machines, saw little difference between the two amusements: "They are really the same thing as you have to put money in to achieve something. With me, I used to put money in [video games] to achieve a higher score. This lead [sic.] me to playing all the time and made me in a happy mood."[156]

Griffiths' findings, which revealed that fruit machine gambling actually reduces pleasant mood states and generates or heightens unpleasant feelings, posed a serious challenge to the **dysphoria-reduction hypothesis**. Although most respondents (73.7%) reported that they were usually in a good mood before a gambling session, fewer (63.2%) claimed to be in a good mood during play, and even fewer (36.8%) felt good afterward. Conversely, while some (42.1%) were sometimes in a bad mood or angry before gambling, more (52.6%) felt this way while gambling and even more (68.4%) were in a bad mood afterward. Gambling did appear to reduce depression for some but only while they were actually gambling: 61.5 percent claimed to feel depressed before gambling, 31.6 percent felt this way during a session, and 52.6 percent said that their depression returned when the session was terminated.

The excitement, arousal, or **sensation-seeking hypothesis** was supported by the fact that while only 42.1 percent claimed that they felt excitement before and 36.8 percent after a gambling session, 63.2 percent felt a "buzz" or a "high" during the session.[157] In the words of one of these youthful subjects, an 18 year-old male,

> I would always be looking forward tremendously to playing machines and (I) couldn't get to them fast enough. . . . [During play] I always got this kind of feeling—being 'high' or 'stoned' would be the best way of describing it. I was very often uncontrollable on my excitable actions, like a five year-old at Christmas time. . . . Since becoming hooked I've never been able to stop playing a machine once I've started.[158]

His findings again led Griffiths to stress that there is no single reason for gambling. Initially, most adolescents begin because their parents or friends do or because gambling offers young people a chance to engage in independent "adult" behavior, often for the first time in their lives. Nevertheless, most of the reasons given centered around the need to escape from unpleasant personal or domestic problems. Griffiths concluded that many players are attracted because fruit machine gambling relieves depression. In time, however, a variety of factors—including social, environmental, emotional, cognitive, and the machines' physical characteristics—may reinforce continued gambling: "Not only were the players overwhelmed by a 'labyrinth of light and sound' but fruit machine playing provided an alternative way to get 'high' or 'stoned' which is exciting, challenging, relieves boredom, *and* offers possible financial rewards."[159] As the addiction develops, a player becomes increasingly more withdrawn and socially isolated until the fruit machine becomes the addicts' best friend:

> An addict can talk to it, shout at it, laugh at it—and it *never* answers back. It can arouse them and occasionally even pays them money for being there. In essence the hard core player 'worships' the fruit machine. They spend all their time either playing the fruit machine or finding ways to finance their playing.[160]

In the words of one addict, "You're having a love affair, and its with a machine."[161]

Quitting is possible but extremely difficult. One 18 year-old male compared his gambling addiction to a drug habit. He was able to begin thinking about quitting only after being accosted by his mother and then turning to his other family members for help:

> [My mum] finally confronted me, and I did something which I'd never thought of doing. . . . I told her everything—and that was the first massive step toward reaching the light at the end of the tunnel. Now that she knew everything I was able to talk to her . . . enabling me to GIVE UP . . . it was sheer will power...with my family's backing to kick the habit. It took me three months to get it out of my system just like a drug. But it was after those three agonizing months I actually began to feel like a person again. . . . I only managed to stay away from the machines by doing other things, even if I didn't want to, just to stop me thinking of [fruit machines].[162]

A 19 year-old male also quit due to the intervention of his parents' who forced him to go to his first Gamblers Anonymous meeting. At first he did not want to go but eventually began to look forward to the meetings. After 14 weeks of attendance he was able to save more than £500. Prior to this he would have stolen this much and more to support his fruit machine addiction. At the time of the study he was still facing a possible jail sentence.

In summary, Griffiths' studies, like Fisher's, demonstrated that even addicted gamblers are motivated to gamble for different reasons. While they were intended as exploratory investigations designed more to generate than to test hypothesis, these studies and their findings do have some bearing on existing motivational theories. They offer some support for **escape** or **tension-reduction theory** since a number of subjects reported that they gambled for these reasons. They provide no support for **small group** and **peer pressure theories** since most of the addicts he observed and who responded to his questionnaire were loners who did not play to impress or interact with others. Since experienced players feel that skill is essential for success, Griffiths also felt that **cognitive factors** such as the illusion of control may also play an important role in fostering persistence among addicted fruit machine gamblers. The findings of these studies also lend fairly strong support to **arousal/sensation-seeking theory** since many of his subjects claimed to experience an indescribable "high" from gambling. However, Griffiths emphasized, "Probably the most important aspect of research into gambling amongst the young is the realization that pathological gambling is *not* just an adult phenomenon."[163]

PART III

QUANTITATIVE APPROACHES

The Role of Survey Research and Statistical Analysis

Chapter 6

STATISTICAL TESTS OF EARLIER IDEAS

SETTING THE STAGE

Statistical studies of gambling, which began to appear in the mid-1960s, generally attempt to determine not only what proportion of a population gambles, but also which demographic groups are the most and least active gamblers and, often, why they are so. Some studies are largely descriptive while others are largely correlational in nature although most incorporate elements of both statistical approaches. In all instances, information for these studies is generally obtained from questionnaire surveys, some of which include sections on the respondents' attitudes toward gambling. The primary purpose of prevalence surveys, which will be discussed in a subsequent volume, is to determine and report rates of both pathological and normative gambling in given populations. Many prevalence studies often include additional correlational data.

Initially, most statistical studies of gambling behavior were designed to test specific hypotheses. The conclusions of correlational studies are typically based on the presence or absence of statistically significant, hence, possibly causal, relationships between the incidence of gambling and certain cultural, demographic, socioeconomic, behavioral, and attitudinal variables. Statistical significance means that the associations that emerge between rates of gambling and other variables are probably not due to chance alone. Research scientists determine significance by subjecting their numerical data to various mathematical tests which are then accepted as rigorous scientific proof of their hypotheses concerning the causes of human behavior. When a correlation meets a standard test of statistical significance, the hypothesis it was designed to test can be accepted, at least temporarily; if significance is not attained, the hypotheses must be rejected.

Nechama Tec: Status Frustration and Aspiration Theory

One of the first quantitative studies of gambling was Nechama Tec's[1] investigation of sports pool (soccer or football) betting in Sweden where such betting is strictly controlled by the national government. Her study was based on information gathered in 1954, 20 years after such betting was legalized. Specifically, her data was taken from previously compiled statistics obtained from a more comprehensive social survey of 812 male sports bettors and nonbettors. "Habitual bettors" who regularly participated in the weekly betting pool made up the largest proportion of the sample while just over one-third were occasional gamblers and nearly one-quarter were nongamblers.

Tec used this data to test some of the popular assumptions about gambling, its motivations, and its effects. Her attempt to correlate gambling with various environmental variables represented a test of psychoanalytic theory while her attempt to discover whether gambling is, in fact, responsible for the many negative social consequences commonly attributed to it represented a test of the moral model and deviance theory. However, her primary goal, an examination of the relationship between gambling and social class, represented a test of the ideas of earlier sociological and economic models, particularly anomie theory with its emphasis on social inequality and the Friedman-Savage hypothesis with its emphasis on hope. Specifically, she attempted to discover not only whether gambling is motivated primarily by the desire for additional wealth, but also whether this desire is more a function of one's absolute income or wealth or of one's wealth and social status relative to others.

In response to those advocating purely economic motivations for gambling, Tec reported that while prize winnings ranged from 50 to 9,999 kroner, "The assumption . . . that players regard gambling as a profitable pastime or way to become wealthy is not borne out by the Swedish data."[2] One-quarter of the regular weekly bettors admitted winning nothing at all while most of those who did win reported winning modest amounts of less than 500 kroner. (The modal annual income of those sampled was 8,000 to 12,000 kroner).[3] Only 16 percent of the gamblers won as much as 500 to 4,000 kroner, one percent won amounts ranging between 4,000 and 9,999 kroner, and none reported any greater winnings. Since most of the prizes were relatively small, Tec suggested that gamblers may play in hopes of winning large amounts, though none may really expect to, and speculated that the hope factor may well constitute gambling's greatest reward.[4] Her ultimate goal in undertaking the study was to prove this hypothesis.

Gambling and Its Consequences

Tec began by investigating the alleged detrimental effects of gambling on the gambler's social and family life. Since gamblers indicated the same

degree of involvement with their friends as did the nongamblers, Tec rejected the hypothesis that gambling leads to the neglect of one's friends. Such
results, she argued, make it "difficult to conclude that consistent wagering
necessarily makes people antisocial."[5] The finding that more nongamblers
than gamblers lived with their parents also refuted the popular notion that
gamblers are more dependent on others. The fact that more gamblers than
nongamblers were married eroded the argument that gamblers are imma-
ture, unreliable, and incapable of assuming adult roles and responsibilities.
Since regular gamblers reported no more domestic difficulties than nongamblers, the study found no evidence to support the contention that gambling
is detrimental to family life.[6]

The overall financial situation of gamblers was investigated to test the
assumption that gambling inevitably leads to financial ruin due to the presumed inability of gamblers to limit the amounts they bet. Tec found that
although those with greater annual incomes bet more frequently and for
slightly higher stakes than those with lesser incomes, the amounts actually
risked were relatively small. Overall, the average weekly bet was three kroner. Only three percent of the sample averaged weekly bets of greater than
15 kroner and none bet more than 20 kroner per week. The survey concluded that, overall, the amounts bet were modest and proportional to
income. These findings meant that "participation in soccer pools could hardly result in financial ruin."[7]

If the assumption that gambling creates an unwillingness to work were
correct, then unemployment rates should be higher among habitual gamblers than occasional and nongamblers. In reality, not only was the incidence
of habitual gambling higher among those who held steady employment than
those who did not, but a higher percentage of gamblers than nongamblers
were employed. Furthermore, if the assumption that gambling causes people
not to seek occupational advancement were correct then fewer gamblers
than nongamblers should be concerned about improving their opportunities
for this. However, the survey found no differences between the educational
and training aspirations of gamblers and non-gamblers, and both groups
expressed similar feelings regarding their future employment opportunities.
In fact, a greater proportion of gamblers than nongamblers expressed dissatisfaction with their current jobs and pay, more gamblers than nongamblers
were already making definite plans to change jobs, and more gamblers than
nongamblers were actually enrolled in adult education courses for the
express purpose of improving their employment situations.[8] Thus, the study
found not only that gamblers tend to be more concerned with self-improve-
ment, but that they also take greater initiative toward this end than nongamblers. Similar conclusions were drawn from later studies of British pools players.[9]

In testing the purported relationship between gambling and anomie, the survey revealed that more habitual or weekly gamblers participated in athletic events, read daily newspapers, were interested in political and foreign events, and voted in the previous national election than nongamblers. Slightly more nongamblers than gamblers were interested in local news and civic events and more nongamblers were actively involved in voluntary associations than gamblers but more gamblers than nongamblers held the highest offices in these associations. The study therefore found "no support for the notion that habitual betting interferes with either interest or participation in political and civic affairs."[10]

Nor did the study find any relationship between the national sports pool and crime. Although betting was unlawful and sports betting had been controlled by an organized criminal element before it was legalized, Tec emphasized that it is a matter of record that "in Sweden underworld operations which had been connected with betting on soccer games were eliminated when the sports pools were legalized."[11] Consequently, the legalization of gambling in Sweden and other countries not only failed to escalate crime, but it also stripped the underworld of a major source of income. Gambling, she insisted, becomes associated with crime only when it is an illegal activity since its demand prompts its supply. Tec took a decidedly antimoralistic stance with her pronouncement that "the weekly soccer pools have failed to produce any harmful effects on Swedish society."[12]

Gambling and Social Class

In attempting to find documentary evidence that gambling is more prevalent in one social stratum than the others, Tec encountered only questionable studies based on imprecise data. A number of studies purporting to broach this topic merely described the gambling patterns of a particular social class or subgroup of that class but failed to draw any comparisons between classes or groups; others were largely speculative. Moreover, many such reports were written not by social scientists, but by advocates of reform. In assessing these reports she wrote, "Most of them have approached their subject as if were self-evident that gambling is a vice and leads to disastrous consequences. From this premise they proceed, attempting to remedy the alleged effects of gambling without first trying to establish the facts about gambling behavior."[13] In the final analysis, no previous studies were able to provide any concrete statistical evidence demonstrating that gambling is any more strongly entrenched in one social class than the others.

Since football or soccer is so popular in Sweden, and since weekly betting on these matches is legal and equally available to all social classes, Tec argued that the Swedish survey data should provide an accurate assessment of the degree to which gambling may actually be a function of class affiliation. The data revealed that, on the basis of occupation, weekly or "habitual" gamblers comprised 60 percent of all lower class, 45 percent of middle class, and 40 percent of upper class gamblers.[14] Nearly identical results emerged after a second test in which class background was correlated with the incidence of habitual gambling. Similar results were obtained through additional tests which correlated rates of habitual gambling with educational levels and incumbency in high offices of voluntary associations. Together these findings led Tec to conclude that "(1) the higher and more advantageous the social position, the less the likelihood to gamble, (2) the lower and the less advantageous the social position, the greater the likelihood to gamble."[15] Hence, the **education hypothesis** predicts that the less formal education people have, the more likely they will be to gamble.

To explain the relationship between social class and gambling that emerged, Tec proposed the **status frustration** or **hope hypothesis** when she maintained that gambling is not motivated by greed but by dissatisfaction with one's present socioeconomic status and hope for a better future. Citing Devereux's earlier assertions of the poor job stability and limited opportunities for educational and occupational advancement that obtain for the lower classes, Tec argued that gambling is not simply a function of class affiliation; it is more accurately related to or differential opportunities for social advancement and improved living standards. Thus, she concluded, gambling will always be more prevalent among those who are dissatisfied with their position in life, whose qualifications and opportunities for advancement in conventional ways are limited, and who perceive gambling as a possible means for advancement; it will be less prevalent among those who are more satisfied with their social position, whose access to conventional ways of advancement is open, and who perceive gambling as an unrealistic means for social advancement.[16]

Elaborating on these premises, Tec went on to offer a more complex explanation based on several popular sociological ideas of the day. According to these lines of thought, not all members of the lower classes will experience equal degrees of dissatisfaction nor, consequently, will they be equally motivated to gamble. Only those in the highest levels of a given class who, by virtue of their proximity to the next higher class, are made more keenly aware of their own deprivation will perceive their lives as unsatisfactory. They will also be the ones who will encounter the most obstacles and experience the most frustration in their attempts to achieve social mobility in conventional ways. Conversely, those occupying the lower strata of the lower class who are further removed from the higher classes will be less exposed to their influence and thus less likely to develop any aspirations for upward mobility. Since gambling is motivated precisely by these aspirations, members of the lower-class "elite" who feel the greatest dissatisfaction and frustration are those who will be most likely to gamble in hopes of achieving the social status to which they so strongly aspire.

Further analysis of the survey data revealed that those who attend church services regularly (small town dwellers of all social classes and upper-class urbanites) are less likely to gamble than those who are less religiously inclined. On the basis of these findings Tec also suggested that exposure to and internalization of Protestant values and norms which are unfavorable to gambling effectively serve to discourage it. According to Tec, then, it is the hopeful gambling by members of the upper-lower class and value-laden avoidance of gambling by members of the middle and upper classes that account for differential rates of gambling among the various social classes.

Tec claimed that her **status frustration hypothesis** was supported in a number of ways by the empirical data obtained through the study.[18] If this hypothesis is correct we should expect to find, for example, more upper and middle-class gamblers to have lower class origins than to have upper or middle-class origins, fewer gamblers among sons of business or farm owners than among those whose parents own no property, fewer gamblers among those who themselves own property than among those who do not, fewer gamblers among the higher income upper classes but more gamblers among the higher income lower classes, and fewer gamblers among the more highly educated of the upper classes but more gamblers among the more highly educated of the lower classes (who would be actively striving for upward mobility). The data do, in fact, confirm these and several other predictions which, according to Tec, all serve to support the contention that those with the highest aspirations but least access to conventional means of social advancement will resort to less conventional and less realistic methods such as gambling. Tec therefore concluded that regular gamblers do not really expect to get rich through gambling as much as they *hope* to get rich in this way. In her own words "continuous wagering keeps alive dreams and hopes of spectacular social advancement because they are constantly revitalized as each stake is laid."[19] A later researcher who drew similar conclusions after conducting a qualitative participant-observational study referred to such gamblers as "dream buyers."[20]

Despite her apparently fresh ideas, however, Tec was not really able to escape the theoretical biases of her mentors. Her true orientation, little different from that of Devereux and other structural-functionalists, was revealed when she referred to gambling as a "safety-valve" institution which serves to reduce the tensions felt by a large segment of society, the upper-lower class.[21] As an important source of relief, she further argued, gambling "diminishes the expression of potentially deviant behavior and can be regarded as an activity which contributes to the continuity of the existing social order."[22] Thus, like Devereux, Tec included both of structural-functionalism's two standard explanations for human behavior–tension-reduction and maintenance of the *status quo*–in her interpretation of gambling.

Critique of Aspiration Theory

At the outset Tec's study suffered from numerous methodological flaws including an initial sampling bias, insufficient numerical data, the lack of statistical significance in correlations from which important conclusions were drawn, and failure to explain inconsistent response rates for different questions. These and other procedural problems have been discussed more fully elsewhere.[23] Of far greater importance is the fact that Tec investigated only one type of gambling–legal weekend football pool betting–to the exclusion of all other forms. As others[24] have pointed out, this means that her conclusions are not generalizable to the overall frequencies, intensities, possible social consequences, or class-based associations of any other types of gambling, legal or illegal, particularly since not all other forms offer the hope of winning amounts large enough to permit social climbing. Moreover, gamblers are not a homogeneous group and their motives undoubtedly vary considerably within as well as between groups. A purely socioeconomic analysis would, of course, fail to take into account other demographic variables such as age, gender, and marital status as well as factors that may be related to individual social, psychological, economic, and cultural circumstances.

Even if her methods were not flawed, the data Tec did draw upon to defend her hypothesis are inadequate. Correlations between the variables she presented in no way demonstrate that the sports betting of upper-lower class males is in any way a direct consequence of their position in the social hierarchy[25] nor, for that matter, even that those occupying this particular echelon are any more greatly distressed by a supposedly heightened class consciousness or status frustration than any others of their class. The mere fact of statistical correlation between two variables does not necessarily imply a causal relationship: an association can be conditional, or caused by some other factor, or it can be entirely coincidental. One of her critics suggested that differential rates of sports betting by these men are more likely to be a consequence of the greater monetary resources they can draw upon in conforming to the subcultural betting norms permeating their entire class than of any thwarted social aspirations.[26] This notion was strongly supported by later research which found that three-fourths of all large pools winners continue to play.[27] Tec's conclusions, and aspiration theory in general, are therefore not only entirely conjectural but they also fail to offer anything in the way of an explanation for the popularity of gambling in the middle and upper classes. Finally, her reference to regular weekly sports bettors as "habitual" gamblers trivializes the issues of problem and pathological gambling.

In the final analysis, then, Tec merely offered another typical structural-functional analysis which, like that of Devereux, portrayed institutionalized gambling as a tension-reduction and system maintenance mechanism. Her general conclusions are therefore subject to the same criticisms as those of Devereux and other structural-functionalists while her specific conclusion that the greater intensity of gambling in the upper-lower class is due to frustrated social aspirations is not demonstrated by the data she presented. Despite her insistence on hard statistical data and scientific rigor to test hypotheses, and contrary to the assumptions of many structural-functionalists, there is no evidence that gambling serves to maintain existing social structural arrangements by defusing class antagonisms.

Nevertheless, at least some of her ideas were partially supported a decade later by a number of gambling studies–mostly of government-sponsored lotteries–in the United States,[28] Canada[29] and the United Kingdom[30] which confirmed that expenditures and taxes on legalized gambling are regressive, meaning that poorer people spend proportionately more of their income on gambling than those with higher incomes. However, the author of a study which found that most large winners are already earning comfortable middle-class livings suggested that lotteries may not be as regressive as is commonly believed.[31] Alternatively, this could also mean that the more affluent win more frequently only because they are able to buy more lottery tickets with proportionately less of their income. This idea is supported by recent research on state lotteries which found that for every 10 percent increase in per capita income, lottery spending decreased by 12 percent. It was also found that the occupations of most winners were characteristic of the lower and lower-middle classes (janitors, factory workers, etc.)[33] and that lottery expenditures decline as education levels increase.[34]

However, Tec's study is not entirely without value. Its greatest contribution is that it "scientifically" refuted many arguments of the moralists and other anti-gambling reformers by showing their beliefs to be based on unsound premises: while those beliefs may accord with the situations of individual problem gamblers, they are certainly not broadly applicable to entire populations of normative gamblers. In her closing paragraphs Tec asked,

> If gambling (1) does not result in the disastrous consequences usually attributed to it, (2) provides for those under socially-induced strain a partial solution to their problems, and (3) reduces potentially deviant behavior (thereby contributing to the continuity of the social order if this continuity is desired), why should gambling not be legalized?[35]

Her report must have enjoyed a thoroughly warm reception by commercial gambling interests.

CULTURAL DETERMINISM: PEER PRESSURE AND THE GAMBLING SUBCULTURE

Cultural determinists argue that human behavior is determined largely by the particular culture or subculture in which people live and whose values they have internalized. Whereas the earlier sociological approaches described gambling as a reaction of the deprived lower, working, and sometimes middle classes to their subordinate positions in society, some social scientists attributed gambling to powerful subcultural influences and peer-group pressures or to pressing personal and social needs stemming from these influences.

In classifying the types of gambling he noted in his patients, Emmanuel Moran,[36] a treatment specialist, was one of the first students of gambling to recognize a subcultural variety. Gamblers in this category come from family, ethnic, or social backgrounds in which gambling constitutes an important in-group activity which is encouraged and reinforced by peer pressure. Since reluctance to gamble would mark one as an outsider, gamblers of this sort are said to gamble out of their need to "fit in" with a particular group. Under these circumstances even heavy gambling is considered culturally normative rather than excessive or pathological. Moran therefore believed that gambling of the subcultural variety will not become pathological in the absence of predisposing individual characteristics.

Although he was the first to identify subcultural gambling as a distinct variety, Moran was not the only theoretician to attribute gambling to peer group influences. Similar conclusions were drawn by an observer of off-track betting through a bookmaker by patrons of an American lower-class neighborhood bar who emphasized the sociability and gregariousness that gambling promotes and the coldness with which nongamblers are met.[37] A working class informant for another researcher succinctly stated his position with the words, "Sure I gamble. I'm a man, ain't I?"[38] Similar "in-group, out-group" explanations for different rates of alcohol consumption by different ethnic and subcultural groups have also been proposed.[39]

Just as peer pressure may encourage gambling in some groups, it may discourage it in others. For example, a large survey of gambling in the United States found far fewer gamblers among fundamentalist Protestants who are less tolerant of the activity than among Catholics or Jews who are more tolerant of the practice and who often employ certain forms of gambling in their fundraising efforts.[40] A study of 186 hospitalized pathological gamblers also reported that Catholics and Jews were overrepresented within its sample.[41] The influence of peer pressure on the betting behavior of individuals has also been reported in studies of racetrack and casino gamblers. Even a small, temporary group of previously unknown peers can influence the individual to bet more cautiously[42] or more recklessly.[43]

Otto Newman: The Culture of the Betting Shop

Another advocate of the subcultural approach was Otto Newman[44] who undertook a study of the betting shops of London's East End. Shortly after the publication of Tec's Swedish study, Newman, one of Tec's harshest critics, attempted to correct some of its faults by conducting a similar study of gambling in Great Britain. In undertaking his study, Newman hoped to test the popular assumptions that gambling (1) is always associated with corruption and illegality, (2) imposes too large a drain on the national economy and is therefore a major social problem, (3) imposes economic hardship at the household level and is therefore an individual problem, (4) is antiredistributive or more prevalent among and harmful to a particular social class, and (5) that it is inherently addictive and therefore injurious to individual reason, will power, and responsibility as inveterate gamblers become more obsessed with it. Newman also hoped to learn whether gambling is motivated primarily by economic concerns or, if it is not a question of economics, what social and psychological needs or "functions" it may serve.

For this undertaking Newman employed a combination of quantitative and qualitative research methods. Like Tec, he used quantitative methods to analyze the information he gleaned from a literature review which represented the first part of his investigation. Like Zola and Herman, he relied on qualitative methods for the second part, a participant observational study in a number of East End betting shops. Most of his conclusions were drawn from his first-hand observations of and associations with the actual bettors who patronize these establishments.

A Review of the Existing Literature

Newman began his investigation with an extensive review of the statistical survey data compiled by various public and private agencies on all available types of gambling. These included dog racing, horse racing, soccer or football pools, lotteries, slot machines, bingo, casino gambling, carnival midway games, traditional public games of skill such as darts, and traditional public games considered not to involve skill such as cribbage and dominoes. His sources provided information on the number of people who gamble, their gambling preferences and frequencies, and the amounts of money wagered. Newman was also able to discriminate among nongamblers, occasional gamblers, and habitual or regular gamblers on the basis of age, gender, marital status, and social class. He therefore claimed to have precisely the kinds of information for his study that were so conspicuously absent from Tec's. However, rather than draw all of his conclusions about gambling from these sources alone as Tec had done, Newman used them to lend focus to his own original study.

The existing literature was able to answer at least some of Newman's original questions. He found that the majority (80%) of all adults in Great Britain do gamble and that men are more likely to do so than women. He also found that since betting became legalized and the betting shops are so closely controlled, the criminal network (illegal bookies, runners, etc.) that once dominated off-track betting have entirely disappeared leaving gambling free of any underworld influences.[45] Any other gambling-related legal infractions were minimal and insignificant.[46] Statistics on gambling expenditures revealed that adult per capita gambling expenditures at the time of the study amounted to only £6.70 per year or 13 pence per week. This represented only one-quarter of one percent of the national labor force and just over one percent of all personal expenditures. The small amount of money spent nationally on gambling relative to other expenditures (nearly one-sixth of that spent for either tobacco or alcohol) was moderate.[47] On the basis of these findings Newman, like Tec, was forced to conclude that legalized gambling is harmful to neither the individual nor society and therefore poses no major problem in Great Britain.[48]

The literature review also revealed that the most popular type of gambling in Great Britain was off-track horse race betting which accounted for nearly 60 percent of all gambling expenditures. Dog racing, at roughly 15 percent, was second in popularity while football or soccer pools, which were the focus of Tec's study, came in a distant third at less than nine percent of all gambling expenditures in Great Britain. Most racetrack betting takes place in establishments commonly referred to as betting offices or betting shops. Specifically, in terms of the amounts and frequencies of track betting, Newman found that 95 percent of all bets, and 90 percent of all the money wagered on horse and dog racing, were placed in Britain's betting shops.[49]

Like Tec, Newman also found the highest rates of gambling among the lower socioeconomic classes. However, unlike Tec who claimed that the heaviest gamblers in Sweden were in the upper levels of the lower class, Newman found that the highest rates of gambling in Britain occurred at the lowest levels of the working class, primarily among manual laborers who earned only 15 to 20 pounds per week in 1970.[50] An examination of the distribution of London's betting shops also confirmed that most are, in fact, located in the city's most impoverished neighborhoods.[51] Newman felt that the knowledge and experience the residents had gained through their long exposure to and intimacy with gambling protected them from undue hardship: "Although manual wage earners tend to predominate . . . especially among the hard-core [gamblers], their superior levels of skill and self-restraint exercised in the interest of prolonged participation, reduce their proportionate losses enabling them to recoup a larger proportion of their stakes."[52] Betting shop gambling could not, therefore, be antiredistributive.

A Field Study of the Betting Shop Environment

Since most gambling in Great Britain was reported to take place in betting shops in areas of greatest deprivation, Newman reasoned that they should be the focus of any serious sociological study of gambling. He therefore initiated his own participant observational study of British betting shops. To gain direct access to Britain's gamblers and the gambling milieu, he initially obtained a position behind the counter at one of these shops in London's East End, the well-known working class part of the city. When he later moved out from behind the counter and became a gambler himself, he was allowed to observe and interview many regular and heavy gamblers, bet with them, and engage them in informal conversations outside the betting office in the streets, cafes, and pubs of the area. For comparative data he frequented two other betting shops in some of the least respectable parts of East London where he also associated with the regular clientele. Finally, he conducted a series of door-to-door interviews on gambling with residents of each of these three areas.

An economic pursuit? On the basis of his observations, interviews, and conversations with London's East End gamblers, Newman found that economics concerns are, in fact, the most commonly voiced reasons for gambling. However, since the regular gamblers he observed invariably lost more than they won and were certainly aware of this fact, Newman questioned whether gamblers themselves actually define it as an economic activity or whether they have merely adopted the cultural definition that has been imposed on it by the greater society in which they live: he wondered, "which is the cause and which the effect?"[53] In either case he deemed the economic incentive to be of only secondary importance in motivating gambling behavior.[54] Newman was clearly not alone in questioning whether the economic interests that gamblers voice is really a valid rationale or merely a convenient rationalization for their gambling.[55]

A structural-functional interpretation. Like Zola, Newman maintained that whatever its degree of importance, the economic factor represents just one of a number of other purposes that gambling serves. In discussing them he closely followed the structural-functionalist example. In the first place, the gambling subculture serves several important personal functions. The influence of **decision theory** is evident in Newman's argument that gambling provides lessons in the utilization of judgement, choice, and decision making involving complex sets of variables: "There seems to be every reason to accept that overwhelmingly the gambler transacts with his social environment in a rational manner, that he exercises optimal deliberation and rational choice."[56] Gamblers are able to further refine their decision-making skills by discussing their choices among a group of betting shop peers. The influence of **interactional theory** was revealed when he suggested that off-track betting also allows the gambler to choose among various institutionalized fantasy roles which enable the "cultivation of talent and development of virtuosity."[57] Although the exercise and development of these talents take place in the context of gambling, the decision making and role-playing skills that one learns provide valuable life experiences which can be transferred to a variety of situations outside the betting shop. Thus, the betting shop also provides a training ground which prepares people for coping with the real world outside.

Although betting shops serve a number of social as well personal functions, not all betting shops necessarily serve the same social functions. One betting shop was said to have an integrative function by introducing newcomers to the gambling group and overseeing their socialization into the gambling lifestyle. In this way the capitalistic middle-class values of competition and achievement are replaced by the working-class values of sharing and cooperation, thereby strengthening the group's social bonds.[58] Newman also drew upon **alienation/anomie theory** when he described gamblers at a second betting shop as members of a group that has withdrawn from mainstream society. He described the betting shop itself as a "retreat in which the disinherited, the social misfit can vent revenge upon his oppressors by denial of validity of external value systems, by desecration of the principle 'deity'– money."[59] A third betting shop was frequented by a group Newman referred to as "frustrated entrepreneurs"[60] who have not yet abandoned the values of greater society. This betting shop created a miniaturized simulation of the capitalistic world by allowing the "Exercise of manipulative and entrepreneurial skills by individuals deprived of facilities for expression of those, due to life situation or personal flaws, yet dominated by [an] ideology of virtue of competitive struggle and achievement."[61] In this environment the "frustrated capitalist" is able to deny his own failure by demonstrating his competence in the alternative environment of the betting shop. Conversely, since any failures that might be experienced in the context of gambling are irrelevant to the external world, they remain confined to the relatively safe environment of the betting shop. Therefore, any failures of this nature can pose no additional threat to one's real world existence.

The true strength of Newman's structural-functional bias was clearly revealed when he asserted that "gambling may well be regarded as a structurally positively-functional component of the social system."[62] He specified that "in all cases it was found that regular interaction within the group does reinforce group cohesion as well as affirm the individual's personal system of values."[63] This bias is also revealed in his description of the betting shop as a place "where collective cohesiveness is constantly refined and redefined."[64] Newman therefore subscribed to the standard structural-functionalist assertion that one of the most important and universal "functions" of all social institutions is the promotion of social solidarity, in this case among members of the betting shop fraternity.

A cultural value. Although Newman was first and foremost a structural-functionalist, he was also a cultural determinist. He repeatedly emphasized that gambling permeated London's East End and that habitués of the different betting shops he studied were essentially the products of their own particular subculture. Newman had, in fact, sharply criticized Tec for failing to consider this possibility which, of course, could not possibly be suggested by an analysis of statistical data alone. He insisted that the East Enders hold a very positive attitude toward gambling and regard it as a "valued and significant feature" and "treasured component"[65] of their lives. The allure of the gambling subculture was fondly recalled by an informant who no longer gambled: "these had been the best days of his life, there was nothing like a racing crowd for generosity, good humour and cheer. No-one ever asked for help and went away empty-handed. What they had, they shared and even when they were all skinned they still had a laugh, they knew how to get the most out of life."[66] According to another informant, "In this area you learn to gamble before you learn to read."[67] Here "the Gambler is the social norm, the Non-gambler the deviant oddity"[68] and the betting shop is the place "where norms are evolved and internalised."[69]

In the end Newman rejected the purely **economic hypotheses** that gambling is simply a quest for money or that it only provides hope of wealth when he found that "gambling is neither an irrational appeal to blind chance, nor individually nor socially disrupting."[70] Since gambling serves so many functions that are not economic, and since all regular betting shop patrons always lose more than they win, he concluded that their inevitable losses merely represent the price they must pay for the enjoyment of these "non-pecuniary satisfactions."[71] It was also his distinct impression that pathological gambling was a problem for only a small minority of all betting shop patrons.[72] Despite his lack of any numerical data he felt comfortable in "dismiss[ing] the charges of addictive pathology and inherent irrationality as unwarranted and largely irrelevant to the situational reality."[73] Furthermore, since he had found no evidence of criminal involvement, like Tec he made the same confident assertion that "conclusively, within all accepted standards of definition, gambling cannot validly be said to constitute a social problem in objective terms."[74] He then went so far as to challenge the entire conception of "social problems" by suggesting that they may be more a reflection of prevalent sociological ideology than of social reality.[75]

A typology of betting shop gamblers. Finally, through his interviews and conversations with his East End informants, Newman also devised a classification of the different types of gamblers and nongamblers he encountered. They include Sportsmen, Rational Gamblers, Handicappers, Professionals, Conmen, Essentialists, Reluctant Gamblers, Reformed Gamblers, Compulsive Gamblers, Nongamblers, Antigamblers, and Bookmakers.

The Sportsman is an occasional gambler who knows very little about picking winners, makes no effort to learn, and often bets on horses that others favor. He does not really expect to win and usually loses but continues to wager his usual limited amount on the outside chance that he might get lucky. The sportsman plays purely for fun.

The Rational Gambler and the **Handicapper** are cut from the same cloth. Both are defined as "A man who, having taken account of all relevant factors and having assigned them to appropriate values and priorities, will endeavor to reach his decision under the set of circumstances most favourable to himself."[76] Such a gambler not only studies the racing form but "also attempts to read between the lines."[77] Both play to win although the handicapper is a somewhat more serious gambler who pays more attention to the condition of the track, the jockeys, the animals, their running positions, and "inside tips" than the rational gambler. Both ascribe their losses to race fixing and misinformation rather than bad luck or their own inadequacies.

The Professional who makes a livelihood from gambling is much less likely to be a gambler than an entrepreneur or paid employee of some gambling enterprise. Although a few gamblers are regularly able to derive an enviable supplementary income from gambling, the idea of the professional gambler is far more a myth than it is a reality.[78] The only "professional" gambler that Newman encountered was not an East Ender. He claimed to earn most of his money playing poker in the Gaming Clubs of West London but supplemented this income by selling insurance on a part-time basis. He also bet on horse and dog races but unlike the rational player and the handicapper, he paid little attention to the racing form and none at all to inside information. His strategies were to play only those horses that appeared to have been deliberately held back in previous races and dropped in class to gain better odds, to ignore races where no such horses were evident, and then, by watching the prerace odds fluctuations, to time his bets to gain the greatest possible odds advantage. Among the other rules he lived by were never to play outside his system and never to chase his losses.

The Conman finds easy marks in neophytes and occasional bettors. Glib, fast-talking, and quick-witted, he gladly gets them to part with their money in return for the "inside information" he swears he has just received from his confederates at the track.

The Essentialist is trying to work out the perfect system by discovering the arcane archetypal "pattern" underlying the racing game. Which horses may be running in which race is of no concern since the key to winning lies in his ultimate discovery of the correct betting "pattern."

The Reluctant Gambler wants to quit, tries to quit, but is unable to quit. The individual upon whom Newman based this characterization was apparently also an alcoholic. When sober he would pontificate on the foolishness of gambling but then go on periodic binges of heavy drinking and gambling.

The Reformed Gambler, once a heavy, irresponsible gambler, has successfully quit gambling and knows he can never place another bet or he will soon go back to his old ways.

The Compulsive Gambler is a self-admitted addict who cannot hold a job, receives public assistance, and spends nearly all his waking hours and welfare money in the betting shop: "It's like a disease," he admits, "you can't get away from it."[79]

The Nongambler and the **Antigambler** have never ventured inside a betting shop nor do they ever intend to do so. Their gambling is strictly limited to occasional raffles and office pools. Although the nongambler never gambles himself, he would not deny others the opportunity to do so; the antigambler is a moralist who feels that all forms of gambling should be outlawed.

The Bookmaker is the paid professional who runs the betting shop. Some bookmakers gamble heavily; others, rarely, if ever.

Critique of Newman

Although the methods Newman employed for his betting shop study were very different from those of Tec, and although he had criticized Tec and the entire structural-functionalist school,[80] his views of gambling and the betting shop as institutions which serve a number of positive "functions" in the community clearly mark him as a structural-functionalist. His interpretations are therefore subject to many of the same criticisms as those of Tec and other structural-functionalists. Unlike most of them however, Newman was able to recognize the fallacy of attributing all the gambling that occurs within an entire population to a single primary "function." Perhaps one of the greatest contributions of his study is embodied in the awkwardly phrased but entirely valid conclusion that

> widely divergent sets of attitudes and behaviour in relation to the activity of gambling were found to prevail. This would suggest that gambling means many things to many people and that sociological concepts of type-situations postulating situational affinity, in which different sets of situational needs and values prevail, rather than in terms of massive, undifferentiated subcultural groups, may more effectively reflect social reality.[81]

In other words, we should recognize the fact that different people gamble for different reasons. Nevertheless, the reasons he proposed were all grounded in the prevailing sociological thought of the day.

Another of Newman's major contributions was his recognition that gambling is an integral part of a particular subculture, in this case, that of London's East Enders. His "when in Rome" attitude toward and description of gambling as a customary part of the everyday life of the community rather than a class-wide reaction to exploitation and deprivation clearly mark him as a cultural determinist. This meant that social scientists were now beginning to see gambling as a *normative* rather than a deviant behavior. It is therefore not surprising that a later investigator who studied the history of gambling among the British working classes also described it as an expression of their subcultural values.[82] It is interesting to note that although a similar orientation toward the study of alcohol use had been strongly recommended decades earlier,[83] it was never put into practice.

It also very much is to his credit that Newman utilized existing numerical data primarily to guide his later research rather than to draw his major conclusions from statistics alone as Tec had done since quantitative studies are devoid of any contextual or cultural meaning. In order to gain an understanding of, and appreciation for, the meaning that gambling holds for the actors themselves, he deemed it essential to immerse himself in the gambling

subculture to the greatest extent possible. As both an observer and a participant, he attempted to explain gambling subjectively, from the point of view
of the actor or cultural insider (the East End gambler) rather than objectively, from that of the cultural outsider (the detached academic). Although a
number of later social scientists employed similar research methods, few
were able to convey the insider's point of view.[84] Newman therefore ranks
among the few cultural determinists ever to explore the world of gambling.

However, the value of Newman's typology is extremely limited precisely
because of his lack of statistical data. It was formulated using the case history method which means that each category of gamblers is represented by
only a single example. With such limited sample size his scheme is not legitimately generalizable to the gambling population at large since one example
does not constitute an entire category. Furthermore, since each category
merely describes one person's present or former gambling habits, the classification alone reveals little if anything about people's motivations for gambling apart from their professed desire for money, a motivation which
Newman himself questioned. Several categories, in fact, discuss nothing
beyond the means that some people employ in obtaining their gambling
money. Overall, his classification revealed only that some people are heavier gamblers than others, some people gamble more or less rationally than
others, and some appear to be unable to control their gambling.

Since we do not know which proportions of the gambling population he
studied may have been "sportsmen," "reformed gamblers," "compulsive
gamblers," or "nongamblers" we know nothing about the true extent of any
individual gambling problems that may exist. This is a point which Newman
had specifically hoped to address when he initiated his study but which he
dismissed despite his intimate association with some obvious pathological
gamblers. Although he may have perceived it as rare he described pathological gambling as a definite problem for some individuals and therefore
should not have rejected it out of hand. It is probable, however, that he acted
in response to his academic background and the prevalent sociological orientations of the day. Well-known mainstream sociologists since the 1940s
had declared the incidence of alcohol problems to be far lower in societies
in which alcoholic beverages have a long established historical tradition and
are well-integrated into the culture but to be much higher in societies lacking
this tradition and where their use is met with attitudinal ambivalence.[85]
Although Newman did not cite this literature since it dealt with drinking
rather than gambling, he was undoubtedly familiar with it. However, he did
cite earlier sociologists[86] who emphasized the ambivalence surrounding gambling in Western society and therefore viewed it similarly. Newman would
therefore not have expected to find any problems associated with gambling
since, as a structural-functionalist, he felt it was so well-integrated into the

East End subculture. Somewhat later Robert Herman, an American contemporary of Newman, did argue that gambling, as like all other forms of play, is "thoroughly interwoven with the rest of the cultural fabric."[87]

FUNCTIONALISM AND THE CROSS-CULTURAL CORRELATES OF GAMBLING

Although anthropologists generally produce richly detailed descriptive or qualitative ethnographic accounts of single cultures, some have conducted correlational studies involving samples of many different tribal groups. Such samples are drawn from the Human Relations Area Files, an archival collection of anthropological materials intended for use in testing a variety of different sociological and psychological motivational hypotheses. Employing sophisticated statistical methods, the authors of such quantitative "cross-cultural" surveys have attempted to determine the reasons for the presence or absence of certain behaviors or customs in these societies by discovering which social, cultural, and physical environmental features accompany them. Gambling has received far less attention than alcohol use by cross-cultural investigators, perhaps because the materials on gambling contained in the Human Relations Area Files are so limited.[88] However, by setting methodological and theoretical precedents, the earlier alcohol studies strongly influenced the direction of later cross-cultural investigations of gambling and other sociocultural phenomena.

Cross-Cultural Perspectives on Alcohol Use

Some of the earliest cross-cultural surveys attempted to isolate the correlates of alcohol use and intoxication in preindustrial societies. In many cases these correlates were then assumed to constitute scientifically derived explanations for this behavior. However, many of these researchers, influenced by the dominant psychoanalytic, behavioral, and sociological theories of the day, interpreted their findings according to their own particular theoretical orientations and biases. As committed functionalists, many cross-cultural investigators contended that their research revealed the ultimate social and psychological "functions" of the various behaviors and customs of tribal peoples. As previously noted, these functions were generally limited to anxiety reduction and/or the promotion of social solidarity.

The first cross-cultural survey ever conducted was undertaken by Donald Horton[89] to prove, through statistical means, the universality of the anxiety-reduction hypothesis. Solely on the basis of the ethnographic record, Horton rated and then compared the general societal level of anxiety, engendered by threats of an insecure food supply, the stress of acculturation, or the threat of warfare, to the degree of insobriety he had also determined for each society. However, as was typical of most functionalists, Horton was decidedly lacking in scientific objectivity: picking and choosing among a number of possible correlates he simply seized upon those that supported his thesis and ignored those that did not. Thus, when he found that people in food gathering societies were heavier drinkers than those in food producing societies, he concluded that alcohol functioned to reduce the high levels of subsistence anxiety which was erroneously assumed to plague all hunter-gatherers. After several abortive attempts, he was eventually able to "prove" that alcohol also functions to reduce sexual anxieties (which psychoanalysts also believed to be universal) as well as the emotional stresses arising from warfare and acculturation pressures. He therefore felt confident in declaring that "the primary function of alcohol use in all societies is the reduction of anxiety."[90]

Despite its methodological flaws, Horton's research set the stage for all cross-cultural studies to follow, a number of which also involved alcohol use. Although they also "proved" that the primary function of drinking was the reduction of anxiety, they were unable to agree on precisely which anxieties it reduces. Thus, while Horton's correlations "proved" that tribal people drink to reduce subsistence, sexual, warfare, and acculturation anxieties, others looked for and found statistically significant positive correlations—which they then interpreted as causal associations—between societal rates of intoxication and informal social structure and social control,[91] dependency conflict,[92] male power concerns,[93] and the fear of harmful supernatural spirits.[94]

Cross-Cultural Perspectives on Gambling

Socialization Anxiety and Environmental Stress

One cross-cultural survey of games of chance was undertaken by anthropologist John M. Roberts and psychologist Brian Sutton-Smith,[95] who were interested in developing a theory of games. They distinguished three fundamental types of games—games of skill, chance, and strategy—that are played throughout the world. Assuming an evolutionary perspective, they speculated that over the course of human cultural development, games of chance were preceded by games of skill whose outcomes depend on sensory-motor dexterity and other physical attributes, and followed by games of strategy whose outcomes depend on mental acuity in decision making. According to the anthropological "age-area principle,"[96] cultural traits that have the widest distribution must be the oldest while those that are least widely distributed must be the most recent. As it turned out, games of skill had the highest frequency of occurrence in the ethnographic record, games of chance occurred less often, and games of strategy had the lowest frequency of occurrence. Of course, games whose outcomes depend on various combinations of these three elements occur in numerous societies.

For their correlational analyses Roberts and Sutton-Smith selected four samples of societies possessing different combinations of these types of games. For example, the first sample compared 82 cultures in which games of chance were present to 89 in which games of chance were absent. A second compared 61 societies lacking games of strategy but possessing games of skill and chance to 67 possessing only games of skill. Similar comparisons were also made between tribal groups whose games incorporated various combinations of skill, chance, and strategy.

The researchers found games of chance to have many statistically significant but widely divergent correlates. For example, analysis of the first sample revealed that "chance" cultures are characterized by:

- the lack of potential for early sexual satisfaction,
- high socialization and sexual socialization anxiety,
- low indices of infantile nurturing consistency, and
- high achievement anxiety

Games of chance occur least frequently in East Eurasian, the Pacific Island, and native South American cultures that are situated in tropical or subtropical rainforest environments. They occur most frequently in the higher latitudes of North America having very harsh, or subtropical bush, or temperate grassland environments. Members of "chance" cultures in this sample are also more likely to:

- subsist by hunting and gathering than by food production,
- live in societies characterized by a band level of social organization rather than tribe, chiefdom, or state levels,
- be nomadic rather than sedentary,
- avoid cousin marriage,
- avoid male genital mutilation,
- segregate young women and menarche, and
- be threatened by warfare

Conversely, most "chance" cultures in the second sample were more common in East Eurasia than elsewhere. Although they subsist through plow agriculture they lack a secure food supply and suffer frequent food shortages. Their members tend to:

- have large state levels of sociopolitical organization
- live in cities and towns where social stratification is based on occupational specialization,
- have a "high god" religious concept,
- no anal explanations for illness,
- few food taboos,
- an Eskimo or Hawaiian rather than Crow, Omaha, or Iroquois kinship systems, and
- permit cousin marriage.

The other two sets of samples yielded equally expansive arrays of correlates, some of which correspond to these findings and some of which differ.

Some examples in the third sample are that "chance" cultures tend to be least prevalent in the Mediterranean and Eastern Eurasian culture areas and most prevalent in North America where very harsh, subtropical bush, or temperate grassland environments prevail. They are characterized by:

- incipient food production methods with a high reliance on hunting and gathering,
- no domesticated food animals,
- no metal working,
- matrilineal family-based communities
- no cousin marriage,
- no male genital mutilation,
- use of Eskimo or Hawaiian kinship terminology,
- wealth-based class stratification,
- no slavery,
- low levels of occupational specialization,
- bride service rather than a bride price or dowry,
- acceptance of homosexuality,
- sexual division of labor (agricultural work is done by males and leather-working is by females),
- anxiety over disobedience in children, and
- an absence of anal explanations for illness.

The fourth sample of "chance" cultures also found that most are located in areas of North and South America having very harsh, or subtropical bush, or temperate grassland environments. They tend to have:

- Eskimo or Hawaiian kinship terminology,
- cities and towns are present,
- state levels of sociopolitical organization,

- nonhereditary political leadership,
- sanctions against premarital sex,
- segregation of girls at menarche
- homosexuality is permitted,
- no negative sanctions against homosexuality,
- high levels of socialization anxiety, sexual socialization anxiety, achievement anxiety, warfare anxiety, and,
- despite the development of intensive plow agriculture, subsistence anxiety is also high since the food supply is insecure and shortages are frequent.

Although their readers may puzzle over the relevance of many of these correlates and see a number of others as clearly contradictory, Roberts and Sutton-Smith contended that their results "in many ways speak for themselves."[97] To them these correlates fell into distinct patterns which lent themselves to obvious interpretation. Like the cross-cultural alcohol studies after which their study was patterned, the authors concluded that the primary function of gambling in tribal societies was the reduction of anxiety generated by a number of uncertainties encountered in daily life. Specifically, they felt that the presence of subsistence and socialization anxiety–particularly in the areas of sex, aggression, and achievement–were "immediately evident"[98] in the first of their data sets:

> The constancy of the presence of the infant's nurturing agent is low, and this early uncertainty is augmented by other situational factors. The chance cultures occur at higher latitudes, where the seasons and weather may be more variable. The chance cultures depend upon hunting and gathering, subsistence techniques which are often characterized by a feast-and-famine sequence. Even the prohibition of first-cousin marriage may lead to greater uncertainty–in finding a spouse. Warfare is prevalent, with all the uncertain rewards and punishments that it implies. There is a hint that contact with the divine may have its uncertainties.[99]

They then went on to suggest that games of chance are a direct consequence of these omnipresent uncertainties:

> If in these cultures there is motivation produced by antecedent conflict, and if there are situational uncertainties which are not easily reduced by the application of either physical skill or strategy . . . , then models of uncertainty, i.e., games of chance, should have appeal.[100]

Their interpretations of the results of the other three data sets were of a very similar nature: although the uncertainties faced by people living in sedentary agricultural societies may be somewhat different from those in nomadic hunting and gathering societies, the authors argued that the specific antecedent conditions to which they are exposed are also anxiety provoking. For example, even in agricultural societies where food supplies are presumably more secure, anxiety may arise over such uncertainties of urban life as concerns with social mobility or the lack of recognition for one's talents where such recognition is a major concern. According to the authors, uncertainty under these circumstances can also arise from concerns with independence, responsibility, marriage, inheritance, and contact with the supernatural. Moreover, both hunter-gatherers and food producers experience the same socialization anxieties, notably those related to aggression, achievement, and particularly sex.

Roberts and Sutton-Smith concluded their study by proposing that games of chance reduce anxiety by providing a ray of hope under conditions of uncertainty:

> It is our provisional formulation then, that games of chance are linked with antecedent conflict, powerlessness in the presence of uncertainty, the possibility of both favorable and unfavorable outcomes within the area of uncertainty, and certain compatible projective beliefs, particularly in the area of religion. The motivations in this situation are assuaged by play with uncertainty models, and the resulting learning may give individuals and groups strength to endure bad times in the hope of brighter futures.[101]

The Positive Social Functions of Gambling

A second cross-cultural analysis of gambling appeared several years later. Its author, functional anthropologist John Price,[102] was apparently attracted more to the social solidarity or structural equilibrium explanation than to the anxiety-reduction approach to gambling. Price, who also espoused a cultural evolutionary perspective, looked for correlations between the presence or absence of gambling and levels of sociopolitical organization. According to the proponents of cultural evolutionism,[103] as human societies evolve they pass through several distinct developmental stages. The simplest level of sociopolitical organization is the band level which is characteristic of hunter-gathers; the next and progressively more complex levels are the tribe, chiefdom, and state. Concomitantly, each stage is accompanied by increasingly greater degrees of social stratification. Price found that gambling and most other kinds of games tend to be rare in the least complex band level societies but fairly common in those at the state level as in classical Egypt, India, and China. This finding led him to conclude that gambling evolves from low levels of intensity to progressively higher levels until it eventually becomes institutionalized.

Price argued that gambling becomes increasingly intensive in more complex societies because it serves a number of beneficial socioeconomic functions. He based this conclusion on the associations he saw between the intensity of gambling and the kinds of subsistence, economic, wealth, and religious systems that accompany it. Specifically, "Intensive agriculture and well developed market systems seem to correlate with gambling."[104] Despite its condemnation in the stricter and more fundamentalistic Christian and Islamic sects, it also appears to flourish in cultures which value material over spiritual pursuits. In those few egalitarian band level societies where gambling does exist, it is available to all people since everyone has equal access to all available resources. However, in more complex nonegalitarian societies where surplus wealth is controlled by a ruling elite, gambling is generally restricted to the upper classes.

Like the play theorists, Price felt that the primary function of gambling among the wealthy is entertainment, but he also insisted that it serves a number of secondary functions. It stimulates the economy by encouraging the production of surpluses to offset gambling debts and by serving as a marketable and taxable commodity where it is commercially available. It also serves as a useful instructional tool by teaching people about capital formation and risk. However, its most consequential secondary function is that it provides a means of redistributing wealth beyond the confines of the kin group.

He also felt that in those complex societies in which intensive gambling is viewed disfavorably, it is opposed because it undermines and therefore threatens the existing social order. Because it cuts across traditional redistribution networks, "It brings in the possibility of the outflow of goods that are not scheduled by the basic social groups of society: families, clans, etc."[105] Thus, while this form of redistribution may be economically beneficial for society as a whole, it excludes those who are accustomed to enjoying exclusive control over wealth and its allocation. It therefore tends to be more accepted in capitalistic societies where competition and individualism are highly valued but censured in communalistic and communistic societies where economic decisions are customarily made by kinship and other primary social groups.

Critique of the Cross-Cultural Method

Apart from several quantitative methodological problems such as a lack of random and systematic sampling and problems with sample sizes which some authors themselves pointed out,[106] cross-cultural studies suffer from a far more serious defect: they all fail to take into account the cultural contexts in which the behaviors they are purporting to explain occur. In many cultures the outcomes of games of chance are believed to result from magical, spiritual, or other supernatural influences, a fact that Roberts and Sutton-Smith[107] themselves acknowledged. For example, gambling for the possessions of the dead is a religious obligation among the Canelos Indians of Amazonian South America. It is their belief that the spirit of the deceased controls the outcome of every throw of the dice and allots the possessions to those he or she favors most. The Canelos also believe that their failure to observe this tradition would deeply offend the spirit who would then send them disease, death, crop failure, famine, and other calamities. Conversely, those who observe this tradition will be rewarded with good fortune and large harvests.[108] From the natives' point of view, then, the gambling that occurs under these circumstances obviously has nothing to do with reducing any of the anxieties that Roberts and Sutton-Smith envisioned. Instead, it "functions" not only as a means of currying favor with the supernatural but, since it determines which relatives and friends will "inherit" which of the dead person's possessions, it also serves as a last will and testament.

By their very nature, statistically-grounded cross-cultural studies treat native cognitions and beliefs as entirely inconsequential since, for the cross-cultural researcher, only the statistically significant and supposedly anxiety-generating correlates of the behaviors under study are held to have any causal influence. In these cases such diverse factors as geography, physical environment, subsistence methods, town or country residence, kinship systems, marriage rules, levels of sociopolitical organization, assumed socialization anxieties, and the presence or absence of anal explanations for illness were considered. Obviously, many of these correlates are purely coincidental and have absolutely no bearing on the natives' motivations for gambling. Moreover, the complete lack of gambling in other tribal cultures whose members face a high degree of risk and uncertainty in their daily lives also repudiates the anxiety-reduction hypothesis. Traditionally, for example, such tribal peoples as the Inuit (Eskimos), Melanesians, and aboriginal Australians who were exposed to physical survival risks on a daily basis never developed any gambling games.[109]

Finally, Price's functional interpretation of gambling as an economic stimulus and redistributive mechanism suffers the same failing as those of the earlier functionally-oriented theorists in that it also assumes the consequences of gambling to be its causes. Although the legalization of lotteries and other forms of gambling by national and regional governments may indeed be motivated by a need for the revenues they generate, this does not explain why people are motivated to gamble.

W. L. Li and M. H. Smith: Analysis of a Gallup Poll

Another early statistical study was conducted by W. L. Li and M. H. Smith who tested some of the same assumptions as Tec. Like Tec, they also analyzed data obtained from an earlier study, in this case a 1971 United States national survey of 1,565 respondents which had been conducted by the Gallup Organization. However, unlike Tec's data which covered only one type of gambling, the Gallup survey covered gambling of many kinds. The hypotheses Li and Smith's study was designed to test included (1) Veblen's **leisure class** contention that those with higher incomes are more likely to gamble, (2) Devereux's **rural-urban residence** or **community-size** proposition that people living in small-towns and rural areas are less likely to gamble than urban dwellers, (3) Tec's proposition that gambling results from **status frustration** or insecurity, and (4) their own **life cycle hypothesis** that gambling and age are inversely related (the older people become, the less likely they are to gamble). The last of these, essentially a sociological test of the **sensation-seeking model**, was based on the premise that a person's need for excitement and stimulation, and hence the appeal of gambling, diminishes with age.[111] Li and Smith reasoned that correlating the propensity to gamble with the income level, community size, age, and status inconsistency (disparity between occupational status and income) of their respondents would constitute satisfactory tests of these hypotheses.

Finding significant positive correlations between gambling and income, and gambling and occupational status, the researchers concluded that these findings clearly confirmed Veblen's original view that gambling is positively related to socioeconomic status and refuted Tec's argument that it is primarily a pursuit of the frustrated lower classes. They suggested that their findings differed from Tec's since her study involved only one kind of wagering, the national soccer pool, and therefore did not adequately represent the entire domain of gambling. The significant correlations that emerged between gambling and age and gambling and residence also confirmed the **life cycle** and **community-size hypotheses**. The weak and statistically insignificant correlation that emerged between gambling and status inconsistency was interpreted as a possible confirmation of the **status frustration hypothesis**.

Critique of Li and Smith

Like Tec's initial study, that by Li and Smith also had a number of flaws. Although they reported that 23 percent of their sample gambled, it is impossible to determine which forms of gambling were most and least popular since they failed to disclose which proportions of their respondents engaged in which forms of gambling. Far more seriously, however, was that their respondents were asked only if they had bet on anything at all in the four weeks immediately prior to the survey. Their responses therefore disclosed nothing about rates of gambling in terms of frequency, duration, persistence, or amounts of money wagered; the data revealed only that more people in higher income categories made some kind of bet at least once in the last month than did people in lower income categories. This finding can in no way be construed as proof of Veblen's thesis that gambling is primarily a leisure class activity. Furthermore, the betting habits of different individuals vary tremendously. Some people place small wagers on the outcome of an occasional round of golf, some regularly place large bets with bookies, and some are habitual slot machine or poker players. Although all of these people would have responded positively to the question on gambling posed by the survey, such qualitatively different sorts of gambling can hardly be treated as quantitative equivalents. Finally, it is impossible to derive an accurate picture of leisure class gambling habits from the arbitrary income categories that were employed in the study. Annual incomes were broken down into only three categories: those below $6,000 were judged to indicate "low" economic status; those between $6,000 and $12,000 indicated "medium" economic status, and those of $12,000 and above were thought to reflect "high" economic status. Even by the economic standards of 1971 when the original survey was conducted, an annual income of only $12,000 could hardly have supported a "leisure class" lifestyle since even six figure incomes were still considered middle class.

However, like Tec's study, Li and Smith's also had some value as it introduced some interesting hypotheses which require further testing. For example, the extent to which gambling may or may not vary with income should be determined on the basis of rates of betting and amounts of money wagered. Their findings that the propensity to gamble appears to vary with age and community size stand in contradiction to psychological drive-reduction theories. In the words of the authors:

> Obviously there are many trivial explanations as to why people gamble. Gambling is often perceived as serving the function of fun, excitement, adventure and, perhaps, escape from a dull, boring life, but what this study has shown is that these psychological explanations may not be sufficient for there are some structural conditions that are significantly related to an individual's propensity to gamble.[112]

Nevertheless, their data revealed only that fewer older people and residents of smaller communities placed a bet in the month prior to the study than younger people or residents of larger communities. In the absence of any additional information, many explanations for these findings are possible but all would be entirely speculative. Since Li and Smith were convinced that gambling is related to income they suggested, for example, that age-related changes in gambling behavior could be due entirely to declining postretirement incomes.[113] However, it could also be that with age comes greater responsibilities which reduce one's interest in gambling and other pursuits that were once popular in youth, or that age restricts one's access to gambling opportunities, or that the experience that comes with age teaches many people that there is actually little profit in gambling. Just as there may be many "trivial" explanations as to why people gamble, there may be just as many as to why they do not.

Chapter 7

LARGE SCALE SOCIOLOGICAL SURVEYS

GAMBLING IN THREE BRITISH URBAN CENTERS

One of the most ambitious and extensive studies, a household survey of 2,000 adult respondents in the United Kingdom, was undertaken from 1968 into the early 1970s to test some of the earlier sociological hypotheses.[1] The study sampled three geographically and culturally distinct urban centers: the steel-working city of Sheffield, the market and administrative center of Swansea, and the suburban community of Wanstead and Wooford which was populated largely by nonmanual laborers who commuted to work in central London. The forms of gambling investigated included sports pools, on-track horse and dog racing, off-track betting, bingo, slot (fruit) machines, raffles, lotteries, card playing at a home or pub, and card playing at a casino. The survey instrument was a long (3,000 item) questionnaire which included questions on gambling frequencies, expenditures, and outcomes for each kind of gambling by household and by individual, the respondent's beliefs and attitudes toward gambling, work, and life in general, the context in which gambling occurred, parental and spousal gambling, and, of course, an array of standard demographic questions such as gender, age, marital status, education, occupation, income, religion, etc. Unlike many other surveys, this one also asked nongamblers the reasons why they did not gamble.

The first part of the study lumped all forms of gambling together to test established hypotheses. Relying entirely on prevalence and frequency statistics, it arrived at one set of conclusions. The second part explored the relationship between different kinds of gambling and various social indicators for the purpose of generating new hypotheses. It included statistics on the volume of gambling in terms of the amounts of money wagered and lost by different groups. Consequently, it also arrived at a number of different conclusions from those of Part 1.

Part 1: Who Gambles?

Univariate Analyses

The United Kingdom study found that far more people engage in some kind of gambling than abstain from all kinds. Fully 1,955 of the 2,000 respondents, or 98 percent of the sample, had staked money on one or more forms of gambling in the year prior to the study.[2] Rates of gambling in different sectors of this population were calculated on the basis of the four primary demographic variables of gender, age, income, and social class. It is important to note that income does not necessarily equate with social status since some respondents from lower working class backgrounds have very high incomes and some upper middle class respondents have very low incomes.

Gambling rates were based on the number of sessions per week, month, or year, rather than the number of games or bets per session. They were categorized as "high," "medium," "low," and "none" according to the kinds of gambling participation and the frequencies of each:

High frequency gamblers included all those who gambled at least two times per week on any one kind of gambling, or once a week on any three kinds, or once every two weeks on any four kinds, or once a month on any five forms of gambling.

Medium frequency gamblers bet once a week on any one form, every two weeks or more on any two forms, once a month on any three kinds, or at least once a year on any four forms.

Low frequency gamblers bet only once a year or more on any single form of gambling.

Nongamblers included those who did not bet at least once a year on even a single form of gambling.[3]

Horse and dog betting, whether on-track or in betting shops, were considered to be "high risk" forms of gambling.

Gender differences. The UK survey found strong gender differences in rates of gambling and, hence, strong support for the **gender hypothesis**. Men, who averaged 123 gambling sessions per year, gamble three to four times more often than women, who averaged 35. Men are also three times more likely to be high frequency gamblers than women and twice as likely to be either medium or high frequency gamblers. Women are only slightly

(1.3 times) more likely to be low frequency gamblers than men but two and one-half times as likely to be nongamblers. Due to the magnitude of sex differences, many subsequent findings were also distinguished on the basis of gender.

Age differences. The study also found that gambling involvement among men dramatically decreases with age. These age-based differences lend support to Li and Smith's **life cycle hypothesis** in some ways but not in others. The survey found that the "youngest" (18-25 years of age) members of society are the most avid gamblers while the "elderly" (66 and older) gamble the least. The other two age categories employed by the researchers included "young middle age" (26-45) and "older middle age" (46-65). Among men, those in the youngest age group gambled an average of 173 times a year, young middle-aged men gambled 126 times a year, older middle aged men averaged 119 times, and elderly men gambled an average of only 57 times each year. With the exception of the elderly, then, these averages all constitute "high frequency" gambling. Therefore, in terms of the authors' frequency rating system, the youngest are no more likely to be "medium" or "high frequency" gamblers than those in either of the middle-aged groups. Although women in all age categories gambled far less frequently than men, a roughly similar trend appeared among them: women in the four age groups gambled an average of 41, 33, 41, 26 times per year, respectively. With the exception of older middle-aged women who were just as involved as the youngest women, the study found, in general, that the younger people are the more likely they are to gamble although the youngest are no more prone to high frequency gambling than anyone else save the oldest members of society.

Income differences. Purely income-based data would appear to provide strong evidence in support of Tec's **aspiration** or **status frustration hypothesis** and against Veblen's **leisure class theory**. According to the study's authors, "The poorest men are clearly far less involved in gambling than the rest"[4] whereas the most affluent women are clearly least involved. The four income categories selected for analysis were "poorest" (£612 or less per year), "poorer" (£613-£999), "more affluent" (£1,000 to £1,432), and "most affluent" (£1,433 or more per year). The poorest men gambled an average of only 66 times a year or roughly once a week. The poorer men gambled an average of 164 times a year or over three times a week; the more affluent, 133 times or about 2.5 time a week; and the most affluent gambled 112 times a year or approximately twice a week. The situation was strikingly different for women who gambled an average of 32, 48, 33, and 24 times per year in each of these income groups, respectively. Although women gamble far less frequently than men, the overall pattern for both sexes is that the most affluent are the least likely to gamble while those in the second lowest income group have the highest gambling rate, just as Tec predicted.

Social class differences. Purely class-based differences in gambling among men would tend to support Tec's **status inequality** observations but neither her **status frustration hypothesis** nor Veblen's **leisure class theory**. In terms of social class differences in rates of gambling among men, the authors found "a clear inverse relationship between high social class and gambling."[5] Social status was divided into four categories–lower working class, upper working class, lower middle class, and upper middle class–on the basis of occupation rather than income. All analyses, irrespective of age or income, showed a definite inverse relationship between rates of gambling and class status. Although the difference in gambling rates between lower and upper middle class men was not striking, upper working class men gambled 20 percent more frequently than either of the middle classes and while lower working class men gambled 40 percent more often. The fact that rates of gambling tend to decrease as levels of education increase among both men and women also corroborates the **education hypothesis, anomie theory**, and Tec's **status inequality** observation.

Among women, however, social class differences in rates of gambling fail to support either of Tec's propositions. Although upper middle class women are the least involved in gambling, the overall trend that occurred among men does not occur among women. In this case, class based rates of gambling describe an inversely "U-shaped" curve with the upper working and lower middle classes more being more involved, and lower working and upper middle classes being less involved.

Religious affiliation. Devereux's **religion hypothesis** was supported by some findings but rejected by others. It found support in the incidence of "high frequency" gambling which was greater among Roman Catholics (36%) than among Anglican (21%) and Nonconformist (17%) Protestants. However, those claiming no religious affiliation also had a fairly high participation rate (23%) while Jews had the lowest of any religion. Moreover, Roman Catholics had a much lower rate of "medium frequency" gambling (27%) than Protestants of any denomination (48%). Finally, the incidence of "high frequency" gambling was greater among men who attended religious services regularly (18%) than among those who did so sporadically (10%). The authors were far less detailed in their discussion of religion and gambling among women. They reported only that "The trend for women on affiliation but not attendance is quite out of line with theories predicting that Protestants would in general tend more to gambling than non-Protestants."[6]

Multivariate Analyses: Age, Income, and Social Class

Multivariate analyses, when combined with the fact that rates of gambling steadily decrease in all successive age groups, provide even stronger support for Li and Smith's **life cycle hypothesis**, at least as far as men are concerned. Although gambling rates were highest in the youngest group of men and tended to decrease with age across all income categories, those in the youngest and poorest group tended to gamble considerably less (71 times a year) than their age mates who earned more money than they did (341, 107, and 120 times a year, respectively) and even somewhat less than the oldest and poorest group of men (73 times a year). The heaviest gamblers in the youngest male group were those in the poorer (252 times a year) and upper working class (341 times a year) categories. Other traits associated with the youngest group of men were upward mobility (attaining a higher social class status than their parents), a motivation to increase income, a propensity toward risk taking, a belief in luck, being single, being an Anglican Protestant, having little involvement in other forms of leisure activities, and having a mother and father who were both regular gamblers. These associations suggested that young men are ambitious and desire social advancement but have few other commitments which would inhibit their gambling until they mature, marry, and assume more responsibilities.

Among women, however, multivariate analyses tend to support Tec's **status inequality** but not her **status frustration hypothesis**. Among the youngest women the average rate of gambling was highest within the lowest income group (at 76 times a year, it was actually higher than for men in this group) and lower working class groups (70 times a year), and steadily decreased with rising social status (70, 46, 18, and 14 times a year, respectively). Except for the oldest lower working class women who were the least involved in gambling (9 times per year), rates of gambling were substantially higher among working class women than those of the middle class across all age groups. These findings suggest that poverty encourages young men to avoid gambling but inspires young women to pursue it.

Hypothesis Testing

Unlike the authors of the United States and Nevada surveys discussed below, the authors of the United Kingdom survey were concerned with hypothesis testing. Although they hoped to test as many of the earlier hypotheses as possible not all were, in fact, testable. For example, the **rural-urban hypotheses** of Devereux and Tec could not be tested since the survey was restricted to urban dwellers. The legalization in 1960 of nearly all forms of gambling in the United Kingdom also ruled out the possibility of testing Devereux's hypothesis that rates of illegal gambling would be higher among the lower classes and elements of society.

The theories that were tested included **anomie**, **alienation**, **decision making**, **working class culture**, **structural-functionalism**, and **risk tak-**

ing. More specifically, **anomie theory** predicts that rates of gambling will be negatively correlated with socioeconomic status. The **action** or **risk-taking hypothesis** predicts that those most oriented toward risk will be the heaviest gamblers. **Alienation theory** predicts that those who have the least autonomy in their employment will be the heaviest gamblers. **Decision making theory**, which is similar to alienation theory, predicts that those who have the least opportunity to make any decisions in their work roles will be the heaviest gambling participants, especially in games such as horse and dog racing which are perceived as involving the greatest element of skill. The **working-class culture hypothesis**, a variant of the subcultural hypothesis advanced by Moran and Newman, assumes that there are cultural as well as economic differences between the working and middle classes among which are major attitudinal differences regarding poverty, delinquency, and the value of education. It also assumes that these differences, which include a penchant for heavy gambling, are instilled during the socialization process. This hypothesis therefore predicts that rates of gambling will be higher among the working classes, particularly among those who adhere most strongly to values of this class. Devereux's **structural-functional** analysis saw gambling as an important "safety valve" institution which functions to preserve the existing social structural order in stratified Western society. His **religion hypothesis** predicts that rates of gambling will be lowest among members of the Protestant middle class and will tend to grow higher as their influence decreased.

Several other propositions were also tested, two of which were concerned more with **deviance theory** in general than with gambling in particular as they sought to test alternative hypotheses. The **home-centeredness hypothesis** predicts that "conjugal role sharing," or the extent to which husbands actively participate in such domestic activities as daily housework and shopping along with their wives, will be inversely related to gambling. The **work-centered leisure hypothesis** predicts that gambling should be least prevalent among those whose free time activities such as studying at home are most closely related to their work. Although they did not designate it as such, the researchers also introduced the **parental gambling hypothesis** which, as a more specific version of the subcultural hypothesis, predicts that people's gambling-related attitudes and behaviors will reflect those of their parents.

As is typical of quantitative sociological research, this study also relied on the presence or absence of statistical correlations to test various hypotheses. In this case the rate of gambling (the dependent variable) was assumed to be influenced by certain socioeconomic and behavioral phenomena (independent or causal variables) selected by the researchers. For example, if Tec's **status frustration hypothesis** were correct, then the upper working class sector of society should have a higher rate of gambling than all other social classes. However, the authors chose to test many of these hypotheses not by correlating objectively determined rates of gambling against such standard objectively determined demographic variables as age, income, and social class, but against various attitudinal variables which were largely subjective and, hence, nonquantifiable by any objective means. Although all trends can be expected to vary with such factors as age, gender, and primary reference group, in Part 1 of the study each theory was tested in its "pure" form with no attempt to control for the influence of these extraneous factors.

Alienation and **anomie theory** were rejected since no direct relationship emerged between gambling and socioeconomic status and the respondents' indications of job autonomy as measured by subjective perceptions of "job effort." However, a negative correlation appeared between gambling and "active community participation" or political involvement among middle class men which the authors felt could possibly be interpreted as an indirect measure of autonomy. **Anomie theory** was partially supported by the finding that social class was inversely correlated with high rates of gambling. That is, the incidence of high frequency gambling tended to decrease as one ascended the socioeconomic ladder: depending on within-class income differences, 21 percent to 37 percent of all lower working class respondents were high frequency gamblers as were 24 percent to 27 percent of the upper working class, 32 percent to 23 percent of the lower middle class, and only 8 percent of the upper middle class respondents. Nevertheless, **anomie theory** was ultimately rejected since this trend failed to materialize among the "high/medium" frequency population. Tec's **status frustration hypothesis**, a variant of anomie theory, was also rejected since the data failed to sustain its prediction that the upper working class should have the highest rate of gambling.

The **working-class culture hypothesis** was also rejected due to the lack of any evidence demonstrating that gambling is a deeply entrenched and highly valued cultural tradition of the working classes. The primary indicator employed to establish such a link–a highly subjective one–was the indication of a strong belief in luck, a trait which the researchers apparently presumed to be more common to the working than to the middle classes. Not only was the "belief in luck" more prevalent among the working classes but, the strongest beliefs in luck among all members of this class were held by those in the lower working class. However, since the upper middle class held stronger luck beliefs than the lower middle class, the expected linear correlation between stronger beliefs in luck and heavier rates of gambling failed to materialize. Instead, the relationship that did emerge described an inversely "U-shaped" curve with more low (54%) and medium frequency (56%) gamblers holding strong beliefs in luck than high frequency (35%) and nongamblers (29%). The same pattern emerged even when the comparison was restricted to the upper and lower working classes.

If working class values are transmitted from parents to their children, another indicator of the **working class culture hypothesis** would be a higher incidence of parental gambling among the working classes. However, analysis of parental gambling also failed to yield the expected class-based results but did support the more narrowly defined **parental gambling hypothesis** since the gambling habits of the respondents and their parents were found to be related in all social classes.

Tests of Devereux's structural-functional **religion theory** produced inconclusive results. Perhaps one reason for this was that since most of the respondents were Protestants (who are expected to gamble less than Catholics or Jews), relatively little comparative data were available. Nevertheless, one analysis (using weighted data) revealed that proportionately more high and medium frequency gamblers were middle class Nonconformist (non-Anglican) Protestants than Roman Catholics or members of other non-Protestant denominations. This finding would serve to refute the prediction that rates of gambling should be lowest among more fundamentalistic Protestants. Moreover, proportionately more middle than working class Nonconformist Protestants were high frequency gamblers. However, after a second analysis (using unweighted data), Devereux's prediction was sustained but only by a narrow margin. A third test which compared middle class Anglican Protestants to middle class Roman Catholics showed the Anglicans to be heavier gamblers than the Catholics.

Decision making theory failed to find conclusive support in some tests but did find limited support in others. According to the study's authors, decision making theory assumes only that the inability to make decisions on the job should be related to the ability to make decisions while gambling. It predicts that gamblers who are allowed to make the fewest decisions on the job will be more likely to prefer games that they feel require skill. One test of this hypothesis was an attempt to correlate four degrees of perceived job autonomy—low to high—with the imputation of skill in gambling. If the hypothesis were correct, then more gamblers with low autonomy on the job should make claims of skill in their preferred form of gambling than those with higher job autonomy. Since the subjects of this test were restricted to horse and dog players (both on-track and betting shop gamblers), the primary reason for the inconclusive findings was that most gamblers from all categories of job autonomy ascribed a great deal of skill to this form of gambling. Nevertheless, one analysis (weighted data) yielded a weak correlation in the expected direction although another (unweighted data) did not. Another test, which correlated subjective degrees of "job interest" of lower working class men with rates of gambling yielded a stronger inverse correlation: those reporting "very low" job satisfaction bet an average of 254 times a year while those with "high" job satisfaction bet an average of 38 times a year. The correlation between these two variables was interpreted as limited support for the decision making theory.

Risk-taking theory was tenuously supported on the grounds that rates of gambling showed a slight tendency to correspond with measures of "action" orientation as determined by responses to questions dealing with the avoidance of, or preference for, risk in daily life. Since risk orientation would not be related to social class, the authors predicted that there should be no relationship between social class and expressions of risk orientation. This prediction was verified by the data. One analysis (weighted data) failed to support the prediction that, irrespective of social class, rates of gambling should be higher among those expressing the greatest preference for risk while another (unweighted data) showed only a modest positive correlation between these variables.

Both the **home-centeredness** and **work-centered leisure hypotheses** were supported. "Conjugal role sharing," the only measure of home-centeredness, showed a strong inverse relationship with gambling involvement. The negative correlation between gambling involvement and "studying at home," the only measure of "work-centered leisure," was also strong.

Part 2: Frequencies and Volumes of Specific Forms of Gambling

The second part of the United Kingdom study, which presented descriptive statistics for and demographic correlates of different kinds of gambling, revealed strong gender differences in gambling preferences and expenditures. Excluding lotteries and raffles, men tended to favor sports pools, off-track betting, pub gaming (generally cards or darts for drinks or small cash stakes), bingo, machine gambling, private card games, bookie betting, private bets, dog racing, and casino gaming in that order. Women tended to prefer sports pools, bingo, private card games, off-track betting, gaming machines, and pub gaming in that order. Very few women participated in on-course betting, bookie betting, casino gaming, dog racing, or private bets. On average, men gambled over three times more often than women (117 vs. 35 times a year) on these kinds of gambling and spent nearly five times as much money on them as did women (1,491 vs. 301 shillings per year). Because the amounts of data for each form of gambling were so voluminous, only the findings for the most popular individual forms of gambling will be summarized.

Sports Pools

The demographics of football pool betting, Britain's most popular form, accorded with Tec's observations of pools betting in Sweden and her **aspiration** or **status frustration hypothesis**; they also tended to support Devereux's **religion hypothesis**. Pools betting is clearly a male dominated form of gambling since twice as many men (52.5%) participated as women (26.3%). Although it is enjoyed by members of all social classes and the differences between them are not great, participation rates for both men and women were highest among the upper working class (57.9% of men; 32.3% of women) and lowest among the upper middle class (43.8% and 18.3%). The greatest variation occurred between the upper working and lower middle classes. Religious affiliation showed some variation since fewer Nonconformist Protestants (23%) than other denominations (48%) were regulars. Those who participated regularly in church services were also more likely to refrain from this form of gambling. Middle-aged and middle income men had the highest participation rates while the poorer had the lowest. Slightly more married men (61%) played regularly than did those whose marriages have ended (44%); participation rates among women also conformed to this pattern. Age appeared to be a factor since relatively few (6%) of the youngest men but substantially more of those in the older age groups (23% to 29%) participated on a regular basis. Participation was lower among those who showed low conventionalism, low risk taking, and low belief in luck. These findings suggested that sports pool betting, which offers at least some opportunity to realize large returns with only a small investment, has gained more respectability among and is more attractive to middle-aged, middle-income, married men with families than among the poor, single, young, or old.

Football pool betting is far more a solitary than a social practice. Although stakes were sometimes shared, this was a far more common occurrence among the youngest men (70%) than the oldest (11%). Of the men who shared, most did so with workmates while most women who shared did so only with their husbands. Nevertheless, most men (75%) and nearly all women were solitary bettors who generally did not discuss their choices and filled out their coupons in the privacy of their own homes.

Relatively little money was used for this form of gambling since the stakes were small, generally ranging from a shilling to a pound with most participants (70%) betting less than five shillings per week. Men, who spent an average of £10.9 per year (1968) of which they lost £7.1, generally bet more than women who spent £4.5 of which £4 was lost. Combined expenditures averaged £8.6 per year with losses of £6. However, because the distribution was skewed by several large expenditures of £100 or more, the median expenditure of about £5 per year (£6 for men; £4 for women) would perhaps yield a more accurate volume estimate.

Analyses of bet sizes appear to support the **life cycle hypothesis** of Li and Smith as well as Veblen's **upper class theory** but to reject Tec's **aspiration hypothesis**. Younger men tended to stake more than older men while the affluent tended to stake more than the poor. In their last bet before being interviewed 86 percent of the respondents in the "poorest" category, 82 percent of the "poorer," 77 percent of the "affluent," and 63 percent of the "most affluent" participants placed bets of less than 6 shillings. Bets of 6 shillings or more were placed by 10 percent of the "poorest" participants, 14 percent of the "poorer," 20 percent of the "affluent," and 33 percent of the most affluent.

The **moralistic** contention that most prize winners squander their money on foolish frivolities and additional betting was not borne out by the data. Only 7 percent to 15 percent of all men who won less than £100 admitted to squandering their money on gifts or spending sprees while only 4 percent of all winners of £100 or more did so. Instead, the disposition of prize money was clearly related to the amount won. In general, prizes of less than £5 were treated no differently than any other pocket money while larger prizes were given special treatment. The overall tendency was for winners of larger amounts to invest their money in savings accounts or home necessities: 80% of those who won £100 or more, 42 percent to 45 percent of those who won between £6 and £99, and 20 percent of those who won £5 or less invested in these ways. While 23 percent to 26 percent of those who won £5 or less rebet their money, only 2 percent of those winning from £6 to £99, and no winners of £100 or more did so. Women disposed of their winnings in roughly the same pattern with the exception that proportionally more women (21%) squandered their prize money than did men (10%) but far fewer rebet it.

The disposition of prize money also appeared to be related to social class but clearly not in accordance with the stereotypical pattern, at least as far as men were concerned. Middle class men were more prone to rebet their winnings than those of the working classes while lower working class men (51%) were more inclined to buy something for the home or save their money than were upper working (35%), lower middle class (30%), or upper middle class (34%) men. However, class-based gender differences are striking. "Women," the authors wrote, "accord to almost a caricature of class stereotypes" in the disposition of their winnings. The tendency to save or spend their prize money on the home steadily declined with decreasing class status (52% upper middle to 14% lower working) as the likelihood of squandering it increased (0% upper middle to 50% lower working). The authors were at a loss to explain why the stereotypical class pattern should be reversed for men while it so clearly obtained for women.

Betting Shops

The second most popular form of gambling in the United Kingdom is racetrack betting, most of which takes place in legal off-track betting shops whose patrons show an overwhelming preference for betting exclusively on the horses (91.1% men; 99.8% of women). Other contests, such as dog racing, boxing, and wrestling, are clearly far less popular. On this basis the authors concluded that "It is plainly not the 'impulse to gamble' which settles randomly on any event staged for gambling purposes. . . . If this were the case, horse-race betting would simply be one of many competing attractions"[8] on which gamblers would stake their money. As it is, the extreme popularity of this single betting shop attraction to the near-exclusion of all others demonstrates that horse race betting is a deeply entrenched Western European cultural tradition, particularly among the English. They therefore felt that "Betting on events outside horse-racing seems most strongly associated with the most regular and the heaviest betters," an observation that, "makes sense in terms of 'gambling impulse' theory—the heavier the gambler, the more prone he is to bet on anything that moves—but not in terms of 'rational' gambling theory—where specialization is the hallmark of the trade."[9]

Gender differences were conspicuous in this arena, as well, since men patronized betting shops more frequently and spent considerably more money in them than women. Only 2 percent of all women sampled regularly patronized the betting shops as opposed to 17 percent of the men. Although their figures suggested that men were eight times more likely to use these shops than women, the authors felt that the true extent of women's participation may have been concealed by proxy betting which an earlier survey found among 36 percent of those sampled. Most of these women preferred to bet through their husbands, neighbors, or other male friends. Men were reported to have spent an average of £111 on off-track betting in 1968 whereas women reported average expenditures of only £5.8 that year.

Typical patterns of betting shop usage failed to support **interactional theories** of gambling since off-track betting, like sports pools betting, is primarily a solitary activity which takes up relatively little of gambler's time. Three quarters of the men bet alone while women tended to bet with others. Those men who did bet with others generally did so with friends while women did so more often with family members. Likewise, betting shop users did not conform to the popular stereotype of the gambler who spends hours at a time making long successions of high stakes bets. Although men tended to spend more time in them than women, and regulars bettors stayed longer than sporadic bettors, most (51% of men and 81% of women) made only one bet of less than five shillings and left within a matter of minutes. Roughly half of the men (48%) and nearly all women (88%) who patronized these shops spent less than five minutes at a time inside them; relatively few (15%) of the men and no women stayed as long as half an hour while over two thirds of the men (36%) and very few women (less than 1%) stayed longer than half an hour. Two or three successive bets were made by 32 percent of the men and 16 percent of the women; 18 percent of the men and only 3 percent of the women bet four or more times in succession. Successive bets were more often made by older (20% to 25%) than younger people (2%) and more were made by both the poorest and the most affluent than by the two middle income groups.

Bet sizes therefore appeared to be associated with income and age but not with successive bets. Small stakes bettors (less than 3 shillings per bet) tended to make slightly more successive bets than others as did some of the heaviest bettors (regulars who generally made more than four successive bets) who tended to wager more than ten shillings per bet. None of the poorest men risked over five shillings per bet whereas 43 percent of the most affluent risked at least that much. Bets larger than ten shillings were most common among more affluent men (50%), younger men (23%), and upper class men (18% vs. 3% in other classes). They were least common among the oldest men of whom only 14 percent risked more than three shillings per bet.

Differential rates of betting shop usage among different demographic groups failed to support either Li and Smith's **life cycle** or Veblen's **leisure class hypothesis**, but they did conform to Tec's **status inequality** or **anomie** prediction and Devereux's **religion hypothesis**. Although the data did not support the ideas that gambling decreases with age or increases with social class, they did reveal that off-track betting is clearly an age- and class-based phenomenon. Older middle aged men were the most frequent patrons (23%) while younger middle aged and the youngest men were less frequent (14% each) and the oldest were the least frequent (9%). Participation rates showed steady increases with decreasing class status (4% upper middle to 32% lower working). Educational differences reflected the same class bias but income differences did not: the poorest and the most affluent used the betting shops about 10 percent less often than those in the middle income groups. Roman Catholics, who went to a betting shop roughly twice as often as Anglican Protestants and three times more often than Nonconformist and other Protestants, were by far the most frequent users. Church attendance and off-track betting were also inversely related to a slight degree. The authors felt that the weakness of this relationship was probably due to the high participation of Roman Catholics.

Betting shop data also failed to support Herman's **functional theory**: whereas Herman found that most on-track bettors played the favorites, the United Kingdom survey found a distinctly different pattern among off-track bettors, the overwhelming majority of whom made riskier bets. Relatively few men (24%) and almost no women (4%) backed the favorites. Likewise, relatively few players of either sex (14% of men; 36% of women) bet on "outsiders" or long shots. Instead, the most typical pattern (54% men; 40% women) was betting on horses "in-between" these two rankings. The authors maintained that playing the favorites implies a reliance on the choices of others (the racing form) and a general tendency to settle for smaller returns in exchange for less risk. They suggested instead that "in-between" playing is the most rational strategy since "it is there that the greatest scope lies for a choice which is both realistic and might 'beat the odds.'"[10] However, the United Kingdom survey also found gender differences among the choices of bets that were similar to Herman's. More women (77%) than men (47%) made "each way" or "show" bets but more men (42%) than women (17%) made strictly "win" bets. These statistics imply that men prefer to take greater risks while women tend to hedge their bets. The authors attributed this difference to the greater confidence that men have in their judgments. However, when choices of horse ranking and betting styles were combined, two "ideal" risk-based betting patterns began to emerge: men tended to bet on more favorites to win while women tended to bet on more "in-between" horses to show. This suggests that men tended to assume greater risk by betting on only one (the favorite wins) of a number of possible outcomes (another horse wins), but to diminish their risk by relying on the more "rational" predictions of the racing form (playing the favorite). Women assumed greater risk by playing against the favorite but reduced it by betting on more than one possible outcome (win, place, or show). Nevertheless, since "in-between" and "show" bets were clearly the most popular choices of both men and women, most players of either sex seemed to prefer safer bets. Preferences for and against combination bets also differed by gender. Riskier combination bets, those with very high payoffs for those who correctly pick all winners in a sequence of races (doubles, triples or trifectas, and other accumulators), were preferred by more men (48%) than women (26%). Consequently, substantially more (61%) women than men (40%) preferred to bet on one race at a time and avoid the combinations.

The authors wrongly predicted that the working classes who were assumed to be more prone to immediate gratification would prefer riskier long shot and more complex combination bets while those in the middle classes who have presumably learned to defer gratification would take fewer risks by playing the favorites and making single race bets. Despite their erroneous assumptions, class-, age-, income-, and volume-based differences were related to preferences for betting type, though in ways precisely antithetical to their predictions. One-quarter of upper middle class players bet on outsiders as opposed to only one-twentieth of those in the lower working class. The opposite pattern appeared for playing favorites since more working class than middle class gamblers did so. Nevertheless, the modal pattern among all social classes was "in-between" betting. The oldest (51%) and the poorest (37%) tended to bet the long shots while middle-aged (37%) and poorer (36%) bettors preferred to play the favorites. However, the oldest and the middle class gamblers tended to make about half as many combination bets as others. The frequency of combination bets was far higher in the lower working class (61%) than the lower middle (25%) and upper middle (34%) classes but among those who did make combination bets the poorest tended to prefer doubles while the most affluent preferred more complex combinations. Still, the most preferred type across all demographic groups was the single bet.

In keeping with the notion of greater rationality in the betting habits of the working classes, the authors found a direct correlation between social class and "win" bets and an inverse correlation between "each way" or "show" bets. That is, working class gamblers made fewer higher risk "win" bets and more lower risk bets of the "each way" kind. It is also not surprising that the lowest stakes gamblers bet on long shots to a significantly greater extent than did higher stakes gamblers who preferred the more rational bet of playing the favorites.

The typical assertions and beliefs of betting shop users were particularly interesting and lend some support to **cognitive** explanations. In the first place, most betting shop users claimed to have broken even over the past year. However, the self-reported annual average losses of only £3.8 by men and £.8 by women appear to have been grossly underestimated. These figures are belied by the fact that they would have generated only £30 million in annual revenues when the betting shops would have required five times that amount just to pay their business expenses. In the second place, since men tended to attribute success to skill and women to luck, gender differences were also quite apparent in terms of gamblers' attributions. Two-thirds (65%) of all the men but only one-fifth (21%) of the women credited their choice of winners to skill whereas only one-quarter (27%) of the men but nearly half (48%) of the women claimed that winning is principally a matter of luck or chance.

Skill- and luck-based attributions also varied by age and class. Younger (81%) and upper working class (76%) bettors also ascribed a greater degree of skill to their choices than did others (53%-67% and 50%-60%, respectively). Members of the upper middle class (50%) tended to rely less on luck or chance than did those of the other classes (54%-67%). The numbers of those attributing their choices to skill steadily increased with both the frequency and volume of betting.

As was the case for pools betting, the ways in which betting shop winnings were spent were determined primarily by the amounts won and followed a pattern similar to that for sports pool prizes. That is, larger amounts were more often used to pay debts, to buy gifts and frivolities, and for savings and home investments whereas smaller amounts were more often pocketed or rebet. Although only regulars rebet their money and squandered it more often than occasionally players, only about one-quarter of them did so. Thus, three times more regulars saved their money or bought things for their homes with it than rebet or squandered it. Overall, only 8 percent of all men and no women rebet their money. Upper middle class bettors were most likely simply to pocket their winnings while those of the lower middle class were most like to save it or make a home investment. Upper working class gamblers were equally likely to pocket or invest their money while lower working class winners were slightly more inclined to save it or buy home furnishings than to pocket or squander it. They were least likely to rebet any money they won.

Devereux's prediction that the middle classes would be more conservative gamblers was contradicted by the pattern of budgeting money for betting that emerged. In fact, very few betting shop patrons ever budgeted or set aside any money for betting: most men (80%) and even more women (85%) simply bet with their ready cash. However, those who did budget money specifically for gambling were generally included among the oldest, the poorer, and working class categories.

Slot Machine Gambling

Although religious affiliation and social class were both influential factors, the United Kingdom survey data on slot machine gambling failed to support either Devereux's **religion** or Tec's **status inequality** or **anomie theory**. In fact, Roman Catholics who spent far less on slot machine gambling than other denominations were among the least involved in terms of both frequency and volume of playing as were the stable working classes whose gambling machine expenditures and participation rates were also among the lowest. Thus, affiliation with the Church of England and upward social mobility along with high conventionalism, medium to high-risk taking proclivities, and an individualistic orientation regarding income increases were listed among the other predictors of slot machine gambling.

The survey also contradicted the commonly accepted idea that slot machine gambling is designed for and encourages solitary playing. Slot machine playing was found to be a predominantly social activity for 80 percent of the males and 90 percent of the females who played regularly. Even among the others none were entirely solitary players. Since the overwhelming majority of all participants preferred playing with others to playing alone, the authors argued that "This seems to rule out the simple 'pathology' view of fruit machine play."[11] They therefore speculated that "If there is an element of compulsion or addiction involved, it is *group* compulsion rather than individual."[12]

CONCLUSIONS

One of the most important findings of the United Kingdom survey was that *gambling is normative.* Since more than three-quarters of all respondents had engaged in at least some kind of gambling in the previous year, it can hardly be considered a "deviant" behavior.

Of equal importance is the fact that *gambling is more a discrete than a unitary phenomenon.* That is, the fact that most gamblers have distinct preferences for and against certain forms of gambling means that they are not indiscriminately drawn to any and all kinds of gambling that happen to be available. For example, nearly half of all men (44%) and over half of all women (57%) who regularly participated in sports pool betting were *not* regularly involved in any other kind of gambling whereas only a very few men (4%) and relatively few women (25%) who were regular betting shop users tended to avoid other forms. From this perspective, betting shop gambling is generally associated with other forms of gambling while pools betting is not. However, very few people (3% to 11%) of either sex who participated in other forms of gambling were also casino gamblers whereas much larger proportions (40% to 57%) of those who engaged in other forms also played the sports pools. From this perspective, pools betting is often associated with other forms of gambling while casino gambling is not.

Differences in gambling preferences are particularly striking when gender differences are considered. Only 5 percent of all women who were regular sports bettors were also off-track bettors while nearly 70 percent of all men who were regular off-track bettors were also sports pool bettors. As previously noted, the United Kingdom survey verified that men are far more likely to be high and medium frequency gamblers than women who are more likely to be nongamblers than men. Thus, the same general pattern held for men although they participated in both forms to a somewhat greater extent than women. Likewise, over half (51%) of all women but only one-fifth (21%) of all men who played bingo did so exclusively. Thus, bingo is generally not associated with other forms of gambling among women but it is among men.

In the final analysis, the authors concluded that the results of their overall findings on gambling in general, which were based on a synthesis of data on all forms, suggested acceptance of a modified social structural theory in which **anomie theory** is combined with Devereux's ideas on **religion** and

Herman's ideas on **decision making**. This conclusion was based on the attempt, despite their insistence on the discrete nature of gambling, to provide a composite of the typical British urban gambler which, in turn, was based on a multivariate analysis of all the data they had amassed throughout the course of their monumental undertaking. They found that the most typical gambler would be a poorly educated single man who attended church sporadically, had low job interest and high job dissatisfaction, had stronger beliefs in luck and parents who gambled, and who had a collective rather than individual orientation toward economic advancement. With the exception of single marital status, their combined data described the average working class male who believes in labor unionization. The authors therefore argued against acceptance of **economic** motivations for gambling in favor of a male-dominated **working class cultural** explanation:

> Economic gain in the purely acquisitive sense . . . does not seem to be a prime determinant of gambling. . . . The pleasure to be derived from gambling, the fascination it exerts, seems more likely in a context which stresses a particular kind of masculine role in both work and leisure. A systematic finding was that even women tended to gamble more the more they come to share the work experience of men.[13]

If this conclusion is valid, it could also be taken as strong support for **social learning theory**.

SUMMARY

Despite the many demographic trends they noted, the authors of the United Kingdom study concluded that the distribution of gambling as a whole revealed a "surprisingly uniform pattern."[14] In terms of sex differences, men are two to three times more likely to be regular and more highly involved gamblers than women. In terms of age differences, the youngest have the highest participation rates but their rates of "high" and "medium" frequency involvement are no greater than any other age group with the exception of the elderly. In terms of class and income differences, the very poor and the upper middle class show less involvement than the other socioeconomic groups although gambling tends to diminish with education. Thus, multivariate analysis of the combined data on all forms of gambling suggested that the typical gambler is motivated less by economic interests than by the desire to share the interests of and identify with a particular segment of society, that of the young working class male.

However, analysis of individual attitudinal variables yielded entirely different conclusions, just as did the data on different kinds of gambling. On the basis of the hypotheses they specifically tested through correlations based on attitudinal variables, the authors also concluded that "broad, class-based theories of gambling are ill-founded"[15] since the social factors which may be responsible for gambling are found in all sectors of society. Specifically, the authors found no support for **anomie theory** in general nor for Tec's **status frustration hypothesis** in particular (they apparently chose to rely solely on class-based data rather than income-based data which showed strong support for this hypothesis). They also found no support for **alienation theory** since no correlation appeared between the propensity to gamble and perceptions of job autonomy. The **working class culture hypothesis** was rejected on the grounds that the respondents' own gambling practices failed to correlate with their belief in luck but the **parental gambling hypothesis** was supported because they did correspond to parental gambling practices in all socioeconomic classes. Veblen's **affluence** or **leisure class hypothesis** must also be rejected on the grounds that rates of gambling among men and women are inversely related to social status and with the exception of the poorest men the most affluent tended to gamble less frequently than the other income groups. The popular notions that young, single, working class men are the heaviest gamblers were upheld but not so strongly as has commonly been assumed since the poorest-youngest group of men were the least involved in gambling. Tests of the structural-functional **religion hypothesis** were inconclusive but the study found tenuous support for Devereux's structural-functional **safety valve**, Herman's **decision making**, and Goffman's **action** or **risk-taking theories**. However, none of the correlations that did emerge between rates of gambling and the variables selected to test these theories was strong enough to constitute decisive confirmation of any of them. Since rates of gambling showed a strong, definite, and steady decrease with age among men and a general tendency to do so among women, the study actually provided the strongest support for Li and Smith's **life cycle theory** even though the authors did not specifically test this hypothesis.

GAMBLING IN THE UNITED STATES AND NEVADA

Another equally ambitious and comprehensive study, a national telephone survey of gambling in America, was sponsored by the United States government conducted at the University of Michigan and overseen by the Commission on the Review of the National Policy toward Gambling.[16] Its chief goals were to determine the "extent" or "amount" of gambling nationwide, to estimate the tax revenues that could be realized through legalization of various forms of gambling and to forecast the social ramifications of such legislation. The researchers also attempted to evaluate people's attitudes toward gambling, to determine rates of compulsive gambling, to discover why some gamblers avoid some types of gambling, and to discover why some people do not gamble at all. Like Li and Smith, they investigated a variety of gambling forms, both legal and illegal. This survey in which more than 2000 adults were sampled, actually represented two distinct comparative surveys since the information obtained from 296 residents of Nevada where nearly all forms of gambling were legal, was analyzed apart from that obtained from 1,796 respondents living elsewhere in the United States where most forms were illegal.

Although the researchers were not overtly concerned with specific hypothesis testing, the large quantities of data they amassed can be used to support or reject a number of existing hypotheses and to introduce some that were previously unconsidered. For example, many gambling authorities have long held to the **availability** or **availability and exposure hypothesis** which predicts that any increase in the sanctioning and availability of gambling will lead to concomitant increases in gambling expenditures, rates of problem gambling, and criminal activities associated with the gambling trade.[17] This hypothesis was supported by the findings that the incidence and volume of nonpathological gambling as well as rates of pathological gambling are directly related to its accessibility. For example, the state of New Jersey had 15 chapters of Gamblers Anonymous in 1978, the year the first Atlantic City casino opened for business. Four years later in 1982 this number had grown to 33. A growth rate of this magnitude was unprecedented.[18] These occurrences have prompted some researchers to assert that "the availability of gambling opportunities will have the effect of impoverishing some dependents, raising the cost to all of us of obtaining a personal loan, and increasing the volume of criminal activity."[19]

General Findings: How Many, How Much, and Where?

The study found that nationally, 61 percent of all adults placed at least one bet in 1974, the year prior to the study. However, 52 percent of those who admitted gambling indicated that they had made only "friendly" bets with friends, relatives, and others in noncommercial settings. Thus, 48 percent had engaged in some form of legal or illegal commercial gambling. In terms of gambling expenditures, an estimated total of $22.4 billion was wagered in 1974. This means that the average American adult spent roughly $150 on various legal and illegal forms of commercial gambling that year. By excluding the 52 percent who claimed not to have participated in commercial gambling of any kind, the researchers estimated that 69 million Americans staked an average of $387 that year.[20] Specifically, over half (55%) of the commercial gambling participants bet less than $50, roughly 20 percent bet between $50 and $200, and 14 percent bet more than $200.[21] More males (68%) gambled than females (55%).

Comparative data from the Nevada survey strongly suggest that the availability of, and early exposure to, gambling opportunities are among the most important determinants of gambling participation. Seventy-eight percent of Nevada's residents made a bet in 1974 in comparison with 61 percent of the national sample. Three-quarters (76%) of the Nevada sample engaged in legal commercial gambling as opposed to less than half (44%) of the national sample. Nevada residents also wagered more money per person than other Americans. The average annual per capita legal gambling expenditure of $665 by Nevada gamblers was nearly two and one-half times the national average of $273 for legal commercial gambling. This means that Nevada residents wagered three times more of their total household income (3.3%) than did the average American (1.1%). However, illegal gambling was markedly reduced in Nevada which had a far lower participation rate (4.3%) than the United States as a whole (11.2%) and substantially lower per capita expenditures for these activities ($257) than other states ($318). Since Nevada has no horse tracks, its residents must travel to other states for on-track betting. Thus, only 3.2 percent of its residents engaged in this form of gambling in comparison with nearly 14 percent of the national sample. Here, too, more males (87%) than females (70%) were gamblers.

The national sample also provided other kinds of evidence which could be interpreted as confirmation of the **availability and exposure hypotheses**. Far more of those who were exposed to gambling in childhood were gamblers than nongamblers when they became adults, and more people gambled in areas where it was available than where it was not. Exposure to gambling in the armed services was also found to be influential since far more armed service veterans became legal (28%) and illegal (37%) gamblers than remained nongamblers (17%).

The researchers also found that the legalization of gambling not only increases overall gambling participation rates, but it also creates more favorable attitudes toward the expansion of gambling. That is, steady and marked increases in gambling were found in states having more forms of legalized gambling. Thus, only four percent of the residents gambled in states in which no forms were legal. This figure rose to 20 percent in those having one to three forms, to 28 percent in those having four to six forms, and to 48 percent in states in which seven or more forms of gambling were legal. They also found that legalization of various forms of gambling tended to affect the attitudes of people with respect to gambling in general. Thus, 40 percent of the respondents in states in which all forms of gambling are illegal indicated that they wanted to maintain this policy. However, the number of those favoring the prohibition of all forms decreased to 21 percent in states in which one form was legal, to ten percent in those in which two forms were legal, and to five percent in those in which three forms were legal. Likewise, the more forms of gambling that were already legal in a state, the more its residents favored the legalization of additional forms.[22]

Frequency Analyses

The study also revealed several distinct regional and demographic differences in people's gambling habits which may have a bearing on many of the hypotheses that have been proposed. In general, although well over half the national population claimed to gamble, less than 50 percent participation was found among the elderly, the least affluent, the most poorly educated, Southerners, Christian fundamentalists, those who have been widowed, and those living in rural areas. The highest gambling rates were found among the young, the more affluent, the better educated, those living in the Northeast, Catholics and Jews, urban and suburban dwellers, and those who have been divorced or separated. Furthermore, more white Americans (62%) gambled than non-whites (52%) although non-whites engaged in illegal forms of gambling to a far greater extent than did white Americans, and men gambled more than women (68% vs. 55%) with the exception of casino gaming (10.2% of women; 8.8% of men) and bingo (21.1% of women; 16% of men).

These findings appear to support Veblen's **leisure class hypothesis** that the more affluent and better educated classes are more likely to gamble and to reject Tec's **status frustration** and **education hypotheses** that gambling represents a quest for upward mobility and should therefore be more common among the less affluent and less well educated. Specifically, rates of gambling were strongly correlated with income and education levels. In the national sample only 24 percent of those who had earned less than $5,000 had made at least one wager in 1974. However, 51 percent of those earning between $5,000 and $10,000, 69 percent of those in the $10 to $15 thousand income bracket, and 76 percent of those making more than $15,000 a year had engaged in some form of gambling activity. The Nevada sample also showed this progression although the differences in participation rates between income categories were less pronounced (63%, 74%, 78%, and 85%, respectively). In terms of legal commercial gambling activities, these income groups had 17 percent, 39 percent, 46 percent, and 54 percent participation rates, respectively, at the national level. In terms of education, 41 percent of high school dropouts, 66 percent of high school graduates, 72 percent of those with some college, and 79 percent of all college graduates gambled. Likewise, the percentages of those who had never gambled were inversely related to educational level (49%, 29%, 22%, and 18%, respectively). These kinds of class differences in the occurrence of casino gambling were also much less pronounced in Nevada than they were nationally.

Rates of gambling within different religious groups lent some support to the **religion hypothesis** which reflects Devereux's ideas on gambling and the Protestant ethic. Gambling was substantially more prevalent among Catholics (80%) and Jews (77%) than among Protestants as a whole (54%). (Were it not for the Catholics' proclivity for bingo, Jews would have had the highest gambling participation rate.) The more conservative fundamentalist sects had the lowest gambling rate of all religious groups (33%) although atheists and those with no religious preference also exhibited a relative low rate (40%). There appears to be a great deal of overlap among certain demographic groups since the highest rate of gambling is found in the more liberal Northeast (80%), America's "Rust Belt," which has relatively more Catholics and Jews, greater affluence, higher education levels, and is more urbanized while the lowest rate is found in the more conservative rural South (40%), America's "Bible Belt," which has more Christian fundamentalists, higher poverty rates, lower education levels, and fewer urban centers.

Moran's **subcultural hypothesis** which attributes the gambling behavior of individuals to peer group influences was supported by different rates of gambling within different ethnic groups. The highest rates were found among Eastern Europeans (81%) and Italians (77%) while African Americans (54%) and "all others" (41%) had the lowest rates. Rates of gambling for Western European, British, Irish, and Spanish Americans fell between these extremes and were fairly uniform (61% to 65%). Although men gambled more than women overall, more women (62%) played bingo than men (52%); although whites tended to gamble more than non-whites, the latter were more active track and casino gamblers.

The **life cycle hypothesis** proposed by Li and Smith was also supported by a strong inverse correlation between age and gambling. Seventy-three percent of the 18-24 year-old category, 69 percent of those 25-44, and 60 percent of those 45-64 years old had participated in some form of gambling while the rate of participation dropped dramatically to 23 percent in the 65+ age group. Similarly, the proportions of those who had never gambled increased with age with the most dramatic increase appearing in the oldest age group (25%, 26%, 33%, and 65%, respectively). The researchers suggested that these age differences may be a function of the large-scale attitudinal shifts among groups of people who are born at different times and under different circumstances, a phenomenon which is generally referred to as the "cohort effect." Thus, the reluctance to gamble by the elderly may reflect the conservative values older Americans had internalized in their youth while the propensity to gamble by the young may reflect more liberal values which began to appear after World War II. Consequently, future generations may not exhibit such extreme differences in rates of gambling by older Americans that existed at the time of this survey.

Finally, in accordance with the findings of Tec and Li and Smith, the correlations that appeared between gambling and residence patterns also supported the **rural-urban residence hypothesis**. Throughout the United States, gambling was found to be less prevalent in smaller towns and rural areas where only 53 percent of the population had gambled the previous year, than in larger urban centers and suburban areas where respectively, 66 percent and 72 percent percent had gambled. Gambling also tends to become more common the closer one lives to a large city. However, participation rates for most forms of gambling (numbers games and horse books excepted) are higher among suburbanites who live from 25 to 50 miles from a large city than they are among those who live less than 25 miles away. As expected, participation drops off dramatically among those living more than 50 miles from a large city. It is important to note that these phenomena could result from the stronger peer influences (the **subcultural** or **religion hypotheses**) and/or the lack of gambling opportunities (the **availability hypothesis**) that are common to rural and small town America.

Volume Analyses

On the other hand, a number of different conclusions can be drawn from analyses of the amounts of money wagered by members of various demographic groups. Volume analyses provided strong support for the **rural-urban residence hypothesis**, some support for the **subcultural hypothesis**, but only weak or no support for the **education**, **life cycle**, and **religion hypotheses**. This occurred because frequencies of gambling within these groups did not generally accord with the amounts of money wagered by their members. For these analyses all gamblers were grouped into three categories according to how much money they had staked in the previous year: heavy (over $200), moderate ($51 to $200), and light bettors (less than $50). Heavy bettors consisted of proportionately more non-whites, males, high school dropouts, those in the 25 to 44 year-old age group, those who were divorced or separated, who earned over $15,000 *and* less than $5,000, who lived in the Northeastern United States, who lived within 25 miles of a large city, and more with Italian and African ethnic backgrounds. Those in the light betting category included proportionately more whites, women, Jews, married *and* single people, those with annual incomes between $10,000 and $15,000, college graduates, Mid-westerners, more of those living 50 or more miles from an urban center, and more of those with British and Irish ancestry. Proportionately the same, or nearly the same, frequencies of Catholics, Protestants, Eastern European, Spanish, and Other Americans were found in the highest volume category as in the lowest.

Veblen's **affluence hypothesis** was supported by analyses of absolute gambling expenditures by different income groups since annual wagers tended to be progressive, meaning that they rose with income. This pattern showed some variation with different types of gambling: upper income groups wagered the most for casino gambling and sporting events, middle income groups spent the most at on-track events, and lower income groups bet the most on numbers, lotteries, bingo, and off-track betting. Nevertheless, combined annual expenditures for all forms of gambling increased fairly steadily from $63.46 per person among the lowest wager earners (under $5,000) through $116.23 ($5,000 to $10,000), $133.99 ($10,000 to $15,000), $203.69 ($15,000 to $20,000), $167.00 ($20,000 to $30,000) to $435.35 a year for the highest income group (over $30,000).

However, neither Veblen's **affluence** nor Tec's **status frustration hypotheses** were supported by correlations between the average bet sizes and income levels. Not only were bet sizes inconsistently related to income but the average bet sizes of different income groups also varied with different forms of gambling. The correlation between income and bet size was linear and positive only among sports bettors. Analyses of most of the other forms of gambling revealed a "U-shaped" curve with larger bets being placed by the highest and lowest income groups and smaller bets by middle income groups. This was particularly true of off-track bettors, bookie bettors, and casino gamblers. However, middle income groups placed the largest bets at racetracks. The fact that the incidence of on-track betting was about the same among the lowest and highest income groups also suggests that the size of one's income is not a determinant of this kind of gambling. In some forms of gambling–particularly bingo, numbers games, and lotteries–average bet sizes tended to decrease with income. Finally, when all forms of gambling were considered, the percentages of annual income that were wagered tended to decline with increases in income (from .62% at the lowest income level to .18% at the highest). Exceptions occurred among sports book bettors whose percent of income bets rose with income level and casino gamblers, among whom this measure took on a "U-shaped" pattern with middle income groups betting the least.

The **affluence hypothesis** was clearly rejected since gambling expenditures relative to income were regressive. That is, lower income groups wagered a greater proportion of their income than higher income groups. As a group, Americans wagered just over one percent (1.1%) of their household income in 1974. However, although the absolute sizes of people's bets steadily rose with their income, the percentages of annual income bet tended to decrease as income rose. In fact, people who earned less than $5,000 bet nearly four times as much of their income (2.53%) as those earning between $20,00 and $30,000 (.67%). Furthermore, this pattern was fairly constant across all types of gambling. The only exceptions were sports book betting in which percentage of income wagered rose with income and casino gambling which followed a "U-shaped" distribution.

Finally, the **affluence hypothesis** was also rejected by loss-to-income ratios which were also regressive (declined with income) since the lowest wage earners lost about three and one-half to four and one-half times more of their income to gambling than did the highest paid segments of the sample. The "takeout" rate (or "house take") refers to the percentage that is retained by gambling operators. More simply, it is a measure of player losses which, relative to income, were most severe among the lower income groups and least severe among the higher income groups. Specifically, those earning less than $5,000 per year lost nearly one-quarter (24.5%) of all the money they bet or .62 percent of their household income. Those in the $5,000 to $10,000 income category lost a somewhat greater proportion of their wagers (27.3%) but only .42 percent of their household income. Gamblers earning between $10,000 and $15,000 a year also lost over one-quarter of the money they bet (26.9%) but only .29 percent of their total income. People in the $15,000 to $20,000 bracket lost less than one-fifth of their total wagers (19.3%) and .23 percent of their annual income while those who earned from $20,000 to $30,000 lost slightly more of the money they bet (20.9%) but only .14 percent of their household income. Finally, those earning more than $30,000 a year lost the smallest share of the money they bet (16.9%) but .18 percent of their income.

Attributions and Attitudes

An examination of the reasons that people gave to explain their own gambling can be interpreted as support for a number of different motivational theories. The options they were given included "Have a good time/enjoyment/recreation," for "Excitement," for the "Challenge," to "Make money," for a "Chance to get rich," to "Pass the time," for "Something to look forward to," "Out of habit," "Because I'm lucky," because they felt they have "a better chance to win than others," and "Some other reason not listed."

The high frequency of entertainment-related attributions tends to support Caillois' **play theory**. When they were asked to specify their main reasons for gambling, most (60%) of the respondents who engaged in legal forms of gambling reported they did so "to have a good time" or for entertainment. The largest number of entertainment-related responses were given by on-track bettors (86%), casino gamblers (78%), sports bettors (62%), and bingo players (62%). Far fewer, though not an inconsequential number, indicated that they gambled "to pass the time." This response, a variant of the "entertainment" motive, was most frequent among off-track bookie bettors (58%) and bingo players (37%) and least frequently given by lottery players (7%), illegal on-track bookie bettors, (5%) and numbers players (5%).

The many money-related responses of lottery players and participants in illegal forms of gambling support an **economic** explanation. Far fewer lottery enthusiasts gave "entertainment" as a response (15%) than indicated that they played in hopes of monetary gain (77%). The same situation occurred among participants in illegal forms of gambling: depending on the form of gambling in question, most expressed money-related reasons (73% to 85%). The fact that most illegal gamblers claimed to do so in hopes of making money also suggests the money motive.

The **sensation-seeking hypothesis** found support in the high frequency of those claiming to gamble for the "excitement" it provides while **alienation** or **decision-making theory** could claim support from the large numbers of those who claimed to gamble for the "challenge" it affords. Substantial proportions of legal on-track, casino, and sports bettors also included the need for the "excitement" (51%, 46%, and 46%, respectively) and "challenge" (40%, 41%, and 50%, respectively) that gambling provides among their principal reasons for gambling but relatively few bingo (20%; 27%) or lottery (23%; 33%) players included these reasons. Many participants of illegal forms of gambling also listed the "challenge" of sports betting (67%) and off-track betting with bookies (60%) among their primary reasons for gambling. All gamblers reported that on-track horse betting provides by far the greatest excitement of any form of gambling. This was followed by cards with friends, casino gambling, slot machines, bingo, sports betting with friends, lotteries, dog tracks, dice, horse betting with a bookie, sports cards, sports betting with a bookie, and numbers playing which is the least exciting, even for numbers players. The researchers therefore suggested that the excitement attributed to any particular form of gambling may derive more from the environment in which it occurs than from the activity itself.

The **sensation-seeking hypothesis** received further but weaker support from the relationships that emerged between the respondents' levels of gambling involvement and (1) their subjectively reported need for excitement, (2) the level of excitement they currently enjoyed, and (3) the degree to which they felt that their excitement needs were being fulfilled which suggests that heavier gamblers may experience a greater need for excitement. Different levels of gambling involvement were defined by different gambling practices. "Non-betting" was the first and lowest level of involvement; "legal betting," which referred only to those who bet with friends and participated in legal forms of commercial gambling, defined moderate involvement; the third and highest level of involvement included those who also participated in "illegal betting." Rated on a scale of 1 (no need) to 8 (high need), the self-reported "need for excitement" index was lowest among nongamblers (3.71), higher among legal gamblers (4.24), and highest among illegal gamblers (4.70). The indices measuring the feeling that they "have excitement" showed a similar progression from no involvement (3.78) through legal betting (4.68) to illegal betting (5.04%). As evidence that heavier gamblers have greater needs for excitement than others, their "fulfillment scores," which measured the degree to which they felt their needs for excitement were being met, progressively decreased from noninvolvement (.89) through moderate involvement (.44) to heavy involvement (.34). However, the relatively low average ratings for this and the other "excitement" indices suggest that sensation seeking may not be a strong motivation for gambling.

Different forms of gambling were also judged to be more "exciting" than others. According to the respondents' ratings, the most exciting form of gambling was on-track horse race betting. Next in order of excitement rating were cards with friends, casino, slot machines, bingo, sports betting with friends, lotteries, dog tracks, dice, horse betting with bookie, sports cards, sports betting bookie, and numbers playing as the least exciting form.

Tec's **aspiration theory** could also claim some support in the rates of "Something to look forward to" choices made by certain gamblers. More lottery players (40%) and sports bettors (31%) indicated that they gambled primarily for this reason than did those who preferred other forms of gambling (2% to 25%).

The **dysphoria reduction hypotheses** could not be tested since none of the response options included in the questionnaire pertained to the alleviation of emotional dysphoria. Moreover, none of the subjects indicated that they gambled "out of habit," because they felt "lucky" or thought they had "a better chance to win than others," or for "some other reason not listed."

Attitudinal data offered some support for the **subcultural** and **religion theories** but the **alienation** and **affluence hypotheses** are only weakly supported. The **subcultural hypothesis** found support in the fact that Northeasterners were most inclined to legalize different forms of gambling whereas Southerners exhibited the strongest antigambling sentiments. In terms of **religion**, Jews were more in favor of legalization than Catholics who favored the idea more than Protestants. Likewise, single and divorced people were more in favor of legalized gambling than those who were married but widowed people were the most strongly against it. **Alienation the-**

ory may have found some support in the strong correlation that appeared between illegal gambling involvement and lack of job satisfaction but no such association materialized when job satisfaction was correlated with legal gambling. Pro-gambling sentiments tended to increase with income but only for some forms of gambling such as slot machines and then only weakly. Other forms of gambling, such as legalized sports books, were less favored by middle income than either higher- or lower income groups. Overall, gambling was so popular among the respondents that the overwhelming majority (80%) favored the legalization of even more kinds and well over half (70%) indicated they would continue to bet even if it were criminalized.

Lack of interest and fear of loss appeared to be the major deterrents of gambling while negative social sanctions appeared to have little bearing on the gambling decisions of most Americans. Among gamblers the most frequently reported reasons for avoiding certain games, whether legal or illegal, were lack of knowledge or interest (77%) and fear of losing (70%); moral and legal concerns were among the least frequently mentioned (7% and 5%, respectively). Among nongamblers the most frequently expressed reasons for refraining from gambling were lack of interest (83%), monetary concerns (64%), moral concerns (48%), and legal concerns (25%). While they may be low in the sample as a whole, the numbers of responses indicating that gambling is deterred by moral (23%) or legal (12%) concerns demonstrates that the behavior of some people will always be guided by their religious and ethical internalizations.

Compulsive Gambling

Unlike the British study, the US survey also attempted to determine rates of compulsive or pathological gambling through a clinical analysis of the interview data. On this basis the researchers estimated that nationally, 1.1 million people, or about 0.77 percent of the adult population were designated as "probable" compulsive gamblers with men outnumbering women by a margin of more than two to one (1.1% to 0.5%). Another 2.33 percent were judged to be "potential" compulsive gamblers (2.7% men; 2% women). However, these rates were much higher in Nevada where 2.62 percent of its residents were classified as probable and another 2.35% as potential compulsive gamblers. Here, too, men outnumbered women in both the probable (3.3% male; 2% female) and potential (3.8% male; 1.1% female) categories. Nevada's higher ratio of probable to potential pathological gamblers suggested that "easy access to gambling facilities results in the actualization of those who are predisposed to compulsive gambling."[23] Since potential pathological gamblers appeared in equal proportions in Nevada and the United

States in general, they also offered the possibility that "those who are predisposed to compulsive gambling are drawn to Nevada by the availability of gambling facilities and once there act out their compulsion."[24]

Those classified as pathological gamblers wagered and lost substantially more money than others. In terms of betting volume, 15 percent of the national sample of probable and 11 percent of the potential pathological gamblers bet over 10 percent of their household income on legal forms of gambling in 1974 whereas only 1.4 percent percent of the general population bet that much. In Nevada, however, fully 93 percent of the probable and 35 percent of the potential pathological gamblers bet over 10 percent of their household income on legal forms of gambling. Although all groups bet much smaller proportions on illegal forms of gambling, the greatest amounts were bet by probable pathological gamblers. In terms of gambling losses, potential compulsive gamblers in the national sample lost twice as much as the general population while probables lost over three times as much: whereas nonpathological gamblers lost an average of $378 per year on legal and $275 on illegal forms of gambling, potential compulsives lost $1,374 on legal and $84 on illegal gambling; probables lost $1,798 and $553, respectively. Moreover, over twice as many potential (86.2%) and probable pathological gamblers (88.9%) as nonpathological gamblers (40.9%) reported that they had lost more than they won. The greatest losses by both pathological groups were sustained at horse tracks and casinos. Surprisingly, Nevada's potential pathological gamblers lost an average of $705 in 1974 which was less than the $1133 average loss among the entire Nevada sample. However, the state's probable pathological gamblers lost an average of $9,970 each, which is nearly nine (8.8) times that of its total sample. Like those in the national sample, nearly twice as many of Nevada's potential (78.3%) and probable (81.7%) pathological gamblers reported net losses for 1974 as did all Nevada respondents (47.6%).

The researchers' claimed that these data confirmed their **availability and exposure hypothesis**, as did self-reported data which demonstrated that probable and pathological gamblers had indeed experienced more childhood and current exposure to gambling than others. Since "easy access to gambling facilities is associated with a higher incidence of compulsive gambling,"[25] the researchers predicted that "widespread legalization of gambling will lead to a significant increase in the incidence of compulsive gambling."[26] Extrapolating from the Nevada data, the researchers estimated that if legalized gambling were to spread throughout the United States to the extent that it existed in Nevada, the number of probable pathological gamblers in the United States would also grow to 2.6%, or from 1.1 million to 3.8 million. The researchers nevertheless warned that the small size of the Nevada sample make these conclusions extremely tenuous.[27]

Self-reports by pathological gamblers provided no support for the **sensa-tion-seeking hypothesis**. Both probable and potential pathological gam-blers reported not only that they needed less excitement than did others, but also that they were already experiencing more excitement in their lives than they wanted. Not surprisingly, probable pathological gamblers expressed a greater need for luck than all others.

Contrary to the opinions of many social and psychological "continuum" or "dimensional" theorists who regard problem gambling merely as an extension of normal gambling, the survey found that *rates of non-compulsive gambling in various demographic groups do not necessarily predict rates of compulsive gambling in those groups.* Indeed, most (79%) compulsive gamblers lived with-in 25 miles of a city, most (74%) were white, and, as noted above, more males than females were found to be pathological gamblers. However, very few (1%) of the pathological gamblers were Jewish while the majority (67%) were Protestants. Most were between 45 and 64 years of age (67%), employed (64%), had some college (57%), earned between $10,000 to $20,000 a year (67%), and lived in the western part of the United States (59%).

SUMMARY

In conclusion, the study as a whole failed to find any strong support for the hypothesis that gambling is a **deviant** activity or an **economic** pursuit of either the more deprived or the more affluent segments of society. On the whole, rates of gambling tended to increase with income, volumes of gam-bling varied with different kinds of gambling thus showing no consistent pat-tern, and the relative volumes of loss decreased with income. Much stronger support was found for the idea that gambling is a form of recreation for peo-ple from all social classes, especially since the stakes of most gamblers are low. Because the incidence of gambling was found to be more closely relat-ed to ethnicity (nationality) and religious affiliation, the survey also support-ed the **subcultural hypothesis**. Since rates of gambling and compulsive gambling were highest among Nevada residents, the study also suggested that significant increases in the incidence of these phenomena would very likely result from the expansion of legalized gambling in other parts of the country as well. Unfortunately, since this survey asked only if the respon-dents had gambled at all in the last year, it failed to obtain any information on how often they may have gambled over that period. However, it did obtain estimates of the amounts of money wagered annually.

CRITIQUE OF THE UNITED KINGDOM AND UNITED STATES SURVEYS

Perhaps the greatest contribution of the early large-scale United Kingdom[28] and United States surveys,[29] a methodological one, is that they highlighted the need to distinguish *frequency* data from *volume* data. They clearly demonstrated that measures of gambling frequency are not at all equivalent to measures of gambling volume even though both variables have been used to estimate, describe, and compare the "extent" of gambling in different populations and demographic groups. One major difference is, of course, definitional: the term "incidence," as employed by the authors of these studies, refers to the number of people within a population or subgroup who have gambled at all within a given time period while "frequency" generally refers to their average number of gambling sessions per week, month, year, etc., throughout that period irrespective of the amounts of money wagered; "volume" has been used in reference to the average size of individual bets as well as to the overall amounts of money staked and lost per session, week, month, year, etc., irrespective of frequency. However, the most important difference is that *the findings and conclusions about the "extent" of gambling that are based on volume analyses are often entirely different from those that are based incidence and frequency analyses.*

Other strengths of the United States and United Kingdom surveys are that both drew upon very large samples, both obtained data on gender differences, both asked their respondents questions specific to their gambling preferences and habits, and both provided highly reliable descriptive statistics. Both studies provided strong evidence in favor of the **gender hypothesis** which predicts that rates of both normative and pathological gambling will be higher among males than females. Furthermore, like Li and Smith, the authors of both studies concluded that gambling does not serve a single primary "function" but is motivated by a number of factors. Another strength of the United States survey was that it related the incidence of gambling to its respondents' religious and ethnic self-identification thereby providing a test of the **subcultural hypothesis**, an area that was ignored by the British study. The United Kingdom study also failed to investigate rates of compulsive gambling.

One of the principal contributions of the United States survey was its introduction of the **availability and exposure hypothesis** and the evidence it presented to support it. Additional and far more compelling evidence for this hypothesis has been provided by more recent studies in the United States, New Zealand, Canada, and the United Kingdom which clearly demonstrate that rates of gambling, gambling expenditures, and lifetime rates of problem and/or pathological gambling are directly related to the availability of gambling opportunities. "Lifetime rates" refer to the percentages of respondents who have ever met the diagnostic criteria for these conditions at any time in their lives. This is often contrasted with "current rates" which refer to the percentages of those who have met these criteria in the recent past, usually within the previous six or 12 months. Because many gamblers move into and out of problem and pathological gambling at different points in their gambling careers, sometimes permanently and sometimes temporarily, current rates are believed to provide more accurate population estimates.

- One study compared the numbers of people contacting South Dakota's gambling treatment centers before, during, and after the legalization of "video lottery" or electronic machine gaming.[30] Its authors reported a significant decrease in the number of inquiries and clients at these centers when the gaming machines were not available.

- A second compared the number of telephone calls to New Zealand's national gambling hotline for periods of six months before and six months after the opening of its second casino in Auckland.[31] During the six-month period prior to the casino opening, the hotline was contacted by 510 first-time callers; during the six months following its opening the number of calls had increased by 62 percent to 826. Moreover, the hotline callers identified specific types of gambling as the cause of their problems: the number of those who named casinos increased from 7 percent in the first period to 34 percent in the second.

- A third was a follow-up prevalence survey of problem gambling in Quebec.[32] At the time of the first study in 1989 in which 1002 adults were sampled, the province had no legal video lottery terminals (VLTs) and no casinos; by 1996, when, 1257 adults were sampled for the replication study, 14,644 VLTs and three casinos were operating. The researchers predicted that these increases in the availability of gambling opportunities would result in more people gambling, larger maximum daily losses, and a higher rate of pathological gambling. Their predictions were realized when the data revealed that significantly more people (63%) had gambled in the year prior to the 1996 survey than had done so in the year prior to the 1989 survey (54%), that the most money lost to gambling in a single day had increased dramatically from an average of $103 to $360, and that the lifetime rate of pathological gambling had risen 75 percent (from 1.2% to 2.1%) representing an average incidence increase of 5,421 new pathological gamblers each year.

• A fourth study evaluated the effects of the opening of a new casino in Hull, Canada.[33] The responses of 457 adults living in or near Hull were compared to those of a control group of 423 living in the Quebec City area. Both groups were surveyed twice: once in 1996 before the casino had opened and again one year later. In contrast to those living in Quebec, the residents of Hull reported significant increases in their casino and machine gambling activities, in the total amount of money spent on casino gaming in the past year, in the maximum amounts of money lost on gambling in one day, and in the number of people they knew who had developed gambling problems over the 12-month study period. At the time of the second survey, three times more Hull residents had gambled at the new casino than had Quebec residents gambled at any casino in the province (65.2% versus 21.9%) and Hull residents had spent more than twice as much money on casino gambling in the previous 12 months as had those living in Quebec (an average of $251.44 versus $113.45). In terms of problem gambling, the lifetime prevalence rate of life at-risk gamblers in the Hull area more than doubled over the 12-month study period (3.3% at pretest, 7.8% at posttest) while that of the Quebec area increase only slightly (3.4% at pretest, 4.4% at posttest).

• Similar studies were conducted before and after the opening of a casino in Niagara Falls, Ontario.[34] Although slight increases occurred in province-wide rates of casino gambling (12% before, 25% after) and associated average monthly expenditures ($6.00 before, $14.45 after), they showed proportionally greater increases in the Niagara Falls area (participation 11% before, 43% after; expenditures $2.26 before, $11.12 after). Likewise, rates of problem gambling remained the same or declined elsewhere in Ontario but showed significant increases in Niagara Falls (0.7% before, 2.3% after). The city's residents also reported substantially higher rates of gambling problems among friends and family members than did those living elsewhere in the province.

• A sixth study examined average weekly gambling expenditures in 7,000 households in the United Kingdom both before and after the introduction of the National Lottery in November of 1994.[35] The researchers found not only that average gambling expenditures more than doubled from £1.45 to £3.81 per week after the lottery was introduced, but also that the proportion of households that spent more than £20 per week on gambling tripled from .8 to 2.5 percent. Levels of excessive gambling also rose dramatically, especially among lower income families: the proportion of households that spent more than ten percent of their total income on gambling increased more than fourfold from 0.4 to 1.7 percent; of those earning less than £200 per week this proportion rose more than fivefold from .6 to 3.2 percent. A geographical analysis also revealed a positive correlation between gambling expenditures in each region sampled and its rates of excessive gambling.

• A seventh study was designed to assess the effect of the introduction of video-poker on rates of pathological gambling in Louisiana.[36] To do so the researchers compared the numbers of Gamblers Anonymous groups in each parish both before and after these machines were legalized in 1992. They found both the absolute number of GA groups as well as the number of these groups per capita to be significantly associated with per capita spending on video-poker in each parish. They also found that the number of GA groups per capita were slightly but positively associated with the number of video-poker establishments per capita in each parish.

• An eighth study, a recent United States national gambling survey which sampled a total of 2,947 adults, reported similar results when it compared the responses of those living within 50 miles of a casino to those living from 50 to 250 miles from a casino.[37] The research team found average per capita casino spending to be nearly three and one-half times higher ($178 versus $52), rates of past year casino gambling to be about twice as great (40% versus 23%), and rates of both problem (2.3% versus 1.2%) and pathological gambling (2.1 versus 0.9%) to be about twice high in communities near a casino than in those more distantly located.

• A ninth study of 1,631 respondents living in seven United States communities near which casinos had recently opened estimated rates of pathological gambling to be over three times greater in them (16%) than elsewhere in the United States (less than 5%).[38]

• In contrast with the most recent United States problem gambling prevalence survey that found only 2.7 percent of the national population to be problem or pathological gamblers,[39] data collected between 1984 and 1998 in Clark County, Nevada, where Las Vegas is located, revealed that 6.6 percent of the county's residents are problem or pathological gamblers.[40]

• Finally, researchers investigating the economic impacts of Native American casinos in Wisconsin[41] reported that nearly four-fifths (79.8%) of the casino patrons they interviewed were residents of that state, 15 percent were from neighboring states, and 5.2 percent were from other states. Of those who lived in Wisconsin, 46.6 percent lived within 35 miles of a casino, 35.8 percent lived between 35 and 100 miles from a casino, and 17.6 percent lived more than 100 miles from a casino. Interestingly, some of the findings of this study were also relevant to other theories: the fact that over half (50.7%) of all casino patrons were over 60 years of age contradicts the **life cycle hypothesis**; the fact that nearly two-thirds (62.6%) were women contradicts the **gender hypothesis**; the fact that two-thirds (66.3%) were married contradicts the **marital status hypothesis**; the fact that the average household income was between twenty and thirty thousand dollars contradicts both Veblen's **affluence** and Tec's **status frustration hypotheses**.

Perhaps the greatest failing of the first United States national survey was that it ignored the question of the frequency with which people gamble, a problem that was stressed in discussing the Li and Smith study. Another serious shortcoming was that its authors also attempted to estimate rates of compulsive gambling at a time when there was little formal knowledge of the disorder, no standard definition for it, and no diagnostic criteria had as yet been developed.[42] Consequently, its estimated rates of pathological gambling were based on attitudinal data which were entirely unrelated to the subjects' actual gambling behaviors[43] and on personality traits which are also evident in many nonpathological and nongamblers.[44] According to one critic, nearly half (44%) of the "at-risk" group identified as potential compulsive gamblers "showed no signs of heavy gambling or any other problems."[45] The study was further criticized on the grounds that the criteria used to define heavy gambling–amount and illegality (spending $50 or more a year on illegal gambling)–are also unrelated to excessive or pathological gambling.[46]

The United Kingdom survey had equally severe shortcomings. Part I of the report focused on the frequency of gambling as determined by average numbers of "sessions" but neglected the intensity of gambling as determined by volume or monetary expenditures and losses. Even the authors themselves recognized this as a serious defect.[47] They also treated the variables of "social class" and "income level" as entirely separate, mutually exclusive phenomena. Whereas income levels were objectively determined by precise sets of numerical parameters, class affiliation was not. Instead, social status was defined entirely by occupation irrespective of income. This produces a paradoxical situation in which some of the "poorest" respondents were accorded upper middle class status while some of the "most affluent" were relegated to the lower working class group[48] solely on the basis of their job titles. It therefore seems more reasonable to suggest that any respondent's present level of income would constitute a far more reliable and valid determinant of social status than his or her occupation, though this may perhaps be more an American than a European attitude. Nevertheless, the authors completely ignored this crucial variable during their own tests of the various hypotheses they chose to investigate. Furthermore, the criteria for determining the incidence of gambling (once a week or twice month for one or more kinds of gambling, etc.) were highly subjective and not necessarily indicative of gambling intensity since they ignore actual gambling expenditures and losses: one bet a week could mean a wager and potential loss of anywhere from a few shillings to hundreds or even thousands of pounds.

Another fault of the United Kingdom survey is that while its authors amassed an incredibly large amount of descriptive data, the methods by which they tested the hypotheses they selected were incredibly weak. In the first place, all forms of gambling were lumped together during these tests so that all were equally weighted: a single gambling "session" could mean the purchase one raffle ticket, a few hours of church bingo, a day at the races, or an entire "lost weekend" in a casino. In the second place, each major hypothesis was tested on the basis of responses to only one or two questions, many of which were attitudinal, subjective, indirect, or otherwise highly questionable indicators of a particular variable. For example, the notion that the strength of the respondents' subjectively reported "belief in luck" should necessarily determine their rates of gambling would clearly not pertain to horse, dog, and poker players who believe that the ability to win is more a matter of skill than of luck. Likewise, the assumption that subjective assessments of "job interest" or "job autonomy" will necessarily provide an adequate test of **alienation** or **decision-making theories** is also doubtful. The authors themselves warned that their findings should be interpreted with extreme caution since the tests they employed were "rudimentary or incomplete, or both."[49]

Consequently, perhaps the only valid conclusion that can be drawn from these studies is that different statistical manipulations can yield entirely different results. This is particularly true of the United Kingdom survey which demonstrated that entirely different gambling practices are associated with different forms of gambling and that entirely different correlations–hence, conclusions–can be drawn from them. Likewise, these studies also demonstrated that conclusions based on the analysis of demographic variables can be entirely different from those based on attitudinal variables and that conclusions based on frequency data can be entirely different from those based on volume data. Thus, just as nearly all existing theories were supported by some correlations, they were also nearly all rejected by others. Nevertheless, our knowledge of this situation in itself should have considerable value in setting the course of future quantitative research since it highlights the need for analytical consistency but methodological diversity. That is, we must decide which factors and which correlations are most appropriate for testing which hypotheses. Additionally, since so many different correlations can produce so many different conclusions, no theory should be accepted or rejected purely on the basis of quantitative data alone: qualitative evidence should also be considered. Finally, as was also one of the primary lessons to be learned from Tec's study of sports pool betting, no theory purporting to explain "gambling" in general should be based on a study of only one form of gambling.

Chapter 8

GAMBLING AND THE GENERAL PUBLIC

The previous chapters dealt primarily with quantitative studies which were designed and undertaken principally to test the emerging socio-logical hypotheses concerning the gambling preferences of certain segments of society. Many of the behavioral and attitudinal surveys that followed were conducted less for the purposes of hypotheses testing and more for purposes of market research or the establishment of public policy guidelines by local governments. That is, since legalized gambling grew so dramatically throughout the 1980s, many studies were undertaken to ascertain not only how many people gambled and how many abstained, but also to discover which kinds of gambling were most appealing to which segments of the population and what social and economic ramifications the expansion of legalized gambling might be having. Nevertheless, not all later studies avoided theoretical issues entirely and, irrespective of their original aim, their findings often turned out to be pertinent to a number of theoretical questions. A number of correlational studies also attempted to discover which demographic and other social or psychological factors are most often associated with normative and problem gambling behavior. These studies were undertaken primarily to enable researchers to predict which categories of people would be most likely to avoid gambling, which would not, and for which gambling would be most likely to become problematic at some point.

THE GAMING INDUSTRY'S GALLUP POLL

A second Gallup Organization telephone survey of 1,564 United States adults (18 years and older) predicted the imminent expansion of legalized gambling throughout the United States.[1] This study, which took place a decade after the first Gallup survey,[2] was sponsored by representatives of the gaming industry who also performed the data analysis. As a market research study its purpose was to assess public sentiments concerning the legalization of various forms of commercial gambling in the United States. Consequently, neither the attitudes toward, nor the extent of, illegal and noncommercial social gambling were investigated.

In comparison with the earlier national survey conducted by the University of Michigan,[3] this study demonstrated that by the early 1980s the public's approval and acceptance of legalized gambling was definitely on the rise. It reported that 82 percent of the respondents favored the legalization of at least one form of gambling in their state to raise revenues. Many (68%) felt that any form of state-sponsored gambling would be preferable to tax increases. Nearly three-quarters (74%) of the respondents now favored the legalization of bingo as opposed to just over two-thirds (68%) of those in the earlier Michigan sample. Slightly fewer (72% vs. 61%) preferred some sort of lottery while roughly half wanted to legalize professional sports betting (48% vs. 31%), casino gambling (51% vs. 40%), and off-track betting (54%; no comparative statistics). The authors considered these results to be "remarkable" considering the antigambling legislation of the day.

Those who favored the expansion of legalized gambling were predominantly middle class Americans who typically bear the brunt of all tax increases. More specifically, over half (52%) had annual incomes of $15,000 or greater and over one-quarter (28.9%) had incomes in excess of $25,000. They were predominantly male and tended to live in the Eastern and Western parts of the country rather than in the South and Midwest. They also tended to be younger (under 30), to be the least well-educated (non-high school graduates), and to be in the middle income range ($15,000 to $24,999 per year). Of course, this overall demographic profile varied with different gambling preferences. Typically, for example, those most in favor of casino gambling were males between 30 and 49 years of age who lived in the East and had annual incomes over $25,000; those most against casino gambling were females 50 years of age and older who lived in the South and had annual incomes below $15,000. In terms of political affiliation 25.8 percent of those who approved of gambling were Republicans, 38.2 percent were Democrats, and 32 percent were Independents. Thus, states having the most liberal constituency would be most likely to legalize gambling.

These results were interpreted as refuting a number of commonly accepted "myths" about socioeconomic status and gambling. The first was that gambling is especially attractive to the poor and therefore tends to victimize those who can least afford it. The authors pointed out instead that those with the lowest incomes were, in fact, those who most strongly opposed the expansion of gambling. The second myth they dispelled was Veblen's supposition that preferences for gambling are the exclusive province of the very

wealthy. Their attitudinal data therefore refuted the contentions of all previous researchers who maintained that rates of gambling are correlated in any
way with income and/or educational levels. The third and most important
myth they claimed to have denounced was that gambling is a deviant pastime pursued by only a minority of the population. Instead, their results
showed gambling to be "a pervasive leisure activity in American life."[4]

However, the authors also found the popular image of gambling as an
instrument of organized crime to be well entrenched. Nearly three-fourths
(71.3%) of their sample either "strongly agreed" or "agreed somewhat" that
legalized gambling would also draw organized crime into their states. As
might be expected, many respondents "strongly agreed" that lotteries
(36.9%) and casino gambling (27.8%) would attract a criminal element.
Surprisingly, although bingo had the highest approval rating of all forms of
gambling, it also had the highest number of respondents (37.7%) who
"strongly agreed" that it was associated with organized crime. Paradoxically,
however, well over half (58.2%) of the respondents felt that legalized gambling would give the individual "a more honest chance" of winning.

The authors drew a number of conclusions from their study. On the basis
of comparative data from the earlier Michigan study, they agreed with the
availability hypothesis that rates of gambling increase with the availability
of gambling opportunities. However, they suggested that further research
would be required before any causal link between the availability of gambling and rates of compulsive gambling could be conclusively established.
Although they insisted that this presumed relationship had not yet been
demonstrated by reliable statistics, they felt that this was an important issue
which the gambling industry itself should address in a responsible way. They
then estimated that if legalized gambling were to expand–and they were sure
that it would–then participation rates would double and perhaps even
quadruple thereby generating gambling revenues of at least double the current $25 billion annual take. They therefore encouraged the gambling indus-
try to undertake positive image-building programs and lobby efforts to
encourage the voting public and state legislatures to repeal their bans on
commercial gambling.

The authors' most obvious interpretive error lay in their tacit assumption
that approval of gambling equates with actual gambling. Just because a certain number of survey respondents may approve of state-sponsored lottery
or bingo in order to minimize their tax burden, this does not necessarily
imply that they would all participate in that form of gambling if it were available. This was clearly demonstrated by the information they obtained on
actual gambling rates. While over four-fifths (82%) of their sample voiced
approval of gambling, less than half this number (40.2%) had actually made
a wager in the previous 12 months. Moreover, less than half (43%) of the

nongamblers indicated that they would probably participate in a state lottery if one were available. This means, of course, that more than half (57%) did not intend to participate. Likewise, one-eighth (12.5%) of the sample had visited casinos (which were then available only in Nevada and New Jersey) in the previous year. While nearly two-fifths (35.9%) claimed they would do so if a casino were readily available, over three-fifths (60.1%) said they would continue to avoid casino gaming. The authors insisted that these findings "in no way vindicate the presumption that the nation is about to come down with a terminal case of gambling fever."[5] Nevertheless, recent prevalence statistics and the explosion of state sponsored lotteries, charitable gambling, Native American casinos or tribal gaming, and other forms of legalized gambling that swept the United States within a few years of their study clearly demonstrate that their predictions concerning the rapid impending growth of the commercial gaming industry were entirely correct.

GAMBLING IN AUSTRALIA

Attitudes and Behavior

In the mid-1980s, a survey of gambling in Australia reported that over three-quarters (76%) of its sample of 1,945 adults 18 years of age and older felt that gambling in moderation was acceptable. Its author, Gordon MacMillan also reported that only 19 percent of the respondents had not gambled on anything in the previous three months. This meant, of course, that over four-fifths (81%) of them had placed some kind of bet within this period. At the time of the survey the kinds of gambling available in order of frequency of participation were the national lottery or Lotto, raffles, state lotteries, instant lotteries, TABs (off-track betting offices), slot machines, art unions, pools, bingo, horse racing, harness racing, casinos, dog racing, and SP betting. Over one-quarter (27%) of the respondents had participated in one form of gambling and the same proportion had participated in two forms. These generally turned out to be national and state sponsored lotteries and raffles "which are available anywhere" and which are "virtually a way of life in Australia," and off-track betting which is available "on what seems like most street corners."[7] A contingent of "hard core" gamblers, largely younger blue collar workers, making up about 5 percent of the sample had wagered on five or more types of gambling including some of the less accessible forms in the previous three months. When asked what forms of gambling they were likely to engage in over the next 12 months, the largest proportion (38%) indicated Lotto followed by state lotteries (16%), instant lotteries (8%), and off-track betting (8%). Although no gender differences emerged, younger people in the 18 to 29 year old age group, those earning between $10,000 and $20,000 annually, and those with a high school education or more expressed greater optimism concerning their ability to win than did other respondents. Over half of those polled approved of the legalization of casinos and slot machines and in most states the approval rating of these forms of gambling has steadily increased over the past several years.

One of the more interesting findings of this study was that more respondents (81%) had placed a bet in the last three months than had indicated their approval of even moderate gambling (76%). This means that even some of those who disapproved of gambling had themselves recently gambled, a fact which suggests that some forms of wagering are not perceived as true "gambling." Unfortunately, although a great deal of information was collected, no comparative numerical data on the extent of gambling among the different age, gender, socioeconomic, or other demographic groups were provided. Consequently, it is impossible to determine whether this study supports of contradicts any of the various gambling theories that have been proposed. However, since MacMillan concluded that "those [gambling activities] that are most accessible are the most popular," it appears to be his view that, more than any other possible variable, **availability** is the strongest determinant of gambling behavior.

Gambling and Religious Affiliation

In the mid-1980s, Wolfgang Grichting[9] surveyed 318 residents (55.7% female; 44.3% male) of the community of Townsville in North Queensland to test several popular assumptions about gambling. Among the things he hoped to determine were whether Australia was indeed a nation of gamblers, whether gambling was indeed more prevalent among the lower classes, and whether Devereux's **religion hypothesis** had any validity. All subjects were asked how frequently and how much money they had wagered in the last year on different forms of gambling including bingo, horse racing, dog racing, toad racing, lotto, cards, casino games, amusement machines, and sports pools. They were then asked about the frequency of their gambling and average amounts of money spent per session. In addition to other standard demographic questions, they were also asked to rate their own religiosity or the degree to which they felt they were committed to their religious beliefs. The community's population was conveniently divided into four predominant religious groups of nearly equal proportions: 26.1 percent Anglican, 26 percent Roman Catholic, 23.8 percent Protestant, and 24.1 percent None/other.

After analyzing his data Grichting concluded that "Australians indeed are a nation of gamblers."[10] His data revealed that 291 (67.9%) of all respondents had gambled, that they had placed an average of 79 bets, and that they had each spent an average of $408 on gambling in the last year. When he distinguished the responses of native born Australians from those who were born in other countries, he found that fully 92 percent of the former had gambled in the last year. This percentage was higher by half than the 61 percent figure reported a decade earlier for the United States.[11] Grichting also found that, on average, those born in Australia not only gambled more frequently than the immigrants (82 vs. 60 times per year) but that they also spent nearly twice as much money on gambling ($436 vs. $225 per capita per year).

He was unable to verify the popular belief that gambling is a pursuit of the lower classes since his data revealed that income is not related to gambling either in terms of frequency or of how much money is spent. Instead, like a number of earlier studies, he found that "The poor and rich gamble similar amounts but the poor spend a larger proportion of their income on gambling."[12] He did find, however, that years of formal education were inversely related to gambling. Unfortunately, apart from several correlation coefficients, Grichting failed to provide any statistical data which would better describe these findings.

Grichting found that the most important factor to influence rates of gambling was religion. It will be recalled that nearly 40 years earlier, Devereux had speculated that gambling would be less common among Protestants who regard it as incompatible with Christian moral precepts and more common among Catholics who condone the practice. Grichting therefore predicted that his own data would show rates of gambling to be highest among Catholics, lower among those with no religious affiliation, and lowest among Protestants. He also predicted that this pattern would be further reflected in his respondents' subjective perceptions of their own religiosity. This meant that the most devout Protestants should gamble the least while the most devout Catholics should gamble the most.

In terms of religion, the gambling population was 22.3 percent Anglican, 28.4 percent Protestant, 24.8 percent Catholic and 24.5 percent none/other. Since their gambling scores were nearly identical, Protestants and Anglicans (who are themselves Protestants) were combined for data analysis. The respondents' religiosity was determined when they were asked to rate themselves according to four degrees of religious commitment: 7.6 percent claimed to be "very religious," 35.3 percent were "quite religious," 34.9 percent were "not very religious," and 22.2 percent were "not religious at all." These categories were then lumped into two larger categories: 42.9 percent were "religious" (the "very" and "quite" religious groups) and 57.1 percent were "nonreligious ("not very/not at all").

Analysis of the data confirmed all Grichting's predictions since, overall, Catholics were the heaviest, the Nonreligious lighter, and Protestants were the lightest gamblers. Furthermore, neither gender nor socioeconomic status had any significant impact on this general pattern. Specifically, 75 percent of Catholics bet on the Melbourne Cup while 62 percent of the Nonreligious and 55% of the Protestants did so; likewise, 25 percent of Catholics engaged in on-track horse race betting while 17 percent of the Nonreligious and 13 percent of the Protestants did so. In terms of intensity, the Catholics also gambled most often and the Protestants least often: the Catholics had each gambled an average of 92 times the previous year, the Nonreligious 81 times, and the Protestants 63 times. Moreover, Catholics who rated themselves as "religious" tended to gamble more often than those who rated themselves as "nonreligious." Conversely, Protestants who considered themselves to be "religious" gambled less frequently than those claimed to be less so. Finally, in terms of annual per capita expenditures, Catholics spent the most money on gambling ($581), the Nonreligious spent an intermediate amount ($448), and Protestants spent the least ($309).

Because he found gambling to be associated far more closely with religion and education than with wealth or gender, Grichting felt it was not a function of any particular demographic status but of a learned "mental attitude."[13] Nevertheless, he did not feel that gambling was not intrinsic to Australians but that it is learned and inculcated by exposure to the social and cultural environment in which they grow up:

> Rather than suggesting that gambling is part of the Australian psyche I believe that it is a consequence of the extremely liberal legislation about gambling in this country. This reflects the prevailing culture which is more readily internalized by the native Australians than by immigrants. In this country there is practically no forbidden gaming provided a license has been obtained. Licensing of course permits the government to tax the activity which may well explain the high incidence of gambling in this nation. . . .[14]

In essence, Grichting, like MacMillan, also appears to have been an advocate of the **availability hypothesis** but unlike MacMillan he added cultural and macroeconomic elements to explain the Australian's penchant for gambling. However, since he found religion to exert such a strong influence over gambling, he concluded that this "forgotten dimension"[15] should be accorded far more attention in our attempts to understand not only gambling but other forms of individual and social behavior, as well.

A THIRD GALLUP POLL

By the late 1980s it was obvious that gambling opportunities and activities were flourishing in the United States. To assess the degree to which the general public was reacting to the expansion of legalized gambling, the Gallup Organization undertook another national survey of 1,208 American adults 18 years of age and older.[16] Of specific interest were their gambling preferences, the volume of their gambling, and their attitudes toward gambling and its social consequences.

General Gambling

The survey reported that in 1989 gambling was a popular and inexpensive activity in the United States. Specifically, it found that nearly three-quarters (71%) of those sampled had gambled that year and that nearly one-third (31%) were regular weekly gamblers. Although 29 percent had not wagered in the previous year, only 10 percent claimed that they had never gambled. Most lifetime abstainers indicated that they avoided it on moral or religious grounds. In comparison with gamblers, abstainers were more likely to be older, more religious, less affluent, to avoid alcoholic beverages, and to live in the South. Most of those who did gamble claimed that it had little effect on their financial situation since most claimed to spend less than $20 at any one time. When asked about the results of their gambling, 24 percent claimed to be ahead, 58 percent behind, 15 percent "even," and 3 percent were unsure. About three-fifths (61%) of all gamblers estimated that a tally of their overall wins and losses throughout the previous year would amount to less than $50. The study therefore concluded that "America is a nation of gamblers who mostly wager small amounts of money on a wide range of games."[17]

The survey also revealed some distinct regional differences in gambling behavior. As already noted, nongamblers were most likely to live in the South than any other region of the country. In fact, the South had twice as many nongamblers (44%) as the North (22%). However, Southerners who did gamble were just as likely to engage in card games, racetrack betting, and sports betting as Northerners. Westerners, 40 percent of whom were regular casino participants, were the heaviest gamblers. They not only gambled more frequently than people from elsewhere, but they also made larger bets.

The general antigambling sentiment that pervades the southern United States was also revealed in an independent examination of regional spending patterns which reported a marked disparity between the amount of money spent on gambling in different parts of the United States.[18] The highest per capita gambling expenditure or handle was found in the Western Mountain region ($6,046) which included Nevada, the state with the nations highest gambling expenditures ($58,670 per capita). Far lower per capita spending rates were reported for the Mid-Atlantic region ($907), New

England ($318), the Midwest ($198), the Pacific states ($184), and the South Atlantic region ($160). The lowest rates were in the South ($94) which included Georgia and North Carolina, the states with the nation's lowest per gambling expenditures ($5).

Gender differences were also quite apparent. Men were far heavier gamblers than women and each sex had its own gambling preferences. Roughly three-fifths (58%) of all men claimed to gamble at least once a month as opposed to two-fifths (41%) of all women. Four-fifths of all gamblers who had ever lost more than $100 on one occasion were men. Men tended to prefer games of skill while women favored games of chance. The most popular gambling activities of males were card games, racetrack betting, and sports betting; most women preferred lotteries, bingo, and other games of luck.

Specific Gambling Activities

Bingo. Bingo, which attracted only 13 percent of all gamblers, was far less popular than other gambling activities. Only 3 percent of all gamblers played bingo on a weekly basis. Most bingo players were female, from the lower socioeconomic classes, Catholic, and lived in the eastern half of the United States. Although occasional players were just as likely to be young adults as senior citizens, weekly players tended to be older. In general, bingo players are likely to participate in other forms of gambling such as card games, racetrack, and betting. They are also just as likely as other gamblers to be heavy bettors and have gambling problems.

Lotteries. Lotteries represented the fastest growing and most popular gambling industry in 1989. Although only 14 states and the District of Columbia had lotteries in the early 1980s, by the time of the study they were being operated in an additional 15 states and three more were in the process of establishing them. Over half (54%) of all the nation's adults had purchased lottery tickets in the 12 months prior to the survey as opposed to only 18 percent who had done so in 1982. Fully two-thirds (66%) of the residents of states that sponsor lotteries were occasional players while nearly one-third (31%) played weekly. As a result of their popularity, lotteries took in more money ($8.4 billion) than any other form of gambling.

On the whole, lottery players did not appear to be heavy gamblers. Each player spent an average of only $5 per week on lottery tickets, which is about the same amount that they spent at racetracks but far less than they spent at casinos. Unlike bingo players, most lottery players limited their gambling to this activity only and most never risked more than $10 in one day. Although more men than women played lotteries, the gender difference was much smaller for this than it was in other forms of gambling. Catholics and those with no religious affiliation participated to a slightly greater extent than Protestants. Southerners were the least avid players, probably because only two southern states (Florida and Kentucky), sponsored lotteries. Lotteries tended to be regarded in a highly favorable light throughout the South since nearly three-quarters (72%) of all southerners surveyed wanted them in their own states. This percentage was nearly the same as that of other Americans who favored them (78%) In opposition to those who claimed that lotteries appeal largely to the lower classes, this study found that the heaviest lottery players were those who earned more than $50,000 per year. However, since lotteries were more popular among high school than college graduates, participation in the activity was inversely related to education.

Games of skill. Sports betting, and card playing, and parimutuel (horse, dog, and jai alai) betting, were included under a single category since they are all games of skill. Moreover, those who enjoyed these games also tended to be weekly players and to risk larger amounts of money than those who preferred games of chance. Two-fifths (40%) of all respondents engaged in at least one of these activities in the previous year and most engaged in more than one. The average participant fit the same demographic profile as the heavy gambler: both were affluent young Catholic males who also drank and smoked. The most commonly expressed motivations for gambling among this group were the enjoyment of risk and the excitement it generates. Although they were less strongly motivated by monetary incentives than those who played lotteries and other games of chance, they won more money overall than other gamblers. One-third (33%) estimated that they had come out ahead over the previous 12 months and 5 percent claimed to be ahead by at least $1,000. Nevertheless, there were still more losers (47%) than winners and the 4 percent who were the heaviest losers ($1,000 or more) lost far more than any lottery player (none of whom lost $1,000 or more).

Sports betting, which was legal only in Nevada, was the most popular game of skill. Whereas 24 percent of all Americans wagered on amateur and professional athletic contests in 1989, 23 percent played cards for money and 17 percent placed parimutuel bets. Altogether, an estimated $20 billion was wagered on professional sports, nearly 10 percent of which was through bookies. The most popular game for sports bettors was American football. Nearly one-tenth (9%) of all adult males placed weekly football bets and nearly twice as many bet on football's Superbowl (14%) as on baseball's World Series (8%). Only lotteries attracted more bettors than professional football.

Casino gaming. The revenues generated by American casinos ($7 billion) were second only to lotteries. Over two-fifths of all adults, many of whom were heavy gamblers, visited a casino within the previous year. However, the demographic characteristics of the average casino gambler were somewhat

different from those of the heavy gambler. In the first place, gender differences were nearly nonexistent since nearly equal numbers of men and
women visited casinos. In the second place, because casinos were legal only
in Nevada and Atlantic City, New Jersey at the time, casino visits usually
involved transportation and possibly lodging expenses. This meant that a
certain degree of wealth was required of most participants. Most casino gamblers were therefore middle aged adults, most of whom had annual incomes
greater than $30,000 and 30 percent of whom earned more than $50,000.
Also related to their respective locations was the fact that most casino patrons
(67%) lived in eastern or western parts of the United States. Because Las
Vegas and Reno are relatively isolated from the large West Coast population
centers, fewer of Nevada's casino patrons were repeat visitors. However, its
proximity to the large urban centers of the East Coast provided Atlantic City
with many more repeat visitors.

Gambling Attitudes and Motivations

On the expansion of legalized gambling. Most Americans favored the legalization of gambling in their states since most regarded it as a harmless pastime. As noted, 78 percent of all respondents favored state lotteries. Although
fewer wanted casinos (55%) and off-track betting (54%), those who favored
these forms of gambling were in the majority. Nevertheless, three-fifths (62%)
felt that the legalization of gambling would cause people to gamble more
than they should. Over half (55%) expressed their disapproval of legalized
sports betting although few believed that the integrity of most athletic com-
petitions–particularly college and most professional team sports–would be
jeopardized by gambling. Notable exceptions were the outcomes of certain
boxing and horse racing events which are traditionally suspected of being
"fixed."

Self-reported reasons for gambling. When the respondents were asked
their personal motivations for gambling (multiple responses were allowed),
the most common response was for entertainment, enjoyment, recreation, or
fun (39%). In descending order of frequency this response was followed by
the desire for money or "to get rich" (27%), for excitement (12%), for the
challenge or competition (11%), as part of one's social life (6%), to make a
game or contest "more interesting" (4%), because "I'm lucky" (1%), and out
of habit (1%). A substantial proportion gave "other" reasons (14%), or indicated that they "didn't know" why they gambled (5%).

On compulsive and problem gambling. Ten percent of the active gamblers
surveyed admitted that they gambled excessively at times. Those most like-

ly to make this admission were the young, members of ethnic minority groups, the less affluent, and the heaviest gamblers who made bets of $100 or more. Nearly the same frequencies of uncontrolled gambling were reported by participants in all forms of gambling including those who only played lotteries.

Theoretical Significance

Although the findings of this study were more descriptive and general than quantitative and specific, they were clearly pertinent to a number of gambling theories. The **gender hypothesis** was again supported by the fact that, with the exception of bingo, males had higher participation rates and tended to be heavier gamblers than females. The study demonstrated to a limited extent that certain demographic groups are attracted to different kinds of gambling: while data on the heaviest gamblers tended to support Li and Smith's **life cycle** and Tec's **status frustration hypotheses**, both of these ideas were refuted by the data on casino gamblers who tended to be older and more affluent than, for example, lottery or bingo players. The **availability and exposure hypothesis** found support in the facts that (1) most casino gamblers lived in the West and the East, the only parts of the country in which casino gambling was legal at the time of the study, and (2) fewer lottery players resided in the South, a region with only two state lotteries. The South, America's Protestant fundamentalist "Bible Belt," is also the region in which the least amount of gambling took place. Since southerners had the highest number of abstainers (as well as teetotalers) and voiced the greatest disapproval of gambling, regional data also provided support for Devereux's **religion** and Moran's **subcultural hypotheses**. The fact that nongamblers tended to be more religious and less affluent than gamblers supported Devereux's **religion** but refuted Tec's **status frustration hypothesis**. The **religion hypothesis** was also supported by the finding that Catholics and those with no religious affiliation tended to gamble more than Protestants. The **moral model** was supported by the finding that most nongamblers objected to gambling on religious grounds. The fact that the greatest percentage of gamblers claimed to gamble for entertainment, recreational or social purposes supported the ideas of the **play** and **interactional theorists**. However, other responses also supported **economic** (to get rich), **sensation-seeking** (for the excitement), and **cognitive** (I'm lucky) hypotheses.

GAMBLING AND AGE IN IOWA

Over 1000 Iowa residents were surveyed in the late 1980s for a final American test of the **life cycle hypothesis**.[19] In addition to the standard demographic and socioeconomic questions, the researchers also solicited information on the scope or number of different kinds of gambling, frequency of gambling, time spent on gambling, and the amounts of money spent on gambling by each respondent. These four components were then combined into a gambling behavior scale or overall gambling index which was then correlated with various age categories (arranged by the decades 18-24, 25-34, 35-44, etc., to 85 and older) and socioeconomic status to determine the rates at which people of different age groups tended to participate in different kinds of gambling. The statistical measures which were taken to control for the influence of socioeconomic status, marital status, employment status, community size, religious affiliation, and gender which are also known correlates of gambling made this one of the most technically sophisticated quantitative studies of gambling ever conducted. (Attitudinal and other correlation data will receive further treatment in a later discussion of the risk factors that are associated with gambling.)

Overall rates of gambling and age were found to be inversely correlated both before and after steps were taken to control for other variables. The researchers discovered that rates of gambling were highest in young adulthood. They then decreased relatively slowly from the youngest age category to the 55-64 year old group at which point they began to decline more rapidly. They also found that although lotteries had the highest participation rates in all age categories, different age groups tended to participate to different degrees in different types of gambling. For example, sports betting was most common among younger (18-44) age groups; rates of casino gambling, stock and bond speculation, racetrack betting, and lottery playing were highest among the middle (35 to 64) age groups; bingo was most prevalent in the younger (18-24) and older (65-74) age categories.

The researchers not only rejected the **anomie** and Veblenian **affluence hypotheses** but, despite the inverse correlation between overall gambling and age, they also rejected the **life cycle hypothesis**. They did so on the grounds that each of these theories would predict a parabolic rather than a linear age-gambling relationship since, according to both anomie and Veblenian theory, most gambling would be expected to occur during an individual's peak earning years of middle age. Despite the emergence of the expected pattern for casino gambling, racetrack betting, speculative investing, and a number of other forms of gambling, it failed to describe the overall pattern of gambling.

To explain the results of their survey the authors advanced a variant of **small-group theory**. They suggested that youthful gambling and other forms of risk-taking may represent experimental forms of role-playing in which all adolescents and young adults engage during their search for an adult identity or public persona. The elderly, whose identities are well-established, have no need for such experimentation or self-presentation. Older people who do gamble may do so only to maintain existing social relationships and, due to their declining mental capacities and lack of concern over financial success, many may choose to restrict their gambling to less intellectually demanding forms such as bingo. According to the **continuity theory** that they proposed, decreases in age-related gambling may also reflect a "cohort-effect" since antigambling sanctions and sentiments have steadily weakened over time. That is, in their youth current members of older age groups may have internalized stronger antigambling values–values which are held for life–than did subsequent generations each of which would have been exposed to successively weaker antigambling values. Such an approach implies, of course, that today's youthful gamblers will be gambling just as much in their old age as they are now.

Gender Differences

A reanalysis of the original Iowa data was later undertaken to determine the existence of any gender differences in gambling behavior.[20] This was possible since of the 1,011 subjects sampled, 45.4 percent were male and 54.5 percent were female. Specifically, the researchers investigated any self-reported gender differences in normative as well as problem gambling behavior. They also looked for any gender differences in the etiology of problem gambling.

Although men scored significantly higher than women on overall gambling behavior, the study found no significant gender differences in terms of problem gambling. As in the original study, overall gambling differences based on the Gambling Behavior Index which compared the scope of gambling, frequency of gambling, and time and money spent on gambling. Specifically, although the scope of gambling was significantly lower for women, no significant gender differences were noted in frequencies of gambling, time spent on gambling, and money spent on gambling. In terms of preferences, lottery playing was most common form of gambling for both men and women while cock or dog fighting was the least common. Males and females were equally likely to engage in lottery play, games played at home, horse and dog racing, and dog and cock fights. Women were significantly more likely than men to play bingo and slightly more likely than men to engage in casino gambling while men were more likely than women to engage in public gambling, sports betting, and speculation in the stock and commodities markets.

In their reanalysis of the original Iowa data, the researchers failed to find any support for the **gender hypothesis**. Since the men and women in their sample were equally likely to report loss of control and adverse consequences from gambling, they concluded that "women gamblers are at equal risk in becoming problem gamblers."

GAMBLING, GENDER, COMMUNITY SIZE, AND INCOME IN NEBRASKA

A telephone survey of 420 adults living in the midwestern state of Nebraska was also conducted in the early 1990s. This study, which was undertaken by D. A. Abbott and S. L. Cramer, was intended as the baseline for a proposed longitudinal or time-series study. Its stated goals were to estimate the extent of gambling participation over the previous twelve month period, to assess people's current attitudes toward gambling and its expansion, and to test Devereux's **rural-urban hypothesis**. However, whereas Devereux felt that any differences in gambling between country and city dwellers would be due to the relative strength of conservative religious values, Abbott and Cramer felt that these differences would be a function of availability as well as religious conservatism. The researchers also compared the gambling rates of those in different income categories. To their credit Abbott and Cramer acknowledged that when subjects receive an unexpected telephone call from a stranger who asks them to provide self-reported data on a sensitive topic like gambling, they may be inclined to be less than truthful in their responses. They therefore advised that their findings be considered only as rough approximations of the true gambling situation.

Overall Participation

Nearly two-thirds (62%) of those polled reported that someone in their household had gambled for money in the past year. Of those who had gambled, 66 percent spent less than $100, 17 percent spent from $100 to $499, 8 percent spent from $500 and $999, 7 percent spent from $1,000 to $4,999, 1 percent spent from $5,000 to $9,999, and 1 percent spent more than $10,000 (mean = $994; median = $121). Well over half (60%) claimed to have broken even over the past year, 25 percent admitted they had lost money, and 15 percent claimed to have won more money than they lost.

Although Nebraska did not have its own state lottery at the time of the study (one has since been approved), those of neighboring states constituted the most popular form of gambling. Thus, 50 percent of all respondents had played a lottery, 43 percent played pull tabs,[23] 36 percent played cards, 34 percent bet on horse races, 32 percent bet on dog races, 27 percent played slot machines, 25 percent were sports bettors, 21 percent were bingo players, 19% had gambled in a casino, 12 percent played keno, and 22 percent had participated in some other gambling activity.

Most respondents restricted their participation to only a few activities. Specifically, 17 percent participated in only one form of gambling, 41 percent wagered on two or three forms, and 42 percent engaged in four or more different kinds of gambling. People's annual gambling expenditures correlated with the number of different activities they pursued. Moreover, those who started gambling in their teen years were more likely to participate in more forms than those who did not start gambling until they were older.

Gender Differences

Participation rates. Like their predecessors, Abbott and Cramer reported some distinct gender differences in the gambling practices of their respondents. Men not only outnumbered women in overall participation rates (60% M vs. 45% F) but more men than women also favored legalized gambling (86% M, 79%F), expressed a desire for more gambling to become available in their own communities (69% M, 54%F), and predicted that their gambling would increase if more gambling were made available (54% M, 40% F). The only forms of gambling in which women had higher participation rates than men were bingo (26% F, 14% M) and dog racing (25% F, 20% M); participation rates for slot machine gambling were nearly identical between the sexes (26% M, 25% F).

Expenditures. With few exceptions, men also spent more than women on all forms of gambling. However, for these measures Abbott and Cramer reported median rather than mean gambling expenditures. They did so because the mean amounts of money that are spent on different forms of gambling tend to be exaggerated by a relatively small number of gamblers who spend exceptionally large amounts. Median annual expenditures for each gambling activity effectively eliminate this "high roller" effect and yield a more realistic picture of how much money the "typical" gambler spends on them. For example, median expenditures for all forms of gambling in the previous year ($153 M, $103 F) were far different from mean expenditures ($1,465 M vs. $448 F). In general, men also outspent women on individual gambling activities. However, women not only had higher annual participation rates in bingo than men, but they also spent much more money on this form of gambling ($96 F, $20 M). Women also spent more than men on horse ($38 F, $28 M) and dog racing ($30 F, $25 M). Although far more men (58%) than women (33%) played pull tabs, the women who did so spent the same amount of money on them as men ($36% M and F).

Community Size Differences

A number of gambling practices were significantly correlated with rural or urban residence, the categories of which were determined by community size. For their analysis. Abbott and Cramer distinguished four categories based on population size: the smaller towns held fewer than 5,000 people; larger towns had between 5,000 and 19,999; smaller cities, between 20,000 and 49,999, and larger cities were populated by more that 50,000 residents. It will be recalled that the **rural-urban hypothesis** predicts that gambling rates and expenditures should increase as a function of population size and proximity to large urban areas.

Participation rates. Because they found no significant differences in overall participation rates among their four community size categories, the researchers were forced to conclude that those living in rural areas were just as likely to gamble as those living in urban areas. Moreover, irrespective of the presence or absence of statistical significance, the absolute figures failed to fall into the predicted pattern: although the smallest towns had the lowest participation rate (48%), gambling was less prevalent in the largest cities (54%) than it was in larger towns (58%). However, those in the largest cities tended to participate in three different gambling activities while those in all smaller communities were most likely to participate in only two. Residents of the smallest towns participated to a significantly greater extent than those of all larger communities only in bingo (27% vs. 19%). Participation rates of small town residents were nearly the same as those of all larger communities for keno (14% vs. 12%, respectively), card games (36% vs. 37%), and pull tabs (41% vs. 45%).

Expenditures. Although the highest per capita gambling expenditures were found among residents of the largest cities (mean = $1,897), no significant differences emerged between those of people living in smaller communities. Moreover, the expected pattern also failed to emerge in smaller communities since per capita expenditures were lower in smaller cities ($312) than they were in either large ($445) or small ($403) towns.

Income Differences

The researchers found that the likelihood of gambling increased with income and that those in the lowest income group spent a substantially greater proportion of their annual income on gambling than those in any other category. In the first place, both the frequency and volume of gambling rose with income. Thus, 40 percent of those earning less than $15,000 per year had gambled for money in the last year. The median expenditure for this group was $134. Those in the $15,000 to $29,000 income bracket had a participation rate of 50 percent and a median expenditure of $158 while 62 percent of those earning between $30,000 and $49,000 gambled in the last year and typically spent $160 per person. The most affluent who earned more than $50,000 per year had a 65 percent participation rate and a median annual expenditure of $242. In the second place, the proportion of annual income spent on gambling tended to decrease with annual income. Thus, the poorest spent significantly more of their household earnings (7.1%) on gambling than did those in the three higher income brackets (3.4%, 1.6%, and 2.4%, respectively).

Despite the slight but insignificant tendency for overall participation rates to increase with income, participation rates in different gambling activities were generally similar across all income categories. For example, the incidence of pull tab gambling was 40 percent among those in the lowest income category, 41 percent in the next two categories, and 43 percent among the most affluent. However, the incidence of lottery playing increased with income across the first three categories then fell among the most affluent (38%, 50%, 57%, 48%, respectively). Another notable exception was in casino gambling which was far more popular in the highest income group (36%) than in the others (15%, 10%, and 18%, respectively). Conversely, bingo was most popular among the poorest (31%), slightly less popular in the next two categories (25% and 20%, respectively), and least popular among the wealthiest (7%).

Attitudes and Opinions

Because most respondents (84%) felt that gambling by family members in the past year had no positive or negative effects on the quality of their domestic situation, gambling was generally seen as a harmless form of recreation. Of those who indicated that gambling did affect their family situation, 6 percent reported that these effects were positive while 10 percent reported that they were negative. Included among the beneficial consequences of gambling were opportunities for increased socialization, entertainment, and increased income; negative consequences included family arguments and loss of household income. The numbers of those reporting such effects were too small to analyze by gender, community size, or income. Nevertheless, there was a tendency for gambling-related domestic problems to increase as income level decreased.

Gamblers were more likely to approve of legalized gambling and its expansion than nongamblers. Thus, 82 percent of the gamblers but only 43 percent of the nongamblers approved of legalized gambling while 63 percent of the former and only 22 percent of the latter wanted to see the state legalize even more kinds of gambling. Nearly half (48%) of all nongamblers favored a state lottery, over one-third (34%) indicated that they would buy lottery tickets if a state sponsored lottery were legalized, and a over one-quarter (26%) indicated that they would engage in other forms of gambling if they had the opportunity to do so.

Theoretical Implications

Abbott and Cramer's general population study demonstrated once again that most people gamble and most do so in a responsible manner for recreational purposes which harms neither themselves nor their families. This finding provides strong evidence for **play theory**, the idea that gambling represents a form of adult recreation. Their findings also provided clear evidence for the **gender hypothesis** since men were found to be heavier gamblers than women in terms of the overall incidence of gambling, the volume of money spent on gambling, and the number of different gambling activities in which they participated. The finding that those who begin gambling at younger ages will participate in more gambling activities as adults supports the **age of initiation hypothesis** which will be discussed in a following section. Findings related to the **rural-urban residence** or **community size hypothesis** were mixed. In terms of incidence, the likelihood of gambling was nearly the same for all respondents irrespective of the size of the communities in which they lived. However, residents of the largest cities spent considerably more money on gambling than those living elsewhere and they were more likely to participate in more kinds of gambling. Nevertheless, none of the other three community size categories were differentiated on these grounds. The authors therefore suggested that differences in gambling preferences between rural and urban dwellers could be a function of either **availability** or **economics** since big city dwellers typically earn more than residents of smaller rural communities. In fact, analysis of income data did provide weak support for Veblen's **leisure class hypothesis**: although both participation rates and median gambling expenditures increased with income level, these differences failed to reach statistical significance. However, the fact that the poorest respondents spent a disproportionate amount of their annual household income on gambling than the more affluent could be interpreted as supporting Tec's **status-frustration** or **aspiration hypothesis**. Thus, Abbott and Cramer also proposed the **economic** explanation that because they are already poor they may feel that they have little to lose and much to gain by gambling. Alternatively, they also proposed a **cognitive** explanation: since the poor typically have less education, they may lack any awareness of the true odds against them and tend to overestimate their chances for winning.

Abbott and Cramer made several predictions about the directions gambling may take in the future. In the first place, they described the existing gender differences they encountered as modest and predicted that they will probably diminish in the future. This will occur not only as a consequence of the increasing availability of gambling, but also as a result of the changes in the gender role socialization process that are now taking place. In the second place, they also suggested that differences in the participation and spending rates of rural and urban dwellers might begin to diminish as smaller communities increasingly come to see gambling as a practical and effective means of stimulating their local economies and, as a consequence, begin to ease some of their existing gambling restrictions. In the third place, despite their acknowledgement that the data alone could not explain why the incidence of gambling was lowest among the poorest respondents, the authors suggested that one reason for this may be their realization that they cannot afford to gamble. However, they felt it more likely that availability plays a larger role since the poor lack ready access to casinos, riverboats, and the lotteries of other states. They therefore predicted that, irrespective of their economic self-perceptions and fiscal responsibilities, the poor, in hopes of surmounting their present economic difficulties, will begin to gamble more as more forms of gambling are legalized. Finally, since so many respondents indicated that the extent of their gambling would probably increase if more opportunities were available, the authors predicted that the incidence of gambling-related personal and family problems will be likely to increase with the expansion of legalized gambling. Since this initial survey represented a baseline for proposed longitudinal research, all of these predictions are likely to be tested in future studies.

Because they did not systematically screen their respondents for problem gambling, Abbott and Cramer recommended that more thorough prevalence studies, incorporating such instruments as the South Oaks Gambling Screen or the Gamblers Anonymous Self-Test, be undertaken in the future. These studies should not only target families that are being adversely affected by gambling but they should also assess the prevalence of pathological gambling. They felt that such studies are necessary so that any changes in gambling behavior that may be having adverse effects can be documented and dealt with in a timely manner. They therefore enjoined that longitudinal research involving a series of studies should take place frequently and regularly, particularly when gambling has expanded as dramatically as it has in the midwestern United States.

LOTTERY PURCHASES IN TWO STATES

Participation Rates in California: A Univariate Analysis

During their literature review of lottery playing, Charles Clotfelter and Philip Cook reanalyzed unpublished market research data from two states. Their primary goal in doing so was to determine which demographic groups were the most avid lottery participants. The researchers found that, despite its many omissions, a body of unpublished data from a 1986 newspaper poll on lottery playing during a one-week period in California provided some information about which demographic groups had the highest participation rates. Their univariate analysis of this data revealed that middle-aged Hispanic Catholic males who are less well-educated laborers were likely to be the state's heaviest lottery players:

Gender. Slightly more males (40%) than females (36%) had purchased lottery tickets in the week prior to the survey. These findings weakly support the **gender hypothesis**.

Age. Interestingly, participation steadily increased with age until retirement when it dropped dramatically (18-39 years, 37%; 30-44, 39%, 45-65, 44%; 65+, 26%). These findings fail to support the **life cycle hypothesis**.

Religion. Catholics had a far higher rate of participation (54%) than Protestants (31%); those claiming no religious affiliation (39%) were only slightly more likely to participate than Protestants while those in "Other" denominations were the least likely to make lottery purchases. These findings support the **religion hypothesis**.

Ethnicity. Hispanics were the most avid players (55%) while Other Whites (35%), Blacks (34%), and Asians (32%) had roughly equivalent participation rates.

Education. Lottery purchases showed a clear correspondence to education level: participation rates were 49 percent among those with less than a high school education, 41 percent among high school graduates, 38 percent among those having some college, and 30 percent among college graduates. These findings support the **status frustration hypothesis**.

Occupation. Lottery purchases also showed a close correspondence to occupation: participation rates were highest (46%) among skilled and unskilled laborers, somewhat less (percentage unspecified) among security and clerical workers, and lowest among advanced professionals (25%), retirees, and students (percentages unspecified). These findings also support the **status frustration hypothesis**.

Income. Average weekly spending in absolute amounts differed very little across income groups (range $2 to $5) although the middle income groups had the highest expenditures ($4 to $5) while those at either extreme (below $10,000 and over $50,000 per year) spent the least (less than $4 per week). However, the amount spent as a percentage of income was highest (2%) in the lowest income category ($10,000 per year) and showed a steady decline across all higher income categories with those in the higher (over $40,000 per year) categories spending a much smaller proportion of their income (less than .5%) on lottery tickets. These findings fail to support the **status frustration hypothesis** but confirm the regressive nature of lottery playing since those who are less affluent spend proportionately more of their income on lotteries than those who are more affluent.

Expenditures in Maryland: A Bivariate Analysis

Clotfelter and Cook then undertook a bivariate analysis of unpublished data on 1984 lottery expenditures in Maryland.[25] They did so because their univariate analysis of the California data was unable to reveal whether the demographic variables that were investigated operated independently of one another or whether one variable was more important than the others. That is, it was unclear whether being poorly educated, or a Hispanic, or a laborer, or a Catholic, was the most influential factor. In Maryland, the most significant variable appeared to be ethnicity since Blacks spent an average of $4.50 more per week on lottery tickets than Whites. The researchers therefore performed two analyses of each of the other demographic characteristics, one for Blacks and one for Whites.

Gender. Males in both groups spent more than females but the gender difference was much greater among Blacks: Black men spent roughly $4 per week more than Black women whereas White men spent about $1 more per week than White women. These findings support the **gender hypothesis**.

Age. Expenditures in both groups were lowest among the elderly and highest during the peak earning or middle years although Blacks in the 40-54 year old age group spent significantly more than their White counterparts. These findings fail to support the **life cycle hypothesis**.

Education. Lottery expenditures among both groups tended to decrease with education but statistically significant reductions were found only among Whites: those lacking a high school diploma spent an average of $5 more per week than college graduates. These findings support the **status frustration hypothesis**.

Income. Data for the entire sample showed that the highest lottery expenditures were made by those in the lowest income category (less than $10,000 per year) while the lowest expenditures were made by those in the middle income ($15,000 to $25,000) group. However, separate analyses on the basis of ethnicity revealed that this pattern was found only among Blacks while expenditures for Whites showed no significant differences between income categories. The researchers therefore concluded that the apparent overall regressivity of lottery spending was an artifact of the spending habits of the Black respondents. These findings fail to support the **status frustration hypothesis**.

Residence. Urban or rural residence was not a factor when the researchers controlled for race, income, and other factors. They therefore found no support for the **rural-urban residence hypothesis**.

NORMATIVE GAMBLING IN MINNESOTA

An explosive growth in the level of gambling in Minnesota accompanied the legalization of new forms of gambling in the early 1990s. Prior to this time pull tabs, a form of charitable gambling along with bingo and raffles, represented Minnesota's most popular and readily available form of gambling since they were sold in nearly all public and private drinking establishments.[26] Although Minnesotans also had legal access to horse racing and high stakes "Indian bingo" at that time, neither of these activities were especially popular. Then, in the early 1990s, a state lottery and Native American casino gaming became available. However, unlike casinos in other states which offer many different forms of gambling, only electronic gaming machines, blackjack, and high stakes bingo were made available in Minnesota's Native American casinos. They nevertheless attracted thousands of visitors from all parts of Minnesota, from other states, and even from other countries. Following the legalization of these newer forms of gambling, annual state-wide gambling expenditures increased dramatically.[27] While the level of lottery playing peaked fairly rapidly after its introduction, Native American casino gaming took somewhat longer to do so since many new buildings, parking lots, and other facilities first had to be constructed, often on previously undeveloped and uncleared reservation lands. Nevertheless, by the end of 1993 seventeen large and opulent gambling casinos had been built and were fully operational in Minnesota.

Although they were conducted for purposes of market research rather than hypothesis testing, several state-wide telephone surveys on gambling behavior were sponsored by the Minnesota State Lottery. A 600 household telephone survey of the public's awareness of how state lottery proceeds were being spent took place in 1991, one year after the initiation of the state lottery and the expansion of tribal casino gaming.[28] A more comprehensive survey of actual gambling behavior took place two years later in June and July of 1993.[29] A similar though less inclusive study was conducted one year later in 1994.[30] Adults in each of the 2,400 households sampled during these surveys were asked questions concerning their attitudes toward gambling and their participation in 12 specific forms. The respondents were asked not only about their lifetime participation, but also about their current participation in the two months prior to each survey. Since these studies were sponsored by state lottery officials who were interested in discovering which segments of the population were the most and least likely to play the lottery and why, a large part of each report was devoted to lottery statistics. Because the findings of both behavioral studies were so similar, those of the first, which was far more comprehensive, will be discussed in greater detail.

Frequency Data

In terms of frequency, 87 percent of all respondents had ever gambled and 71% had done so within the last two months. The average Minnesota gambler had participated at one time or another in four different gambling activities, the most common being the state lottery which was played by nearly two-thirds of all respondents. Table 8-1 demonstrates that current participation rates for various activities yield a different order of preference than lifetime rates.

Since all rates listed in Table 8-1 were taken from the 1993 study, it must be noted that the 1994 study showed a sharp increase in lifetime tribal casino gaming (46%) and concomitant but slight decreases in lottery (61%) and pull tab (45%) participation. Nevertheless, the table suggests that while many people may experiment with different gambling activities, with the exception of lottery players relatively few become regular participants. A more accurate picture of a population's gambling rates and preferences would therefore appear to be provided by its current rather than lifetime levels of involvement.

Table 8-1. MINNESOTA'S GAMBLING PREFERENCES
AS DETERMINED BY PARTICIPATION RATES[31]

Lifetime		Current (past two months)	
Activity	*Rate*	*Activity*	*Rate*
MN lottery	63%	MN lottery	50%
Card games	53%	Pull tabs	18%
Pull tabs	51%	MN tribal casino	18%
Bingo	42%	Card games	15%
Social betting	39%	Social betting	12%
Sports betting	37%	Non-MN lotteries	7%
MN tribal casinos	36%	Bingo	5%
Non-MN lotteries	31%	Sports betting	5%
Non-MN casinos	31%	Dice/tavern games	4%
Horse racing	31%	Non-MN casinos	2%
Dice/tavern games	17%	Dog racing	1%
Dog racing	16%	Horse racing	0%

Although most Minnesotans gambled, certain demographic groups did so more than others and each had its own preferences. Here, too, however, the incidence of casino gambling showed dramatic increases over time. Nevertheless, the demographic groups having the highest levels of gambling involvement were:

Males. Overall gender differences were slight since only a few more males (90%) than females (85%) have ever gambled. Males showed higher rates of participation in all forms of gambling with the exception of bingo (48% F; 35% M). Gender differences were greatest in dice (24% M; 11% F) and sports betting (49% M; 25% F) but least pronounced in horse racing (32% M; 30% F), the Minnesota lottery (68% M; 58% F), and pull tabs (55% M; 47% F). However, while the incidence of casino gaming for both males and females increased between the 1993 and 1994 studies, that for women (29%, 1993; 42% 1994) showed a much sharper increase than that for men (44% 1993; 50% 1994).

Young adults. The highest incidence of gambling was found among young adults 18-24 years of age while the lowest were found among senior citizens over 65. The youngest, those in the 18-20 year-old group, had the highest current (85%) and the second highest lifetime (92%) participation rates. Interestingly, there was no difference between the lifetime rates of males and females in this age group. Those in the second youngest or 21-24 year-old group had the highest lifetime (94%) and second highest current (83%) gambling rates. Incidence measures tended to show a slight but steady decrease with age through the 55-64 year-old group (86% lifetime; 72% current) and then dropped sharply among those 65 and older (74% lifetime; 43% current). Senior citizens also participated in fewer gambling activities than younger Minnesotans: as a group, they had engaged in an average of three different gambling activities in their lives as opposed to an average of five for the youngest respondents and four for all others. Gambling preferences were also related to age: social betting, the lottery, card games, sports betting, pull tabs, and Native American casino gambling in that order were the most popular forms of gambling among the very young. Lotteries, pull tabs, and cards were the most popular games for older adults while bingo, cards, and the state lottery were the favorite activities of senior citizens. However, the 1994 study showed a significant rise in casino gambling among all adults over 35. The sharpest increase occurred among the elderly whose participation rate for casino gaming nearly doubled in just one year (21%, 1993; 40%, 1994). These statistics confirmed earlier research which found that most lottery winners (80%) were in the middle and older (40 and above) age categories.[32]

The affluent. Those living in lower income households were considerably less likely to gamble than those in the middle and upper income brackets. Both lifetime (74%) and current (55%) rates of participation were lowest among those earning less than $10,000 per year and only slightly higher (77% lifetime; 56% current) among those earning between $10,000 and $15,000. Participation rates became higher (87% lifetime; 72% current) in the $15,000 to $20,000 income bracket after which they tended to show a gradual but steady rise through the $40,000 to $50,000 bracket (95% lifetime; 81% current). However, they then showed a slight drop among those earning more than $50,000 per year (91% lifetime; 77% current). Like the elderly, low income residents also bet on fewer activities (an average of 4) in their lifetimes than the more affluent (an average of 6) and their gambling preferences differ. Those in the lowest income category were least likely to have engaged in any form of gambling apart from bingo. Card games were least popular among the poor but most popular among the wealthy. The most affluent also the most likely to engage in sports, racetrack, social, out-of-state lottery, and casino gambling. Likewise, the incidence of tribal casino gaming in 1993 was significantly higher among the wealthiest (47%) than the less affluent (19%-40%). While this income group still had the highest rate in 1994 (53%), the large

gap that once existed between this group and those earning between
$10,000 and $50,000 had now narrowed considerably (38%-51%).
Although the poorest group (below $10,000) still had the lowest 1994
incidence of casino gaming (26%), the second lowest rate (38%) was
now found in the second highest income group ($40,000 to $50,000).
These statistics also confirmed earlier research which found that most
lottery winners were in the more affluent social classes.[33]

The better educated. Those with the least amount of formal education are the
least likely to gamble. Only 78 percent of all respondents with less
than a high school education had participated in gambling at some
time in their lives as opposed to 88 percent of those with more education. The pattern presented by current participation rates, while similar, is even more marked: it was lowest among those with less than a
high school education (55%), higher among those who completed high
school (74%), and slightly higher among those having some college
(77%). The current participation rate then showed a sharp drop among
those having college degrees. However, since most Minnesotans who
lacked a high school education were over 65 years old, it should be
noted that their low rates of gambling may have been related to age or
income rather than education. The least well educated preferred bingo
while those with a high school or more education preferred the lottery.
High school graduates were also the most likely to play pull tabs while
those with some college were most likely to engage in lottery and
Native American casino gaming. Those with college degrees were
least likely to play pull tabs or bingo but the most likely to play cards,
bet on horse races, and visit a nonlocal casino. Here, too, the incidence of tribal casino gaming rose dramatically with levels of education: the incidence of casino gaming in 1993 was lowest among those
having the least formal education (17%), second lowest among the
most highly educated (35%), and higher among those with intermedi-
ate levels of education (39% and 41%). By 1994, 40 percent of those
who lacked a high school diploma, 49 percent of high school graduates, and 52 percent of those with some college had visited a Native
American casino. However, those with the most education were the
least likely to have done so (39%) in 1994. Again, these statistics supported the earlier study of lottery winners which found that most (50%
to 60%) had a high school education while those with the least amount
of formal education (0 to 8 years) were the least frequent winners (6%
to 9.4%).[34]

Urban dwellers. Although regional differences in participation rates were
slight, residents of the Twin Cities metropolitan area were more likely

to gamble than those living elsewhere. Participation rates varied from highs of 89 percent lifetime and 76 percent current in the Metro area to lows of 82 percent lifetime and 62 percent current in the northwest quadrant of the state. Examination of regional differences in gambling preferences also revealed that with only two exceptions, proportionally more residents of the Twin Cities metropolitan area participated in all forms of gambling than those who lived elsewhere in the state. Bingo was significantly more popular in the agricultural southwest while pull tabs were more popular in central Minnesota's pine forest and lakes region which is highly dependent on tourism. Central Minnesota, which lies adjacent to the Metro area had the second highest participation rates in the state (86% lifetime; 71% current). Regional data on tribal casino gaming also showed that lifetime participation rates in 1993 were highest in the urban Metro region (41% vs. 24% to 38% elsewhere). However, by 1994 they had shown such dramatic increases throughout the state that rates in some regions (39% to 49%) were higher than that of the urban Metro area (47%).

Volume Data

Although the lottery was the state's most popular gambling activity in terms of participation rates, Native American casino gaming and pull tabs were far more popular in terms of sales volumes. State-wide expenditures for tribal gaming were estimated to be $2 billion in 1992, pull tab sales came to roughly $1 billion, and lottery sales came to just under $300 million. Thus, although many residents played the lottery, they spent relatively little of their money on it. Overall, all those who played the lottery within the previous two months made an average of five purchases for which they typically spent $1.33 per week. Unfortunately, no other volume analyses were reported.

Lottery Purchases

The popularity of the lottery tended to decrease with age but to increase with education and income. Lifetime participation rates for lottery purchases among various demographic categories varied as follows:

Gender. More men (68%) than women (58%) had ever bought lottery tickets.

Age. Senior citizens were least likely to play the lottery. Only 31 percent of those over 65 years of age had ever played the lottery as opposed to

64 percent of those in the 18-20 year age group and from 66 percent to 74 percent of those 21-64 years of age.

Education. The least well-educated were the least likely to make lottery purchases. Two-fifths (41%) of those with less than a high school education made lottery purchases as opposed to roughly two-thirds of high school graduates (66%), those with some college (68%), and a college degree or more education (61%).

Income. The poorest residents were least likely to play the lottery and spent the least amount of money on it. Lottery purchases were made by only 42 percent of those who earned less than $10,000 per year, 51 percent of those earning between $10,000 and $15,000, and 57 percent of those in the $15,000 to $20,000 range. Nearly three-quarters (71% to 74%) of those earning between $20,000 and $50,000 had made lottery purchases while slightly fewer (68%) of those earning more than $50,000 per year did so. Low-income residents also played less frequently than those with higher incomes. Only 8 percent of those who earned less than $20,000 annually made one or more lottery purchase per week as opposed to 19 percent of those with higher incomes. The poorest residents who earned below $10,000 per year spent an average of $.52 per week on lottery purchases while those earning between $10,000 and $15,000 spent $.98 per week. Those in higher income brackets spent between $1.39 and $1.79 per week. The most affluent Minnesotans, those earning more than $50,000 a year, averaged nearly two dollars ($1.98) on lottery purchases per week. This income group comprised one-quarter (25%) of the state's population but made 42 percent of all lottery purchases. At the other end of the income spectrum, those earning less than $20,000 also made up roughly one-quarter (23%) of the population but were responsible for only 13 percent of all lottery purchases.

Residence. Residents of the Twin Cities metropolitan area were most likely to make lottery purchases while those in the agricultural southwestern part of the state were the least likely to do so. The Twin Cities area also had the highest incidence of "frequent" players and the lowest incidence of "nonplayers."[35]

Attitudinal Data

All respondents were asked about their attitudes toward gambling in general and the lottery in particular. Whereas only 19 percent of all respondents opposed all forms of gambling on moral or religious grounds, 78 percent had no objections to it and 3 percent were uncertain as to its morality. Not only were most of those who voiced these objections were in the older (45-65+) age groups, but the younger the respondents, the less likely they were to hold these feelings. They were then asked why they did or did not play the lottery. Most (74%) of those who did so claimed to do so for "fun and excitement." Nearly half (47%) claimed to do so because "the proceeds go to a good cause" while a relatively small minority (17%) felt that it would be a "good way to make money." Of the 37 percent who had never played the lottery, most felt that the "games rely too much on chance" (84%). This reason was followed by claims that the lottery was "not interesting or exciting" (77%), that the "odds of winning [were] too great," (74%), that they "don't enjoy gambling" (72%), that the "proceeds don't go to a good cause" (40%), that they were "opposed to gambling for moral or religious reasons" (39%), that they "can't afford to play the lottery" (37%), that the "games are not honest" (24%), and that they would "rather visit a casino or play pull tabs" (19%).

Theoretical Implications

Frequency data for both gambling in general and lottery playing in particular demonstrate distinct **gender** differences with males being heavier gamblers overall than females with the exception of those in the youngest (18-20) age group. Li and Smith's **life cycle hypothesis** found support in the fact that older people tend to gamble less than younger people. Veblen's **leisure class theory** was supported by evidence that rates of gambling tend to increase with education and income. Devereux's **rural-urban residence hypothesis** was supported by evidence that residents of the Twin Cities metropolitan area have higher participation rates for nearly all forms of gambling than any other region of the state. The **availability and exposure hypothesis** appeared to garner strong support from the dramatic increase across all demographic groups in the incidence of Native American casino gaming, which was relatively new to Minnesota. However, it must also be noted that this increase was accompanied by decreases in the state's two other most popular forms of commercial gambling. Since this hypothesis predicts that all forms of gambling should rise when new forms become available, it is contradicted by these findings. Nevertheless, the sharp rise in casino gambling among the state's older residents suggests that this form of gambling could become problematic for many senior citizens who may be looking for novel ways of spending time and dispelling the boredom of retirement. It is unfortunate that information on gambling sales volumes received so little treatment since earlier studies in the United States and the

United Kingdom clearly showed that conclusions based on volume data can be quite different from those based on frequency data.

The respondents' attitudes had some relevance for several psychological theories. Although a few older Minnesotans still subscribed to the early **moral model** of gambling, the belief that gambling is sinful has largely fallen by the wayside. It is also likely to become less commonplace in the future since the proportions of respondents holding this impression tended to decrease in progressively younger age groups. Because most lottery participants played for entertainment and excitement purposes, the **play** and **sensation-seeking theories** found some support in the attitudinal data. However, **cognitive theory** did not. From an economic perspective, lotteries offer poorer chances of winning than any other gambling activity. The Minnesota State Lottery was no exception since in 1992 only 57.8 percent of all the money spent on lottery purchases was returned to the players[37] as opposed to the 70 percent to 80 percent return on pull tab purchases.[38] Because so few respondents believed that they could make money by playing the lottery, the attitudinal data failed to support the hypothesis that gambling is fostered by the irrational beliefs people have about their ability to win.

Chapter 9

SPECIAL POPULATIONS:
YOUTHFUL GAMBLERS

As noted in the introductory chapter, most of the early research into the motivations for gambling focused exclusively on men, and particularly on pathological gambling among white, middle-class, middle-aged, men seeking treatment. More recently, however, growing numbers of researchers are turning their attention to normative, problem, and pathological gambling among children, adolescents and young adults. Far fewer studies have focused exclusively on gambling among women, the elderly, and specific ethnic groups. Other special populations such as homosexuals, the homeless, institutionalized groups, and military personnel have been largely ignored even though some of these groups have been found to have higher rates of substance abuse.[1]

Participation Rates

Gambling is clearly a popular normative rather than a deviant behavior among young people and it is not uncommon for children to begin gambling for money while they are still very young. This may have serious ramifications in later life since research on other potentially addictive behaviors has found that early involvement is likely to produce addiction in adulthood.[2]

A review of the earliest literature on the incidence of youthful gambling reported that from nearly half (49.3%) to nearly all (91%) of all children and adolescents sampled in Canada, India, the United Kingdom, and the United States have gambled for money at some time in their lives and that from nine percent to 39 percent were regular gamblers.[3] A subsequent survey of high school students in Atlantic City, New Jersey found that 64 percent had gambled at the city's casinos. More specifically, 42 percent of 14-year-olds sampled, 49 percent of 15-year-olds, 63 percent of 16-year-olds, 71 percent of 17-

year-olds, 76 percent of 18-year-olds, and 88 percent of 19-year-olds admitted to casino gambling. Many did so repeatedly, often on a weekly basis, and most (79%) did so with their parents' knowledge.[4] A study of nearly 900 New Jersey high school students reported that 91 percent had gambled at least once in their lives, 86 percent had done so within the past year, and 32 percent gambled one or more times per week throughout the past year.[5] A survey of 1,612 high school students in Quebec City found that only 2.2 percent of those who had ever gambled had not done so in the past year. The researchers therefore stressed that of all the young people they sampled, "very few stopped gambling once they started."[6]

More recent research has revealed similar trends among the youth of North America. For example, 86 percent of New York[7] and 89.7 percent of Minnesota[8] adolescents have gambled. Researchers in Oregon reported that of 1,000 adolescents between 13 and 17 years of age, 75 percent had gambled at least once in their lives, 66 percent had gambled in the past year, 13.3 percent gambled weekly, and 4 percent gambled daily. Although it is illegal for them to do so, 39 percent have played the Oregon Lottery and 30 percent did so in the past year. Over one-third (35%) were able to make their own lottery purchases while half (50%) obtained their tickets from members of their own family. Nearly one-fifth (19%) had gambled in a casino and over one-tenth (12%) had done so in the past year. A few (less than 1%) had gambled on the internet. Boys and older subjects were significantly more likely to gamble than girls or younger subjects.[9] A study of 3,426 junior and senior high school students in Quebec City reported that 87 percent had ever gambled, 77 percent had done so within the last year, and 13 percent regularly gambled one or more times per week. Of 817 Montreal students enrolled in grades seven, nine, and 11, over four-fifths (80.2%) reported gambling at least once in the past year and more than one-third (35.1%) did so weekly. The average age at which they began gambling was 11.5 years. The most popular forms of gambling in this sample were card games (56.2%), lotteries (52.4%), bingo (35.2%), sports betting (34%), electronic gaming machines (31.8%), sports lottery tickets (30.3%), and games of skill. Although casino gambling is illegal for those in this age group, 7.5 percent of the sample had done so. Although females were just as likely to have gambled in the past year as males (78.8% F; 81.5% M), males were twice as likely as females to be regular weekly gamblers (46% M; 22.5% F). Females were more likely than males to have played bingo and purchased lottery tickets during the past year but participation rates of males exceeded those of females in all other forms of gambling.[11] A questionnaire survey administered to 200 adolescents (97 males; 102 females; 1 gender unknown) between 12 and 18 years of age living in southern California found that although 41 percent felt that legalized gambling would be appropriate for teenagers, 83 percent of the males and 61 percent of the females had gambled at least once. Nearly half (44%) of the gamblers but only one-quarter (26%) of the nongamblers reported that at least one of their parents gambled. In order of preference the most common forms of gambling were sports betting (60.6%), cards (42.3%), lotteries (40.1%), horses (39.4%), and casinos (16.5%). This study also found that the likelihood of gambling increased with age. The largest reported wager and loss were both $200; the largest reported win was $500. Most subjects made the highly unlikely claim that they won more often than they lost.[12] Far higher participation rates were reported in a survey of 935 Windsor, Ontario high school students (age 14 to 19 years): 96.2% had gambled at some time in their lives and 90.8 percent had done so in the past year. Once again, it was found that the likelihood of gambling increases with age.[13] A United States national telephone survey of 534 adolescents (16 and 17 years of age) reported that about two-thirds had gambled in the past year. Although they tended to favor card games and instant lotteries some had also engaged in racetrack and casino gambling. About two percent admitted that they had lost more than $100 in one day. Of these, roughly two-thirds were male.[14]

A suburban New York high school survey of 318 students in grades 9 through 12 reported that nearly three-quarters (72.6%) had ever gambled. In addition to card games, sports betting, and games of skill, a number of the subjects had also participated in such illegal forms of gambling as casino gaming, lotteries, scratch-off cards, Quick Draw (a form of keno found primarily in drinking establishments), and parimutuel betting. Some claimed to have lost more than $300 dollars over the past two weeks. Here, too, a number of gender differences were noted: far more girls (36.1%) than boys (17.9%) had remained abstinent, those who did gamble did so far less frequently than boys (26.2% of the boys and 6.9% of the girls had gambled more than ten times in the previous 12 months), and boys tended to start gambling at a younger age than girls. Although the likelihood of gambling tended to increase with age, 65 percent of the boys and 43.7 percent of the girls started gambling before entering high school. This study also found that the most frequent gamblers were the most frequent alcohol users.[15] A very large survey of 11,736 Louisiana school children and adolescents in grades 6 through 12 found that only 14 percent had never gambled and that 16.5 percent played the lottery on a weekly basis. This study also found that the heaviest gamblers were the heaviest tobacco, alcohol, and other drug users.[16] An even larger survey of 13,549 adolescents in grades seven, nine, ten, and twelve living in Canada's Atlantic provinces found that 70.3 percent of the respondents had gambled at least once during the year prior to the study. In order of preference the most common forms of gambling were scratchtabs which were played by over half (55.9%) of the sample, card games (32.9%), lotteries (32.9%), sports betting (26.4%), bingo (26.2%), gaming machines (14.8%), and Sport Select (14.6%), a specialized lottery game.[17]

Recent surveys in Australia and the United Kingdom reveal that gambling is a popular pastime among adolescents in these countries, as well. A study of 1,017 Australian adolescents and young adults between 14 and 25 (average 17) years of age found that more than three-quarters (75.5%) were active gamblers most of whom (67.7%) gambled with family members.[18] A recent survey of 204 boys between the ages of 11 and 16 in Birmingham, England found that 42 percent had purchased their own instant lottery stratchcards. The researcher also found a significant relationship between the scratchcard purchasing behavior of the parents and that of their children.[19] Finally, a similar study of 256 children between the ages of 13 and 15 in Devon County, England reported that 56 percent had played the National Lottery on-line game and 54 percent had purchased instants scratchcards. Household participation and income were the strongest predictors of scratchcard gambling.[20]

Gambling is a surprisingly common and well established activity among younger children, as well. A survey of British adolescents reported that the average age at which gambling began was eight years nine months for girls and eight years three months for boys.[21] The large Louisiana student survey mentioned above found that 86 percent of those sampled had gambled and that the average age at which they started gambling was 11.2 years.[22] The previously mentioned adolescent survey of a New York suburb found that over half (58.4%) of the subjects admitted to gambling before the ninth grade and nearly one-quarter (24.6%) claimed to have started in grade six or earlier.[23] A small survey of 104 Montreal school children in grades four, six, and eight (51 males and 53 females aged 9 to 14) found that 70 percent had gambled while 53 percent regularly gambled once a week or more.[24] Although more males than females had ever gambled (78% M; 60% F) and were regular gamblers (58% M; 47% F), these gender differences were not statistically significant. The researchers therefore speculated that the previously reported gender differences might become more pronounced in later adolescence. Moreover, the tendency to gamble did not change with age since no significant age-related prevalence differences were found although the older children tended to risk more money than younger children, particularly among males. A simulated gambling experiment utilizing a computerized blackjack game revealed that males not only tended to gamble for higher stakes than females but that they also tended to win more. Of all gamblers, 27 percent felt that they gambled more than they wanted and 13 percent felt that they gambled too much. Males, who accounted for most of those in both categories, comprised 84 percent of those who gambled more than they wanted and 100 percent of those who indicated that they gambled too much. Interestingly, the highest proportion of those who indicated that their gambling was excessive were the youngest, those in grade four, of whom 43 percent felt that they gambled more than they wanted and 29 percent that they gambled too much. In contrast, only four percent of the sixth graders and nine percent of the eighth graders felt that their gambling was excessive. Of equal interest was the finding that the older children become, the less likely they are to fear being caught for gambling.

Similar findings were reported in a larger and more extensive study of 1,320 of Quebec's primary school students in grades four through six who ranged between eight and 12 years of age.[25] The survey found that 86 percent had gambled for money at some time in their lives and that more than 40 percent were regular bettors who gambled at least once a week. Of the weekly gamblers 8.4 percent played cards, 8.2 percent bet on sports, and 7.7 percent played lotteries. The study also confirmed earlier findings that the likelihood of gambling increases with age since 80.5 percent of those nine or younger, 85.2 percent of those 10 years of age, 87.6 percent of those 11 years old, and 94 percent of those 12 or older had done so. Rates of weekly gambling, which ranged from 39.8 percent in the youngest, through 36.7 percent and 40.5 percent respectively in the 10 and 11 year groups, to 48.2 percent among the oldest children, also increased with age. The most popular forms of gambling among these children were lotteries (61.1% participation), bingo (55.5%), card games (53.3%), sports betting (47.9%), betting on "specific events" (32.3%), slot or video poker machine gambling (28.6%), and games of skill (10.7%). Over one-third of the children (37.2%) admitted that they had risked something that was dear to them including some surprisingly large sums of money: 11.4 percent had wagered more than $15 in a single day, 8.3 percent bet between $10 and $15, 19.5 percent bet between $5 and $10, and 38.5 percent bet from $1 to $5 in one day. The money they used for gambling came from a variety of sources including allowances (62.5%), employment (57.6%), gifts (51.8%), and borrowing (7.9%); some (1.6%) admitted to stealing their gambling money. Most children—70.9 percent of the youngest to 85.6 percent of the oldest—gambled with their parents. Because more boys (89.7%) gambled than girls (81.9%), and because boys tended to gamble with their parents more so than girls, the researchers suggested that boys might be more greatly influenced by modeling or social learning than girls. They therefore suggested that future studies should investigate the degree to which parental influence and modeling might exacerbate gambling behavior, particularly among boys. Although this study was not intended to assess the prevalence of pathological gambling among children of this age group, the researchers felt that such studies are warranted by the fact that some of their young subjects already appeared to be developing potentially serious gambling problems. Findings and conclusions of a similar nature were also reported in a later study of 477 Montreal secondary school children ranging in age from 9 to 14[26] and a much larger survey of 3,426 junior and senior high school students in Quebec.[27] Virtually all (98%) of the seventh and eighth graders sampled in an Alberta survey had gambled within the previous 12 months.[28]

Problem Gambling

As a result of their early exposure to gambling, increasing numbers of children and adolescents are encountering gambling problems. It has been found, for example, that greater proportions of problem (26.4% to 36%) than nonproblem gamblers (7% to 10%) in Quebec had their first gambling experience in adolescence.[29] A United States study of adult members of Gamblers Anonymous in a mid-Atlantic state found that the average age at which they started gambling for money was 13: 37 percent of the sample began by age 10, 47 percent between 11 and 18, and only 14 percent after the age of 19.[30] Similar findings were reported in a study of adolescent gambling in Oregon where far more problem and pathological gamblers started gambling while they were still in grade school (31.67%) than after they had completed grade school (16.8%).[31] A study of fruit machine gambling among British adolescents found that those who were addicted started playing at an average age of 9.2 years while nonaddicted players did not start until they were 11.3.[32] Other studies have similarly reported that many of the pathological gamblers they sampled embarked on their gambling careers in their pre- or early teens[33] and nearly all had begun gambling for money by their mid or late teens.[34] A Montreal student survey found that rates of pathological gambling varied inversely with grade level: 4.7 percent of seventh grade students, 5.7 percent of ninth grade students, and 3.1 percent of eleventh grade students were identified as pathological gamblers. Moreover, younger students started gambling at an earlier age than older students: seventh graders started gambling at an average age of ten years and two months; ninth graders, at 11 years and six months; and eleventh graders, at 13 years and two months.[35]

These findings strongly suggest that the earlier in life people start to gamble, the more likely they are to become problem gamblers. This **age of initiation hypothesis** has also been referred to as the "early start phenomenon."[36] However, the findings of most of these studies were obtained retrospectively, by asking their subjects to try to recall the age at which they started gambling. Longitudinal studies designed to monitor the gambling behavior of cohorts from grade school into adulthood are necessary not only to verify this hypothesis but also to expand our limited knowledge of gambling among the very young.

Pertinent to this issue as well as to the **gender hypothesis** were two very large school surveys conducted in 1992 and 1995, each of which sampled nearly all the sixth, ninth, and twelfth grade students then enrolled in Minnesota's public school system.[37] The 126-item Minnesota Student Survey which was used in them included questions on gambling frequency as well as two potential problem gambling areas: within the past year had the respondents ever felt bad about the amount of money they bet, and had they felt they would like to stop betting money but didn't think they could. Of the 168,919 students sampled in 1992, 61,311 were sixth graders. Gambling was not only more common among the boys in this group but they also gambled more often than girls: only 29.7 percent of the sixth-grade boys but 54.0 percent of the girls had never gambled, 38.0 percent or the boys vs. 31.4 percent of the girls gambled on a less than monthly basis, 17.5 percent vs. 9.2 percent gambled monthly, and 14.8 percent vs. 5.4 percent were daily or weekly gamblers. Rates of problem gambling were also higher among the boys. It is puzzling that of those who claimed never to have gambled, .6 percent of both the girls and boys responded positively to one problem gambling question and .1 percent of each gender responded positively to both problem gambling questions. In all other frequency categories, however, two to four times more boys than girls responded positively to one or both problem gambling questions. Three years later 65,094 of the total 75,900 students surveyed were ninth graders, many of whom would also have participated in the 1992 sixth grade sample. Although the frequency of gambling and rates of problem gambling of both sexes increased over this three-year period, those for boys had risen more sharply than those for girls. Among older students who were in the ninth grade in 1992 and the twelfth grade in 1995, overall gambling frequencies and rates of problem gambling remained fairly constant with slight increases for boys and slight decreases for girls.

Similar results were obtained during the 1998 Minnesota school survey which sampled 78,582 students aged 14 to 17 enrolled in grades nine and twelve. This survey found not only that rates of daily gambling were eight times greater among boys than girls and that gambling frequencies were much higher in some ethnic groups (Hispanic, Black, and Native American) than others (Caucasian and Asian). The researcher was particularly concerned by the high frequency of illegal gambling activities by underage youth. Nearly 25 percent of the boys had purchased lottery tickets and ten percent had engaged in casino gambling. Some reported that they gambled in casinos on a regular weekly (4%) or daily (3%) basis.[38]

As will be shown in greater detail in the volume on epidemiology, prevalence rates of problem and pathological gambling in North America are nearly always higher among adolescents and young adults than they are among older adults. It has been estimated, for example, that from 24 percent[39] to 32 percent[40] of the teenagers in some North American locales are regular or heavy gamblers and that 5.7 percent[41] to 6.7 percent[42] and, depending on the criteria used, perhaps even as many as 8.8 percent[43] to 9.5 percent[44] of some adolescent populations are pathological gamblers.[45] However, rates of problem gambling may be even higher in some minority populations. A comparative study of youthful gambling in northern Minnesota reported that 9.6 percent of Native American adolescents exhibited symptoms of pathological gambling as opposed to only 5.6 percent of their non-Indian peers. The Native American adolescents also experienced an earlier onset and greater severity of gambling problems.[46]

Several possible explanations for this phenomenon have been offered. Some researchers have suggested that the higher rates of gambling and probable pathological gambling among youth may be a reflection of the fact that most young people may experiment with gambling in their late teens and early twenties just as they do with alcohol, other drugs, and other adult behaviors but "grow out" of their heavy involvement in these activities as they mature.[47] Conversely, the high rates of problem and pathological gambling that have been reported among adolescents may also be a consequence of the type of gambling screen that is administered. For example, while most adolescent surveys have employed a version of the South Oaks Gambling Screen known as the SOGS-RA,[48] a recent United States national survey of 534 adolescents 16 and 17 years of age employed the newer NORC DSM Screen or NODS. It found that only two percent of these youths could be classified as at-risk gamblers while approximately 1.5 percent were designated as either problem or pathological gamblers. However, the study's authors pointed out that if the adult financial criteria had been omitted from the questionnaire, the percentage of problem and pathological gambling in this sample would have doubled.[49] Likewise, the previously mentioned large adolescent survey in Canada's Atlantic provinces found strikingly different rates of at-risk and probable pathological or problem gambling when they were defined by different criteria. The more conservative or "narrow" SOGS-RA definition identified 3.8 percent as at risk and 2.8 percent as problem gamblers while a less conservative or "broad" definition yielded estimates of 8.2 percent and 6.4 percent, respectively. Here, too, males had much higher rates of at-risk (5.6% narrow; 10.8% broad) and problem gambling (3.5% narrow; 9.6% broad) than females (2.1% narrow, 5.5% broad at-risk; 0.9% narrow, 3.0% broad problem).[50] Of this group, 12 percent met the DSM-IV criteria for pathological gambling.

A study of the attitudes and knowledge of youthful gambling found that many North American parents are relatively unaware of the extent of their children's gambling activities and of the negative consequences they may have.[51] It found that most parents tend to overestimate the age at which their children start gambling, most believe that gambling is a socially acceptable activity, many feel that it is a good recreational activity for families, and a number are convinced that gambling habits develop only in adulthood. Consequently, parents tend to be unconcerned about their children's gambling activities and few make any attempt to control them. These findings suggest that the relaxed attitudes and general lack of knowledge that parents have with respect to their children's gambling behavior may be a important factor in accounting for the high rates problem and pathological gambling among the youth of North America.

Gambling problems among the youth of Europe and elsewhere are also on the rise. Although several studies have reported on the popularity of lotteries among British children and adolescents,[52] only one has investigated the degree of problem gambling associated with this form of gambling. Its authors found that over three-fifths (64%) of British youths between the ages of 11 and 15 played the National Lottery occasionally, nearly half (48%) played regularly, and about one-seventh (14%) played weekly. Substantial proportions were concerned about the amount of money they spend on the lottery (17%) and had developed gambling problems as a result of their participation (6%). This study also found that while most of these children (71%) bought tickets through their parents, some (17%) were able to make their own illegal purchases.[53]

Slot or fruit machine gambling by children and adolescents under the age of 18 in the United Kingdom has been particularly prevalent ever since the 1968 Gaming Act made it legal for them to do so. Since these machines are now freely available in British amusement arcades, cafes, fish and chips shops, youth clubs, sports centers, and pubs, fruit machine gambling has become the most common form of gambling among British school children.[54] As a result, many children of both sexes begin gambling by the age of eight or nine and from 65 percent to 90 percent have gambled by their early teens.[55] Surveys of youthful fruit machine players have reported that as many as 13 percent to 18 percent showed signs of pathological gambling.[56] Over four-fifths (82%) of all adolescent callers to the United Kingdom National Telephone Gambling Helpline report problems with fruit machines.[57] It has also been reported that fruit machine addicts now account for 50 percent of all new members of Gamblers Anonymous in the United Kingdom and that half of these are children and adolescents[58] many of whom claim to have started playing by the age of eleven.[59]

Since they were first legalized in 1986, slot machines in the Netherlands have found their way into bars, snack bars, and canteens as well as amusement arcades where they are available to the adolescents and young adults of that country. Their presence is believed to be responsible for the "explosive" growth in the number of young people who have requested professional help for pathological gambling since that time. Between 1986 and 1987 slot machine addiction accounted for 60 percent of all reported cases of compulsive gambling; 20 percent of all those who sought treatment were between 16 and 20 years of age and half (50%) were below 25.[60] Slot machines are also thought to be responsible for the high rates of pathological gambling among children and adolescents in Spain which also exceed those of adults.[61] A study of problem gambling among electronic gaming machine (EGM) players in Australia found "A significant relationship between age and pathological machine gambling . . . with the younger age groups more likely to develop an EGM gambling problem."[62] These findings, which appear to confirm the **availability and exposure** and **age of initiation hypotheses**, have prompted investigators to undertake research intended to test these and other hypotheses.

A Review of Gambling Among American Youth

The first comprehensive review of the literature on teen age gambling in the United States was undertaken by psychologist Durand Jacobs.[63] Jacobs' review focused on six different published and unpublished studies of students (grades 9 through 12) attending 14 high schools in the four states of California, Connecticut, New Jersey, and Virginia. Altogether 2,777 students were administered similar questionnaires which elicited information on demographic background, stressful life experiences, and psychological adjustment. A final section asked questions concerning the respondents' history of, initial reactions to, and extent of involvement with gambling, chemical substance use, and overeating. All respondents were rated on their potential for addiction.

The studies Jacobs reviewed, all of which were conducted between 1984 and 1988, reported that Americans tend to start gambling at an early age. Roughly a third (from 27% to 41% percent; median 36%) of the students sampled had gambled for money before the age of 11 while over four-fifths (70% to 88%; median 82%) had done so before the age of 15. More than half of the students surveyed claimed to have gambled within the past 12 months. In terms of their gambling preferences, the largest proportion (45%) played card games with their family and friends; a nearly equal proportion (43%) had played state lotteries; over one-third (34%) had bet on games of skill such as pool, bowling, etc.; and nearly one-third (30%) had engaged in sports betting. Other kinds of gambling were bingo (played by 22% of the sample), dice games (not in a casino; 16%), horse and dog track betting (13%), numbers games with a bookie (9%), casino gambling (8%), commercial card rooms (4%) and jai-alai (2%).[64] Ironically, it is illegal for minors under the age of 18 to gamble in all the states in which these surveys were conducted.

Jacobs felt that youthful gambling is not a harmless pastime. On the basis of their responses, from four to six percent of these high school students, about three times the adult average of 1.4 percent, were classified as pathological gamblers according to DSM-III criteria.[65] One-fifth of those who gambled indicated that their gambling was either "out of control" or that they would like to quit but could not. From two to 12 percent had sought out Gamblers Anonymous or professional treatment for their gambling problems. Thirteen percent admitted having committing illegal acts to obtain gambling money or pay gambling debts and 12 percent said that their gambling had damaged family relationships.

Whereas children of alcoholic parents have been the subjects numerous studies, Jacobs broke new ground when he investigated the problems experienced by adolescent children of problem gamblers. Of 844 high school students sampled, 52 reported having at least one parent who was a problem gambler. Compared to their peers, the children of problem gamblers demonstrated a distinct array of psychosocial correlates: as a group they experienced a greater involvement with overeating, a higher degree of emotional dysphoria, a lower quality of life, twice the frequency of suicide attempts, and higher rates of tobacco, alcohol, and other drug use. Moreover, the incidence of parental divorce was twice as high among this group as among the others.

Although Jacobs initiated some highly innovative research and presented some valuable descriptive data, he was unable to escape the temptation to force his data into the procrustean beds of the **tension-reduction** and **family systems models**. On the basis of his findings he proposed a link between problem gambling parents and an elevated risk for dysfunctional behaviors among their children. However, Jacobs read more into his analysis than the data warranted when he went on to surmise that the parents turn to gambling and other potentially addictive behaviors in a maladaptive attempt to cope with the stresses and problems they are otherwise unable to face. This hypothesized parental stress was then presumed to have adverse effects upon the children which would, in turn, lead them down the path to addiction:

> What is suggested by these findings are intergenerational effects wrought by highly stressed, preoccupied, inconsistent, and often absent parents who have provided seriously flawed parenting, sex, social, and occupational role models for their children. The results of this study indicate that deficiencies in the home life of children [of problem gamblers] become evident among such youths by their greater involvement in a number of potentially addictive health threatening behaviors, coupled with a consistent pattern of inadequate stress management and inferior coping skills.
>
> One cannot resist the conclusion that without early and competent intervention, children of problem gamblers: (a) will be seriously disadvantaged when attempting to solve their present and future problems of living, and (b) as a consequence are themselves high risk candidates for developing one or another form of dysfunctional behavior, including an addictive pattern of behavior.[66]

His conclusions led Jacobs to recommend an ambitious array of prevention measures intended to reduce the incidence of gambling and pathological gambling among America's youth. He suggested that a comprehensive
prevention program involving public education, self-evaluation, the teaching
of social and coping skills, problem-solving strategies, and stress management should be instituted for all children before they enter junior high
school. A pilot program which incorporated many of these suggestions was,
in fact, tested among Canadian high school students in Quebec. However,
contrary to Jacobs' aspirations, the results were disappointing. Although the
students' general knowledge of gambling and its consequences increased
dramatically after its presentation, a follow-up study six months later found
that their attitudes, behaviors, and skills surrounding their own gambling
remained essentially unchanged. Furthermore, none could recall any of the
coping skills they had been taught.[67]

Critique. Jacobs' ideas thus appear to have been tempered more by his
own theoretical convictions as a psychologist and his public policy biases as
a prevention advocate than by the logical conclusions of his findings. In the
first place, such sweeping generalizations about the causes and consequences
of problem gambling were not at all justified by his data, particularly since
they were based on a sample size of only 52. In the second place, he failed
to realize that experimental drinking, drug use, and risk taking among adolescents are not inexorably precipitated by the need to manage stress and do
not inevitably lead to addiction. At best his findings merely suggested some
interesting hypotheses which require a great deal of further testing. It is
therefore to his credit that Jacobs recommended the initiation of longitudinal
studies designed to identify precisely which environmental circumstances are
the direct causes of dysfunctional adolescent behavior.[68] It would not be
unreasonable to suggest that such studies should also attempt to determine
precisely which sorts of adolescent behavioral responses are directly attrib-
utable to problem gambling in the parental generation as opposed to other
intra- or extra-familial influences such as overprotective parents, rebellious-
ness, social learning, and peer pressure.

Reviews of Gambling Among British Youth

Since many studies of youthful gambling are designed to obtain little more
than prevalence rates, they tend to present statistics which are largely
descriptive rather than correlational. Thus, through their reviews of the published and unpublished literature on gambling among the youth of Great
Britain, Sue Fisher[69] and Mark Griffiths[70] found that estimates by various
researchers of the number of young people who play arcade machines one

or more times a week ranged from six percent to 37 percent and averaged around 25 percent. Estimates of those who play most frequently (at least four times a week), ranged from two percent to five percent and averaged 3.5 percent. Although these figures represent a substantial number of the nation's youth, Fisher rightfully insists that the frequency of gambling alone "does not automatically imply negative consequences."[71] Instead, amusement arcades and the gambling that takes place in them may constitute important points of social interest in Britain's adolescent subculture.[72]

Overall gambling expenditures may provide a more realistic appraisal of the incidence of problem gambling among children than the frequencies with which they play arcade machines. Fisher's own research revealed that children can feed from £30 to £60 ($55.50 to $111 US; £1 = $1.85 US) into a machine during each hour of continuous play.[73] It is important to note that this represents the total amount played or the "handle" and not the amount lost which is an entirely different measure: those who win more than they lose can put this much money into a machine and still come out ahead.[74] An investigation of all forms of gambling among adolescents 13 and 14 years of age reported that boys spent an average of £38.45 while girls spent an average of £9.52 per year on these activities. The highest amount reported was £260 per year.[75] Another study which asked its youthful respondents how much money they spent on fruit machines per week found that 71 percent spent less than £1, 17 percent spent from £1 to £2, and 12 percent spent over £2.[76] Unfortunately, this study failed to indicate how many spent more than these amounts or precisely how much more. Several of the studies Fisher reviewed reported a strong correlation between the frequency of gambling and the amount of money spent per session.[77] One of these, for example, found that 15 percent of those who played once a week or more (22% of the sample) spent more than £3 per session while ten percent spent £5. In contrast, 33 percent of those who played four or more times a week spent over £10 per session or nearly £50 per week on gambling.[78] In relative terms, one study reported that 35 percent of all fruit machine players spent only a "very small proportion" of their money on gambling while 40 percent spent half or more of their income in this way.[79] Again, no information was presented on precisely what proportion of their incomes the heaviest gamblers spent. A more recent survey of 26 dependent (addicted) and 41 non-dependent fruit machine players reported that the machine addicts gambled an average of 5.5 times per week and spent an average of £66 while the latter played three times and spent only about £5 each week.[80]

To obtain the money they use for gambling some young people exhibit behaviors which are indicative of incipient to severe gambling problems. Among those that have been reported are borrowing money, obtaining money from strangers by selling one's knowledge of the machines, using school lunch money, truancy, theft, the sale of possessions including those of others, and drug dealing.[81] Similar activities are also known to occur among North American adolescents.[82] Griffiths' research among young fruit machine players revealed that 12 percent of those he interviewed as they were leaving an amusement arcade admitted that they had stolen gambling money;[83] a later survey by Fisher[84] revealed that fully 21 percent of regular arcade visitors had stolen money or used their school lunch or transportation money to play fruit machines. In her review Fisher acknowledged that while all of these behaviors may occur in contexts that are unrelated to gambling, she felt that they may be symptomatic of excessive involvement if children engage in them for the purpose of playing these machines. She added that since the actual degree to which these and similar behaviors may occur in the general population is not yet known, further research will be required to determine their true extent. However, criminal justice statistics indicate that four percent of all juvenile thefts are known to be directly related to machine gambling.[85]

Mark Griffiths[86] later found that the heaviest fruit machine players spend *all* their money on them. His initial survey of 50 adolescent fruit machine players was the first to provide any estimate of the prevalence of pathological gambling in this population. He found that fully 18 percent of the sample were pathological gamblers according to standard medical (DSM-III-R) criteria.[87] All had started gambling at an earlier age than the others (9.2 vs. 11.3 years), they now played the machines at every opportunity, and they regularly spent all the money they had on them. Their funding sources included any money they had earned through full- or part-time employment, money they had received as Christmas and birthday gifts, school lunch money, and any money they could borrow from friends or steal from their parents; all had accrued gambling debts and had missed school or work to play the machines.[88] Although most nonaddicted and all addicted fruit machine players in his sample were males who started playing significantly earlier in life, Griffiths judiciously suggested that age and gender may or may not be causative factors in the development of pathological gambling.

One of the studies Fisher reviewed included a functional analysis of amusement arcades along with its statistical description.[89] For British youth, the amusement arcade serves an important social function by providing a place for them to gather away from the vigilant eyes of their parents and other adult authority figures. Thus, it not only offers the thrill of gambling, but also provides an arena for engaging in such adult activities such as smoking, flirting with members of the opposite sex, and similar daring exploratory behaviors in a relatively nonthreatening social environment. The physical environment is not so innocuous, however, since illegal and risky activities such as fighting, drug dealing, the fencing of stolen goods, requests to steal, and solicitations for other illegal activities occur often enough to lend an air of intrigue and danger to the surroundings. Even the perception that going to an arcade might be hazardous adds to their allure. Fisher contended that since the actual extent of these potential hazards are unknown, further research into the safety of the arcade environment is warranted.

Although some investigators believe gambling-related delinquency to be minimal,[90] the results of studies intended to determine the extent of stealing, for example, are few and inconclusive. One reported a significant relationship between the amounts of money spent on gambling machines, frequencies of play, and the propensity to steal. Specifically, it found that only four percent of those who play once a month or less or who play £1 or less have stolen to play, while 38 percent of those who play at least four times a week and 25 percent of those who spend an average of £5 to £10 per session have stolen. Fully 67 percent of the children who spend more than £10 per session have stolen money for gambling purposes.[91] Interestingly, irrespective of how much they spend on gambling, those who play in such places as cafes and fish and chips shops are more likely to steal to fund their habit than those who play in amusements arcades. A study of 100 delinquent males at a youth correctional facility found that 60 percent played fruit machines on a regular basis and that 23 percent of them had stolen money to finance their gambling.[92] Other studies have reported that three percent to eight percent of their respective samples of children who were not confined had admitted to stealing in order to gamble.[93] One study reported that some young people have also resorted to drug pushing and prostitution for the specific purpose of financing a fruit machine habit.[94]

Interestingly, Griffiths[95] cited several United States studies which found that arcade video games are also potentially addictive and that some children who play them exhibit some of the behavioral symptoms of drug and gambling addictions including theft, the use of school lunch money, truancy, etc., to support this habit.[96] Others have found that the frequency of visits to nongambling video arcades is significantly correlated with the frequencies of gambling, pathological gambling, missing school to gamble, and the use of tobacco and other drugs.[97] The previously mentioned survey of British delinquents at a youth correctional facility also found that 60 percent of the sample played video games on a regular basis and that 21.7 percent of them had stolen money to do so.[98] Griffiths himself encountered and described a young pinball machine player who met six of the nine (DSM-III-R) criteria for dependency.[99] He suggested[100] that a possible explanation for video game and fruit machine addiction might be found in Amsel's **frustration theory** which postulates that persistence derives from frustration over the failure to achieve a seemingly attainable goal.[101]

Since most young people frequent the amusement arcades to socialize with their friends as well to play the machines, and since playing them is largely a social event, playing alone may also be symptomatic of a gambling problem. The extent of normative arcade involvement for most young people is, according to one study,[102] established by the peer group and any involvement which threatens to exceed the preestablished limitation tends to be discouraged by social pressures. There are some loners, however, who are not part of a group and whose involvement is therefore not checked by peer influences. As many as 24 percent of the boys and from ten percent to 17 percent of the girls in some samples were solitary players.[103] While this in itself does not constitute conclusive evidence of a gambling addiction, the latter study found a positive correlation among frequency of play, the amount of money staked, and playing alone.

A United Kingdom National Survey: Fruit Machines and Lottery Scratchcards

Fisher's own later (1997) and much larger survey of 9,774 British adolescents between the ages of 12 and 15 not only replicated a number of earlier findings but also made some new contributions to our understanding of adolescent gambling.[104] The **gender hypothesis** was supported by her finding that nearly twice as many pathological gamblers were male (65%) as were female (35%).[105] She also reported that far more of those identified as pathological gamblers also had higher rates of tobacco, alcohol, and other illegal drug use, and claimed to feel bad about their use, than did other children. Not surprisingly, they were also more likely than others to have played fruit machines or made lottery purchases on three or more days of the previous week.[106] Moreover, the parents of problem gamblers were more likely to be gamblers, to gamble more than their children thought they should, to demonstrate a lack of concern or voice approval regarding their children's gambling whether legal or illegal, and to purchase lottery tickets with their children.[107]

Those identified as pathological gamblers were also significantly more likely than others to engage in other illegal or dishonest behaviors. Because of their gambling they were more likely to misuse their school transportation or lunch money, to engage in truancy, to steal from family members and others, to "fall out" with their family and lie to them, to spend more on gambling than intended, to sell their possessions to gamble or pay gambling debts, to borrow money, and to have spent more than £10 in a single day on gambling. However, her study revealed that pathological gamblers were more likely than others to engage in dishonest behaviors that were *not relat-*

ed to gambling. Specifically, she found that problem gamblers were significantly more likely to misuse their school transportation or lunch money to steal from family and nonfamily for reasons other than gambling.[108]

Fisher also found that National Lottery scratchcards have become the second most popular form of commercial gambling for this age group despite the fact that their sale to minors under 16 years of age is prohibited by law. The idea that fruit machines are the most popular form of gambling among young people and that they pose the greatest risk for gambling problems were confirmed when she found that three-quarters (75%) of her subjects had played them and that nearly two-thirds of those identified as pathological gamblers were addicted to fruit machines. However, 47 percent of those sampled had purchased scratchcards with their own money and 40 percent had used their own money to purchase National Lottery Draw tickets.

She suggested that when the National Lottery was instituted it "tapped into the existing market for youth fruit machine gambling"[109] by exploiting the gambling proclivities of regular players. If this were indeed the case, she ventured, there should be substantial overlap between those identified as pathological fruit machine gamblers and those identified as pathological lottery players, especially those who bought scratchcards. Her analysis revealed that of the 5.6 percent identified as pathological gamblers, 62 percent (3.4% of the entire sample) had problems with fruit machines. It also revealed that 17 percent of the pathological gamblers (3.4% of the sample) reported problems with National Lottery scratchcards and 21 percent (1% of the sample) claimed to have problems with both fruit machines and scratchcards.[110] Fisher interpreted these findings as support for her hypothesis, a variant of the **availability and exposure hypothesis** and suggested that "the National Lottery has, to date, directly increased the estimated prevalence of problem gambling among British youth by some 18 percent."[111] She also found that while most children watch the weekly televised lottery draw with their parents or other family members, those who were identified as pathological scratchcard players were significantly more likely than others to watch these broadcasts alone. She judiciously acknowledged that while these observations do not constitute proof of a causal relationship between lottery advertising and problem gambling in children, they do justify the need for further research in this area.[112]

Fisher further tested the **availability and exposure hypothesis** by comparing the rate of pathological gambling in seaside locations to the national rate. She made this comparison since most of the amusement arcades are located in seaside communities where, by implication, fruit machines are more readily accessible to children. This hypothesis received additional confirmation by her finding that the prevalence of problem gambling was 44 percent higher among children living in seaside communities than it was nationally.[113]

Scratchcard Gambling Among Adolescent Boys in the United Kingdom

Psychologist Mark Griffiths[114] conducted a less extensive investigation of scratchcard gambling among 204 boys ranging in age from 11 to 16 years attending two secondary schools in the United Kingdom. However, his sample was clearly not representative of the general adolescent population of the United Kingdom since it was not only limited to males, but it was also composed largely of ethnic minorities of Afro-Caribbean and Asian ancestry having low socioeconomic status. Nevertheless, he found that 55 percent of his respondents had played scratchcards since their introduction less than three years earlier in 1995. Although 16 is the legal age for purchasing scratchcards, 42.2 percent of the entire sample had made their own purchases. This meant that 38 percent were able to purchase these cards illegally. Griffiths identified those who bought their own cards as "gamblers." Of this group, 44 percent spent between £2 and £5 per week, six percent spent between £6 and £15, and 3.5 percent spent more than £15 per week on them; 15 percent admitted that they had broken the law to obtain money for scratchcards.

The rate of pathological gambling among this sample of adolescents was nearly five times higher than the estimated national rate of one percent. Nearly five percent (4.9%) of the entire sample and twelve percent (11.6%) of those identified as gamblers met the DSM-IV criteria for pathological gambling by scoring four or more positive responses. Another 18.1 percent of the sample and 43 percent of the gamblers scored between one and three. Thus, nearly three-fifths (57.8%) of the entire sample but only one-fifth (19.1%) of those identified as gamblers exhibited no signs of problem gambling.

Like Fisher, Griffiths also found significant relationships between the gambling habits of his subjects and those of their parents. Adolescent boys whose parents regularly bought scratchcards were not only more likely to buy scratchcards themselves, but they were also more likely to meet the DSM-IV criteria for pathological gambling. However, he also found that those who played scratchcards with friends were more likely to experience gambling problems than those who played alone or with family members.

Describing scratchcards as "paper fruit machines,"[115] Griffiths attributed their strong appeal to a combination of **behavioral** and **cognitive psychological** elements inherent in the structural characteristics of this form of gambling. In the first place, scratchcards have a short "event frequency." That is, the payout interval is short since the time between the purchase of a winning ticket and payment of the prize is only a matter of seconds. Because it represents a continuous form of gambling, any winnings can be bet again almost immediately since replay intervals are determined only by the amount of time it takes to scratch the covering from the face of a card. Consequently, the period of loss is also so short that financial costs are given little consideration. Because the rewards are presented intermittently, continued play is reinforced on a variable-ratio schedule. In the second place, scratchcards are printed to insure a higher occurrence of "near misses" than chance alone would allow and, as noted in the first volume of this series, nearly winning can be just as reinforcing as actually winning. They have therefore been described as "heartstoppers" owing to the high level of excitement that is generated by the illusion of almost winning a large prize.[116] Griffiths felt that because it incorporates this combination of structural characteristics, "it is not hard to see how scratchcard gambling could become a repetitive habit."[117]

He further speculated that pathological scratchcard gambling could also be a consequence of sociological influences. It could either represent a temporary fad or, owing to the greater **availability** and wider social acceptance of gambling now than in the past, it could reflect a **cohort effect** with today's youngsters holding different attitudes toward gambling than their elders. He insisted, however, that neither possibility can be accepted in the absence of longitudinal research designed to track rates of problem scratchcard gambling over time and assess its long-term effects. Like Fisher, he also suggested that further research be undertaken to determine whether or not there is, indeed, an association between fruit machine and scratchcard gambling.

Adolescents, Video Games, and Dysfunctional Families

R. I. F. Brown and Seonaid Robertson[118] administered a questionnaire survey to 380 Scottish school children and adolescents from 11 to 18 years of age in an attempt to discover what relationships, if any, exist among home computer game playing, arcade video game playing and slot machine playing. The ten-page questionnaire they developed included a battery of questions on leisure time activities as well as a standard Addiction Involvement Scale. The project was inspired by a preliminary study which revealed that 11.1 percent of a smaller sample (n=134) of children from 12 to 16 years of age who played video games often played until their money was gone and often borrowed money to continue to play. Brown and Robertson interpreted these results as evidence that "a sizeable percentage of the general population of school children may have a significant addiction to video gaming alone."[119] This suggested the possibility that video games might act as a "gateway or precursor"[120] to addictive slot machine gambling.[121]

The researchers observed several general demographic trends in their study population. They found, for example, that boys tend to play more than girls, that those who play only gambling games tend to be younger than those who play only video games, and among those who play only gambling games, fewer are from skilled working class or entrepreneurial backgrounds than from other socioeconomic groups.

They also found significant differences among various categories of players in terms of the amounts of time spent in playing these games. Those who began to play these games at an earlier age spend a much greater proportion of their free time in these activities, and engage in them for longer periods per session, than do those who started later. Analysis revealed that the average age at which adolescents began playing each type of game was ten years. Of particular interest is the finding that those who began to play all types of games before this age are those who now spend the greatest amount of leisure time playing gambling machines. Those in this category spend nearly three-quarters (71%) of their free time playing slot machines while those who started after the age of ten spend little more than one-tenth (10.6%) of their spare time on them.

In general, those who play home computer games, those who play alone, and those who began playing at an earlier age also tend to spend far greater amounts of free time than others at these activities. More specifically, those who have access to home computer games spend much more of their free time playing them than they do in playing video and gambling games outside the home. They also spend more time playing these games than do their peers who play video or slot machine games exclusively outside the home. Lone players also tend to spend more time on these games than those who play socially. For example, those with home computers who play alone spend nearly half (49.7%) of their free time playing these games while those who play with friends spend less than one-fifth (18.8%) of their free time on this activity. Likewise, those who play video arcade games alone also spend over twice as much time on them (53%) as those who play in groups (25%). However, when they are playing video games outside the home, those who enjoy playing all types of games in groups spend more than five times as long per playing session than those who play outside video games alone. This suggested to the researchers that video game playing outside the home is primarily a social activity.

Brown and Robertson stressed that their primary concern in conducting their research was not with whether adolescents can become addicted gamblers nor with the extent of adolescent addiction since these phenomena are already well-documented. However, results of the Addiction Involvement Scale confirmed that children and adolescents can, indeed, become addicted to nongambling electronic games since the scores of at least some of those who played computer and arcade video games exclusively were as high as those of addicted drinkers, gamblers, and overeaters.

They also stressed that their findings are so far preliminary since a detailed multivariate analysis of their data has not yet been undertaken. Nevertheless, another concern was to attempt to find evidence of a relationship between the playing of electronic video games and the fruit machines that are available to children in the United Kingdom. They felt that the information they gathered so far allowed them to propose a developmental scheme in which television and video games can lead to problem fruit machine gambling:

> Young machine-gambling addicts will be found to have vulnerability to video and computer games as well as to gambling, probably previous to their involvement with gambling machines; and these vulnerabilities spring from a common base in an attachment to electronic video devices formed at an early critical period when the young child was left in the company of a television as its major stimulus and companion for a long period of time.
>
> It is suggested that the vulnerability is first produced when the young child, at a critical point in its development, spends long periods with television as its main stimulus or sole company, or when it finds the figures on television more encouraging and less hostile and intrusive than its parents. The television becomes a caretaker and/or a companion figure, and a positive attachment is developed to it. This builds in a familiar precedent or template for later relationships with electronic robot figures. So these figures become one of the child's preferred caretaker/attachment figures.[122]

Brown and Robertson ultimately traced the origin of problem machine gambling among contemporary youth to childhood social deprivations wrought by dysfunctional family environments. They argued that in the absence of positive parental caregiving, children will develop an attachment to electronic gaming devices, the only company they know, which serves as a surrogate mother. They further suggested that under such circumstances very young children will first be attracted to passive television viewing. Later, due to their preconditioned involvement with the video screen, they will progress to interactive video games. To support this highly conjectural scenario, the authors invoked Harry Harlow's well-known studies of juvenile rhesus monkeys that preferred contact with cloth-wrapped mother figures over bare wire effigies, presumably in an effort to satisfy their innate need for social contact. Like Harlow's monkeys, then, "The vulnerable gambler-to-be, deprived of real human relationships with their healthy mix of security/comfort and stimulations, satisfies these needs in attachment to robot figures and especially to the most lifelike."[123] Finally, in the continual maladaptive quest to satisfy their thwarted needs for satisfactory human relationships, these neglected children will graduate to gambling machines with their more powerful monetary reinforcements. In this way "the television orphan has become the gambling machine addict."[124]

Critique. Like Fenichel, Bergler, Galdston, and so many other psychoanalytical theorists of a bygone era, Brown and Robertson argued that pathological machine gambling stems from an unfulfilled longing for parental love and attachment. Obviously, like the earlier psychoanalytic approaches, this explanation is highly procrustean since it also attempts to fit a very limited body of data into a preexisting mold, that of family systems theory, which, as of this writing, is enjoying an extremely high but perhaps undeserved degree of popularity. Although the data the researchers did present may have been entirely valid and highly useful in describing certain behavioral characteristics of a particular population, their unwarranted theoretical explanation appeared to draw more support from inferences based on the principles of imitative magic and the doctrinaire precepts of pop psychology than from any empirical data. Its authors presented no information about the respective home environments of their different types of subjects since they have absolutely no factual knowledge of this: they merely presumed to have these insights. Furthermore, the world of "high tech" amusements is highly appealing to children from all family backgrounds. Nevertheless, the authors implied that it not possible for children from loving and caring families to become preoccupied with television, video games, or gambling machines but once again they offered no concrete evidence of this. Clearly, far more substantial research will be required before their ideas can be seriously entertained, much less accepted. Fortunately, the authors themselves appeared to be aware of this fact.

Children, Video Games, and Intermittent Reinforcement Schedules

Because the hypothetical connection between video game playing and gambling had not yet been established, Rina Gupta and Jeffrey Derevensky[125] set out to test the **gateway hypothesis**. The ideas and methods they adopted in formulating their study were drawn heavily from psychological learning and cognitive theories. They first noted that excessive video game playing has a number of features in common with other addictions. Not only is there a strong learning component but, like many gamblers, many video game enthusiasts report that they experience both excitement and stress relief from these activities. Thus, video games can also serve to reduce the intensity of certain drive states. Nevertheless, the most compelling feature of many commercial video games, the investigators maintained, lies in the variable-ratio reinforcement schedules that are programmed into them. Video games typically involve randomly placed hazards which players learn to avoid during a series of trials. Such "addictive" reinforcement schedules which are extremely powerful in establishing and sustaining repetitive behaviors are little different from those of gambling games. Like the fruit machines which adjoin them in British amusement arcades, video games are further reinforced through their intense visual and auditory stimuli, their fast action, and the immediate feedback they provide.

The purpose of their research was to test the hypothesis that video games, owing to the sense of control they impart to players, may serve as a precursor to other forms of gambling. Their study was designed to compare the perceptions and behaviors of high and low frequency video game players. Specifically, the investigators focused on their subjects' risk-taking strategies, attributions of skill, and the degree to which they recognize the element of chance in video games and in an actual gambling situation. While gambling games provide merely an illusion of control, the interactive nature of video games offers a strong degree of actual control which permits a player's performance to improve as each new challenge is overcome. They therefore suggested that playing skill, which is acquired through familiarity and experience, "establishes a sense of mastery as randomness turns into order."[126] Because most children and adolescents would lack sophisticated problem-solving abilities and have little awareness of the laws of probability, Gupta and Derevensky therefore predicted that when these youngsters enter into a gambling situation they take with them the same sense of control that video games have instilled. If so, then the more experienced video game players could be expected to have a false sense of confidence which would inspire them to gamble more frequently and to take greater risks than their less experienced peers.

To test this hypothesis Gupta and Derevensky recruited 104 Montreal school children and adolescents between nine and 14 years of age (51 males; 53 females) who were judged to be either low or high frequency video game players. Low frequency players (n=55) were required to play video games no more than two days per week and a maximum of one hour per session while high frequency players (n=49) were required to play no less than five days a week and a minimum of 1.5 hours per session. All subjects were first administered a questionnaire designed to elicit their perceptions, attitudes, and behaviors with respect to gambling and video game playing. Their gambling behavior was then observed and recorded as they played a computerized blackjack game with an initial imaginary stake of $100. As an incentive they were offered a chance to win movie certificates.

Video game behavior. Analysis of the questionnaire data revealed that, overall, the subjects perceived video games as requiring more skill than luck. Nevertheless, over half (54%) of them believed that video games involved at least some luck. High frequency video game players of both genders were significantly more likely to visit amusement arcades than low frequency players although high frequency males visited them significantly more often than high frequency females. High frequency players believed themselves to be more skillful than low frequency players but they also expressed a desire to be even more skillful. Both low and high frequency males considered themselves to be more skillful and expressed a desire to attain even higher levels of skill than their female counterparts.

Gambling behavior. Most (70%) of the sample reported past gambling activities and a many (53%) gambled at least once a week. High frequency video game players of both genders were significantly more likely to have gambled in the past and to currently gamble once a week or more than were low frequency players. Although high frequency males were no more likely to have ever gambled than low frequency males, they were two and one-half times more likely to be weekly gamblers (63% vs. 25%). Twice as many high than low frequency females had ever gambled but five and one-half times as many high frequency females were weekly gamblers (55% vs. 10%). No significant differences emerged between high frequency males and females or between low frequency males and females in either their past or current gambling behavior.

Skill and luck attributions. Likewise, most (70%) of the subjects believed that gambling involves a great deal of luck while many (56%) believed that it also involves a great deal of skill. However, far more (87%) believed that it involves at least some skill. The researchers contended that these findings demonstrate that despite their realization that luck is an important factor in gambling, most of their subjects held to the illusion that skill is also important in gambling.

Perceptions of gambling skill. No differences in self-perceptions of gambling skill emerged between either males and females or between high and low frequency video game players. However, the high frequency players expressed a greater desire for improved gambling skills. Moreover, significantly more high than low frequency video game players (23% vs. 7%) indicated that gambling made them feel more important.

Largest wagers. With respect to the largest amount of money ever risked at once, no significant differences appeared between high and low frequency players. When these data were analyzed by gender there were also no differences between high and low frequency males but high frequency females wagered significantly larger amounts on average than their low frequency peers ($5 vs. $2).

Gambling motivations. The reasons given for gambling were enjoyment (74%), excitement (49%), to pass time (25%), to win money (22%), and for peer approval (1%). Although no other gender differences emerged, significantly more males (30%) than females (19%) gambled for excitement. Interestingly, far more of those who gambled (47%) than those who did not (10%) indicated that they played video games for excitement.

Experimental gambling. Observations of the subjects behavior during the blackjack test revealed that, in terms of their gross wagers, high frequency video game players risked significantly more money on average than low frequency players ($493 vs. $381.20). Table 9-1 reveals that this pattern was particularly strong among males but not females among whom low frequency players wagered more than high frequency players. Although high frequency males wagered nearly twice that of high frequency females, low frequency males and females wagered nearly identical amounts overall.

Table 9-1. AVERAGE GROSS WAGERS BY VIDEO GAME PLAYERS[127]

	Males	*Females*
High Frequency	$607.07	$355.86
Low Frequency	$387.54	$377.13

No significant differences emerged in gross winnings between high and low frequency players until the data were broken down by gender. High frequency males won significantly more than low frequency males ($292.83 vs. $191.35) while low frequency females won more than high frequency females ($176.66 vs. $149.54) although this difference was not significant. Subjects in all categories ended up losing more than their original stake.

Interpretation. In summary, although these findings reaffirmed that males are more likely to gamble than females, they also demonstrate that high frequency video game players of both genders gamble more often and report that gambling makes them feel more important than low frequency players. Interestingly, high frequency female video game players were not only more likely to be gamblers than low frequency males, but they were also more likely to be weekly gamblers. High frequency females also risked greater amounts of money than their low frequency peers. Although high frequency players and all males took greater risks while gambling, they were no more successful at it than low frequency players and females. Thus, although they perceive gambling as involving a certain degree of skill, they exhibit less caution while gambling.

Gupta and Derevensky therefore claimed that these findings established a firm link between video game playing and gambling in children. Specifically, they concluded that the frequency of video game playing is directly related to greater risk taking while gambling, particularly among males. Success at video games, over which players have a relatively high degree of control, imparts a sense of confidence and security which carries over into the gambling situation. Thus, the belief that gambling makes them feel important may encourage high frequency players to gamble. The belief that they can exercise the same degree of control over gambling situations that they do over video games may then encourage them to assume greater risks. In the investigators' own words,

> This illusion of control suggests that the players' cognitions may be driven by intermittent schedules of reinforcement in the game, similar to those found in video games. More specifically, since the players are expecting reinforcement to occur at any time, when it finally does occur, they believe has something to do with their ability to control outcomes, despite the number of times reinforcement did not take place. It appears as though they get so caught up in the excitement of the game (physiological arousal) that their ability to think rationally is lost.[128]

Critique. This initial empirical study appears to have established a genuine link between video game playing and gambling. However, its sample size renders its findings highly tentative and, as a consequence, they cannot be considered conclusive in the absence of further confirmation. Moreover, the nature of the link that was proposed remains highly speculative, as the authors themselves acknowledged when they wrote, "It should be noted that causality cannot be established from this study [since] it still remains unclear whether experience with video-games leads one to gamble or whether both activities attract the same children due to their shared properties."[129] Indeed, people were gambling and experiencing gambling-related problems long before the appearance of video games. Nevertheless, this study provides a firm basis for some highly warranted additional research in this area. Gupta and Derevensky[130] suggested not only that similar studies of children should involve different forms of gambling, but also that the issue of causation will be resolved only through longitudinal studies.

Chapter 10

SPECIAL POPULATIONS: FEMALE, ELDERLY, AND NATIVE NORTH AMERICAN GAMBLERS

GAMBLING AND PROBLEM GAMBLING AMONG WOMEN

A Feminist Perspective

Henry Lesieur and Sheila Blume[1] were among the first gambling researchers to turn their attention to gambling problems among women. In his first descriptive study of 50 female GA members from throughout the United States, Lesieur[2] reported on a number of their background characteristics. Alcoholism was far more common in the parental generation than was compulsive gambling (28% of his subjects reported an alcoholic father and 10% an alcoholic mother; 10% reported a compulsive gambling father and 4% a compulsive gambling mother). Relatively few (16%) had never married, nearly one-third (30%) were divorced or separated, one (2%) was widowed, and over half (52%) were currently married. Of those who had ever married, many had husbands who had problems themselves: 16 percent of the husbands were pathological gamblers, 28 percent alcoholics, eight percent drug addicts, eight percent mentally ill, ten percent "womanizers," and 18 percent were "workaholics." Nearly half (44%) of these women suffered chronic loneliness due to the fact that their husbands' jobs kept them away from home. Nearly one-third (29%), most of whom were married to alcoholics, lived in a physically or sexually abusive relationship. Over half claimed that they began to gamble as a means of escape from their lonely, discordant, and abusive relationships. All (100%) of these women were initially attracted to gambling because of the "action" it offered. In fact, many of the women they interviewed found the need to stay "in action" so intense that they would go for days without sleeping or eating and get up to relieve themselves when they could no longer avoid it.

These women revealed a somewhat different gambling pattern than is common among men. Most prefer legal types of gambling such as cards, slot and video poker machines, horse race betting, and lotteries. Men, who prefer horse racing, sports betting, and dice games, are far less concerned about their legality.[3] Like all pathological gamblers, women go through several phases in the development of their gambling careers. Despite their tendency to favor legalized forms of gambling, fully 68 percent of the women sampled had engaged in illegal activities to support their gambling habit. Women are more likely to engage in check forgery, embezzlement, operating small-time card games, running "con games," and prostitution to support their gambling habit than men who prefer theft, embezzlement, tax evasion, tax fraud, "hustling," and fencing stolen goods. Far more women (70%) than men (24%) had sought professional help for their problem before joining GA.

Many of the women surveyed had a number of other problems in addition to their gambling difficulties. Over one-quarter (26%) experienced serious depression or had attempted suicide (12%) even before they started gambling. Many experienced other addictive problems: nearly half (48%) were either substance abusers or drug addicts, nearly one-quarter (24%) were compulsive spenders, one-fifth (20%) were compulsive overeaters, and some (12%) were sexually addicted. The symptoms of paranoia described by one-quarter of the sample (26%) may have been related to their fear of retribution by various creditors or to their drug abuse. Similar findings have been reported by others.[4]

Lesieur and Blume later found that although nearly all (93% to 98%) who seek treatment in Gamblers Anonymous are male, epidemiological surveys have demonstrated that about one-third of all potential and probable pathological gamblers in the United States are females.[6] This means that "women who have gambling problems are a chronically underserved group."[7] One reason for this, they suggested, is the prevalence of the stereotypical but socially acceptable "Damon Runyon" image of the gambler as a flashy, well-dressed, big spending male. Because female gamblers do not fit this colorful image, they are stigmatized. Lesieur and Blume reported that, as a rule, female compulsive gamblers are more likely to be clandestine loners than group participants who gamble openly. Those who have joined Gamblers Anonymous are also more likely to be single, separated, or divorced than their male counterparts and, hence, have fewer social supports available to them.

Adopting a feminist perspective, Lesieur and Blume attributed pathological gambling among women primarily to its ability to reduce the overwhelming problems and tremendous stresses that are unique to women and which they routinely encounter in their daily lives. They cited evidence that depression is more common among women than men in general, that because women feel more responsible for the welfare of others they become more distressed and concerned than men over the problems of family members and friends, and that they experience higher levels of overall life stress than men. They contended that many of these problems can be traced to sexist attitudes that prevail in the workplace as well as the home. These male-dominated environments give women a negative self-image and cause them to suffer lower self-esteem than most men. Through gambling, the authors maintained, women are able to escape their work-related responsibilities, their abusive domestic relationships, their demanding social role requirements as wife, mother, homemaker, and caretaker, and the intense guilt that derives from their failure to live up to the expectations of others.

Lesieur and Blume therefore described female pathological gamblers as "victims of the social stereotypes and limitations imposed upon women."[8] Consequently, they argued, "It is not surprising then that one effect of stressful life events in the lives of female pathological gamblers studied was to resort to some means of escape as a method of coping."[9] The relief they experience by gambling arises primarily from the "escape" and the "action" that it conveniently provides. However, some women find that by allowing them to compete in a male-dominated world, gambling offers a means of "empowerment" that is ordinarily denied them:

> It is possible that a sense of inadequacy in being traditionally female (produced by poor socialization experiences and failed relationships) may have propelled these women to compete in a stereotypically male domain–gambling. If a female could be successful in this male turf, then she might acquire a sense of personal power that would counteract a poor self-esteem.[10]

Critique. The greatest contribution of gender-oriented gambling research is that it highlights the degree to which female pathological gamblers have been underrepresented in treatment populations and, hence, underserved by existing treatment facilities. Apparently, many clinicians have failed to recognize that women, too, can become pathological gamblers. Lesieur and Blume suggested that this oversight could be corrected by screening for gambling problems all women who enter treatment for other addictive and emotional problems. In one treatment population, for example, the South Oaks Gambling Screen[11] disclosed that six percent of 133 women admitted for alcoholism and drug dependence also had gambling problems.[12] In another it was found that although women started gambling significantly later in life (32.4 years) than men (20.4 years), the progression of pathological gambling in women occurred twice as fast as it did in men.[13]

Unfortunately, those who undertake gender-oriented research appear to fall short of the mark in their attempts to explain why women become pathological gamblers. In the final analysis, Lesieur and Blume adopted the **drive-reduction theories** of behavioral psychology, the **alienation** and **anomie**

theories of early sociological thought, and the dysfunctional family explanation of later **family systems theorists** in their attempt to explain pathological gambling among women. Somewhat earlier Blume[14] had also proposed very similar explanations to explain alcoholism among women.

Thus, the major difference between Lesieur and Blume's explanations and those of their predecessors is not that the causes of pathological gambling among women are basically any different from those of men; like their predecessors they contended that the "escape" and "action" provided by gambling afford relief from all of life's problems and frustrations. They merely suggested that the *kinds* of problems and frustrations that drive women to drink and gamble excessively are perhaps different from those that drive men to gamble and drink excessively. Consequently, the same criticisms that apply to the drive-reduction, alienation, and dysfunctional family hypotheses reviewed earlier also apply to their feminist explanation.

Even if earlier criticisms of the drive-reduction approach could somehow be dismissed, the argument that Lesieur and Blume advanced to support it is contradictory to the epidemiological facts of addiction. Basically, they argued that it should come as no surprise that women turn to alcohol and gambling because they lead harder, crueler lives than men. To support this contention they cited previous research which concluded that, overall, women experience more emotional and personal problems than men. If these problems are the ultimate cause of addictive behaviors, then both alcoholism and pathological gambling should occur more frequently among women, yet the incidence of both is substantially higher among men. Therefore, if women do indeed experience harsher lives and more problems than men, then two other possibilities exist: (1) either women are inherently better able to cope with their problems than men or (2) factors other than stress, depression, low self-esteem, and other emotional or personal difficulties are of primary importance in the etiology of addictive behaviors. Although the authors failed to address either of these possibilities, a later study designed to investigate the role of self-esteem in the etiology of behavioral addictions found no relationship between low self-esteem and gambling in either women or men.[15]

Moreover, some of their own statistical data on the antecedent emotional and environmental conditions experienced by the women in their sample clearly fail to support their thesis. For example, only one-quarter of their subjects reported premorbid symptoms of depression. Thus, fully three-quarters of their sample were *not* depressed prior to the onset of pathological gambling. This means that in most cases of pathological gambling, something other than depression must be the cause of the problem. The statistics provided on stress do provide some support for their thesis since all women who were married reported a lonely or troubled marital relationship. Nevertheless, despite the fact that the degree of marital problems experienced by each subject was not and probably could not be quantified (exactly how much stress and depression are required for the development of pathological gambling?), 16 percent of the sample were never married and therefore could not claim any degree of marital discord as a cause. Unfortunately, whether such antecedent conditions as parental alcoholism or some other natal family dysfunction can be called upon to explain these exceptions is impossible to determine from the data provided. Even if the majority had reported antecedent depression or claimed to have grown up in a dysfunctional family, no causal relationship between these circumstances and the later development of pathological gambling is demonstrated; only a temporal one. Like those who would attribute the sunrise to the rooster's crowing, Lesieur and Blume are therefore guilty of the logical fallacy of *post hoc ergo propter hoc.* Their sensation-seeking explanation finds the strongest support in the data they provided since it indicated that all the women sampled claimed to have been initially attracted to gambling by its "action." However, a later study of arousal and sensation-seeking in female fruit machine gamblers found no correlation between heart rate measures and subjective arousal levels since heart rates increased only in those who were winning. Moreover, the researchers found marked negative correlations between sensation-seeking scores and gambling frequencies as well as between self-reported arousal levels and gambling frequencies. They were therefore forced to conclude that gambling alone was not enough to induce arousal in their subjects and that sensation-seeking was negatively associated with this form of machine gambling.[16]

Finally, like many similar studies, Lesieur and Blume drew their entire sample from a population of subjects who were already self-admitted pathological gamblers. The number of women in the general population who experience equal degrees of domestic and emotional turmoil but do not become pathological gamblers is therefore unknown. Obviously, many women (and men) experience stress-filled lives but only a small percentage become pathological gamblers. The same argument applies to their alienation or "empowerment" hypothesis. There are doubtless many other women who also feel exploited, unappreciated, and confined by traditional gender role expectations who do not become pathological gamblers. However, the premises of their "empowerment" and drive-reduction explanation were presented as axiomatic even though they were neither evaluated nor substantiated. Consequently, the alleged influences of alienation and stress in motivating pathological gambling in women are assumed more than they are demonstrated. Their use of so many qualifiers—"it is *possible* that. . .," "*may* have propelled. . .," "*might* acquire. . .," etc.—in their alienation or "empowerment" hypothesis demonstrates that even they regard this explanation as highly tentative and in need of far more extensive empirical research.

A later study investigated the purported relationship between loneliness or alienation and gambling among women among a convenience sample of women in Australia.[17] Although no differences were found between the loneliness scores of gamblers and nongamblers, those of problem gamblers were significantly higher than those of others in the sample. The researchers nevertheless acknowledged that they found no evidence to suggest that women were "driven" to gambling by either loneliness or alienation. They suggested instead that feelings of isolation and alienation may become more pronounced in women as they lose control over their gambling. However, they insisted that the question of whether loneliness is a predisposing factor or a consequence of gambling among women can only be resolved through longitudinal research.

Female Pathological Gamblers in Las Vegas

After being struck by the conspicuous absence of data on female pathological gamblers, two other researchers undertook a questionnaire survey of 52 women who were members of Gamblers Anonymous in Las Vegas.[18] In terms of demographics they found that most of these women were Caucasian, married, had children, and were in their 30s and 40s. Many were Catholic (39%), nearly as many were Protestant (31%), while relatively few were Jewish (6%). In terms of family history, most (96%) had siblings, the parents of nearly a third (31%) had been divorced by the time they were 15, the same number had suffered the death of a close friend or family member within two years of their joining GA, and over two-fifths (42%) had an alcoholic parent and at least one parent who gambled excessively. Roughly a third claimed to have been physically abused by their parents (33%) and to have been sexually abused in childhood (29%).

A substantial number admitted to having mental problems before joining the group. Over two-thirds (69%) had considered suicide while nearly one-quarter (23%) had attempted it. Nearly one-quarter (23%) admitted being dually-addicted to alcohol or other drugs and holding membership in other 12-step groups. Nearly two-thirds (65%) had consulted a mental health professional and almost half (46%) had sought marriage or family counseling. Interestingly, these professionals had failed to diagnose a gambling problem in nearly three-quarters (72%) of the cases. Well over half (62%) were unaware that compulsive gambling was considered a disease before they began attending GA meetings.

In terms of their gambling behavior, nearly all (90%) of the women indicated that they were addicted to video poker machines and that they had played them for as long as seven to 25 or more hours consecutively. Over two-fifths (21%) recalled having gambling sessions which lasted 24 hours or more. To support their gambling habits many had wiped out their family savings (87%), exceeded or "maxed-out" their credit card limits (76%), written bad checks (73%), pawned their valuables (60%), stolen from their employers (37%), considered prostitution (27%) or actually became prostitutes (10%), and had resorted to blackmail or extortion (6%). One-quarter (25%) were forced to declare bankruptcy because of their gambling.

Rather than attempting to use this information to test any specific hypotheses, the authors' stated purpose was merely to gather descriptive statistics on this particular group in order to raise the general awareness of problem gambling. However, their report must have been warmly received by Nevada gambling interests since, by pointing out how "destructive and demoralizing"[19] compulsive gambling can be, they gave the distinct impression that they hoped their findings would be used to promote an antigambling agenda among public policy decision makers and the general public in *other* parts of the country. Toward this end they also predicted that the same kinds of problems that their respondents had experienced would spread throughout the United States with the expansion of legalized gambling.

Gambling Among Female Club Members in Australia

In their effort to remedy the need for gender-specific gambling research, Nerilee Hing and Helen Breen compared the data obtained from the 1,257 females sampled during a telephone survey of 3,000 registered members of various clubs in Sydney, Australia to that of the 1,743 males sampled.[20] While their study did not investigate all aspects of female gambling, it did focus on gender differences in various gambling activities, gaming machine play, and problem gambling. According to the researchers, "Registered clubs in Australia are voluntary, not-for-profit organizations established by people sharing a common interest to pursue or promote that interest."[21] The interests shared by the members of these clubs encompass such activities as sports, community interests, occupational interests, and common religious and ethnic interests. In addition to the annual dues paid by each member, these clubs derive their revenues through the sale of alcohol, food, and various forms of entertainment including such gambling opportunities as raffles, bingo, keno, off track betting, and gaming machines. Since 1956, when gaming machines were first legalized in Australia, these clubs have become the largest providers of gaming machines in the country, the state of New South Wales, and perhaps even the entire world: by 1998 these clubs controlled 74 percent of all gaming machines in the state, 40 percent of those in the country, and 9.1 percent of those worldwide. These machines generate tremendous operating revenues for the clubs as well as tax revenues for the state. Although only the members of such clubs were sampled, they were asked about the extent of their participation in and preferences for 13 different forms of gambling at a number of venues including clubs, casinos, racetracks, off-course betting offices or TABS, hotels, and private locations.

The researchers undertook their study to test several hypotheses inferred or suggested by previous research. The first was that women would tend to prefer bingo, lotto, lotteries, sports pools, and gaming machines to a greater extent than male club members. The second was that participation rates of females would differ from those of males in different forms of gambling. The third, based on studies suggesting that women play gaming machines as a form of escape, was that women would tend to maximize their machine playing time to a greater degree than men. Their fourth hypotheses to be tested was rates of problem gambling, as determined by SOGS scores, would be lower among females than males.

Data analysis confirmed the first three hypothesis. The first was confirmed by the finding that more females than males expressed preferences for bingo, lotto, lotteries, sports pools, and gaming machines while more men than women claimed to prefer TAB betting, on-course betting, casino table games, keno, and other forms of gambling. The second hypothesis was also confirmed by the findings that actual participation rates for males and females were indeed different for different forms of gambling: men engaged more frequently than women in on-course betting, TAB betting, keno, casino table games, and gaming machines while women had higher participation rates for bingo. Interestingly, although women expressed a greater preference for gaming machines than men, they did not actually play them more frequently than men. However, the third hypothesis was confirmed by the finding that when women did play gaming machines, they not only played for longer periods than men but they also employed various strategies to maximize their playing time and minimize their losses to a greater extent than males: women tended to play lower denomination (two and five cent) machines while men played those requiring coins or credits of higher denominations (10 cent, 20 cent, $1, and $2) and they seldom risked more than one coin or credit per play time while men did so more frequently. Consequently, although playing sessions lasting over an hour were more common among women than men, women spent less money on gaming machines both per session and per week than men. However, the reasons for these playing patterns were unclear since no significant differences emerged between the reasons males and females gave for playing these machines. The fourth hypothesis, which predicted that rates of problem gambling would be lower among females than males, was not supported. Although proportionately more males (4.1%) than females (3.0%) had SOGS scores of 5 or more, this difference was not statistically significant.

On the basis of their findings Hing and Breen offered several suggestions for further research. Because the gambling preferences and frequencies of females differ from those of males it is important to determine whether these differences are caused by the structural characteristics of different forms of gambling or to changing social norms related to gender role expectations. They also felt it important to discover why women tend to employ strategies to maximize machine playing time and minimize loss while males do not. Since women appear to spend less money but more time gambling than men, they also felt that future studies should be designed to determine whether the social and economic impacts of machine gambling also differ for males and females. They also suggested that qualitative studies would be better able to answer these questions than quantitative studies. Finally, because problem gambling rates of males and females were statistically equivalent they concluded that this finding was contradictory to earlier studies in which rates of problem gambling were consistently found to be significantly higher among men than women. Because they chose a convenience sample of club members rather than a randomized general population sample, they suggested that this discrepancy could be due to sampling error. However, they also suggested the possibility that women are now beginning to experience gambling problems to a greater extent than they did in the past due to the steadily increasing availability and accessibility of gaming machines. It will therefore be important to discover the extent to which gambling problems are associated with gaming machines and other forms of gambling. Unlike the SOGS which assesses gambling in general, newer screening instruments should be designed to assess the degrees to which problem gambling is associated with specific forms of gambling.

Related research by later researchers compared differences in the length of time it takes for pathological gambling to develop in machine gamblers and in those who prefer other forms of gambling. After questioning 44 pathological gamblers they found that the average latency period between regular gambling involvement and the onset of pathological gambling was much shorter among machine gamblers (1.08 years) than others (3.58 years). Because gender was not related to latency the researchers concluded that the speed at which pathological gambling develops is determined by the gambling environment and the structural characteristics of gaming machines.[22]

GAMBLING AMONG THE ELDERLY

Most of what we know about gambling among senior citizens has been gleaned from general population surveys in which the respondents are grouped according to various age categories. However, the lack of consistency in how these groupings have been defined in terms of the age ranges they encompass renders any attempt at comparison extremely difficult. What these studies have revealed is that, in the past at least, gambling tended to be less prevalent in the oldest than younger age groups irrespective of how the age categories were defined. Beyond that, relatively little is known about the extent of gambling among the elderly in recent years which, with the advent of charitable, tribal, riverboat, offshore, internet gaming, and national lotteries, have witnessed a tremendous expansion of gambling opportunities for all age groups. Perhaps the greatest shortcoming in the literature is that no previous study has focused on the consequences of gambling among the elderly. Additionally, although the authors of some of the earlier studies offered tentative explanations for their findings of low frequency gambling among the elderly, those they proposed were usually entirely speculative and based on whichever motivational theory a particular author happened to favor at the time. Few studies have been undertaken with the specific goal of determining why those senior citizens who do gamble choose to do so and why those who do not choose to abstain. Consequently, no matter how intuitively attractive any such explanations may seem, in the absence of any conclusive proof they are still entirely speculative and, hence, of questionable scientific merit.

As discussed in the first volume of this series,[23] one of the most popular theoretical explanations for gambling is the **arousal** or **sensation-seeking hypothesis**, the idea that gambling is motivated by the intense thrill, excitement, and emotional arousal or "action" it provides. Glen Walters' **gambling lifestyle theory**, which was based on his observations of prison inmates, is one such example.[24] However, the subjects of many other studies designed to test this proposition have been college students and other youthful gamblers while age did not constitute a variable in many of those conducted among general populations. As a consequence, their findings are not relevant to gambling among senior citizens. Moreover, the fact that sensation-seeking scores, as determined by standard psychometric instruments such as Zuckerman's Sensation-Seeking Scale[25] tend to diminish significantly with age[26] would suggest that the need for emotional arousal is probably not a strong motivator for gambling among the elderly.

Some theoreticians who favor the arousal motive agree that the elderly will be less likely to gamble than the young. As noted in Chapter 6 of this volume, this idea was first explored by W. L. Li and M. H. Smith[27] who based their **life cycle hypothesis** on the finding that gambling and age are inversely correlated. It will be recalled that this hypothesis was initially based on the premise that gambling is motivated by the need for stimulation and excitement and that, as people mature, their inclination to gamble will steadily diminish along with their need for arousal. Similarly, the findings of the United Kingdom household survey (discussed in Chapter 7) provided some support for the **life cycle hypothesis** with its finding that the youngest members of society are the most avid gamblers while the elderly are the least avid: the elderly not only gambled much less frequently than other age groups, but they also bet the least amount of money when they did gamble.[28] Additional support for the **life cycle hypothesis** was provided by the first United States national[29] and Iowa[30] surveys which also reported a strong inverse correlations between gambling and age. Similar results were reported in market research conducted annually by the Minnesota State Lottery[31] and studies of slot machine gambling in Germany.[32] Many of the epidemiological studies that have been undertaken to ascertain rates of problem and pathological gambling in various populations have revealed similar trends in age-related gambling behavior and rates of problem gambling. In general, these investigations found that those in the youngest age groups are most likely to have gambled and to have experienced gambling problems while those in the oldest age groups are least likely to have done so.[33] However, with their focus on prevalence data, their authors offered no explanations for these trends.

While most of these studies appeared to confirm that the elderly do, in fact, tend to gamble less frequently than those in younger age groups, there was no agreement as to how to account for these findings. Although Li and Smith initially interpreted their data as confirmation of the **sensation-seeking hypothesis**, they were also convinced that gambling is also related to income and therefore suggested that any age-related decreases in gambling could also be due entirely to declining post-retirement monetary resources.[34] The authors of the United Kingdom survey refrained from speculating on any of the possible causes for their age-related findings since they did not specifically set out to test the **life cycle hypothesis**. Rather than attribute their findings to the hypothetical need for arousal, the authors of the United States national survey suggested that the age differences they found may be a reflection of the different attitudes toward gambling that are held by different generations, a phenomenon known as the "cohort effect."[35]

Despite the popularity of the **life cycle hypothesis** with its prediction that gambling frequencies will steadily decrease with age, not all theoreticians advocate it nor do all studies support it. For example, despite their finding of an inverse correlation between overall gambling and age, the authors of the Iowa survey[36] rejected the **life cycle hypothesis** when they found that different certain forms of gambling were associated with different age groups. They therefore offered a variant of **small-group interactional theory** first proposed by Erving Goffman[37] and favored by a number of later investigators.[38] They did so in the belief that in their quest to establish an adult identity, young adults engage in certain forms of gambling as a means of experimental role-playing and self-presentation. Older adults, whose identities are already established, gamble for social purposes. The **continuity theory** they also proposed attributed age-related decreases in overall gambling levels to the stronger antigambling sentiments that existed in the past. Thus, like the authors of the United States national survey, they predicted that the current gambling levels of younger age cohorts will not decrease as they grow older. A reanalysis of market research data on lottery gambling in two states report- ed that participation rates steadily *increased* with age until retirement when it dropped off dramatically.[39] At least one epidemiological study, a follow-up survey of New York adults, contradicted the **life cycle hypothesis** when it found that respondents under 30 years of age were the least frequent gam- blers while those between 30 and 54 were the most frequent.[40]

Continuity theory, the idea that the values internalized in youth will be held for life, has found support in studies reporting that the oldest respon- dents are the most likely to abstain from gambling for religious or moral rea- sons. A recent national Gallup survey found that in comparison with gam- blers, abstainers were more likely to be older, more religious, less affluent, to avoid alcoholic beverages, and to live in the South.[41] Attitudinal data obtained by the Minnesota State Lottery also revealed that most of those who objected to gambling on religious or moral grounds were in the older age groups; conversely, the younger the respondents, the less likely they were to hold a negative attitude toward gambling.[42] However, only time will tell whether or not the more liberal attitudes of the young will persist into their senior years.

Some recent studies are finding that gambling involvement among senior citizens is actually on the rise. One of the few studies specifically designed to investigate social activities of senior citizens surveyed the activities directors of various senior citizen centers including assisted care facilities, nursing homes, and church groups serving a total 6,975 older Americans.[43] Finding that senior citizens play bingo and go to casinos more frequently than they engage in other kind of social activities, the researchers concluded that gam- bling constitutes the most important organizationally-sponsored activity of this population. Unfortunately, although the researchers claimed that senior citizens are "gambling in numbers unlike any other time in the history of this country,"[44] they were unable to document any changes in the gambling fre- quencies of senior citizens in recent years. Fortunately, other studies have documented these changes. The second United States national gambling sur- vey reported that although past-year gambling rates have decreased among young adults (18-44 years of age) and increased only slightly among middle- aged adults (45-65), the rate for senior citizens (65 and older) doubled between 1975 and 1998.[45] Market research conducted by the Minnesota State Lottery found that although the advent of tribal gaming in the early

1990s was accompanied by significant increases in casino gambling among all adults over the age of 35, the sharpest rise occurred among the elderly whose participation rate for casino gaming nearly doubled in just one year.[46] Likewise, rates of gambling in different age groups were measured before the opening of a casino in Niagara Falls, Ontario and compared to those after it had been in operation for one year. Those of older Ontario residents more than doubled while those of older Niagara Falls residents nearly tripled. However, increases in some of the other age groups were equal to or even greater than these, especially in they youngest.[47] Nevertheless, these findings strongly support the **availability and exposure hypothesis** which predicts that any increase in the availability of gambling will lead to higher rates of normative and pathological gambling and which has been reported and advocated by others.[48] The sharp rise in casino gambling among the state's older residents also suggests that this form of gambling could become problematic for many senior citizens who claim to gamble as a novel way of spending time, dispelling the boredom of retirement, and socializing with their peers.[49]

Despite the contradictory findings of many studies, the majority of those that have taken age differences into consideration have concluded that gambling frequencies do, indeed, show a general tendency to decrease with age. Consequently, the **life cycle hypothesis** cannot yet be discarded. Nevertheless, alternative explanations for this tendency are also conceivable: just as there are many possible reasons why people gamble, there may be just as many as to why they do not. It is possible that with age comes greater responsibilities which reduce one's interest in gambling and other pursuits that were once popular in youth, or that advancing age restricts one's access to gambling venues, or that through the experience that comes with age many people eventually learn that there is actually little profit in gambling. Conversely, it has been suggested that because their incomes are smaller and more fixed than those of younger people who are still in the labor force, the elderly should feel poorer and should therefore be *more* likely to gamble than younger people.[50] It has also been suggested that regular gamblers tend to regard gambling merely as a form of entertainment, a sentiment that, as we have already seen in Chapter 2, is shared by many economists.[51] Thus, those who were weekend gamblers for many years while they were working often continue to enjoy recreational gambling on a daily basis when they retire, generally betting smaller amounts on the favorites.[52] However, the United Kingdom study[53] found that the oldest racetrack bettors preferred the long shots to the favorites.

In the final analysis we must acknowledge that very little is known about gambling among the elderly. This, as some researchers have noted, is because "the older adult gambler has yet to be examined or systematically studied, despite a growing number of older adults who regularly frequent the increasing number of casinos. . . ."[54] and who are specifically targeted by casino marketing directors. While statistical data alone may reveal the frequencies of gambling within different age and other demographic groups, most quantitative studies are incapable of ascertaining the reasons for either gambling or abstaining. Consequently, we still do not know to what extent gambling among those senior citizens who do gamble is a consequence of availability, access, experience, psychological factors, social forces, economics, depression, loneliness, the need for excitement, or any of the other myriad explanations for gambling that have ever been proposed. We also have very little information on the consequences that the increased availability of gambling may be having on the elderly. The paucity of data on the motivations, practices, and ramifications related to gambling among senior citizens represents a conspicuous void in the literature which can only be corrected with research oriented specifically toward this population. Fortunately, at least one such study has already been undertaken.

Gambling Among Older Adults in Oregon

One of the most detailed studies of gambling and the elderly was a prevalence survey in which 1,512 Oregon residents 62 years of age and older were interviewed by telephone during the summer of 2000.[55] The subjects were not only asked about their gambling behavior, but they were also screened for gambling problems, substance abuse problems, and depression. Their responses were grouped according to gender and age in categories spanning five-year intervals with the exception of the youngest (62 to 64) and oldest (80+) groups.

Past-year gambling. The study found that three-quarters (74.7%) of the respondents had engaged in at least one form of gambling at some point in their lives and that over half (58.2%) had gambled during the previous 12-month period. Past-year gambling rates steadily declined with age with the sharpest drop occurring in the oldest (80+) category. Proportionately more men (62.5%) than women (54.8%) were active gamblers.

Problem and pathological gambling. Previous research had found that while Oregon's *lifetime* rate of combined problem and pathological gambling had not changed significantly between 1997 (5.0%) and 2000 (4.6%), the *current* (past-year) combined rate showed significant decreases in both the state's general population (from 3.3% to 2.3%) and among those 65 and older (from 0.8% to 0.5%).[56] However, since 18 of the 1,512 subjects 62 years of age and older were so identified, the current combined rate for this population in 2000 was 1.2% (0.9% problem; 0.3% probable pathological). Although current rates of problem and probable pathological gambling among males (1.4% and 0.5%, respectively) were more than twice those of females (0.6% and 0.2%, respectively), these differences were not statistically significant. Current rates of problem and probable pathological gambling were highest in the 65 to 69 year old group (2.0% and 0.3%, respectively) and lower in the 62 to 64 (1.2% and 0.6%) and 70 to 74 (1.4% and 0.3%) year age groups. Current gambling problems were not found in any subjects 75 years of age and older. In terms of residence, combined rates of problem and pathological gambling were more than twice as high in counties with large urban centers (1.8%) than in those that are predominantly rural (0.7%).

Gambling preferences. Lotteries, casino gaming, and charitable gambling were among the most preferred forms of gambling among older people. Of those who had gambled in the past 12 months, 56.3 percent played traditional (nonvideo) lottery games, 50.1 percent went to casinos, 30.8 percent participated in charitable gambling excluding bingo, 18.9 percent played noncasino video poker, and 10.6 percent played non-Indian bingo. The most preferred forms of casino gaming were slot machines and line games (29.5%) followed by card games (6.1%), video poker (5.5%), "other" casino games (4.2%), keno (1.8%), bingo (1.6%), dice (0.7%), and roulette (0.5%). Men tended to prefer keno, roulette, sports betting, games of skill, and the stock market while women preferred slot machines, charitable gambling, and bingo. Nearly equal numbers of men and women participated in lottery games, video poker, cards, dice, and racetrack betting.

Gambling associates. Senior citizens prefer to gamble with others. Over one-third (37.7%) of the sample gambled with a spouse or partner, one-quarter (25.1%) gambled alone, and one-fifth (21.1%) gambled with friends. Far fewer gambled with other family members (13.0%), co-workers (1.3%), or other individuals or groups (1.9%). Men were somewhat more likely than women to gamble with spouses (46.4% M; 30.2% F) while women were likely more than men to gamble with friends (24.1% F; 17.6% M) or other family members (18.3% F; 6.7% M). Roughly equal percentages of males and females gambled alone (26.3% M; 24.1% F), with co-workers (1.1% M; 1.4% F), or with others (2.0% M; 1.9% F).

Time spent on gambling. When senior citizens gamble, they usually do so only several times a month and for brief periods of less than two hours at a time. Older adults gambled an average of 3.8 days per month during the previous 12 months. While engaged in their preferred form 43.2 percent claimed to gamble for one hour or less; 27.2 percent, for one to two hours; 22.1 percent for three to five hours; 4.1 percent, for six to 12 hours; and only 3.4 percent reported that they their gambling episodes last for 12 hours or more. Differences between males and females were generally slight although males outnumbered females by nearly two to one (4.6% vs. 2.4%) among those who gamble for periods in excess of 12 hours.

Gambling expenditures. Older adults generally restrict their losses but some risk fairly sizeable amounts of money. The average monthly amount spent on gambling was $58.78 with women tending to spend slightly more than men ($62.80 vs. $54.80). However, those identified as problem and pathological gamblers spent an average of $304.50 per month on gambling. For most respondents (74.6%) the largest bets ever made were less than $100 but some had risked up to $1,000 (22.1%), from $1,000 and $10,000 (3.1%), and a few (0.2%) staked more than $10,000 on a single bet. Most of the smaller bets were made by women while most of the larger bets were by men: no bets over $10,000 and only a small number of those over $1,000 were made by women. Those identified as problem and pathological gamblers also tended to make larger bets.

Self-reported motivations for gambling. When asked their reasons for gambling, most respondents (59.6%) reported that they did so for entertainment or fun. Far fewer claimed to do so to socialize (11.6%), to win money (6.7%), for excitement/challenge (6.4%), out of curiosity (4.1%), to support worthy causes (2.8%), as a hobby (2.2%), as a distraction from problems (0.8%), or for "other" reasons (5.8%). Gender differences were not significant in most categories. However, all of those who indicated that they gambled for distraction from their problems were female. Most (78.9%) of those identified as problem or pathological gamblers indicated that they also gambled for fun or entertainment; only one male claimed to gamble for excitement and only one female claimed to do so to escape problems.

Parental problem gambling. Gambling problems in the parental generation were nearly four times more common among those identified as problem and pathological gamblers than among others. Only 4.2 percent of the non-problem gamblers but 15.8 percent of those identified as problem/pathological gamblers indicated having at least one parent with gambling problems. Interestingly, in every case the parent was the father.

Age of gambling initiation. The age of the first gambling experience appears to be associated with current age and gender. Older respondents tended to start gambling later in life than younger respondents: the average age of the first gambling experience was 34.4 years in the 80+ group but 29.3 years in the 62-64 group. Males also started gambling earlier than females: the average age for men was 24.5 years while that for women was 37.1 years. The first gambling experience of most men involved cards, dice, or sports betting while most women were introduced to gambling at a casino.

Alcohol, tobacco, and other drug use. Although nearly half (47.8%) of all older adults used alcohol, relatively few (12.2%) used tobacco products or illegal drugs (0.6%). Although regular alcohol use remained fairly constant across all age categories, tobacco use tended to decline with age. However, of those identified as problem or pathological gamblers, two-thirds (66.7%) used tobacco on a daily basis while surprisingly few (4.8%) were daily drinkers. Although some of the nonproblem gamblers (0.5%) admitted past year difficulties with alcohol, none of the problem or pathological gamblers did so. Approximately ten percent of the subjects used sedatives, antidepressants, and antianxiety drugs on a weekly or daily basis. A few (1.1%) used these drugs without a physician's prescription.

Depression. Relatively few (5.2%) of the subjects met the criteria for current clinical depression which affected slightly more women (6.0%) than men (4.4%). However, levels of depression among males tended to show slight but steady increases with age (from 1.3% to 6.9%), a trend that did not occur among females. Nearly one-third (29.1%) of this group also used prescription drugs. Interestingly, only three (16.6%) of the 18 individuals identified as problem or pathological gamblers were also identified as suffering from depression.

Health and happiness. Problem and pathological gamblers appear to be just as healthy but less happy than nongamblers. Although more of the former than the latter estimated their health to be poor or fair, more of the former also estimated their health to be excellent. Only five percent of the entire sample but 27.8 percent of the problem and pathological gamblers claimed to be "not very satisfied" with the way they spent their time.

Demographic variables: employment, education, marital status, religion, and income. No data on racial or ethnic affiliation were provided. As might be expected, however, most of the subjects in this study were retired (82.5%) and married (61.4%) or widowed (28.5). Most had completed high school or also had some college training (62.1%). The modal income level for this population was less than $15,000 per year (22.1%). Slightly fewer earned from $15,000 to $25,000 (19.9%), from $25,000 to $35,000 (16.5%), from $35,000 to $50,000 (17.9%), and from $50,000 to $75,000 (13.6%). Over ten percent

(10.2%) had annual incomes in excess of $75,000. Only a few were Jewish (0.7%) or Buddhist (0.4%) while most were Protestant (53.4%), Catholic (13.4%), followed by "Other" religious paths (19.2%), or had no religious preference (12.7%). Unfortunately, no comparable demographic data specific to nonproblem, problem, and pathological gamblers was provided. However, both groups were described as having similar distributions in terms of marital status and roughly equal proportions of problem/pathological and nongamblers claimed that they either "could not make ends meet" (2.1%), earned "just enough, no more" (16.1%), earned "enough with a little extra sometimes" (43.0%), or "always had money left over" (38.8%).

Theoretical significance. Data on gambling among Oregon's older adults are relevant to at least some of the hypotheses that have been proposed to explain normative and excessive gambling. Specifically, the **gender hypotheses** was weakly supported by the findings that more men than women gambled and experienced gambling problems in the past year. The fact that only females claimed to gamble to escape their problems would seem to suggest that at least some women may have different motivations for gambling than men. However, this idea is also contradicted by the findings that no significant gender differences were reported in any of the other motivational categories. The **life cycle hypothesis** was also weakly supported by the finding that past-year gambling rates declined with age and dropped off most sharply in the oldest age group. However, it was not supported by the data on problem and pathological gambling. The **rural-urban residence hypothesis** found support by the observation that rates of problem and pathological gambling in urban areas were more than twice as high as those in rural areas. The **parental gambling hypothesis** found support in the fact that the occurrence of problem gambling in the parental generation was almost four times greater among problem and pathological than among nonproblem gamblers. **Continuity theory** was supported by the finding of a cohort effect as the age of initiation into gambling tended to increase with the present age of the respondents. Because so few respondents claimed to gamble for excitement, and because so few problem and pathological gamblers regularly used alcohol or other drugs or showed any signs of depression, neither the **sensation-seeking hypothesis**, the **dysphoria reduction hypothesis**, nor the **co-addiction hypothesis** were supported.

Unfortunately, the study's small sample size and resulting lack of relevant data specific to problem and pathological gamblers also made it impossible to test a number of other possibilities. For example, the **age of initiation hypothesis** could not be tested since no data on the first gambling experiences of these subgroups was provided. Likewise, the absence of any demographic data distinguishing nonproblem from problem/pathological gamblers also prevented any insights into such **social structural theories** as the **affluence, education, status inequality**, and **religion hypotheses**. The **ethnicity hypothesis** could not be tested since no mention was made of the racial or ethnic affiliation of any of the respondents. Replication studies involving much larger sample sizes should eliminate problems of this nature. The greatest importance of this study lies in the fact that it represents a beginning attempt to rectify our lack of knowledge concerning gambling among the elderly.

GAMBLING AMONG NATIVE NORTH AMERICANS

A review of the literature on gambling among Native North American populations was conducted to assess the prevalence rates of problem gambling in these groups and compare them to those of general populations, as well as to identify any features that may be associated with problem and pathological gambling among Native Americans.[57] Gambling played an important role in the traditional life of many Native American groups but excesses were rare because its original purposes, like those of tobacco, were primarily ceremonial and often religious in nature. Among contemporary Native groups, however, the commercialization of gambling, like that of tobacco, has had some adverse consequences. Although the researchers conducted searches in eight electronic databases and other sources, they were able to locate relatively few relevant source materials, a number of which remain unpublished.

The reviewers found that far more Native Americans experience gambling problems than non-Natives. Only four studies pertained to adolescent gambling and their authors employed different research methods and assessment criteria to determine rates of problem gambling severity in the populations they studied. Consequently, their estimates ranged from 9.6 to 21 percent for pathological and from 10.1 to 25 percent for "at risk" or problem gambling among Native American adolescents and from 3 to 5.6 percent for pathological and 2.2 to 9.6 percent for "at risk" or problem gambling in comparable non-Native populations. Thus, Native American adolescents are about five times more likely to experience gambling problems than their non-Native counterparts. Adult estimates were also provided by only five studies. Once again the different research methods and assessment criteria employed yielded a divergence of general population estimates ranging from 2.8 to 22 percent for pathological gambling and from 4.6 to 19 percent for problem gambling. Estimated rates for comparable non-Native populations ranged from 0.5 to 7.3 percent for pathological and from 1.3 to 14 percent for problem gambling. Thus, Native American adults are 2.2 to 15.69 times more likely to have gambling problems than non-Natives.

Adolescents

A number of demographic and behavioral features were also found to be associated gambling problems among Native Americans. The correlates of problem gambling among adolescents, which appeared in only one unpublished Canadian study, included:

- **Gender.** More problem gamblers are male than female.

- **Age.** Problem gamblers tended to be younger (13.5 years) than non-problem gamblers (14.3 years).

- **School grade.** Problem gamblers tended to be in a lower grade in school (7.4) than nonproblem gamblers (8.3).

- **Age of initiation.** Problem gamblers were significantly more likely to have started gambling at a younger age (10 years) than nonproblem gamblers (12 years).

- **Siblings.** Problem gamblers were more likely to have older brothers (1.3) than nonproblem gamblers (1).

- **Household composition.** Problem gamblers lived in homes with fewer non-relatives (.01) than nonproblem gamblers (.11).

- **Employment.** Problem gamblers worked more hours per week (4.4) than nonproblem gamblers (3.3).

- **Gambling preferences.** Problem gamblers engaged in a wider variety of gambling forms than nonproblem gamblers.

This study also reported that adolescent problem gamblers were more likely than nongamblers to use alcohol, tobacco, and other drugs as well as to have been the victims of theft or vandalism, struck in anger, purposely injured, survived the death of friends or family members, had a family member commit suicide, participated in sports, engaged in ceremonial fasting, had friends who had dropped out of school, and to have parents who gamble.

Adults

The correlates of problem gambling among adults were investigated in five studies. Some compared Native American problem and pathological gamblers to Native American nonproblem gamblers; others compared Native American gamblers to non-Native gamblers. In addition to the observations that problem and pathological gamblers spent more time and money on gambling, comparisons of Native American problem/pathological to Native American nonproblem revealed that:

- **Age.** Problem gamblers were younger (30 or less vs. 38 years).

- **Gender.** Problem gamblers were more likely to be female.

- **Marital status.** Problem gamblers were less likely than nonproblem gamblers to be married.

- **Income.** Problem gamblers tended to have lower incomes.

- **Age of initiation.** Problem gamblers started gambling at a younger age (17 vs. 20 years).

- **Education.** Problem gamblers were more likely to have attended boarding schools.

- **Gambling preferences.** Problem gamblers (a) participated in a wider variety of gambling types and (b) showed a distinct preference for bingo.

- **Residence.** Problem gamblers were more likely to live on reservations.

- **Family gambling.** Problem gamblers were more likely to have fathers, brothers, sisters, spouses, other relatives, and friends who also have gambling problems.

- **Stress level.** Problem gamblers tended to score higher on measures of grief.

- **Self-reported motivations.** Problem gamblers were more likely to claim to gamble to socialize with friends and to satisfy their curiosity.

Comparisons of Native to non-Native American problem/pathological gamblers revealed the following associations:

- **Gender.** Native Americans were more likely than non-Natives to be female.

- **Age.** Native Americans were more likely to be under 30.

- **Education.** Native Americans were less likely to have completed high school.

- **Marital status.** Native Americans were less likely to be married.

- **Income.** Native Americans were likely to have lower annual incomes (less than $25,000).

- **Gambling preferences.** Native Americans participated in a wider variety of gambling types. However, they spent more money on lotteries and bingo but less on casinos and card games.

- **Self-reported motivations.** Native Americans were more likely to claim to gamble for fun or entertainment, money, excitement or challenge, solitude, to escape problems, or as a hobby.

Because so few studies of Native American gambling have been conducted, and because of the wide variation in estimated rates of problem and pathological gambling in these populations, this review clearly highlights the need for far more research among them. Its authors recommended that a primary goal of future research will be to determine why rates of problem and pathological gambling are so much higher among Native Americans than their non-Native counterparts. They acknowledged that although the correlations they outlined are not necessarily causal, the exact nature of these relationships remains unknown and must therefore be clarified. For example, although stress appears to be associated with Native American problem gambling, it is presently impossible to determine whether gambling is a consequence of stress or whether stress is a consequence of gambling. Likewise, although problem gambling appears to be associated with living on reservations, the ways in which reservation life may contribute to the development of gambling problems is also unknown. Is problem gambling caused by the current lack of entertainment, educational, and employment opportunities on reservations or is it a consequence of past abuses suffered in childhood at the hands of boarding school authorities? Why are female problem gamblers more common among Native Americans than non-Natives? Why do Native Americans prefer bingo over other forms of gambling? In short, the authors insisted, more qualitative research is necessary to determine the nature and strength of cultural influences on the behaviors and other specific factors associated with gambling in Native American populations.

Chapter 11

PROBLEM GAMBLING CORRELATES
AND RISK FACTORS

Many studies of the psychosocial, behavioral, demographic, environmental, personality, and other background correlates and antecedents of such behaviors as drinking and drug use have been undertaken in an effort to determine which past or present conditions are associated with these activities. While some of these correlates are thought to be consequences of these behaviors, others are thought to be causal and therefore to serve as "predictors" or "risk factors" for them. It must be emphasized, however, that risk factors should be considered only as possible influences that may or may not contribute to the onset or maintenance of a disorder. For example, heavy and problem drinking is correlated with, and therefore possibly influenced or "predicted" by, such demographic circumstances as being young, male, and single.[1] In contrast, such correlates such as being old, female, and married are referred to as "protective factors" since they are believed to mitigate against its development.

Likewise, a number of demographic and psychosocial correlates of gambling behavior have also emerged, some of which have already been discussed. As previously noted, rates of gambling and problem gambling are typically higher among males than females, among the young than the old, among the single, divorced, and widowed than the married, and among Catholics and Jews than Protestants. A recent study of Minnesota adolescents found that Hispanic, Black, Native American, and mixed race students gambled significantly more frequently than Asian and Caucasian students.[2] A survey of Texas youth also found significant differences in the gambling frequencies of different ethnic groups.[3] Therefore, the most frequently cited demographic "predictors" of gambling are age, gender, socioeconomic background, marital status, ethnic minority status, and religious affiliation. Those for problem gambling among Native American populations were discussed in the previous chapter. In some populations, however, no significant gender differences in the incidence of pathological gambling can be found.[4] In others, gambling was found to be influenced more by degree of religious devotion than by denominational affiliation. Specifically, the frequency of gambling among Las Vegas residents was found to be associated not only with their denominational affiliation, but also with the importance of religion in their lives and the frequency with which they attended religious services. However, irrespective of their denominational preferences, the amount of money they gambled was related to their frequency of attendance at religious services and the importance of religion in their lives.[5] Similarly, a United States national survey designed to assess the influence of religion on problem gambling found an inverse relationship between frequency of attendance at religious services and gambling problems (frequent attenders reported having fewer gambling problems) but no relationship between the importance of faith in a deity and problem gambling.[6]

Previously mentioned findings supporting the **availability and exposure** and **age of initiation hypotheses** have prompted a number of investigators to undertake research intended to discover the psychosocial, behavioral, and demographic correlates or predictors of gambling and problem gambling among young people. In the process, a number of early sociological hypotheses were tested. For example, although a slightly greater percentage of British children who prefer fruit machines are from working class than other socioeconomic backgrounds, no significant association between social class and the propensity to gamble has been reported.[7] The age at which one is introduced to gambling has also been suggested as a critical risk factor which could contribute to the development of problem gambling: it has been found that children who started gambling before the age of nine are more likely to gamble "very frequently," or at least four times a week.[8] However, some studies have found that, instead of chronological age, the earlier young people start gambling in terms of school grade, the more likely they are to become problem and pathological gamblers.[9]

Family and peer influences may constitute important psychosocial risk factors for gambling among children and adolescents. As noted in the previous chapter, young people commonly start gambling in their own homes with parents and other relatives.[10] A number of studies have also noted a strong association between individual gambling and peer gambling.[11] Although these studies suggest that young people are therefore more likely to gamble if their parents and friends gamble, we still do not know the extent to which family and peer pressures may contribute to the development of problem gambling.

Other commonly reported correlates of problem gambling are gender (male), alcohol/tobacco/other drug use, eating disorders, parental indifference to their children's gambling, parental problem gambling/substance abuse, ethnic minority status, juvenile delinquency/antisocial behavior/theft, misuse of school lunch or transportation money, increased sexual activity, poor scholastic performance, and psychological distress.[12] It has also been suggested that such stressors as the death of a parent, physical or sexual abuse in childhood, and living in single-parent homes may also constitute important risk factors.[13] However, a large study of 9,744 British adolescents found no significant differences between ethnic groups but suggested that children living in single parent households were more likely than others to have gambling problems.[14] More recentlty, Sue Fisher reported that the location of one's residence can also constitue a risk factor for problem gambling. Specifically, she found that children living in British seaside communities, where most amusement arcades are located and fruit machines are therefore more accessible, are significantly (40%) more likely to develop gambling problems than those living in inland communities which have fewer arcades. She added that children whose parents have gambled on fruit machines or the National Lottery scratchcards in the past week are twice as likely to develop gambling problems as others while the odds for those whose gamble with their parents' knowledge and approval are increased by 50 percent.[15]

A number of these hypotheses were tested in a survey by Henry Lesieur and Robert Klein[16] who sampled 892 New Jersey high school students. This study, in which 5.7% of the sample were deemed to be pathological gamblers, found statistically significant correlations between adolescent pathological gambling and gender, parental problem gambling, lower grade averages, and gambling frequency. Specifically, signs of pathological gambling were exhibited by: 9.5 percent of the males but only 2 percent of the females; 17 percent of those who identified one or both parents as excessive gamblers but only 5 percent of those who did not; 17 percent of those receiving grades below "C" average, 7 percent of "C" students, 4 percent of "B" students, and 6% of "A" students; and 11 percent of those who gambled once a week or more as opposed to only 3 percent of those who gambled less frequently. Significant but weak correlates were type of neighborhood and religion. Those identified as pathological gamblers were more likely to describe their neighborhoods as "worse off" (18%) than "better than average" (6%). However, contrary to the findings and expectations of others, Catholics and Jews in this study were less likely to show signs of pathological gambling than were members of Protestant and other religious denominations. Specifically, 6 percent of the Protestant and 17 percent of the students claiming "Other" religious affiliations (including Eastern Orthodox, Muslim, and no religious preference) were classified as pathological gamblers as opposed to only 3 percent of those who identified themselves as Jewish and 5 percent as Catholic. Pathological gambling was not significantly correlated with age, with either single or two parent households, parental occupation or socioeconomic status, parental ownership or rental of the family home, or proximity to Atlantic City. Consequently, this study failed to provide any support for the popular **social class**, **religion**, **availability**, and **age of initiation hypotheses**.

Some researchers have therefore suggested that "high frequency gambling in adolescence may be part of a constellation of deviant behaviors that are exhibited by some males, including frequent alcohol use, physical violence, vandalism, shoplifting, and truancy to name a few."[17] The author of one recent study which found an association between the severity of gambling problems and unsafe sex practices in 134 substance abusers concluded that problem gambling may be a risk factor for HIV in this population.[18] The author of another concluded that the use of false identification and lying about one's age to procure beverage alcohol were risk factors for problem gambling among the youth of Canada's Atlantic provinces.[19] Not surprisingly, researchers investigating the influence of personal attitudes on gambling behavior found that subjective norms related to gambling predicted the intention to gamble while intentions to gamble in turn predicted gambling frequency and problem gambling.[20]

A number of environmental conditions have also been investigated as possible predictors of gambling behavior. One of the earliest of such studies examined the influence that family size, birth order, and gender might have on the risk-taking behavior of children. Family size was the only variable to be implicated when it was found that children from larger families made riskier choices in laboratory experiments than those from smaller families.[21] Currently, however, such environmental correlates as parental problem gambling and/or substance abuse, tyrannically domineering parents, physical and/or sexual abuse in childhood, early parental loss, spousal loss or rejection, and other painful life traumas or stressors are the most frequently cited risk factors. For example, while national rates of physical and sexual abuse range from one percent to two percent,[22] rates as high as 29%[23] to 32.5%[24] have been reported for pathological gamblers. However, a history of these kinds of traumatic abuse appear to be far more common among females (60%) than males (16%).[25]

One consequence of physical and emotional abuse is posttraumatic stress disorder, a chronic state of hedonic and cognitive dysphoria which can affect both males and females and which may in some cases be a precursor to addiction. While physical and sexual abuse are believed to constitute common risk factors for women, men are believed to be placed at heightened risk for addiction by "shell shock," a stress disorder first observed in combat veterans. Some researchers have therefore posited the existence of a Learned Helplessness or Addictive Response Syndrome in which addictive behaviors are preconditioned by any highly traumatic event or series of events which produce posttraumatic stress disorder.[26] Such a condition is believed to render susceptible individuals vulnerable to addiction since they are likely to lose control over any chemical substance or behavior that offers immediate relief.

Different populations have been the focus of different correlational studies. Although many have surveyed young to mature adults,[27] a number have examined children, adolescents, and young adults[28] while others have explored special populations such as females[29] and certain ethnic groups.[30] The previously described cross-cultural study of games of chance focused on the correlates of gambling in non-Western tribal societies.[31] The findings of several representative correlational studies will be outlined below.

THE UNITED STATES NATIONAL SURVEY

Although the first United States national survey[32] enumerated a number of factors that were found to be associated with heavy gambling, none were said to be "predictive." Nevertheless, to further our knowledge of problem gambling, data from the study were analyzed in two different ways: the first involved levels of gambling involvement; the second involved clinically determined rates of pathological gambling. As noted previously, low to high levels of involvement were initially described as "nonbetting, "legal betting," and "illegal betting." The researchers then added a fourth level, "heavy illegal betting," to designate the highest level of involvement. Rates of compulsive gambling were based on a clinical analysis of subjects' responses to series of 18 questions which were specifically included to identify "probable" and "potential" pathological gamblers.

Progressively higher levels of involvement were found to be associated with unsatisfactory domestic relationships, employment problems, mobility, and alcohol use. More specifically, high involvement was strongly related to spousal disagreements over money matters, divorce, a lack of understanding between spouses, and a higher incidence of (unspecified) problems among children. It was also associated with such employment-related problems as job dissatisfaction, days of work missed, hours of work missed due to lateness, frequency of job changes, and garnishment of wages. The fact that those who were more heavily involved in gambling tended to reside in one location for shorter periods than those who were less involved was interpreted as an indication of instability. Finally, gamblers drank alcohol four times more frequently than nongamblers with the heaviest gamblers being the heaviest drinkers. Moreover, rates of alcohol consumption varied with gambling preferences. The lightest drinkers were bingo players who drank an average of 48 days a year. They were followed by lottery players (62 days/yr), on-track horse race bettors (71 days/yr), casino gamblers (73 days/yr), numbers players and dog track bettors (76 days/yr), sports bettors (83 days/yr), college sports bettors (95 days/yr), illegal sports bettors (109 days/yr), and illegal horse bettors who were the most frequent drinkers (110 days/yr).

In terms of demographics, analysis of the data on rates of compulsive gambling revealed a number of associations. Most "probable" compulsive gamblers were in the 45 to 64 year-old age category while most "potentials" were in the 25 to 44 age group. This is consistent with the idea that pathological gambling is a progressive disorder that increases in severity over time. Whites were underrepresented in both the "probable" and "potential" groups while blacks were slightly overrepresented among "potentials" and other minorities were overrepresented among "probable" compulsive gamblers. The authors suggested that this may reflect a trend toward upward mobility within the minority community. High school graduates made up an unusually high proportion of "potentials" while college graduates made up an inordinate number of "probables." Although most of those in either group were employed, retired people were overrepresented in the "probable" category while the unemployed showed a high rate of "potential" pathological gambling. More people in both groups lived in or near large cities and more lived in the Northeast than elsewhere. Catholics and those with Italian and Spanish ancestry were overrepresented in both categories while Jewish and Irish Americans were not. The researchers suggested that different concentrations of these populations in the different parts of the country may explain these findings.

Although the study's investigation of pathological gamblers did appear to support theoretical issues related to family disruption, a number of correlates related to employment performance stand in direct contradiction to the expectations of many gambling theorists. A number of hypotheses related to family stability problems were supported by findings that both probable and potential compulsive gamblers had more spousal disagreements about finances, higher divorce and remarriage rates, higher mobility, higher spending rates, and their children had more problems than the general population. However, both groups also reported a higher rate of self-employment, greater job satisfaction, fewer days of work missed, and fewer late days. Furthermore, although compulsive gamblers lost eight to 15 times more money than nonproblem gamblers, they had roughly the same rates of debt and wage garnishments. The researchers suggested either that fewer employment problems may result from more self-employment or, because pathological gambling is a progressive condition, the gambler's job performance may not begin to deteriorate until its later stages.

THE UNITED KINGDOM THREE COMMUNITY SURVEY

In their quest to discover some of the social indicators or "predictors" of gambling behavior, the authors of the United Kingdom survey specifically attempted to determine not only why some people choose to gamble while others do not, but also what factors determine the frequency and volume of gambling among those who do. They did so by a computerized interactional factor analyses which yielded the presence or absence of a variety of correlations between different forms of gambling and a large number of possible demographic, socioeconomic, and attitudinal variables.[34] Gambling was treated as the dependent variable while the personal and social factors, either in isolation or as constituents of various constellations, were treated as independent variables. It must be stressed that unlike most other studies, the United Kingdom survey attempted to discover the best predictors of normal or social gambling rather than those of abnormal or pathological gambling. In doing so, its authors not only investigated gambling in general, but they also differentiated among various kinds of gambling.

Sports betting. The authors concluded that gender is probably the best predictor of sports pool betting since men participated three times more frequently than women and spent more than twice as much on this form of gambling. The strongest trait constellation predictive of abstention for men was infrequent pub attendance with no history of parental gambling. No similar grouping of traits emerged to predict participation among men. The most likely predictors among women were having ten years or more in the same job with no prospects of promotion and holding a strong belief in luck. The least likely among women was a weak belief in luck.

Betting shop patronage. Gender was also the strongest predictor of betting shop usage since men bet five times more frequently than women and spent ten times as much per year in them. The best predictors of high frequency off-track betting among men were lower working class status, low job interest, high risk-taking orientation, and only an elementary school education. The best predictor of heavier betting expenditures was the claim of having "enough" free time. Analysis of average betting sizes suggested that the most likely high stakes bettors would be younger middle aged, more affluent, upper working class men. Whether men decided to bet at all was best predicted by having at least one parent who was a regular gambler, no regular hobbies, being more affluent, being in any social class other than lower middle, having attended either elementary or secondary school only, and low job interest. The men who were least likely to gamble were those whose parents were not regular gamblers, whose leisure time was marked by a strong family orientation, and who were better educated. Among women the single best predictor of abstinence was old age while the best predictors of participation were low job interest and high belief in luck.

Gaming. The strongest predictors of pub, casino, or private gaming among men were parental gambling, age, and income. More specifically, the highest frequencies of these forms of gambling were found among those whose mother and father both gambled (45.5%), the youngest (45%), and the more affluent (32.1%) and most affluent (32.4) men. The lowest frequencies of these kinds of gambling were found among the elderly (5.8%), the poorest (9.8%), and those among whom neither parent gambled (15.4%). The next best predictors were spending either the least or the most amount of time on hobby activities and being upwardly mobile. The strongest predictors of any participation at all in these forms of gaming were an individualistic orientation and the lack of an elite education. For women, the best predictors were high rates of TV watching, which the authors were at a loss to explain, and parental gambling.

Slot machines. Age rather than gender was the principal predictor of slot machine gambling in terms of both frequency and volume of play. Although only ten percent of all men and only two percent of all women played these machines on a regular basis, as many as one-third of all males and one-fifth of all females played them at least occasionally. Fully 20 percent of the youngest males were regular players as opposed to ten percent of the younger and only four percent of older men. Slot machine expenditures steadily decreased from an average of £37 per year among the youngest to £7 per year among the oldest players. They also showed a steady decrease with greater formal education. Although the most affluent men spent more on slot machines than the other groups, the poorest and wealthiest women spent more than those in the middle two groups: upper middle class women averaged only £3 per year. Surprisingly, the highest average expenditure of £136 per year occurred among men whose marriages had been terminated. A maximum expenditure of £1 per session was exceeded by only 12 percent of males and three percent of females. In fact, most players (66% of men; 76% of women) never spent more than five shillings per session. Those whose usual expenditures did exceed more than five shillings tended to be young men who were regular players; those who spent more than £1 per session were among the most affluent who played in private clubs and casinos.

Although the second strongest predictor of slot machine playing among both men and women was parental gambling, a number of other associations were related to preferences for entertainment. Regular participation in sports, dining out, pub and club attendance, cinema and theater attendance, and similar forms of entertainment were all closely associated with slot machine playing. The authors noted that participation in these forms of entertainment, which tend to attract the young, may also be a function of age and/or availability since and slot machines are commonly found in the establishments—restaurants, pubs, clubs, cinemas, etc.—that provide these forms of entertainment. In keeping with the age-relatedness of this form of gambling were the inverse correlations between slot machine playing and political involvement, community involvement, and leisure orientations around work and family life, all of which tend to develop with maturity. Interestingly, involvement in on- or off-track betting was definitely not associated with slot machine gambling. Other predictors of frequent slot machine gambling among men were being single and sporadic attendance at football matches, factors which may also be related to young adulthood with its relative lack of responsibility.

Bingo. As a rule, parental gambling and gender turned out to be two of the strongest predictors of participation in gambling in general as well as many specific forms. The most notable exception to these rules was club bingo which the authors expected to be confined largely to women since other studies had reported that among those who have ever played club bingo, women outnumbered men by margins as high as 2.5 to 1 (15% vs. 6%, respectively). However, in their study they found nearly equal proportions of male and female participants although the average annual bingo expenditures and losses of women did exceed those of men. Rather than gender, social class turned out to be the strongest predictor of bingo participation since it was confined almost exclusively to the working classes who enjoyed such other working class leisure pursuits as pub going and football (soccer). Other predictors of bingo were parental gambling, a strong belief in luck, and being in the "poorer" income category, and job dissatisfaction. Recent voluntary job changes, high but thwarted ambition, low job autonomy, old age, and a low incidence of TV watching were also associated with bingo playing by men while full-time employment, middle age, low education, and claims of having too much leisure time were associated with bingo playing by women.

All forms. Univariate analysis of the combined data revealed that gender was the only real predictor of gambling in general since men, who gambled an average of 123 times per year, did so nearly four times more often than women, who averaged only 35. The cumulative results of all forms of gambling failed to yield any other significant predictors in terms of either frequency of participation or volume of expenditures. Among the more suggestive variables were parental gambling, job-related factors, pub-going, and interest in football.

Multivariate analysis, in which the data for men and women were analyzed separately, yielded somewhat more fruitful results. The strongest predictor of gambling among men was irregular church attendance, a finding which lends some support to Devereux's **religion hypothesis** but which contradicts all other social structural theories. In accordance with this hypothesis were the findings that Roman Catholics had the highest gambling participation rates (67%), Anglicans the next highest (36%), and Nonconformist Protestants the third highest (27.5). However, the fact that all "Others," including Jews, had the lowest participation rates (12%), tended to weaken Devereux's position. The authors therefore pointed out it would probably be more correct to say that frequent church attendance would be predictive of nongambling.

Additional factors that tend to deter gambling among men are middle class social status, better education, disbelief in luck, marriage, higher job interest, involvement in community and political activities, and infrequent TV watching. Interestingly, high risk-taking was also associated with a low incidence of gambling which demonstrates that risk-taking is not necessarily a measure of one's proclivities for the types of risks involved in gambling. Since this cluster of traits describes the Protestant entrepreneurial middle classes, the authors felt that these results were "emphatically in line with Devereux's theorization."[35] Other indicators of low or nonparticipation were being married, social class stability, a long time at the same job, very low incomes, a collective approach toward increasing one's income, and conjugal role-sharing. Since this constellation describes working class men over 45 years of age, the authors suggested that "being thoroughly settled in a job and *not* experiencing social mobility in middle age makes for exceptionally low participation in gambling."[36]

Aside from sporadic church attendance, the next strongest predictor of active participation by men was parental gambling. This was followed by low involvement in hobbies, job dissatisfaction, stronger beliefs in luck, and entertainment seeking. Multivariate analysis of data on only those men who did gamble found that job-related factors and being single were among the strongest predictors of gambling.

Among women the strongest predictors of gambling were parental gambling, age (any age other than elderly), and having paid employment outside the home. The oldest women and housewives were the least likely to gamble. Middle-class women who attended church regularly and had a "home-centered" orientation also had low rates of gambling.

THE IOWA STUDY

The Iowa study group also tested some of the other psychosocial and demographic correlates of gambling and problem gambling that had been suggested by previous studies.[37] Although the study solicited information about all types of gambling, the researchers focused on lottery playing, the most popular form of gambling in Iowa at the time of the study. The 1,011 subjects sampled were asked questions on the frequency of their lottery of play since its inception in Iowa, in the last seven days, when play would be most likely for them, the amounts of money typically spent on the lottery, whether they felt that chance or skill was involved in winning, their reasons for playing, whether they had ever lost control over their gambling, and if any undesirable consequences had ever resulted from their gambling. The survey also included questions designed to elicit the sociodemographic and certain personality characteristics of the respondents.

Gambling of any kind was found to correlate with a number of different variables. Predictors of gambling, those variables that showed a significant positive association with it, included impulsiveness, competitiveness, big spending, lottery playing, the amount of money spent on lottery playing, alcohol use, interest in sports, childhood and recent exposure to gambling, residential mobility, full-time employment, Catholic or Jewish religious affiliation, being male, and being a military veteran. Negative correlates included age, education level, church attendance, and religious affiliation. Neither income, marital status, occupation, rural or urban residence, nor community size correlated with gambling.

Problem gambling was defined by self-admitted loss of gambling control and having experienced such negative consequences of gambling as borrowing money or resorting to illegal activities to pay for gambling or gambling debts, loss of time from work or school because of gambling, and being criticized for gambling. Loss of control was positively correlated with lottery playing, the amount of money spent on lottery playing, self-centeredness, competitiveness, big spending, impulsiveness, childhood exposure to gambling, alcohol use, residential mobility, renting one's home, Judaism, and never having been married. Gender, community size, rural or urban residence, employment, education, Protestantism, Catholicism, and prior military service were not correlated with loss of control while age and income showed negative correlations. Slight but significant positive correlations emerged between problem gambling as determined by self-admitted negative consequences and the amount of money spent on lottery playing, big spending, residential mobility, multiple marriages, widowhood, non-Caucasian ethnicity, Judaism, and military experience. Age and marriage were the only negative correlates while no correlation appeared between the experience of negative consequences and any of the other variables.

On the basis of a regression analysis of their data, the authors ranked the predictors of gambling and problem gambling. The best predictor of problem gambling was the belief that lottery outcomes were not random or chance events. That is, those who consulted astrological charts or kept track of winning numbers were most likely to have gambling problems. The best predictors of impaired gambling control were Judaism, impulsiveness, low income level, childhood exposure to gambling, the previous week's lottery expenditures, alcohol use, and a change in residence within the previous five years. Adverse consequences of gambling were predicted by being Jewish, weekly lottery expenditures, loss of control, being unmarried, number of marriages, changes in residence, being widowed, and military service. The best predictors of gambling of any kind were the amount of money spent on lotteries during the previous week, and past and present lottery play. The next best predictor was being Jewish with current and childhood exposure to other gamblers, alcohol use, Catholicism, and lower educational levels being third in importance.

From their factor analysis and tests of significance the authors found that more respondents (76%) reported gambling than loss of control gambling, and that more reported loss of control gambling (26%) than adverse consequences (6%). They therefore concluded that problem gambling is a progressive phenomenon involving three distinct sequential phases: gambling, loss of control gambling, and unfavorable consequences resulting from gambling. They interpreted these findings to mean not only that problem gambling is preceded by nonproblem gambling, but also that lottery playing and other kinds of recreational gambling do not inevitably lead to problem gambling.

Gender Differences. A reanalysis of these data attempted to discover any possible gender differences in the etiology of problem gambling. To do so, the researchers subjected their original data to a multivariate analysis to distinguish the correlates or predictors of problem gambling among women from those of men.[38] Specifically, the researchers correlated problem gambling with three kinds of variables: social structural or "past experience" variables, associational variables, and attitudinal variables. The social structural variables included age, educational level, previous military service, religious affiliation, childhood exposure to gambling, residential mobility, and frequency of marriage. Curiously, such measures of social status as income, occupation, home ownership, etc., were not considered, nor were such variables as marital status, rural or urban residence, or community size. Associational variables that were tested included the amount of money spent on lottery play, team lottery play, level of alcohol consumption, current exposure to gambling, and the amount of money spent on leisure activities. Attitudinal variables that were tested included a series of questions designed to determine the degree of the respondents' civic personality (maturity, responsibility, etc.), whether or not they described themselves as big spenders, and their gambling related attitudes or cognitions as determined by whether they believed that lottery play is a matter of chance or skill and whether or not the odds of winning a lottery can be improved by such means as consultation of astrological charts, keeping track of winning numbers, and picking one's own numbers.

Analysis revealed a number of gender differences in the risk factors for problem gambling. Specifically, none of the social structural or "past experience" variables were associated with problem gambling among men. However, those that were determined to be risk factors for women included previous military service, a lack of either Catholic or Protestant religious affiliation, exposure to gambling in childhood, residential mobility, and frequency of marriage. The associational variables that predicted problem gambling among both sexes were alcohol consumption and the amount of money spent on lotteries. Team lottery play was found to be a risk factor for women while current exposure to gambling was a risk factor for men. For both men and women the only attitudinal risk factors associated with problem gambling were describing one's self as a big spender and believing that lottery play is not simply a game of chance (i.e., there are ways to beat the odds). Thus, this correlational analysis found no evidence for the **life cycle** or **religion hypotheses** but provided some evidence supporting **cognitive psychological theory**.

Gambling Among New Jersey College Students

A correlational study of youthful gambling was conducted by Michael Frank[39] who undertook a three-year investigation of the gambling behavior of 636 undergraduates attending a college near Atlantic City, New Jersey. This study included a series of interview questions designed to determine which segments of this population were most likely to gamble. It also included the South Oaks Gambling Screen (SOGS)[40] which was used to identify, and determine the frequency of, problem and pathological gambling within this population.

Since Frank found no relationship between gambling and a number of social and demographic variables, he concluded that casino gambling is neither an age- nor class-based phenomenon.[41] Specifically, he found that three-fifths (59%) of his sample had gambled within the previous year, almost half (42%) in the past six months, and one-quarter (24%) had gambled within one month of the survey. He also found that while a large proportion (66%) of those who gambled were under 21, the minimum legal age limit for casino gambling, a nearly identical proportion (68%) of those who did not gamble were also under 21. Since he found no association between gambling and such demographic and social variables such as gender, employment status, family size, parental marital status, parental home ownership, parental income, or parental education level, he concluded that these were not determining factors.

On the basis of the students' gambling preferences and betting habits, Frank also concluded that for most of these young people "gambling is, in fact, recreational and controlled."[42] Most of the subjects (64%) preferred slot machine gambling although some claimed blackjack (28%) and roulette (6%) as their games of preference. Maximum bets rarely exceeded $5 although some (8%) reported that their usual bets were $25. Nearly one-quarter of the sample (24%) indicated that the largest bets they had ever placed exceeded $25. Most staked no more than $50 per session although seven percent staked more than $100. Although most of the students reported that they also drank while they gambled, they averaged only 1.4 drinks per gambling session.

There were nevertheless some for whom gambling could pose a definite problem. Interestingly, when asked about their gambling success in terms of overall wins and losses, most respondents (66%) reported that they were either breaking even or that they were actually ahead of the game. This is a statistical impossibility, however, since the odds advantages that are built into all casino games favor the house. He interpreted this as demonstrating that most gamblers hold an erroneous cognitive bias concerning their gambling outcomes. Roughly four percent of the respondents reported regular gambling on a weekly or more frequent basis and four percent also reported gambling alone. Although these respondents may represent those who are "at risk" of eventually becoming problem gamblers, only seven of those who were included in both groups were also heavy bettors. According to data obtained from the SOGS questionnaire, six percent could be regarded as potential or probable pathological gamblers, a percentage which Frank considers to be "alarmingly high" in comparison with that of the general population.[43]

Frank argued that lottery playing and speeding tickets are among the best predictors of casino gambling for these students. His first conclusion was based on the finding that nearly 75 percent of the students who gambled in a casino within the previous year also played the lottery while only 59 percent of the nongamblers played the lottery. Since casino gamblers were also more likely to have been apprehended for exceeding speed limits while driving an automobile than nongamblers, Frank suggested that another predictor of gambling is the tendency to violate speed laws. He interpreted these findings as indicating a general propensity toward risk-taking by gamblers and suggesting the existence of "underlying personality differences between gamblers and nongamblers."[44]

Gambling Among Minnesota College Students

Another survey of gambling among American college students was conducted on three campuses in different regions of Minnesota.[45] One of the principal purposes of the study was to assess the relationship between gambling and drug use on Minnesota's campuses; another was to determine the extent of any regional differences in these behaviors. The survey, which included questions on demographics, frequency of gambling and amounts spent, licit (tobacco and alcohol) and illicit drug use, and the South Oaks Gambling Screen,[46] was administered to a total of 1770 undergraduates: 373 students attended the University of Minnesota's Twin Cities campus (UMTC) located in the Twin Cities metropolitan area in the southeastern part of the state, 868 attended the University of Minnesota's Duluth campus (UMD) in the northeast, and 529 attended Moorhead State University (MSU) in the northwest.

In terms of demographics, a number of gender differences materialized since the sample included fairly equal numbers of males and females. However, no ethnic differences emerged since the subject population was predominantly White. Freshmen, sophomores, juniors, and seniors were also equally represented except on the UMTC campus where seniors comprised roughly half the sample. Most respondents on all campuses were 19 to 22 years of age, some were older (roughly one-third at UMTC were over 22), and the remainder were under 18 years of age. The major findings of the study are summarized in Table 11-1 which reveals that rates of gambling among college students are highest in Duluth and lowest in the Twin Cities while Moorhead State has the highest incidence of problem gambling.

Table 11-1. GAMBLING, PROBLEM GAMBLING, AND DRUG USE ON THREE MINNESOTA CAMPUSES

	UMTC	UMD	MSU
Gambling frequency			
Past 12 months			
Total	77.7%	89.2%	84.5%
Males	83.4%	92.5%	88.3%
Females	76.1%	85.9%	82.6%
Monthly or less			
Total	68.4%	77.1%	73.3%
Males	65.6%	73.5%	69.2%
Females	72.6%	81.6%	77.3%

Continued on next page

	UMTC	UMD	MSU
Weekly or daily			
Total	9.4%	12.1%	11.2%
Males	17.8%	19.0%	19.2%
Females	3.6%	4.2%	5.3%

Type of gambling, past 12 months

	UMTC	UMD	MSU
Cards with friends			
Total	29.5%	41.9%	36.9%
Males	50.3%	55.4%	52.3%
Females	15.2%	26.3%	26.6%
Cards at a casino			
Total	29.2%	42.5%	34.6%
Males	43.9%	57.4%	50.5%
Females	18.3%	26.3%	24.0%
Bet on animals (horse or dog racing, cockfights, etc.)			
Total	6.7%	10.4%	9.6%
Males	10.8%	15.2%	15.9%
Females	3.0%	5.2%	5.6%
Bet on sports			
Total	23.1%	38.5%	29.9%
Males	41.4%	56.3%	53.7%
Females	13.7%	18.4%	17.4%
Dice for money			
Total	7.8%	16.0%	13.8%
Males	12.1%	19.6%	20.1%
Females	4.1%	11.9%	9.5%
Lottery			
Total	56.0%	65.2%	60.5%
Males	58.6%	67.5%	67.8%
Females	55.8%	63.3%	55.6%
Bingo for money			
Total	10.2%	18.7%	20.0%
Males	12.1%	17.0%	19.6%
Females	9.6%	20.8%	20.1%
Machines			
Total	50.1%	71.3%	61.1%
Males	54.1%	72.4%	63.6%
Females	49.2%	70.7%	59.9%
Games of skill (pool, golf, bowling, etc.)			
Total	17.7%	31.8%	22.3%
Males	33.8%	45.9%	39.3%
Females	5.6%	16.4%	9.9%
Pull tabs			
Total	19.8%	28.5%	33.3%
Males	17.2%	32.5%	37.4%
Females	21.8%	24.3%	30.3%

Continued on next page

	UMTC	UMD	MSU
High risk stocks/investments			
Total	3.2%	5.8%	3.6%
Males	5.1%	9.1%	5.6%
Females	2.0%	2.0%	2.3%

Gambling losses, past 12 months

	UMTC	UMD	MSU
None			
Total	46.0%	36.1%	41.2%
Males	45.2%	33.4%	39.3%
Females	46.2%	39.6%	42.6%
Less than $10			
Total	20.1%	23.7%	21.8%
Males	14.8%	17.9%	14.2%
Females	24.4%	29.1%	26.1%
$10 to $49.99			
Total	17.4%	23.1%	23.7%
Males	19.4%	23.5%	22.3%
Females	16.2%	23.4%	25.1%
$50 to $99.99			
Total	8.8%	7.3%	6.3%
Males	9.7%	10.0%	9.5%
Females	7.6%	4.2%	4.3%
$100 or more			
Total	7.7%	9.8%	7.1%
Males	11.0%	15.3%	14.7%
Females	5.6%	3.7%	2.0%

SOGS Scores

	UMTC	UMD	MSU
Zero			
Total	77.2%	66.9%	70.5%
Males	69.4%	59.2%	59.8%
Females	81.7%	75.7%	78.0%
1 or 2			
Total	18.5%	25.3%	22.9%
Males	24.2%	29.4%	27.1%
Females	15.2%	20.6%	20.1%
3 or 4			
Total	2.9%	4.8%	3.6%
Males	4.5%	6.8%	7.9%
Females	2.0%	2.7%	0.7%
5 or more			
Total	1.3%	2.9%	3.0%
Males	1.9%	4.6%	5.1%
Females	1.0%	1.0%	1.3%

Continued on next page

Licit Drug Use

Never use	15.8%ny	10.3%	10.8%
Twice monthly or less	42.1%	36.6%	40.3%
Weekly or more often	42.1%	53.1%	49.0%

Illicit Drug use

Never use	70.8%	63.6%	76.6%
Twice monthly or less	22.8%	27.4%	16.6%
Weekly or more often	6.4%	9.0%	6.8%

Correlates of gambling frequency and problem gambling. Gambling frequency and SOGS scores were correlated with a number of variables including age, gender, problem gambling in a parent, class standing, (i.e., Fr, So, Jr, or Sr), current course load, grade point average, hours of weekly employment, past year income, amount of disposable income per month, credit card debt, licit drug use frequency, and illicit drug use frequency. The variables most strongly correlated with weekly or daily gambling on all three campuses were gender, licit drug use, having a disposable income of $200 or more per month, illicit drug use, and parental problem gambling. Those most strongly correlated with SOGS scores were parental problem gambling, illicit drug use, licit drug use, and gender. More specifically, for example, on two campuses (UMD and MSU) the sons and daughters of problem gamblers were 12 times more likely to score as pathological gamblers on the SOGS than others. At MSU males were also 12 times more likely to be problem gamblers than females while the chances were four times greater for those with disposable incomes of at least $200 a month.

Correlates of Pathological Gambling Down Under

For comparative data, a retrospective survey of 85 consecutively-admitted patients was conducted at a major Australian treatment unit.[48] In addition to standard demographic data, the questionnaire was also designed to elicit information on their gambling behavior before it had become a problem and for the six months immediately prior to their seeking treatment. Far more men (89%) than women (11%) were included in the sample. Over a third (34.5%) had been introduced to gambling by their parents. As determined by education level and employment, most of the subjects came from lower socioeconomic backgrounds. Only four percent had a university education, 30 percent had attended a technical school, and 66 percent had a secondary school education; 19 percent held professional positions, 62 percent were employed in a non-professional capacity, and 19 percent were unemployed.

Gambling preferences tended to fall into certain patterns. All but one of the women indicated that they were addicted to slot machines. Before gambling had become a problem for them, most men (58%) bet exclusively on horses, 29 percent played machines only, 2 percent played in illegal casinos, and 11 percent preferred other kinds of gambling. However, after gambling had become a problem there was a definite shift away from horses toward illegal casino gambling and away from a single form of gambling toward a variety of forms. Specifically, just 20 percent continued to bet exclusively on horses, 17 percent played only machines, and 12 percent gambled only in illegal casinos. The remaining 51 percent had graduated to a combination of several forms of gambling. As problem gambling progressed among this population, the median bet size increased from $10 per bet in the nonproblem period to $200 per bet.

As part of a prevalence study of pathological gambling in New Zealand, several demographic characteristics were also examined.[49] A number of significant differences were found between those identified as problem and probable pathological gamblers from the entire sample of 4,053 respondents. Specifically, the most salient distinguishing features of the troubled gamblers were gender (male), parental problem gambling, ethnicity (non-Caucasian), age (under 30), marital status (single), household size (larger), and employment status (unemployed). The troubled gamblers also preferred continuous forms of gambling, the most favored of which were racetrack (horse and dog) betting and gaming machines, while the nonproblem gamblers tended to prefer noncontinuous forms such as lotteries, Lotto drawings, and raffles.

Correlates of Active Slot Machine Gambling in Germany

Reviews of the literature on slot machine gambling in Germany[50] revealed that roughly 10.2 percent of adults (registered voters over 18 years of age) were "active" gamblers who had played within the past three months. Of these .7 percent were described as "intensive" gamblers who played at least five hours a week. Several definite demographic trends were observed. In terms of:

Gender: Over four times as many males (17.3%) as females (4.2%) were active gamblers.

Age: Participation rates steadily decreased with age.
26.6%, 18 to 19 years
19.0%, 20 to 29 years
11.8%, 30 to 39 years

9.9%, 40 to 49 years
6.6%, 50 to 59 years
3.1%, 60 and older

Education: Participation among males tended to decrease with
educational level.
19.4%, vocational school without an apprenticeship
18.8%, vocational school with apprenticeship
16.3%, high school
17.6%, college
7.9%, university

Occupation: Participation among males also tended to decrease with
occupational level.
29.7%, never employed
20.1%, unskilled labor
22.2%, skilled labor
12.1%. clerical/civil servant
13.6%, self-employed

Employment: Participation was far greater among the unemployed than
the employed
33.0%, unemployed
22.3%, in training
19.0%, employed
6.7%, retired

Marital Status: Active participation was also much higher among single
(19.7%) than married (8.1%) respondents.

Income: Gambling rates and income were inversely correlated
71%, less than DM 1,000 per month
60%, more than DM 6,000 per month

Stress: One-quarter (26%) of the intensive gamblers reported that feelings
of stress were associated with their gambling.

Correlates of Pathological Gambling Severity in Maryland

Another group of researchers studied patients in treatment in an attempt
to determine which factors might be associated with, and therefore responsi-

ble for, the most severe gambling problems.[51] Questionnaires that were administered to all pathological gamblers who received care in three Maryland treatment centers between 1983 and 1989 revealed that most of the respondents were quite similar in terms of demographic background: they tended to be male Caucasian high school graduates from small family backgrounds who were married, middle class, middle aged, and employed. The incomes of these individuals were also uniformly distributed: 27 percent had annual incomes of $10,000 or less; 21.8 percent fell between $10,000 and $20,000; 20 percent made from $20,001 to $30,000; 13 percent, from $30,001 to $40,000; and 12 percent earned over $40,000.

A large proportion reported that their parents had been abusive drinkers, drug users, or gamblers who had died at a relatively young age and a substantial proportion were themselves the victims of various kinds of abuse. Specifically, 37.9 percent had parents who were "plagued" by alcohol or gambling problems: 37.3 percent reported paternal alcohol abuse while 27.3 percent reported paternal and 8 percent maternal gambling problems. In 50.3 percent of the cases, the mother had died before the subject was 18 years-old while 14.2 percent reported the death of the father before this age. More than 41 percent reported having been physically or sexually abused in childhood, over 26 percent had a drug problem, 50.8 percent abused alcohol, 15 percent had experienced some form of eating disorder, and 25 percent had attempted suicide. Nearly half (48%) had sought prior treatment on an outpatient basis while 22 percent had previously been inpatients. Over 20 percent reported legal problems and 13 percent had been incarcerated.

The authors of the study speculated that such a history "may indicate inadequate resistance to indulgence and early loss of parental support and guidance"[52] and may therefore contribute to a more severe gambling problem. To test this hypothesis they first calculated each subject's gambling severity rating by dividing the size of a person's gambling debt by his or her annual income with higher scores indicating greater severity. They then employed a *logit analysis*, a complex categorical statistical analysis which describes a ratio or percentage comparing the probability that an event will occur to the probability that it will not, to determine the most likely predictors of problem gambling severity.

Their analysis determined that the strongest predictor of high gambling severity was death of the mother before the subject was 18 years old; next in order of strength were having a high school education, past physical or sexual abuse, and a past or present drug abuse problem. Interestingly, however, the *severity* of problem gambling was inversely related to a history of drug abuse. The authors speculated that early death of the mother could exacerbate any ensuing gambling problems since "the earlier the emotional bond is broken, the more the gambler may have been deprived of early emotional support, and the more the gambler may have a need to find a source of security, be it financial or otherwise."[53] They went on to venture that heavy gambling following physical or sexual abuse "may be seen as an attempt to recoup lost self-esteem" and that high school graduates are more likely to become more involved in gambling than drop-outs since they "appear to be more venturesome and risk-seeking than those who did not attain that level."[54] Finally, they argued that drug abuse and gambling severity are inversely related because serious gamblers require clarity of thought. They insisted that "The more the gambler gets involved with drugs, the more befogged that person's focus of attention becomes . . . and the less the ability to get highly involved with serious gambling. . . . Those patients with the more severe gambling problems tend to steer clear of drug usage and dependence."[55] But what if this is not the case? Perhaps, the authors speculated, "The spending of money to satisfy the need for drugs depletes the compulsive gambler of his means for satisfying his gambling addiction" and "The needs of the drug and gambling addiction compete and conflict"[56] thereby forcing the most severe gambling addicts to rationally order their priorities. Then, too, they added, multiple addictions could appear sequentially with the gambling addiction eventually becoming so strong that it replaces drug addiction.[57] Apparently the authors found it unthinkable that the reason for the inverse correlation between gambling severity and drug abuse might remain unknown.

Correlates of Adolescent Fruit Machine Addiction

His review and synthesis of the literature on adolescent gambling prompted Mark Griffiths[58] to propose a "risk factor model" of slot or fruit machine addiction. The comprehensive list of risk factors he compiled, which incorporated many ideas of earlier theoreticians, included:

1. male gender
2. early age of initiation to gambling (about 8 years)
3. playing for reasons other than winning money
4. an early big win
5. began playing with parents or by one's self
6. feeling depressed before gambling
7. feeling excitement while gambling
8. irrationality while playing
9. attracted to the "aura" of the machines
10. attributing success to skill
11. poor scholastic achievement

12. engaging in other potentially addictive behaviors
13. lower socioeconomic class background
14. parental gambling/other addictive problems
15. history of delinquency (theft, truancy, etc.) in order to gamble

As noted elsewhere, other researchers have also suggested that ethnic minority status, psychological distress, and early traumatic experiences such as the death of a parent and physical or sexual abuse in childhood may also be important risk factors. Griffiths was careful to emphasize that none of these factors alone necessarily indicates problem gambling but those who experience or exhibit a number of these factors will be more likely to become addicted to gambling. In this respect, his scheme was similar to that of personality theorists who attempted to associate problem gambling certain clusters of personality traits.

Griffiths also listed a number of possible cues or warning signs to help parents, educators, and prevention specialists detect gambling problems. They include:

1. abruptly declining scholastic standards
2. leaving the home every evening and evasiveness about one's activities
3. abrupt personality changes (moodiness, defensiveness. etc.)
4. unexplained disappearances of money from the home
5. inability to account for the money received from sales of possessions
6. discontinuation of previously enjoyed activities
7. reduced ability to concentrate
8. adoption of a "couldn't care less" attitude
9. lack of attention to personal appearance or hygiene

To this list should probably be added the inability to account for money obtained from sources other than borrowing, employment, the sale of possessions and gifts, etc. Moreover, since periodic wins are always possible, the list should also include the unexpected appearance of larger than normal sums of money and the inability to account for them.

Griffiths noted that while many of these individual behaviors are common to all adolescents, the sudden appearance of a number of them in a young person should alert parents and school officials to the possibility that a serious gambling problem is developing. This is particularly important in light of the findings of a recent Canadian study of parental knowledge and attitudes about youthful gambling which found that because parents still know very little about it they are in dire need of such educational measures.[59] It should be noted that although Griffiths gave special attention to fruit machine gambling in the United Kingdom, his list of cues should be equally useful in detecting problems with other forms of gambling that may be popular among young people in other parts of the world. He and a colleague later reported on the risk factors common to adolescent fruit machine, lottery, scratchcard, video game, and internet gamblers.[60]

Correlates of Gambling-Related Suicide in Australia

A unique study of gambling-related suicide investigated the correlates of 44 cases that occurred between 1990 and 1997 in the State of Victoria, Australia.[61] That gambling was a factor in these cases is known from the suicide notes left by the victims, testimonies of their survivors, the fact that the victims had previously sought professional help for a gambling problem, and had written records of heavy gambling or gambling-related debts immediately prior to the suicide. The researchers claimed that although the coroner's reports they reviewed did not unequivocally state that gambling was the primary cause, they were confident that it either "acted as a catalyst or played a relevant role in the suicide."[62]

The demographic correlates that emerged from the analysis of the coroner's case records included gender and occupational (socioeconomic) status. Far more were male (88.6%) than female (11.4%). This eight-to-one ratio of males to females, which was nearly twice that of the four-to-one ratio of suicides in the general population, meant that males were greatly overrepresented in this sample. Far more of the victims had been skilled (32.6%) and unskilled laborers (27.9%) or were unemployed (23.3%) than had held professional positions (2.3%), managerial positions (4.7%), were self-employed (4.6%), or were retired (4.6%). Thus the greatest number of suicides (83.9%) were either working class or unemployed.

A number of mental or emotional problems were also revealed. Nearly one-third (31.8%) of the cases suffered from depression prior to or at the time of death. Three (6.8%) claimed to have been suffering intense bereavement over the loss of a loved one. One-fourth were described as either heavy drinkers (13.6%), former alcohol and other drug abusers (6.8%), or current drug users (4.5%). However, only 15 percent of these cases had elevated postmortem blood alcohol levels as compared to 33 percent to 46% of suicides that were not gambling-related. Nearly one-third (31.8%) had made previous suicide attempts. Not surprisingly, financial difficulties and large gambling debts were found in every case. In terms of stress, over one-third (34%) had been having problems in their domestic relationships and four (9/1%) had experienced problems related to their employment. One-quarter of the cases had previously sought help for their gambling problems either from a professional treatment provider or a self-help group such as GA. However, low treatment compliance and poor attendance were typical.

Criminal activities were also a factor in eight (18.2%) of these cases. To finance their gambling one had stolen money from his parents, another had multiple convictions for fraud, a third had embezzled money from the club for which he had been the treasurer, a fourth had stolen money from a business account he held jointly with a friend, two had stolen from their employers, and two had forged checks and bank withdrawals.

Not surprisingly, the researchers concluded that the most probable immediate cause of suicide among these cases was depression triggered by acute financial and/or legal crises resulting from gambling. The greatest period of risk occurs immediately after a severe loss when the extent of their gambling-related debts and/or criminal offenses are most likely to be exposed. Their findings further indicated that male gender, low socioeconomic status, difficulties in domestic relationships, a history of seeking help, and previous suicide attempts may also be risk factors. Contrary to the findings of others, however, they found that chemical dependence did not appear to be a factor since relatively few of these cases exhibited elevated blood alcohol levels at the time of death. Although retrospective data obtained from relatives suggested that low self-esteem and introversion may also be contributing factors, the researchers warned that such data may be distorted by either the survivors' attempts to "explain" the suicide or their fear of stigmatization.

Correlates of Gambling Among North American Juveniles

Roughly ten years after his initial literature review of adolescent gambling which included six studies of American youth conducted between 1984 and 1988 (see previous chapter), Durand Jacobs expanded his review to include nine United States and six Canadian studies conducted between 1989 and 1999. He now found that the median number of those in the United States who had gambled at all in the previous 12 months had increased from 45 percent to 60 percent. Thus, "juvenile gambling throughout the United States has increased significantly over the past decade and a half."[64] However, the average age at which the respondents had begun gambling remained 12 years. The Canadian studies yielded comparable results with an average age of commencement of 12 years but a slightly higher past year gambling average of 66 percent. On the basis of these studies Jacobs concluded not only that nearly seven out of every ten junior and senior high school students throughout North America had gambled for money in the past year, but also that "minors . . . have managed to penetrate and participate to some degree in every form of social, government sanctioned, and illegal gambling available in their home communities and places where they travel."[65] The most popular forms of gambling among adolescents were card, dice, and board games with other family members; games of skill with peers; sports betting with peers and through bookmakers; bingo; and lotteries. Males start gambling earlier in life, participate in more forms, gamble more frequently, risk more money, and experience more problems than females. Males also tend to prefer games of skill and sports betting while females prefer games of chance but participation rates in parimutuel betting and electronic machine gambling are roughly equal.

Jacobs called upon the **gateway** or **precursor hypothesis** to explain increasing rates of adolescent gambling by arguing that the legalization of even one form constitutes a stepping-stone that leads to other forms of gambling, both legal and illegal. Just as the authors of the first United States national gambling survey[66] found that the overall gambling rates of adults were higher in states in which some forms were legalized (see Chapter 7), Jacobs found higher overall gambling rates among adolescents in jurisdictions having government sponsored lotteries: the median frequency of adolescents who had gambled during the past year was 45 percent in states without lotteries but 66 percent in states and provinces that had lotteries. Jacobs explained this phenomenon, which he referred to as the "Pied Piper effect,"[67] by suggesting that government sponsorship, support, and promotion of state and provincial lotteries creates an ambiance of social tolerance toward gambling which gives adolescents the impression that gambling in any form is acceptable. This impression is further reinforced by the permissive attitudes and behavior of parents and other older relatives who often introduce children to gambling, as well as by lottery vendors who are willing to sell to minors. Although Jacobs judiciously admitted that no direct causal association between lotteries and increasing rates of adolescent gambling has yet been established, he nevertheless maintained that "the circumstantial evidence clearly points in that direction."[68]

Further analysis provided strong support for the **availability and exposure hypothesis**. Rather than differentiate "at-risk/potential pathological" from "problem/probable pathological" gamblers as the authors of all epidemiological studies have done and as he did in his initial review, Jacobs lumped the two categories into a single group which he referred to as those with Serious Gambling-Related Problems or the SGRP group. He found not only that more children were gambling now than in the past, but also that more were now experiencing gambling-related problems: the average proportion of United States children in the SGRP group increased from ten to 14 percent between 1988 and 1998; in Canada an average of 15 percent were categorized as SGRP. These findings led Jacobs to conclude that, "as increasing numbers of juveniles participate in an expanding array of gambling opportunities around them, an increasing number of them will experience serious gambling-related problems."[69]

The correlations Jacobs found between problem gambling and other demographic, behavioral, and psychosocial variables were also relevant to a number of other motivational hypotheses. Although he found no relationship between current age and problem gambling, he did find a correlation between the age of commencement of gambling and problem gambling. Thus, the fact that far more of those in the SGRP group started gambling before the age of 12 than did those with no gambling problems supports the **early start hypothesis**. His finding that the SGRP groups contained three to five times more boys than girls supports the **gender hypothesis**. The **parental gambling hypothesis** was supported by the observation that those in the SGRP group reported two to three times the levels of parental gambling and excessive gambling than others. In comparison with those having no gambling problems, the SGRP group also reported higher rates of illegal activities and involvement with the police, truancy and poorer school performance, and such psychological problems as unhappiness, depression, and anxiety. The **rural-urban residence** or **community size hypothesis** found support in the observation that those in the SGRP group are more likely to live in cities than in suburban or rural areas. In accordance with the **continuous forms hypothesis**, Jacobs also found that those in the SGRP group preferred such continuous interactive games as video arcade games, gaming machines, poker, games of skill, and sports betting. The **co-addiction hypothesis** found support in the fact that the SGRP group had twice the rate of tobacco and alcohol use and two to four times the rate of other drug use as those with no gambling problems. Jacobs attributed these correlations to the psychological needs of these individuals to reduce stress and escape reality. He did so because the most frequent self-reported reasons for gambling given by those in the SGRP were excitement, the prospect of winning money, because they are "good at it," to escape, to find distraction from their problems, boredom, loneliness, depression, to feel more powerful or in control, shyness, and to make friends. Those in this group were also more likely to report such dissociative reactions as losing track of time, feeling like a different person, feeling as though they were outside themselves, feeling as though they were in a trance, and experiencing memory blackouts while gambling.

Because Jacobs believed that North America will see an even greater expansion of gambling and gambling expenditures than currently exist, he predicted that rates of underage gambling would grow to 80 percent in coming years. He believed that boys will engage in even greater levels of sports betting with their peers in school and high stakes poker games in their homes. Outside the home they will seek out bookmakers for sports betting and they will be drawn to sports oriented lottery games that appear to require skill, scratch offs, and electronic gaming machines. Both boys and girls will be attracted to interactive video lottery terminals and more girls will take up gambling as a recreational diversion. Jacobs was also convinced that children will start gambling at continually younger ages as more forms of gambling are legalized and parental attitudes toward gambling become even more relaxed. As a consequence, the future will see increasingly higher levels of children with serious gambling-related problems. Moreover, unlike others who believe that children and adolescents eventually "mature out" of their heavy gambling involvement, Jacobs suggested that these problems may persist as they grow up thereby raising adult rates of pathological gambling, as well. He insisted, however, that only prospective cohort studies will be able to verify his predictions.

Chapter 12

CRITIQUE OF QUANTITATIVE STUDIES

DEMOGRAPHIC STUDIES

Taken together, the quantitative studies reviewed in this section reveal a number of important facts about gambling. They conclusively demonstrate, for example, that gambling is *not* a deviant behavior; on the contrary, it is quite normative since an overwhelming majority of people gamble. They also demonstrate that males tend to gamble more than females overall, that gambling is very common among children and adolescents, that people living in or near larger population centers tend to gamble more than those living in smaller population centers, that young people tend to gamble more than the elderly, and that people tend to gamble more when they have more opportunities for doing so. Thus, these studies refute the **deviance hypothesis** but support the **gender**, **rural-urban residence**, **life cycle**, and **availability and exposure hypotheses**.

However, demographic studies are descriptive rather than explanatory. That is, they can tell us *what* is happening but not *why* it is happening. As some researchers have pointed out, although the pictures of gambling participation painted by demographic studies may be useful for descriptive and marketing purposes, they are nevertheless incomplete for those seeking to understand the motivations underlying gambling behavior.[1] As the authors of the Australian telephone survey readily admitted, "Indeed, the quantitative methodology used precludes an explanatory discussion."[2] While such studies may reveal which segments of the population are engaging in which forms of gambling or which are the heaviest gamblers and which are the lightest, they fail to distinguish which individuals in any socioeconomic group gamble for which particular reasons. Figures alone do not reveal why young people gamble more than older people, why men gamble more than women, why gambling is more prevalent in cities than in small towns, or even why members of one socioeconomic class may gamble more or less than any other, and all attempts to explain such findings are entirely speculative. This is because the behaviors they are attempting to assess are completely divorced from the individual, social, and cultural settings in which they occur. By their very nature, demographic analyses are incapable of isolating any of the less tangible social, emotional, cognitive, and biological factors that may influence individual gambling decisions. Thus, analyses of this sort ignore such crucial influences as subcultural norms and peer pressure that may encourage or discourage gambling, anxiety and depression that gambling may alleviate, the strength of people's beliefs in their ability to win, and individual differences in the needs for relaxation and stimulation that gambling may meet. Studies based on secondary data, like those of Tec, Li and Smith, and others, are especially vulnerable to this criticism.

Another criticism is that the determinations of many demographic studies are not only inferential and inconclusive, but they are often contradictory. Even some of the more recent demographic studies have arrived at entirely different conclusions from others and therefore support entirely different hypotheses. Although a number of such studies have suggested that gambling is positively related to socioeconomic status and income, a number of others did not. Thus, one study claims that gambling is a matter of marital status and another claims that marital status has no bearing on the issue; some say that it is a matter of community size while others maintain it is not. One study finds that gambling is a high income phenomenon, another attributes it to low socioeconomic status, and a third finds no association between social class and gambling. Consequently, one reviewer felt that any such relationship has yet to be established.[3] Still others have reported that different forms of gambling are favored by different income groups. In New York City, for example, it was found that low-income gamblers preferred numbers games, middle-income gamblers preferred sports and racetrack betting, and high-income gamblers preferred casino gaming.[4] According to another reviewer, "This mosaic of gambling preferences implies that the correlation between social-economic status and gambling depends upon which gambling game is under scrutiny."[5]

At times the different kinds of data obtained by a single study can be used to support *and* reject a hypotheses at the same time. For example, the findings of the first United States national survey demonstrate that gambling rates increase with income, that the amounts of money wagered by people in different income categories falls into a "u-shaped" curve with those in the middle-income bracket staking the least, and that the proportion of their earnings that people lose decreases with income. These findings mean that the Veblenian **affluence hypothesis** is supported by measures of incidence, is not supported by measures of volume, and is rejected by measures of loss. In the final analysis, we still don't know whether gambling is motivated more by poverty or affluence.

One of the most frequently voiced criticisms of statistical surveys in general is that despite their claims of scientific rigor and objectivity, they are often quite subjective and therefore highly inconsistent from one to the next. In the first place many quantitative studies are subjective in terms of which forms of gambling will be investigated and which will not and, therefore, which forms will be held to represent gambling in general and which will not. Once that decision has been made, the researchers are left to decide which variables will be selected for study, which will be correlated with which others, which hypotheses will be accepted or rejected on what grounds, and how the class boundaries of such interval variables as age, income, and rates of gambling will be determined. Thus, there is little agreement among different gambling researchers as to how "heavy," "regular," "moderate" or "occasional," and "nongamblers" will be defined.[7] At what point should one be considered a heavy, moderate, or light gambler? Is someone who once gambled but now abstains a nongambler? Does an occasional gambler gamble once, twice, or three times a week? A month? A year? Should researchers investigate their subjects' lifetime or current gambling practices? Should "current" gambling be defined as that which has occurred within the past two months, the past six months, or the past year?

Another common fault of many statistical surveys is that their reliability, hence, their validity, may be questionable since their conclusions are based on self-reported data which is often highly subjective and erroneous. Some questionnaire items touch upon sensitive issues of a highly personal and perhaps even unlawful nature. Many respondents are reluctant to be entirely truthful in answering since they feel their responses could be self-incriminatory. The validity of any conclusions based on information that is false or likely to be false is therefore suspect. A study which attempted to ascertain the extent to which young people may be exhibiting dependence on amusement arcade video and electronic gaming machines in the United Kingdom vividly illustrates these points.[8] In the first place, this study was criticized for asking its youthful respondents to give their own name as well as the full names, addresses, and telephone numbers of their parents.[9] In attempting to elicit information about dependency, the study asked only about the amounts of time and money the respondents spent on these machines. Its critic pointed out that even though some children may play these machines for long periods and spend large amounts of money on them they are not, in and of themselves, indicators of dependency. Moreover, the children were asked only how much of their own money they spent on these machines and nothing about money they may have diverted from other sources such as their school lunch money, and no correlations were drawn between such variables as frequency of gambling and amounts of money spent. Finally, since this study failed to report specifics on the most heavily involved gamblers, it was criticized for diverting attention away from precisely those individuals it was intended to investigate and who are at the highest risk of developing gambling problems.[10] Some researchers are therefore not at all reluctant to admit that the self-reported data obtained for their studies constitutes one of their major weakness.[11]

Sampling biases are also common. The design of many studies assures that certain segments of the population under investigation will not be sampled. For example, telephone surveys exclude those who do not have telephones or who are not at home at the time of the survey. The former are likely to be from low income groups while the latter are likely to be at work. As one researcher acknowledged, military personnel, the institutionalized, non-English speakers, those such as the hearing impaired who are physically incapable of being interviewed by telephone, and those who may be unavailable due to business or vacation trips will also be excluded.[12] Likewise, school surveys include only students who are officially enrolled and in class at the time of the survey. As another noted, "Those students who are truant, have dropped out of school, or who are absent [are] excluded and they may be more likely to gamble than students still attending school. This potential sample bias increases with each advancing grade, such that the 12th grade estimate is most likely to be affected by this potential sample bias."[13] Modern industrial advancements also contribute to this problem. The recent technological innovation of "caller I.D." allows prospective respondents to screen all their incoming calls. Many people, tired of being constantly bombarded by sales pitches from countless telemarketers, are now refusing to answer calls originating outside their immediate area or from numbers which cannot be identified.

Another common failing of many quantitative surveys pertains to the constraints they place on their range of responses. Not every possible response option that might apply to some—or sometimes many—items is always included in a formally structured questionnaire. Failure to include certain possibilities could bias the survey results by channeling the subjects' responses in directions they might not normally take. For example, the present author once participated in an attitudinal telephone survey which failed to include a "no opinion" response for any of its questions whereupon the interviewer attempted to force a choice of one of the options listed on the questionnaire. One of the most egregious examples of the artificial limitations imposed by a gambling survey instrument is found in the first United States national and Nevada studies.[14] Although the questionnaire's designers provided a list of possible reasons for gambling from which their respondents were instructed to choose, and an "other" category was also provided, none of the available options suggested the possibility that some people might gamble as a means of reducing tension, anxiety, or depression. Consequently, this otherwise frequently proposed motivation for gambling is mentioned nowhere in their report. At best this oversight prevented a very important theoretical issue– the reduction of emotional dysphoria–from being tested; at worst, it invalidated all conclusions based on this part of the survey.

Quantitative studies are far more useful in generating new hypotheses (which then require further testing) and in disproving existing hypotheses (by eliminating or disproving the influence of one or two key variables) than they are in verifying them: even a highly significant correlation between two variables does not eliminate the possible influence of other factors which may not even have been considered. For example, after finding a strong positive correlation between annual gambling expenditures and bankruptcy rates an investigator might be strongly tempted to conclude that gambling is a leading cause of bankruptcy or, conversely, that bankruptcy is a leading cause of gambling. However, this finding alone would not preclude the influence of such important concurrent factors as the expansion of legalized gambling, a depressed economy, and growing unemployment rates. Nevertheless, such crucial social and economic considerations are entirely ignored in simple correlational studies.[15] Therefore, as noted above, even if such correlations are found to occur with any degree of regularity, statistical studies by their very nature are unable to provide much useful information as to the reasons for their occurrence.

As has been repeatedly observed, many advocates of quantitative research attempt to evade this problem by offering a number of "possible explanations" for their findings which are, nevertheless, purely conjectural. Although this problem is common to many of the studies reviewed, it was particularly apparent in some more than others. Thus, a possible explanation of the propensity for single and divorced people to gamble is that they have fewer responsibilities and more time and money for it.[16] Likewise, widows and older people in general, who also have fewer responsibilities and more free time, are said to be among the least likely to gamble since it is possible that they lack the resources for it that they once enjoyed during the relative affluence of middle age.[17] It is possible that men are more likely to gamble than women since men are raised to be more competitive. The reason women who do gamble tend to prefer different games than men may also be due to the influence of gender role socialization.[18] Possible explanations as to why city dwellers gamble more than small town and rural people are that urbanites may have greater access to gambling opportunities and younger people may make up a greater proportion of the population. The endorsement of gambling by some religions and its condemnation by others may provide a possible explanation for differences in the gambling behavior by members of different denominations[19] or it may be due to the greater availability of gambling opportunities in areas where these groups make up higher percentages of the population.[20] As seen above, the authors of the Iowa survey[21] offered no less than five possible explanations for the age-based differences in rates of gambling that they reported: experimental role-playing, needs for social contact, diminished mental capacity, the influence of socialization, and the cohort-effect of continuity theory. The authors of the Maryland study offered no less than three to account for their finding that substance abuse is inversely related to the problem gambling severity: the need for a clear head while gambling, the need for gambling money, and sequential addiction. Many such "possible explanations" are highly plausible and some, in fact, may even be true. Nevertheless, no matter how intuitively attractive they may seem, in the absence of any conclusive proof of them they are still entirely speculative and, hence, of no scientific merit.

After dismissing the conjectural conclusions of such studies one critic wrote, "it would seem that systematic empirical investigations based upon observations of gambling within its social and interpersonal context and of gamblers inside their own natural environment, may well offer the best hope of elucidating causes accounting for the widespread persistence of gambling as well as disclosing some of the social functions gambling does serve."[22] "In particular," another wrote, "we need *ethnographic research*."[23] Similar though more detailed concerns were expressed by another prominent theoretician who suggested that gambling theory will progress no further unless more meaningful descriptions of gambling in its natural settings are undertaken. Here the social aspects of gambling must be emphasized to determine the degree to which one's gambling associates contribute to the development or curtailment of gambling problems. Specifically, how important are the social aspects of gambling? Does one's circle of gambling friends become so important that people will continue to gamble despite adverse consequences? Is problem gambling a consequence of peer pressure or the attitudes and expectations of one's gambling confederates or does it develop because the gambler does not belong to a social group whose members help each other control their impulses? Such important questions cannot be answered by only a few studies of specific forms of gambling; all gambling forms and venues must be investigated.[24]

In essence, these critics all suggested that in the future the causes and consequences of gambling and problem gambling should be investigated from the point of view of the gambler rather than that of the statistician. As this was precisely the direction taken by a number of later sociologists (see Chapter 5), their advice has not fallen on deaf ears.

CORRELATIONAL AND RISK FACTOR STUDIES

The utility of amassing any body of purportedly predictive or causal correlates of gambling and pathological gambling is questionable. This is because correlations by themselves do not denote causal relationships. Of all the source materials reviewed for this series, the authors of only a few acknowledged this fact. In evaluating their own research, for example, one research team wrote, "This study is, of course, correlational in nature; therefore, cause and effect conclusions cannot be legitimately drawn."[25] There are several good reasons for this. According to one critic of correlational studies, "Verification of alleged causal relations is difficult unless the instruments of observation elicit objective evidence and assure its replicability."[26] This fundamental tenet of scientific inquiry is one of which far too many gambling researchers seem to be unaware.

Another important consideration, as noted above, is that all the data for these and all other statistical studies which attempt to gather detailed information on sensitive topics from large groups of subjects is based on unverifiable and often highly unreliable self-reports. This is particularly true of surveys targeting children and adolescents since, as at least some researchers have acknowledged, respondents who are not of legal gambling age may want to avoid incriminating themselves.[27] Others have openly conceded that their self-reported findings "may well be taken with a pinch of salt"[28] since boys are likely to exaggerate their involvement while girls may understate theirs. Consequently, and as noted previously, the truth and accuracy of self-reported data and, hence, the validity of such surveys are always in doubt.

Given these incontrovertible facts, a number of specific points regarding various attempts to isolate the predictors of gambling behavior must also be made. Many criticisms of the larger and more comprehensive United Kingdom and United States surveys, as well as many other quantitative studies, have already been discussed and need not be repeated here. It nevertheless bears repeating that the many different correlations that have been found between gambling and other sociodemographic and attitudinal variables have resulted in a plethora of entirely different "predictors." In this sense, the conclusions of these studies are little different from those of the earlier personality theorists who developed long lists of personality traits which were then presumed to be responsible for this behavior.

The authors of the first United States national and Nevada surveys[29] assumed that participation in illegal forms of gambling represented a heavier level of gambling involvement than participation in legal forms. While this may have been true in Nevada where nearly all forms of gambling were legal when the study was conducted in the 1970s, it may not necessarily have been true elsewhere where nearly all forms were illegal. Moreover, the researchers themselves raised the "chicken and egg" question when they admitted "It is impossible to determine whether gambling is the cause or a result of these factors."[30] The research team also cautioned that the rates of pathological gambling they presented should not be taken as conclusive but only as suggestive since, at the time of the study, the amount of research on pathological gambling was extremely limited and the phenomenon was poorly defined. Since compulsive gambling was assumed at that time to represent an environmentally determined personality disorder, they felt that the survey instrument may have identified an unknown number of false positives through its failure to distinguish it from other personality disorders. They also suggested that multivariate analyses, which they did not perform, should be able to resolve a number questions pertaining to the relative influence of certain correlates.

Some study populations are far too restricted as was the case with Michael Frank's investigation of New Jersey college students.[31] To suggest that a study of the gambling habits of a sample of undergraduate psychology students all attending the same college could be in any way representative of, and generalizable to, any other population is unreasonable. The characteristics of this sample would be far too homogeneous compared to those of the general population since most of the subjects would have been very similar in terms of age and social background. On this basis alone the study's conclusions that age, income, and social class are not associated with casino gambling have no relevance outside this narrowly defined group. Furthermore, to suggest that lottery playing, speeding, or any other social or behavioral correlate is necessarily "predictive" of casino gambling is misleading: no doubt nearly 100 percent of those who gamble love their mothers but this highly significant correlation would never be interpreted as suggesting that loving one's mother is a valid predictor of gambling.

However, research of this sort does have some merit. In the first place, it has value as a purely descriptive study of a particular population. Since most of the respondents who do gamble in the casinos of Atlantic City are below the legal age, it is particularly revealing of the ineffective age controls that are currently in place and the relaxed attitude of the casino management toward screening their patrons. Additionally, the degree of influence that the **age of initiation** into gambling may or may not have on the development of later gambling problems is a question which warrants a great deal more attention than it has received. Specifically, comparative studies of the prevalence of pathological gambling in different age groups are needed. However, it will do little good to investigate only those who are already pathological gamblers since the times at which they developed gambling problems will no doubt encompass many age categories. To answer this question it will be necessary to determine what percentage of the general population that began gambling in childhood eventually developed gambling problems and compare this figure to the percentage of those who developed similar problems but did not start gambling until they were adults. Future surveys should therefore include questions designed to elicit this information.

Some subpopulations of larger surveys are also too limited. Like the United Kingdom and United States national surveys, the Iowa studies[32] also drew from a large overall sample but some subgroups were so grossly underrepresented that any correlations drawn from them are in no way generalizable to an entire population. For example, since Judaism was correlated positively with all degrees of gambling it was therefore considered to be one of the best predictors of gambling and problem gambling. However, the fact that only four of the survey's 1,011 subjects were Jewish renders this conclusion meaningless. Furthermore, it is questionable, as the authors themselves admitted, whether their conclusions that normal gambling precedes problem gambling and that it does not inevitably lead to problem gambling—as meticulously authenticated by the most sophisticated statistical measures, analyses, and tests—are really revelations of any major scientific importance. It is to their credit that the researchers later acknowledged that some of the associations resulting from their multivariate analysis were based on very small numbers which rendered their findings far more suggestive than conclusive.[33]

Like the authors of the United Kingdom survey, those of the Iowa studies pointed out that the correlations that did emerge could conceivably be used to support any of several earlier theories. Those between gambling or problem gambling and such variables as income, education, and employment could be, and have been, interpreted as supporting **deprivation** or **anomie theory**; correlates such as exposure to gambling and military service suggest **social learning** factors; others could be taken as support for **personality theory**. Since marriage is negatively correlated with negative consequences while bachelorhood and widowhood are positively correlated, these variables imply a **social control mechanism** in which the natural inclinations of potential problem gamblers are restrained in the presence of marriage partners but unleashed in their absence. However, it is also to their credit that, at least initially, the authors acknowledged that the associations they found do not necessarily demonstrate any cause and effect relationship. They also conceded that although their results were generally consistent with previous gambling surveys, they actually have little bearing on the question of problem gambling. They therefore suggested that future research into its development, as well as the relationship between lottery playing and later problem gambling, should be conducted as longitudinal studies of specific cohort groups. Similar long-term, prospective cohort studies into the natural history of alcohol and drug problems, which investigate the possible causative conditions and events surrounding the onset of abuse as it occurs or fails to occur, have already proven to be highly suggestive.[34]

Like most correlational and other quantitative studies of abusive behaviors, the Iowa and Maryland studies, as well as some of those of youthful addicts, were retrospective. In studies of this nature the predictors of any abusive behavior such as alcohol, drug, or gambling dependence are typically sought by looking back over the subject's lives and trying to surmise which earlier conditions or life experiences preceded and, hence, may have been responsible for the present condition. The typical result of such studies is that lists of correlational variables—which may not be in any way related to the behavior in question—are compiled as "possible" causative influences. After reviewing a number of correlational studies of drug addiction, one prominent specialist concluded,

> these data do not justify the conclusions, drawn by some authorities, that drug addiction "causes" juvenile delinquency, that blacks and Puerto Ricans are more commonly drug addicts because they are black or Hispanic, and that poverty and drug use are invariably linked. Significant correlations like those reported . . . are deceptive because they imply causality without in any way proving it.[35]

This criticism is equally applicable to correlational studies of gambling. In addition to their failure to distinguish mere associations from genuine causal relationships, it has been noted that many gambling studies fail to investigate the age at which their subjects were exposed to the risk factors they claim to have discovered, the degree to which they were exposed to them, and the age at which they began to experience gambling problems.[36] Consequently,

> from an etiological standpoint, these methodological limitations make it impossible to determine whether suspected risk factors might "cause" pathological gambling or problem gambling, or whether they are only correlated or associated with these behaviors. Thus, much of the evidence presented or implied in the literature as causal to pathological and problem gambling is, by commonly accepted etiological standards, better defined merely as evidence for an association.[37]

Some gambling studies present additional problems. In the first place, if nonproblem gambling always precedes problem gambling, it seems rather strange that such factors as renting one's home, widowhood, multiple marriages, low or middle income, white or non-white ethnicity would be predictive of problem gambling but not of normative gambling. In the second place, all correlational studies also raise the proverbial "chicken or egg" question: is any correlation a cause or an effect of the behavior in question? Some researchers do not even bother to distinguish between antecedent and subsequent conditions but lump them together in their lists of risk factors. In Griffiths' scheme, for example, gender and social class are clearly antecedent conditions whereas a sudden drop in grade point average and adolescent theft or truancy for the express purpose of playing fruit machines are clearly consequences of an established or developing gambling habit. In the third place, as noted above, not all correlations are necessarily causal relations. In addition to being consequential they can also be coincidental or conditional (a consequence of some other unnamed influence). For example, finding a statistically significant correlation between problem gambling and team lottery play among the females they surveyed, the authors of the Iowa study concluded that "What distinguishes women from men is that their *team play appears to be a cause of their problem gambling* while this is not the case for men."[38] They then went on to venture the explanation that "Team play connotes a special support for women who gamble, they gamble with others, and this can lead to problem gambling."[39] Similarly, a more recent correlational study of leisure time activities and gambling among Australian adolescents suggested that for both boys and girls greater amounts of unstructured leisure time predicted higher frequencies of gambling.[40] Gambling frequency, in turn, was the strongest predictor of problem gambling. The authors also offered some gender-based predictors. For boys gambling was predicted by greater amounts of time spent socializing with friends and greater involvement in organized sports. However, problem gambling among boys was predicted by lower levels of "masculine" adolescent activities with their male peers, greater involvement in cognitive activities such as board games, and a greater commitment to hobbies involving collecting. Lower levels of involvement in "feminine" adolescent activities also predicted problem gambling among girls but the more time they spent studying, the less likely they were to gamble. On the basis of their findings the authors offered the speculative explanation that socializing with one's peers "may increase risk through access to gambling venues yet simultaneously increase protection through a sense of belongingness."[41] To underscore the potential absurdities to which such associations might lead, one critic wondered whether wearing clothes might seriously be considered as a risk factor for relapse since most treated addicts are dressed when they "slip."[42] Finally, the multitude of correlational studies that have sought to isolate the psychosocial and demographic predictors of drug use and gambling have demonstrated only substantial heterogeneity in the kinds of factors that are associated with their onset. Contrary to the findings of many studies, for example, some researchers have been unable to find any evidence that socioeconomic status or drug use are predictive of adolescent gambling.[43] As in personality studies of these behaviors, no single conclusive causative factor or set of factors has emerged. Thus, as some gambling researchers have cogently observed, "A single set of empirical correlations can always be explained by several–often very different–causal models."[44]

Moreover, it may not be reasonable to view a discontinuous form of gambling like lottery playing in the same light as continuous forms such as electronic gaming machines since the latter, which involve many rapidly repeated cycles of bets and outcomes, are believed to pose far greater risks than the former, in which there is a considerable delay between the time a bet is made and its outcome is known.[45] For example, a recent study of 1,376 adults seeking treatment for problem gambling in Winnipeg, Canada found electronic gaming machines to be the most common form of gambling in this sample while lotteries and bingo were rare.[46] Nevertheless, a recent correlational study which attempted to assess the impact of gambling on suicide in Louisiana found that rates of suicide were positively correlated not only with rates of unemployment but also with per capita lottery expenditures in the state's 64 parishes. However, no correlation was found between suicide rates and video poker expenditures.[47] The clear implication is that while lottery play and unemployment are associated with–and therefore responsible for– higher suicide rates, electronic gaming machines are not. Conversely, a study of the health-related correlates of lottery gambling in the United Kingdom found no relationship between lottery expenditures and poor mental health.[48]

Inconsistent usage of the terms that are bandied about in any discipline pose a perennial research problem. As one astute critic observed, "Clearly prevalence will vary according to the operational definitions employed."[49] The same could be said of problem gambling "severity." In light of this observation, the findings of the Maryland study are interesting and would be worthy of further inquiry if a different measure of severity were employed. In the first place, gambling severity in this study was based entirely on the single criterion of debt to income ratio which, by itself, constitutes a questionable determinant of gambling involvement. According to the United States survey researchers,[50] debt levels among the potential and probable pathological gamblers they identified were little different from those of the general population. Thus, as some specialists have pointed out, "severity should be measured not only by financial parameters, but the effects on other aspects of living: work, family and the extent to which they are prepared to go to obtain gambling money."[51] Others have compiled long lists of indicators, including many "soft signs" of compulsive gambling such as superior intelligence, high energy levels, history of athletic and scholastic excellence, love of risk, love of spending, etc.,[52] all of which must be considered in any assessment of the severity of the problem. Since their development the South Oaks Gambling Screen[53] and the DSM-IV diagnostic criteria,[54] which are based on a many such factors, have become standard instruments for determining gambling involvement. In the second place, since the list of possible causes that the study's authors have compiled to explain their findings are purely conjectural, they have no scientific merit and are therefore entirely unwarranted. It is always dangerous to presume that any statistical relationship is necessarily a causal one but it is foolhardy to attempt to account for such relationships by concocting spurious, fanciful "possible explanations" for them. The conjecture, for example, that the lack of parental security through early maternal loss may be responsible for the most serious gambling problems is scarcely different from the notions of the early psychoanalysts who, despite their lack of any empirical evidence, likewise confidently ascribed problem gambling to various psychological insecurities. The assertion that high school graduates tend to be more venturesome than drop-outs is not a matter of fact but of opinion since the authors provided no concrete evidence of this. The same is true of the highly speculative contention by the authors of the Iowa gender study that women who engage in team lottery play limit their social networks only to other gamblers and therefore must be lacking in ties to the more conventional community.[55] Furthermore, it has been shown that co-addictive drug and alcohol problems are not uncommon among compulsive gamblers. Despite the fact that more than half of their own sample claimed to have drug and alcohol problems the authors merely shrugged this off as a statistically insignificant phenomenon as it relates to the *severity* of problem gambling. Finally, their list of guesses as to why drug use was inversely correlated with gambling severity reveals only that they have absolutely no idea why this relationship exists. Clearly, as these authors themselves have recommended, far more conclusive research is warranted.

In summary, the relevance of many demographic and psychosocial factors that happen to correlate with gambling or any other potentially addictive behavior is unknown. While it is true that there may be some direct relationship between these factors and addiction, it is also true that the exact nature of these associations has never been conclusively established. In fact, some researchers have been unable to find any correlations between gambling severity and such demographic variables as age, gender, or educational level or such personality dimensions as sensation-seeking.[56] Others have been unable to find any significant demographic or behavioral correlates–including gambling behavior and drug use–which might distinguish pathological from nonpathological gamblers.[57] Nevertheless, by designating them as risk factors or predictors, many researchers insist on ascribing tremendous importance to the many different correlations they have found merely because their analytical procedures established them as statistically significant. However, just as the observation that a very high percentage of addicts may have loved their mothers in childhood in no way suggests that "mother love" should be given serious consideration as a predictor of addiction, neither should one's gender, social class, place of residence, or the climate in which they happen to live. It must be remembered that, at best, any such correlates can be regarded only as possible partial contributing factors.

Furthermore, it has been pointed out that, by themselves, environmental models of pathological gambling are inadequate because they fail to answer a very basic question: why is it that of all the people who share a particular psychosocial history, such as childhood abuse, being raised in a single parent household, or experiencing any number of other traumas, only a few become pathological gamblers while most do not? For this reason an alternative view has been proposed by biopsychiatrists suggesting that "*biologically* based predispositions [may] interact with psychosocial history and other environmental factors to determine ultimate behavioral outcome."[58] In doing so they clearly did not mean to dismiss the importance of any environmental factors; they merely wished to propose the possibility that a biological predisposition may be of equal importance. Biological and multicausal models of pathological gambling will therefore be the focus of the next volume in this series.

Chapter 13

CONCLUDING SUMMARY

This volume has reviewed the most influential theories that have been advanced by various social scientists to explain why people gamble and continue to do so even when they consistently lose more than they win. They include early "armchair" speculations and later empirical studies: the former represent a more philosophical approach adopted by scholars who believed that any questions that might be raised about the human penchant for gambling can be answered largely through the exercise of reason alone with no need for empirically derived knowledge; the latter include qualitative or observational studies and quantitative or statistical surveys. Qualitative studies involve three basic research methods: observation of actual gamblers in their respective gambling environments, participant observation in which the researchers themselves become active gamblers and members of particular gambling groups, and unstructured or open-ended interviews with current and former gamblers. Quantitative studies involve the administration of structured questionnaires to larger samples of respondents selected from various populations and statistical analysis of the data that is obtained through them. Most social scientists attribute gambling to one or more particular features of the social or subcultural environment in which the gambler lives.

Early "Armchair" Theories

Early social scientists believed that gambling was inextricably linked to social class. In his **affluence** or **leisure class theory**, Thorstein Veblen argued that the degree to which people gamble is positively related to their income and social class. He therefore saw gambling as a pursuit of the idle rich who engage in the pastime as a means of displaying their wealth through conspicuous consumption which, in turn, serves as a symbolic affirmation of their exalted social status.

Later armchair sociologists, who recognized that gambling is also a common practice among the lower classes, contended that gambling is inversely related to income and social status. For them, gambling represents one of the few possible means available to the masses to help them escape a meaningless working class life of drudgery and tedium. Although they saw it as a deviant, antisocial, or criminal behavior, they were convinced that gambling persists because it serves some positive social function: **alienation theorists** saw gambling as a way for the poverty-ridden working classes to make some decisions of their own and have at least some control over their lives; **anomie** or **deprivation theorists** argued that gambling offers the possibility of financial independence and social advancement; **structural-functional theorists** were convinced that gambling functions either to reduce societal levels of stress and anxiety or to maintain the social structure by strengthening existing social bonds.

Edward Devereux incorporated many of these ideas into his own explanation of gambling in Western society. Although it is strongly condemned, Devereux argued that gambling persists because it benefits all social classes. It not only offers hope, excitement, and opportunities for choice and decision to the masses but, as society's "safety valve," it also allows them to release some of the frustration they feel at being denied access to other means of acquiring wealth. It is condoned by society's elite not only because it keeps the masses in a perpetual state of impoverishment thereby insuring their continued exploitation, but also because it provides a convenient scapegoat for the social inequities inherent in capitalism. For Devereux, then, gambling serves both to release tension and to maintain the *status quo*.

Devereux also proposed the **rural-urban residence** or **community size hypothesis** which predicts that gambling will be less prevalent in smaller rural areas and more so in larger urban areas. This could, in turn, be explained by the **religion hypothesis** which predicts that gambling should be less prevalent where the Protestant work ethic is strongest and more prevalent where this orientation is weaker. However, even in urban areas gambling should be less prevalent among the entrepreneurial middle classes whose members attend religious services regularly and adhere most closely to the tenets of the Protestant ethic.

Structural-functional theories of human behavior have been criticized not only on the grounds that they are untestable but also because they all too often treat the consequences of an activity as its "function" or cause. Furthermore, they generally fail to acknowledge that gambling is not characteristic of any one social class but is popular in all. Finally, they attribute gambling to one aspect or another of highly stratified and industrialized capitalistic societies even though it was also highly popular in tribal and preindustrial societies in which rigid social stratification and capitalism were unknown.

Economic Theories

Early economists assumed that the primary motivation for gambling and other forms of risk-taking was the prospect of monetary gain. Advocates of **rational choice**, **expected value**, or **expected utility theories** assume that people are rational decision makers who consider all facts and possible outcomes before making any economic decision and that they will then choose the option which promises the greatest likelihood of success. A number of mathematical formulas incorporating initial costs, potential payoffs, and outcome probabilities have been formulated to describe the rational decision-making process and to distinguish choices that are more rational from those that are less so: choices having greater probabilities of gain are rational while those with greater probabilities of loss are irrational.

Adam Smith introduced a cognitive element to rational choice theory by recognizing that many people overvalue their chances of winning and undervalue their chances of loss. Thus, estimates of their own probabilities of success are based more on subjective than objective considerations. He also pointed out that two parties in the same venture might have different probabilities of gain or loss. For example, the odds of casino and lottery games always favor the house and never the player.

Later economists factored the risk-taker's base wealth into their equations. Thus, the poor, for whom a dollar holds more subjective value than it does for the wealthy, will be less likely to risk their money than the wealthy. Others noted that most expected value theories failed to acknowledge the fact that many people make economic decisions, such as gambling and buying insurance, that are likely to decrease their base wealth and are therefore irrational. This behavior was explained by the fact that gambling offers hope for otherwise unattainable levels of wealth while insurance offers protection and security against any sudden catastrophic losses. Thus, the poor should be more likely to play lotteries to make social advancements than the wealthy who are already occupying the highest social strata. However, the wealthy who have far more to lose are more likely to protect their wealth through insurance than are the former who have relatively little to lose. The middle classes, who want to protect what they have and acquire even more, will be likely to buy both lottery tickets and insurance.

Some **Marxian economic theorists** argue that gambling benefits the ruling class since it offers yet another means through which the working class can be exploited. Gambling not only funnels additional wealth to those who are already wealthy but, by offering the promise of wealth to a small minority of the masses, it also mitigates against organized revolutionary activities. Others argue that gambling is detrimental to the ruling class because it not only reduces the surplus labor pool upon which capitalism depends for its profits, but it also deprives workers of the discretionary income they would otherwise spend on consumer goods which the upper and middle classes manufacture and sell to them so profitably.

Rational choice or expected value theories have been criticized on the grounds that they do not describe reality. They cannot explain gambling by those who are already wealthy, the irrational economic decisions made by casino gamblers whose chances of loss far outweigh their chances of gain, "hunch" and "long shot" bets which are based more on superstition and wishful thinking than on reason, or the self-destructive persistence of pathological gamblers. These theories and the formulas that derive from them also fail to take into account unforeseeable contingencies which do not remain constant and which cannot therefore be mathematically expressed. Marxian theories are in error because they assume that gambling is necessarily restricted to the working classes when, as Veblen and Dostoevsky pointed out, it is a pastime of the wealthy, as well. They also assume that it is a product of capitalistic economic systems and the class struggles they create when, in fact, it is also popular in egalitarian tribal societies in which capitalism does not exist.

Since the expected value of commercial gaming is always negative, some economists feel that factors other than the maximization of wealth are involved in people's decisions to gamble. They have therefore started viewing some forms of gambling as consumptive rather than productive activities. For example, while the desire for wealth may motivate lottery purchases, casino gamblers are consumers of a form of entertainment which they purchase through their losses. Viewed in this way, neither the wealth nor the entertainment motive can be considered irrational.

Tests of "Armchair" Theories

In their quest to test the theories of their predecessors, later social scientists began to conduct field studies to make first-hand observations of gamblers and gambling. However, most of these field researchers were unable to disengage themselves from the ideas of their mentors but continued to interpret their observations according to various armchair theories. They therefore continued to see gambling as serving one or more positive social functions:

- Irving Zola studied illegal off-track betting among a group of men in a lower class New England bar. He concluded that while the desire to make their own decisions may be a secondary motivation for gambling, the primary motivations are to affirm social solidarity (structural functional theory), to acquire prestige among a core group of fellow bettors by winning and explaining their betting choices (alienation theory), and to vent their hostility against a common enemy, an unjust "system" which is personified by the bookie they are continually trying to beat (tension-reduction).

- Robert Herman studied betting by men and women of all social classes at a large California racetrack. He felt that betting among both lower and middle class men is motivated primarily by the chance it offers not for the wealth, but for rational decision making (alienation theory). Among lower class women it functions as an "escape hatch" by providing a respite from the boredom of daily life (tension reduction); among middle class women who bet on advice of others it demonstrates their desire for dependence (psychoanalytic theory). It offers the upper classes an opportunity to display their wealth through conspicuous consumption (leisure class theory).

Others reviewed the existing literature on gambling to question and challenge the assumptions of their predecessors:

- Joseph Scimecca classified various types of gamblers to show that not all are neurotic or socially deviant. Professional gamblers, percentage gamblers, and cheaters gamble for money; economic gamblers also gamble for money but lack the skills necessary for success; compulsive gamblers are neurotics who want to lose; thrill gamblers seek excitement and boredom relief; functional gamblers occupy lower social strata and see gambling as a means of self-expression, social advancement, and expressing social solidarity. Scimecca was one of the first sociologists to recognize that different gamblers have different motivations and that gambling is a normative behavior.

- Henry Lesieur examined both the positive and negative "functions" of pathological gambling. His goal was to emphasize that by focusing on either the positive or negative consequences of gambling, social scientists may be advancing a moral stance either for or against it. He also demonstrated that the "beneficial" consequences of pathological gambling cannot be its causes since they are grossly outweighed by its negative consequences.

The Researcher's Perspective

Among those who interpreted gambling from the detached perspective of the objective social scientist are **small-group interactional theorists** who see gambling as a means of role-playing. According to advocates of this approach the gambling environment offers a stage upon which gamblers, as actors, are allowed to play a role of their own choosing by adopting a desired identity and presenting this idealized persona to their gambling peers. They may, for example, attempt to present the quality of always being able to retain their composure and remain calm in times of stress. As functionalists, small-group interactionists contend that gambling functions to meet the gambler's personal need for self-expression.

- Erving Goffman argued that people gamble not for money but to impress others. Gambling, which provides a means of gauging one's true character under stressful conditions, involves four phases: squaring off, the initial decision to gamble; determination, the means chosen; disclosure, the outcome; and settlement, the exchange of stakes. During this sequence the actors are able to judge their own character as well as that of others. "Action" derives not only from the excitement of risk but also from the test of character it provides. Displays of character, a resource that can be risked, won, and lost, are more important than money and therefore constitute the primary motivation for all risky behaviors.

- David Oldman also argued that gambling is motivated by the desire to assume an identity one cannot otherwise present. He reasoned that since the odds of any casino game always favor the house, gamblers themselves realize the futility of trying to win. Nevertheless, habitual gamblers lose and when their losses accumulate they deal with their financial problems in the only way they know: they continue to gamble. Thus, habitual or compulsive gambling does not indicate a personality defect but defective gambling strategies and money management skills.

- John Rosecrance argued that persistent gambling is sustained not by economic rationality, psychological pathology, or the game itself, but by the social networks that develop among cliques of regular gamblers who bond together to create their own social worlds. These bonds are strengthened through the sharing of critical betting information and decision-making procedures, mutual money lending, shared contingencies such as heavy losses, and the absence of social interaction, common interests, and emotional support in times of stress.

Family dynamics. **Transactional** and **family systems theorists** contend that pathological gambling and other addictive behaviors are caused by dysfunctional family relationships. Some argue that these behaviors represent a self-fulfilling prophecy by parents or other family members who have continually expressed negative opinions and expectations of the addict. Still others believe that gamblers and their spouses are merely playing a maladaptive role-playing "game" through which they can manipulate and control each other. For example:

- Robert Ingram combined elements of psychoanalytic and family systems theories to formulate his **transactional script theory**. Individuals who have been criticized since childhood will adopt the "life script" of a loser and act accordingly while those who have been praised will adopt that of winner. Gamblers know they must inevitably lose due to the built-in house advantage if they participate in commercial gaming and betting activities. Those who do so must therefore want to lose to fulfill the negative expectations they have internalized.

- W. H. Boyd and D. W. Bolen felt that gambling is not a cause but an effect of marital dysfunction. They noted that compulsive gamblers often adopt the "sick" or "scapegoat" role as those who are blamed for all the family's hardships. Their wives adopt the "well" or "martyr" role as they assume more family responsibilities and make more of its decisions. However, Boyd and Bolen also observed that while they are in therapy, gamblers and their spouses often exhibit an alternation of symptoms. This occurs because the wife enjoys her newfound authority which she fears losing when her husband quits gambling. At this time her own emotional deterioration forces him back into the "sick" role in an effort to save the marriage.

Other psychoanalytically-oriented family systems theorists claim that some women are interested in maintaining their husbands' abstinence from gambling not because they are afraid they will lose, but because they may win. The reason for this, it is presumed, is that a large win would jeopardize the dominance these women secured while their husbands were losing. Similarly, the husbands, all of whom have unresolved dependency needs, fear winning since they could not bear independence from their wives. A similar situation is believed to exist between parents of pathological gamblers and their children. Abstinence is therefore essential for all parties in the control game.

Small group and **family systems theories** are essentially **functional theories** since they generally claim that gambling functions either to strengthen social bonds, to preserve existing social relationships, or to reduce tension. They are therefore subject to many of the same criticisms as other functional theories. Unfortunately, few advocates of these theories provide any empirical evidence which might verify their claims: all too often they offer only personal opinions that have been molded by a preexisting theoretical orientation. Thus, many suffer from the "false cause" fallacy by attributing the reasons for gambling to such consequences as role-playing or support group formation. Furthermore, small group interactional explanations cannot account for solitary forms of gambling such as lottery and slot machine play in which no social interaction takes place. It is difficult to accept the position adopted by family systems theorists that pathological gambling is a control game since it cannot account for pathological gambling among those who are not married or do not live with their parents. It is also difficult to accept the position that pathological gambling actually serves to hold marriages together when divorce rates are so high among pathological gamblers and the parents of pathological gamblers. Those cases in which marriages do not dissolve could also be explained by religious proscriptions against divorce. Even if gambling in some cases does function to hold families together, this would not explain how the problem originated. In fact, since their focus is always on the consequences of gambling, none of these approaches reveals anything about the ultimate origin of pathological gambling or any other addiction.

Play Theory. Early **play theorists** believed that the need for recreation or play is a biological instinct or drive. Gambling, an adult form of play, offers excitement, amusement, a challenge, and an escape from the reality of routine daily life. The "action" of gambling describes both the emotional arousal it generates and the escape from reality it provides. When the pursuit of either arousal or escape through any form of recreation becomes a compulsion, the activity has become pathological. Some contemporary social scientists have combined the elements of play theory with those of various sociological theories:

- Vicki Abt and her colleagues merged **play theory** with **interactional**, **structural-functional**, and **consumer theories** to explain the appeal of nonpathological gambling. They insisted that by enabling gamblers to assume new identities, casino and racetrack gambling create distinct social worlds with their own symbolic meaning systems. Unlike interactional theorists, they felt that gambling permits the expression of one's true personality rather than an idealized imitation. Thus, people gamble not for money, but for fun, excitement, safe risk, hope, and escape from a world of despair into an alternative social reality. Gambling losses pay for this form of entertainment.

- Jon Altman examined gambling among native Australians. Both gambling and cash were unknown to them prior to European contact but were readily adopted. Because the winnings from their marathon card

games were constantly redistributed and often given back to losers so
they could continue to play, Altman concluded that the primary function of gambling was entertainment. However, since the sharing of winnings conformed to their original pattern of gift giving and resource
redistribution, he also suggested that gambling functioned as a mechanism for culture change by aiding the transition from a subsistence to a
cash economy.

• Robert Herman felt that **play theory** combined with **interactional theory** offered a much better explanation for gambling than psychoanalytic theory since this approach is based on reality rather than speculation.
Gambling is not only fun, but it also functions as a socialization mechanism since the risk-taking, rule-following, role playing, and character displays it involves prepare the gambler for the real world.

• James Smith and Vicki Abt added an element of **drive-reduction theory** by claiming that gambling functions to reduce an acquired drive for
status and prestige rather than an instinctive drive for recreation. Play
functions as a socialization mechanism through which our cultural values are learned and passed on. The Western capitalistic values of wealth-
building, risk-taking, competitiveness, aggression, independence, and
success are incorporated into many children's games. Those who lack
the size and strength required for success in physical competition will
seek alternative means, such as gambling, for expressing these qualities.

The Gambler's Perspective

Although observational methods allow some insights that are denied armchair theorists, they fail to "get inside the head" of the gambler. In their quest
to do so, a number of researchers employed participant observational techniques by becoming gamblers themselves while others conducted in-depth
interviews with current and former gamblers. All attempted to understand
and explain problem or compulsive gambling. Their conclusions, made from
the point of view of the gambler, are substantially different from those
derived from armchair speculation and observational research alone.

• Thomas Martinez and Robert LaFranchi studied cardroom gamblers to
discover why some continued when they consistently lost. They identified four types with different motivations. Action players play for tension
relief and seem not to care if they lose to give the impression that they
can afford it. Losers bet wildly hoping to win, attribute their losses to bad

luck, lose control, and persist to gain recognition and bolster a low self-image. Winners play skillfully while break-evens have not yet honed their skills. Both know that emotional control is crucial to winning, appear to have an internal locus of control orientation with which they approach all aspects of their lives, and play for the fun and challenge it offers.

• David Hayano insisted that cardroom gamblers play not to lose but to stay in action. The gambler's persona is not a cause of gambling but a way to intimidate and mislead others. Compulsive gambling is due to poor playing skills, poor money management, false beliefs, and an external locus of control orientation: "sickies" or "degenerates" can't quit when they are ahead; "berserkos" or "desperados" are uncontrolled players who don't care if they lose. Normally controlled gamblers who bet wildly after a "bad beat" are "on tilt." This is not a permanent compulsion but a temporary mental state to which even seasoned professionals can succumb.

• John Rosecrance felt that regular and part-time racetrack bettors gamble for social and entertainment reasons. Pros support themselves by disciplined betting, serious players are semiprofessionals who lack the discipline of the pros, bustouts are undisciplined bettors who play long shots. Interactional theory can explain persistent gambling but cognitive and attribution theories explain problem or compulsive gambling. This temporary "on tilt" condition is due to a shift in the gambler's attributions of causality and locus of control orientation following a traumatic "bad beat" or "fluke." Problem gambling is therefore reversible with the help of one's gambling peers.

• Basil Browne felt that problem gambling results from frustration and poor emotional control rather than poor playing and money management skills. He also invoked the "on tilt" state, which can include blackouts or dissociative states, to explain the temporary periods of wild betting that can affect all gamblers. "Tilt" can be induced by "bad beats" as well as intoxication, long playing sessions, long losing streaks, unbeatable games, "escape" gambling, playing with "short money," and "needling" or provocation by others. To avoid "tilt" one should avoid these circumstances, avoid all intoxicants, ignore "needling," and do "emotion work" to maintain control.

The **"on tilt" theory** of problem gambling has been criticized on several grounds. It's proponents studied only cardroom poker players and racetrack bettors who attribute success to skill. While frustrated card players and hand-icappers may go "on tilt" it would be unlikely among those who play lotteries, slot machines, and other games of pure chance in which "bad beats" do not occur. Neither Rosecrance nor any of his key informants felt they had a gambling problem while Browne admitted that his were professionals employed by the cardroom rather than committed gamblers who would be more likely to experience problem gambling. Therefore, none would be able to discuss the problem from first-hand experience. Finally, social scientists are clearly not trained or equipped to identify and explain compulsive or pathological gambling solely on the basis of their observations and interactions with active gamblers: since a temporary display of irrational betting behavior does not necessarily indicate pathological gambling, it does not warrant such a diagnosis.

While advocates of the "on tilt" explanation viewed compulsive gambling as the result of single discrete incidents such as "bad beats," others felt that it involved a long developmental process which could be otherwise identified:

• Henry Lesieur, who held in-depth interviews with self-admitted compulsive gamblers, felt that compulsive gambling is long-term **"chasing"** to recoup all past losses. He described the progression of strategies compulsive gamblers employ to pay off old debts and raise fresh gambling money: during the "attainment of money stage" the gambler taps personal savings and spouse's assets; the "moving or juggling of money stage" involves borrowing from one source to pay another; the "closure stage" is one of desperation, wild betting, and sometimes suicide. Lesieur later suggested that going "on tilt" may represent the first stage in the career of the compulsive gambler.

• Richard Rosenthal attempted to reconcile the ideas of Lesieur and "on tilt" theory by suggesting that a "bad beat" may trigger chasing in those who hope to reverse their misfortune all at once. However, he also added elements of psychodynamic theory by suggesting that pathological gambling can often be traced to some previous life trauma which would then act as a precursor to irrational betting. "Bad beats" may therefore incite feelings of shame, humiliation, and injustice which the "on tilt" gambler is also attempting to alleviate.

• Sue Fisher and Mark Griffiths found that young fruit machine players have different motivations: "arcade kings," who play for gains in character, have the highest levels of skill, status, and emotional control; "rent-a-spacers" are teenage girls whose main goal is to socialize; "action-seekers" play for thrills, excitement, and to "get a buzz";

"machine beaters" play for the sense of achievement and control winning can give but often lose emotional control and all their money; "escape artists" gamble to escape a troubled home life. A desire for action, control, and escape, in conjunction with the physical characteristics of fruit machines, can lead to seriously addictive playing.

Statistical Tests of Early Ideas

Quantitative or statistical studies, which involve sample surveys of larger populations, are designed to discover overall frequencies of gambling, which subpopulations are the most and least avid gamblers, and sometimes to obtain attitudinal data. Some are descriptive while others are correlational. Statistically significant correlations between two variables are often interpreted as being causally related. The earliest large scale gambling surveys were designed to test specific motivational theories.

- Nechama Tec studied Swedish sports pool betting to test the economic motivation. Because gambling is more common among the lower than the upper classes, Tec proposed her **status frustration** or **hope hypothesis** which contends that gamblers are motivated by dissatisfaction with their present status and hope for a better future. However, not all members of the lower classes are dissatisfied: only those in the upper-lower class who are in closest proximity to the middle class. In addition to a number of methodological problems, Tec's study has been criticized for drawing sweeping conclusions about gambling in general from a study of one specific form.

While many sociologists attributed gambling to social class affiliation, others saw it as a consequence of subcultural influences and peer pressure. Emmanuel Moran was among the first to propose a **subcultural hypothesis** in which gambling is necessary to "fit in" with one's primary reference group while failure to gamble is the mark of an outsider.

- Otto Newman found that, according to existing statistics, gambling was not a deviant behavior since 80 percent of all adults gambled and that off-track betting, the most popular form, was most frequent in the lower-lower class. Field research in London's East End betting shops revealed that although money was the most commonly voiced reason for gambling, it also had other motivations: it affords entertainment, training for the real world, an escape, independent decision making, and it reinforces in-group cohesion. Most importantly, it was a highly valued part of East End subculture. His typology also revealed that different people have different motivations for gambling.

Cross-Cultural Studies

Cross-cultural studies were developed by anthropologists to test various psychological and sociological theories using quantitative methods. To do so they sample many different tribal groups looking for correlations between certain customs or behaviors and any social, cultural, or environmental features. Any such relationships are then presumed to be causal. Early cross-cultural studies, which attempted to determine the primary function of alcohol use in preindustrial societies, found significant correlations between societal levels of intoxication and anxieties stemming from uncertainties surrounding subsistence, warfare, sex, dependency conflict, male powerlessness, informal social structure and social control, and fear of the supernatural. They therefore concluded that the primary function of alcohol was to reduce these anxieties. Several cross-cultural studies of gambling have also been conducted:

- John Roberts and Brian Sutton-Smith developed a theory of games, of which they identified three types. They believed that, over time, games of skill would have appeared first, then games of chance followed by games of strategy. Games of skill are most common in the world, games of chance less common, and games of strategy least common. The correlations they found between games of chance and an array of other cultural traits led them also to conclude that the primary function of games of chance is the reduction of anxiety aroused by socialization, subsistence, and other environmental stressors. They do so by offering hope in the face of uncertainty.

- John Price found that gambling becomes more common as levels of social organizational complexity increase. If gambling evolves from low levels of intensity to progressively higher levels until it is institutionalized, then it must serve some positive functions in complex societies. He felt that it serves primarily as a form of entertainment, secondarily as a means of redistributing wealth beyond the kinship group, and to a lesser extent it encourages surplus production to pay debts and provides a means of teaching people about capital and risk.

The strongest criticism of cross-cultural studies is that the behaviors they seek to explain are entirely removed from their cultural context. In many societies, for example, gambling has religious meanings which correlational studies could not possibly recognize. In these instances, it has nothing to do with either the reduction of anxiety or maintaining social equilibrium: it serves as a means of communicating with the supernatural. Furthermore, as functional analyses, they also assume the consequences of gambling to be its causes.

- W. L. Li and M. H. Smith reanalyzed data from an earlier Gallup survey. Positive correlations between gambling and status, income, residence, and age supported the **affluence** and **community size hypotheses** as well as their own **life cycle hypothesis** which predicts that gambling rates will decrease with age. Tec's **status frustration hypothesis** found only weak support in an insignificant correlation between gambling and status inconsistency. The study was criticized on the grounds that it asked only if the respondents had made at least one bet in the last month, but by focusing on elements of social structure it challenged a number of psychological theories.

Large Scale Surveys

In the 1970s, large gambling surveys involving thousands of respondents were undertaken in the United Kingdom and United States Their purpose was to test a number of earlier theories, to develop some newer hypotheses, and to determine which demographic groups were the most and least avid gamblers. The United States survey also attempted to determine rates of compulsive gambling to compare that of the nation to that of Nevada where gambling was legal.

- The United Kingdom survey studied a variety of gambling activities, frequencies, expenditures, outcomes, and attitudes. Among its many findings were that gambling is a normative rather than deviant behavior and that it is a discrete rather than a unitary phenomenon in that people are drawn to specific forms of gambling rather than to any or all forms. The typical gambler is a young, poorly educated, single, working-class male who seldom attends church, is dissatisfied with his job, whose parents gambled, and who believes in luck. The **working-class subcultural hypothesis** can better explain the popularity of gambling than any economic or class-based ones.

- The United States/Nevada survey strongly supported the **availability hypothesis**. Unlike the United Kingdom survey, gambling in the United States correlated positively with income and education.

Frequency data also supported the **religion, subcultural, life cycle, and community size hypotheses**; volume data supported the **community size** and **subcultural** but not the **education, life cycle, status frustration,** nor **religion hypotheses**. Attitudinal data supported the **economic, play, arousal, alienation, anomie, aspiration, subcultural,** and **religion** but not the **moral or deviance hypotheses**. Rates of normative gambling in a demographic group do not necessarily predict its rates of problem gambling.

Both studies are commendable for their large sample sizes and for examining gender differences, all forms of gambling, individual gambling preferences, and attitudinal data. Since far more men gamble than women, both provide strong support for the **gender hypothesis**. They also demonstrate that gambling does not have any single "function" but is motivated by a variety of reasons. The United States survey tested the **subcultural hypothesis** and attempted, although crudely, to estimate rates of compulsive gambling while the United Kingdom survey did not. The former failed to explore the frequency with which people gamble while the latter failed to include volume data in the first part of the study. The United Kingdom study's use of job descriptions rather than income levels to determine social class affiliation is also questionable.

Possibly the most important contribution of these surveys is that they highlight the need to distinguish frequency from volume data since the resultant correlations can be highly contradictory. They also demonstrate that different demographic variables and practices are associated with different forms of gambling which makes any general conclusions difficult: just as most existing motivational theories were supported by some correlations, they were also rejected by others. Because different correlations can yield different conclusions, (1) no theory of "gambling" should be based on a study of only one form and (2) motivational theories should be accepted or rejected on the basis of qualitative as well as quantitative data.

Gambling and the General Public

Whereas most previous quantitative studies were designed primarily for purposes of hypothesis testing, later general population surveys also began to obtain descriptive statistical data for public policy and market research purposes. The findings of many such studies are relevant to a variety of theoretical issues.

- A Gallup survey to assess public opinion found that by the 1980s most United States residents favored gambling over new taxes to raise public revenues. Contrary to sociological thought, lower income groups were most opposed to gambling, it was not correlated with education or income, and it was not a "deviant" activity of only a few. While the authors felt that greater availability would generate more gambling, they were unconvinced that it would increase rates of compulsive gambling. They were criticized for assuming that gambling attitudes would predict gambling behavior.

• An Australian survey in the mid 1980s also found not only that most respondents favored gambling, but also that even more had placed a bet within the last three months. This suggests that some forms are not perceived as "true" gambling. The fact that the most readily accessible forms were the most popular would seem to support the **availability hypothesis**.

• Another found that Australia was "a nation of gamblers" since nearly all native born Australians had bet within the previous year. They not only gambled more frequently than immigrants, but they also bet nearly twice as much money. Neither income nor gender were related to gambling rates but the **education, cultural, religion,** and **availability hypotheses** were strongly supported.

• A third Gallup survey in the late 1980s found the United States to be "a nation of gamblers." Most subjects had gambled in the previous year and nearly a third gambled weekly. The 10 percent who abstained did so for moral or religious reasons: most were older, poorer, more religious, and Southern. The **subcultural, religion,** and **availability hypotheses** were also supported by a number of other regional differences. The study not only supported the **gender hypothesis** but it also revealed that men and women prefer different types of gambling. Self-reported reasons for gambling supported the **play, interactional, economic, sensation-seeking,** and **cognitive hypotheses**.

• An Iowa survey in the late 1980s found that gambling rates decrease with age but rejected the **life cycle hypotheses** since most should occur during the peak earning years. Heavier gambling among the young may represent role-playing during the search for an adult identity; older people, who already have an established identity, have no need for such self-presentation. Decreases in gambling among older people may also reflect a "cohort effect" and those who gamble may do so only to maintain existing social relationships. The **gender hypothesis** was supported by overall rates of gambling but not by rates of problem gambling.

• A Nebraska survey in the early 1990s obtained baseline data for a longitudinal study. It rejected the **rural-urban hypothesis** since it found that rural dwellers were just as likely to gamble as urbanites. Attitudinal data supported **play theory** while descriptive data provided strong support for the **gender hypothesis** and confirmed that men and women have different preferences. Gambling frequencies and expenditures failed to correlate significantly with income. The finding that those who begin gambling at a younger age engage in more forms as adults supported the **age of initiation hypothesis**. The researchers offered several speculative explanations for their findings.

• Reanalysis of market research data on lottery playing in California and Maryland provided support for the **gender** and **religion**, mixed support for the **status frustration**, and no support for the **life cycle** and **rural-urban residence hypotheses**.

• Market research sponsored by Minnesota lottery officials in the early 1990s supported the **gender, life cycle, affluence, rural-urban residence,** and **availability hypotheses**. The state witnessed dramatic increases across all demographic groups in the frequency of Native American casino gaming since its introduction. Attitudinal data supported **game** and **arousal theories** but not the **moral model**.

Special Populations

In the late 1980s and early 1990s a number of gambling researchers turned their attention away from general population surveys and began to focus on particular demographic groups, primarily children and adolescents.

Gambling is quite common among young people. Studies in different countries have found that from half to nearly all children and adolescents have gambled for money on lotteries, card games, bingo, sports events, electronic gaming machines, and even in casinos. A surprising number of young people are regular gamblers who have made some surprisingly large bets. In accordance with the **gender hypothesis**, boys are more avid gamblers than girls. Many young people begin gambling with their parents and continue to gamble with their parents' approval although many parents are unaware of either the extent of their children's involvement or its potential ramifications. Serious consequences could ensue later in life since few youngsters stop gambling once they start and, according to the **age of initiation hypothesis**, early involvement in gambling is likely to produce pathological gambling in adulthood. Studies have demonstrated that, indeed, most adult pathological gamblers started gambling in childhood or adolescence.

Some young people are already showing signs of serious gambling problems such as being unable to quit and stealing money for gambling. In fact, epidemiological studies have shown that prevalence rates of problem and pathological gambling are higher among adolescents and young adults than they are among older adults, and higher among boys than girls. Since the legalization of fruit machines in the United Kingdom in 1968, many children of both sexes begin gambling by the age of eight or nine; fruit machine addiction among adolescents is now a serious problem in that country. Similar phenomena have been reported in the Netherlands, Australia, and Spain since slot machines were legalized in those countries.

These findings, which clearly support the **availability and exposure and age of initiation hypotheses**, have prompted some researchers to test these and other sociological theories further.

- Durand Jacobs synthesized data on teenage gambling from four states. About two thirds started before the age of 11 and four-fifths before they were 15; from four percent to six percent met the criteria for pathological gambling. Children of problem gamblers exhibited a distinct array of other problems including overeating, emotional dysphoria, a lower quality of life, twice as many suicide attempts, higher parental divorce rates, and higher rates of tobacco, alcohol, and other drug use. Jacobs attributed problem gambling in adolescents to the stresses he presumed their parents must be under.

Surveys of adolescent gambling in the United Kingdom have been mostly of a descriptive nature with an emphasis on its negative consequences.

- Sue Fisher and Mark Griffiths reviewed the literature on adolescent fruit machine gambling. Estimates of the percentages of youth who played at least once a week ranged from six percent to 37 percent; from two percent to five percent played at least four times a week and spent an average of £50 to £66 per week on these machines. They exhibit a variety of behavioral symptoms of addictive gambling including borrowing, selling one's knowledge of the machines, using school lunch money, theft, the sale of possessions including those of others, drug dealing, prostitution, and truancy.

- In Mark Griffiths' later sample of 50 fruit machine players, 18 percent met the criteria for pathological gambling. All started between age nine and 11, played whenever they could, regularly spent all their money on gambling, had gambling debts, and missed school or work to play. Their money came from jobs, allowances, gifts, borrowing, and theft: two-thirds of those who spent more than £10 per week on them have stolen money to play. Griffiths suggested that one possible explanation for fruit machine addiction might be Amsel's "frustration theory" which postulates that persistence derives from frustration over the failure to achieve a seemingly attainable goal.

• R. I. F. Brown and S. Robertson explored the relationship between video game and slot machine playing since school children often become addicted to video games alone. Those who played video games before the age of ten now spend three-quarters of their leisure time playing gambling machines while those who started when they were older spend only one-tenth of their spare time on them. Thus, video games may serve as a **"gateway"** or precursor to slot machine addiction. They then offered the highly speculative explanation that slot machine addiction can ultimately be traced to the early childhood social deprivations common to dysfunctional family environments.

• R. Gupta and J. Derevensky also explored the **gateway hypothesis** since video games and slot machines both involve learning curves, stress relief, excitement, variable-ratio reinforcement schedules, visual and auditory stimuli, fast action, and instant feedback. However, video games offer a high degree of personal control while gambling offers only an illusion of control. When video gamers gamble, the strong sense of control they have retained will cause them to gamble more often and take greater risks. The responses of high and low frequency video game players to a computerized blackjack game were interpreted as confirmation of this hypothesis, especially among males.

• Michael Frank conducted a correlational study of students at a college near Atlantic City. Since no relationships emerged between casino gambling and a number of social and demographic variables, he concluded that gambling is neither an age- nor class-based phenomenon. These findings were criticized since the subjects were similar in age and socioeconomic background. Because lottery play and speeding tickets correlated positively with casino gambling, Frank argued that these factors were among the best predictors of casino gambling. The gambling of most was recreational but six percent met the criteria for problem or pathological gambling.

• A larger survey of students on three Minnesota campuses found the variables most closely associated with both gambling frequencies and problem gambling to be parental problem gambling, licit and illicit drug use, gender (male), and disposable incomes larger than $200 per month: the sons and daughters of problem gamblers were 12 times more likely than others, males were 12 times more likely than females, and those with disposable incomes of $200 or more a month were four times more likely than others to be pathological gamblers.

Some researchers investigated gambling among women but tended to focus more on pathological than normative gambling.

- Henry Lesieur surveyed 50 female pathological gamblers in Gamblers Anonymous. He found that many lived in abusive relationships and started gambling as a coping mechanism to escape their domestic problems. Many were depressed, had attempted suicide, and had other addictive problems even before they started gambling. All were initially attracted to gambling because of the "action" it offered.

- Lesieur and Sheila Blume later found that female pathological gamblers constitute an underserved treatment population. They attributed the disorder to the sexist attitudes and low self-esteem women face in a male-dominated workplace as well as to life stresses that are not only unique to women but which are also far more intense than those experienced by men. While most women turn to gambling to escape these problems and their other demanding responsibilities, some women may find gambling empowering. These speculative explanations were criticized for reflecting popular feminist rhetoric which is not supported by empirical evidence.

- A survey of 52 female GA members in Las Vegas did not test specific hypotheses but provided descriptive statistics on female pathological gamblers. Apart from standard demographic data, the researchers focused on the negative consequences–debt, criminal activities, bankruptcies, suicide attempts, prostitution, etc.–of pathological gambling among their subjects. Their antigambling agenda was apparent in their warning that gambling would have the same results wherever it is legalized.

Little is known about gambling among the elderly. Much of what we do know has been taken from surveys of general populations in which it was found that levels of gambling involvement and rates of problem gambling tend to decrease with age. Most explanations for these findings are entirely speculative since no studies aimed isolating the reasons for either gambling or abstaining by senior citizens have ever been undertaken. For example, advocates of the **sensation-seeking hypothesis**, the **life cycle hypothesis**, and the **gambling lifestyle theory** contend that gambling is motivated by the need for emotional arousal or excitement. Since the strength of this need is believed to decrease with age, few senior citizens feel the need to gamble to reduce this drive. Advocates of **economic theories** argue that because gambling is related to income, retired people living on fixed incomes will be less likely to risk losing the money they do have. Advocates of **continuity theory** believe that the low rates of gambling found among senior citizens is a consequence of the "cohort effect" with the strong antigambling sentiments of the past still prevailing among today's senior citizens. Advocates of **small group interactional theory** believe that since the self-identities of older adults are already established, they have no need to gamble as a means of impressing others. Advocates of the **availability and exposure hypothesis** are convinced that as more gambling opportunities arise, senior citizens will be more likely to gamble and to experience the negative consequences of doing so. Some studies have, in fact, documented increases in the frequencies of gambling among older people following the introduction of lotteries and casinos. However, the lack of research focusing exclusively on gambling among the elderly means that neither these nor any other possible explanations can yet be accepted.

Even less is also known about gambling among ethnic minorities. The only groups that have received any serious attention at all are Native North Americans among whom only limited research has been undertaken. The few studies that have been conducted reveal that among Native Americans prevalence rates of problem and pathological gambling are far higher among both adolescents and adults than among their non-Native peers, higher among the younger members of both the adolescent and adult samples, and higher among adolescent males than females but lower among adult males than females. Native American problem and pathological gamblers begin gambling at a younger age and are more likely to have first degree relatives with gambling problems than nonproblem gamblers. In comparison with non-Natives, they are more likely to be single, to have attended boarding schools, to have less than a high school education, to earn less money, to live on reservations, and to report higher levels of stress. Although the reasons for them is not known, these findings provide support for the **ethnicity, life-cycle**, **age of initiation**, **parental gambling**, **marital status**, **status inequality**, **education**, and **dysphoria reduction hypotheses** but no support for the **rural-urban residence hypothesis**. Support for the **gender hypothesis** is mixed since the gender ratio of adult problem and pathological gamblers contradicts that of adolescents.

Problem Gambling Correlates and Risk Factors

A number of psychosocial, behavioral, demographic, and environmental factors have frequently been found to be associated with addictive behaviors. While some result from these behaviors, others precede them and may contribute to their onset and development. Some researchers are therefore convinced that if we can determine which of these antecedent conditions are most closely associated with these addictions, we will be better able to predict who is at greater and lesser risk for developing them later in life.

These observations and convictions have prompted researchers to seek out the specific correlates or predictors of problem gambling. Although results differ, the most commonly reported demographic risk factors are age (young), gender (male), socioeconomic background (lower), marital status (not married), ethnic minority status, and religion (Catholic and Jewish). Environmental factors include family size, parental problem gambling or substance abuse, domineering parents, physical or sexual abuse in childhood, early parental loss, spousal loss or rejection, and other severe traumas leading to posttraumatic stress disorder. Behavioral correlates include tobacco/drug/alcohol use and eating disorders. In addition to these, the most commonly cited behavioral risk factors for problem gambling among adolescents are age of initiation (starting to gamble before the age of 9), physical violence, the use of false identification, lying about one's age, juvenile delinquency/antisocial behavior, increased sexual activity, unsafe sex, and poor scholastic performance.

Some of these possibilities were tested by Henry Lesieur and Robert Klein who surveyed 892 New Jersey high school students, 5.7 percent of whom were pathological gamblers. The finding that nearly five times more pathological gamblers were males than females clearly supported the **gender hypothesis**. Problem gambling also correlated with parental gambling, gambling frequency, and lower grade point averages. However, no evidence was found to support the **social class, availability, age of initiation,** or **religion hypotheses**. In fact, Protestants were more likely to be pathological gamblers than Catholics or Jews. Others have therefore suggested that problem gambling in adolescence may be part of a constellation of deviant behaviors exhibited by some males.

Various other populations including children, young adults, mature adults, females, and certain ethnic groups have also been the focus of correlational studies by researchers attempting to discover the strongest predictors of gambling and problem gambling.

- The United States national survey found high gambling involvement to be associated with such environmental factors as unsatisfactory domestic relationships, divorce, alcohol use, mobility, and employment problems including job dissatisfaction, more work missed, frequent job changes, and wage garnishment. Demographic factors were age (most probable compulsive gamblers were 45 to 64; most potentials, 25 to 44), high school or more education, ethnic minority status, retired or unemployed, Northeastern and urban residence, Catholic religion, and Spanish ethnicity. Compulsive gambling was associated with self-employment, greater job satisfaction, and less work missed.

• The United Kingdom survey found the strongest predictor of gambling in general to be gender (male). Sports betting is best predicted by gender; betting shop use, by gender, lower working-class status, low job interest, and elementary school education; high stakes off-track betting, by gender, younger middle age, upper working-class status, and more affluence; bingo, by working-class status and parental gambling; casino gaming, by parental gambling, youth, and affluence; and slot machine gambling, by youth and parental gambling. The best predictors for males were irregular church attendance and parental gambling; for females, parental gambling and any age other than elderly.

• The best predictors of normative gambling identified by the Iowa study are impulsiveness, competitiveness, lottery play, big spending, alcohol use, interest in sports, childhood and recent exposure to gambling, residential mobility, full-time employment, Catholic or Jewish religion, male gender, and being a military veteran; negative correlates include age, church attendance, education level, and religion. Not correlated with gambling are income, marital status, occupation, rural or urban residence, and community size.

• The Iowa study found the best predictors of problem gambling to be the belief that lotteries are not random, self-centeredness, competitiveness, impulsiveness, childhood exposure to gambling, big spending, alcohol use, mobility, renting one's home, being single, and Judaism. The best "past experience" risk factors for women are prior military service, neither Catholic nor Protestant religion, mobility, early exposure to gambling, and frequency of marriage, none of which apply to males. For both sexes the best predictive variables were alcohol use and lottery expenditures. Team lottery play was a risk factor for women; current exposure to gambling was one for men.

• An Australian study of patients in treatment for pathological gambling found that most were men, had lower socioeconomic backgrounds, had only secondary school education, were employed in nonprofessional positions, and a third were introduced to gambling by their parents. Most women were addicted to slot machines. Before gambling became a problem, most men bet on horses or played machines exclusively; afterward, they gravitated toward a variety of forms and illegal casino gambling.

• A New Zealand survey found problem and pathological gambling to be associated with gender (male), parental problem gambling, ethnicity (non-Caucasian), age (under 30), marital status (single), employment status (unemployed), and household size (larger). Troubled gamblers preferred such continuous forms as racetrack betting and electronic machines, while nonproblem gamblers preferred such noncontinuous forms such as lotteries, Lotto, and raffles.

• A correlational study of slot machine gamblers in Germany confirmed several demographic trends. Most active gamblers were young, single, male, had attended a vocational school, were never employed or were unskilled laborers, were currently unemployed, earned the least income, and reported being stressed.

• A clinical study in Maryland found most pathological gamblers to be married, middle class, middle-aged, employed male Caucasian high school graduates from small family backgrounds. The strongest predictors of gambling severity were death of the mother before the subject was 18, high school education, past physical or sexual abuse, and a past or present drug problem. The researchers speculated that gambling represents the search for security and/or self-esteem. They also offered an array of conjectural explanations for the negative correlation between gambling severity and drug abuse.

• Mark Griffiths' **risk factor model** of adolescent fruit machine addiction includes male gender, early initiation, playing for reasons other than money, an early big win, began playing alone or with parents, depression before gambling, excitement while gambling, irrationality while playing, attraction to the machines' "aura," attributing success to skill, poor scholastic achievement, other potentially addictive behaviors, lower socioeconomic status, parental gambling or other addiction, and theft or truancy to gamble. Griffiths added a list of possible early warning signs to detect a serious gambling problem if several of these signs suddenly appear together.

- A study of gambling-related suicides in Australia found the most likely immediate cause to be depression due to gambling-related financial crises. Other risk factors were gender (male), occupational status (working-class and unemployed), domestic relationship problems, and previous suicide attempts. Because so few had elevated blood alcohol levels, the researchers also concluded that chemical dependency was not a risk factor for suicide. Although low self-esteem and introversion may also have been involved, they felt that these psychological factors may represent convenient rationalizations by relatives to "explain" the suicide or escape stigmatization.

Critique of Quantitative Studies

Quantitative studies conclusively demonstrate a number of facts about gambling. They show that it is not a deviant but an entirely normative behavior since most people gamble, that males are more frequent and heavier gamblers than females, that gambling is common among children and adolescents, that city dwellers gamble more than country dwellers, and that people will gamble more when there are greater opportunities for doing so. They therefore refute the **deviance hypothesis** but support the **gender**, **rural-urban residence**, and **availability and exposure hypotheses**.

Although general population surveys can identify which segments of a population gamble, to what extent they gamble, and their gambling preferences, they are incapable of revealing the reasons why people gamble. They have therefore been criticized because they cannot isolate the social, emotional, cognitive, and biological variables that may influence the decision to gamble. More specifically, they cannot measure peer pressure, subcultural norms, anxiety, depression, expectations, individual physiological differences, and other less tangible factors that many see as crucial to understanding the motivations for gambling.

Correlational studies have also been criticized on a number of grounds. Because of their frequently conflicting results, the validity of many hypotheses remains in doubt. For example, some associate gambling with particular demographic groups while others do not. One possible reason for this is that there has been no consistency in drawing class boundaries for such cardinal variables as age, income, education, etc., and no agreement as to how "moderate," "regular," or "heavy" gambling should be defined. Another possible reason is that some studies investigating only one form of gambling have generalized their findings and conclusions in an attempt to explain all forms. Others have investigated a variety of forms but still do not find the same correlations or draw the same conclusions.

The reliability and validity of such studies are also questionable. In addition to potential sampling biases in which certain groups can be over- or underrepresented, the conclusions of statistical surveys are based on unverifiable self-reported data. Because their subjects' responses can change with their mood state and personal circumstances at the time of the survey, they are not replicable. The retrospective nature of these studies–their attempt to associate previous life experiences with present conditions–often results in a laundry list of "possible" causes. Consequently, the many correlational studies that have been conducted have yielded a multitude of different "predictors" or "risk factors," none of which has yet been conclusively demonstrated to be causal. Many questionnaires also include items of a highly personal and perhaps even self-incriminatory nature which many people–particularly young people–may not be inclined to answer honestly. Highly structured questionnaires do not always include a full range of possible answers and therefore channel the subjects' responses in particular directions. Such influences would bias the results of any study.

Even if these problems were accounted for, quantitative studies are still incapable of explaining their findings and correlations because they are divorced from the social and cultural settings in which gambling occurs. As already noted, although statistics may be able to determine which segments of a population gamble more or less than others, figures alone are incapable of explaining why this occurs. Consequently, the relevance of the many demographic, environmental, and psychosocial factors that happen to correlate with gambling is unknown. However, far too many researchers offer "possible explanations" for their findings which are nevertheless purely conjectural and therefore of no scientific merit.

A number of critics are convinced that these shortcomings can be rectified only with other methods of research. Some feel that qualitative ethnographic and long-term prospective cohort studies of gambling hold the greatest promise. Others suggest that the predisposition for pathological gambling may have biological underpinnings which quantitative studies are incapable of discovering, an issue that will be explored in the next book in this series.

APPENDIX

SUMMARY OF ETIOLOGICAL THEORIES OF GAMBLING

Psychodynamic Approaches

Psychoanalytic Theory. Any inclination for gambling is symptomatic of a personality fixation at an early stage of psychosexual development.

Personality Theory. Gambling is a manifestation of a particular basic personality type. Earlier personality theorists assumed that environmental factors determined the individual's basic personality; more recent theorists, focusing on neurochemical and other physiological imbalances, have begun to explore individual biological differences.

Power Theory. A personality theory which assumes that gambling is motivated by low self-esteem and the need for achievement.

Dependency Conflict Theory. A personality theory which assumes that gambling is motivated by unconscious needs for independence.

Behavioral Psychological Approaches

Learning Theory. All behaviors represent learned responses to various environmental stimuli; addictions are habits that have been acquired through repeated reinforcement of those behaviors.

The Continuous Form Model. Continuous forms of gambling such as casino and machine gaming which involve rapidly repeated cycles of bets, outcomes, and rebets will be more addicting than noncontinuous forms such as lotteries in which the outcome does not immediately follow the bet.

The Skinnerian, Reinforcement, or Operant Conditioning Model. All behavioral responses that are rewarded will be reinforced; those that are no longer rewarded or are punished will be extinguished.

Drive-Reduction or Need-State Theories. Gambling reduces the intensity of certain drives or needs.

• *Play Theory.* Gamblers do not gamble for money, they gamble for fun. Some theorists see play as an instinctive drive or basic survival need while others see it as a learned or acquired drive. In either case, the drive is satisfied through gambling. Others see gambling as a socialization mechanism through which cultural values are transmitted and reinforced to successive generations.

• *The Tension-Reduction, Dysphoria-Reduction, or Escape Hypothesis.* Gambling reduces or relieves unpleasant hedonic or emotional states.

• *The Arousal or Sensation-Seeking Hypothesis.* Gambling is motivated by the intense thrill and excitement or "action" it provides.

• *Risk-Taking or Action Theory.* Similar to arousal theory, risk-taking theory assumes that those with the strongest risk orientation will be the heaviest gamblers.

• *The Dual-Effect Hypothesis.* Addictive behaviors can simultaneously reduce tension and increase arousal.

• *The Dual-Reinforcement Hypothesis.* Gambling is reinforced by the emotional reward of "action," which is delivered on a fixed-interval schedule with each wager, *and* by monetary rewards which are delivered on a variable-ratio schedule with each win.

The Pavlovian or Classical Conditioning Model. Associational learning through which a reflexive response to one cue or stimulus can be unintentionally elicited by an unrelated stimulus. The gambling response can be elicited by certain associated cues such as a croupier's call or track announcements.

• *Behavior Completion Mechanism Theory.* A fusion of the tension-reduction and classical conditioning models. A strong gambling-related cue stimulates a drive to gamble; any interruption of the sequence of behaviors that usually follow will produce a state of heightened tension and anxiety which can only be relieved by gambling.

- *Cognitive Approaches.* Gamblers persist even when they are losing because of the erroneous beliefs about winning and rationalizations of loss they maintain.

- *Attribution Theory.* Investigates the reasons and rationalizations gamblers give for their successes and failures. Those who ascribe the outcomes of events to such agencies as luck or fate are externally oriented; those who ascribe outcomes to their own skill are internally oriented.

- *The Illusion of Control Hypothesis.* Gamblers become more confident and will take greater risks when they are encouraged to believe that their own actions and choices can influence the outcome of chance-related outcomes.

- *The "Big Win" or "Early Win" Hypothesis.* Gamblers who win large amounts or smaller amounts consistently early in their careers will attribute their success to their own personal talents which leads them to expect similar success in the future. Such an orientation will serve to encourage persistence when they are losing as well as the initiation of new gambling sessions.

- *The Superstition Hypothesis.* Gamblers persist because of their conviction that luck can be influenced through magical thinking and ritualistic performances.

- *Social Learning or Modeling.* People acquire certain behaviors by imitating those they admire and regard as role models.

- *Frustration Theory.* Persistence derives from frustration over the failure to achieve a seemingly attainable goal.

Social Science Approaches

Social Structural Models. Gambling is in one way or another related to social class.

- *Leisure Class or Affluence Theory.* As a form of conspicuous consumption, gambling represents a visible status symbol among members of the upper classes.

Deviance Theory. Gambling, which is controlled by a vast criminal network, is one of many of immoral and antisocial behaviors typical of the unprincipled lower classes.

Structural-Functional Models. Gambling serves some positive social purpose, usually tension-reduction and/or the promotion of social solidarity.

  • *Alienation/Decision Making Theory.* Gambling allows members of the powerless working classes to make at least some of their own decisions and exercise at least some degree of control over their own lives.

  • *Anomie, Deprivation, or Status Inequality Theory.* Gambling offers an alternative means of social and economic advancement for members of the impoverished lower classes.

  • *Rural-urban Residence/Community Size Hypothesis.* Gambling will be relatively more prevalent in larger urban centers but less so in smaller towns and rural areas.

  • *The Religion Hypothesis.* Those who subscribe to the Protestant ethic and attend religious services on a regular basis will be less likely to gamble than those who do not. Protestants will therefore be less likely to gamble than either Catholics or Jews. The religion hypothesis was also used to explain the community size hypothesis since the Protestant ethic is presumed to be stronger in smaller rural towns and weaker in larger urban areas.

  • *The Ethnic Minority or Ethnicity Hypothesis.* Ethnic minorities will be more likely to gamble and develop gambling problems than those in the predominant ethnic group.

Economic Theories. People risk something of value to acquire something of greater value.

  • *Value-Maximizational or Utility Theory.* Gamblers are rational decision makers who assume only those risks which have the lowest potential cost and the highest probability of reward.

  • *The Regressivity Hypothesis.* Gambling taxes and losses are disproportionately higher among low-income groups who can least afford it.

- *Rational Addiction Theory.* Because the risks of addiction are low, the initial decision to engage in any potentially addictive behavior is a rational choice based on the expected costs and benefits of doing so.

- *Consumption Theory.* Gambling is a consumer service that must be purchased. Akin to play theory, theory maintains that the true reward of gambling lies in the enjoyment and satisfaction it offers the customer. Because gamblers who frequent commercial gaming establishments expect to lose, their losses represent the cost of this amusement. The gambler's goal is to minimize this cost.

- *Marxian Theory.* Gambling is just another means through which the bourgeois ruling class continues to exploit the proletarian masses.

Goffman's Small-Group Interactional Theory. Gambling provides an arena for role playing in which gamblers can act out their wish-fulfillment fantasies by assuming other identities through which they can exhibit idealized behavioral and personality traits. The primary goal of gambling is not to accrue money, but to acquire "character" and prestige.

Rosecrance's Interactional Theory. The gambling venue constitutes a distinct social world. As gamblers become increasingly committed to gambling, their social life increasingly centers around their gambling associates. Gamblers persist despite the losses they incur for the reward of social interaction with others who share this commitment.

Transactional or Family Systems Theory. Gambling is caused by strained, dysfunctional family relationships.

- *Transactional Script Theory.* Gamblers persist despite their losses to fulfill negative parental expectations. They want to lose because in early childhood they adopted the "life script" of loser as a result of their parents' harsh criticism of their failures and repeated predictions that they would grow up to be losers.

- *Family Systems Theory.* Gambling is a result rather than a cause of family discord. Gamblers and their significant others are playing different roles in a maladaptive social interactional game which they find rewarding.

"On Tilt" Theories. Problem gambling is a transient, often short-term condition brought about by unexpected and devastating losses or "bad

beats" which induce a state of emotional disequilibrium. This temporary loss of normal emotional control leads to poor judgment, irrational betting, chasing, and even greater losses. Since the condition is temporary it is correctable. The period of uncontrolled betting ceases with the return of normal emotional control.

Chasing. Compulsive gambling is a long-term condition brought about by the need to keep gambling in order to get even for all past losses. As gamblers chase their previous losses, they escalate the size and frequency of their bets, often betting and losing money slated for other purposes and then borrowing or stealing more to continue gambling. The more they gamble, the more they lose, and the more money they need to pay old debts and continue to chase in the futile quest to get even.

The Continuum or Dimensional Model. Many social and behavioral scientists insist that there are no qualitative differences between pathological and normative gamblers. Excessive gambling is therefore defined as that point along a graduated continuum of lesser to greater involvement at which financial and social problems are encountered.

Statistically-Based Models

Quantitative studies, which are generally based on questionnaire data, look for associations between gambling and various sociodemographic, environmental, and behavioral variables. Statistically significant correlations are assumed to be causal.

The Status Frustration/Hope/Aspiration Hypothesis. Closely related to anomie or status inequality theory, the status frustration hypothesis posits that gambling is motivated not by greed but by dissatisfaction with one's present socioeconomic status and hope for a better future. It will be most prevalent among those who are in the upper levels of a given social class and hope to move up to the next higher social class.

The Education Hypothesis. Related to the status inequality hypothesis, the education hypothesis predicts that the less formal education people have, the more likely they will be to gamble and to experience gambling problems.

The Subcultural Hypothesis. Gambling or its avoidance is largely determined by the subcultural values which people have internalized. In cultural contexts in which gambling is highly valued, it will be motivated by the need to "fit in" with one's primary reference group.

The Working-Class Culture Hypothesis. A variant of the subcultural hypothesis, the working-class culture hypothesis assumes that there are cultural and attitudinal as well as economic differences between the working and middle classes. One of these is a working-class fondness for gambling. This hypothesis therefore predicts that gambling frequencies will be higher among the working classes, particularly among those who adhere most strongly to values of this class.

The Life Cycle Hypothesis. Because the need for stimulation diminishes with age, the older people become the less likely they will be to gamble.

Continuity Theory. Related to the life cycle hypothesis, this approach suggests that a person's attitudes toward gambling are internalized in youth and maintained for life. Age-related gambling reflects a "cohort-effect": older people gamble less frequently because of the antigambling values that were prevalent in their youth; later generations gamble more frequently because antigambling sanctions and sentiments have steadily weakened over time.

The Age of Majority Hypothesis. Predicts that rates of gambling among adolescents will show rapid and dramatic increases when they reach legal gambling age.

The Home-Centeredness Hypothesis. Predicts that "Conjugal role sharing," or the extent to which husbands participate in such domestic activities as housework and shopping along with their wives, will be inversely related to gambling.

The Work-Centered Leisure Hypothesis. Predicts that gambling should be least prevalent among those whose free time activities such as studying at home are most closely related to their work.

The Parental Gambling Hypothesis. Another variant of the subcultural hypothesis, this hypothesis predicts that people's gambling-related attitudes and behaviors will reflect those of their parents. The risk of becoming a pathological gambler will also be greater for those having at least one parent who was a pathological gambler.

The Availability or Availability and Exposure Hypothesis. Predicts that any increase in the sanctioning and availability of gambling will lead to concomitant increases in gambling expenditures, rates of problem gambling, and criminal activities associated with the gambling trade.

The Gender Hypothesis. Predicts that rates of both normative and pathological gambling will be higher among males than females. Also, males and females gamble for different reasons.

The Marital Status Hypothesis. Married people will be less likely to gamble and to develop gambling problems than single, divorced, or widowed people.

The Age of Initiation or "Early Start" Hypothesis. The earlier in life people start to gamble, the more likely they are to develop gambling problems.

The Gateway or Precursor Hypothesis. Heavy video game involvement in childhood serves as a "gateway" or "stepping-stone" to electronic gaming machine addiction later in life. Similarly, the legalization of one form of gambling, such as government sponsored lotteries, is a "stepping-stone" to other forms of gambling, both legal and illegal.

The Risk Factor Model. Those who experience or exhibit a number of risk factors are more likely to become addicted to gambling than those who do not.

The Social Control Hypothesis. Being married is negatively correlated with pathological gambling while being single or widowed is positively correlated. Thus, the natural inclinations of potential problem gamblers are suppressed in the presence of marriage partners but expressed in their absence.

The Co-Addiction Hypothesis. Those who adopt one addictive or potentially addictive behavior or substance are likely to adopt others.

Medical or Disease Models

Pathological gambling is a medically diagnosable and treatable disorder. It may be either psychological or biological in origin.

Evolutionary Theory. Risk-seeking and the emotional arousal it incites are instinctive needs. They arose from the life-threatening hazards our pre-human ancestors encountered in their constant struggle for survival.

Repeated exposure to situations that provoked the involuntary "fight or flight" reaction eventually established a biological need for such experiences. Today, gambling is an intellectual substitute for the physical conflicts and risks our forebears were required to seek out and overcome to meet their survival needs.

Pathological Gambling as a Medical Syndrome (Moran). Pathological gambling is identifiable by a concurrence of one or more of the following phenomena: concern that gambling is excessive, an urge to gamble, loss of control over gambling, disturbances to family functioning. There are several varieties of pathological gambling, each of which has its own motivation.

Compulsive Gambling as a Psychological Illness (Custer). All addictions and the withdrawal symptoms that sometimes accompany them are purely psychological, resulting from the intense pleasure, relief, or escape they provide. Despite their outward demeanor, compulsive gamblers are lonely, anxious, depressed, insecure, and lacking in self-esteem.

The Heritability Hypothesis. The predisposition for pathological gambling is a genetically determined trait and therefore transmissible from parent to child.

Multicausal Theories

Pathological gambling and other addictions are caused by a variety of influences, including both hereditary biological and environmental learning factors.

The Sensation-Seeking or Arousal Hypothesis. Potential addicts are born with a greater than normal biological need for excitement which they learn to satisfy through such stimulating behaviors as drug use and gambling.

Opponent-Process Theory. Like sky-divers, pathological gamblers do not become addicted to the initial unpleasant emotions that their behavior arouses, but to the highly enjoyable opposite emotional reactions that automatically ensue to diminish or counteract them.

Reversal Theory. People who are stressed or anxious gamble to relax; those who are bored gamble for excitement. Their motivations for gambling can undergo rapid reversals during the course of a gambling session.

Pathological gambling develops when anxiety itself becomes a powerful internal associational cue that further stimulates the gambling response.

The General Theory of Addictions/Addictive Personality Syndrome. This approach represents an ambitious attempt to explain *all* addictions. According to its advocates, some people are born either overaroused or underaroused, both of which they find unpleasant and will attempt to alleviate. Those who feel rejected, inferior, and have low self-esteem will, under certain circumstances, resort to gambling and other addictive behaviors as a means of escaping into a make-believe world of wish-fulfillment fantasy.

A Parsimonious Need-State Model. There are two fundamental types of pathological gamblers who can be motivated by either psychological or biological causes. They are the chronically depressed who gamble to relieve this condition and the chronically understimulated who gamble for excitement. The temporary relief that gambling provides is followed by an even stronger rebound need state which the gambler again attempts to relieve through further gambling.

Learned Helplessness Theory. Addiction is a direct consequence of chronic negative affect (low self-esteem, depression, guilt, anxiety, etc.) which, in turn, is a direct consequence of self-blame which, in turn, is a direct consequence of a learned internal locus of control orientation which, in turn, is a direct consequence of one's past life experiences and traumas. Learned helplessness, which also takes such forms as posttraumatic stress syndrome or "shell shock," affects only those who are genetically predisposed for it.

The Synoptic Model. Rather than immoral, deviant, or sick, gambling is a normal social activity. As a form of entertainment, it is motivated either by internal psychological factors, external social factors, or the particular structure of a game and the challenge it offers. Nonconventional or excessive gambling results from the individual's inability to follow the rules and conventions of normative gambling.

NOTES

SERIES INTRODUCTION

1. Lesieur 1990; 1992; cf. Lorenz and Politzer 1990.
2. Lesieur 1988c.
3. See Barker and Britz 2000; Ladouceur, Boisvert, Pépin, Loranger, and Sylvain 1994; Lesieur 1990; Meyer and Stadler 1999 for more detailed discussions.
4. E.g., Shaffer 1989, p. 1; Tarter and Schneider 1976, pp. 80-82.
5. Cited by Wagner 1972, p. i.
6. Aristotle 1953, p. 98.
7. Hopper 1970, p. 360.
8. Quoted by Rosecrance 1988b, p. 107.
9. Rosecrance 1988b, pp. 96-100.
10. E.g., Blaszczynski, McConaghy, and Frankova 1989; Bolen and Boyd 1968; Brown 1987c; Cressey 1971; Custer and Custer 1978; Lemert 1953; Lesieur 1979; 1984; 1987; 1993; Livingston 1974a; Maurer 1974; Roebuck 1967.
11. Abt, Smith, and Christiansen 1985, p. ix.
12. Ibid.
13. For reviews and examples, see Bell 1976; Clotfelter and Cook 1989, pp. 47-48; Inglis 1985; Orford and McCartney 1990; Reid 1985; Shaffer and Gambino 1989; Tarter and Schneider 1976; Turner, Ialomiteanu, and Room 1999, p. 56.
14. E.g., Abt, Smith, and Christiansen 1985; Caldwell 1985a, p. 18; Campbell 1976; Kusyszyn 1976; 1984; 1990; Rosecrance 1986a; 1988b; Smith and Abt 1984.
15. Abt, Smith, and Christiansen 1985, p. 136.
16. E.g., Blaszczynski, Buhrich, and McConaghy 1985; Brown 1987a; 1993; Coventry and Brown 1993, p. 543; Custer and Milt 1985, p. 28; Dickerson 1977a; 1984; 1987; 1989; Ferrioli and Ciminero 1981; Gaboury and Ladouceur 1993; Galdston 1960, p. 555; Jacobs 1986; Koller 1972; Kusyszyn 1972; Larkin and Griffiths 1998; Leary and Dickerson 1985; Lesieur and Rosenthal 1991; Lester 1979, p. 106; Marks 1990; Miller 1980; Moran 1970a; 1970b; Orford 1985; Rosenthal 1993; Shaffer 1989, p. 7; 1996; 1997; Shaffer, Stein, Gambino, and Cummings 1989, p. xv; Thorson, Powell, and Hilt 1994; Tyndel 1963; Victor 1981, p. 280.
17. American Psychiatric Association 1980; 1987, 1994.
18. World Health Organization 1991; 1992.
19. Cf. Fisher 1993a, p. 413.

20. Brown 1993, p. 265.
21. Dickerson 1991, p. 317.
22. E.g., Custer and Milt 1985; Jacobs 1986.
23. McConaghy 1980.
24. Orford 1985.
25. Glasser 1976.
26. Brown 1993, p. 251.
27. Becker and Murphy 1988, p. 676; Peele and Brodsky 1975; Wittman, Fuller, and Taber 1988.
28. Goddard 1993, p. 48.
29. Goodman 1990, p. 1403; Herman 1967, p. 103; Livingston 1974a, p. 3; Marks 1990, p. 1391; Shaffer 1989, pp. 12, 28; 1996; 1997.
30. Shaffer 1989.
31. Ibid., p. 6, note 3.
32. Walker 1985.
33. Cornish 1978; Dickerson 1989; Kroeber 1992; Orford 1985; Orford and McCartney 1990; Walker 1992c, p. 151.
34. Büringer and Konstanty 1992; Törne and Konstanty 1992.
35. McCormack 1994.
36. Oldman 1978.
37. Dickerson 1984; 1985; 1989.
37. Burglass 1989, p. 206.
39. Gilovich and Douglas 1986, p. 229.
40. Shaffer and Hall 1996; Shaffer, Hall, and Vander Bilt 1997; Moore 2001a; 2001b.
41. Atlas and Peterson 1990; Browne 1989; Dickerson 1989, p. 158; Rosecrance 1986b; 1988b, p. 117; Walker 1992c, p. 151.
42. Rosenthal 1989, pp. 118-119.
43. Abt, Smith, and Christiansen 1985.
44. Rosenthal 1989, p. 120.
45. Custer and Milt 1985, p. 25.
46. Rosenthal 1989, p. 120.
47. Fisher 1999; Walker 1985.
48. Greene 1982; Walker 1992c.
49. Bühringer and Konstanty 1992.
50. Dickerson 1984; 1985.
51. Miller, P. 1980, p. 268.
52. Custer and Custer 1978.
53. E.g., Kallick, Suits, Dielman, and Hybels 1976; 1979; Volberg and Steadman 1988.
54. Haberman 1969, p. 164.
55. Lesieur and Heineman 1988.
56. Lesieur, Blume, and Zoppa 1986.
57. McCormick 1993, p. 333.
58. Elia and Jacobs 1991.
59. Lesieur and Rosenthal 1991, p. 18.

60. Feigelman, Kleinman, Lesieur, Millman, and Lesser 1995.
61. Spunt, Lesieur, Hunt, and Cahill 1995.
62. Spunt, Lesieur, Liberty, and Hunt 1996.
63. Shepherd 1996.
64. Daghestani, Elenz, and Crayton 1996.
65. Miller and Westermeyer 1996.
66. McCormick, Russo, Ramirez, and Taber 1984.
67. Lesieur 1988a.
68. Yaffee, Lorenz, and Politzer 1993.
69. Lesieur 1988a.
70. Lesieur 1993, p. 501.
71. Linden, Pope, and Jonas 1986; Lesieur 1988b.
72. Lesieur 1988b.
73. Ramirez, McCormick, Russo, and Taber 1983.
74. McCormick, Russo, Ramirez, and Taber 1984.
75. Adkins, Rugle, and Taber 1985.
76. Ciarrocchi and Richardson 1989.
77. Lesieur and Klein 1987.
78. Ciarrocchi, Kirshner, and Fallik 1991.
79. Schwarz and Lindner 1992.
80. Bland, Newman, Orn, and Stebelsky 1993.
81. Steinberg, Kosten, and Rounsaville 1992.
82. Gambino, Fitzgerald, Shaffer, Renner, and Courtnage 1993.
83. Specker, Carlson, Edmonson, Johnson, and Marcotte 1996.
84. E.g., Bergh and Külhorn 1994b; Blaszczynski and McConaghy 1989; Blaszczynski, Buhrich, and McConaghy 1985; Blume 1994; Blume and Lesieur 1987; Bondolfi, Osiek, and Ferrero 2000; Ciarrocchi 1987; Coyle and Kinney 1990, p. 35; Custer and Milt 1985; Feigelman, Wallisch, and Lesieur 1998; Feigelman, Kleinman, Lesieur, Millman, and Lesser 1995; Galdston 1951; Graham and Lowenfeld 1986; Greenson 1948; Hall, Carriero, Takushi, Montoya, Preston, and Gorelick 2000; Harris 1964; Ibàñez, Mercadé, Aymami Sanromà, and Cordero 1992; Kagan 1987; Langenbucher, Bavly, Labouvie, Sanjuan, and Martin 2001; Lejoyeux, Feuche, Loi, Solomon, and Ades 1999; Lesieur and Blume 1990; 1991; McCormick, Taber, and Kruedelbach 1989; McCormick 1993; Martinez-Pina, Guirao de Parga, Fuste i Vallverdu, Planas, Mateo, and Auguado 1991; Marty, Zoppa, and Lesieur 1985; Miller and Westermeyer 1996; Moran 1970a; 1970b; Orford 1985; Peele 1985; Petry 2000a; 2000b; 2001; Robins, Helzer, Weissman, Orvaschel, Gruenberg, Burke, and Regier 1984; Roy, Smelsen, and Lindeken 1996; Shepherd 1996; Slutske, Eisen, True, Lyons, Goldberg, and Tsuang, 2000; Spunt, Lesieur, Hunt, and Cahill 1995; Spunt, Lesieur, Liberty, and Hunt 1996; Spunt, Dupont, Lesieur, Liberty, and Hunt 1998; Taber, McCormick, and Ramirez 1987; Taber, Russo, Adkins, and McCormick 1986; Templer, Kaiser, and Siscoe 1993; Tyndel 1963; Vitaro, Ferland, Jacques, and Ladouceur 1998.
85. Oliveira and Silva 2000.

86. Briggs, Goodin, and Nelson 1996.
87. Becoña 1993.
88. Kroeber 1992, pp. 86-87.
89. Rosenthal 1992, p. 76.
90. Lesieur 1993, p. 511.
91. Custer and Custer 1978.
92. Miller, P. 1980, p. 267.
93. Ciarrocchi 1987, p. 25; Slutske, Eisen, True, Lyons, Goldberg, and Tsuang, 2000.
94. Moran 1970c, p. 67.
95. Lesieur 1989, p. 231; Lesieur, Blume, and Zoppa 1986, p. 33.
96. Ciarrocchi and Richardson 1989, p. 63.
97. Rosenthal 1970.
98. E.g., Madsen 1974; Seixas, Omenn, Burk, and Eggelston 1972.
99. Saunders and Wookey 1980, p. 1.
100. Brown 1987b.
101. Freud 1950 [1928]; see also Abraham 1960; Bergler 1936; 1943; 1958; Rado 1926; Rosenthal 1987; Simmel 1920.
102. Skinner 1974; see also Dickerson 1979; 1984; Knapp 1976.
103. E.g., Dickerson 1991; 1993; Dickerson and Adcock 1987; Gaboury and Ladouceur 1988; 1989; Ladouceur and Gaboury 1988; Griffiths 1990a; 1990d; 1993d; Ladouceur and Gaboury 1988; Ladouceur, Gaboury, Dumont, and Rochette 1988; Walker 1985; 1988; 1992a; 1992b; 1992c; 1992d.
104. E.g., Devereux 1949; Goffman 1967; 1969.
105. E.g., Moran 1970a; Newman 1972a; Zola 1963.
106. E.g., Carlton and Goldstein 1987; Carlton and Manowitz 1987.
107. E.g., Carlton and Goldstein 1987; Jacobs 1986; 1988; 1989a; McCormick 1987; Roy, Adinoff, Roehrich, Lamparski, Custer, Lorenz, Barbaccia, Guidotti, Costa, and Linnoila 1988.
108. E.g., Kallick, Suits, Dielman, and Hybels 1976; 1979; Volberg 1993; 1994; Volberg and Steadman 1988; 1989.
109. E.g., Blaszczynski and McConaghy 1987; Ciarrocchi and Richardson 1989; Hraba, Mok, and Huff 1990; Specker, Carlson, Edmonson, Johnson, and Marcotte 1996.
110. E.g., Downes, Davies, David, and Stone 1976; Newman 1972a; Price 1972; Roberts and Sutton-Smith 1966; Tec 1964.
111. Lesieur 1993; Mark and Lesieur 1992; Specker, Carlson, Edmonson, Johnson, and Marcotte 1996; Rosenthal 1987, p. 42; Strachan and Custer 1993.
112. France 1902, p. 380.
113. Dickerson 1984, p. 39.
114. Laundergan, Schaefer, Eckhoff, and Pirie 1990, pp. 15-16, 41; Legarda, Babio, and Abreu 1992, p. 769; Lesieur 1988b; Lesieur and Blume 1991; Sommers 1988, p. 484; Volberg and Steadman 1988; 1989.
115. Strachan and Custer 1993, p. 235.

CHAPTER 1
GAMBLING AND SOCIAL STRUCTURE

1. Campbell 1976, p. 218.
2. Bolen 1976, pp. 13-15.
3. Veblen 1931 [1899].
4. E.g., Tylor 1958 [1871], pp. 78-83.
5. Veblen 1931 [1899], p. 36.
6. Dostoevsky 1972 [1866], pp. 17-18.
7. Ibid., p. 17.
8. Ibid., p. 18.
9. Li and Smith 1976, p. 204.
10. Downs, Davies, David, and Stone 1976, p. 39.
11. Newman 1972a, p. 7.
12. Tec 1964, p. 105.
13. E.g., Bloch 1951; Davis 1956, p. 15; Dentler 1967, p. 369; Landis 1945, p. 279; Maurer 1950, p. 114; Peterson 1951, pp. 6 ff.; Quinn 1912, p. 1; Weinberg 1960, p. 285.
14. Tec 1964, pp. 19, 105-106.
15. Newman 1972a, p. 222.
16. Frey 1984.
17. E.g., Bloch 1951.
18. E.g., Campbell 1976, p. 227; Herman 1967, pp. 101-102; Newman 1972a; Scodel 1964; Zola 1963, p. 360.
19. See Smith, Preston, and Humphries 1976 for a brief review.
20. E.g., Bloch 1951; 1962; Clinard 1963.
21. Bloch 1951, pp. 217-218.
22. Herman 1967, pp. 102-103.
23. Smith and Abt 1984, p. 125.
24. Merton 1938.
25. Bloch 1951, p. 218; cf. Myrdal 1944, p. 985; Tec 1964, p. 108.
26. Devereux 1949.
27. Cf. Bloch 1962; Devereux 1968; Thorner 1956.
28. Devereux 1949, p. 643.
29. E.g., Tec 1964; Clotfelter and Cook 1989.
30. Devereux 1949, pp. 109, 594.
31. Newman 1972a, p. 11.
32. Ibid., p. 15.
33. Furnham 1985.
34. Greenberg, Lewis, and Dodd 1999.
35. E.g., Herman 1967.
36. Schissel 2001.
37. Abt, Smith, and Christiansen 1985, p. 23.
38. Cornish 1978.

39. Lesieur 1984.
40. Cornish 1978; see also Fleming's 1978 historical review.
41. Abt, Smith, and Christiansen 1985, p. 22.
42. Scott 1968.
43. Ibid., p. 118.
44. Ibid.

CHAPTER 2
GAMBLING AND ECONOMICS

1. E.g., Blanche 1950, p. 77; Brenner 1986; Brenner and Brenner 1990; Clotfelter and Cook 1989, p. 73; Davis 1956, p. 77; Devereux 1949, pp. 781-782; Sumner and Keller 1927, p. 739.
2. E.g., Brenner 1986; Cornish 1978; Furnham 1985; Tec 1964.
3. Lea, Tarpy, and Webley 1987, p. 271.
4. Clotfelter and Cook 1989, p. 73.
5. Brenner 1986, p. 128.
6. Scarne 1961.
7. Scarne 1975.
8. Brenner, Lipeb, and Bikanda 1993.
9. Newman 1972a, p. 227.
10. Eadington 1987, p. 264.
11. Friedman and Savage 1948, pp. 297-298.
12. Lea, Tarpy and Webley 1987, p. 277; Slovic and Lichtenstein 1968, p. 2.
13. Clotfelter and Cook 1989, p. 20.
14. Bernoulli 1954 [1738].
15. Smith, A. 1937 [1776].
16. Slovic and Lichtenstein 1968, p. 3, after Edwards 1955.
17. Scott 1968, p. 84.
18. E.g., Edwards 1955; Philips and Amrhein 1989; Slovic and Lichtenstein 1968; Yaari 1965.
19. von Neumann and Morgenstern 1944.
20. Friedman and Savage 1948.
21. Brunk 1981, p. 344.
22. Brenner 1986; Brenner and Brenner 1990.
23. Eadington 1987, p. 266.
24. See also Corney and Cummings 1992.
25. Munson 1962; see also Coombs and Pruitt 1960; Payne 1975.
26. Pryor 1976.
27. Brenner, Lipeb, and Bikanda 1993, pp. 187-188.
28. Ibid., p. 190.
29. Slovic 1969.
30. Brunk 1981.

31. Eadington 1973, p. 13; cf. Cornish 1978, p. 93.
32. Eadington 1976.
33. E.g., Cornish 1978; Machina 1982; Quiggin 1985; 1987.
34. Rosecrance 1988b, p. 64.
35. Cornish 1978, pp. 92; cf. Walters 1994a, pp. 166-167.
36. Slovic and Lichtenstein 1968.
37. Eadington 1987, p. 265.
38. Cohen 1970, p. 450; Eadington 1973, pp. 31-49.
39. Cornish 1978, p. 97.
40. Ibid.
41. E.g., Mobilia 1993.
42. E.g., Becker and Murphy 1988.
43. Orphanides and Zervos 1995, p. 741.
44. Moran 1970c, p. 64.
45. Wagenaar, Keren, and Pleit-Kuiper 1984, p. 167.
46. Keren and Wagenaar 1985, p. 154.
47. E.g., Coombs and Pruitt 1960; Edwards 1955; Griffith 1949; Kahneman and Tversky 1979; 1984; McGlothlin 1956; Snyder 1978; Tversky and Kahneman 1974.
48. E.g., Abt, Smith, and Christiansen 1985, p. 11; Eadington 1973, pp. 33, 38; 1987; 1999; Ignatin and Smith 1976, pp. 72-73; Lea, Tarpy and Webley 1987, p. 267; Wagenaar, Keren, and Pleit-Kuiper 1984.
49. Eadington 1987, p. 269.
50. Ibid.
51. Ibid., p. 264.
52. Ibid., p. 266.
53. Ignatin and Smith 1976, p. 81, footnote.
54. Frey 1984, p. 112.
55. Fuller 1974, pp. 36-37.
56. Ibid., p. 37.
57. Hogan 1986.
58. Walker 1992c, p. 88.
59. Dickerson, Walker, Legg England, and Hinchy 1990, p. 174.
60. Caldwell 1985b, p. 265.
61. Dickerson, Bayliss, and Head 1984, cited by Caldwell 1985b, p. 265.
62. Bergler 1943; 1949; Smith and Preston 1984.
63. Aasved and Schaefer 1995, p. 317; Aasved and Laundergan 1993, pp. 305-306; 311; Eadington 1999; 2000; Walker 1992c, p. 89.
64. Lea, Tarpy and Webley 1987, p. 278; cf. Eadington 1987, p. 266.
65. Walker 1985, pp. 146-147; cf. 1992c, p. 88.

CHAPTER 3
TESTS OF "ARMCHAIR" THEORIES

1. Dixey 1987.
2. Campbell 1976, p. 219.
3. Ibid., p. 227.
4. Zola 1963.
5. Rosecrance 1988b, p. 59.
6. Ocean and Smith 1993.
7. Herman 1967.
8. Ibid., p. 97.
9. Fabricand 1965; Griffith 1949; McGlothlin 1956; Mukhtar 1977; Snyder 1978; Weitzman 1965.
10. McGlothlin 1956.
11. Herman 1967, p. 99.
12. Ibid., pp. 101-102.
13. Ibid., p. 101.
14. Scott 1968.
15. Herman 1967, p. 102.
16. Ibid., p. 103.
17. Ibid.
18. Ibid.
19. Ibid.
20. Smith and Abt 1984, p. 125.
21. Herman 1967, p. 104.
22. Scimecca 1971.
23. Ibid., p. 56.
24. Lesieur 1984, pp. 250-257.
25. E.g. Newman 1975.

CHAPTER 4
THE RESEARCHERS' POINT OF VIEW

1. Aasved 2002, pp. 25-27.
2. Goffman 1959; 1967; 1969.
3. Goffman 1967, pp. 218-237.
4. Ibid., pp. 5ff.
5. Ibid., p. 239.
6. Newman 1972b, p. 6.
7. Newman 1972a, p. 157.
8. Zola 1963.
9. Scott 1968, pp. 113-114.
10. Zurcher 1970.

11. Abt, McGurrin, and Smith 1985, p. 82.
12. Holtgraves 1988, p. 80.
13. Ibid., p. 81.
14. Spanier 1994, pp. 167-168.
15. Holtgraves 1988.
16. Scodel 1964.
17. Dostoevsky 1972 [1866], p. 158.
18. Gamblers Anonymous, no date, p. 20.
19. Holtgraves 1988; Miller 1986.
20. Oldman 1974; 1978.
21. Oldman 1978, p. 357.
22. Lesieur 1984; Oldman 1978, p. 368.
23. Oldman 1978, p. 359.
24. Ibid., pp. 358-359.
25. Ibid., p. 366.
26. Ibid., p. 365.
27. Ibid., p. 365.
28. Ibid., p. 369.
29. Ibid., p. 366.
30. Ibid., p. 367.
31. Ibid.
32. Ibid., pp. 369-370.
33. Ladouceur and Gaboury 1988; Ladouceur and Mayrand 1986; 1987; Ladouceur, Mayrand, and Tourigny 1987; Ladouceur, Tourigny, and Mayrand 1986.
34. Walker 1992c, p. 86.
35. Oldman 1974, p. 118.
36. Ibid.
37. Walker 1992c, p. 86.
38. Ibid., p. 85.
39. Rosecrance 1986a; 1988b.
40. E.g., Smith and Preston 1984.
41. E.g., Hayano 1982; Herman 1967; Newman 1968; 1975; Oldman 1978; Scott 1968.
42. Rosecrance 1986a.
43. Ibid., p. 358.
44. Ibid.
45. Rosecrance 1988b.
46. Rosecrance 1986a, pp. 365-366.
47. Rosecrance 1988b, p. 86.
48. Cf. Hayano 1982.
49. Rosecrance 1986a, p. 368.
50. Rosecrance 1988b, p. 86.
51. Ibid., p. 374.
52. Rosecrance 1986a, p. 374; cf. Ocean and Smith 1993.
53. Rosecrance 1988b, pp. 84-85.

54. E.g., Berne 1972; Steiner 1969; 1971; Cahalan 1970.
55. Ingram 1985.
56. Boyd and Bolen 1970; Gaudia 1987; Lorenz 1987.
57. Boyd and Bolen 1970.
58. Ibid., p. 82.
59. Ibid., pp. 89-90.
60. Lorenz 1987; Lorenz and Shuttlesworth 1983.
61. Lorenz 1987, p. 76.
62. Custer and Milt 1985; Lesieur 1984; Wexler 1984.
63. Lorenz 1987, pp. 76-79.
64. Scodel 1964.
65. Ibid., p. 125.
66. Lorenz 1987.
67. Ibid., p. 80.
68. Ibid.
69. Ibid.
70. Ibid., pp. 79-80, emphasis added.
71. Rosecrance 1986a, p. 365.
72. Walker 1992b, pp. 487-488.
73. Jacobs 1989b; 1993.
74. Lorenz 1987, p. 80.
75. Custer and Custer 1978.
76. Ciarrocchi and Richardson 1989, pp. 52, 57.
77. McCormick and Taber 1987, pp. 20-21.
78. Lesieur 1989, pp. 234-236.
79. France 1902, p. 407.
80. Huizinga 1950, p. 13.
81. Caillois 1961.
82. E.g., Kusyszyn 1976; 1984.
83. Smith and Abt 1984; cf. Griffiths 1989.
84. E.g., Herman 1976a, p. 1; 1976b; Kusyszyn 1976; 1978; 1984; 1990; Kusyszyn and Rutter 1985, p. 63; Lester 1979; Smith and Abt 1984.
85. Scott 1968.
86. Abt, Smith, and Christiansen 1985; Abt, Smith, and McGurrin 1985.
87. Abt, Smith, and McGurrin 1985, p. 64.
88. Ibid., p. 64.
89. Abt, Smith, and Christiansen 1985, p. 202.
90. Ibid., p. 135.
91. Altman 1985.
92. Dodd 1985.
93. Herman 1976b, p. 214; cf. Lester 1979, p. 1.
94. Herman 1976b, pp. 213-214, emphasis in original.
95. Smith and Abt 1984.
96. Ibid., p. 123.
97. Ibid., p. 124.
98. Keill 1956, pp. 88-89, quoted by Fisher 1993c, p. 398 and Griffiths 1989, p. 71.

CHAPTER 5
THE GAMBLER'S POINT OF VIEW

1. Martinez and LaFranchi 1969.
2. Ibid., p. 52.
3. Ibid., p. 33.
4. Ibid., p. 35.
5. Ibid., p. 34.
6. Ibid.
7. Ibid., p. 52.
8. Ibid., p. 35.
9. Ibid., p. 33.
10. Ibid., p. 34.
11. Ibid.
12. Ibid., p. 33.
13. Hayano 1982.
14. Ibid., p. 148.
15. Ibid., p. 151.
16. Ibid., pp. 150-151.
17. Ibid., pp. 102-105.
18. Ibid., p. 6.
19. Ibid., p. 104.
20. Ibid., pp. 65-68.
21. Ibid., p. 106.
22. Ibid., pp. 10-11, 18.
23. Ibid., p. 36.
24. Ibid., pp. 113 ff.
25. Ibid., p. 127.
26. Ibid., pp. 26-28.
27. Ibid., p. 74.
28. Ibid., p. 28.
29. Ibid., p. 104.
30. Ibid., p. 105.
31. Ibid., p. 57.
32. Ibid., p. 47.
33. Ibid., p. 48.
34. Ibid., p. 103; cf. the "action player" described by Martinez and La Franchi 1969.
35. Ibid., p. 185.
36. Ibid., p. 52.
37. Ibid., p. 28.
38. Ibid., pp. 94-96.
39. Ibid., p. 97.
40. Ibid., pp. 105-106.
41. Oldman 1974, p. 418.
42. Hayano 1982, p. 106; cf. Cohen 1970, p. 455.
43. Ibid, p. 110.

44. Ibid., p. 106.
45. Ibid., pp. 140-141.
46. Rosecrance 1986a.
47. Rosecrance 1986b; 1988b, pp. 128-137.
48. E.g., McCormick and Taber 1988; McCormick, Taber, and Kruedelbach 1989. Learned helplessness theory will be discussed in greater detail in a future volume of this series.
49. Rosecrance 1988b, p. 8.
50. E.g., Martinez and LaFranchi 1969; Scimecca 1971.
51. Rosecrance 1986c.
52. Ibid., p. 79; cf. Scott 1968.
53. Oldman 1974.
54. Scott 1968.
55. Ibid., p. 97.
56. Rosecrance 1986b; 1988b.
57. E.g., Rotter 1966, p. 1; Lefcourt 1983.
58. Lefcourt 1966, p. 191.
59. Rosecrance 1986b, p. 468.
60. Ibid., p. 469.
61. Ibid., p. 466; cf. Rosecrance 1986c, p. 89; 1988b, pp. 126-127.
62. Ibid., p. 128.
63. Ibid., p. 466.
64. Ibid., p. 131.
65. Ibid.
66. Ibid., p. 473.
67. Rosecrance 1986a.
68. Rosecrance 1986c, p. 91.
69. Rosecrance 1988b, p. 135.
70. Ibid., p. 466.
71. Rosecrance 1988a; 1988b; 1989.
72. Browne 1989.
73. Ibid., p. 7.
74. Stein 1993, p. 630.
75. Browne 1989, p. 12.
76. Ibid., p. 11.
77. Ibid., p. 12.
78. Ibid., p. 19; cf. Baron and Dickerson 1999.
79. Ibid., p. 17.
80. Lesieur 1988c, p. 27; 1989, p. 232.
81. Ibid.
82. Browne 1989, p. 6.
83. Ibid.
84. Rosecrance 1989, p. 152.
85. Levy and Feinberg 1991, p. 44.
86. Browne 1989, p. 20, endnote 3.

87. Hraba, Mok, and Huff 1990, p. 357.

88. E.g., Gilovich 1983, Gilovich and Douglas 1986.

89. Aasved and Schaefer 1995.

90. Shaffer 1996, p. 463.

91. Livingston 1974b, p. 51.

92. Nadler 1985, p. 48.

93. Kusyszyn 1978, p. 1100.

94. Lesieur 1984.

95. Dostoevsky 1972 [1866], p. 191.

96. Lesieur 1984, p. xi.

97. Ibid., p. 248.

98. Lesieur 1989, p. 233; Lesieur and Rosenthal 1991, p. 31.

99. Lesieur 1984, pp. 214-216.

100. Ibid., p. 217; Lesieur 1979.

101. Lesieur 1984, pp. 217 ff.

102. Cf. Lesieur 1993, pp. 506-509; Meyer and Fabian 1993, pp. 518-519.

103. Fenichel 1945, p. 178; Menninger 1938.

104. Dickerson 1984, p. 81.

105. Browne 1989, p. 5.

106. Ibid.

107. Bergh and Külhorn 1994a, pp. 268-269.

108. Beaudoin and Cox 1999.

109. E.g., Oldman 1978; Rosecrance 1985, 1986a, 1986b; Browne 1989.

110. Knapp 1987, pp. 298-290.

111. Rosenthal 1995.

112. Ibid., p. 368.

113. Ibid., p. 371.

114. Ide-Smith and Lea 1988.

115. Huxley and Carroll 1992.

116. Fisher 1993b; 1993c.

117. Griffiths 1991b.

118. Martinez and LaFranchi 1969.

119. Fabian 1995, p. 251.

120. Fisher 1993b; Griffiths 1990a.

121. Downes, Davies, David, and Stone 1976, p. 193.

122. Griffiths 1990b, p. 122.

123. Fabian 1995, p. 251.

124. Fisher 1993b; 1993c; Griffiths 1990a; 1990b; 1990c; 1991b; 1993a; 1993c.

125. Fisher 1993b, p. 458.

126. Cf. Griffiths 1991b, p. 316.

127. Fisher 1993b, p. 462.

128. Fisher 1993c, pp. 400-401.

129. Fisher 1993b, p. 462; cf. Griffiths 1990a, p. 36.

130. Griffiths 1991b, p. 317.

131. Griffiths 1990a, p. 36; 1990b, p. 123.

132. Fisher 1993b, p. 463.
133. Griffiths 1991b, pp. 314, 318.
134. Fisher 1993b, p. 467.
135. Griffiths 1991b, p. 317.
136. Fabian 1995; Griffiths 1993c.
137. See also Fisher 1995.
138. Fisher 1993b, p. 469.
139. Griffiths 1991b, p. 317; cf. 1991a; 1993b.
140. Fisher 1993c, p. 400.
141. Ibid., p. 471.
142. Griffiths 1990b.
143. American Psychiatric Association 1987.
144. Griffiths 1990b, p. 119.
145. Ibid., p. 120.
146. Ibid.
147. Ibid., p. 121.
148. Ibid.
149. Ibid., p. 122.
150. Ibid.
151. Ibid.
152. Griffiths 1993d.
153. Ibid., p. 43.
154. Ibid., p. 35; see also Griffiths 1993e, p. 391.
155. Griffiths 1993d, p. 37.
156. Ibid., p. 40.
157. Ibid., p. 39.
158. Ibid., pp. 39-40.
159. Ibid., p. 42.
160. Ibid., p. 42.
161. Ibid.
162. Ibid., p. 40; Griffiths 1993e, pp. 394-395.
163. Griffiths 2000, p. 81.

CHAPTER 6
STATISTICAL TESTS OF EARLIER IDEAS

1. Tec 1964.
2. Ibid., p. 10.
3. Ibid., p. 86.
4. Cf. Campbell 1976, p. 223; Newman 1972a, pp. 227-228.
5. Tec 1964, p. 19.
6. Ibid., p. 21.
7. Ibid., p. 22.

8. Ibid., pp. 23-25.

9. Gallup 1972; Smith and Razzell 1975.

10. Tec 1964, p. 27.

11. Ibid., pp. 29-30.

12. Ibid., p. 32.

13. Ibid., p. 51.

14. Ibid., pp. 47, 52.

15. Ibid., p. 50.

16. Ibid., pp. 61-62.

17. Ibid., pp. 89-103.

18. Ibid., pp. 70-87.

19. Ibid., p. 108.

20. Campbell 1976, p. 223.

21. Tec 1964, pp. 114, 115.

22. Ibid., p. 117.

23. Newman 1972a, pp. 16-17.

24. Cornish 1978, p. 114; Li and Smith 1976; Weinstein and Deitch 1974.

25. Newman 1972a, p. 17.

26. Ibid.

27. Smith and Razzell 1975.

28. E.g., Abbott and Cramer 1993; Brinner and Clotfelter 1975; Brown, Kaldenberg, and Brown 1992; Clotfelter 1979; Heavey 1978; Herring and Blesdoe 1994; Kallick, Suits, Dielman, and Hybels 1976; Mikesell 1991; Rosen and Norton 1966; Spiro 1974.

29. E.g., Lemelin 1977; McLoughlin 1979; Vaillancourt and Grignon 1988.

30. E.g., Downes, Davies, David, and Stone 1976; Newman 1972b.

31. Kaplan 1988, p. 172.

32. Suits 1982; cf. Clotfelter and Cook 1989; Kaplan 1989.

33. Brenner 1983; Brenner and Brenner 1990, p. 28.

34. Borg 1988; Brenner 1985; Clotfelter and Cook 1989; Livernois 1987; Mikesell 1989.

35. Tec 1964, p. 117.

36. Moran 1970a, p. 594.

37. Zola 1963.

38. Campbell 1976, p. 225.

39. E.g., Bales 1962; Snyder 1955; 1962.

40. Kallick, Suits, Dielman, and Hybels 1976, p. 6.

41. Ciarrocchi and Richardson 1989, pp. 53, 61.

42. Knox and Stafford 1978; McCauley, Stitt, Woods, and Lipton 1973.

43. Blascovich, Ginsberg and Howe 1976; Blascovich, Veach, and Ginsburg 1973.

44. Newman 1972a.

45. Newman 1975, p. 543.

46. Newman 1972a, p. 226.

47. Ibid., p. 226.

48. Ibid., p. 64; cf. Newman 1975, p. 543.

49. Ibid., p. 99.

50. Ibid., pp. 71-72, 85.

51. Ibid., pp. 108-109.

52. Newman 1975, p. 543.

53. Newman 1972a, p. 158.

54. Ibid.

55. See Bergler 1943; 1949; Smith and Preston 1984.

56. Newman 1975, pp. 544-545.

57. Newman 1972a, p. 157.

58. Ibid., p. 158.

59. Ibid.

60. Ibid., p. 144.

61. Ibid., p. 158.

62. Ibid., p. 230.

63. Ibid., p. 160.

64. Newman 1972b, p. 6.

65. Newman 1972a, p. 222.

66. Ibid., pp. 200-201.

67. Ibid., p. 213.

68. Ibid., p. 124; Newman 1968, p. 2; cf. Newman 1975, p. 545.

69. Newman 1972b, p. 6.

70. Newman 1972a, p. 159.

71. Ibid.

72. Ibid., p. 226.

73. Newman 1975, p. 544.

74. Ibid., p. 545.

75. Ibid., p. 549.

76. Newman 1972a, p. 172.

77. Ibid.

78. Cf. Hayano 1982.

79. Newman 1972a, p. 204.

80. Ibid., p. 11.

81. Ibid., p. 160.

82. Maguire 1987.

83. Bacon 1943.

84. Notable exceptions are Hayano 1982; Lesieur 1984; and Rosecrance 1982, 1986a, 1986c.

85. E.g., Bacon 1962 [1945]; Bales 1946; 1962; Myerson 1940; Snyder 1958; 1962; Ullman 1958.

86. E.g., Bloch 1962; Devereux 1949.

87. Herman 1976a, p. 1.

88. Price 1972, p. 163.

89. Horton 1943.

90. Ibid., p. 223.

91. Field 1962.

92. Bacon, Barry and Child 1965.
93. McClelland, Davis, Wanner, and Kalin 1966.
94. Schaefer 1976.
95. Roberts and Sutton-Smith 1966.
96. Wissler 1923.
97. Roberts and Sutton-Smith 1966, p. 141.
98. Ibid., p. 142.
99. Ibid.
100. Ibid.
101. Ibid., p. 143.
102. Price 1972.
103. E.g., Steward 1955.
104. Price 1972, p. 164.
105. Ibid.
106. Roberts and Sutton-Smith 1966, p. 141.
107. Ibid., p. 133.
108. Karsten 1935, pp. 468-470.
109. Price 1972, p. 158.
110. Li and Smith 1976.
111. Ibid., p. 191.
112. Ibid., p. 204.
113. Ibid.

CHAPTER 7
LARGE SCALE SOCIOLOGICAL SURVEYS

1. Downes, Davies, David, and Stone 1976.
2. Ibid., p. 94.
3. Ibid., p. 57.
4. Ibid., p. 90.
5. Ibid., p. 91.
6. Ibid., p. 199.
7. Ibid., p. 113.
8. Ibid., p. 129.
9. Ibid., p. 130.
10. Ibid., p. 131.
11. Ibid., p. 188.
12. Ibid.
13. Ibid., p. 210.
14. Ibid., p. 199.
15. Ibid., p. 79.
16. Commission on the Review of the National Policy Toward Gambling 1976; Kallick, Suits, Dielman, and Hybels 1976; 1979.

17. E.g., Arcuri, Lester, and Smith 1985; Campbell and Lester 1999; Clotfelter and Cook 1989; Culleton and Lang 1985; Deland 1950; Elia and Jacobs 1993; Lester 1994; Moran 1970a; 1970b; 1970c; Orford 1985; Ploskowe 1950.
18. Arcuri, Lester, and Smith 1985, p. 937.
19. Clotfelter and Cook 1989, p. 126.
20. Kallick, Suits, Dielman, and Hybels 1979, pp. 1, 93-95.
21. Ibid., 1, 8.
22. Commission on the Review of the National Policy Toward Gambling 1976, pp. 70-71.
23. Kallick, Suits, Dielman, and Hybels 1979, p. 454; cf. Commission on the Review of the National Policy Toward Gambling 1976, p. 74.
24. Ibid.
25. Kallick, Suits, Dielman, and Hybels 1979, p. 448.
26. Ibid., pp. 76-77; 454.
27. Ibid., p. 448.
28. Downes, Davies, David, and Stone 1976.
29. Commission on the Review of the National Policy Toward Gambling 1976; Kallick, Suits, Dielman, and Hybels 1976; 1979.
30. Carr, Buchkoski, Kofoed, and Morgan 1996.
31. Sullivan, McCormick, and Sellman 1997.
32. Ladouceur, Jacques, Ferland, and Giroux 1999.
33. Jacques, Ladouceur, and Ferland 2000.
34. Room, Turner, and Ialomiteanu 1999.
35. Grun and McKeigue 2000.
36. Campbell and Lester 1999.
37. Gerstein, Murphy, Toce, Hoffmann, Palmer, Johnson, Larison, Chuchro, Bard, Engelman, Hill, Buie, Volberg, Harwood, Tucker, Christiansen, Cummings, and Sinclair 1999, pp. 66-67.
38. Stitt, Nichols, and Giacopassi 2000.
39. Gerstein, Murphy, Toce, Hoffmann, Palmer, Johnson, Larison, Chuchro, Bard, Engelman, Hill, Buie, Volberg, Harwood, Tucker, Christiansen, Cummings, and Sinclair 1999.
40. Strow 1999, cited by Stitt, Nichols, and Giacopassi 2000, p. 437.
41. Thompson, Gazel, and Rickman 1995, pp. 21-23.
42. Culleton 1989, p. 26.
43. Nadler 1985; Orford 1985, p. 42.
44. Culleton 1989, p. 27.
45. Sommers 1988, p. 478.
46. Orford 1985, p. 41.
47. Downes, Davies, David, and Stone 1976, p. 250, note 12.
48. Ibid., pp. 92-93.
49. Ibid., p. 87.

CHAPTER 8
GAMBLING AND THE GENERAL PUBLIC

1. Klein and Selesner 1982.
2. See Li and Smith 1976.
3. Commission on the Review of the National Policy Toward Gambling 1976; Kallick, Suits, Dielman, and Hybels 1976; 1979.
4. Klein and Selesner 1982, p. 7.
5. Ibid.
6. MacMillan 1985.
7. Ibid., p. 254.
8. Ibid., p. 255.
9. Grichting 1986.
10. Ibid., p. 56.
11. Kallick, Suits, Dielman, and Hybels 1979.
12. Grichting 1986, p. 57.
13. Ibid., p. 57.
14. Ibid., p. 56.
15. Ibid.
16. Hugick 1989.
17. Ibid., p. 32.
18. La Fleur 1991, pp. 197-210.
19. Mok and Hraba 1991.
20. Hraba and Lee 1996.
21. Ibid., p. 98.
22. Abbott and Cramer 1993.
23. See Aasved and Schaefer 1995 for a description of pull tab gambling.
24. Clotfelter and Cook 1989, pp. 96-100.
25. Ibid., pp. 100-104.
26. See Aasved and Schaefer 1995.
27. See, e.g., Bouza 1990; Larson, Hill, Pile, and Reckers 1992; Reckers, Coleman, and Mains 1993.
28. Feeney 1991.
29. Feeney 1994a.
30. Feeney 1994b.
31. Adapted from Feeney 1994a.
32. Kaplan 1987, p. 173.
33. Ibid., p. 172.
34. Ibid., p. 173; Kaplan 1988, p. 175.
35. Feeney 1991.
36. Downes, Davies, David, and Stone 1976; Commission on the Review of the National Policy Toward Gambling 1976; Kallick, Suits, Dielman, and Hybels 1976; 1979.
37. Minnesota State Lottery 1992.
38. Aasved and Laundergan 1993, pp. 305-306; Aasved and Schaefer 1995.

CHAPTER 9
SPECIAL POPULATIONS: YOUTHFUL GAMBLERS

1. Shaffer, Hall, and Vander Bilt 1997, p. 12.
2. E.g., USDHHS 1994.
3. Griffiths 1989.
4. Arcuri, Lester, and Smith 1985, pp. 936-937.
5. Lesieur and Klein 1987.
6. Ladouceur and Mireault 1988, p. 6.
7. Volberg 1998.
8. Winters, Stinchfield, and Fulkerson 1990; 1993a.
9. Carlson and Moore 1998.
10. Ladouceur, Boudreault, Jacques, and Vitaro 1999 .
11. Gupta and Derevensky 1998b.
12. Buchta 1995.
13. Govoni, Rupcich, and Frisch 1996.
14. Gerstein, Hoffmann, Larison, Engleman, Murphy, Palmer, Chuchro, Hill, Toce, Johnson, Bard, Buie, Volberg, Harwood, Tucker, Christiansen, Cummings, and Sinclair 1999, pp. 58-59.
15. Kassinove, Doyle, and Milburn 2000.
16. Westphal, Rush, Stevens, and Johnson 2000.
17. Hing and Breen 2000.
18. Moore and Ohtsuka 1997.
19. Griffiths 2000.
20. Pugh and Webley 2000.
21. Ide-Smith and Lea 1988, p. 115.
22. Westphal, Rush, Stevens, and Johnson 2000.
23. Kassinove, Doyle, and Milburn 2000.
24. Derevensky, Gupta, and Della Cioppa 1996.
25. Ladouceur, Dubé, and Bujold 1994.
26. Gupta and Derevensky 1997.
27. Ladoudeur, Boudreault, Jacques, and Vitaro 1999.
28. Adebayo 1998.
29. Ladouceur 1993b, p. 382; Volberg 1994, p. 240.
30. Dell, Ruzicka, and Palisi 1981.
31. Carlson and Moore 1998.
32. Griffiths 1990c.
33. Custer 1982; Livingston 1974a; Ramirez, McCormick, Russo, and Taber 1983, p. 427.
34. Ciarrocchi and Richardson 1989, p. 57; Jacobs 1989b, p. 252; Stinchfield and Winters 1994.

35. Gupta and Derevensky 1998b, p. 327.
36. Fisher 1993a, p. 286.
37. Stinchfield, Cassuto, Winters, and Latimer 1997.
38. Stinchfield 2000.
39. Ladouceur and Mireault 1988.
40. Lesieur and Klein 1987.
41. Lesieur and Klein 1987; Jacobs 1989b, pp. 256-257; 1993, p. 434.
42. Gaboury and Ladouceur 1993, p. 447; Shaffer, LaBrie, Scanlon, and Cummings 1994.
43. Winters, Stinchfield, and Fulkerson 1993a.
44. Winters, Stinchfield, and Kim 1995.
45. See also Govoni, Rupcich, and Frisch 1996; Gupta and Derevensky 1998b; Ladouceur, Boudreault, Jacques, and Vitaro 1999; Lesieur, Cross, Frank, Welch, White, Rubenstein, Moseley, and Mark 1991; Poulin 2000; Shaffer and Hall 1996; Shaffer, Hall, and Vander Bilt 1997; Volberg 1998; Westphal, Rush, Stevens, and Johnson 2000; Wynne, Smith, and Jacobs 1996.
46. Zitzow 1996a.
47. E.g., Gupta and Derevensky 1998b, p. 338; Lesieur 1989, p. 237; Shaffer and Hall 1996, p. 209; Stinchfield 2000, p. 170; Stinchfield, Cassuto, Winters, and Latimer 1997, pp. 44-45; Winters, Stinchfield, and Kim 1995, p. 167; Winters and Anderson 2000.
48. Lesieur and Blume 1987; Winters, Stinchfield, and Fulkerson 1993b.
49. Gerstein, Hoffmann, Larison, Engleman, Murphy, Palmer, Chuchro, Hill, Toce, Johnson, Bard, Buie, Volberg, Harwood, Tucker, Christiansen, Cummings, and Sinclair 1999, pp. 59-60.
50. Hing and Breen 2000.
51. Ladouceur, Jacques, Ferland, Giroux 1998.
52. E.g., Fisher and Balding 1996; Moran 1995.
53. Wood and Griffiths 1998.
54. Fisher 1991, p. 224; 1992, p. 264; 1993a, p. 280; 1999, pp. 517, 531; Griffiths 1989, p. 76; 1990b, p. 114; 1990c, p. 194; 2000, p. 80; Huxley and Caroll 1992.
55. Fisher 1993c, 1993d; 1999; Ide-Smith and Lea 1988.
56. Griffiths 1990a; 1990c.
57. Griffiths, Scarfe, and Bellringer 1999, p. 86.
58. Moody 1987; 1990, p. 109.
59. Griffiths 1988; 1990b.
60. Hermkens and Kok 1990.
61. Becoña 1997.
62. Kweitel and Allen 2000, p. 167.
63. Jacobs 1989b; see also Jacobs 1993.
64. Jacobs 1989b, p. 252; 1993, pp. 433-434; see also Lesieur and Klein 1987, p. 129.
65. American Psychiatric Association, 1980.
66. Jacobs 1993, p. 436.
67. Gaboury and Ladouceur 1993.
68. Jacobs 1993, p. 437.

69. Fisher 1993d, p. 417.
70. Griffiths 1990b, p. 115.
71. Fisher 1993c, p. 419.
72. Cf. Griffiths 1991b.
73. Fisher 1993d, p. 419.
74. It has been reported that German youths can lose between 33.6 DM and 72 DM (or between $21 and $45; 1.60 DM = $1 U.S.) on a single machine in one hour and that some play several machines simultaneously (Fabian 1995, p. 251).
75. Ide-Smith and Lea 1988, p. 115.
76. Graham 1988.
77. NHTPC 1988; Spectrum Children's Trust 1988; Waterman and Atkin 1985.
78. NHTPC 1988.
79. Graham 1988.
80. Carroll and Huxley 1994, p. 1074.
81. Arcuri, Lester, and Smith 1985; Fisher 1992; 1993a; 1994; 1995; 1999; Fisher and Griffiths 1995; Griffiths 1989; 1990b; 1990c; 1993d; Huxley and Carroll 1992.
82. Kearney, Roblek, Thurman, and Turnbough 1996; Ladouceur and Mireault 1988; Westphal, Rush, Stevens, and Johnson 2000.
83. Griffiths 1990b, p. 117.
84. Fisher 1995.
85. Yeoman and Griffiths 1996a; 1996b.
86. Griffiths 1990c.
87. American Psychiatric Association 1987.
88. Cf. Griffiths 1993d.
89. Graham 1988.
90. Ibid.
91. NHTPC 1988; cf. Griffiths 1990c.
92. Huff and Collinson 1987.
93. Barham and Cormell 1987; Spectrum Children's Trust 1988; NHTPC 1988, cited by Fisher 1993d; Griffiths 1990b.
94. Barham and Cormell 1987, cited by Griffiths 1989, p. 77.
95. Griffiths 1990b, p. 117.
96. E.g., Anderson and Ford 1986; Cory 1983; McClure and Mears 1984; see also Abbott, Palmisano, and Dickerson 1995; Brown and Robertson 1993.
97. Ladouceur and Dubé 1995.
98. Huff and Collinson 1987.
99. Griffiths 1992.
100. Griffiths 1991b, p. 351.
101. Amsel 1958.
102. Graham 1988.
103. Ibid.; NHTPC 1988.
104. Fisher 1999.
105. Ibid., p. 519.
106. Ibid., pp. 524-525.
107. Ibid., pp. 525-526.

108. Ibid., pp. 524-526.
109. Ibid., p. 531.
110. Ibid., pp. 519, 531-532.
111. Ibid., p. 532.
112. Ibid., p. 527.
113. Ibid., pp. 529, 532.
114. Griffiths 2000.
115. Ibid., p. 82.
116. Moran 1979.
117. Griffiths 2000, p. 83.
118. Brown and Robertson 1993.
119. Ibid., p. 453.
120. Ibid., p. 455.
121. Cf. Brown 1989; Fisher 1994; Griffiths 1991a.
122. Brown and Robertson 1993, pp. 466-467.
123. Ibid., pp. 467-468.
124. Ibid., p. 468; cf. Brown 1989; Fisher and Griffiths 1995, p. 244.
125. Gupta and Derevensky 1996.
126. Ibid., p. 379.
127. Adapted from Gupta and Derevensky 1998b, p. 386.
128. Gupta and Derevensky 1998b, p. 389.
129. Ibid., p. 391.
130. Ibid.

CHAPTER 10
SPECIAL POPULATIONS: FEMALE, ELDERLY, AND NATIVE NORTH AMERICAN GAMBLERS

1. Lesieur and Blume 1991.
2. Lesieur 1988a.
3. Cf. Lindgren, Youngs, McDonald, Klenow, and Schriner 1987, p. 160.
4. Ciarrocchi and Richardson 1989.
5. Lesieur and Blume 1991.
6. E.g., Kallick, Suits, Dielman, and Hybels 1976, p. 74; Volberg and Steadman 1988.
7. Lesieur and Blume 1991, p. 182.
8. Ibid., p. 190.
9. Ibid., p. 191.
10. Ibid., p. 191.
11. Lesieur and Blume 1987.
12. Lesieur, Blume and Zoppa 1986.
13. Tavares, Zilberman, Beites, and Gentil 2001.
14. Blume 1982; 1985.
15. Greenberg, Lewis, and Dodd 1999.
16. Coventry and Constable 1999.
17. Trevorrow and Moore 1998.
18. Strachan and Custer 1993.
19. Ibid., p. 238.

20. Hing and Breen 2001.
21. Ibid., p 49.
22. Breen and Zimmerman 2002.
23. Aasved 2002, pp. 85-105.
24. Walters 1994a; 1994b.
25. Zuckerman 1975.
26. Kuley and Jacobs 1988.
27. Li and Smith 1976.
28. Downes, Davies, David, and Stone 1976.
29. Commission on the Review of the National Policy Toward Gambling 1976; Kallick, Suits, Dielman, and Hybels 1976; 1979.
30. Mok and Hraba 1991.
31. Feeney 1991; 1994a.
32. Bühringer and Konstanty 1992; Törne and Konstanty 1992.
33. E.g., Abbott and Volberg 1991; 1992; 1996; Becoña 1993; Dickerson, Baron, Hong, and Cottrell 1996; Gerstein, Murphy, Toce, Hoffmann, Palmer, Johnson, Larison, Chuchro, Bard, Engelman, Hill, Buie, Volberg, Harwood, Tucker, Christiansen, Cummings, and Sinclair 1999; Laundergan 1996; Laundergan, Schaefer, Eckhoff, and Pirie 1990; Volberg and Abbott 1994.
34. Li and Smith 1976, p. 104.
35. Commission on the Review of the National Policy Toward Gambling 1976; Kallick, Suits, Dielman, and Hybels 1976; 1979.
36. Mok and Hraba 1991.
37. Goffman 1959; 1967; 1969.
38. E.g., Abt, McGurrin, and Smith 1985; Holtgraves 1988; Newman 1972a; 1972b; Oldman 1974; 1978; Rosecrance 1986a; 1988b; Scott 1968; Spanier 1994; Zola 1963; Zurcher 1970.
39. Clotfelter and Cook 1989.
40. Volberg 1996.
41. Hugick 1989.
42. Feeney 1991; 1994a; 1994b.
43. McNeilly and Burke 2001.
44. Ibid., p 26.
45. Gerstein, Murphy, Toce, Hoffmann, Palmer, Johnson, Larison, Chuchro, Bard, Engelman, Hill, Buie, Volberg, Harwood, Tucker, Christiansen, Cummings, and Sinclair 1999, pp, 9-10.
46. Feeney 1994b.
47. Room, Turner, and Ialomiteanu 1999, p. 1457.
48. E.g., Arcuri, Lester, and Smith 1985; Clotfelter and Cook 1989; Culleton and Lang 1985; Deland 1950; Elia and Jacobs 1993; Lester 1994; Moran 1970a; 1970b; 1970c; Orford 1985; Ploscowe 1950.
49. McNeilly and Burke 2000.
50. Brenner 1986; Brenner and Brenner 1990.
51. E.g., Eadington 1973, 1987; 1999; Ignatin and Smith 1976; Lea, Tarpy and Webley 1987; Wagenaar, Keren, and Pleit-Kuiper 1984.

52. Rosecrance 1986b.
53. Downes, Davies, David, and Stone 1976.
54. McNeilly and Burke 2001, p. 21.
55. Moore 2001a.
56. Volberg 2001, pp. 16-18.
57. Wardman, el-Guebaly, and Hodgins 2001.
58. Hewitt and Auger 1995.

CHAPTER 11
PROBLEM GAMBLING CORRELATES AND RISK FACTORS

1. E.g., USDHHS 1990, pp. xxii, 23.
2. Stinchfield 2000.
3. Wallisch 1966.
4. Zitzow 1996b.
5. Diaz 2000.
6. Hoffman 2000.
7. Fisher 1993d, p. 413.
8. Ibid., p. 412; cf. Fisher 1993a, p. 283.
9. Carlson and Moore 1998; Hewitt and Augur 1995; Govoni, Rupchich, and Frisch 1996; Wallisch 1996; Winters, Stinchfield, and Fulkerson 1993a.
10. E.g., Jacobs 1989a; 1989b; 2000.
11. E.g., Gupta and Derevensky 1996; 1998; Jacobs 1989a; Wynne, Smith, and Jacobs 1996; Stinchfield and Winters 1998.
12. E.g., Arcuri, Lester, and Smith 1985; Barnes, Welte, Hoffman, Dintcheff 1999; Blanco, Ibañez, Saiz-Ruiz, Blanco-Jerez, and Nuñes 2000; Carlson and Moore 1998; Ciarrocchi and Richardson 1989; Cornish 1978; Dell, Ruzicka, and Palisi 1981; Downes, Davies, David, and Stone 1976; Fisher 1993a; 1999, pp. 529-530, 532; Govoni, Rupcich, and Frisch 1996; Griffiths and Wood 2000; Gupta and Derevensky 2000; Huff and Collinson 1987; Jacobs 1989b; 1993; 2000; Kassinove, Doyle, Milburn 2000; Ladouceur and Mireault 1988; Ladouceur, Dubé, and Bujold 1994; Ladouceur, Boudreault, Jacques, and Vitaro 1999; Lesieur and Klein 1987; Petry 2001; Stinchfield 2000; Stinchfield, Cassuto, Winters, and Latimer 1997; Vitaro, Ladouceur, and Bujold 1996; Wallisch 1993; 1996; Westphal, Rush, Stevens, and Johnson 2000; Winters, Stinchfield, and Fulkerson 1990; 1993a; Winters, Stinchfield, and Kim 1995, p. 167.
13. Ciarrocchi and Richardson 1989; Petry 2001; Specker, Carlson, Edmonson, Johnson, and Marcotte 1996.
14. Fisher 1999, p. 519.
15. Ibid., p. 529.
16. Lesieur and Klein 1987.
17. Stinchfield, Cassuto, Winters, and Latimer 1997, p. 45; Stinchfield 2000, p. 170; see also Winters and Anderson 2000.

18. Petry 2000a.
19. Poulin 2000.
20. Moore and Ohtsuka 1997.
21. Jamieson 1969.
22. National Center on Child Abuse and Neglect 1981.
23. Ciarrocchi and Richardson 1989, p. 57.
24. Specker, Carlson, Edmonson, Johnson, and Marcotte 1996, p. 79.
25. Ibid., p. 76.
26. McCormick and Taber 1988; McCormick, Taber, and Kruedelbach 1989; Taber 1993, p. 282; Taber, Collachi, and Lynn, 1986, p. 39.
27. E.g., Abbott and Volberg 1996; Bühringer and Konstanty 1992; Ciarrocchi and Richardson 1989; Colsher and Wallace 1990; Ellermann 1948; Furnham 1985; Grichting 1986; Gurnack and Thomas 1989; Hendriks, Meerkerk, Van Oers, and Garretsen 1997; Hugick 1989; Li and Smith 1976; Mok and Hraba 1991; Moore and Ohtsuka 1997; 1999b; Rogers and Webley 2001; Smart and Ferris 1996; Volberg and Abbott 1994; Volberg, Reitzes, and Boles 1997; Yaffe, Lorenz, and Politzer 1993.
28. E.g., Barnes, Welte, and Dintcheff 1992; Barnes, Welte, Hoffman, and Dintcheff 1999; Browne and Brown 1994; Griffiths 1989; 2000; Gupta and Derevensky 1998; 2000; Ide-Smith and Lea 1988; Ladouceur, Boudreault, Jacques, and Vitaro 1999; Moore and Ohtsuka 1997; 1999a 2000; Petry 2001; Poulin 2000; Proimos, DuRant, Pierce, and Goodman 1998; Stinchfield 2000; Stinchfield, Cassuto, Winters, and Latimer 1997; Vitaro, Ladouceur, and Bujold 1996; Volberg 1998; Weschler and Thum 1973; Westphal, Rush, Stevens, and Johnson 2000; Windle 1993; Winters, Stinchfield, and Fulkerson 1993a.
29. Dritschel and Pettinati 1989; Harrison, Hoffman, and Edwall 1989.
30. E.g., Cervantes, Gilbert, Snyder, and Padilla 1990-1991; Lubben, Chi, and Kitano 1989; Volberg and Abbot 1997; Wardman, el-Guebaly, and Hodgins 2001; Zitzow 1996a; 1996b.
31. Roberts and Sutton-Smith 1966.
32. Kallick, Suits, Dielman, and Hybels 1976; 1979.
33. Downes, Davies, David, and Stone 1976.
34. Among the possible predictive correlates of gambling that the U.K. survey researchers investigated were: area (community), sex, age, marital status, religious affiliation, religiosity (the importance of religion in one's life), church attendance (apart from wedding, funerals, and christenings), conventionalism, proclivity for "risk-taking," strength of one's "belief in luck," annual household income, education level, current socioeconomic grouping, intergenerational social mobility, number of dependent children, household size, parental gambling, job autonomy, job effort, job interest, prospects for promotion, number of years in the same job, past job preferences, job change reasons, means of increasing income, women's (wive's) work, free time availability, conjugal role sharing, political/community activity, frequency of study, active home leisure, active child leisure, hobbies, attendance at sporting events, pub going, frequency of going out for entertainment, and extent of TV-watching.

35. Downes, Davies, David, and Stone 1976, p. 202.
36. Ibid., p. 204.
37. Hraba and Lee 1995; Hraba, Mok, and Huff 1990.
38. Hraba and Lee 1996.
39. Frank 1993.
40. Lesieur and Blume 1987.
41. Frank 1993, p. 390.
42. Ibid., p. 391.
43. Ibid., p. 392.
44. Ibid., p. 390.
45. Winters, Bengston, Stinchfield, and Dorr 1996.
46. Lesieur and Blume 1987.
47. Adapted from Winters, Bengston, Stinchfield, and Dorr 1996.
48. Blaszczynski and McConaghy 1987.
49. Abbott and Volberg 1996; Volberg and Abbott 1994.
50. Bühringer and Konstanty 1992; Törne and Konstanty 1992.
51. Yaffee, Lorenz, and Politzer 1993.
52. Ibid., p. 663.
53. Ibid., p. 673.
54. Ibid.
55. Ibid.
56. Ibid., p. 674.
57. Ibid.
58. Griffiths 1995; see also Griffiths and Wood 2000.
59. Ladouceur, Vitaro, and Côté 2001.
60. Griffiths and Wood 2000.
61. Blaszczynski and Farrell 1999.
62. Ibid., p. 105.
63. Jacobs 2000.
64. Ibid., p. 120.
65. Ibid., p. 123.
66. Commission on the Review of the National Policy Toward Gambling 1976; Kallick, Suits, Dielman, and Hybels 1976; 1979.
67. See also Jacobs 1994.
68. Jacobs 2000, p. 126.
69. Ibid., p. 134.

CHAPTER 12
CRITIQUE OF QUANTITATIVE STUDIES

1. Clotfelter and Cook 1989, p. 106.
2. Hing and Breen 2001, p. 65.
3. Dickerson 1985, p. 140.
4. Fund for the City of New York 1972.

5. Light 1977, p. 895.
6. Kallick, Suits, Dielman, and Hybels 1979.
7. Fisher 1993d, p. 416.
8. Graham 1988.
9. Fisher 1993d, p. 414.
10. Ibid., pp. 414-415.
11. E.g., Griffiths 2000, p. 90.; Stinchfield 2000, p. 171.
12. Moore 2001b.
13. Stinchfield 2000, p. 171.
14. Commission on the Review of the National Policy Toward Gambling 1976; Kallick, Suits, Dielman, and Hybels 1976; 1979.
15. Cf. Meyer and Stadler 1999, pp. 40-41.
16. Li and Smith 1976.
17. Kallick, Suits, Dielman, and Hybels 1976.
18. Lindgren, Youngs, McDonald, Klenon, and Schriner 1987.
19. Mok and Hraba 1991.
20. Kallick, Suits, Dielman, and Hybels 1979.
21. Mok and Hraba 1991.
22. Newman 1972a, p. 19.
23. Lesieur 1989, p. 226.
24. Walker 1992c, p. 238.
25. Campbell and Lester 1999, p. 127.; cf. Wardman, el-Guebaly and Hodgins 2001, p. 97.
26. Voget 1975, p. 469.
27. Clarke and Rossen 2000, p. 10.
28. Ide-Smith and Lea 1988, p. 115.
29. Kallick, Suits, Dielman, and Hybels 1976; 1979.
30. Kallick, Suits, Dielman, and Hybels 1979, p. 70.
31. Frank 1993.
32. Hraba, Mok, and Huff 1990; Mok and Hraba 1991.
33. Hraba and Lee 1996, p. 98.
34. E.g., Bagnall 1991; Rydelius 1981; Schuckit 1988; Vaillant 1983.
35. Nathan 1980, pp. 244-245.
36. Committee on the Social and Economic Impact of Pathological Gambling and the Committee on Law and Justice 1999.
37. Ibid., p. 112.
38. Hraba and Lee 1996, p. 95, emphasis added.
39. Ibid., p. 98.
40. Moore and Ohtsuka 2000.
41. Ibid., p. 167.
42. Sutton 1993.
43. Barnes, Welte, Hoffman, and Dintcheff 1999.
44. Meyer and Stadler 1999, p. 40.
45. E.g., Beaudoin and Cox 1999; Dickerson 1977b; 1979; 1984; 1991; 1993; Dickerson and Adcock 1987; Kroeber 1992; Fabian 1995; Oliveira and Silva 2001.

46. Wiebe and Cox 2001.
47. Campbell, Simmons, and Lester 1999.
48. Reid, Woodford, Roberts, Golding, and Towell 1999.
49. Dickerson 1989, p. 157.
50. Kallick, Suits, Dielman, and Hybels 1979, p. 438.
51. Blaszczynski and McConaghy 1987, p. 267.
52. Custer and Milt 1985, pp. 240-257.
53. Lesieur and Blume 1987; 1993.
54. American Psychiatric Association 1994.
55. Hraba and Lee 1996, p. 99.
56. Dickerson, Walker, Legg England, and Hinchy 1990.
57. Oliveira and Silva 2000.
58. Carlton and Manowitz 1987, p. 275.

REFERENCES

Aasved, M. J. (2002). *The psychodynamics and psychology of gambling: The gambler's mind.* Springfield, IL: Charles C Thomas.

Aasved, M. J. and Laundergan, J. C. (1993). Gambling and its impacts in a northeastern Minnesota community: An exploratory study. *Journal of Gambling Studies 9*(4), 301-319.

Aasved, M. J. and Schaefer, J. M. (1995). "Minnesota Slots": An observational study of pull tab gambling. *Journal of Gambling Studies 11*(3), 311-341.

Abbott, D. A. and Cramer, S. L. (1993). Gambling attitudes and participation: A midwestern survey. *Journal of Gambling Studies 9*(3), 247-263.

Abbott, M. W. and Volberg, R. A. (1991). *Gambling and problem gambling in New Zealand.* Research Series No. 12. Wellington: New Zealand Department of Internal Affairs.

Abbott, M. W. and Volberg, R. A. (1992). *Gambling and problem gambling in New Zealand: A report on phase two of the national survey.* Wellington: Department of Internal Affairs.

Abbott, M. W. and Volberg, R. A. (1996). The New Zealand national survey of problem and pathological gambling. *Journal of Gambling Studies 12*(2), 143-160.

Abbott, M., Palmisano, B., and Dickerson, M. (1995). Video game playing, dependency, and delinquency: A question of methodology? *Journal of Gambling Studies 11*(3), 287 301.

Abraham, K. (1960). The psychological relation between sexuality and alcoholism. In Bryan, D. and Strachey, A. (Trans). *Selected papers of Karl Abraham.* New York: Basic Books.

Abt, V., McGurrin, M. C., and Smith, J. F. (1985). Toward a synoptic model of gambling behavior. *Journal of Gambling Behavior 1*(2), 79-88.

Abt, V., Smith, J. F., and Christiansen, E. M. (1985). *The business of risk: Commercial gambling in mainstream America.* Lawrence, KS: University of Kansas Press.

Abt, V., Smith, J. F., and McGurrin, M. C. (1985). Ritual, risk, and reward: A role analysis of race track and casino encounters. *Journal of Gambling Behavior 1*(1), 64-75.

Adebayo, B. (1998). Gambling behavior of students in grades seven and eight in Alberta, Canada. *Journal of School Health 68*(1), 7-11.

Adkins, B., Rugle, L., and Taber, J. (1985, November). *A note on sexual addiction among compulsive gamblers.* Paper presented at the First National Conference on Gambling Behavior, National Council on Compulsive Gambling, New York.

Altman, J. (1985). Gambling as a mode of redistribution and accumulating cash among aborigines: A case study from Arnhem Land. In Caldwell, G., Haig, B., Dickerson, M., and Sylvan, L. (Eds.) *Gambling in Australia* (pp. 50-67). Sydney: Croom Helm.

American Psychiatric Association (1980). *Diagnostic and statistical manual of mental disorders, third edition (DSM-III).* Washington, D.C.: American Psychiatric Association.

American Psychiatric Association (1987). *Diagnostic and statistical manual of mental disorders, third edition, revised (DSM-III-R).* Washington, D.C.: American Psychiatric Association.

American Psychiatric Association (1994). *Diagnostic and statistical manual of mental disorders, fourth edition (DSM-IV).* Washington, D.C.: American Psychiatric Association.

Amsel, A. (1958). The role of frustrative non-reward in non-continuous reward situations. *Psychological Bulletin 55*, 102-119.

Anderson, C. A. and Ford, C. M. (1986). Affect of the game player: Short-term effects of highly and mildly aggressive video games. *Personality and Social Psychology Bulletin 12*, 390-403.

Arcuri, A. F., Lester, D., and Smith, F. (1985). Shaping adolescent gambling behavior. *Adolescence 20*, 935-938.

Aristotle (1953). *The ethics of Aristotle*, Thompson, J. A. K. (Ed. and Trans.) London: Allen and Unwin.

Atlas, G. D. and Peterson, C. (1990). Explanatory style and gambling: How pessimists respond to losing wagers. *Behaviour Research and Therapy 28*, 523-529.

Bacon, M. K., Barry, H., III, and Child, I. L. (1965). A cross-cultural study of drinking. *Quarterly Journal of Studies on Alcohol, Supplement No. 3.*

Bacon, S. D. (1943). Sociology and the problems of alcohol. *Quarterly Journal of Studies of Alcohol 4*, 402-445.

Bacon, S. D. (1962 [1945]). Alcohol and Complex Society. In Pittman, D. J. and Snyder, C. R. (Eds.) *Society, Culture and Drinking Patterns*. New York: John Wiley and Sons.

Bagnall, G. (1991). Alcohol and drug use in a Scottish cohort: 10 years on. *British Journal of Addiction 86*(7), 895-904.

Bales, R. F. (1946). Cultural differences in rates of alcoholism. *Quarterly Journal of Studies on Alcohol 6*(4), 480-499.

Bales, R. F. (1962). Attitudes towards drinking in the Irish culture. In Pittman, D. J. and Snyder, C. R. (Eds.) *Society, Culture, and Drinking Patterns*. New York: John Wiley and Sons.

Barham, B. and Cormell, M. (1987). *Teenage use of amusement arcades in Bognor Regis*. Bognor Regis: West Sussex Institute of Higher Education.

Barker, T. and Britz, M. (2000). *Joker's wild: Legalized gambling in the twenty-first century*. Westport, CT: Praeger.

Barnes, G. M., Welte, J. W. and Dintcheff, B. (1992). Alcohol misuse among college students and other young adults: Findings from a general population study in New York State. *International Journal of the Addictions 27*(8), 917-934.

Barnes, G. M., Welte, J., Hoffman, J. H., and Dintcheff, B. A. (1999). Gambling and alcohol use among youth: Influences of demographic, socialization, and individual factors. *Addictive Behaviors 24*(6), PP. 749-767.

Baron, E. and Dickerson, M. (1999). Alcohol consumption and self-control in gambling behaviour. *Journal of Gambling Studies 15*(1), 3-15.

Beaudoin, C. M. and Cox, B. J. (1999). Characteristics of problem gambling in a Canadian context: A preliminary study using a DSM-IV-based questionnaire. *Canadian Journal of Psychiatry 44*(5), 483-487.

Becker, G. S. and Murphy, K. V. (1988). A theory of rational addiction. *Journal of Political Economy 96*(4), 675-700.

Becoña, E. (1993). The prevalence of pathological gambling in Galicia (Spain). *Journal of Gambling Studies 9*(4), 353-369.

Becoña, E. (1997). Pathological gambling in Spanish children and adolescents: An emerging problem. *Psychological Reports 81*(1), 275-287.

Bell, R. C. (1976). Moral views on gambling promulgated by major American religious bodies. In Commission on the review of the national policy toward gambling (Eds.) *Gambling in America*, Appendix 1. Washington, D.C.: U.S. Government Printing Office.

Bergh, C. and Külhorn, E. (1994a). The development of pathological gambling in Sweden. *Journal of Gambling Studies 10*(3), 261-274.

Bergh, C. and Külhorn, E. (1994b). Social, psychological and physical consequences of pathological gambling in Sweden. *Journal of Gambling Studies 10*(3), 275-285.

Bergler, E. (1936). On the psychology of the gambler. *American Imago 22*, 404-441.

Bergler, E. (1943). The gambler: a misunderstood neurotic. *Journal of Criminal Psychopathology 4*, 370-393.

Bergler, E. (1949). *The basic neuroses: Oral regression and psychic masochism.* New York: Grune and Stratton.

Bergler, E. (1958). *The psychology of gambling.* New York: International University Press.

Berne, E. (1972). *What do you do after you say hello? The psychology of human destiny.* New York: Grove Press.

Bernoulli, D. (1954 [1738]). Exposition of a new theory on the measurement of risk. *Econometrica 22*, 23-36.

Blanche, E. E. (1950). Gambling odds are gimmicked. *Annals of the American Academy of Political and Social Science 269 (May)*, 77-80.

Blanco, C., Ibañez, A., Saiz-Ruiz, J., Blanco-Jerez, C., and Nuñes, E. V. (2000). Epidemiology, pathophysiology and treatment of pathological gambling. *Cns Drugs 13*(6), 397-407.

Bland, R. C., Newman, S. C., Orn, H., and Stebelsky, G. (1993). Epidemiology of pathological gambling in Edmonton. *Canadian Journal of Psychiatry 38*(2), 108 112.

Blascovich, J., Ginsburg, G. P., and Howe, R. C. (1976). Blackjack, choice shifts in the field. *Sociometry 39*(3), 274-276.

Blascovich, J., Veach, T. L., and Ginsburg, G. P. (1973). Blackjack and the risky shift. *Sociometry 36*(1), 42-55.

Blaszczynski, A. and Farrell, E. (1999). A case series of 44 completed gambling-related suicides. *Journal of Gambling Studies 14*(2), 93-109.

Blaszczynski, A. P. and McConaghy, N. (1987). Demographic and clinical data on compulsive gambling. In Walker, M. (Ed.) *Faces of gambling: Proceedings of the Second National Conference of the National Association for Gambling Studies (1986).* Sydney, Australia: National Association for Gambling Studies.

Blaszczynski, A. P. and McConaghy, N. (1989). Anxiety and/or depression in the pathogenesis of addictive gambling. *International Journal of the Addictions 24*(4), 337-350.

Blaszczynski, A. P., Buhrich, N. and McConaghy, N. (1985). Pathological gamblers, heroin addicts and controls compared on the EPQ 'addiction scale'. *British Journal of Addiction 80*(3), 315-319.

Blaszczynski, A. P., McConaghy, N., and Frankova, A. (1989). Crime, antisocial personality and pathological gambling. *Journal of Gambling Behavior 5*(2), 137-152.

Bloch, H. A. (1951). The sociology of gambling. *American Journal of Sociology 57*, 215 221.

Bloch, H. A. (1962). The gambling business: An American paradox. *Crime and Delinquency 8*(4), 355-364.

Blume, S. B. (1982). Psychiatric problems of alcoholic women. In Solomon, J. (Ed.) *Alcoholism and clinical psychiatry* (pp. 179-193). New York: Plenum.

Blume, S. B. (1985). Women and alcohol. In Bratter, T. E. and Forrest, C. G. (Eds.) *Alcoholism and substance abuse: Strategies for clinical intervention* (pp. 623-638). New York: The Free Press.

Blume, S. B. (1994). Pathological gambling and switching addictions: Report of a case. *Journal of Gambling Studies 10*(1), 87-96.

Blume, S. B. and Lesieur, H. R. (1987). Pathological gambling in cocaine abusers. In Washton, A. M. and Gold, M. S. (Eds.) *Cocaine: A clinician's handbook.* New York: The Guilford Press.

Bolen, D. W. (1976). Gambling: Historical highlights and trends and their implications for contemporary society. In Eadington, W. R. (Ed.) *Gambling and society: Interdisciplinary studies on the subject of gambling* (pp. 7-38). Springfield, IL: Charles C Thomas.

Bolen, E. W. and Boyd, W. H. (1968). Gambling and the gambler: A review and preliminary findings. *Archives of General Psychiatry 18*(5), 617-630.

Bondolfi, G., Osiek, C., and Ferrero, F. (2000). Prevalence estimates of pathological gambling in Switzerland. *Acta Psychiatrica Scandinavica 101*(6), 473-475.

Borg, M. O. (1988). The budgeting incidence of a lottery to support education. *National Tax Journal 41*, 75-86.

Bouza, A. V. (1990). *Gambling in Minnesota.* St. Paul: Minnesota Department of Gaming.

Boyd, W. and Bolen, D. (1970). The compulsive gambler and spouse in group psychotherapy. *International Journal of Group Psychotherapy 20*(1), 77-90.

Breen, R. B. and Zimmerman, M. (2002). Rapid onset of pathological gambling in machine gamblers. *Journal of Gambling Studies 18*(1), 31-43.

Brenner, G. (1986). Why do people gamble? More Canadian evidence. *Journal of Gambling Behavior 2*(2), 121-129.

Brenner, R. (1983). *History: The human gamble.* Chicago: University of Chicago Press.

Brenner, R. (1985). *Betting on ideas.* Chicago: The University of Chicago Press.

Brenner, G. (1986). Why do people gamble? More Canadian evidence. *Journal of Gambling Behavior 2*(2), 121-129.

Brenner, R., and Brenner, G. A. (1990). *Gambling and speculation: A theory, a history, and a future of some human decisions.* Cambridge: Cambridge University Press.

Brenner, G., Lipeb, M., and Bikanda, P. (1993). The lottery player in Cameroon: An exploratory study. *Journal of Gambling Studies 9*(2), 185-190.

Briggs, J. R., Goodin, B. J., and Nelson, T. (1996). Pathological gamblers and alcoholics: Do they share the same additions? *Addictive Behaviors 21*(4), 515-519.

Brinner, R. E. and Clotfelter, C. T. (1975). An economic appraisal of state lotteries. *National Tax Journal 28*(4), 395-404.

Brown, R. I. F. (1987a). Classical and operant paradigms in the management of compulsive gamblers. *Behavioural Psychotherapy 15*, 111-122.

Brown, R. I. F. (1987b). Dropouts and continuers in Gamblers Anonymous: Part 3. Some possible specific reasons for dropout. *Journal of Gambling Behavior 3*(2), 137-151.

Brown, R. I. F. (1987c). Pathological gambling and associated patterns of crime: Comparisons with alcohol and drug addiction. *Journal of Gambling Behavior 3*(2), 98-114.

Brown, R. I. F. (1989). Gaming, gambling, risk-taking, addictions, and a developmental model of man-machine relationships. In Klabberg, J., Croowall, H. de Jong, and Scheper, W. (Eds.) *Simulation gaming.* Oxford: Pergamon Press.

Brown, R. I. F. (1993). Some contributions of the study of gambling to other addictions. In William R. Eadington and Judy Cornelius (Eds.) *Gambling behavior and problem gambling* (pp. 241-272). Reno, Nevada: Bureau of Business and Economic Research, College of Business Administration, University of Nevada.

Brown, R. I. F. and Robertson, S. (1993). Home computer and video game addiction in relation to adolescent gambling: Conceptual and developmental aspects. In Eadington, W. R. and Cornelius, J. (Eds.) *Gambling behavior and problem gambling* (pp. 451-471). Reno, Nevada: Bureau of Business and Economic Research, College of Business Administration, University of Nevada.

Brown, D. J., Kaldenberg, D. O., and Brown, B. A. (1992). Socioeconomic status and playing the lotteries. *Sociology and Social Research 76*(3), 161-167.

Browne, B. (1989). Going on tilt: Frequent poker players and control. *Journal of Gambling Behavior 5*(1), 3-21.

Browne, B. A. and Brown, D. J. (1994). Predictors of lottery gambling among American college students. *Journal of Social Psychology 134*(3), 339-347.

Brunk, G. G. (1981). A test of the Friedman-Savage gambling model. *Quarterly Journal of Economics 96*(2), 341-348.

Buchta, R. M. (1995). Gambling among adolescents. *Clinical Pediatrics 34*(7), 346-348.

Bühringer, G., and Konstanty, R. (1992). Intensive gamblers on German-style slot machines. *Journal of Gambling Studies 8*(1), 21-38.

Burglass, M. E. (1989). Compulsive gambling: Forensic update and commentary. In Shaffer, H. J., Stein, A., Gambino, B., and Cummings, J. N. (Eds.) *Compulsive gambling: Theory, research, and practice* (pp. 205-222). Lexington, MA: Lexington Books.

Cahalan, D. (1970). *Problem drinkers: A national survey.* San Francisco: Jossey-Bass.

Caillois, R. (1961). *Man, games, and play,* Barash, M. (Trans.) New York: The Free Press.

Caldwell, G. (1985a). Some historical and sociological characteristics of Australian gambling. In Caldwell, G., Haig, B., Dickerson, M., and Sylvan, L. (Eds.) *Gambling in Australia* (pp. 18-27). Sydney: Croom Helm.

Caldwell, G. (1985b). Poker machine playing in NSW and ACT clubs. In Caldwell, G., Haig, B., Dickerson, M., and Sylvan, L. (Eds.) *Gambling in Australia* (pp. 261-268). Sydney: Croom Helm.

Campbell, F. F. (1976). Gambling: A positive view. In Eadington, W. R. (Ed.) *Gambling and society: Interdisciplinary studies on the subject of gambling* (pp. 218-228). Springfield, IL: Charles C Thomas.

Campbell, F. and Lester, D. (1999). The impact of gambling opportunities on compulsive gambling. *Journal of Social Psychology 139*(1), 126-127.

Campbell, F., Simmons, C., and Lester, D. (1999). The impact of gambling on suicidal behavior in Louisiana. *Omega - Journal of Death & Dying. Vol 38*(3), 235-239.

Carlson, M. J. and Moore, T. L. (1998). *Adolescent gambling in Oregon: A report to the Oregon Gambling Adddiction Treatment Foundation.* Salem, OR: Oregon Gambling Addiction Treatment Foundation.

Carlton, P. L. and Goldstein, L. (1987). Physiological determinants of pathological gambling. In Galski, T. (Ed.) *The handbook of pathological gambling* (pp. 111 122). Springfield, IL: Charles C Thomas.

Carlton, P. L. and ManowWiebe and Cox 2001.itz, P. (1987). Physiological factors as determinants of pathological gambling. *Journal of Gambling Behavior 3*(4), 274 285.

Carr, R. D., Buchkoski, J. E., Kofoed, L., and Morgan, T. J. (1996). "Video lottery" and treatment for pathological gambling. A natural experiment in South Dakota. *South Dakota Journal of Medicine 49*(1), 30-32.

Carroll, D. and Huxley, J. A. A. (1994). Cognitive, dispositional, and psychophysiological correlates of dependent slot machine gambling in young people. *Journal of Applied Social Psychology 24*(12), 1070-1083.

Cervantes, R., Gilbert, M. J., de Snyder, N. S., and Padilla, A. (1990-1991). Psychosocial and cognitive correlates of alcohol use in younger adult immigrant and U.S.-born Hispanics. *International Journal of the Addictions 25*, 687-708.

Ciarrocchi, J. (1987). Severity of impairment in dually addicted gamblers. *Journal of Gambling Behavior 3*(1), 16-26.

Ciarrocchi, J. and Richardson, R. (1989). Profile of Compulsive gamblers in treatment: Update and comparisons. *Journal of Gambling Behavior 5*(1), 53-65.

Ciarrocchi, J. W., Kirschner, N. M., and Fallik, F. (1991). Personality dimensions of male pathological gamblers, alcoholics, and dually addicted gamblers. *Journal of Gambling studies 7*(2), 133-141.

Clarke, D. and Rossen, F. (2000). Adolescent gambling and problem gambling: A New Zealand study. *New Zealand Journal of Psychology 29*(1), 10-16.

Clinard, M. (1963). *Sociology of deviant behavior.* New York: Holt, Reinhart, and Winston.

Clotfelter, C. T. (1979). On the regressivity of state-operated 'Number' games. *National Tax Journal 32*(4), 543-547.

Clotfelter, C. T. and Cook, P. J. (1989). *Selling hope: State lotteries in America.* Cambridge, MA: Harvard University Press.

Cohen, J. (1970). The nature of gambling. *Scientia 105,* 445-469.

Colsher, P. L. and Wallace, R. B. (1990). Elderly men with histories of heavy drinking: Correlates and consequences. *Journal of Studies on Alcohol 51*(6), 528-535.

Commission on the Review of the National Policy Toward Gambling (1976). *Gambling in America.* Washington, D.C.: U.S. Government Printing Office.

Committee on the Social and Economic Impact of Pathological Gambling and the Committee on Law and Justice (1999). *Pathological gambling: A critical review.* Washington, D.C.: National Academy Press.

Coombs, C. H. and Pruitt, D. G. (1960). Components of risk in decision making: Probability and variance preferences. *Journal of Experimental Psychology 60*(5), 265-277.

Corney, W. J. and Cummings, W. T. (1992). Poker tournament attributions. In Eadington, W. R. and Cornelius, J. A. (Eds.) *Gambling and commercial gaming: Essays in business, economics, philosophy, and science* (pp. 499-504). Reno, Nevada: Bureau of Business and Economic Research, College of Business Administration, University of Nevada.

Cornish, D. B. (1978). *Gambling: A review of the literature and its implications for policy and research.* London: Home Office Research Study 42.

Cory, L. T. (1983). Pac-man as a playmate. *Psychology Today 17*(1), 58.

Coventry, K. R., and Brown, R. I. F. (1993). Sensation seeking, gambling and gambling addictions. *Addiction 88*(4), 541-554. Reprinted (1993) as, Sensation seeking in gamblers and nongamblers and its relation to preference for gambling activities, chasing, arousal and loss of control in regular gamblers. In Eadington, W. R. and Cornelius, J. (Eds.) *Gambling behavior and problem gambling* (pp. 25-49). Reno, Nevada: Bureau of Business and Economic Research, College of Business Administration, University of Nevada.

Coventry, K. R and Constable, B. (1999). Physiological arousal and sensation-seeking in female fruit machine gamblers. *Addiction 94*(3), 425-430.

Coyle, C. and Kinney, W. (1990). A comparison of leisure and gambling motives of compulsive gamblers. *Therapeutic Recreation Journal 24*(1), 32-39.

Cressey, D. (1971). *Other people's money.* Belmont, CA: Wadsworth Publishing.

Culleton, R. P. (1989). The prevalence rates of pathological gambling: A look at methods. *Journal of Gambling Behavior 5*(1), 22-41.

Culleton, R. P. and Lang, M. H. (1985). *Supplementary report on the prevalence rate of pathological gambling in the Delaware Valley in 1984.* Camden, NJ: Rutgers/Camden Forum of Policy Research and Public Service.

Custer, R. L. (1982). An overview of compulsive gambling. In Carone, P. A., Yolles, S. F., Kieffer, S. N., and Krinsky, L. W. (Eds.) *Addictive disorders update: Alcoholism/drug abuse/gambling* (pp. 107-124). New York: Human Sciences Press.

Custer, R. L. and Custer, L. F. (1978, December). *Characteristics of the recovering compulsive gambler: A survey of 150 members of Gamblers Anonymous.* Paper presented at the fourth annual Conference on Gambling, Reno, Nevada.

Custer, R. L. and Milt, H. (1985). *When luck runs out.* New York: Warner Books.

Daghestani, A. N., Elenz, E., and Crayton, J. W. (1996). Pathological gambling in hospitalized substance abusing veterans. *Journal of Clinical Psychiatry 57*(8), 360-363.

Davis, C. B. (1956). *Something for nothing.* New York: Lippincott.

Deland, P. S. (1950). The facilitation of gambling. *Annals of the American Academy of Political and Social Science 269* (May), 21-29.

Dell, L. J., Ruzicka, M. F., and Palisi, A. T. (1981). Personality and other factors associated with the gambling addiction. *International Journal of the Addictions 16,* 149-151.

Dentler, R. R. (1967). *Major American Social Problems.* Chicago: Rand McNally.

Derevensky, J. L., Gupta, R., and Della Cioppa, G. (1996). A developmental perspective of gambling behavior in children and adolescents. *Journal of Gambling Studies 12*(1), 49-66.

Devereux, E. C. (1949). *Gambling and the social structure: A sociological study of lotteries and horseracing in contemporary America.* Doctoral dissertation, Harvard University.

Devereux, E. C. (1968). Gambling in psychological and sociological perspective. *International encyclopedia of the social sciences 6,* 53-62.

Diaz, J. D. (2000). Religion and gambling in sin-city: A statistical analysis of the relationship between religion and gambling patterns in Las Vegas residents. *Social Science Journal 37*(3), 453-458.

Dickerson, M. G. (1977a). 'Compulsive' gambling as an addiction: Dilemmas. *Scottish Medical Journal 22,* 251-252.

Dickerson, M. G. (1977b). The role of the betting shop environment in the training of compulsive gamblers. *Behavioural Psychotherapy 5,* 3-8.

Dickerson, M. G. (1979). FI schedules and persistence at gambling in the UK Betting Office. *Journal of Applied Behavioral Analysis 12,* 315-323.

Dickerson, M. G. (1984). *Compulsive gamblers.* London: Longman.

Dickerson, M. G. (1985). The characteristics of the compulsive gambler: A rejection of a typology. In Caldwell, G., Haig, B., Dickerson, M., and Sylvan, L. (Eds.) *Gambling in Australia* (pp. 139-145). Sydney: Croom Helm.

Dickerson, M. G. (1987). The future of gambling research - Learning from the lessons of alcoholism. *Journal of Gambling Behavior 3*(4), 248-256.

Dickerson, M. G. (1989). Gambling: A dependence without a drug. International Review *Journal of Psychiatry 1,* 157-171.

Dickerson, M. G. (1991). Internal and external determinants of persistent gambling: Implications for treatment. In Heather, N., Miller, W. R., and Greeley, J. (Eds.) *Self control and the addictive behaviors* (pp. 317-328). Australia: Maxwell Macmillan Publishing.

Dickerson, M. G. (1993). Internal and external determinants of persistent gambling: Problems in generalizing from one form of gambling to another. In Eadington, W. R. and Cornelius, J. A. (Eds.) *Gambling behavior and problem gambling* (pp. 3-24). Reno, Nevada: Institute for the Study of Gambling and Commercial Gaming, College of Business Administration, University of Nevada.

Dickerson, M. and Adcock, S. (1987). Mood, arousal and cognitions in persistent gambling: Preliminary investigation of a theoretical model. *Journal of Gambling Behavior 3*(1), 3-15.

Dickerson, M. G., Bayliss, D. and Head, P. (1984). *Survey of a social club population of poker machine players.* Unpublished research paper.

Dickerson, M., Baron, E., Hong, S.-M., and Cottrell, D. (1996). Estimating the extent and degree of gambling related problems in the Australian national population: A national survey. *Journal of Gambling Studies 12*(2), 161-178.

Dickerson, M., Walker, M., Legg England, S., and Hinchy, J. (1990). Demographic, personality, cognitive and behavioral correlates of off-course betting involvement. *Journal of Gambling Studies 6*(2), 165-182.

Dixey, R. (1987). It's a great feeling when you win: Women and bingo. *Journal of Leisure Studies 6*(2), 199-214.

Dodd, R. as told to Vaughan, R. (1985). Aboriginal gambling and self-determination in Queensland. In Caldwell, G., Haig, B., Dickerson, M., and Sylvan, L. (Eds.) *Gambling in Australia* (pp. 46-49). Sydney: Croom Helm.

Dostoevsky, F. (1972 [1866]). *The gambler,* Terras, V. (Trans.) Chicago: University of Chicago Press.

Downes, D. M., Davies, B. P., David, M., and Stone, P. (1976). *Gambling, work and leisure: A study across three areas.* London: Routledge and Kegan Paul.

Dritschel, B. H. and Pettinati, H. M. (1989). The role of female occupation in severity of alcohol related problems. *American Journal of Drug and Alcohol Abuse 15*(1), 61 72.

Eadington, W. R. (1973). *The economics of gambling behavior: A qualitative study of Nevada's gaming industry.* Research Report Number 11. Reno, Nevada: Bureau of Business and Economic Research, University of Nevada.

Eadington, W. R. (1976). Economic aspects of Nevada's gaming industry. In Eadington, W. R. (Ed.) *Gambling and society: Interdisciplinary studies on the subject of gambling* (pp. 138-158). Springfield, IL: Charles C Thomas.

Eadington, W. R. (1987). Economic perceptions of gambling behavior. *Journal of Gambling Behavior 3*(4), 264-273.

Eadington, W. R. (1999). The economics of casino gambling. *Journal of Economic Perspectives, 13*(3), 173-192.

Eadington, W. R. (2000). Personal communication to the author, June 5.

Edwards, W. (1955). The prediction of decisions among bets. *Journal of Experimental Psychology 51*(3), 201-214.

Elia, C. and Jacobs, D. F. (1993). The incidence of pathological gambling among Native Americans treated for alcohol dependence. *International Journal of the Addictions 28*(7), 659-666.

Ellermann, M. (1948). Social and clinical features of chronic alcoholism. *Journal of Nervous and Mental Disease 107*(6), 556-568.

Fabian, T. (1995). Pathological gambling: A comparison of gambling at German-style slot machines and "classical" gambling. *Journal of Gambling Studies 11*(3), 249-263.

Fabricand, B. P. (1965). *Horse Sense.* New York: David McCay.

Feeney, D. (1991). *A survey of the public's knowledge of lottery beneficiaries.* Roseville, MN: Minnesota State Lottery.

Feeney, D. (1994a). *Gambling in Minnesota. Who? What? Where?* Roseville, MN: Minnesota State Lottery.

Feeney, D. (1994b). *Gambling behavior and attitudes.* Roseville, MN: Minnesota State Lottery.

Feigelman, W., Wallisch, L., and Lesieur, H. R. (1998). Problem gamblers, problem substance users, and dual-problem individuals: An epidemiological study. *American Journal of Public Health 88*(3), 467-470.

Feigelman, W., Kleinman, P. H., Lesieur, H. R., Millman, R. B., Lesser, M. L. (1995). Pathological gambling among methadone patients. *Drug and Alcohol Dependence 39*(2), 75-81.

Fenichel, O. (1945). *The psychoanalytic theory of neurosis.* New York: Norton.

Ferrioli, M. and Ciminero, A. R. (1981). The treatment of pathological gambling as an addictive behavior. In Eadington, W. R. (Ed.) *The gambling papers: Proceedings of the Fifth National Conference on Gambling and Risk Taking.* Reno, Nevada: Bureau of Business and Economic Research, College of Business Administration, University of Nevada.

Field, P. B. (1962). A new cross-cultural study of drunkenness. In Pittman, D. J. and Snyder, C R. (Eds.) *Society, culture, and drinking patterns.* New York: John Wiley and Sons.

Fisher, S. (1991). Governmental response to juvenile fruit machine gambling in the U.K.: Where do we go from here? *Journal of Gambling Studies 7*(3), 217-247.

Fisher, S. (1992). Measuring pathological gambling in children: The case of fruit machines in the U.K. *Journal of Gambling Studies 8*(3), 263-285.

Fisher, S. (1993a). Gambling and pathological gambling in adolescents. *Journal of Gambling Studies 9*(3), 277-288.

Fisher, S. (1993b). The pull of the fruit machine: A sociological typology of young players. *The Sociological Review 41*(3), 446-474.

Fisher, S. (1993c). Towards a sociological understanding of slot machine gambling in young people. In Eadington, W. R. and Cornelius, J. (Eds.) *Gambling behavior and problem gambling* (pp. 395-403). Reno, Nevada: Bureau of Business and Economic Research, College of Business Administration, University of Nevada.

Fisher, S. (1993d). The use of slot machines by young people in the U.K.: The present evidence. In Eadington, W. R. and Cornelius, J. (Eds.) *Gambling behavior and problem gambling* (pp. 405-430). Reno, Nevada: Bureau of Business and Economic Research, College of Business Administration, University of Nevada. Revision of (1991) Governmental response to juvenile fruit machine gambling in the U.K.: Where do we go from here? *Journal of Gambling Studies 7*(3), 217-247.

Fisher, S. (1994). Identifying video game addiction in children and adolescents. *Addictive Behaviors 19*(5), 446-473.

Fisher, S. (1995). The amusement arcade as a social space for adolescents: An empirical study. *Journal of Adolescence 18*(1), 71-86.

Fisher, S. (1999). A prevalence study of gambling and problem gambling in British adolescents. *Addiction Research 7*(6), 509-538.

Fisher, S. and Balding, J. (1996). Under sixteens find the Lottery a good gamble. *Education and Health 13*, 65-68.

Fisher, S., and Griffiths, M. (1995). Current trends in slot machine gambling: Research and policy issues. *Journal of Gambling Studies 11*(3), 239-247.

Fleming, A. M. (1978). *Something for nothing: A history of gambling.* New York: Delacorte Press.

France, C. J. (1902). The gambling impulse. *American Journal of Psychology 13*(3), 64 407.

Frank, M. L. (1993). Underage gambling in New Jersey. In Eadington, W. R. and Cornelius, J. (Eds.) *Gambling behavior and problem gambling* (pp. 387-394). Reno, Nevada: Bureau of Business and Economic Research, College of Business Administration, University of Nevada.

Freud, S. (1950 [1928]). Dostoevsky and parricide. In Strachey, J. (Ed.) *Collected papers, Vol. 5: Miscellaneous papers 1888-1938* (pp. 222-242). London: Hogarth Press and The Institute of Psychoanalysis.

Frey, J. H. (1984). Gambling: A sociological review. *Annals of the American Academy of Political and Social Science 474* (July), 107-121.

Friedman, M. and Savage, L. J. (1948). The utility analysis of choices involving risk. *Journal of Political Economy 16*, 279-304.

Fuller, P. (1974). Introduction. In Halliday, J. and Fuller, P. (Eds.) *The psychology of gambling.* New York: Harper and Row.

Fund for the City of New York (1972). *Legal gambling in New York: Discussion of numbers and sports betting.* New York: Fund for the City of New York.

Furnham, A. (1985). Attitudes to, and habits of, gambling in Britain. *Personality and Individual Differences 6*(4), 439-502.

Gaboury, A. and Ladouceur, R. (1993). Preventing pathological gambling among teenagers. In Eadington, W. R. and Cornelius, J. (Eds.) *Gambling behavior and problem gambling* (pp. 443-450). Reno, Nevada: Bureau of Business and Economic Research, College of Business Administration, University of Nevada.

Galdston, I. (1951). The psychodynamics of the triad: Alcoholism, gambling, and superstition. *Mental Hygiene 35*, 589-598.

Galdston, I. (1960). The gambler and his love. *American Journal of Psychiatry 35*, 553-555.

Gallup (1972). *Gambling in Britain.* London: Social Surveys (Gallup Poll) Ltd.

Gambino, B., Fitzgerald, R., Shaffer, H., Renner, J., and Courtnage, P. (1993). Perceived family history of problem gambling and scores on SOGS. *Journal of Gambling Studies 9*(2), 169-184.

Gamblers Anonymous (No date). *Gamblers Anonymous pamphlet (3rd edition).* Los Angeles: G. A. Publishing.

Gaudia, R. (1987). Effects of compulsive gambling on the family. *Social Work 32*(3), 254 256.

Gerstein, D., Murphy, S., Toce, M., Hoffmann, J., Palmer, A., Johnson, R., Larison, C., Chuchro, L., Bard, A., Engelman, L., Hill, M. A., Buie, T., Volberg, R., Harwood, H., Tucker, A., Christiansen, E., Cummings, W., and Sinclair, S. (1999). *Gambling Impact and Behavior Study: Final Report to the National Gambling Impact Study Commission.* University of Chicago: National Opinion Research Center.

Gilovich, T. (1983). Biased evaluation and persistence in gambling. *Journal of Personality and Social Psychology 44*(6), 1110-1126.

Gilovich, T. and Douglas, C. (1986). Biased evaluations of randomly determined gambling outcomes. *Journal of Experimental and Social Psychology 22*(3), 228-241.

Glasser, W. (1976). *Positive addictions.* New York: Harper and Row.

Goddard, L. L. (1993). Alcohol and other drug abuse literature, 1980-1989: Selected abstracts. In Goddard, Lawford L. (Ed.) *An African-centered model of prevention for African-American youth at high risk* (pp. 47-56). Center for Substance Abuse Prevention (CSAP) Technical Report No. 6. Rockville, MD.: U.S. Department of Health and Human Services, Public Health Services, Substance Abuse and Mental Health Services Administration.

Goffman, E. (1959). *The presentation of self in everyday life.* Garden City, NJ: Doubleday.

Goffman, E. (1967). *Interaction ritual: Essays on face-to-face behavior.* New York: Anchor Books.

Goffman, E. (1969). *Where the action is.* London: Allen Lane.

Goodman, A. (1990). Addiction: Definition and implications. *British Journal of Addiction 85*, 1403-1408.

Govoni, R., Rupcich, N., and Frisch, R. (1996). Gambling behavior of adolescent gamblers. *Journal of Gambling Studies 12*(3), 305-317.

Graham, J. (1988). *Amusement machines: Dependency and delinquency.* Home Office research study no. 101. London: HMSO.

Graham, J. R. and Lowenfeld, B. H. (1986). Personality dimensions of the pathological gambler. *Journal of Gambling Behavior 2*(1), 58-66.

Greenberg, J. L., Lewis, S. E., and Dodd, D. K. (1999). Overlapping addictions and self-esteem among college men and women. *Addictive Behaviors 24*(4), 565-571.

Greene, J. (1982). The gambling trap. *Psychology Today 16*, 50-55.

Greenson, R. R. (1948). On gambling. The Yearbook of Psychoanalysis 4, 110-123. Orig. 1947. *American Imago 4*, 61-77.

Grichting, W. L. (1986). The impact of religion on gambling in Australia. *Australian Journal of Psychology 38*(1), 45-58.

Griffith, R. M. (1949). Odds adjustments by American horse-race bettors. *American Journal of Psychology 62*(2), 290-294

Griffiths, M. D. (1988). Adolescent gambling: Report of a workshop. *Society for the Study of Gambling Newsletter, 14*, 1719.

Griffiths, M. D. (1989). Gambling in children and adolescents. *Journal of Gambling Behavior 5*(1), 66-83.

Griffiths, M. D. (1990a). The cognitive psychology of gambling. *Journal of Gambling Studies 6*(1), 31-42.

Griffiths, M. D. (1990b). Addiction to fruit machines: A preliminary study among young males. *Journal of Gambling Studies 6*(2), 113-126.

Griffiths, M. D. (1990c). The acquisition, development and maintenance of fruit machine gambling in adolescence. *Journal of Gambling Studies 6*(3), 193-204.

Griffiths, M. D. (1990d). The role of cognitive bias and skill in fruit machine gambling. In Lea, S. E. G., Webley, P., and Young, B. M. (Eds.) *Applied economic psychology in the 1990s, Vol 1* (pp. 228-253). Exeter: Washington Singer Press.

Griffiths, M. (1991a). Fruit machine addiction: Two brief case studies. *British Journal of Addiction 86*(4), 465.

Griffiths, M. (1991b). The observational study of adolescent gambling in UK amusement arcades. *Journal of Community and Applied Social Psychology 1*, 309-320.

Griffiths, M. (1992). Pinball wizard: The case of a pinball machine addict. *Psychological Reports 71*, 160-162.

Griffiths, M. (1993a). A study of the cognitive activity of fruit machine players. In Eadington, W. R. and Cornelius, J. (Eds.) *Gambling behavior and problem gambling* (pp. 85-109). Reno, Nevada: Bureau of Business and Economic Research, College of Business Administration, University of Nevada.

Griffiths, M. (1993b). Problem factors in adolescent fruit machine gambling: Results of a small postal survey. *Journal of Gambling Studies 9*(1), 31-45.

Griffiths, M. (1993c). Fruit machine gambling: The importance of structural characteristics. *Journal of Gambling Studies 9*(2), 101-120.

Griffiths, M. (1993d). Factors in problem adolescent fruit machine gambling: Results of a small postal survey. *Journal of Gambling Studies 9*(1), 31-45.

Griffiths, M. (1993e). Fruit machine addiction in adolescence: A case study. *Journal of Gambling Studies 9*(4), 387-399.

Griffiths, M. (1995). Towards a risk factor model of fruit machine addiction. *Journal of Gambling Studies 11*(3), 343-346.

Griffiths, M. (2000). Scratchcard gambling among adolescent males. *Journal of Gambling Studies 16*(1), 79-91.

Griffiths, M. and Wood, R. (2000). Risk factors in adolescence: The case of gambling, videogame playing, and the internet. *Journal of Gambling Studies 16*(2-3), 199-225.

Griffiths, M., Scarfe, A., and Bellringer, P. (1999). The UK National Telephone Gambling Helpline—Results on the first year of operation. *Journal of Gambling Studies 15*(1), 83-90.

Grun, L. and McKeigue, P. (2000). Prevalence of excessive gambling before and after introduction of a national lottery in the United Kingdom: Another example of the single distribution theory. *Addiction 95*(6), 959-966.

Gupta, R. and Derevensky, J. (1996). The relationship between gambling and video-game playing behavior in children and adolescents. *Journal of Gambling Studies 12*(4), 375-394.

Gupta, R. and Derevensky, J. (1997). Familial and social influences on juvenile gambling behavior. *Journal of Gambling Studies 13*(3), 179-192.

Gupta, R. and Derevensky, J. (1998). Adolescent gambling behavior: A prevalence study and examination of the correlates associated with problem gambling. *Journal of Gambling Studies 14*(4), 319-345.

Gupta, R. and Derevensky, J. L. (2000). Adolescents with gambling problems: From research to treatment. *Journal of Gambling Studies 16*(2-3), 315-342.

Gurnack, A. M. and Thomas, J. L. (1989). Behavioral factors related to elderly alcohol abuse: Research and policy issues. *International Journal of the Addictions 24*(7), 641-654.

Haberman, P. W. (1969). Drinking and other self-indulgences: Complements or counter attractions? *International Journal of the Addictions 4*(2), 157-167.

Hall, G. W., Carriero, N. J., Takushi, R. Y., Montoya, I. D., Preston, K. L., and Gorelick, D. A. (2000). Pathological gambling among cocaine-dependent outpatients. *American Journal of Psychiatry 157*(7), 1127-1133.

Harris, H. (1964). Gambling addiction in an adolescent male. *Psychoanalytic Quarterly 33*, 513-525.

Harrison, P. A., Hoffman, N. G., and Edwall, G. E. (1989). Differential drug use patterns among sexually abused adolescent girls in treatment for chemical dependency. *International Journal of the Addictions 24*(6), 499-514.

Hayano, D. M. (1982). *Poker faces: The life and work of professional card players.* Berkeley: University of California Press.

Heavey, J. F. (1978). The incidence of State Lottery Taxes. *Public Finance Quarterly 6*(4), 415-425.

Hendriks, V. M., Meerkerk, G.-J., Van Oers, H. A. M., Garretsen, H. F. L. (1997). The Dutch instant lottery: Prevalence and correlates of at-risk playing. *Addiction 92*(3), 335-346.

Herman, R. D. (1967). Gambling as work: A sociological study of the race track. In Herman, R. D. (Ed.) *Gambling.* New York: Harper and Row.

Herman, R. D. (1976a). *Gamblers and Gambling.* Lexington, MA: Lexington Books.

Herman, R. D. (1976b). Motivations to gamble: The model of Roger Caillois. In Eadington, W. R. (Ed.) *Gambling and society: Interdisciplinary studies on the subject of gambling,* pp; 207-217. Springfield, IL: Charles C Thomas.

Hermkens, P. and Kok, I. (1990). Gambling in the Netherlands: Developments, participation, and compulsive gambling. *Journal of Gambling Studies 6*(3), 223-240.

Herring, M. and Blesdoe, T. (1994). A model of lottery participation–Demographics, context and attitudes. *Policy Studies Journal 22*(2), 245-257.

Hewitt, D. and Augur, D. (1995). *Firewatch on aboriginal adolescent gambling.* Edmonton, Alberta: Nechi Training, Research and Health Promotion Institute.

Hing, N. and Breen, H. (2001). Profiling Lady Luck: An empirical study of gambling and problem gambling amongst female club members. *Journal of Gambling Studies 17*(1), 47-69.

Hoffmann, J. P. (2000). Religion and problem gambling in the U.S. *Review of Religious Research 41*(4), 488-509.

Hogan, R. (1986). The working class gamble: Frontier class structure and social control. *Research in Law, Deviance and Social Control 8*, 131-148.

Holtgraves, T. M. (1988). Gambling as self-presentation. *Journal of Gambling Behavior 4*(2), 78-91.

Hopper, V. F. (1970). *Chaucer's Canterbury tales (selected), An interlinear translation.* Woodbury, NY: Barron's Educational Series.

Horton, D. (1943). The functions of alcohol in primitive societies: A cross-cultural study. *Quarterly Journal of Studies on Alcohol 4*, 199-320.

Hraba, J., and Lee, G. (1995). Problem gambling and policy advice: The mutability and relative effects of structural, associational, and attitudinal variables. *Journal of Gambling Studies 11*(2), 105-121.

Hraba, J., and Lee, G. (1996). Gender, gambling, and problem gambling. *Journal of Gambling Studies 12*(1), 83-101.

Hraba, J., Mok, W. P., and Huff, D. (1990). Lottery play and problem gambling. *Journal of Gambling Studies 6*(4), 355-377. Reprinted (1993) as Tonight's numbers are ... Lottery play and problem gambling. In Eadington, W. R. and Cornelius, J. (Eds.) *Gambling behavior and problem gambling* (pp. 177-196). Reno, Nevada: Bureau of Business and Economic Research, College of Business Administration, University of Nevada.

Huff, G. and Collinson, F. (1987). Young offenders, gambling and video game playing. *British Journal of Criminology 27*(4), 401-410.

Hugick, L. (1989). Gambling on the rise: Lotteries lead the way. *The Gallup Report 285*, 32-41.

Huizinga, J. (1950). *Homo ludens: A study of the play-element in culture.* New York: Roy Publishers.

Huxley, J. and Carroll, D. (1992). A survey of fruit machine gambling in adolescents. *Journal of Gambling Studies 8*(2), 167-179.

Ibàñez, A. G., Mercadé, P. V., Aymami Sanromà, M. N., and Cordero, C. P. (1992). Clinical and behavioral evaluation of pathological gambling in Barcelona, Spain. *Journal of Gambling Studies 8*(3), 299-310.

Ide-Smith, S. G. and Lea, S. E. G. (1988). Gambling in young adolescents. *Journal of Gambling Behavior 4*(2), 110-118.

Ignatin, G. and Smith, R. (1976). The economics of gambling. In Eadington, W. R. (Ed.) *Gambling and society: Interdisciplinary studies on the subject of gambling* (pp. 69 91). Springfield, IL: Charles C Thomas.

Inglis, K. (1985). Gambling and culture in Australia. In Caldwell, G., Haig, B., Dickerson, M., and Sylvan, L. (Eds.) *Gambling in Australia* (pp. 5-17). Sydney: Croom Helm.

Ingram, R. (1985). Transactional script theory applied to the pathological gambler. *Journal of Gambling Behavior 1*(2), 89-96.

Jacobs, D. F. (1986). A general theory of addictions: A new theoretical model. *Journal of Gambling Behavior 2*(1), 15-31.

Jacobs, D. F. (1988). Evidence for a common dissociative-like reaction among addicts. *Journal of Gambling Behavior 4*(1), 27-37.

Jacobs, D. F. (1989a). A general theory of addictions: Rationale for and evidence supporting a new approach for understanding and treating addictive bahviors. In Shaffer, H. J., Stein, S. A., Gambino, G., and Cummings, T. N. (Eds.) *Compulsive gambling: Theory, research, and practice* (pp. 35-64). Lexington, MA: Lexington Books.

Jacobs, D. F. (1989b). Illegal and undocumented: A review of teenage gambling and the plight of children of problem gamblers in America. In Shaffer, H. J., Stein, S. A., Gambino, G., and Cummings, T. N. (Eds.) *Compulsive gambling: Theory, research, and practice* (pp. 249-292). Lexington, MA: Lexington Books.

Jacobs, D. F. (1993). A review of juvenile gambling in the United States. In Eadington, W. R. and Cornelius, J. (Eds.) *Gambling behavior and problem gambling* (pp. 431-441). Reno, Nevada: Bureau of Business and Economic Research, College of Business Administration, University of Nevada.

Jacobs, D. F. (1994). Evidence supporting the "Pied Piper Effect" of lottery promotion and sales on juvenile gambling. Paper presented at the Eighth National Conference on Gambling Behavior, Seattle, WA.

Jacobs, D. F. (2000). Juvenile gambling in North America: An analysis of long term trends and future prospects. *Journal of Gambling Studies 16*(2-3), 119-152.

Jacques, C., Ladouceur, R., and Ferland, F. (2000). Impact of availability on gambling: A longitudinal study. *Canadian Journal of Psychiatry. Vol 45*(9), 810-815.

Jamieson, B. D. (1969). The influences of birth order, family size, and sex differences on risk-taking behavior. *British Journal of Social and Clinical Psychology 8*(1), 1-8.

Kagan, D. M. (1987). Addictive personality factors. *The Journal of Psychology 121*(6), 533-538.

Kahneman, D. and Tversky, A. (1979). Prospect theory: An analysis of decision under risk. Econometrica 47, 263-291.

Kahneman, D. and Tversky, A. (1984). Choices, values, and frames. *American Psychologist 39*, 341-350.

Kallick, M., Suits, D., Dielman, T., and Hybels, J. (1976). Appendix 2: Survey of American gambling attitudes and behavior. In *Gambling in America*. U.S. Department of Justice. Washington, D.C.: U.S. Government Printing Office.

Kallick, M., Suits, D., Dielman, T., and Hybels, J. (1979). *A survey of American gambling attitudes and behavior*. Ann Arbor, Michigan: Survey Research Center, Institute of Social Research, University of Michigan.

Kaplan, H. R. (1987). Lottery winners: The myth and reality. *Journal of Gambling Behavior 3*(3), 168-178.

Kaplan, H. R. (1988). Gambling among lottery winners: Before and after the big score. *Journal of Gambling Behavior 4*(3), 171-182.

Kaplan, H. R. (1989). State lotteries: Should the government be a player. In Shaffer, H. J., Stein, S. A., Gambino, G., and Cummings, T. N. (Eds.) *Compulsive gambling: Theory, research, and practice* (pp. 187-204). Lexington, MA: Lexington Books.

Karsten, R. (1935). *The head-hunters of western Amazonas: The life and culture of the Jibaro Indians of eastern Ecuador and Peru.* Commentationes Humanarum Leterarum, Vol. VII, No. 1. Helsingfors, Finland: Centraltryckeriet.

Kassinove, J. I., Doyle, K. A., Milburn, N. G. (2000). Gambling and alcohol use in adolescence. *Journal of Social Behavior & Personality 15*(1), 51-66.

Kearney, C. A., Roblek, T., Thurman, J., and Turnbough, P. D. (1996). Casino gambling in private school and adjudicated youngsters: A survey of practices and related variables. *Journal of Gambling Studies 12*(3), 319-327.

Keill, N. (1956). The behavior of five adolescent poker players. *Journal of Human Relations 5*, 79-89.

Keren, G. and Wagenaar, W. A. (1985). On the psychology of playing blackjack: Normative and descriptive considerations with implications for decision theory. *Journal of Experimental Psychology: General 114*(2), 133-158.

Klein, H. H. and Selesner, G. (1982). Results of the first Gallup Organization study of public attitudes toward legalized gambling. *Gaming Business Magazine*, November, 5-7, 48 49.

Knapp, T. J. (1976). A functional analysis of gambling behavior. In Eadington, W. R. (Ed.) *Gambling and society: Interdisciplinary studies on the subject of gambling* (pp. 276 294). Springfield, IL: Charles C Thomas.

Knapp, T. J. (1987). Book review of The chase: Career of the compulsive gambler by Henry R. Lesieur. *Journal of Gambling Behavior 3*(4), 288-291.

Knox, R. E. and Safford, R. K. (1976). Group caution at the race track. *Journal of Experimental Social Psychology 12*, 317-324.

Koller, K. M. (1972). Treatment of poker-machine addicts by aversion therapy. *The Medical Journal of Australia 59*, 742-745.

Kroeber, H.-L. (1992). Roulette gamblers and gamblers at electronic game machines: Where are the differences? *Journal of Gambling Studies 8*(1), 79-92.

Kuley, N. B. and Jacobs, D. F. (1988). The relationship between dissociative-like experiences and sensation seeking among social and problem gamblers. *Journal of Gambling Behavior 4*(3), 197-207.

Kusyszyn, I. (1972). The gambling addict versus the gambling professional: A difference in character? *International Journal of the Addictions 7*, 387-393.

Kusyszyn, I. (1976). How gambling saved me from a misspent sabbatical. In Eadington, W. R. (Ed.) *Gambling and society: Interdisciplinary studies on the subject of gambling* (pp. 255-264). Springfield, IL: Charles C Thomas.

Kusyszyn, I. (1978). "Compulsive" gambling: The problem of definition. *International Journal of the Addictions 13*(7), 1095-1101.

Kusyszyn, I. (1984). The psychology of gambling. *Annals of the American Academy of Political and Social Science 474* (July), 133-145.

Kusyszyn, I. (1990). Existence, effectance, esteem: From gambling to a new theory of human motivation. *International Journal of the Addictions 25*, 159-177.

Kusyszyn, I. and Rutter, R. (1985). Personality characteristics of male heavy gamblers, light gamblers, nongamblers, and lottery players. *Journal of Gambling Behavior 1*(1), 59 63.

Kweitel, R. and Allen, F. (2000). Electronic gaming machines: Is there a problem? *North American Journal of Psychology* 2(1), 167-178.

Ladouceur, R. (1993b). Prevalence estimates of pathological gamblers in Quebec, Canada. In Eadington, W. R. and Cornelius, J. (Eds.) *Gambling behavior and problem gambling* (pp. 379-384). Reno, Nevada: Bureau of Business and Economic Research, College of Business Administration, University of Nevada.

Ladouceur, R. and Dubé, D. (1995). Prevalence of pathological gambling and associated problems in individuals who visit non-gambling video arcades. *Journal of Gambling Studies* 11(4), 361-365.

Ladouceur, R. and Gaboury, A. (1988). Effects of limited and unlimited stakes on gambling behavior. *Journal of Gambling Behavior* 4(2), 119-126.

Ladouceur, R. and Mayrand, M. (1986). Charactéristiques psychologiques de la prise de risque monétaire des joueurs et des non-joueurs à la roulette. *International Journal of Psychology* 21(415), 433-443).

Ladouceur, R. and Mayrand, M. (1987). The level of involvement and the timing of betting in roulette. *The Journal of Psychology* 121(2), 169-176.

Ladouceur, R. and Mireault, C. (1988). Gambling behaviors among high school students in the Quebec area. *Journal of Gambling Behavior* 4(1), 3-12.

Ladouceur, R., Dubé, D., and Bujold, A. (1994). Gambling among primary school students. *Journal of Gambling Studies* 10(4), 363-370.

Ladouceur, R., Mayrand, M., and Tourigny, Y. (1987). Risk-taking behavior in gamblers and nongamblers during prolonged exposure. *Journal of Gambling Behavior* 3(2), 115 122.

Ladouceur, R., Tourigny, Y., and Mayrand, M. (1986). Familiarity, group exposure, and risk taking behavior in gambling. *Journal of Psychology* 120(1), 45-49.

Ladouceur, R., Vitaro, F., and Côté, M.-Λ. (2001). Attitudes, knowledge, and behavior toward youth gambling: A five-year follow-up. *Journal of Gambling Studies* 17(2), 101-116.

Ladouceur, R. Boudreault, N. Jacques, C. and Vitaro, F. (1999). Pathological gambling and related problems among adolescents. *Journal of Child & Adolescent Substance Abuse* 8(4), 55-68.

Ladouceur, R., Gaboury, A., Dumont, M., and Rochette, P. (1988). Gambling: Relationship between the frequency of wins and irrational thinking. *Journal of Psychology* 122(4), 409-414.

Ladouceur, R., Jacques, C., Ferland, F., and Giroux, I. (1998). Parents' attitudes and knowledge regarding gambling among youths. *Journal of Gambling Studies* 14(1), 83-90.

Ladouceur, R., Jacques, C., Ferland, F., and Giroux, I. (1999). Prevalence of problem gambling: A replication study 7 years later. *Canadian Journal of Psychiatry* 44(8), 802-804.

Ladouceur, R., Boisvert, J.-M., Pépin, M., Loranger, M., and Sylvain, C. (1994). Social cost of pathological gambling. *Journal of Gambling Studies* 10(4), 399-409.

La Fleur, T. (1991). *La Fleur's 1991 North American gambling abstract.* Boyds, MD: TLF Publications.

Landis, C. (1945). Theories of the alcoholic personality. In Jellinek, E. M. (Ed.) *Alcohol, science, and society.* New Haven, CT: Quarterly Journal of Studies on Alcohol.

Langenbucher, J., Bavly, L., Labouvie, E., Sanjuan, P. M., and Martin, C. S. (2001). Clinical features of pathological gambling in an addictions treatment cohort. *Psychology of Addictive Behaviors* 15(1), 77-79.

Larkin, M. and Griffiths, M. (1998). Response to Shaffer (1996), The case for a 'Complex Systems' conceptualisation of addiction. *Journal of Gambling Studies* 14(1), 73-82.

Larson, M., Hill, L., Pile, D., and Reckers, S. (1992). *High stakes: Gambling in Minnesota.* St. Paul: Minnesota Planning Office.

Laundergan, J. C. (1996). *Gambling and problem gambling among low and moderate income residents of the Twin Cities seven county Metro Area: Age and income differences.* St. Paul: Minnesota Department of Human Services, Mental Health Division.

Laundergan, J. C., Schaefer, J. M., Eckhoff, K. F., and Pirie, P. L. (1990). *Adult survey of Minnesota gambling behavior: A benchmark, 1990.* Duluth, MN: University of Minnesota Center for Addiction Studies.

Lea, S. E. G., Tarpy, R. M., and Webley, P. (1987). *The individual in the economy: A textbook of economic psychology.* London: Cambridge University Press.

Leary, K. and Dickerson, M. (1985). Levels of arousal in high and low frequency gamblers. *Behaviour Research and Therapy 23*, 635-640.

Lefcourt, H. (1966). Belief in personal control: A goal for psychotherapy. *Journal of Individual Psychology 22*, 185-195.

Lefcourt, H. (1983). The locus of control as a moderator of variable stress. In Lefcourt, H. H. (Ed.) *Research with the locus of control construct, Vol. 2* (pp. 253-269). New York: Academic Press.

Legarda, J. J., Babio, R., and Abreu, J. M. (1992). Prevalence estimates of pathological gambling in Seville (Spain). *British Journal of Addiction 87*, 767-770.

Lejoyeux, M., Feuche, N., Loi, S., Solomon, J., and Ades, J. (1999). Study of impulse-control disorders among alcohol-dependent patients. *Journal of Clinical Psychiatry 60*(5), 302-305.

Lemelin, C. (1977). Les effets redistributifs des loteries québebécoises. *L'Actualité Economique 53*, 468-475.

Lemert, E. (1953). An isolation and closure theory of naive check forgery. *Journal of Criminal Law, Criminology, and Police Science 44*, 296-307.

Lesieur, H. R. (1979). The compulsive gambler's spiral of options and involvement. Psychiatry: *Journal for the study of Interpersonal Processes 42*, 79-87.

Lesieur, H. R. (1984). *The chase: Career of the compulsive gambler.* Cambridge, MA: Schenkman Publishing Co.

Lesieur, H. R. (1987). Gambling, pathological gambling, and crime. In Galski, T. (Ed.) *The handbook of pathological gambling* (pp. 89-110). Springfield, IL: Charles C Thomas.

Lesieur, H. R. (1988a). Altering the DSM-III criteria for pathological gambling. *Journal of Gambling Behavior 4*(1), 38-47.

Lesieur, H. R. (1988b). The female pathological gambler. In Eadington, W. R. (Ed.) *Gambling research: Proceedings of the Seventh International Conference on Gambling and Risk Taking* (pp. 230-258). Reno, Nevada: Bureau of Business and Economic Research, College of Business Administration, University of Nevada.

Lesieur, H. R. (1988c). Report on pathological gambling in New Jersey. In *Report and recommendations of the Governor's Advisory Commission on Gambling.* Trenton: New Jersey Governor's Advisory Commission on Gambling.

Lesieur, H. R. (1989). Current research into pathological gambling and gaps in the literature. In Shaffer, H. J., Stein, S. A., Gambino, G., and Cummings, T. N. (Eds.) *Compulsive gambling: Theory, research, and practice* (pp. 225-248). Lexington, MA: Lexington Books.

Lesieur, H. R. (1990). *Compulsive gambling: Documenting the social and economic costs.* Paper presented at Gambling in Minnesota: An Issue for Policy Makers. Humphrey Institute of Public Affairs, University of Minnesota, Minneapolis, December, 1990.

Lesieur, H. R. (1992). Compulsive gambling. *Society 29*(4), 43-50.

Lesieur, H. R. (1993). Female pathological gamblers and crime. In Eadington, W. R. and Cornelius, J. (Eds.) *Gambling behavior and problem gambling* (pp. 495-515). Reno, Nevada: Bureau of Business and Economic Research, College of Business Administration, University of Nevada.

Lesieur, H. R. and Blume, S. B. (1987). South Oaks Gambling Screen (SOGS), A new instrument for the identification of pathological gamblers. *American Journal of Psychiatry 144*, 1184-1188.

Lesieur, H. R. and Blume, S. B. (1990). Characteristics of pathological gamblers identified among patients on a psychiatric admissions service. *Hospital and Community Psychiatry 41*(9), 1009-1112.

Lesieur, H. R. and Blume, S. B. (1991). When lady luck loses: Women and compulsive gambling. In van den Bergh, N. (Ed.) *Feminist perspectives on treating addictions* (pp. 181-197). New York: Springer.

Lesieur, H. R. and Blume, S. B. (1993). Revising the South Oaks Gambling Screen in different settings. *Journal of Gambling Studies 9*(3), 213-223.

Lesieur, H. R. and Heineman, M. (1988). Pathological gambling among youthful multiple substance abusers in a therapeutic community. *British Journal of Addiction 83*(7), 765-771.

Lesieur, H. R. and Klein, R. (1987). Pathological gambling among high school students. *Addictive Behaviors 12*(2), 129-134.

Lesieur, H. R. and Rosenthal, R. J. (1991). Pathological gambling: A review of the literature. *Journal of Gambling Studies 7*(1), 5-39.

Lesieur, H. R., Blume, S. G., and Zoppa, R. M. (1986). Alcoholism, drug abuse, and gambling. *Alcoholism: Clinical and Experimental Research 10*(1), 33-38.

Lesieur, H. R., Cross, J., Frank, M., Welch, M., White, C., Rubenstein, G., Moseley, K., and Mark, M. (1991). Gambling and pathological gambling among university students. *Addictive Behaviors 16*, 517-527. Reprinted (1993) in Eadington, W. R. and Cornelius, J. (Eds.) *Gambling behavior and problem gambling* (pp. 473-492). Reno, Nevada: Bureau of Business and Economic Research, College of Business Administration, University of Nevada.

Lester, D. (1979). *Gambling today.* Springfield, IL: Charles C Thomas.

Lester, D. (1994). Access to gambling opportunities and compulsive gambling. *International Journal of the Addictions 29*(12), 1611-1616.

Levy, M. and Feinberg, M. (1991). Psychopathology and pathological gambling among males: Theoretical and clinical concerns. *Journal of Gambling Studies 7*(1), 41-53.

Li, W. L. and Smith, M. H. (1976). The propensity to gamble: Some structural determinants. In Eadington, W. R. (Ed.) *Gambling and society: Interdisciplinary studies on the subject of gambling* (pp. 347-370). Springfield, IL: Charles C Thomas.

Light, I. (1977). Numbers gambling among blacks: A financial institution. *American Sociological Review 42*(6), 892-893.

Linden, R. D., Pope, H. G., and Jonas, J. M. (1986). Pathological gambling and major affective disorder: Preliminary findings. *Journal of clinical psychiatry 47*(4), 201-203.

Lindgren, H. E., Youngs, G. A., Jr., McDonald, T. D., Klenow, D. J., and Schriner, E. C. (1987). The impact of gender on gambling attitudes and behavior. *Journal of Gambling Behavior 3*(3), 155-167.

Livernois, J. R. (1987). The redistributive effects of lotteries: Evidence from Canada. *Public Finance Quarterly 15*, 339-351.

Livingston, J. (1974a). *Compulsive gamblers: Observations on action and abstinence.* New York: Harper and Row.

Livingston, J. (1974b). Compulsive gambling: A culture of losers. *Psychology Today 7*(10), 51-55.

Lorenz, V. C. (1987). Family dynamics of pathological gamblers. In Galski, T. (Ed.) *The handbook of pathological gambling* (pp. 71-88). Springfield, IL: Charles C Thomas.

Lorenz, V. C. and Politzer, R. M. (1990). *Final report on the task force on gambling addiction in Maryland.* Report to the Maryland Department of Health and Mental Hygiene. Baltimore, MD.

Lorenz, V. C. and Shuttlesworth, D. E. (1983). The impact of pathological gambling on the spouse of the gambler. *Journal of Community Psychology 11*, 67-76.

Lubben, J. E., Chi, I., and Kitano, H. H. L. (1989). The relative influence of selected social factors on Korean drinking behavior in Los Angeles. *Advances in Alcohol and Substance Abuse 8*(1), 1-17.

McCauley, C., Stitt, C. L., Woods, K., and Lipton, D. (1973). Group shift to caution at the race track. *Journal of Experimental Social Psychology 9*(1), 80-86.

McClelland, D. C., Davis, W. N., Wanner, E., and Kalin, R. (1966). A cross-cultural study of folk-tale content and drinking. *Sociometry 29*, 308-333.

McClure, R. F. and Mears, F. G. (1984). Video game players: Personality characteristics and demographic variables. *Psychological Reports 55*, 271-276.

McNeilly, D. P. and Burke, W. J. (2000). Late life gambling: The attitudes and behaviors of older adults. *Journal of Gambling Studies 16*(4), 393-415

McNeilly, D. P. and Burke, W. J. (2001). Gambling as a social activity of older adults. *International Journal of Aging & Human Development 52*(1), 19-28.

McConaghy, N. (1980). Behavior completion mechanisms rather than primary drives maintain behavioral patterns. *Activitas Nervosa Superior (Praha) 22*, 138-151.

McCormack, P. J. (1994). *Minnesota's programs for troubled gamblers.* St. Paul. MN: Senate Counsel and Research.

McCormick, R. A. (1987). Pathological gambling: A parsimonious need state model. *Journal of Gambling Behavior 3*(4), 257-263.

McCormick, R. A. (1993). Disinhibition and negative affectivity in substance abusers with and without a gambling problem. *Addictive Behaviors 18*(3), 331-336.

McCormick, R. A. and Taber, J. I. (1987). The pathological gambler: Salient personality variables. In Galski, T. (Ed.) *The handbook of pathological gambling* (pp. 9-39). Springfield, IL: Charles C Thomas.

McCormick, R. A. and Taber, J. I. (1988). Attributional style in pathological gamblers in treatment. *Journal of Abnormal Psychology 97*, 368-370.

McCormick, R. A., Taber, J. I., Kruedelbach, N. (1989). The relationship between attributional style and post-traumatic stress disorder in addicted patients. *Journal of Traumatic Stress 2*(4), 477-487.

McCormick, R. A., Russo, A. M., Ramirez, L. F., and Taber, J. I. (1984). Affective disorders among pathological gamblers seeking treatment. *American Journal of Psychiatry 141*(2), 215-218.

McGlothlin, W. H. (1956). Stability of choices among uncertain alternatives. *American Journal of Psychology 69*, 604-615.

Machina, M. (1982). "Expected Utility" analysis without the independence axiom. *Econometrica 50*(2), 277-323.

McLoughlin, K. (1979). The lotteries tax. *Canadian taxation 1 (Jan.)*, 16-19.

MacMillan, G. E. (1985). People and gambling. In Caldwell, G., Haig, B., Dickerson, M., and Sylvan, L. (Eds.) *Gambling in Australia* (pp. 253-260). Sydney: Croom Helm.

Madsen, W. (1974). *The American alcoholic: The nature-nurture controversy in alcoholism research and therapy.* Springfield, IL: Charles C Thomas.

Maguire, J. A. (1987). Against the odds: The survival of English working class gambling since 1800. *ARENA Review 11*, 37-42.

Mark, M. E. and Lesieur, H. R. (1992). A feminist critique of problem gambling research. *British Journal of Addiction 87*(4), 549-565.

Marks, I. (1990). Behavioural (non-chemical) addictions. *British Journal of Addiction 85*, 1389-1394.

Martinez, T. H. and LaFranchi, R. (1969). Why people play poker. *Trans-Action* (July August), 30-35, 52.

Martinez-Pina, A., Guirao de Parga, J. L., Fuste i Vallverdu, R., Serrat Planas, X., Martin Mateo, M., and Moreno Auguado, V. (1991). The Catalonia survey: Personality and intelligence structure in a sample of compulsive gamblers. *Journal of Gambling Studies 7*(4), 275-

299. Reprinted (1993) in Eadington, W. R. and Cornelius J. (Eds.) *Gambling behavior and problem gambling*. Reno, Nevada: Bureau of Business and Economic Research, College of Business Administration, University of Nevada.

Marty, H., Zoppa, R., and Lesieur, H. (1985). Dual addiction: Pathological gambling and alcoholism. In Eadington, W. R. (Ed.) *Proceedings of the Sixth National Conference on Gambling and Risk-Taking*. Reno, Nevada: Bureau of Business and Economic Research, College of Business Administration, University of Nevada.

Maurer, D. D. (1950). The argot of the dice-gambler. *Annals of the American Academy of Political and Social Science 269* (May), 114-133.

Maurer, D. D. (1974). *The American confidence man*. Springfield, IL: Charles C Thomas.

Menninger, K. A. (1938). *Man against himself*. New York: Harcourt, Brace, and World.

Merton, R. K. (1938). Social structure and anomie. *American Sociological Review 3*, 672 682.

Meyer, G. and Fabian, T. (1993). Pathological gambling and criminal behavior. In Eadington, W. R. and Cornelius, J. (Eds.) *Gambling behavior and problem gambling* (pp. 517-529). Reno, Nevada: Bureau of Business and Economic Research, College of Business Administration, University of Nevada.

Meyer, G. and Stadler A. (1999). Criminal behavior associated with pathological gambling. *Journal of Gambling Studies 15*(1), 29-43,

Mikesell, J. L. (1989). A note on the changing incidence of state lottery finance. *Social Science Quarterly 70*, 513-521.

Mikesell, J. L. (1991). Lottery expenditure in a non-lottery state. *Journal of Gambling Studies 7*(2), 89-98.

Miller, M. A. and Westermeyer, J. (1996). Gambling in Minnesota. *American Journal of Psychiatry 153*(6), 845.

Miller, P. M. (1980). Theoretical and practical issues in substance abuse assessment and treatment. In Miller, W. R. (Ed.) *The addictive behaviors: Treatment of alcoholism, drug abuse, smoking, and obesity* (pp. 265-290). Oxford: Permagon.

Miller, W. R. (1986). Individual outpatient treatment of pathological gambling. *Journal of Gambling Behavior 2*(2), 95-107.

Minnesota State Lottery (1992). *1992 Minnesota State Lottery annual report*. Roseville, MN: Minnesota State Lottery.

Mobilia, P. (1993). Gambling as a rational addiction. *Journal of Gambling Studies 9*(3), 121-151.

Mok, W. P. and Hraba, J. (1991). Age and gambling behavior: A declining and shifting pattern of participation. *Journal of Gambling Studies 7*(4), 313-335. Reprinted (1993) in Eadington, W. R. and Cornelius, J. (Eds.) *Gambling behavior and problem gambling*, p. 51-74, Reno, Nevada: Bureau of Business and Economic Research, College of Business Administration, University of Nevada.

Moody, G. E. (1987). *Parents of young gamblers*. Paper presented at the Seventh International Conference on Gambling and Risk Taking, Reno, Nevada.

Moody, G. E. (1990). *Quit compulsive gambling*. Northampton, U.K.: Thorsons.

Moore, T. L. (2001a). *Older adult gambling in Oregon: An epidemiological survey*. Salem, OR: Oregon Gambling Addiction Treatment Foundation.

Moore, T. L. (2001b). *The prevalence of disordered gambling among adults in Oregon: A secondary anaylsis of data*. Salem, OR: Oregon Gambling Addiction Treatment Foundation.

Moore, S. M. and Ohtsuka, K. (1997). Gambling activities of young Australians: Developing a model of behavior. *Journal of Gambling Studies 13*(3), 207-236.

Moore, S. M. and Ohtsuka, K. (1999a). Beliefs about control over gambling among young people, and their relation to problem gambling. *Psychology of Addictive Behaviors 13*(4), 339-347.

Moore, S. M. and Ohtsuka, K. (1999b). The prediction of gambling behavior and problem gambling from attitudes and perceived norms. *Social Behavior & Personality 27*(5), 455-466.

Moore, S. and Ohtsuka, K. (2000). The structure of young people's leisure and their gambling behaviour. *Behaviour Change 17*(3), 167-177.

Moran, E. (1970a). Varieties of pathological gambling. *British Journal of Psychiatry 116*, 593-597.

Moran, E. (1970b). Gambling as a form of dependence. *British Journal of Addiction 64*, 419-428.

Moran, E. (1970c). Pathological gambling. *British Journal of Hospital Medicine 4*(1), 59 70. Reprinted (1975) *British Journal of Psychiatry, Special Publication No. 9*, 127, 416-428.

Moran, E. (1979). An assessment of the report of the Royal Commission on Gambling 1976 1978. *British Journal of Addiction 74*(1), 3-9.

Moran, E. (1995). Majority of secondary school children buy tickets. *British Medical Journal 311*, 1225-1226.

Mukhtar, M. A. (1977). Probability and utility estimates for racetrack bettors. *Journal of Political Economy 85*, 803-815.

Munson, R. F. (1962). Decision-making in an actual gambling situation. *American Journal of Psychology 75*, 640-643.

Myerson, A. (1940). Alcohol: A Study of Social Ambivalence. *Quarterly Journal of Studies on Alcohol 1*(1), 13-20.

Myrdal, G. (1944). *An American dilemma*. New York: Harper.

Nadler, L. B. (1985). The epidemiology of pathological gambling: Critique of existing research and alternative strategies. *Journal of Gambling Behavior 1*(1), 35-50.

Nathan, P. E. (1980). Etiology and process in the addictive behaviors. In Miller, W. R. (Ed.) *The addictive behaviors: Treatment of alcoholism, drug abuse, smoking, and obesity.* Oxford: Pergamon Press.

National Center for Child Abuse and Neglect (1981). *National study of the incidence and severity of child abuse and neglect.* Department of Health and Human Services Publication OHDS 81-303929. Washington, D.C.: U.S. Government Printing Office.

NHTPC (National Housing and Town Planning Council) (1988). *The use of arcades and gambling machines: A national survey.* London: NHTPC.

Newman, O. (1968). The sociology of the betting shop. *British Journal of Sociology 19*, 17 35.

Newman, O. (1972a). *Gambling: Hazard and reward.* London: The Athelone Press.

Newman, O. (1972b). The gambling problem. *Social Service Quarterly 46*, 3-6.

Newman, O. (1975). The ideology of social problems: Gambling, a case study. *Canadian Review of Sociology and Anthropology 122*, 541-550.

Ocean, G. and Smith, G. J. (1993). Social reward, conflict, and commitment: A theoretical model of gambling behavior. *Journal of Gambling Studies 9*(4), 321-339.

Oldman, D. (1974). Chance and skill: A study of roulette. *Sociology 8*(3), 407-426.

Oldman, D. (1978). Compulsive gamblers. *Sociological Review 26*, 349-370.

Oliveira, M. and Silva, M. (2000). Pathological and nonpathological gamblers: A survey in gambling settings. *Substance Use & Misuse 35*(11), 1573-1583.

Oliveira, M. and Silva, M. (2001). A Comparison of Horse-Race, Bingo, and Video Poker Gamblers in Brazilian Gambling Settings. *Journal of Gambling Studies 17*(2), 137-149.

Orford, J. (1985). *Excessive appetites: A psychological view of addictions.* New York: John Wiley and Sons.

Orford, J. and McCartney, J. (1990). Is excessive gambling seen as a form of dependence? Evidence from the community and the clinic. *Journal of Gambling Behavior 6*(2), 139-152.

Orphanides, A. and Zervos, D. (1995). Rational addiction with learning and regret. *Journal of Political Economy 103*, 739-758.

Payne, J. W. (1975). Relation of perceived risk to preferences among gamblers. *Journal of Experimental Psychology: Human Perception and Performance 104*(1), 86-94.

Peele, S. (1985). *The meaning of addiction: Compulsive experience and its interpretation.* Lexington, MA: Lexington Books.

Peele, S. and Brodsky, A. (1975). *Love and addiction.* New York: Signet.

Peterson, V. W. (1951). *Gambling: Should it be legalized?* Springfield, IL: Charles C Thomas.

Petry, N. M. (2000a). Gambling problems in substance abusers are associated with increased sexual risk behaviors. *Addiction 95*(7), 1089-1100.

Petry, N. M. (2000b). Psychiatric symptoms in problem gambling and non-problem gambling substance abusers. *American Journal on Addictions 9*(2), 163-171.

Petry, N. M. (2001). Comparison of problem-gambling and non-problem-gambling youths seeking treatment for Marijuana abuse. *Journal of the American Academy of Child and Adolescent Psychiatry 40*(11), 1324-1331.

Phillips, J. G. and Amrhein, P. C. (1989). Factors influencing wagers in simulated blackjack. *Journal of Gambling Behavior 5*(2), 99-111.

Ploskowe, N. (1950). Obstacles to the enforcement of gambling laws. *Annals of the American Academy of Political and Social Science 269* (May), 1-8.

Poulin, C. (2000). Problem gambling among adolescent students in the Atlantic provinces of Canada. *Journal of Gambling Studies 16*(1), 53-78.

Price, J. A. (1972). Gambling in traditional Asia. *Anthropologica 14*(2), 157-180.

Proimos, J., DuRant, R. H., Pierce, J. D., and Goodman, E. (1998). Gambling and other risk behaviors among 8th- to 12th-grade students. *Pediatrics 102*(2), 323.

Pryor, F. L. (1976). The Friedman-Savage utility function in cross-cultural perspective. *Journal of Political Economy 84*, 821-834.

Pugh, P., and Webley, P. (2000). Adolescent participation in the U.K. national lottery games. *Journal of Adolescence 23*(1), 1-11.

Quiggin, J. (1985). The economics of gambling. In Caldwell, G., Haig, B., Dickerson, M., and Sylvan (Eds.) *Gambling in Australia.* Sydney: Croom Helm.

Quiggin, J. (1987). Lotteries: an economic analysis. In Walker, M. (Ed.) *Faces of gambling: Proceedings of the Second National Conference of the National Association for Gambling Studies (1986)* (pp. 127-138). Sydney, Australia: National Association for Gambling Studies.

Quinn, J. P. (1912). *Gambling and gambling devices.* Akron, OH: The New Werner Company.

Rado, S. (1926). The psychic effects of intoxicants: An attempt to evolve a psychoanalytic theory of morbid cravings. *International Journal of Psychoanalysis 7*, 396-413.

Ramirez, L. F., McCormick, R. A., Russo, A. M., and Taber, J. I. (1983). Patterns of substance abuse in pathological gamblers undergoing treatment. *Addictive Behaviors 8*(4), 425-428.

Reckers, S., Coleman, S., and Mains, S. (1993). *Minnesota gambling 1993.* St. Paul: Minnesota Planning Office.

Reid, S. A. (1985). The churches' campaign against casinos and poker machines in Victoria. In Caldwell, G., Haig, B., Dickerson, M., and Sylvan, L. (Eds.) *Gambling in Australia* (pp. 195-216). Sydney: Croom Helm.

Reid, S., Woodford, S. J., Roberts, R., Golding, J. F., and Towell, A. D. (1999). Health-related correlates of gambling on the British National Lottery. *Psychological Reports.* Vol 84(1), 247-254.

Roberts, J. M. and Sutton-Smith, B. (1966). Cross-cultural correlates of games of chance. *Behavior Science Notes 1*(1), 131-144.

Robins, L. N., Helzer, J. E., Weissman, M. M., Orvaschel, H., Gruenberg, E., Burke, J. D., and Regier, D. (1984). Lifetime prevalence of specific psychiatric disorders in three sites. *Archives of General Psychiatry 41*, 949-958.

Roebuck, J. (1967). *Criminal typology.* Springfield, IL: Charles C Thomas

Rogers, P. and Webley, P. (2001). "It could be us!": Cognitive and social psychological factors in UK National Lottery play. *Applied Psychology: An International Review 50*(1), 181-199.

Room, R., Turner, N. E., and Ialomiteanu, A. (1999). Community effects of the opening of the Niagara casino. *Addiction 94*(10), 1449-1466.

Rosecrance, J. (1982). *The degenerates of Lake Tahoe: A study of persistence in the social world of horse race gambling*. Ph.D. Dissertation, University of California, Santa Barbara.

Rosecrance, J. (1985). Compulsive gambling and the medicalization of deviance. Social Problems 32(3), 275-284.

Rosecrance, J. (1986a). Why regular gamblers don't quit: A sociological perspective. *Sociological Perspectives 29*, 357-378.

Rosecrance, J. (1986b). Attributions and the origins of problem gambling. *The Sociological Quarterly 27*, 463-477.

Rosecrance, J. (1986c). You can't tell the players without a scorecard: A typology of horse players. *Deviant Behavior 7*(1), 77-97.

Rosecrance, J. (1988a). Active gamblers as peer counselors. *International Journal of the Addictions 23*, 751-756.

Rosecrance, J. (1988b). *Gambling without guilt*. Pacific Grove, CA: Brooks/Cole Publishing.

Rosecrance, J. (1989). Controlled gambling: A promising future. In Shaffer, H. J., Stein, S. A., Gambino, G., and Cummings, T. N. (Eds.) *Compulsive gambling: Theory, research, and practice* (pp. 147-160). Lexington, MA: Lexington Books.

Rosen, S. and Norton, D. (1966). The lottery as a source of public revenues. *Taxes 44*, 617 625.

Rosenthal, R. J. (1970). *Genetic theory and abnormal behavior*. New York: McGraw-Hill.

Rosenthal, R. J. (1987). The psychodynamics of pathological gambling: A review of the literature. In Galski, T. (Ed.) *The Handbook of pathological gambling* (pp. 41-70). Springfield, IL: Charles C Thomas.

Rosenthal, R. J. (1989). Pathological gambling and problem gambling: Problems of definition and diagnosis. In Shaffer, H. J., Stein, S. A., Gambino, G., and Cummings, T. N. (Eds.) *Compulsive gambling: Theory, research, and practice* (pp. 101-125). Lexington, MA: Lexington Books.

Rosenthal, R. J. (1992). Pathological gambling. *Psychiatric Annals 22*(2), 72-78.

Rosenthal, R. J. (1993). Some causes of pathological gambling. In Eadington, W. R. and Cornelius, J. (Eds.) *Gambling behavior and problem gambling* (pp. 143-148). Reno, Nevada: Bureau of Business and Economic Research, College of Business Administration, University of Nevada.

Rosenthal, R. J. (1995). The phenomenology of 'bad beats': Some clinical observations. *Journal of Gambling Studies 11*(4), 367-372.

Rotter, J. B. (1966). Generalized expectancies for internal versus external control of reinforcement. *Psychological Monographs 80*, 1-28.

Roy, A., Smelson, D., and Lindeken, S. (1996). Screening for pathological gambling among substance misusers. *British Journal of Psychiatry 169*(4), 523.

Roy, A., Adinoff, B., Roehrich, L., Lamparski, D., Custer, R., Lorenz, V., Barbaccia, M., Guidotti, A., Costa, E., and Linnoila, M. (1988). Pathological gambling: A psychobiological study. *Archives of General Psychiatry 45*(4), 369-373.

Rydelius, P.-A. (1981). Children of alcoholic fathers: Their social adjustment and their health status over 20 years. *Acta Paediatrica Scandinavica*, Supplement 286.

Saunders, D. M. and Wookey, P. E. (1980). Behavioral analyses of gambling. *Behavioural Psychotherapy 8*, 1-6.

Scarne, J. (1961). *Scarne's complete guide to gambling*. New York: Simon and Schuster.

Scarne, J. (1975). *Scarne's new complete guide to gambling*. London: Constable.

Schaefer, J. M. (1976). Drunkenness and cultural stress: A holocultural test. In Everett, M. W., Waddell, J. O., and Heath, D. B. (Eds.) *Cross-cultural approaches to the study of alcohol: An interdisciplinary perspective*. The Hague: Mouton.

Schissel, B. (2001). Betting against youth—The effects of socioeconomic marginality on gambling among young people. *Youth & Society, 2*(4), 473-491.

Schuckit, M. A. (1988). Physiological and psychological factors as predictors of alcoholism risk. In Galanter, M. (Ed.) *Recent developments in alcoholism, Volume 6* (pp. 311 322). New York: Plenum.

Schwarz, J. and Lindner, A. (1992). Inpatient treatment of male pathological gamblers in Germany. *Journal of Gambling Studies 8*(1), 93-109.

Scimecca, J. (1971). A typology of the gambler. *International Journal of Contemporary Sociology 8*, 56-71.

Scodel, J. A. (1964). Inspirational group therapy: A study of Gamblers Anonymous. *American Journal of Psychotherapy 18*(1), 115-125. Reprinted (1967) in Herman, R. D. (Ed.) *Gambling.* New York: Harper and Row.

Scott, M. B. (1968). *The racing game.* Chicago: Aldine Publishing Co.

Seixas, F. A., Omenn, G. S., and Burk, D. (1972). Nature and nurture in alcoholism. *Annals of the New York Academy of Sciences, Vol. 197*, May 25.

Shaffer, H. J. (1989). Conceptual crises in the addictions: The role of models in the field of compulsive gambling. In Shaffer, H. J., Stein, S. A., Gambino, G., and Cummings, T. N. (Eds.) *Compulsive gambling: Theory, research, and practice* (pp. 3-33). Lexington, MA: Lexington Books.

Shaffer, H. J. (1996). Understanding the means and objects of addiction: Technology, the internet, and gambling. *Journal of Gambling Studies 12*(4), 461-469.

Shaffer, H. J. (1997). The most important unresolved issue in the addictions: conceptual chaos. *Substance Use & Misuse 32*(11), 1573-1580.

Shaffer, H. J. and Gambino, B. (1989). The epistemology of "addictive disease": Gambling as predicament. *Journal of Gambling Behavior 5*(3), 211-229.

Shaffer, H. J. and Hall, M. N. (1996). Estimating the prevalence of adolescent gambling disorders: A quantitative synthesis and guide toward standard nomenclature. *Journal of Gambling Studies 12*(2), 193-214.

Shaffer, H. J., Hall, M. N., and Vander Bilt, J. (1997). *Estimating the prevalence of disordered gambling behavior in the United States and Canada: A Meta-analysis.* Boston: Harvard Medical School Division on Addictions.

Shaffer, H. J., LaBrie, R., Scanlon, K. M., and Cummings, T. N. (1994). Pathological gambling among adolescents: Massachusetts Gambling Screen (MAGS). *Journal of Gambling Studies 10*(4), 339-362.

Shaffer, H. J., Stein, S. A., Gambino, B., and Cummings, T. N. (1989). Introduction. In Shaffer, H. J., Stein, S. A., Gambino, G., and Cummings, T. N. (Eds.) *Compulsive gambling: Theory, research, and practice* (pp. xv-xviii). Lexington, MA: Lexington Books.

Shepherd, R.-M. (1996). Clinical obstacles in administrating the South Oaks Gambling Screen in a methadone and alcohol clinic. *Journal of Gambling Studies 12*(1), 21 32.

Simmel, E. (1920). Psychoanalysis of the gambler. *International Journal of Psychoanalysis 1*, 352-353.

Skinner, B. F. (1974). *About behaviorism.* New York: Alfred A. Knopf.

Slovic, P. (1969). Differential effects of real versus hypothetical payoffs on choices among gambles. *Journal of Experimental Psychology 80*(3), 434-437.

Slovic, P., and Lichtenstein, S. (1968). Relative importance of probabilities and payoffs in risk-taking. *Journal of Experimental Psychology Monograph 78*(3, Part 2), 1-18).

Slutske, W. S., Eisen, S., True, W. R., Lyons, M. J., Goldberg, J., and Tsuang, M. (2000). Common genetic vulnerability for pathological gambling and alcohol dependence in men. *Archives of General Psychiatry. 57*(7), 666-673.

Smart, R. G. and Ferris, J. (1996). Alcohol, drugs and gambling in the Ontario adult population, 1994. *Canadian Journal of Psychiatry 41*(1), 36-45.

Smith, A. (1937 [1776]). *The wealth of nations.* New York: The Modern Library.

Smith, J. F. and Abt, V. (1984). Gambling as Play. *Annals of the American Academy of Political and Social Science 474* (July), 122-132.

Smith, R. W. and Preston, F. (1984). Vocabularies of motives for gambling behavior. *Sociological Perspectives 27*, 325-348.

Smith, R. W., Preston, F., and Humphries, H. L. (1976). Alienation from work: A study of casino card dealers. In Eadington, W. R. (Ed.) *Gambling and society: Interdisciplinary studies on the subject of gambling* (pp. 229-246). Springfield, IL: Charles C Thomas.

Smith, S. and Razzell, P. (1975). *The pools winners.* London: Caliban Books.

Snyder, C. R. (1955). Studies of drinking in Jewish culture. IV. Culture and sobriety. A study of drinking patterns and sociocultural factors related to sobriety among Jews. Chapter 4. Ingroup-outgroup relations. *Quarterly Journal of Studies on Alcohol 16*(4), 700-742.

Snyder, C. R. (1958). *Alcohol and the Jews.* Glencoe, IL: The Free Press.

Snyder, C. R. (1962). Culture and Jewish sobriety: The ingroup-outgroup factor. In Pittman, D. J. and Snyder, C. R. (Eds.) *Society, culture, and drinking patterns.* New York: John Wiley and Sons.

Snyder, W. (1978). Decision-making with risk and uncertainty: The case of horse racing. *American Journal of Psychology 91*(2), 201-209.

Sommers, I. (1988). Pathological gambling: Estimating prevalence and group characteristics. *International Journal of the Addictions 23*, 477-490.

Spanier, D. (1994). *Inside the Gamblers mind.* Reno: University of Nevada Press.

Specker, S. M., Carlson, G. A., Edmonson, K. M., Johnson, P. E., and Marcotte, M. (1996). Psychopathology in pathological gamblers seeking treatment. *Journal of Gambling Studies 12*(1), 67-81.

Spectrum Children's Trust (1988). *Slot machine playing by children.* Special Report.

Spiro, M. H. (1974). On the tax incidence of the Pennsylvania Lottery. *National Tax Journal 27*(1), 57-61.

Spunt, B., Lesieur, H., Hunt, D., and Cahill, D. (1995). Gambling among methadone patients. *International Journal of the Addictions 30*(8), 929-962.

Spunt, B., Lesieur, H., Liberty, H. J., and Hunt, D. (1996). Pathological gamblers in methadone treatment: A comparison between men and women. *Journal of Gambling Studies 12*(4), 431-449.

Spunt, B., Dupont, I., Lesieur, H., Liberty, H. J., and Hunt, D. (1998). Pathological gambling and substance misuse: A review of the literature. *Substance Use & Misuse 33*(13), 2535-2560.

Stein, S. (1993). The role of support in recovery from compulsive gambling. In Eadington, W. R. and Cornelius, J. (Eds.) *Gambling behavior and problem gambling* (pp. 627 640). Reno, Nevada: Bureau of Business and Economic Research, College of Business Administration, University of Nevada.

Steinberg, M. A., Kosten, T. A., and Rounsaville, B. J. (1992). Cocaine abuse and pathological gambling. *American Journal on Addictions 1*(2), 121-132.

Steiner, C. (1969). The alcoholic game. *Quarterly Journal of Studies on Alcohol 30*(4), 920 938.

Steiner, C. (1971). *Games alcoholics play: The analysis of life scripts.* New York: Grove Press.

Steward, J. (1955). *Theory of Culture Change.* Urbana: University of Illinois Press.

Stinchfield, R. (2000). Gambling and correlates of gambling among Minnesota public school students. *Journal of Gambling Studies 16*(2-3), 153-173.

Stinchfield, R. D. and Winters, K. C. (1994). *Treatment effectiveness of six state-supported compulsive gambling treatment programs in Minnesota.* Minneapolis: University of Minnesota, Center for Adolescent Substance Abuse.

Stinchfield, R. D. and Winters, K. C. (1998). Gambling and problem gambling among youths. *Annals of the American Academy of Political Science 566*, 172-185.

Stinchfield, R., Cassuto, N., Winters, K., and Latimer, W. (1997). Prevalence of gambling among Minnesota public school students in 1992 and 1995. *Journal of Gambling Studies 13*(1), 25-48.

Stitt, B. G., Nichols, M., and Giacopassi, D. (1999). Perceptions of the extent of problem gambling within new casino communities. *Journal of Gambling Studies 16*(4), 433 451.

Strachan, M. L. and Custer, R. L. (1993). Female compulsive gamblers in Las Vegas. In Eadington, W. R. and Cornelius, J. A. (Eds.) *Gambling behavior and problem gambling* (pp. 235-238). Reno, Nevada: Bureau of Business and Economic Research, College of Business Administration, University of Nevada.

Strow, D. (1999, May 24). Study pinpoints prevalence of problem gambling. *Las Vegas Sun.*

Suits, D. B. (1982). Gambling as a source of revenue. In Brazer, H. E. and Laren, D. S. (Eds.) *Michigan's fiscal and economic structure.* Ann Arbor: University of Michigan Press.

Sullivan, S. G., McCormick, R., and Sellman, J. D. (1997). Increased requests for help by problem gamblers: data from a gambling crisis telephone hotline. *New Zealand Medical Journal 110*(1053), 380-383.

Sumner, W. G. and Keller, A. G. (1927). *The science of society, Vol. 2.* New Haven, CT: Yale University Press.

Sutton, S. (1993). Is wearing clothes a high risk situation for relapse? The vase rate problem in relapse research. *Addiction 88*(6), 725-727.

Taber, J. I. (1993). Addictive behavior: An informal clinical view. In Eadington, W. R. and Cornelius, J. A. (Eds.) *Gambling behavior and problem gambling* (pp. 273-286). Reno, Nevada: Bureau of Business and Economic Research, College of Business Administration, University of Nevada.

Taber, J. I., Collachi, J. L., and Lynn, E. J. (1986). Pathological gambling: Possibilities for treatment in northern Nevada. *Nevada Public Affairs Review 2*, 39-42.

Taber, J. I., McCormick, R. A., and Ramirez, L. F. (1987). The prevalence and impact of major life stressors among pathological gamblers. *International Journal of the Addictions 22*, 71-79.

Taber, J. I., Russo, A. M., Adkins, B. J., and McCormick, R. A. (1986). Ego strength and achievement motivation in pathological gamblers. *Journal of Gambling Behavior 2*(2), 69-80.

Tarter, R. E. and Schneider, D. U. (1976). Models and theories of alcoholism. In Tarter, R. E. and Sugerman, A. A. (Eds.) *Alcoholism: Interdisciplinary approaches to an enduring problem.* Reading, MA: Addison-Wesley.

Tavares, H., Zilberman, M. L., Beites, F. J., and Gentil, V. (2001). Brief communications: Gender differences in gambling progression. *Journal of Gambling Studies 17*(2), 151-159.

Tec, N. (1964). *Gambling in Sweden.* Totawa, NJ: Bedminster Press.

Templer, D. I., Kaiser, G., and Siscoe, K. (1993). Correlates of pathological gambling propensity in prison inmates. *Comprehensive Psychiatry 34*(5), 347-351.

Thompson, W., Gazel, R., and Rickman, D. (1995). *The economic impact of Native American gaming in Wisconsin.* Milwaukee, WI: The Wisconsin Policy Research Institute.

Thorner, I. (1956). Ascetic protestantism, gambling, and the one-price system. *American Journal of Economics and Sociology 15*, 161-172.

Thorson, J. A., Powell, P. C., and Hilt, M. (1994). Epidemiology of gambling and depression in an adult sample. *Psychological Reports 74*(3), 987-994.

Törne, I. V., and Konstanty, R. (1992). Gambling behavior and psychological disorders of gamblers on German-style slot-machines. *Journal of Gambling Studies 8*(1), 39-58.

Trevorrow, K. and Moore, S. (1998). The association between loneliness, social isolation, and women's electronic gaming machine gambling. *Journal of Gambling Studies 14*(3), 263-284.

Turner, N., Ialomiteanu, A., and Room, R. (1999). Checkered expectations: Predictors of approval of opening a casino in the Niagara community. *Journal of Gambling Studies 15*(1), 45-70.

Tversky, A. and Kahneman, D. (1974). Judgment under uncertainty: Heuristics and biases. *Science 185*, 1124-1131.

Tylor, E. B. (1958 [1871]). *Primitive culture, Volume 1*. New York: Harper Torchbooks.

Tyndel, M. (1963). Gambling: An addiction. *Addictions 10*, 40-48.

Ullman, A. D. (1958). Sociocultural backgrounds of alcoholism. *Annals of the American Academy of Social and Political Science 315*, 48-54.

USDHHS (U.S. Department of Health and Human Services) (1990). *Seventh special report to the U.S. Congress on alcohol and health from Secretary of Health and Human Services*. Washington, D.C.: U.S. Department of Health and Human Services.

USDHHS (U.S. Department of Health and Human Services) (1994). *Preventing tobacco use among young people: A report of the Surgeon General*. Washington, D.C.: U.S. Department of Health and Human Services.

Vaillancourt, F. and Grignon, J. (1988). Canadian lotteries as taxes: Revenues and incidence. *Canadian Tax Journal 36*, 369-388.

Vaillant, G. E. (1983). *The natural history of alcoholism: Causes, patterns, and paths to recovery*. Cambridge, MA: Harvard University Press.

Veblen, T. (1931 [1899]). *The theory of the leisure class*. New York: Viking Press.

Victor, R. G. (1981). Gambling. In Mulé, S. J. (Ed.) *Behavior in excess: An examination of the volitional disorders* (pp. 271-281). New York: The Free Press.

Vitaro, F., Ladouceur, R., and Bujold, A. (1996). Predictive and concurrent correlates of gambling in early adolescent boys. *Journal of Early Adolescence 16*(2), 211-228.

Vitaro, F., Ferland, F., Jacques, C., and Ladouceur, R. (1998). Gambling, substance use, and impulsivity during adolescence. *Psychology of Addictive Behaviors 12*(3), 185-194.

Voget, F. W. (1975). *A history of ethnology*. New York: Holt, Rinehart, and Winston.

Volberg, R. A. (1993). Estimating the prevalence of pathological gambling in the United States. In Eadington, W. R. and Cornelius, J. A. (Eds.) *Gambling behavior and problem gambling* (pp. 365-378). Reno: University of Nevada Press.

Volberg, R. A. (1994). The prevalence and demographics of pathological gamblers: Implications for public health. *American Journal of Public Health 84*(2), 237-241.

Volberg, R. A. (1996). *Gambling and problem gambling in New York: A 10-year replication survey, 1986 to 1996*. Report to the New York Council on Problem Gambling.

Volberg, R. A. (1998). *Gambling and problem gambling among adolescents in New York*. Report to the New York Council on Problem Gambling.

Volberg, R. A. (2001). *Changes in gambling and problem gambling in Oregon: Results from a replication study, 1997 to 2000*. Northampton, MA: Gemini Research.

Volberg, R. A., and Abbott, M. W. (1994). Lifetime prevalence estimates of pathological gambling in New Zealand. *International Journal of Epidemiology 23*(5), 976-983.

Volberg, R. A., and Abbott, M. W. (1997). Gambling and problem gambling among indigenous peoples. *Substance Use & Misuse 32*(11), 1525-1538.

Volberg, R. A. and Steadman, H. J. (1988). Refining prevalence estimates of pathological gamblers. *American Journal of Psychiatry 145*(4), 502-505.

Volberg, R. A. and Steadman, H. J. (1989). Prevalence estimates of pathological gambling in New Jersey and Maryland. *American Journal of Psychiatry 146*(12), 1618-1619.

Volberg, R. A., Reitzes, D. C., and Boles, J. (1997). Exploring the links between gambling, problem gambling, and self-esteem. *Deviant Behavior 18*(4), 321-342.

von Neumann, J., and Morgenstern, O. (1944). *Theory of games and economic behavior*. Princeton: Princeton University Press.

Wagenaar, W. A., Keren, G., and Pleit-Kuiper, A. (1984). The multiple objectives of gamblers. *Acta Psychologica 56*(1-3), 167-178.

Wagner, W. (1972). *To gamble or not to gamble.* New York: World Publishing.

Walker, M. B. (1985). Explanations for gambling. In Caldwell, G., Haig, B., Dickerson, M., and Sylvan, L. (Eds.) *Gambling in Australia* (pp. 146-162). Sydney: Croom Helm.

Walker, M. B. (1988). Betting shops and slot machines: Comparisons among gamblers. In Eadington, W. R. (Ed.) *Gambling research: Proceedings of the Seventh International Conference on Gambling and Risk Taking, Volume 3* (pp. 65-82). Reno, Nevada: Bureau of Business and Economic Research, College of Business Administration, University of Nevada.

Walker, M. B. (1992a). A sociocognitive theory of gambling involvement. In Eadington, W. R. and Cornelius, J. A. (Eds.) *Gambling and commercial gaming: Essays in business, economics, philosophy, and science* (pp. 371-398). Reno, Nevada: Bureau of Business and Economic Research, College of Business Administration, University of Nevada.

Walker, M. B. (1992b). The presence of irrational thinking among poker machine players. In Eadington, W. R. and Cornelius, J. A. (Eds.) *Gambling and commercial gaming: Essays in business, economics, philosophy, and science* (pp. 485-498). Reno, Nevada: Bureau of Business and Economic Research, College of Business Administration, University of Nevada.

Walker, M. B. (1992c). *The psychology of gambling.* Oxford: Pergamon Press.

Walker, M. B. (1992d). Irrational thinking among slot machine players. *Journal of Gambling Studies 8*(3), 245-261.

Wallisch, L. S. (1993). *Gambling in Texas: 1992 Texas survey of adolescent gambling behavior.* Austin, TX: Texas Commission on Alcohol and Drug Abuse.

Wallisch, L. S. (1996). *Gambling in Texas: 1995 Surveys of adult and adolescent gambling behavior.* Austin, TX: Texas Commission on Alcohol and Drug Abuse.

Walters, G. D. (1994a). The gambling lifestyle: I. Theory. *Journal of Gambling Studies 10*(2), 159-182.

Walters, G. D. (1994b). The gambling lifestyle: II. Treatment. *Journal of Gambling Studies 10*(3), 219-235.

Wardman, D., el-Guebaly, N., and Hodgins, D. (2001). Problem and pathological gambling in North American Aboriginal populations: A review of the empirical literature. *Journal of Gambling Studies 17*(2), 81-100.

Waterman, J. and Atkin, K. (1985). Young people and fruit machines. *Society for the Study of Gambling Newsletter,* No. 7.

Weinberg, K. (1960). *Social problems of our times.* Englewood Cliffs, N.J.: Prentice Hall.

Weinstein, D. and Deitch, L. (1974). *The impact of legalized gambling: The socioeconomic consequences of lotteries and off-track betting.* New York: Praeger.

Weitzman, M. (1965). Utility analysis and group behavior: An empirical study. *Journal of Political Economy 73*, 18-26.

Weschler, H. and Thum, D. (1973). Teen-age drinking, drug use and social correlates. *Quarterly Journal of Studies on Alcohol 34*(4), 1220-1227.

Westphal, J. R., Rush, J. A., Stevens, L., and Johnson L. J. (2000). Gambling behavior of Louisiana students in grades 6 through 12. *Psychiatric Services 51*(1), 96-99.

Wexler, S. (1984, December). *A chart on the effects of compulsive gambling on the wife.* Paper presented at the Sixth National Conference on Gambling and Risk-Taking, Atlantic City, New Jersey.

Wiebe, J. M. D. and Cox, B. J. (2001). A profile of Canadian adults seeking treatment for gambling problems and comparisons with adults entering an alcohol treatment program. *Canadian Journal of Psychiatry 46*(5), 418-421.

Windle, M. (1993). A retrospective measure of childhood behavior problems and its use in predicting adolescent problem behaviors. *Journal of Studies on Alcohol 54*(4), 422 431.

Winters, K. and Anderson, N. (2000). Gambling involvement and drug use among adolescents. *Journal of Gambling Studies 16*(2-3), 175-198.

Winters, K. C., Stinchfield, R. D., and Fulkerson, J. (1990). *Adolescent survey of gambling behavior in Minnesota: A benchmark*. St. Paul: Minnesota Department of Human Services, Mental Health Division.

Winters, K. C., Stinchfield, R. D., and Fulkerson, J. (1993a). Patterns and characteristics of adolescent gambling. *Journal of Gambling Studies 9*(4), 371-386.

Winters, K. C., Stinchfield, R. D., and Fulkerson, J. (1993b). Toward the development of an adolescent gambling severity scale. *Journal of Gambling Studies 9*(1), 63-84.

Winters, K. C., Stinchfield, R. D., and Kim, L. G. (1995). Monitoring adolescent gambling in Minnesota. *Journal of Gambling Studies 11*(2), 165-183.

Winters, K. C., Bengston, P. L., Stinchfield, R. D., and Dorr, D. (1996). *1995 college gambling survey: University of Minnesota Twin Cities, University of Minnesota Duluth, and Moorhead State Universtity*. St. Paul: Minnesota Department of Human Services, Mental Health Division. Published (1998) as Prevalence and risk factors of problem gambling among college students. *Psychology of Addictive Behaviors 12*, 783-793.

Wissler, C. (1923). *Man and culture*. New York: Thomas Y. Crowell.

Wittman, G. W., Fuller, N. P., and Taber, J. I. (1988). Patterns of polyaddictions in alcoholism patients and high school students. In Eadington, W. R. (Ed.) *Gambling research: Proceedings of the Seventh International Conference on Gambling and Risk Taking*. Reno, Nevada: Bureau of Business and Economic Research, College of Business Administration, University of Nevada.

Wood, R. and Griffiths, M. (1998). The acquisition, development and maintenance of lottery and scratchcard gambling in adolescence. *Journal of Adolescence 21*, 265-273.

World Health Organization (1991). *The international classification of diseases, 9th revision, clinical modification; ICD-9-CM, fourth edition, volume 1, diseases, tabular list*. Washington, D.C.: DHHS Publication No. (DHS) 91-1260, U.S. Dept. of Health and Human Services, U.S. Govt. Printing Office.

World Health Organization (1992). *International statistical classification of diseases and related health problems, tenth revision, ICD-10, volume 1*. Geneva: World Health Organization.

Wynne, H. J., Smith, G. J., and Jacobs, D. F. (1996). *Adolescent gambling and problem gambling in Alberta*. Report to the Alberta Alcohol and Drug Commission.

Yaari, M. E. (1965). Complexity in the theory of choice under risk. *Quarterly Journal of Economics 89*(2), 278-290.

Yaffee, R. A., Lorenz, V. C., and Politzer, R. M. (1993). Models explaining gambling severity among patients undergoing treatment in Maryland: 1983 through 1989. In Eadington, W. R. and Cornelius, J. A. (Eds.) *Gambling behavior and problem gambling* (pp. 657-667). Reno, Nevada: Bureau of Business and Economic Research, College of Business Administration, University of Nevada.

Yeoman, T. and Griffiths, M. (1996a). Adolescent machine gambling and crime. *Journal of Adolescence 19*(1), 99-104.

Yeoman, T. and Griffiths, M. (1996b). Adolescent machine gambling and crime. *Journal of Adolescence 19*(2), 183-188.

Zitzow, D. (1996a). Comparative study of problematic gambling behaviors between American Indian and non-Indian adolescents within and near a northern plains reservation. *American Indian & Alaska Native Mental Health Research 7*(2), 14-26.

Zitzow, D. (1996b). Comparative study of problematic gambling behaviors between American Indian and non-Indian adults in a northern plains reservation. *American Indian & Alaska Native Mental Health Research 7*(2), 27-41.

Zola, I. K. (1963). Observations on gambling in a lower-class setting. *Social Problems 10,* 353-361.

Zuckerman, M. (1975). *Manual and research report for the Sensation Seeking Scale (SSS).* University of Delaware.

Zurcher, L. A. (1970). The friendly poker game: A study of an ephemeral role. *Social Forces 49*(2), 173-186.

INDEX

A

Abbott, D. A., 220–225

Abt, Vicki, 70, 89–90, 92–94, 335–336

Action, 68–70, 72, 77, 88–89, 95–100, 104, 108, 111–112, 122, 129–130, 173, 176, 186, 259, 263, 265–267, 272, 333, 335–339, 346–347, 355

Action hypothesis (*see* Risk–taking hypothesis)

Action players, 95–97, 99–100, 336

"Action seekers," 129–130, 338

Addict/addiction/addictive, 8–16, 33, 46, 49, 59, 72, 79 80, 82, 86–88, 114, 120, 130–136, 148, 153–154, 184, 237, 242, 245–253, 255–258, 263–266, 268, 289–290, 304, 307–308, 312, 323–324, 326–327, 333–335, 339, 345–347, 349, 351, 354–355, 358, 361–363
definitional issue, 8–11

Addiction Involvement Scale, 255–256

Addictive personality syndrome, 363

Addictive response syndrome (*see* Learned helplessness theory)

Affluence theory (*see* Leisure class/affluence theory)

Age–area principle, 158–159

Age differences, 145, 149, 165–172, 174, 177, 180–182, 185–186, 189–191, 198, 203, 207, 209–211, 213–219, 224, 226–227, 230–243, 245–246, 250, 265, 271–281, 286–288, 291–300, 303–306, 312, 314, 316, 318–319, 321, 323, 326, 341, 343–352, 360

Age of initiation/hypothesis, 224, 237, 242, 246, 280, 282–283, 287, 289, 307, 310, 312–313, 321, 323, 344–346, 348–349, 351, 361

Age of majority hypothesis, 360

Agôn, 88–89

Alcohol use/alcoholism, 9, 11–14, 147, 154–158, 239, 244, 247, 252, 263, 265–268, 279–280, 282, 286–287, 289–291, 296–300, 306, 309–310, 312, 323, 326, 340, 345, 349–350, 352
primary function, of 157–158, 340

Alia, 88

Alienation theory, 26–28, 31, 33, 55–57, 60, 64, 68, 151, 172–174, 186, 194–196, 204, 265 268, 329, 332, 342, 357

Altman, Jon, 90–91, 335–336

American Psychiatric Association, 8

Amusement arcades, 126–136
status hierarchy of, 127–130

Amusements with prizes, 126

Anomie theory, 26, 28–29, 32–33, 55, 64, 68, 97, 102, 140, 142, 151, 171–174, 180, 183–184, 186, 198, 218, 265–270, 281, 322, 329, 342, 348, 357, 359

Antigambler, 154

Anxiety/anxiety reduction (*see* Dysphoria reduction)

"Apprentices," 128

"Arcade kings," 127–130

Aristotle, 6

"Armchair" theorists,
Devereux, Edward, 30–33, 56, 143–146, 165, 171–173, 175, 177, 180, 183–184, 186, 190, 210–211, 217, 220, 235, 295, 329
Veblen, Thorstein, 23–25, 165–166, 170–171, 178, 180, 186, 189, 192, 203, 207, 218, 224, 235, 315, 328, 331

"Armchair" theory, 19, 23–51, 55, 62, 94, 105, 328–332, 336

DSM–III; DSM–III–R; DSM–IV, 8, 130,
244, 247, 250–251, 254, 326
Dual–effect hypothesis, 355
Dual–Reinforcement hypothesis, 355
Dysphoria (anxiety, tension, stress) reduction, 29–30, 33, 35, 57–58, 95–96, 100,
132, 136, 144–146, 157–158, 161–162, 164,
166, 195, 246–248, 258, 264–267,
283–284, 289 290, 305, 307–309, 312,
315, 317–318, 329, 332, 334, 336,
340–341, 346–349, 351 352, 355–357,
362–363
Dysphoria–reduction hypothesis, 134, 136,
157–158, 161–162, 164, 280, 348, 332,
355

E

Early start hypothesis (*see* Age of initiation
hypothesis)
Early win hypothesis, 356
Economic gambler, 63, 332
Economic theories, 19, 27, 36–51, 76, 122,
151–152, 185, 217, 224, 330–331, 348,
357–358
  Base wealth 41, 330
  Consumer/consumption, 47–48, 331,
  335, 358
  Expected utility/value, 28, 37–46,
  330–331, 357
  Marxian, 27, 30–31, 49–50, 330–331, 358
  Rational addiction, 46, 357
  Regressivity, 146, 192–193, 222–223,
  227–228, 357, 357–358
  Subjective expected utility/value, 40–41
  Value–maximizational, 28, 37–38, 42–43,
  46–47, 50–51, 357
Economic theorists
  Bernoulli, Daniel, 39–40
  Friedman, Milton, 41–43
  Fuller, Peter, 49–50
  Morgenstern, Otto, 41
  Savage, L. J., 41–43
  Smith, Adam, 40–41, 44, 330
  von Neumann, John, 41
Educational differences, 141, 143–144, 146,
168, 171, 173, 180, 185, 189–192, 207–208,
210 212, 215, 225–228, 232, 234,
279–284, 287, 291–297, 299, 303,
305–307, 317, 322, 326, 341–343, 348,
350–352

Education hypothesis, 143, 146, 171, 189, 191,
235, 257, 281, 348, 359
Electronic gaming machines/players, 3, 200,
228, 238, 241, 246, 269–271, 301,
311–312, 316, 325, 344, 346, 351, 354, 361
"Emotion work," 116–118, 337
Employment status, 95, 107–108, 121, 131,
141, 198, 218, 279, 282, 291, 294–296,
299, 303 306, 308–309, 318, 322, 325,
350–352
Ephemeral roles, 70
Erroneous/False/Irrational beliefs, 40, 47,
71–72, 75, 79, 97, 100, 104, 110, 120, 122,
124, 127, 236, 259–260, 262, 297–299,
315, 330, 337, 350, 356
Escalation of stakes, 74, 104, 122, 124
"Escape artists," 130, 132, 339
"Escape hatch," hypothesis 27–28, 30–33,
59–60, 332
Essentialist, 154
Ethnic differences, 189–192, 198–199, 217,
226–228, 237, 243–244, 254, 268–269,
279, 281 286, 288, 290–291, 286, 291,
296, 300, 304, 306, 308, 323, 348–351,
357
Ethnicity hypothesis, 281, 348–350, 357
Ethnographic research, need for, 319
Ethnoscientific research method, 106
Exhaustion phase of family breakdown,
82–83, 87
Expected utility/value theories of risk–tak-
ing, 28, 37–46, 330–331, 357
  Bernoulli, 39–40
  Elementary, 38–39
  Friedman–Savage, 41–44, 140
  von Neumann and Morgenstern, 41
External locus of control orientation (*see*
Locus of control orientation, external)

F

"Face work," 69, 102
Family breakdown, phases of
  denial, 82, 84, 86
  exhaustion, 82–83, 87
  stress, 82, 87
  growing, 83
Family dynamics (*see* Family systems/trans-
actional theory)

and "religiosity"/religious commitment, 210–212, 220, 274, 287, 295–296, 329, 341, 343, 350

and religious affiliation, 32, 144, 147, 168, 171–173, 175, 177, 180, 183–184, 186, 189–192, 195–196, 198–199, 210–215, 217–218, 220, 226, 235, 268, 279–280, 286–288, 291, 295–298, 318, 322, 329, 344, 349–350

and residence, 32, 165, 172, 189, 191, 198, 288–290, 296–297, 312, 314, 327, 341, 350

and residential mobility, 290, 296–298, 350

and self-esteem, 61, 265–266, 307, 310, 337, 347, 351–352, 354, 362–363

and self-presentation, 68, 73–74 219, 274

and sensation-seeking, 88–89, 101, 134, 136, 165, 194–195, 198, 217, 236, 267, 272 273, 280, 326, 343

and skill, 35, 46, 57, 62–64, 70–71, 77, 88–89, 93, 95, 97–100, 103–104, 109–110, 114 116, 118–119, 127–129, 132–133, 136, 148, 150, 158–159, 161, 173, 175, 182, 204, 214–215, 238–239, 241, 246, 248, 259–260, 262, 277, 296, 298, 301, 307, 311–312, 337–338, 340, 351, 356

and social class/status, 23–29, 31–34, 60–61, 64, 95, 102, 140–151, 155, 165–166, 169 178, 180–183, 185–186, 189–190, 198, 203, 207, 210, 212, 214–215, 217–218, 232, 254, 256, 287, 289, 292–295, 297–298, 303, 306, 308–310, 314–315, 321, 324, 327–332, 339, 341, 343, 346, 348–352, 356–360

and social mobility, 56, 143–144

and status frustration, 140, 143–147, 165, 170–174, 177, 186, 189, 192, 203, 217, 224, 226–228, 339, 341–342, 344, 359

and subculture, 145, 147–148, 151–152, 155–157, 173, 190–191, 195, 198–199, 249, 315, 328, 339–343, 352, 359–360

and suicide, 4, 66–67, 83, 86, 117, 124, 247, 264, 268, 306, 309–310, 325, 338, 345, 347, 352

and superstition, 31, 50, 62–64, 125, 331, 356

and the Protestant ethic, 6–7, 30–32, 35, 144, 190, 329, 357

and truancy, 131

as adult activity/behavior, 129, 135

as amusement/entertainment/recreation, 31, 48, 76, 88–92, 107, 123, 153, 163, 166, 193–194, 198, 216, 223–224, 235–236, 244, 261, 269, 275, 278, 284, 297, 299, 313, 331, 335–337, 339–340, 346, 358, 363

as appeal to Fate, 64

as behavioral survival, 24

as challenge, 98, 100, 128, 134, 193–194, 278, 284, 335, 337, 363

as character display, 69–71, 73–74, 88, 92, 96, 98–101, 128, 333, 335–336, 338, 358

as compulsory, 102

as decision making, 27–28, 30–32, 55, 57–61, 70, 77, 128, 151, 153, 158, 172–173, 175–176, 185–186, 194, 204, 330, 332–333, 339, 357

as deviant behavior, 23, 25–28, 30, 32–33, 35, 58, 62, 64, 73, 95, 102, 148–149, 153, 173, 184, 198, 208, 289, 314, 329, 332, 339, 341–343, 349, 352, 357, 363

as "discrete" phenomenon, 184–185, 341

as disease or illness, 64, 73, 83

as divination, 24

as drive-reducing, 29, 58, 87–88, 92–93, 136, 157–158, 160–162, 166, 258, 265–267, 335–336, 348, 355

as ego-enhancing, 128, 130

as empowerment, 264, 267

as escape/"escape hatch", 27–28, 30–33, 59–60, 73, 88, 90, 98, 101, 130, 132, 136, 166, 263–264, 266, 270, 278, 280, 284, 312, 329, 332, 335, 337, 339, 347, 355, 362

as experimental behavior, 219, 244, 248, 250

as expression of conspicuous consumption, 24–25, 61, 328

as expression of masculinity, 64

as hobby, 278, 284

as immoral, 5–8, 59, 61, 67, 95, 102, 140–142, 146, 154, 179, 196, 211, 213, 217, 235 236, 274, 332, 343, 357

as irrational behavior, 37, 39–42, 45, 47–48, 50–51, 59, 64, 152–153, 330